Tradition, pluralism and identity

Contributions to Indian Sociology

OCCASIONAL STUDIES

1. T.N. MADAN, ed., 1976. *Muslim communities of South Asia: Society and culture* (vol. 6, 1972). New Delhi: Vikas.*

2. SATISH SABERWAL, ed., 1978. *Process and institution in urban India: Sociological studies* (vol. 11, no. 1, 1977). New Delhi: Vikas. Second impression (New Delhi: Vikas), 1978.*

3. T.N. MADAN, ed., 1982. *Way of life: King, householder, renouncer: Essays in honour of Louis Dumont* (vol. 15, nos. 1 & 2, 1981). New Delhi: Vikas; Paris: Maison des Sciences de l'Homme. Second impression (New Delhi: Vikas), 1982. Second edition (Delhi: Motilal Banarsidass), 1988.

4. VEENA DAS, ed., 1986. *The word and the world: Fantasy, symbol and record* (vol. 19, no. 1, 1985). New Delhi: Sage.

5. McKIM MARRIOTT, ed., 1990. *India through Hindu categories* (vol. 23, no. 1, 1989). New Delhi: Sage. Fifth impression, 1998.

6. T.N. MADAN, ed., 1995. *Muslim communities of South Asia: Culture, society and power* (Revised enlarged edition) (vol. 6, 1972). New Delhi: Manohar (First published by Vikas).*

7. PATRICIA UBEROI, ed., 1996. *Social reform, sexuality and the state* (vol. 29, nos. 1 & 2, 1995). New Delhi: Sage. Third impression, 1998.

*Out of print.

Tradition, pluralism and identity

In honour of T.N. Madan

Edited by

Veena Das
Dipankar Gupta
Patricia Uberoi

CONTRIBUTIONS TO INDIAN SOCIOLOGY • OCCASIONAL STUDIES 8

Sage Publications
New Delhi Thousand Oaks London

First published in 1999 by

Sage Publications India Pvt Ltd
32, M-Block Market, Greater Kailash–I
New Delhi 110 048

Sage Publications Inc
2455 Teller Road
Thousand Oaks, California 91320

Sage Publications Ltd
6 Bonhill Street
London EC2A 4PU

Published by Tejeshwar Singh for Sage Publications India Pvt Ltd, typeset by Siva Math Setters, Chennai, and printed at Print Perfect, Mayapuri Phase–II, Delhi.

Library of Congress Cataloging-in-Publication Data

Tradition, pluralism and identity: in honour of T.N. Madan/edited by Veena Das, Dipankar Gupta, Patricia Uberoi.

p. cm. (cloth)—(Contributions to Indian Sociology. Occasional studies;.8)

Includes bibliographical references and index.

1. Sociology—India—History. 2. Social structure—India—History. 3. India—Social conditions. 4. Ethnology—India. I. Das, Veena. II. Gupta, Dipankar, 1949– III. Uberoi, Patricia. IV. Title. V. Series.

HM477.I4 T73   301'.0954—dc21   1999   99–046675

ISBN: 0–7619–9381–9 (US-hb)
81–7036–850–2 (India-hb)

Sage Production Team: Aruna Ramachandran, Shashi Sharma and Santosh Rawat

Contents

Preface 7

1. *Tradition, pluralism, identity: Framing the issues* 9
VEENA DAS

2. *The imagined landscape: Patterns in the construction of Hindu sacred geography* 23
DIANA L. ECK

3. *Caste and purity: A study in the language of the Dharma literature* 47
PATRICK OLIVELLE

4. *Secularism, unicity and diversity: The case of Haracandi's grove* 75
FREDERIQUE APFFEL-MARGLIN

5. *The politics of moral practice in psychotherapy and religious healing* 95
ARTHUR KLEINMAN *and* **DON SEEMAN**

6. *The issue of 'right to food' among the Hindus: Notes and comments* 111
R.S. KHARE

7. *The female family core explored ethnosociologically* 137
McKIM MARRIOTT

8. *The diaspora comes home: Disciplining desire in* DDLJ 163
PATRICIA UBEROI

9. *Indian diaspora, globalisation and multiculturalism: A cultural analysis* 195
RAVINDRA K. JAIN

10. *What did Bernier actually say? Profiling the Mughal empire* 219
STANLEY J. TAMBIAH

11. *Rejecting violence: Sacrifice and the social identity of trading communities* 245
LAWRENCE A. BABB

12. *Caste and politics: The presumption of numbers* 267
DIPANKAR GUPTA

13. *Gifting and receiving: Anglo-Indian charity and its beneficiaries in Madras* 283
LIONEL CAPLAN

14. *Arabs, Moors and Muslims: Sri Lankan Muslim ethnicity in regional perspective* 307
DENNIS B. McGILVRAY

15. *Secularism out of its place* 359
PAUL R. BRASS

16. *The Babri Masjid and the secular contract* 381
HAROLD A. GOULD

17. *The twilight of certitudes: Secularism, Hindu nationalism and other masks of deculturation* 401
ASHIS NANDY

18. *Self as other: Amar Singh's diary as reflexive 'native' ethnography* 421
LLOYD I. RUDOLPH

T.N. Madan: A biographical note and bibliography 451

About the editors and contributors 461

Index 465

Preface

This volume of essays, the eighth in the *Contributions to Indian sociology* Occasional Studies series, is presented to honour the work of Triloki Nath ('Loki') Madan: scholar, colleague and friend. Contributors are scholars from different parts of the world who have known Triloki well, who are located in academic institutions with which he has been closely associated in the course of his distinguished career, and whose own research bears on the themes of tradition, pluralism and identity that have been a consistent emphasis in T.N. Madan's own writings over several decades. T.N. Madan is one of the few sociologists of India who have been able to combine the use of Indological and other textual sources, and anthropological fieldwork. The papers presented here draw on a similar range of source materials and, like Madan's own work, seek to add to the ethnography of the region as well as to the clarification of theoretical and conceptual issues in the social sciences.

The majority of the essays in this volume were originally published in a special issue of *Contributions to Indian sociology* (volume 32, number 2 [1998]), the professional journal of South Asian sociology and social anthropology of which T.N. Madan had been the distinguished editor for twenty-five years from 1967 to 1991. To these have been added essays by two of the co-editors of this volume which, for want of space, had been held over from the original journal issue. While Veena Das presents an overview of the essays and a framework for understanding the guiding themes of the volume, Dipankar Gupta takes up the issue of the supposed intersection of caste identities and contemporary electoral politics with an empirical study of voting behaviour in the three states of Maharashtra, Uttar Pradesh and Bihar. Also added, with permission, are two previously published papers by Ashis Nandy and Lloyd I. Rudolph. The former, in his characteristic feisty style, addresses the problem of Indian 'secularism', the central focus of T.N. Madan's recently published and much acclaimed book, *Modern myths, locked minds: Secularism and fundamentalism in India* (1997). The latter seeks inspiration from Madan's several methodological discussions of the challenges of doing anthropological fieldwork among 'one's own people' to present a reading of the diary of a Rajasthani nobleman as an example of 'reflexive "native" ethnography'. Also included are a bibliography of T.N. Madan's major publications and a brief biographical note.

We express our thanks to our distinguished contributors, whose essays individually and collectively carry forward discussions on themes that are critical to the project of the sociology of India; to Aradhya Bhardwaj, Editorial Assistant to the Sociology Unit of the Institute of Economic Growth, for the labour she has put into the production of this volume; to the Institute of Economic Growth for much-needed infrastructural support; and to the editorial team of Sage Publications, some of whom were closely associated with T.N. Madan in his capacity as former editor of *Contributions to Indian sociology*.

Editors

1

Tradition, pluralism, identity: Framing the issues

Veena Das

The essays in this volume honour the outstanding contributions of Professor T.N. Madan to the development of sociology and social anthropology in South Asia. They engage the linked themes of tradition, pluralism and identity to which his work has made seminal contributions. The idea of tradition has many strands—one can see that in recent years it has become intertwined with notions of memory, invention and identity politics—giving it a life in many a scholarly treatise and in public culture. Is there, then, a purity to the concepts of tradition, pluralism and identity, which have been put into play in this volume? For instance, is pluralism something external to tradition, or something internal to it? When aligned with the notion of modernity, do we think of tradition as standing in an antagonistic relation to modernity, refusing mutual translatability, or do we emphasise *circulations* within a tradition—between generations, different sexual geographies and different ways of evolving strategies of survival? I take these three concepts to suggest that human imagination conceives of culture in the plural—i.e., the possibility of exile, of there being an 'elsewhere', is what makes tradition *possible*. Thus, a tradition must struggle with the pain of recognising itself in change and not only in staticity. In what manner does the displacement of tradition, the relations forged between tradition and modernity and the encounter with the other—whether in the mode of travel, of colonialism, or in the imagination—leave a mark on tradition as it is encoded in everyday life? These issues have crystallised in the papers in this volume, taking the discussion of tradition in many unexpected and new directions.

Although the meaning of tradition has become mired in anxieties about its appropriation, especially in the project of reorganisation of the polity in the present context in India, Madan's interest in these issues is a long-standing one. One can discern in his writings three different spheres in which the problem of tradition is engaged. First is the sphere of everyday life, best encapsulated in the figure of the householder, which has fascinated him since his early writings on household and family (Madan 1965). By marking out the practices of the householder as those of '*non-renunciation*', Madan (1987) places the creation of everyday life not within some universal notion of family and household, but as embedded in the particularity of the civilisational tradition of Hinduism. This is, of course, particularly important in the lives of the Kashmiri Pandits among whom he completed his first field project. Second, tradition figures as a problematic in the organisation of polity and the creation of a public culture, as evidenced in Madan's recent provocative writings on secularism and fundamentalism in contemporary India (Madan 1997). Third, he also writes of tradition as the scholarly practices from within which a discipline gets its founding orientations: his many contributions to the history of sociology in India and his engagement with anthropology at home testify to his abiding concern with these issues (see Madan 1982a, 1982b, 1994).

I

Tradition, domesticity and everyday life

The site of the domestic as the place in which tradition is instituted has been recognised in much of the social science literature in India. In Madan's work this becomes evident in the importance he attaches to the figure of the householder. Both in his work on Kashmiri Pandits as well as in his reflections on the cultural texts (including modern literary productions), the securing of the moral in everyday life is a complicated affair. This cannot be attributed only to pressures of modernity—even the traditional concerns with purity and pollution in the domestic context are seen as fraught with questions of doubt. It is to this theme that Patrick Olivelle speaks in his essay, 'Caste and purity: A study in the language of the Dharma literature'. He demonstrates with consummate skill that there is a distinction between purity as it applies to persons (*śuci*) and as it applies to things or non-persons (*śuddhi*) in the Dharma texts. The concepts of purity as applied to persons, Olivelle suggests, relate to various transitions through which individual bodies come to be linked to the social body. Concerns with purity and impurity when applied to persons appear as ways of managing boundaries, on the lines of Mary Douglas's (1966) classic work on this theme. The various examples given by Olivelle show, though, that it is through the grammar of purity that external criteria come to be connected to internal states such as that of anxiety. In the context of Madan's remarks about his Kashmiri Pandits being in a state of *śanka* or doubt about their ritual behaviour, one can see that purity or *śuci* links the external and the internal states of a person through a different grammar than, say, the grammar of belief.[1] Tradition is to be understood here as forming a habit memory, expressed in bodily styles and virtues, and not as a system of representations alone.

Two other papers take up the theme of domesticity: McKim Marriott in 'The female family core explored ethnosociologically' and Patricia Uberoi in 'The diaspora comes home: Disciplining desire in *DDLJ*'. Marriott develops his formulations on the ethnosociology of the Hindus by concentrating on the female roles and

[1] I use the term grammar here in the Wittgensteinian sense of philosophical grammar. See Das (1998).

activities in the domestic core. Making a creative use of the rich ethnography produced by women anthropologists on the South Asian family in recent years, he argues that the distribution of roles and the movements between the different positions women occupy can be mapped on the tripartite structure of matching/unmatching, marking/unmarking and mixing/unmixing. For those convinced that Marriott's schemes capture the essential structural features within which all roles and relationships can be plotted, his paper is a serious demonstration that female activities, whether within the household or outside it, move along a limited range of possibilities and that this is what makes households in South Asia recognisable as *South Asian*. To others, an important problem remains. I might try to put the problem, following a puzzle from Wittgenstein (1953), in the following way:

> It is, of course, imaginable that two people belonging to a tribe unacquainted with a game should sit at a chess board and go through the moves of a game of chess; and even with all the appropriate mental accompaniments. And if *we* were to see it we should say they were playing chess. But now imagine a game of chess translated according to certain rules into a series of actions which we do not ordinarily associate with a *game*—say into yells and stamping of feet. And now suppose those two people to yell and stamp instead of playing the form of chess that we are used to: and this in such a way that their procedure is translatable by suitable rules into a game of chess. Should we still be inclined to say that they were playing a game? What right should one have to say so? (Wittgenstein 1953: par. 200).

In other words, a set of actions can always be made to accord with a rule or to contradict it, provided we can give ourselves sufficient leeway in deciding what constitutes obeying a rule, as Wittgenstein demonstrated in his later work. Thus when Marriott assumes that the multidimensional logic he proposes constitutes the *distinctive culture* of the region, the question still remains whether such a definition of culture can be sustained. What is the place of rules in relation to customs, habits and examples, which make the rule livable? These are issues that require sustained debate, but Marriott demonstrates that female practices in the household may be seen as offering a variation on tradition as defined by male roles and relationships. It will be interesting to see how such an ethnosociology, which can translate all actions performed by Hindus over time and space as being in accord with the paradigm proposed by Marriott, may be useful in engaging the vexing questions on pluralism and identity in contemporary India.

The question of tradition presents itself in the paper by Uberoi in the face of the problem of its *dislocation* from its imagined home. The importance of the diasporic imagination in the invention of tradition in places away from home has received much attention in recent years. Uberoi asks, instead, how the home society imagines the place of the diaspora in the invention of tradition? Selecting two recent popular Hindi films with apparent similarity in their treatment of the homecoming diasporic male, she detects an important difference in the manner in which their 'Indianness' is evoked in the sphere of the domestic. Without going into the details of her analysis, I want to point to the interesting issue she raises on the globalisation of desires and sexual practices. There is a complex sexual geography within which the regulation of desires and bodily practices (very much a concern of the state) is seen to index important sites of conflict. The cinematic resolution of these conflicts in the two films functions to calm the anxiety about diaspora and Indianness at the site of the domestic. In the subtext of one of the films, Uberoi says, women speak as critics of the culture of kinship in which there is no place for them as subjects of their own desire. In the case of men, the very sacrifice of their desire serves to enhance their agency as the ones who can author and maintain the traditions of their society. In the second film, it is the problematic desire for diaspora itself which is performed. Uberoi pays rather less attention to the *cinematic*, assuming that the plot and the dialogue can represent how such contradictions are addressed, without reference to image or soundtrack. An interesting move she makes, though, is to interweave the dialogue in the film with the voices of the film stars outside the strict frame of the film though still in the wider context of cinema, as in interviews given to film magazines. Thus the relation between the *star* on the screen and the *type* as it appears in various interviews she cites, becomes a way of addressing how a new medium, such as cinema, can be made to carry the conversation on tradition, both in moments of location and dislocation. Perhaps the question of sexual geography lends itself especially to such a treatment. It is clear that such conflicts over sexual geographies will continue, as witnessed in the recent furore over films such as *Fire* for suggesting a non-normative 'Indian', and more specifically 'Hindu', sexuality.

These essays on the site of the domestic show that pluralism may be both internal to tradition, as in the different male and female ways of inhabiting the domain of kinship seem to suggest, and external to it. This requires attention to circulations *within* a tradition but, as I suggested earlier, also to the possibility of exile, of there being an 'elsewhere' on which tradition may also be constituted. The pain of recognising oneself in change is anchored on new mediums such as cinema, though other regions of the imaginary may also become important sites for this recognition and acknowledgement to occur. The relation between location and dislocation raises important challenges to our understanding of the old problem of continuity and change with regard to tradition.

II
Geography, tradition and identity

The locativity of tradition is analysed in several papers in this volume. If we think of location as the set of cultural practices through which communities create boundaries, then sacred geography provides a rich ground on which to explore the creation of tradition. In Diana Eck's paper, 'The imagined landscape: Patterns in the construction of Hindu sacred geography', we get a dense description of such practices as pilgrimage, the production of sacred texts and the creation of local mythologies. An important feature of this sacred geography, for Eck, is that instead of uniqueness, it values the duplication and replication of sacred space in many different local imaginaries. Thus, sacred landscape does give depth to the idea of nationhood but, as Eck is careful to show, there are many such imaginaries which constitute the grounds on which the belongingness of different kinds of groups is created and performed. 'But the "imagined landscape" of India', she says, 'is not singular, even from the many perspectives clustered under the name "Hindu". And it is important to recognise at the outset that many regional, tribal, and religious groups have never ascribed to this cosmology, either consciously or by tacit assent and have their own "imagined landscapes".... Above all, the past 1,000 years of India's history have also included the flowering of an extensive Indo-Muslim culture with its own mental composition of the land, and with its own imagined landscape....' Eck goes on to describe the intertwining of many of these imagined landscapes in the lived-history and lived-reality of these places. Social and cultural processes occurring on a national and global scale, however, have the potential to alter the manner in which the consciousness of those living in these places is mobilised to create new senses of locality and belonging. The appropriation of the Ramjanmabhumi–Babri Masjid controversy into such global and national projects provides an important example of how local structures of feeling undergo reformulation and even distortion in the denials of difference that they enact as part of their political rituals.

In his important paper on this theme, 'The Babri Masjid and the secular contract', Harold A. Gould provides a fascinating local history of the Faizabad–Ayodhya complex through an analysis of a series of political and legal events. Such an event-centred history shows the complex ways in which locality is created in the context of the wider socio-political processes and the reverse inscription of locality into national events. The destruction of the Babri Masjid has rightly become an important marker in the political debates about secularism and communalism in India, but it also marks a particular way in which locality is violently reconfigured. Gould's method of analysis shows the complex configurations through which locality and memory are co-produced. The political project of creating a hegemonic view of the past through claims over tradition completely dismantles the naive notion that one could ever discern a 'world-view' in some simple way from the locativity of traditions. Thus if the invention of tradition in its dislocation is an important theme for understanding the relation between tradition, pluralism and identity, the violent reconfiguration of locality is equally important for understanding these themes.

The relation between location and tradition are posed directly, of course, in diaspora studies. Instead of looking at diaspora as a new phenomenon, Ravindra K. Jain in his paper on diaspora 'Indian diaspora, globalisation and multiculturalism: A cultural analysis' proposes an organic link between immigration and settlement abroad in the 19th century and migration to industrially advanced societies in the 20th century. Examining the triadic relation between settlement societies, civilisations and the order imposed by colonial regimes, Jain makes use of Furnivall's (1948) discussion of pluralism and especially his notion that plural societies have no common will. There is enough evidence in Jain's discussion, though, that Furnivall's formulation is too simple—that the mutually constitutive relations between civilisational processes and settlement societies (a variant of the relation between great tradition and little tradition)—yield a different frame for the understanding of Indian diaspora. Though new anxieties have arisen about the cultural texts produced in diasporic communities and the relation these bear to their immediate societies and to social formations back home, Jain's analysis invites us to trace the genealogies of such concerns as hybridity, boundaries and multiculturalism in the continuities and ruptures in the formulation of tradition. Whether or not one agrees with Jain's magisterial dismissal of problems of identity as belonging to social psychology, his analysis provides fresh insights into the relation between plurality and tradition through questions of location.

III
In relation to the modern

We now come to one of the most stable oppositions in the social science literature—viz., the opposition between tradition and modernity. Students of Indian society and culture have shown the complex relation between tradition and modernity since the 1960s. Yet the staging of such questions in those earlier decades is decidedly different from the way that the problem presents itself in the last decade of the 20th century, when confidence in such notions as progress and development has been shaken. Particularly important are questions on pluralism, and whether modernity increases pluralism or reduces it by processes of homogenisation and rationalisation. Two papers in this volume, by R.S. Khare and Lionel Caplan, ask how traditional ideas of gift and exchange are to be understood in relation to modern projects of ensuring social justice and human rights in the context of hunger and poverty in India. Khare, in his paper 'The issue of "right to food" among the Hindus', starts with the premise that the discourse on human rights in India is 'culturally alien and socially rootless'. He concedes, though, that the massive public distribution system, through which the state has organised the distribution of subsidised food for the poor, is an important though not a sufficient resource for poor families to survive. In the absence of economic opportunities, the poor have to depend on both, norms of kinship solidarity and entitlements over the state, in order to meet the food needs of the household. Thus norms of gift and exchange have to be seen in alignment with entitlements created by the state. From the perspective of the poor, it is the struggle with daily survival through which questions of minimum rights or human dignity are posed. Khare shows that there are several participating moral economies which provide overlapping networks in which traditional ideas of religious debts, provider-protector economic locations and social duties are deployed. Thus traditional notions of welfare seem to stand in a complex relation to entitlements created by the modern state. In seeking the right to food for all Indians, Khare concludes, 'both Indian traditions and democracy, though horses of different breed, must stay yoked together until they learn to pull as a team.'

Lionel Caplan, in 'Gifting and receiving: Anglo-Indian charity and its beneficiaries in Madras', takes up similar issues—how may ideas of charity be understood in relation to gift-giving in the Indian context? His focus is on poor Eurasians and the organisation of Anglo-Indian charity. Caplan too assumes that in India the poor must take individual responsibility for their plight, and thus charitable institutions come to play a major role in the survival strategies of the poor. His essay shows that some processes in the organisation of charity are similar to those observed in other countries—e.g., the separation between the deserving poor and the lazy, slothful poor. The former are considered fit recipients of charity while the latter either have to be converted into the deserving poor or are abandoned. Though modelled on principles of impersonality and organisational rationality, the Christian organisations engaged in the work of charity seem to have evolved a much more personal style of administration in which Anglo-Indian philanthropists can ensure a close and long-term relationship with their beneficiaries.

In both the essays on this theme we see how the traditional ideas of gift cross over to the modern bureaucratic organisations. Though a close relationship between tradition and modernity in the conduct of public institutions in India is evident, these essays also point to the need for more grounded ethnographic work in this area. For instance, it is not at all clear as to what are the processes through which poor households procure food in the course of the year, what proportion of the total household needs of food is met through the public distribution system, and what by the other means operating in traditional moral economies. By aligning the domestic to the public institutions of state and civil society in such areas as exchange of food and of goods, Khare and Caplan open a new window to the understanding of these issues in the contemporary context.

Two other essays in the volume seem to me to address the issue of tradition in its encounter with modernity: the difference in their orientation to these questions is instructive. Frédérique Apffel-Marglin describes practices of forestry in terms of the antagonistic relation between tradition and modernity. She sees indexing and referentiality as signs of the modern, while multiplicity-generating practices are, for her, the sign of the traditional. The separation between subjects and objects under the constitution of modernity, as Latour (1993) among others has argued, would make the labour of purification typical of the modern. Apffel-Marglin argues that this indexing pushed scientific forestry towards the practices of monocultivation and destroyed the diversity of ecologies sustained by traditional practices. Refusing the easy distinction between sacred and profane as organising the idea of tradition, she shows the varied practices cutting across these divisions in organising the relations between men, women and nature. It would be interesting to see if a similar description of the *practices* rather than the idealised notions of modernity might make this antagonism between tradition and modernity more layered than it is at the moment.

The paper by Arthur Kleinman and Don Seeman, 'The politics of moral practice in psychotherapy and religious healing', pulls us in that direction. In this essay the authors argue that even in its purely technical construction of efficacy, biomedicine has been unable to escape the soteriological concern with healing, to which it is heir. The contrast between psychotherapy and religious healing is not formulated in this essay by the opposition between 'standardised representation of the world' and the 'diversity-generating practices' of tradition, as in Apffel-Marglin's formulation. Instead, Kleinman and Seeman argue that in the Western orientation to the moral there is a fear of the 'loss of the human', the anxiety that the dangerous potential of selfishness and evil in human nature would destroy the capacities to be human. If we compare this with the orientation to suffering and healing in locally grounded moral worlds, we find that the anxiety is not about the loss of some implicit idea of the *human*, but about what is at stake in relationships in the concrete worlds of social actors. Once we shift our gaze to the level of these concrete lived worlds we can see that both biomedicine and religious systems of healing can reify suffering. It is thus in the connections *and* in the discontinuities in the religious and medical ideas of healing and suffering that notions of efficacy are tested. Pluralism is achieved, then, within the complex interrelationships between tradition and modernity—whether in the case of claiming entitlements over the resources of the state or in the case of determining efficacy in healing. Tradition cannot be seen as a residue of pure habit any more than modernity can be seen as forming a complete rupture with the past. Further, both these papers show that we cannot think of modernity as that which comes *after* tradition: in the process of being instituted, it both forms and is formed by the particularity of the contexts in which it comes to be located. It is useful to look at three other essays on the construction of caste identity in the context of locality, for they engage with issues of tradition and modernity on the *locus classicus* for discussing issues of identity in India.

Dipankar Gupta in 'Caste and politics: The presumption of numbers' argues that despite the widespread belief that electoral victories are strongly dependent upon the numerical strength of the castes in a region, the scrutiny of election results does not bear this out. By undertaking a cross-regional comparison, he demonstrates that alliances among castes are not based upon the logic of caste hierarchy, but rather on the secular concerns that go to make up politics. Since the resurgence of identity politics is seen in many parts of the world as a response to the over-rationalisation of life, Gupta urges us to pay close attention to local context—for what might appear to be a case of identity politics reveals on scrutiny many other factors overriding primordial loyalties. Lawrence A. Babb's analysis of the processes through which a new Agravāl identity is sought to be forged in Rajasthan in 'Rejecting violence: Sacrifice and the social identity of trading communities' is in fact a demonstration of the processes through which caste identities are currently being negotiated. Babb shows the resilience of the symbol of sacrifice as a creative force for the production of new identities. He gives a subtle portrayal of how the Agravāl legend that he has studied is sought to be modified and represented in modernist terms—showing how caste identity comes to be placed within the larger political culture of reform and progressive values. We do not find here a straightforward antagonism between tradition and modernity—it is rather the knotting of traditional themes with modern concerns that gives caste its new formations.

Dennis B. McGilvray raises these very issues of pluralism and identity in his three-way comparison of the formation of Muslim identity in Tamilnadu, Kerala and Sri Lanka. He brings the logic of space to bear on formation of caste identity as he shows how divergent cultural styles, ethnic identities and political strategies evolve out of the compulsions of historically distinct events that impact upon locality in distinct ways. The ethnographic portrait of the everyday life of a local Muslim community, closely juxtaposed with Hindu Tamil neighbours in the tumultuous politics of the 1990s in Sri Lanka, shows how local-level relations may be severely distorted—the difficulties of maintaining pluralism stem here not from local hostilities but from the violent production of ethnic identities in the on-going civil war in Sri Lanka. The production of identity in the contemporary world is complicated by the logic of space and the flow of national and transnational technologies and images into local societies. But such issues are not new. Attention to the historical dimension of these flows raises important questions about translation, not only from one place to another, but also across time.

IV
Translations of culture

Stanley J. Tambiah's paper 'What did Bernier actually say? Profiling the Mughal empire' provides an important frame for posing the question of translation. His reading of the travel account of India written by Francoise Bernier in the 17th century provides interesting analogies for framing the issues that concern us today. First, Bernier wrote within the tradition of European political discourse and the axioms about the Orient that he proposed on the basis of 'eyewitness' accounts were in fact inherited from his predecessor's accounts. Second, his formulations on the Mughal 'despotism' had a pedagogic function especially with regard to the importance of private property—its absence in the Orient is what political philosophers in this period saw as responsible for 'tyranny, slavery, injustice, beggary, and barbarism'. Despite such didactic formulations, however, Tambiah argues that Bernier provides evidence of the manner in which arrangements of mutual accommodation were made with a variety of chieftains so that, in administrative terms, the empire was more like a galactic assembly rather than a despotic rule. Thus political practice and theory in India recognised a variety of political constellations and assemblages which accommodated communitarian differences. Tambiah offers this as a different kind of resource for the organisation of memory, a different region of the past, as it were, which is endangered today in the hegemonic projects of creating a singular tradition for a Hindu nation.

An important theme in Tambiah's paper is the proposition that what one writes, even when based upon sensory knowledge, is formed by the tradition within which one writes. Madan has reflected on this set of questions directly in asking how Indian sociology and anthropology might recover the capacity to write from within their own tradition. But what is 'one's own tradition' is not easy to decipher from a set of textual practices alone. For Madan, India is the land not only of *karma*, caste and renunciation, but also of moral responsibility to the present. This responsibility is marked both by a curiosity and a compulsion to seek what is at stake for him in being an Indian anthropologist. Lloyd I. Rudolph engages this aspect of Madan's work most directly in his essay 'Self as other: Amar Singh's diary as reflexive "native" ethnography'.

Rudolph revisits Madan's famous formulation on ethnographic work within one's own society as making the familiar strange, though he had earlier described it as 'living intimately with strangers' (see Madan 1975). In Madan's rendering of this alteration, the 'otherness' towards which he had gestured in the title of his essay was merely a bow to anthropological orthodoxy. In my own reading of Madan's contributions to this theme over the years, I see a palpable tension in his work between tradition as a discipline formulated across different countries and different historical contexts and as located within India.[2] It is the tension and conversation between these two positions that gives enormous power to his disciplinary and social critique. Rudolph's essay on Amar Singh's diary relates the concerns articulated by Madan to a reading of this diary which records events from 1898 to 1942. He argues that this is an example of an early form of ethnographic writing of the kind proposed by Madan, for it is not based upon travel and encounter with the other, but rather with rendering the 'self as other'. Many interesting questions arise in this context. Is locality configured as a didactic site, as in Bernier's account? What is the nature of curiosity that renders the familiar strange? How is identity constructed in the act of writing? Why is the act of recording more about recording social events than one's feelings, emotions and conflicts? How should we see the relation between ethnography and the autobiographical (as distinct from the authorial) voice? Indian sociologists and anthropologists have engaged with these questions in ways that are quite different from the manner in which questions of reflexivity and criticism have been posed in recent discussions in American anthropology. Thus the discipline itself displays a plurality of traditions. It would be interesting to see if, following Madan's lead, one could formulate multiple genealogies of the intersection between ethnography and autobiography as Rudolph attempts in his essay.

V

Tradition and regret: The theme of loss

Already in his reflections on anthropological enquiry, Madan had conveyed a sense of loss, a structure of feeling, in which he argued that non-Western societies

[2] For a stimulating discussion of these issues, see Peirano (1998).

have had their traditions tampered with and eroded or reinvented, sometimes with the help of anthropologists and historians (see Madan 1994: 160–61). This feeling developed later into a full-fledged critique of both secularism and fundamentalism in his much-discussed book *Modern myths, locked minds: Secularism and fundamentalism in India* (Madan 1997). With this book Madan fully engages the relation between anthropology and public culture. Not surprisingly, it has been praised for opening up issues in the spirit of a public exercise of reason *and* critiqued for understating the dangers of the repudiation of a secular polity, especially for political minorities in India. Ashis Nandy in his paper, 'The twilight of certitudes: Secularism, Hindu nationalism and other masks of deculturation', makes a strong case for the evolution of a public culture which is not alien to or dismissive of the way of life of ordinary citizens. He sees secularism as a tired ideology with little to offer in the resolution of the political conflicts that have surfaced with the rise of Hindu nationalism. Paul R. Brass, on the other hand, in 'Secularism out of its place', feels that secularism is a pragmatic solution to the conflicts and tensions between different religious communities rather than an ideology: the danger he sees is that of 'double talk', the tendency on the part of the elite to give formal allegiance to secularism while in practice denying political rights to minorities. Nandy openly avows that his interest is polemical, for what is at stake for him is not academic agreement or disagreement but public intervention. Brass's prose is marked by hyperbolic and didactic statements, rather than a careful weighing of evidence. Thus, the styles in which this debate is engaged signal the mirroring of emotive public concerns in sociological analysis. It is not accidental, then, that 'common sense' holds an important place in this discussion—references are made to 'traditional social and psychological checks against communalism' (Nandy) or to Gandhian ideals amounting to 'nothing but a pipe dream in a country where politicians make a living out of instigating ethnic and religious conflicts' (Brass)—with little attention to the manner in which the everyday life of communities as well as political culture in India is now mired in wider global processes.[3]

It appears that on both sides of the debate on secularism and communalism, there has been rather less attention paid to the manner in which everyday life is

[3] I do not know what to make of such tropes as that of 'abject degrading poverty, illiteracy, and ill health for the overwhelming majority of the people in India and a life of ease and comfort for the corrupt political and bureaucratic classes' used by Brass as a diagnostic category for the ills of India, because it pays little attention to the differentiated picture in the country. Thus literacy rose spectacularly in the states of Kerala, Himachal Pradesh, Punjab, Karnataka, Tamilnadu and even in some districts such as Jaspur in Madhya Pradesh, while continuing to languish in the badly administered states of Bihar, Uttar Pradesh and Rajasthan. Similarly the story of immunisation against childhood diseases shows important differences in controlling infectious childhood diseases in the different states in India. As for the corruption of bureaucrats and politicians—it is not sustainable at the scale at which it occurs without a global economy in which multinational concerns, arms dealers and failures of international law co-produce such corruption. Such facts do not lend themselves to prophetic statements of the kind preferred by Brass, because they require us to be critical in the way in which a physician needs to exercise critical judgement in the process of diagnosis. I owe the distinction between prophetic and therapeutic judgement to the work of Rhinehart Kosseleck.

shaped by media and publicity. What are the different kinds of *publics* created through the discourses on Hindutva, for instance? Is humiliation the dominant public emotion that shapes mass subjectivities in contemporary India? Nandy's paper gestures in these directions, but takes for granted that his formulations on everyday life and citizenship are self-evident.

On the other side, Brass may well be right that he has never met any politician in India who has criticised Hinduism publicly, but does that adequately engage the argument about tradition and loss? It is difficult to imagine that Brass is unaware of the dismissal of all non-European traditions as mere mythologies by reputed philosophers even today.[4] It seems to me that Madan tried to open these questions, and that a further step in this direction would be to demonstrate how legal and political arrangements relate to the evolution of public cultures and the formation of mass subjectivities. Neither the hyperbolic rhetoric of Brass, nor the appeals to some kind of innocence of local moral worlds by Nandy, is sufficient to meet the challenge posed by the complex interweaving of transnational, national and local communities through which subjectivities are produced and circulated today. The question is how this debate might be joined. And this point of uncertainty is a good point to leave as a signpost for future discussions.

It is not conventional for *festschrifts* to include polemical papers but I imagine that Madan's ideas on these themes do provoke strong opinions and emotions. This is a tribute to the many areas he has opened up for discussion in the academic and public spheres in India. My concluding thought is that the vitality of the papers in this volume shows that the many conversational communities with which Madan has been seriously engaged attest to the intellectual vigour he has brought to teaching and research. It is an honour to invite the reader to meander among the many pathways he has opened on questions that are of deep and abiding concern in both the academic life and the political culture of India.

REFERENCES

DAS, VEENA. 1998. Wittgenstein and anthropology. *Annual review of anthropology* 27: 171–95.

DOUGLAS, MARY. 1966. *Purity and danger: An analysis of the concepts of pollution and taboo*. London: Penguin.

FURNIVALL, J.S. 1948. *Colonial policy and practice: A comparative study of Burma and India*. New York: New York University Press.

HUSSERL, E. 1970. *The crisis of European sciences and transcendental phenomenology* (ed. and trans. David Carr). Evanston: North-Western University Press.

LATOUR, BRUNO. 1993. *We have never been modern*. Cambridge, MA: Harvard University Press.

MADAN, T.N. 1965. *Family and kinship: A study of the Pandits of rural Kashmir*. Bombay: Asia Publishing House.

——. 1975. On living intimately with strangers. *In* André Béteille and T.N. Madan, eds., *Encounter and experience: Personal accounts of fieldwork*, pp. 131–56. New Delhi: Vikas Publishing House.

[4] See for instance Husserl (1970) for the view that Indian thought represents the religious-mythical attitude. See also Mohanty's (1992) discussion of the dismissal by Heidegger and Rorty of philosophical claims made on behalf of Indian thinkers as not amounting to philosophy, without any knowledge of the thinkers they seek to dismiss.

MADAN, T.N. 1982a. Anthropology as the mutual interpretation of cultures: Indian perspectives. *In* Hussain Fahim, ed., *Indigenous anthropology in non-Western countries*, pp. 4–18. Durham, NC: Carolina Academic Press.

——. 1982b. Indigenous anthropology in non-Western countries: An overview. *In* Hussain Fahim, ed., *Indigenous anthropology in non-Western countries*, pp. 260–68. Durham, NC: Carolina Academic Press.

——. 1987. *Non-renunciation: Themes and interpretations of Hindu culture*. Delhi: Oxford University Press.

——. 1994. *Pathways: Approaches to the study of society in India*. Delhi: Oxford University Press.

——. 1997. *Modern myths, locked minds: Secularism and fundamentalism in India*. Delhi: Oxford University Press.

MOHANTY, J.N. 1992. *Reason and tradition in Indian thought: An essay on the nature of Indian philosophical thinking*. Oxford: Clarendon Press.

PEIRANO, MARIZA G.S. 1998. When anthropology is at home: The different contexts of a single discipline. *Annual review of anthropology* 27: 105–71.

WITTGENSTEIN, LUDWIG. 1953. *Philosophical investigations*. New York: Macmillan.

2

The imagined landscape: Patterns in the construction of Hindu sacred geography

Diana L. Eck

This is a study of the grammar of signification in the 'imagined landscape' of India, a landscape constructed of the pilgrimage places (tīrthas) *and pilgrimage networks that have long served to create a complex sense of place—locally, regionally, and nationally. Here I provide an overview of the patterns of signification that have generated this symbolic landscape characterised by its polycentricity, pluralism, and duplication. I look at the intricate interrelation of myth and landscape, in which myth 'takes place' in thousands of shrines and in the culturally-created mental 'map' of Bhārata. The symbolic language of the body-cosmos, the* avatarana *from heaven to earth, the multiple patterns of four-*dhāms *and self-manifest* svayambhū *images—all contribute to the shaping of this imagined landscape.*

In first glimpsing the city of Banaras, many a western viewer has compared it to Mecca or Jerusalem as the great centre of Hindu holiness. The British civil servant Norman Macleod typified this response when he wrote in the 1860s:

> Benares is to the Hindoos what Mecca is to the Mohammedans, and what Jerusalem was to the Jews of old. It is the 'holy' city of Hindostan. I have never seen anything approaching to it as a visible embodiment of religion; nor does anything like it exist on earth (Macleod 1870: 20).

The singling out of a centre toward which an entire religious community turns in collective memory or in prayer made sense to Macleod, as it does for many who have been schooled in the habits of thought shaped by western monotheistic consciousness. Even in India there are many people—in previous centuries and in ours—who would concur on the profound significance of Banaras (Kāshī, Vārānasī). Through the centuries, this city has been elaborately articulated both textually and ritually as a *tīrtha*, a sacred ford. But is Banaras 'the' sacred city of Hindus, as Mecca is to Muslims, the centre, the hub, toward which the faithful turn? Closer study makes us wary of such comparisons, for singularity is not the primary marker of the city's significance; indeed, everything about 'the' holy city is duplicated elsewhere, set amidst a pattern of symbolic signification that makes

Banaras not unique, but inextricably part of a wider landscape shaped by the duplication and repetition of its features. It is not the centre, but one of multiple centres in a polycentric landscape, linked with the tracks of pilgrimage.

As I began my own work on Banaras over twenty years ago, I too was embedded in the consciousness Macleod so well represents: a scholar eager to study an ancient and important city and to understand it in the framework of its supposed uniqueness. Only gradually did I discover the cumulative evidence that undermined my own presuppositions. Among its pre-eminent theological claims is that Kāshī is a place where death brings liberation: *Kāshyām maranam muktih.* And yet Kāshī is clearly said to be one of seven cities that bestow moksha (*mokshadāyaka*), including Ayodhyā, Mathurā, Hardvār, Kānchī, Ujjain, and Dvārakā. Kāshī is said to be the earthly manifestation of Shiva's *jyotirlinga*, the *linga* of light, and yet so are at least eleven other places, several of them ardently contested, that constitute the twelve *jyotirlingas.* And quite beyond these twelve are countless other *lingas* celebrated as *jyotirlingas.* Kāshī is circled by a famous circumambulatory route called the *panchkroshī* pilgrimage, with five stops along the circuit. Gradually, I discovered that the *panchkroshī* is not a particular pilgrimage, but a type of five-fold pilgrimage that is also found in Ayodhyā, in Omkāreshvar on the Narmadā, on Mount Brahmagiri in Maharashtra, and in dozens of other places. Kāshī and its *jyotirlinga*, Kāshī Vishvanāth, are also duplicated, with cities and temples all over India called the 'Kāshī of the South', the 'Kāshī of the North', or the 'Secret Kāshī'. Temples of Kāshī Vishvanāth are everywhere, from Mount Ābu in Rajasthan to Tirupparankunram in Tamilnadu. And, of course, the river Gangā is multiplied into the famous 'seven Gangās', including the Narmadā, Godāvarī, and Kāverī rivers, each of which lays claim to the heavenly origin and gracious power of the Gangā of north India.

At first, I tried to resist the complexities of my own peripheral vision, still interested in establishing what makes this one place special, different from the rest. Gradually, it became clear to me that Kāshī could be understood only in the context of a much wider system of meanings in which significance is marked not by uniqueness, but by plurality and duplication. Those things that are deeply important are important enough to be widely repeated. This paper is part of a larger project in which I am exploring the grammar of signification in the pilgrimage landscape of India, an 'imagined landscape' in which networks of pilgrimage places have generated a powerful sense of land and location.[1] Here, I would like to provide an overview of the patterns of sanctification that have created and continue to create

[1] The work nearing completion for publication, *India: The sacred geography of Rose-apple island,* is based on textual traditions of *tīrtha māhātmyas* and ritual traditions of pilgrimage. The term 'imagined landscape' will call to mind some analogies with Benedict Anderson's *Imagined communities* (1983) in which he makes a powerful case for the role of the imagined community in nation-making. In his final chapters he also investigates the role of map-making and modern cartography as representative of a 'colonial style of thinking about its domain'. My project in this book has been to investigate forms of 'map-making' and myth-making indigenous to India through which Hindus have constructed a religious landscape.

a symbolic landscape characterised primarily by its polycentricity, pluralism, and duplication.

The ancient traditions of Buddhist, Jain, and Brahmanical Hindu cosmology have in common a cosmos of ring-shaped islands and seas, centred at Mount Meru, a peak not of granite and snow, but envisioned as the pericarp of a lotus of four petals, its southern petal being India.[2] The river Gangā, the Himālayas, and the many *tīrthas* of India that are duplicated in the landscape are part of this cosmology, which has spread a kind of 'geographical Sanskritisation' in its construction of the imagined landscape of India. The great myths of the Hindu tradition 'take place' in this landscape, and many regional and even tribal traditions have subscribed to this understanding, by attaching the significance of local places and gods to wider Hindu mythic and epic themes: Gangā fell from heaven in this place, Devī slew the bull-demon Mahisha here on this hillock, the Pāndavas stopped here on their journey, or Rāma, Sītā, and Lakshmana stayed here during their forest sojourn.

But the 'imagined landscape' of India is not singular, even from the many perspectives clustered under the name 'Hindu'. And it is important to recognise at the outset that many regional, tribal, and religious groups have never ascribed to this cosmology, either consciously or by tacit assent and have their own 'imagined landscapes'. Some have actively resisted being subsumed in the imagined landscape with its patterns of duplicated mountains, rivers, and *tīrthas*. Above all, the past 1,000 years of India's history have also included the flowering of an extensive Indo-Muslim culture with its own mental composition of the land, and with its own imagined landscape—a land enlivened with the heritage of kings and kingdoms, palaces and gardens, heroes and saints. Especially, the intricate Muslim traditions of devotion associated with the Sufis and intertwined with traditions of Hindu and Sikh *bhakti* have created a landscape of shrines and *dargahs*, with their own cycles and networks of pilgrimage. There are many places where what we have come to call 'Muslim', 'Hindu', 'Sikh', or 'Christian' traditions through the retrojective labelling of history have a lived-history and lived-reality all their own in which devotion has not subscribed to the boundaries of what we call the 'religions'. The *dargah* of Moin-ud-din Chishti in Ajmer, for example, attracts both Hindu and Muslim pilgrims, as does the *dargah* of Saiyid Abd al-Qadir Shahul Hamid Nagoori in Nagore in Tamilnadu, and its virtual neighbour the Catholic shrine of Our Lady of Vailankanni, which participates in a ritual idiom that is shared throughout the pilgrimage networks of Tamilnadu. The Golden Temple at Amritsar has long been the destination of pilgrims both Hindu and Sikh. Local examples of the confluence and layering of religious traditions around sacred sites abound.

Our concern in this paper, however, is with the construction of a pluralistic and widespread Hindu imagined landscape through the process of duplication and multiplication. The contestation over the Rām Janmabhūmi in Ayodhyā in

[2] A full discussion of this cosmology cannot be included in this paper, but is the subject of 'Rose-apple island: India in the lotus of the world', another chapter of the forthcoming work (see note 1).

the past decade raises sharply the question of the meanings of uniqueness and of plurality in the symbolisation of Hindu sacred geography. Slogans pledging to build Rāma's temple 'at that very place' (*hum mandir vahīn banāyenge*) participate in a discourse that is both familiar and yet dissonant if we view it in the wider context of India's complex sacred landscape. The *māhātmyas* and *sthala purānas* of Hindu India's thousands of *tīrthas* do indeed extol and praise 'this very place', and even employ the poetic licence commonly called *arthavāda* to amplify the greatness and glory of 'this very place'. However, these are always set in the context of a wider peripheral vision in which *tīrthas* and their *māhātmyas* are not unique, but ultimately numberless, limited not by the capacity of the divine to be present, but by the capacity of human beings to discover and to apprehend the divine presence. The dissonance, of course, arises from a discourse of exclusivity and uniqueness, more typical of the monotheistic traditions of the west, now arising in a Hindu context in which patterns of religious meaning have traditionally been constructed on the mythic presuppositions of divine plurality and plenitude.

I

Pilgrimage and the storied landscape

For at least 2,000 years, pilgrimage to the *tīrthas* (*tīrthayātrā*) has been one of the most widespread of the many streams of practice that have come to be called 'Hindu'. The *tīrthas* are intricately related to a vast corpus of stories, ancient and modern. These *tīrtha māhātmyas* and *sthala purānas* tell how they became holy and how one will benefit from visiting them. Looking at both pilgrimage literature and pilgrimage sites, what are some of the ways in which holiness is articulated? How does the language of pilgrimage with its 'grammar of sanctification' create a landscape out of this vast corpus of places and their stories?

Wendy Doniger observes in her book, *Other people's myths*:

> A myth cannot function as a myth in isolation; it shares its themes, its cast of characters, even some of its events with other myths. This supporting corpus glosses any particular myth, frames it with invisible supplementary meanings, and provides partially repetitious multiforms that reinforce it in the memory of the group (1995: 31).

Her observations about Hindu myth are equally true of Hindu sacred places—the *tīrthas*, *pīthas*, and *dhāms*. They do not stand alone, in isolation. Even those in the most remote places, in the farthest mountain reaches of the Himālayas, where the rivers rise and the shrines are snowbound half the year, are not isolated, but part of a complex fabric of reference and signification that constitutes a cumulative landscape replete with its own 'invisible supplementary meanings'.

Many Indian scholars have noted the significance of the network of pilgrimage places in construing a sense of Indian 'nationhood', not as a nation-state in the modern usage of the term, but as a shared, living landscape, with all its cultural and regional complexity. For example, T.V. Rangaswamy Aiyengar, introducing the Sanskrit text of the *Tīrthavivecana khanda*, Lakshmīdhara's 12th century digest of pilgrimage places, writes: 'Long before wise statesmanship attempted or accomplished Indian unification, Akhand Hindusthan had sprung from the wanderings of pilgrims'. Aiyengar wrote in the early 1940s in the last years of the Indian independence movement and several decades before new forms of political Hindu nationalism had made scholars more aware of the political resonance, and indeed the exclusionism, of such expressions. He was writing of a 12th century context, but as a scholar also participated in a 20th century context in which pilgrimage to the *tīrthas* had scarcely diminished in importance but had grown considerably with the expansion of mass transportation.

The very idea that the imagined landscape cast by the network of India's *tīrthas* has contributed immensely to the construal of an indigenous Hindu sense of 'nationhood' is articulated today in a political context so charged with the contemporary disputation about 'Hindu nationalism' that it is difficult, but all the more important, to investigate what it has meant historically and what it still means today in the context of Hindu pilgrimage. It is indisputable that an Indian imaginative landscape has been constructed in Hindu mythic and ritual contexts, most significantly in the practice of pilgrimage. The vast body of Hindu mythic and epic literature is not free-floating literature of devotional interest to the Hindu and of scholarly interest to the structuralist, comparativist, or psychoanalytically minded interpreter. Hindu mythology is profusely linked to India's geography—its mountains, rivers, forests, shores, villages, and cities. It 'takes place', so to speak, in thousands of shrines and in the culturally-created mental 'map' of Bhārata.

Just as myth is linked to the land, so the land is alive with mythic meanings and stories. The Vindhyas are not just low-lying hills, but mountains which bowed humbly to the sage Agastya as he approached on his way south, vowing to remain in such a posture until he returned, which he never did. Just as the Gangā is said to have descended from heaven to earth to give life to the dead and purification to the living, the Narmadā is said to rise from the very body of Shiva, and the Godāvarī is said to be the Gangā, falling to earth not in the Himālayas, but on Brahmagiri in the western ghats. The journey of the Pāndavas and the forest sojourn of Rāma, Sītā, and Lakshmana are elaborately inscribed in the land, to such an extent that numberless local shrines and temples subscribe, as it were, to the meta-narrative, linking their own place to the drama as one of the halting places of the five Pāndavas or as one of the kitchens of Sītā. The *līlās* of Krishna are remembered in *līlāsthalas*, the 'places of the Lord's play', dotted throughout the landscape of Braj (see Eck 1981a).

Mapping the land of India has not been simply the domain of the cartographers of empire who have created maps in which Bombay, Banaras, and Rāmeshvaram are equally dots on the map, as Benedict Anderson suggests. In a range of Hindu traditions, map-making has been the domain of both cosmologists and mythmakers, and it is arguable that the imagined landscape they have created is far more culturally powerful than that displayed on the Bartholomew's map of India. The imagined landscape bears imprints of meaning: the self-manifest eruptions of the gods, the footprints of the heroes, the divine origins of the rivers, the parts of the body of Devī. Geography is overlaid with layer upon layer of story. In a broad sense, each village, river, and hillock has a story. Some of them are local, some are linked through their stories to several other regional shrines, and some are linked through these stories to a network of shrines all over India.

Most important, however, is the fact that the landscape is a *system* of reference in which each *tīrtha* functions as part of a whole fabric of *tīrthas*. It is the linking, the network, the duplication, the substitution of *tīrthas* that cumulatively constitute a landscape. Indeed, the internally complex sacred geography of a city like Kāshī is impossible to decipher without placing it in this landscape-system. What, then, are the systematic elements that constitute this landscape? What are those elements that are repeated, duplicated, and classified into networks so as to construe a wider landscape? What are the 'sets' of the system—some ancient, others more recent—that participate in creating a landscape knit together by its repetitions and homologies? My examples here are drawn deliberately from a wide variety of sources—textual and ritual, ancient and modern, from the Rig Veda to the ephemeral pamphlets of today's *tīrthas*, from so-called classics of literature to folk art and wall paintings. What is of interest and significance are the ways of systematising meaning, the symbolic structures by which a sacred landscape is constructed and inhabited.

There are many discernible strategies through which the sacred features of this landscape are established, many distinctive ways in which the divine presence has been experienced, named, and storied. For example, elements of the symbolic landscape descended from heaven to earth, like the rivers, or were retrieved from the sea by the gods, like the coastlands. The divine erupted from the earth like the many *jyotirlingas*, or clung spontaneously to the earth and could not be moved by human hands, like the image of Ranganāthaswāmī at Shrīrangam or the *linga* at Gokarna. The body of the divine was distributed throughout the land by the dismemberment of Satī, evoking the ancient language of the body-cosmos as symbolised by the *yajna*. The gods and temples of the Tamil south are located in the 'five landscapes' of nature—mountain, forest, countryside, seashore, and wilderness. All these ways of speaking of divine presence begin to constitute an imagined landscape, patterned with sacred places.

Duplication is one of the transitive strategies that creates a pluralism of interrelated parts. A piece of the Himālayas is transported to Saurashtra or Tamilnadu; the Gangā falls in Maharashtra or gushes from underground in Orissa; a temple of Kāshī Vishvanāth is re-created in the south or in the west; a *linga* is brought from the Himālayas to the shores of the southern sea. To paraphrase Doniger, this supporting corpus of *tīrthas* glosses every particular *tīrtha*, frames it with invisible supplementary meanings, and provides partially repetitious multiforms that reinforce and amplify its significance from the local to the translocal.

This systematic structuring of the landscape of India is, of course, based on a cosmology in which the entire universe is construed as a system, with its multiple ring-shaped islands and ring-shaped seas, each with its own rivers and mountains.

The *bhuvana kosha* sections of the Mahābhārata and the Purānas constitute a 'directory of the universe', a cosmology and geography.[3] Appropriately, these texts often begin with the story of creation and then proceed to explain the structure of the entire universe. This cosmology is instructive for us in that it establishes a 'systematic geography' in which geographical features are noteworthy not for their uniqueness, but for their repetition in the ordered, systemic whole. As the *bhuvana kosha* texts begin their descriptions of the universe, we are in the imaginative realm of the mythic universe: seven ring-islands circled by ring-shaped seas, variously filled with sugarcane juice, wine, and milk, extending out as far as the mind can reach to the mountains called Lokāloka, the 'world–unworld' divide. Each of these ring-islands features its own systematic geography: each has seven mountain ranges, seven holy rivers, and so forth. Thus Jambudvīpa, our own 'Rose-apple Island' in the centre of the universe, participates in a framework of geography already established in the wider universe. Each of the four petals of this lotus-shaped island centred on Mount Meru has its own set of seven mountain ranges, seven rivers, its distinctive trees and peoples. The pattern of seven rivers is repeated in Bhārata, the southern petal. However, as the *bhuvana kosha* texts move into the description of this India-petal, they move gradually but surely from the realms of mythic geography with their seas of wine and milk to the very particular imagined landscape of peninsular India.

It is essential to investigate the many mythic and ritual strategies for the construction of India's intricately-storied sacred geography if we are to understand the complexity of this imagined landscape and glimpse the power that it has had and continues to have for the many peoples who today call themselves 'Hindu'. In doing so, we implicitly ask whether the lifting up of single *tīrthas* within this complex landscape for unique, singular treatment—as has been the case with the exclusivity of attention to the Rām Janmabhūmi in Ayodhyā, the Kāshī Vishvanāth temple in Vārānasī, or the Krishna Janmasthān in Mathurā—does not run wholly against the grain of a cumulative tradition in which plurality, not exclusivity, is the marker of significance.

II
Beginning at Girnār

A dramatic series of peaks, known today as Girnār, rises from the rolling agricultural land of Gujarat's Saurashtra peninsula. This is one of many places from where we might begin exploring the interconnectedness of India's pilgrimage patterns. Girnār, sometimes called Raivatakagiri in the Sanskrit Purānas, is a mountain shrine including both Jain and Hindu temples, though most of the Gujarati pilgrims would find the either–or distinction of 'Jain' or 'Hindu' an unfamiliar way

[3] A partial listing of the *bhuvana kosha* accounts is as follows: Agni Purāna 108; Bhāgavata Purāna V. 16–19; Brahmā Purāna 18–19; Devī Bhāgavata Purāna VII. 5–7; Garuda Purāna 54–55; Kūrma Purāna 43–44; Linga Purāna I. 48–49; Mahābhārata Bhīshma Parva VI. 6–8; Mārkandeya Purāna 54–56; Matsya Purāna 113; Vāmana Purāna 13; Vāyu Purāna 34; Vishnu Purāna II. 2.

of designating identity. The Hindu temples, one on each peak, are dedicated to the Goddess Ambā, Gorakhnāth, Dattātreya, and Mahākālī. At the base of the mountain are thirteen Ashokan rock edicts, warning against large festivals and animal sacrifices, taking note of the significance of this place some three centuries B.C.E. Indeed, the pilgrim track up the peaks is so well established that it has long since been made into a giant, steep, winding stone staircase, some 10,000 steps in length. This is an ancient pilgrimage, and it participates in a complex skein of meanings. It is one of countless hilltop and mountain-top shrines all over India, many dedicated prominently to forms of Devī, like the many Ambās scattered through the hill country of Gujarat and Rajasthan.

In the textual and ritual language of Girnār we see the use of a number of motifs that are widely employed in the description of Hindu sacred geography. But first, the story: According to a local penny-paperback *māhātmya*, Girnār or Girinārāyana was Pārvatī's brother. Both Pārvatī and Girinārāyana were the children of Himālaya, the mountains personified. Like other mountains in his mythic moment, Girnār originally had wings. Only after Brahmā commissioned Indra to stabilise the earth by cutting off the wings of the mountains did they become known as *achala*, literally 'the immoveable ones'. As the local story goes, when Indra came after Girnār to cut off his wings, Girnār got permission from his father to hide in the sea, but Pārvatī yearned for him and implored the gods to find him. Vishnu, Shiva, and the other gods discerned Girnār's hiding place and sang praises to the sea. For their praises, they received a boon: they asked the sea to retreat a certain distance. So it is, according to the *māhātmya*, that Girnār, a piece of the Himālayas, now rises abruptly from the farming land of Saurashtra, some distance from the seacoast. In order to protect her brother, Pārvatī herself came from the Himālayas to dwell on Girnār as Ambā, the mother of all the earth.

The Himālayas are *devālaya*, the 'abode of the gods', filled with temples and *tīrthas*. The transposition of Himālayan peaks to other parts of India is a widespread motif, creating an entire landscape dotted with mountains transported from the snowy north. Girnār is not the only piece of the Himālayas to be found elsewhere in India and thus to partake of this symbolic duplication. In Tamilnadu, for instance, the two hills of Pālani are said to have been carried from the Himālayas by the *asura* Idumban, who bore them on either end of a long shoulder pole. On the larger of the two hills is one of the six famous shrines of Murugan or Skanda. The hills of Tirumalai bearing the shrine of Shrī Venkateshvara are also acclaimed as transposed Himālayan peaks. Ganesha Rock at Tiruchirapallai in Tamilnadu is called Dakshina Kailās, the Kailās of the South. One of the three hills at Kālahasti in southern Andhra Pradesh is also called Kailās. Mount Gandhamadana, the Himālayan peak in the Badrīnāth area of the far north, is also situated the full span of India to the south at Rāmeshvaram.

The sacred land that emerged from the sea is another motif with wide resonance in Hindu sacred geography. Along the coasts of India there are stretches of land as well as individual *mūrtis* that are said to have emerged from the sea, having long been lost in the waters. The most extensive use of this mytheme is all along the west coast of India from present-day Goa to Trivandrum, a coastland said to have been retrieved from the sea by Parashurāma, one of the avatāras of Vishnu. According to the popular series of myths associated with the river Gangā's descent from heaven to earth, the princely ascetic Bhagīratha led the river across north India to the sea, where her waters filled the seas to overflowing and submerged part of the seacoast, especially the west coast with its lush green low-lying lands and its myriad temples. The sages propitiated Parashurāma to help rescue the land from the sea again.[4] There are many tellings of the tale. Parashurāma stood on the hills of the western ghats and drew back his bow. At the very threat of the great arrow of Parashurāma, the sea god Varuna recoiled in fear and agreed to withdraw from the coastlands. In other tellings, Parashurāma actually shot the arrow, or hurled his battle axe, or threw a sacrificial ladle—and in so doing claimed the land he was able to cover with the strength of his mighty arm.

However the tale is told, people along the western coast say that this is 'Parashurāma Kshetra', the land of Parashurāma. Some say Parashurāma Kshetra is Kerala; others say that it extends from Kanyā Kumārī to Gokarna in what is today northern Karnataka, or that it extends further still up the Konkani coast. In any case, there are countless temples that link themselves to this story: the hill in present day Mangalore where Parashurāma performed austerities; the place at the top of the ghats near Udipi where he stood to shoot the arrow; or the *linga* at Gokarna that was reclaimed after he made the sea retreat.

The *mūrtis* of many shrines are also said to have been retrieved from the sea, to say nothing of the related themes of the retrieval of *mūrtis* from submersion in rivers and tanks, or the retrieval of *mūrtis* that had long been buried in the earth. The theme of the submergence and reappearance of shrines is a major part of the mythology of Dvārakā, the westernmost *tīrtha* in India today, sitting on the seacoast on the Saurashtra peninsula of Gujarat. Dvārakā is a busy pilgrimage town dominated by the great temple of Krishna Dvārakādhīsh, but the ancient Dvārakā, the capital of Lord Krishna in his later years, is said to have been submerged by flood. Not surprisingly, many other important shrines in India are linked to the disappearance of the ancient image of Krishna at Dvārakā. Not the least among them, of course, is Dvārakādhīsh itself. But other places also claim the presence of Dvārakā's ancient Krishna as their own—among them the image of Krishna at Dakor in Gujarat, the image of Krishna at Udipi in Karnataka, at Guruvāyūr in Kerala, and even at Jagannāth Purī in Orissa on the coast of the Bay of Bengal.

The descent of the Gangā from heaven to earth is another widespread symbolic motif recapitulated here at Girnār. Part way up the steep path of stairs to the summit of Girnār's first peak is an ashram and a spring called Gomukhī Gangā. Of course, the Gangā as a whole is duplicated throughout India, with seven major

[4] According to some legends, Parashurāma, the great warrior who was also a Brahmin, gave away the entire earth as a gift to a king. Then, having nowhere to live, he had to reclaim land from the sea.

'Gangās' and numberless other rivers called Gangā, as we shall discuss later. Here at Girnār, however, one particular facet of the river's course is duplicated: Gomukh, the Cow's Mouth, where the Gangā emerges from beneath a glacier in the Uttar Khand area of the Himālayas. Gomukh also has numerous duplications. For instance, on the top of Brahmagiri in Maharashtra, the Godāvarī river has its own Gomukh at the very source of the river. In many temple tanks, the spring filling the tank will issue from a Gomukh spout in the shape of a cow's head: at Gomukh Kund on the steep slope of Mount Ābu or at Manikarnikā Kund in the Himālayan town of Gupta Kāshī, for example. And, of course, the spout that carries the waters of the *abhisheka* out of inner sanctum of a Shiva temple is often called Gomukh, signalling the sanctity of these waters.

Returning again to Girnār, the pilgrims who begin their journey up the ten thousand stair steps at three or four in the morning make four stops along their journey, which they refer to as the *chār dhām*, the 'four *dhāms*' of Girnār: Gomukhī Gangā, Ambājī, Gorakhnāth, and Dattātreya. At each of these stations on the pinacle hills of Girnār, they receive a *sindhūr* stamp on their hands or arms, the signet of having reached each *dhām*. As we will see, the term *dhām* means 'divine abode', and the term 'four *dhāms*' is widely used to signify a pilgrimage of the completed whole. Most widely, it refers to the circumambulatory pilgrimage around the whole of Bhārata's four *dhāms*: Badrināth in the north, Purī in the east, Rāmeshvaram in the south, and Dvārakā in the west: a pilgrimage of encompassment that is widely patterned into India's Hindu landscape.

In this one place, very much a regional pilgrimage place, we begin to glimpse something of the vast systematisation of India's pilgrimage geography through the use of powerful and widely shared symbols. Nothing stands isolated, but each place, each *tīrtha* participates in the references and resonances of a wider system of meanings. Just by beginning in Girnār and examining the ways in which this singular set of peaks in Gujarat participates in a complex grammar of sanctification, we begin to see the patterning of the landscape. There is duplication and transposition—of the Gangā, the Himālayas, the four *dhāms*. There is disappearance and discovery—of Girnār itself, the coastlands of Gujarat, and the whole coast of western India. And beginning at Girnār, we encounter yet another great fact of Indian sacred geography: that there are many overlapping worlds, like the Hindu and Jain shrines on the mountainside—a virtually identical arduous mountain pilgrimage, visiting the 'same' places, and yet calling them by distinctive names and bringing with them distinctive meanings. Beginning at Girnār suggests in a modest way the potential fruitfulness of exploring the interconnected references of the language of place and pilgrimage.

III
Body language: The body of God

No image is as evocative as the body in suggesting the systemic whole—interrelated, with distinctive differences, and yet an organic unity. It is not surprising that the body-cosmos is widely employed in the patterning of India's sacred landscape. The world created in the imaginative vision of vedic, upanishadic, and purānic creation myths is construed as whole, emerging from the unitary *garbha* or egg, in some cases imaged as a cosmic body. It is what I have called an 'organic ontology' in which the symbolism of the body (and, variously, of the seed or the plant) is employed to create an entire worldview (see Eck 1981b for a fuller explication of this organic ontology). The Rig Veda X. 90 image of Purusha—the cosmic person dismembered into the time, space, and order of this world—is profusely employed throughout the purānic corpus in hundreds of mythic transformations. In one example of purānic mythopoesis, Vishnu is himself the Hiranyagarbha, the 'golden egg', containing the whole unmanifest world within his body, and when the world becomes manifest through creation it emerges to become a transformed externalisation of this interior world. In a well-known story, the sage Mārkandeya describes the many *tīrthas* of India as he visits them inside the body of Vishnu, discovering only when he accidentally falls out of Vishnu's mouth that he has been inside, rather than outside in the manifest world (Matsya Purāna 165–66). The bards of the Mahābhārata, in introducing the subject of *tīrthas*, also use the body-image: 'Just as certain parts of the body are called pure, so are certain parts of the earth and certain waters called holy' (Mahābhārata XIII. 3. 16).

In the religious landscape of India, the image of the body is frequently utilised to suggest the wholeness and interrelatedness of the land. The anthropomorphic construal of a whole land as 'mother' or 'father' land is not so unusual, but the extensive systematisation of India's landscape is distinctive and has given force to the symbolism of the body-cosmos. One need only recall the vedic and purānic homologies of sun-eye, mind-moon, veins-rivers, hair-trees, etc., to imagine how naturally the earth's *tīrthas* would have a place in this body. The most striking instance of this is the system of *pīthas*, the 'seats' of the Goddess said to be the various parts of the body of the Goddess, distributed throughout India. As in the mythopoeic image of the Purusha, distributed throughout the cosmos, the distribution of Satī or Shakti creates a paradigmatic system. Like the body, it is a dynamic and fluid system, not a rigid or static one. Just which *pīthas* are part of the group is far less significant than the fact that there is a grouping in which, ultimately, every devī may be said to participate.

The story is contained in the complex myth of Daksha's sacrifice, told in both the Mahābhārata and the purānas. Most of the early versions of the myth focus on the exclusion of Shiva from Daksha's cosmic *yajna*. When Shiva obliterates the sacrificial arena and then restores it by his mercy, all knees are bent and praises directed toward Shiva.[5] Later versions of the myth, however, are directed toward the apotheosis and distribution of Shakti, the Goddess.[6] When the

[5] The most extensive Shiva-centred version of the myth of Daksha's *yajna* is in the Shiva Purāna, where it occupies the entirety of section II of the Rudra Samhitā. It includes many elements also found in shorter compass in the Linga Purāna (I. 99–100); the Bhāgavata Purāna (IV. 2–7); the Skanda Purāna (I. 1.1–5); the Vāyu Purāna (30); and the Padma Purāna (I. 5–11).

[6] This telling is found in the Devībhāgavata Purāna VII. 30 and the Kālikā Purāna 15–18.

enraged Satī gives up her life because of Shiva's exclusion from the *yajna*, it is she who is ultimately praised. In some of these tellings of the tale, the grieving Shiva carries Satī's body all around India, and where the pieces of her body finally fall, the Shakta *pīthas* are manifest. Indeed, the whole of India becomes, as it were, the dismembered body of the Goddess. Two purānas—the Kālikā Purāna and the Devībhāgavata Purāna—describe, each in its own way, the relation of limbs to land: at Hridaya *tīrtha* in Bihar is her heart; at Bhadrakālī in Nāsik is her chin; at Kurukshetra is her ankle; in Vārānasī is her left earring; in the far north-east in Kāmākhyā is her *yoni*, at Kanyā Kumārī in the far south is her back. In some listings of the *pīthas*, there are fifty-one, in others 108. In its dynamic workings 'on the ground', however, this system is open to a multitude of subscribers who would identify their local devī with Mahādevī through the body-cosmos of the Shākta-*pīthas*, creating as many Hindu claimants to the body of the Goddess as claimants to fragments of the true cross in medieval Europe.

As J.N. Tiwari documents in his historical study of the Goddess, the seemingly endless textual lists of multiple devīs long precede the imaginative vision of Mahadevī's body-cosmos (1985: 2, 13–20, 21–40). In a sense, however, these lists of devīs also begin to cast a mental map of devīs with countless local names—east and west, north and south. The groupings of *pīthas*—whether four, fifty-one, or 108—have been documented by D.C. Sircar in some of the earliest Tantric texts in the 8th or 9th centuries, reaching their most elaborate form with the *Pīthanirnaya* in the 17th century. By this time, the body-land construed by the myth of the dismemberment of the goddess Satī was surely well known, with the parts of the devī-body linked to the *pīthas* of countless locales (Sircar 1973).

In this perspective, the whole of India adds up to the body of the Goddess, for dismemberment and distribution is a form of universalisation. Satī, distributed in the landscape, is not dead, but alive, not broken, but whole. As one Hindu nationalist writer put it in the 1920s, '. . . India is not a mere congeries of geographical fragments, but a single, though immense organism, filled with the tide of one strong pulsating life from end to end' (Mookerji 1921: 39). Some historians, political scientists, and interpreters of the modern period in India have traced the language of 'Bhārat Mātā' to Bankim Chandra Chatterjee's 'Bande Mātaram', its early 20th century usage in the opposition to the partition of Bengal and in the subsequent rise of new forms of Hindu nationalist politics, but such a view of its history lacks a longer historical perspective. It is clear that the identification of devīs with the land has much older roots in the symbolisation of the body-cosmos as inscribed in the land through its system of devī shrines. A considerable history of pilgrimage to the multitude of India's hilltop, cave, and cliff-side devīs preceded the use of the rhetoric of the mother-land in 20th century Hindu nationalism.

The building of Bhārat Mātā temples, first in Banaras, then in Hardvār and elsewhere, displays in concrete form the imaginative vision implicit in the body-cosmos. The simplicity of the Banaras temple makes the point in a powerful way: the marble relief map of India is the *mūrti*, so to speak, which visitors to the temple circumambulate, in what amounts to a two-minute four-*dhām* pilgrimage.

In the more recent Hardvār temple, a key-pad next to the map permits one to light up the four *dhāms*, the seven moksha-giving cities, the twelve *jyotirlingas*, a group of *shākta pīthas*. A bountiful Bhārat Mātā stands above the scene, holding a handful of grain and a pot of water. In New Delhi at the headquarters of the Vishva Hindu Parishad, a niche in the courtyard displays a different version of the image: the Goddess Durgā superimposed on a relief map of India. Such images which so clearly 'read' the relation of land/devī are disquieting in the context of the politicisation of Hindu symbolism in today's India, but it is important to recognise that this body-cosmos is not a new image, but a very old and pervasive one, which is precisely why its power can be so effectively deployed.

The body-landscape is expressed in a multitude of other ways as well—literary and artistic, classical and popular, from the well-known interior visualisations of the Tantric traditions to the esoteric interpretations of the *panchkroshī* pilgrimages as corresponding to the various concentric 'sheaths' or *koshas* of the human body. 'On the ground' in the *tīrthas* of India, such conceptions are also visible. In Ujjain, for example, at Shiva's great Mahākāla temple, there is an enormous wall painting portraying Shiva, in giant anthropomorphic form, blue and four-armed, superimposed on a map of India. The twelve *jyotirlingas*, the *lingas* of light, are marked on this body-map montage—his head in the Himālayas near Kedārnāth and his feet astride peninsular south India near Rāmeshvaram. Although the twelve are not identified with parts of the divine body, the message pairing the whole of India with the whole of Shiva is clear. Ujjain, the home of the Mahākāleshvar *jyotirlinga*, is close to dead-centre in India and explicitly uses the language of the *nābhi*, the navel, to describe its centrality and sanctity. Local *māhātmyas* credit the Varāha Purāna: 'Shiva is honoured under the name of Mahākāla in Nābhidesha, the "Land of the Navel".'

At one of the *jyotirlingas*, the northernmost Kedārnāth, a local story typifies regional uses of the body-image to create a landscape: the primary site of Kedārnāth is but one of Five Kedārs. After the great war of the Mahābhārata, so the story goes, the Pāndavas struck out into the Himālayas to seek purification for the sin of killing their own kin in battle. They had come to the mountains before, when Arjuna scaled the heights of heaven to receive divine weapons from Shiva. Now the battle was over, the weapons had been used, and the Pāndavas were seeking purification for the sin of fratricide. When they approached Shiva at Kedārnāth, he took the form of a bull and dove headlong into the earth. Thus, the portion of Shiva that can be seen in the rocky out-cropping of the Kedārnāth *linga* is but one of five parts of Shiva; the whole encompasses a large region of the Himālayas, where his body-parts protrude at five places—Tunganāth, Madhyameshvar, Rudranāth, Kalpeshvar, and Kedārnāth.

To conclude this discussion of the body as a patterning system, we should also recall that the imaging of space as the manifest body of the divine is found not only in geography, but in the symbolic space of temples, which are architectural 'embodiments' of the divine. The homology of body–temple–land–universe can be extensively illustrated in textual and ritual, historical and modern sources. The important point here is that this body-cosmos creates a system of meanings in which India's *tīrthas* also participate.

IV
Avatarana: *Divine descent*

Divine descent from heaven to earth creates yet another system of meanings. The words *avatarana*, *avatāra*, and *tīrtha* come from the same verbal root [*tr*] meaning 'to cross over'. The language of crossing creates a world of descending and ascending, linking heaven and earth, this world and yonder. The most famous of the divine descents are the *avatāras* of Lord Vishnu, but the notion of descending, *avatarana*, is common to many gods, and of course to the rivers. *Tīrthas* are literally the 'crossings' or 'fords' where one crosses the other way—to the far shore of river, or to the far shore of the heavens. While many *tīrthas* are, indeed, river-fords, they have become, more significantly, spiritual fords. The language of crossing has a wide symbolic reference: from the descending and ascending flow of life between this world here below and the worlds of heaven above to the ultimate crossing of the 'river' of birth and death to the 'far shore' of liberation. *Tīrthas* are fords because there such crossings may be made.

The rivers are the great descenders. Many of India's great rivers, the Gangā foremost among them, are said to have crossed over from heaven to earth. According to the popular story, the Gangā was originally a divine river streaming across the heavens. Through the asceticism and prayers of the sage-king Bhagīratha, she agreed to descend from heaven to earth to raise the dead ancestors of the Ikshvaku line of kings. To break the force of her fall, Gangā fell first upon the hair of Lord Shiva in the Himālayas and then flowed across the plains of north India. Other sacred rivers, such as the Godāvarī and the Narmadā, repeat this pattern of divine descent. The Narmadā flows from the body of Shiva at Amarakanthak in the hills of eastern Madhya Pradesh. The Godāvarī, brought to earth by the prayers of the sage Gautama, descended on the top of Brahmagiri in the western ghats of what is today Maharashtra. Today the Godāvarī makes her official appearance in a mountain-top well; a short distance away is a small shrine housing a long ripple of rock, the very hair of Shiva that broke her fall from heaven. Further down the mountain, a cliff-side shrine is called Gangādvār, the 'Door of the Gangā', a name which is also used for Hardvār, where the Gangā enters the plains of India in the north. The Godāvarī is often called Gangā Godāvarī and Dakshina Gangā. As a saying attributed to the Brahmā Purāna puts it: South of the Vindhya mountains the Gangā is called Gautamī (after the sage Gautama), while north of the Vindhyas she is called Bhāgīrathī (after the sage Bhagīratha). The two rivers are symbolically the same river—repeated, duplicated in two geographical settings. And so it is that temple tanks all over south India are called Shiva Gangā, and wells, like that at Viraja in Orissa, are said to be linked directly through underground streams with the Gangā.

In investigating how systems of geographical meaning are constructed, India's rivers are important, for they are not simply individual rivers, but are part of a system of rivers. They are linked together in groups—like the seven Gangās. They commonly issue from the 'same' place—the Gomukh. They are knotted together in braids—like the many *trivenīs* or 'triple-braids' where a confluence of two rivers is joined by a third, the deep symbolic waters of the underground Sarasvatī, which long ago vanished from her visible, earthly riverbed. The best known *trivenī* is at Prayāga, but there are other *trivenīs* all over India that express the triple confluence of rivers. In sum, India's rivers are joined by the inter-referential symbolic language of their heavenly origins, their sources, confluences, and mouths. Indeed, wherever waters drip from a pot above a *linga* of Shiva in the sanctum of a temple or are poured lavishly upon the shaft of the *linga*, the *avatarana* of the Gangā might be said to be ritually repeated.

The idea that India's sacred rivers are fundamentally seven in number—all purifying and heavenly in origin—is very old in Indian lore. The river hymns of the Rig Veda speak of the seven 'mother-rivers' or the seven Sindhus, calling them all by the name of the mightiest, the Sindhu, now called the Indus. They are called 'goddess-waters' and are praised as purifying, nourishing, cleansing, never-sleeping. The heavenly waters are released by Indra from Vritra's blockade as mother cows might be freed from the pen to nourish their young, suggesting even in ancient times what has become a well-known homology: that of rivers and cows, waters and milk.[7] The seven rivers in these early times are identified with the 'five rivers' of the Punjab (literally, the 'land of the five rivers') plus the Sindhu and the Sarasvatī. These were all rivers of north-west India, the first land of the Aryan seers.

The Gangā and the Yamunā rivers of the plains of central north India were eventually incorporated into this group of seven. When the extensive mythology of the Gangā was elaborated, the notion of the seven divine rivers continued in the popular myth of her descent from heaven: the Gangā herself split into seven branches—three flowing east, three flowing west, and one, the Bhāgīrathī, flowing south into India. These seven Gangās watered not only India, but in this vision of things, the whole inhabited earth. Still later came the notion of what are today called the *sapta nadī*, the 'seven rivers' of India, sometimes called the 'seven Gangās': Gangā, Yamunā, Sindhu, Narmadā, Godāvarī, Krishnā, Kāverī.[8] This group of seven rivers is invoked into ritual waters of Hindu worship all over India and, today, all over the world in the temples and homes of the Hindu diaspora. Many of the rivers are said to have been individually constituted by seven tributaries or to have split into seven streams. For example, as the Gangā forms in the Himālayas

[7] The comparison to mother cow's milk and mother's milk is made in X. 9 and X. 75, for instance, and Indra's role in forging the channels of the rivers is noted in X. 47 and X. 49.

[8] See the *Kalyān Tīrthānk* (1957) for a listing of the seven rivers. Some contemporary formulations preserve the Sarasvatī instead of the Krishnā, as in the invocation of rivers in ritual found in the *Nitya Karma Vidhi* (1977: 56): *Gange ca Yamune caivā Godāvarī Sarasvatī; Narmade Sindhu Kāverī jale' smin samnidhim kuru.*

it is said to have seven tributaries, representing the waters that were dispersed as the heavenly river flowed through the tangled mass of Shiva's hair. In the Tamil south, the Kāverī river is said to split into seven mouths at its delta as its flows out into the Bay of Bengal.

The rivers of India provided a litany of names by which the mind's eye traced the land. The whole scheme of seven sacred rivers with their headwaters in seven ranges of mountains came to constitute an important part of a systematic geography—a thoroughly ordered imaginative world extending from the outer reaches of the imagination to the rivers and mountains of India's present topography. As Radhakumud Mookerji wrote in an essay on *Nationalism in Hindu culture* published in 1921: 'As the mind of the devotee calls up in succession the images of these different rivers defining the limits of his country, it naturally traverses the entire area of his native land and grasps the image of the whole as a visible unit and form' (1921: 21). Even when local rivers substitute for one or more of the seven, as they often do, the mental construction of an imagined landscape watered by divine rivers remains. The specific rivers may change, but the structure of duplication and its resonances links these rivers, however enumerated, into an ordered whole coextensive with the locale, the region, the land of Bhārata, and even the wider universe.

V
The Four Dhāms—*A four-fold dwelling*

If the word *tīrtha* conveys a sense of crossing, the term *dhām* (Sanskrit *dhāman*) contains the meanings of dwelling, clearing, and light. When *dhām* is used, it suggests not so much that we 'cross over' to the divine, but that the divine dwells amongst us, right here. Jan Gonda, who has studied in detail the uses of this term in the ancient vedic literature (Gonda 1976), writes that a *dhāman* may be described as both the location and the refraction of the divine, a place where it manifests its power and where one experiences its presence.[9] The very notion of a *dhāman*, a divine abode, conveys to us that the sacred takes form, is located, and is apprehended. In the vedic ritual context this meant, for example, that the fire god Agni's *dhāman* was the fire altar, the place where the *tejas* or luminous power of Agni was manifest.[10]

[9] Gonda speaks of a *dhāman* as the '"location", of a numen, of divine power, of a deity, i.e. not only or merely a "holder" or "receptacle" of divine power, a place, being or phenomenon in which a divinity sets or locates itself, functions or manifests itself, or displays its power, or where its "presence" is experienced, but also a particular way of presenting or revealing itself, of locating or "projecting" a mode of its nature and essence, a hypostasis or refraction in which it is believed to be active' (1976: 19ff). He notes that the suffix '*man*' denotes some 'power concept' as in numen; *karman*, *bhuman*—a locative power. He further explores the close relation of *nāman* and *dhāman*, name and place. Gonda compares this to the Hebrew sense of God's 'glory' as present in the temple. God's name dwells in a place. 'On this place I put my name' (Deut. 12.5, I Kings 9.3).

[10] See his discussion, for instance of Rig Veda 10.45.2: 'We know thy *dhāmani*, O Agni, distributed in many places . . .' (1976: 24ff).

As the term comes to use in the systematisation of sacred geography, there are four famous *dhāms* in India, sited at the four compass points of the land. The modern proliferation of *stutis, māhātmyas*, and ritual enactments of the *chār dhām* motif is one of the most extensive ways in which a systematic geography has been construed. The standard four claim virtually unanimous agreement. In the north is Badrīnāth, the Himālayan shrine now associated with Vishnu, sitting on the banks of the Ālakanandā river, one of Gangā's tributaries, within a few miles of the Tibetan border. In the east is Purī, the abode of Krishna Jagannāth whose temple on the Bay of Bengal is one of the largest temple complexes in all of India. In the south is Rāmeshvaram, the Shiva *linga* said to have been dedicated by Rāma, Sītā, and Lakshmana after having defeated the demon Rāvana in Lankā.[11] In the west is Dvārakā, the latter-day capital of Lord Krishna, where Krishna dwells as Dvārakādhīsh.

The *chār dhām yātrā* is one of the most popular in India, for it takes pilgrims on a circumambulation of the whole country.[12] There are still Hindu pilgrims—sannyasins, widows, householders, and others—who have walked the *chār dhām* pilgrimage on foot, but today it is most commonly undertaken by chartered bus, even by 'video-coach'. The imagined landscape of a circuit of India can be seen even in the pilgrimages described by the sages Pulastya and Dhaumya in the Mahābhārata, some two thousand years ago, though their specificity about the *tīrthas* of the south is extremely sketchy. While the individual *dhāms* have been visible in purānic textual sources for at least a thousand years, and perhaps longer, the notion of the *chār dhām* is not one we find in the older purānic literature. The traffic of the devout—north, south, east, and west—is present, but not under this particular name, at least as far as I am aware. Nonetheless, today's pilgrimage tracts speak of the *chār dhām* as 'established during prehistorical ages'.[13] For those in the Hindi-speaking regions in particular, this is a very popular pilgrimage, as can be affirmed from the presence of Hindi language publications in the heart of Tamilnadu at Rāmeshvaram.

One of the myriad Hindi booklets on the *Chāron Dhām Yātrā* begins with a discourse on the religious nature of the land of Bhārata, with its great sages who filled the world with peace and its unbroken tradition of reverence for *tīrthas*, even in times of subjugation. It understands the four-*dhām* pilgrimage to be an expression of this Indian religiousness. The guidebook tells us, 'Some people come to Badrināth after having already visited the three other *dhāms*. And some,

[11] In some of the many mythic versions of the origins of Rāmeshvaram, the *linga* is established by Rāma and his party before crossing the 'bridge' to Lankā.

[12] There are, of course, other forms of what has been called *digvijaya*, the 'conquering of the four directions', for example, four *pīthas* said to have been established by Shankarāchārya in his tour around India. The *mathas* or monasteries somewhat correspond to the four *dhāms*: Dvārakā in the west; Jyoshimatha near Badrīnāth in the north; Purī in the east; and Sringeri (as well as Kanchipuram) in the south. As A.K. Shastri puts it in his book *A history of Sringeri*, 'The idea of establishing these *mathas* in four different corners of India was to bring about national integration which Sankara perhaps had then in his mind (1982: 4).

[13] For instance, N. Singh, in the introduction to *The call of Uttrakhand* (n.d.).

at the time of their pilgrimage to Badrīnāth, set their minds on taking water from Shrī Gangotrī to offer in the temple at Rāmeshvaram'.[14] As is usually the case with pilgrimage in India, there is little rigidity about the precise form the circuit takes. It depends on one's own *bhāvana*, the disposition of the heart. Badrīnāth is the hardest to get to, since the others are easily accessible by train and Badrīnāth requires a road journey into the mountains. Until recently it was a long and arduous journey by foot, but now there is a motorable road all the way. Even so, it is not an easy journey. At one point, the author of this pilgrim tract reveals a schema for thinking about the *chār dhām*: Badrī is the *dhām* of the Satya Yuga, the perfect age of the beginnings. Rāmeshvaram is the *dhām* of the Tretā Yuga, when Rāma reigned on earth. Dvārakā is the *dhām* of the Dvāpara, when Krishna held forth. With the Mahābhārata war and the death of Krishna began the Kali Yuga, a difficult age for human religiousness. Jagannāth Purī is the *dhām* of the Kali Yuga.

As we have come to expect, the *chār dhām yātrā* is a complete pilgrimage—four-fold, as signalled by the four directions—and is widely duplicated in local and regional pilgrimages. Many of the same Hindi pamphlets published in Hardvār that celebrate the four *dhāms* of India also praise the four *dhāms* of the Himālayas: Badrīnāth, Kedārnāth, Gangotrī, Yamunotrī. In rural Chitrakut where Rāma, Sītā, and Lakshmana are said to have halted in a forest ashram there are also four *dhāms* to be visited. We have already noted the four *dhāms* of Girnār in Saurashtra, and Ann Gold's research in Ghatiyali in Rajasthan cites a local *chār dhām yatra* in a village in which few people aspired to visit the four *dhāms* of India. In Ghatiyali, the exact four may vary. 'More important than who are named,' writes Gold, 'is the popularity of the concept' (Gold 1988: 36).

VI
Svayambhū: *Self-manifest divinity*

The language of the divine as 'self-manifest' in the natural environment also contributes to the symbolic grammar of sanctification that casts a landscape. The term *svayambhū*, 'self-existent', is used to describe countless places and images in which the divine is said to have appeared miraculously, or some would say naturally: without human intervention or supplication. '*Apne āp prakat hui*', they say in Hindi. 'It appeared here of its own accord.' The notion that agency in establishing the presence of the divine is not human, but divine, is widespread. These natural manifestations are not established by human hands or by royal patronage, but are the spontaneous eruptions of the divine, whether as Shiva, Vishnu, Devī, or a local divinity.

One of the commonly shared myths of self-manifestation is that of the *jyotirlinga*, the '*linga* of light', appearing from below, spanning earth, the sky, and the heavens above.[15] The term *jyotirlinga* is used to describe the appearance

[14] *Chāron Dhām Mahātmya* (n.d.: 12).

[15] The myth is told twice at the beginning of the Shiva Purāna: I. 5–12; II. 1.6–9. See also Linga

of many of India's most powerful Shiva *lingas*–especially the group of twelve stretched throughout India, cited in both the Linga Purāna and Shiva Purāna. Some of the *jyotirlingas*—Kedārnāth in the Himālayas, Vaidyanāth in Bengal, and Tryambakeshvar in Maharashtra, for instance—are outcroppings of rock around which temples have been constructed. Some are *pārthiva lingas*, temporary 'earth *lingas*' fashioned of clay by a devotee. In *jyotirlinga* myths, these simple earthen *lingas* provide the occasion of devotion for Shiva to step forth into that very place with his full presence. At the request of his devotee, Shiva pledges to be forever present there, and the *pārthiva linga* is transformed from the most transient to the most transcendent of images—the world-spanning shaft of light.

Geographically, these twelve are located throughout the length and breadth of India, linked to the fractionless (*nishkala*) luminous form of Shiva. As we have seen, a modern painted image in the Ujjain temple of Mahākāleshvar shows the body of Lord Shiva superimposed on the map of India. In introducing the twelve, the author of a popular Hindi pamphlet on the *jyotirlingas* draws his own conclusions: 'From all over India these twelve *jyotirlingas* have come to be especially important, and in this our symbolic, religious, and national sense of unity is vested' (Jayasval n.d.: 2). He cites the twelve: In the north is Kedār. In the Gangetic plain is Kāshī Vishvanāth and, further east in Bihar, Vaidyanāth. Along the Narmadā river in central India are Mahākāl and Omkāreshvar. At the headwaters of the Godavarī is Tryambak. Nearby in the Deccan and along the western ghats are Ghushmeshvar and Bhīma Shankar. In the far west in Saurashtra are Somnāth and Nāgesh. In the east, along the river Krishna, is Mallikārjuna. And in the far south is Rāmeshvaram.

Shiva is often cast in five-fold form—homologised to the five sounds of the syllable Om, and so it is that many of these *jyotirlingas* spread beyond their temples to a wider embodiment in the land. Kāshī Vishvanāth, for instance, is really the *panchkroshātmaka linga*, a geographical embodiment taking five days to circumambulate. In Kedār, the 'five Kedārs' extend the divine embodiment of Shiva throughout the high mountain country of the Himālayas. Ujjain, like Kāshī, is a city of many temples where the real *jyotirlinga* of light is not so much the single icon of Mahākāleshvar, but a whole area, a *kshetra* or field, with its own *panchkroshī* pilgrimage. Omkāreshvar's temple is on an island in the Narmadā river, the whole of which is inscribed with a 'circumambulatory' trail called the *panchkroshī* pilgrimage in which pilgrims literally trace out the syllable Om with their feet as they walk the path. From the temple of Tryambak in Maharashtra, pilgrims climb a steep bluff to the top of the five-peaked mountain called Brahmagiri. Repeating the five-fold symbolic structure we have seen, these five peaks are said to be the five faces of Shiva, and the whole mountain is called Shiva *svarūpa*—Shiva himself. In all these places, the five-fold presence of Shiva is inscribed in the landscape.

Purāna 17. 17–21; Kūrma Purāna I. 25.62–111; II. 31.1–31; Skanda Purāna I. 3.1.1–2; I. 3.1.6; I. 3.2.9–15; VII. 3.34; Vāyu Purāna 55.1–68. I have discussed the *jyotirlingas* in 'Shiva and Shakti in the land of India' (Eck 1982).

Special stones are also self-manifest images of the divine. Keep in mind that in consecrated images—made by the hands of the artisan—divine presence is established and the *prāna*, the breath of life, imparted to the image in the rites of *prāna pratishthā*. A *svayambhū* image, however, has no need of *prāna pratishthā*. Symbolically speaking, the divine breath is already there and has been there from time immemorial. Certain stones are always *svayambhū*. The *shālagrāmas* found in the Gandakī river in Nepal are natural manifestations of Vishnu, sacred without so much as a mantra of invocation. And so are the stones found along the beaches of Dvārakā called *Dvārakā chakras*, the 'wheels of Dvārakā' pure white stones imprinted with intricate wheels, the emblems of Vishnu. Likewise, *bāna lingas*, the smooth stones found in the bed of the Narmadā river, are natural embodiments of Shiva.

Beyond these natural manifestations, there are countless local stones, rocks, outcroppings, and *mūrtis* that are called *svayambhū* by the acclamation of those who worship them. For example, the small jet black image of Krishna as Rādhā Raman in Brindāvan, the smooth stone form of Kāmākhya Devī in Assam or Vaishno Devī in Kashmir, or the local folk image of Draupadi at the cult centre of Gingee in Tamilnadu are all spoken of as *svayambhū* (for the latter see Hiltebeitel 1988: 66–67). Self-manifest images are especially powerful in attracting pilgrims, whether locally, regionally, or nationally. Our point here, however, is not to enumerate the multitude of such divine manifestations, but to call attention to the grammar of sanctification through which a landscape is created. The language of self-manifestation participates richly in the creation of an imagined landscape.

VII
Pratishthā: *Sanctification by adhesion*

The final mode of sanctification we will explore here is related to patterns of self-manifestation: the divine is manifest not through eruption, but through spontaneous adhesion. When an image of the divine is established in a temple, the rites of consecration include not only *prāna pratishthā*, but also the attachment of the image to its pedestal in the *garbha griha*, binding stone upon stone with the strongest of adhesives. But certain powerful images, we are told, adhere spontaneously to the earth. Here is yet another symbolic device through which a divine landscape is construed.

All over India there are *mūrtis* and *lingas* said to have adhered fast to this place or that by spontaneous natural fusion of divinity to place. For instance, the hills of Pālani in Tamilnadu, which Idumban carried on a shoulder pole from the Himālayas, are said to have stuck to the earth the moment he put them down. In the many myths of this sort found in local *māhātmyas* or *sthala purānas*, someone puts the image down, and it cannot be moved again by any amount of muscle or effort. At Vaidyanāth in Bihar, the local *māhātmya* tells the story: The powerful Rāvana was returning from the Himālayas to Lankā with a *linga* given to him by

Shiva as a reward for great *tapas*. Rāvana had been told, however, that he must not put the *linga* down en route. The gods were understandably fearful that if Rāvana established such a powerful *linga* in Lankā his *asura* kingdom would become even stronger. As a result, they conspired to have him put the *linga* down on the way. By design of the gods, Rāvana experienced the acute feeling of having to relieve himself, and he set the *linga* down to attend nature's call. When he returned to pick it up again, it would not budge. Vaidyanāth today claims to be one of the twelve *jyotirlingas* and attracts pilgrims from all over north India.

A similar story is told of the Gokarna *linga* hundreds of miles to the south-west along the coast of Karnataka. As Rāvana travelled with the *linga*, evening came and he had to perform his ritual duties, for he was a piously observant *asura*. Therefore he gave the *linga* to a boy—actually Ganesha in disguise—to hold while he bathed in the ocean and performed his evening rites. But the image proved too heavy, and Ganesha put it down. When he returned, Rāvana tried so hard to remove the *linga* forcibly from the place where it stuck that he twisted it. The form of the Gokarna *linga* today is that of a piece of solid reddish rock, twisted like an old stump.

At Shrīrangam, the island shrine of Vishnu at Tiruchirapallai in Tamilnadu, it is said that Vishnu's image as Ranganāthaswami had been given to Vibhīshana, Rāvana's brother, by the royal household of Rāma in Ayodhyā. Again, Vibhīshana was told not to put the image down. Even so, when he came to the beautiful Kāverī river he was overwhelmed with the desire to bathe. He gave the image to a Brahmin boy, again Ganesha in disguise, and the boy agreed to hold it for him, under the condition that Vibhīshana would come promptly if he called for him three times. When Vibhīshana was under water, taking his dips in the Kaverī river, the boy called out. Of course, Vibhīshana could not hear. The boy put down the image of Ranganāthaswami, and so it is that the image has been worshipped in the island temple of Shrīrangam ever since.

A final example may be found at Rāmeshvaram. Here it is said that Rāma sent Hanumān to the Himālayas, or alternatively to Kāshī, to bring a *linga* to establish in honour of Shiva at the site called Setu, the 'bridge', where Rāma's armies had crossed the sea to Lankā to fight the armies of Rāvana and retrieve Sītā. When the auspicious hour for consecrating the *linga* arrived, however, Hanumān had not yet returned. Thus Sītā fashioned a *linga* of sand and the rites of consecration proceeded. When Hanumān finally returned, he wanted to replace the sand *linga* with the fine stone *linga* from the north. Try as he did, however, even wrapping his tail about it to pull with all his might, Hanumān was unable to remove the sand *linga*. So the fine Himālayan stone *linga* was established as well, side by side with the sand *linga* that could not be moved.

A 17th century version of divine adhesion to the land also attends the establishment of Krishna as Shrīnāth-jī in Rajasthan. During the reign of the emperor Aurangzeb, the Pushti Mārgī devotees placed the image in a cart and took it from its site at Mount Govardhana in Braj, seeking a safe place in Rajasthan to establish a temple. According to legend, the cart got stuck in the mud at the place north of Udaipur known today as Nāthdvāra. No human effort could make the wheel move, and the mishap was taken as a sign that the image of Shrīnāth-jī wanted to stay right there where the great Nāthdvāra temple exists today.

The multitude of such stories suggest a kind of chosenness, a divine selection that powerfully creates a local sense of 'place'. Whereas many of the *svayambhū* images of the self-born divine are held to have been manifest in response to the unstinting devotion of *bhaktas*, here the principle of selection seems to be ascribed to the affinities of the god. It is a divine reversal of the *ishtadevatā* principle, for here the divine power does the choosing. In many of these stories it seems that the fusion of god and earth could, in principle, take place anywhere. If twilight had come a few minutes later, Rāvana could have stopped for his *samdhyā* rituals along the coast of Kerala or near the mouth of the Kāverī. But once the contact with earth has been made, god is there to stay.

VIII
Myth on earth

This brief survey has explored the ways in which patterns of sanctification have created a strong sense of the imagined landscape—locally, regionally, or on an all-India basis. Whether the divine is present on earth by divine descent, divine eruption, or divine adhesion, these forms of sanctification participate in the creation of a landscape of polycentricity and duplication, no matter how deeply the heart's devotion may be attached to a particular place or manifestation of the divine.

Both mythology and topography provide for people and cultures the 'maps' of the world. Obviously, to speak of an 'imagined landscape' is not to speak of something fanciful, for the imagined landscape is the most powerful landscape in which we live. No one really lives in the India displayed on the Bartholomew's map, nor in any other two-dimensional graph of the world. Such a map can locate our hometown, or the route we followed from Rishikesh to Gangotrī, or the rail line from Rāmeshvaram to Madurai, and there is no question of its utility. But all of us, individually and culturally, live in the mappings of our imagined landscape, with its charged centres and its dim peripheries, with its mountain tops and its *terrae incognitae*, with its powerful sentimental and emotional three-dimensionality, with its bordered terrain and the loyalty it inspires, with its holy places, both private and communally shared.

The extent to which mythology and topography overlap or diverge in the shaping of an imagined landscape is a critically important question for students of religion, culture, and politics today. Does the land, with its rivers and mountains, bear the powerful symbolic charge of myth? Are the myths and the gods people live by linked to the land in which they live? What kind of worldview is shaped by the maps and the myths of the imagined landscape? The question of location has been a continuing issue in the Jewish tradition, for example, which is highly locative and yet has had a long history of adapting to the realities of singing the Lord's song in a foreign land. The culture of China has also had a strongly locative sensibility, with a clear sense of both centre and periphery. More 'ecumenical' traditions like Buddhism, Christianity, and Islam have travelled widely across cultural regions, developed multiple cultural forms, continually composing a more universal mapping of the world.

In India, the inscribing of the land with the prolixity of Hindu myth is so vast and complex that it composed a radically locative worldview. The profusion of divine manifestation is played in multiple keys as the natural counterpart of divine infinity, incapable of being limited to any name or form, and therefore expressible only through multiplication and plurality. The land–god homologies create a multitude of imagined landscapes, lived-in maps, among the many peoples who might speak of themselves as Hindus, but they have in common an imagined landscape constituted by such homologies whatever they may be in personal, local, regional and national terms. The challenges of diaspora have loosened the locativity as Hindu communities reconstitute temples and negotiate new identities in new lands. And yet to some extent, the experience of reconstituting Hindu communities in the west has created yet a further duplication of the patterns of sanctification found in India—the Kāshī Vishvanāth temple in Flint, Michigan; the Shrī Venkateshvara temple in Pittsburgh; the Shree Meenakshi temple in Houston; and the whole of south India's sacred geography recapitulated in the Shiva–Vishnu temple of Lanham, Maryland.

The imagined landscape may coincide with the kind of imagined community Benedict Anderson speaks of as a 'nation', or it may not. Many of the tensions described as 'communal' in modern India arise from the challenges of bringing into being the imagined community of a multireligious, secular nation-state in the context of multiple, though overlapping imagined landscapes. The Indian national anthem, *Jana Gana Mana*, names an imagined landscape, reciting the evocative names of the regions of India, circling from the Punjab, to the south, and back to Bengal, and reciting the names of mountains and rivers—the Vindhya and Himālayas, the Yamunā and Gangā. Even as the mind's eye circles India, people of multiple communities will imagine different, but overlapping landscapes. 'Vindhya, Himāchala, Yamunā, Gangā . . .' will be evocative in very different ways to those of the north and south, to Hindus, Muslims, and secular environmentalists. This paper has attempted to illumine some of the particular ways in which it is evocative for Hindus because of the elaborate patterns of inscribing myth on earth.

REFERENCES

AIYENGAR, T.V. RANGASWAMY. n.d. *Tīrthavivecana khanda.*

ANDERSON, BENEDICT. 1983. *Imagined communities.* London: Verso.

Chāron Dhām Mahātmya. n.d. Hardvār: Harbhajan Singh and Sons.

DONIGER, WENDY. 1995. *Other people's myths.* Chicago: University of Chicago Press.

ECK, DIANA L. 1981a. India's *tīrthas*: Crossings in sacred geography. *History of religions* 20, 4.

———. 1981b. The dynamics of Indian symbolism. *In* Peter Berger, ed., *The other side of God*, pp. 157–81. New York: Doubleday.

ECK, DIANA L. 1982. *Shiva and Shakti in the land of India.* Gambier, Ohio: Larwill Lectures in Religion Series.

GOLD, ANN GRODZINS. 1988. *Fruitful journeys: The ways of Rajasthani pilgrims.* Berkeley: University of California Press.

GONDA, JAN. 1976. *The meaning of the Sanskrit term Dhāman.* Amsterdam: N.V. Noord-Hollandsche Uitgevers Mattschappij.

HILTEBEITEL, ALF. 1988. *The cult of Draupadi.* Chicago: University of Chicago Press.

JAYASVAL, RAMKISHAN. n.d. *Jyotirlinga Mahimā.* Baravah: Rajahamsa Prakashan.

Kalyān Tīrthānk. 1957. vol. 31, 1. Gorakhpur: The Gita Press.

MACLEOD, NORMAN. 1870. *Days in north India.* Philadelphia: J.B. Lipincott & Co.

MOOKERJI, RADHAKUMUD. 1921. *Nationalism in Hindu culture.* London: Theosophical Publishing House.

Nitya Karma Vidhi. 1977. Bareli: Samskriti Samsthan.

RADHAKUMUD, MOOKERJI. 1921. *Nationalism in Hindu culture.* London: Theosophical Publishing House.

SHASTRI, A.K. 1982. *A history of Sringeri.* Dharwad: Karnataka University.

SINGH, N. n.d. *The call of Uttrakhand.* Hardvar: Randhir Book Sales.

SIRCAR, D.C. 1973 [1950]. *Sakta pithas.* Banaras: Motilal Banarsidass.

TIWARI, J.N. 1985. *Goddess cults in ancient India.* Delhi: Sundeep Prakash.

3

Caste and purity: A study in the language of the Dharma literature

Patrick Olivelle

The caste system, according to the currently prevalent view, is based on purity, each caste being located on a hierarchical gradation of purity, a thesis laid out most compellingly by Louis Dumont. It has generally been assumed that purity is the basis of hierarchy in ancient India. This paper examines the ancient texts on Dharma relating to purity and social hierarchy and finds that the texts establish no link between the two and that they rarely, if ever, refer to purity as an abstract condition or state. The language of purity itself is multifaceted, containing numerous terms with significant differences in meaning, and it makes a clear distinction between persons and things. With respect to persons, the vocabulary clearly indicates that the focus is not on any permanent, or even transitory, condition of purity but rather on the transition from impurity to purity, on the recovery of lost purity; the dynamic meaning dominates the use of the major Sanskrit terms for pure.

With this volume on the theme of tradition, pluralism, and identity, we celebrate the lifelong achievements of Professor T. N. Madan both as scholar extraordinaire and wonderful human being, a man who is as secure in his own identity when he is talking with a villager in Kashmir as when he is addressing a scholarly audience in Texas. The Indian tradition down the centuries, however, has managed pluralism primarily within the context of interlocking group identities, the most basic of which is caste. And the caste system, according to the currently prevalent view, is based on purity, each caste being located on a hierarchical gradation of purity. The higher the caste the greater the degree of purity.

This thesis was laid out most boldly and most compellingly by Louis Dumont in his seminal work *Homo hierarchicus*, first published in 1966. Purity, according to Dumont, is the basis of hierarchy in traditional India and is, therefore, the ideological principle behind the caste system. Quigley (1993: 1), in his critique of the Dumontian thesis, acknowledges that the prevalent view among both Hindus and outside observers considers castes to be 'hierarchically ranked on a purity–pollution scale'. Madan (1989: 365) himself states that 'according to traditional

Acknowledgements: I want to thank James L. Fitzgerald, who read this paper carefully and gave valuable suggestions and criticisms.

caste ideology, which is obviously the brainchild of Brahmins, the key to the rank order lies in the notion of ritual purity.'

Dumont's thesis has not gone unchallenged. In a 'Review symposium' published just four years after the appearance of *Homo hierarchicus* and organised by Madan with contributions from ten scholars,[1] several critiqued the central point of Dumont's thesis that caste is based on purity. McKim Marriott's (1990) efforts to construct an 'Indian ethnosociology' using what he terms 'Hindu categories' are in large part directed against Dumont. In the same volume Nicholas Dirks undertakes a frontal attack on Dumont's thesis, claiming that in his own ethnographic work he has 'found that purity and pollution are not the primary relational coordinates which endow hierarchy with its meaning and substance' (Dirks 1990: 61). In his recent book Quigley (1993) likewise challenges the premise that caste is based on the gradation of ritual purity.

The connection between caste and purity that is at the heart of Dumont's thesis, furthermore, appears not to be based on ethnographic data. This is a point asserted repeatedly by reviewers, and it is the basis for Dirks' (1990) critique. Madan (1971: 9) remarks that the ethnologists 'complain of his [Dumont's] attitude to empirical evidence' and acknowledges Dumont's 'devaluation of the ethnographic datum', but he notes:

> What distinguishes this work from the usual social anthropological discussions of caste is that it does not proceed from fieldwork to a model of how the system works. Instead it begins with a cardinal explanatory principle—hierarchy—and boldly sets out to build a model thereon, throughout maintaining the position that theory or ideology overrides and encompasses ethnography.... Models, therefore, are not to be judged as true or false but as possessing more or less explanatory power.

Yet Dumont cannot invoke the principle of hierarchy and its basis in purity totally a priori; they must be derived in some way from the evidence of how the Indian society functions or from the native social ideology. So, if not ethnography then what is the source of such evidence? Some think that his source is Sanskrit texts. Berreman (1971: 22–23) explicitly states that Dumont 'relies heavily on some classical Sanskrit texts while ignoring others' and concludes that his thesis 'conforms well to the theory of caste purveyed in learned Brahmanical tracts. But it bears little relationship to the experience of caste in the lives of the many millions who live it in India.' Von Fürer-Haimendorf (1971: 24) notes Dumont's 'expertise in classical Indology'.

Are the classical texts of Brahmanism, then, the inspiration behind Dumont's 'model' of the caste system? These texts, especially the technical literature on

[1] Madan (1971). Besides Madan, the reviewers were E. Leach, G.D. Berreman, C. von Fürer-Haimendorf, R.S. Khare, V. Das, J.S. Uberoi, J.C. Heesterman, D. Kantowsky, and M. Singer, with a response by Dumont. Especially critical of Dumont's thesis are Berreman, Veena Das, and Uberoi. For a recent defence of purity as the basis of caste from a psychoanalytic perspective, see Dundes (1997).

Dharma (*Dharmaśāstra*), however, recognise only the division of human society into four *varṇas*. Their social ideology is based on *varṇa* and not on caste (*jāti*), castes being subsumed under *varṇa* ideology as hybrid forms. Leach (1971: 15) appears to hint that Dumont's ideology is borrowed from the Brahmanical theory of *varṇa* when he remarks on

> Dumont's insistence that the structure of *jati* organization which is "out there", external to the observer, is integral with the structure of *varna* hierarchy. . . . As anthropological outsiders we need to pay close attention to the *varna* system because it helps to make sense of the facts on the ground and, in turn, continually forces the facts on the ground into a coherent pattern.

Brahmanical scholarship is consistent on this point, and the technical literature on Dharma continues to focus on *varṇa* as the basis of Indian society throughout the medieval period and right up to modern times.

In Dumont's (1980: 66–91) own treatment of *varṇa*, however, he states clearly that although *varṇa* and *jāti* are both based on hierarchy divorced from 'power', the *varna* hierarchy is not based on the pure and the impure (1980: 66, 73). So, according to Dumont, on this crucial point the two systems of social hierarchy in India diverge. And yet he acknowledges that much of the caste ideology, which Madan (1989: 365) calls 'the brain-child of Brahmins', is derived from the *varṇa* ideology. We are then faced with not just a theoretical or ideological problem but with a historical question: when and how did caste ideology of purity/impurity emerge out of the *varna* hierarchy?[2] The historical question is raised by Madan (1971: 12): 'It is not clear, however, at what time Dumont believes the crucial structural elements of the caste system, as presented by him, to have crystallized.' Is it plausible, furthermore, that the same Brahmin intelligentsia that kept purity out of the *varṇa* hierarchy would have made it the cornerstone of the caste hierarchy?

Even though, as Dumont himself acknowledges, *varṇa* hierarchy is not based on a gradation of purity/impurity, nevertheless the same Brahmanical social thinking that developed the *varṇa* ideology also placed great emphasis on purity, creating intricate and minute rules on pollution and purification. These rules and the ideology underlying them have not been subjected to thorough scholarly scrutiny.

An important way to get a handle on that ideology, I think, is to study the vocabulary of purity/impurity in these texts. Scholars regularly use Sanskrit equivalents in dealing with purity under a tacit assumption that this will somehow take us closer

[2] Another question is the ideological basis of the *varṇa* hierarchy, a question Dumont never fully answers except to draw a distinction between 'dignity' and 'power' and the separation of status from power. The mythical legitimisation of the *varṇa* division is, of course, contained in the Puruṣa Hymn of the Ṛg Veda (10.90) which portrays the creation of the four *varṇas* from four parts of the creator's body and posits thereby a biological (racial/genetic?) basis for *varnas*. The early vedic texts, however, indicate that raw power was a central ingredient in *varṇa* hierarchy, illustrated by the metaphor of food and eater, the lower *varnas* being the 'food' of the upper *varnas* (see Smith 1990).

to the reality on the ground.[3] Yet, there is no single term in Sanskrit for either the substantives 'purity/impurity'[4] or the adjectives 'pure/impure'. The existence of a large number of terms in a language for a broad area of human experience is prima facie evidence for that area being central to that culture and for its nuanced and often technical treatment by that culture. It is interesting to note, however, that, despite the enormous amount of writing on the concept of purity in India, there has been no sustained and detailed study of the Sanskrit (or other vernacular) terms for 'pure/impure'. That is what this paper attempts to do within the confines of the ancient Dharma texts in an attempt to uncover the complex ways in which they deal with the category today subsumed under 'purity'. This is an exercise in philology in the best sense of the word, a philological study that is context-sensitive and therefore refuses to reify anything,[5] least of all words, and examines the changing patterns of word usage that opens a window into the changing reality of the social world lying behind the language. Such a study may also throw some valuable light on the ongoing scholarly debate about the caste system and contribute to the cross-cultural study of purity and pollution, to which I will return in the concluding section of this paper.

I
The vocabulary of pure/impure

The principal terms for pure/impure in the Dharma literature belong to seven families,[6] some of which contain several individual terms with their own nuances and technical meanings. For convenience I introduce each family under its most prominent representative in the order I treat them.[7]

1. *śuci—śauca, aśuci, āśauca*
2. *śudhyati (śodhayati, śodhana)—śuddhi, śuddha, aśuddha*

[3] See, for example, Marriott (1990: 33). Madan himself is concerned about the use of the modern English term 'purity' to describe the lived reality of Indian life:

> I use deliberately, but only as far as seems reasonable, the Sanskrit words *śubha* and *śuddha* instead of 'auspiciousness' and 'purity'. The former two words or derivatives from the same are in use in most languages of India. My hesitation in using the two English words throughout the chapter arises from the fact that they have become omnibus words and conceal more than they reveal (Madan 1988: 49–50).

[4] The abstract term 'purity', as we will see, is absent in the vocabulary of Dharma texts.

[5] Marriott's (1990) use of the term 'Hindu' is misleading, pointing as it does to a reified and unchanging substance or category. There is a similar reified use of 'Hindu' with reference to food in Khare (1992), about which I have written elsewhere (Olivelle 1995). On the context-sensitive nature of Indian culture, see Ramanujan (1990).

[6] I have ignored a few terms, such as *kalmaṣa*, which in the Dharma literature always refers to moral turpitude or sin: **A** 1.22.4; 1.24.25; 1.28.18; 1.29.1 (the last three repeat the same expression); **B** 2.4.5; **Va** 28.6 (same as **B**); **M** 4.260; 12.18; 12.22; **Vi** 1.36; 23.60; 52.14; **Y** 3.218.

[7] So as not to make matters more complex than they already are, I have not treated separately compound terms, such as *viśuddhi* and *pariśuddhi* (and other compounds with the prefixes *vi-*, *pari-*, etc.). These, as far as I can tell, do not add new meanings or nuances, except to make the term more intensive. So *pariśuddha* or *viśuddha* may mean 'purified to an extraordinary degree'.

3. *prayata—aprayata*
4. *pūyate (pūta, apūta)—pavitra, pāvana*
5. *ucchiṣṭa*
6. *medhya—amedhya*
7. *mala (amala/nirmala)*

Let me make a few general comments before proceeding to a more detailed analysis of each term. First, a grammatically negative term (e.g., *aśuci* or *amedhya*) is not always simply the opposite of the positive; negatives often develop their own semantic overlay, creating highly technical meanings. This is a common phenomenon in Sanskrit as witnessed by the well-known term *ahiṃsā*, whose meaning goes well beyond what may be expected from the simple negative of *hiṃsā*.

Since there is considerable semantic overlap between several of these terms, the use of one in a particular text or context may not always be of special significance. Often the selection may be based on the exigencies of metre (in verses), or on alliteration and other 'sound effects'. There is the danger of 'reading too much' into a word. In this study, I have tried to survey a broad sampling of cases before determining whether nuances and technical meanings are attached to particular terms in particular contexts or by particular authors.

In my discussion of individual terms, I will focus on several significant questions. Does a term refer: (*a*) to a person or to a thing; (*b*) to a condition (that is, to a person or thing *being* pure, or more generally to the abstract 'purity') or to a transition (that is, a person or thing *becoming* pure, the recovery of lost purity); (*c*) to what we have come to call 'ritual purity', to common cleanliness, or to the areas of morality and criminal law (four areas that are not always as cleanly distinguished in our sources as in our own minds); (*d*) to an individual in his own existential being or to a class or group (or to an individual as part of a group)? The resolution of these questions, I believe, is important not only to our understanding of ancient Indian world views and ritual practices, but also to the ongoing debate on the role of purity in caste identity and hierarchy.

For a diachronic study of the terms for pure/impure we need both an absolute and a relative chronology of the Dharma texts. Unfortunately, as is the case with most ancient Indian literature, we cannot place certain or accurate dates against any of these texts. In footnote 8 I give a tentative chronology that may be of some help for those unfamiliar with this literature.[8]

[8] Kane (1968) gives the following chronology: Gautama 600–400 B.C.E.; Āpastamba 450–350 B.C.E.; Baudhāyana 500–200 B.C.E.; Vasiṣṭha 300–100 B.C.E.; Manu 2nd century B.C.E to C.E. 2nd century (I would place him closer to the later than the former date); Viṣṇu 300 B.C.E–C.E. 100 (the current inflated text C.E. 400–600); Yājñavalkya C.E. first two centuries; Nārada C.E. 100–300; Vaikhānasa C.E. 300–400. This sort of chronology is a mere house of cards without too much supporting evidence. My own opinion is that, whatever may be said about the original versions, with regard to the texts as we have them now, Āpastamba is the oldest, followed by Gautama, Baudhāyana (although this text has undergone extensive additions), and Vasiṣṭha, all probably composed between the 4th and 1st centuries B.C.E. Then come Manu, Nārada, Yājñavalkya, Viṣṇu, and Vaikhānasa in no particular order (see Lariviere's comments, N, vol. 2, pp. xix–xxii; Manu is probably the oldest of this

Within the confines of this paper it is not possible to discuss fully and in detail every occurrence of these terms in the Dharma literature. I will confine myself to presenting illustrative examples for each major meaning or nuance, relegating to the charts attached to each family of terms the exhaustive listing of the evidence.

1. *Śuci*

The term *śuci* is an adjective derived from the verbal root *śuc* and in its earliest usage meant 'shining, bright, white'. By the time of the early Dharma texts the term had acquired its traditional meaning of 'pure', although more literal meanings continued to coexist.[9] As its primitive meaning indicates, *śuci* alludes to a positive quality (bright, pure) in a subject, and its dynamic meaning refers to the regaining of this lost quality. In contrast, we will see that *śuddhi* refers directly to the getting rid of impurities, the positive quality being indicated indirectly as the result of such purification. For the sake of clarity, I give below four significant areas in the semantics of *śuci*.

1. An important distinction our texts make is between the purification of persons and of things, such as vessels, seats, or a piece of ground.[10] *Śuci* is the most common term for 'pure' with reference to persons.[11] When a text wants to make this distinction clear, it invariably uses *śuci* (or its derivative *śauca*: see section 1.2) for persons and *śuddhi* for things. The use of separate terms points to an ideological distinction between persons and non-persons in the area of purity.

Gautama is the first author to use the expression *dravyaśuddhiḥ* ('purification of things'). He introduces the section (**G** 1.29–34) on the different methods for cleansing articles made of metal, clay, wood, and so forth with this expression (**G** 1.29) and distinguishes that from personal purification, *śauca* (**G** 1.35), a topic he deals with in the very next section (1.35–45). This distinction is brought out most clearly by Manu. In the first chapter he gives a table of contents which lists *śaucam* and *dravyāṇāṃ śuddhiḥ* (**M** 1.113) as two separate entries, the former referring to personal purification and the latter

group), all of them composed well into the common era, although Viṣṇu contains sections belonging to an old *sūtra* text.

[9] Kālidāsa, in his *Ṛtusaṃhāra* (1.2), for example, calls 'summer' the hot season, *śuci*. References in the Dharma texts to god as *śuci* probably have the meaning of bright or shining: **A** 1.22.7; **B** 1.104; 1.13.2. Interestingly, the word 'pure' itself is derived from the Indo-European root for fire, from which is derived the Greek *pyra* and English 'pyre' and 'fire', as well as the Sanskrit *pūyate* (see section 4 on *pūyate*).

[10] In this study I make the broader distinction between persons and 'non-persons', the latter including animals, objects, activities (e.g., rites), bodily discharges, and detached parts of the human body, such as hair and nails. Within the category of 'person' I include 'pure' used with reference to the human body (*śarīra*) or bodily parts (*aṅga*), such as hands and mouth.

[11] *Āpastamba*, possibly the earliest Dharma text, uses *prayata* (see section 3) in preference to *śuci* with regard to personal purity, using the latter mostly in its second meaning. This *may* indicate a development of the purity vocabulary within the Dharma tradition. It may, however, be simply a matter of personal preference or idiosyncrasy, or even a regional difference in the vocabulary.

to the cleansing of things. In the body of the text he maintains this distinction with a verse that concludes his discussion of personal purification and introduces the next topic, the purification of things: *eṣa śaucasya vaḥ proktaḥ śārīrasya vinirṇayaḥ / nānāvidhānāṃ dravyāṇāṃ śuddheḥ śṛṇuta nirṇayam* // ('I have explained above the settled practice regarding the purification of the body. Listen now to the settled practice regarding the cleansing of things') (**M** 5.110). This distinction is also evident in a rule that prohibits vedic recitation when a person finds that 'the ground where the recitation takes places is unclean or he himself is impure': *svādhyāyabhūmiṃ aśuddhām ātmānaṃ cāśucim* (**M** 4.127).

Throughout the Dharma literature, the term for 'pure' within the sections on personal purification is invariably *śuci*. Even outside these sections, *śuci* most frequently refers to the purity of persons rather than of things (see Figure 1: A.l.a–b).

Śuci is not used *exclusively* with reference to people, however, although this is its primary sense. It has a broader application; animals, clothes, mines, and water are said to be *śuci*. The most frequent use of *śuci* outside the context of persons, however, occurs in the set phrase *śucau deśe* ('in a clean [or cleansed] place') with reference to the area where a ritual act is to take place (see Figure 1: A.2.b).

2. The connection of *śuci* with persons carries over into the area of morality and personal character. Thus, in many contexts, especially in the appointment of ministers and other public officials, *śuci* is used with the meaning of 'upright', 'honest', 'loyal', 'trustworthy'—that is, a man of character and integrity. The king 'should appoint Āryas who are upright and honest to protect his subjects' (*āryañ chucīn satyaśīlān prajāguptaye nidadhyāt* [A 2.26.4]). The king himself, as well as his ministers, officials, supervisors of mines and gambling houses, ambassadors, judges, and witnesses in a court should be *śuci* upright (Figure 1: A.1.c).
3. In the area of criminal justice *śuci* means 'innocent', although this meaning is recorded only in the somewhat late texts of Manu and Nārada. A man who has undergone an ordeal successfully is said to be *śuci* (**M** 8.115). A king's power is demonstrated by that fact that his word can make a guilty person (*aśuci*) innocent (*śuci*), and vice versa (**N** 18.49).
4. When *śuci* is used with the first meaning, it most frequently indicates 'purification' or 'becoming pure' rather than 'being pure'; that is, *śuci* indicates that a person has *become* pure through some purificatory activity (see Figure 1: A.l.a). This usage, together with its counterpart in *śuddhi* (see section 2.1), shows that the concern of Dharma authors was with the constant struggle to recover lost purity rather than with some abstract notion of 'purity' that may attach to persons or groups.

This dynamic meaning is most evident in the expression *śucir bhavet* ('he becomes pure') coming at the end of the description of purificatory rituals. Thus, after he has bathed in and drunk a mixture of cow's urine, cowdung,

Figure 1

A. śuci

1. Person:
   a. becoming pure: **A** 2.18.6 (?); **G** 1.40; 9.2; 26.21; **B** 1.6.15; 1.8.23; 1.8.24; 1.8.25; 1.11.38; 1.11.41; 2.5.18; 4.2.8; **Va** 3.41; 10.31; 23.31; 29.21; **M** 2.51; 2.107; 2.176; 4.35; 5.106; 5.143; 8.87 (twice); **Y** 1.131; 1.195; 1.225; 2.99 (?); 3.21; 3.26; 3.51; **Vi** 22.89; 23.49; 23.55; 66.15; **N** 12.87; 20.17; **Vkh** 1.3; 2.11.
   freed from sin: **Y** 3.245; 3.257; 3.303.
   b. being pure: **B** 1.10.5 (twice); **M** 5.106; **Y** 1.187; **Vi** 22.89 (thrice).
   c. morally upright: **A** 2.15.11; 2.25.13; 2.26.4; **G** 11.4; **B** 2.14.6; **Va** 2.9; **M** 2.109; 2.115; 5.106; 7.22; 7.31; 7.38; 7.60; 7.62; 7.63; 7.64; 8.77; 9.188; 9.335; **Y** 1.28; 1.121; 1.309; 1.312; 1.322; 1.355; 2.191; **Vi** 3.71; 29.10; **N** 1.133; 1.209; **Vkh** 3.5 (?).
   d. criminally innocent: **M** 8.115; **N** 18.49 (twice).
   e. god: **A** 1.22.7; **B** 1.10.4 & 1.13.2.
2. Non-persons:
   a. becomes pure: **Va** 12.15.
   b. is pure:
   place (*śucau deśe*): **A** 1.11.23; 2.4.23; 2.18.6; **G** 1.36; **B** 1.8.11; 2.5.21; **M** 2.222; 3.206; 5.68; **Y** 1.18; 1.227; **Vi** 61.17: **Vkh** 3.5.
   others: **B** 1.9.2; 1.9.3; 1.9.6; 1.13.1 (re. sacrifice); 1.13.4; 3.5.2; 3.9.2; **Va** 3.47; 14.27; 21.14; 28.8; **M** 5.130; 5.131; 9.70; **Y** 1.187; 1.191; 1.192; 1.193; **Vi** 23.49; 23.50; 23.52; **N** 18.42.

B. śauca

1. Purification:
   a. person: **A** 2.15.12; **G** 1.35; 1.42; 9.25; 9.71; 14.44; **B** 1.6.2; 1.6.15; 1.7.1 (twice); 1.8.1; 1.8.3; 1.8.4; 1.8.11; 1.8.52; 1.8.53; 1.14.19; 2.4.5; 2.11.24; 2.15.11; 3.1.25; 3.1.26 (twice) **Va** 4.35; 4.37; 6.17; 6.19; 11.28; 12.17; 19.47; 28.6; **M** 1.113; 2.61; 2.69; 3.126; 3.192; 4.93; 4.148; 4.175; 5.94; 5.97; 5.98; 5.100; 5.106 (twice); 5.110; 5.137; 5.139; 5.140; 5.146; 7.145; 9.11; **Y** 1.15; 1.17; 1.71; 1.98; 1.209; 1.232; 3.29; **Vi** 22.26; 22.89 (twice); 22.93; 23.42; 60.24; 60.26; 91.18; **Vkh** 2.9 (twice); 3.4.
   b. thing: **B** 1.14.16; **Va** 3.48; 3.53; **M** 5.114; 5.118 (twice); 6.53; **Vi** 23.34 (divine image).
2. Virtue: **G** 8.23; 10.51; **Va** 6.23; 11.35; **M** 3.235; 6.92; 10.63; 12.31; **Y** 1.122; 3.66; 3.137; 3.313; **Vi** 2.16; **Vkh** 1.4; 2.4.

C. aśuci

1. Person:
   a. impure: **G** 16.46; **B** 1.6.14; **Va** 4.38 (? sinner); 5.6; **M** 4.71; 4.127; 4.142; 4.143; 5.75; 5.76; 5.79; 5.81; 5.84; 5.86 (?); **Y** 1.135; 1.149; 3.30; **Vi** 96.26; **Vkh** 2.14; 3.3; 3.4;
   b. morally bad (sinner): **A** 1.21.12; 1.21.19; 1.29.14; 1.29.15; 1.29.17; 1.29.18; 2.12.22; **G** 9.11; 9.16; 23.22; **B** 1.10.5; 2.2.15; 2.2.23; 2.2.24; **N** 14.24.
   c. guilty: **N** 18.41; 18.49 (twice).
2. Non-persons:
   a. impure (adj.): **B** 1.9.6; **Va** 4.23; 14.30; **M** 4.124; **Y** 1.149; **Vi** 70.17; 98.70; **N** 18.42; **Vkh** 3.5.
   b. filthy substance (noun): **A** 1.2.29; **M** possibly 5.86; **Vi** 5.106; 60.13; **N** 5.6.

D. āśauca (aśauca)

Period of impurity: **G** 2.3; 14.1; 14.23; 14.29; 16.18; **B** 1.11.1; 1.11.18; 1.11.19; **Va** 4.9; 4.16; 4.23; 4.31; 4.34; 4.36; 23.24; **M** 5.59; 5.61; 5.62; 5.74; 5.80; 5.97 (twice); 11.183; **Y** 3.6; 3.18; 3.27; **Vi** 19.13; 19.18; 20.32; 21.1; 22.1; 22.6; 22.7; 22.8 (twice); 22.10; 22.11; 22.12; 22.13; 22.14 (twice); 22.15; 22.16; 22.17; 22.18; 22.19; 22.21; 22.33; 22.35 (thrice); 22.38; 22.39; 22.40; 22.47; 22.56; 27.5; **Vkh** 2.11; 2.14; 3.8.

milk, curd, ghee, and a decoction of Kuśa grass, 'a man who has been bitten by a worm is purified' (*kṛmidaṣṭaḥ śucir bhavet:* **B** 1.11.38). More commonly, however, the verb *bhavet* is dispensed with and the prescription of the rite concludes with just *śuciḥ*—'after bathing he becomes pure' (*snātvā śuciḥ:* **M** 2.176); 'after bathing the father becomes pure' (*upaspṛśya pitā śuciḥ:* **M** 5.62); and with regard to food particles stuck to the teeth, 'a man becomes pure by simply swallowing them' (*nirgirann eva tac chuciḥ*: **G** 1.40; **B** 1.8.25; **Va** 3.41).

The dynamic meaning is also prevalent whenever *śuci* is used *adjectivally*. Thus, when a text states that a '*śuci* Brahmin' should do something, it does not mean that a 'pure Brahmin' (static meaning) should do it but that a Brahmin 'having become or made himself pure' should do it, and refers to a purificatory rite such as bathing or sipping water that would precede any ritual act. Thus, when Manu (**M** 4.35) describes what a vedic student should do when he recites the veda: *klptakeśanakhaśmaśrur dāntaḥ śuklāmbaraḥ śuciḥ* ('having cut his hair, beard and nails, keeping himself subdued, wearing white clothes, *pure*'), the term *pure* as an attribute of the student while studying indicates that he should *make himself pure* before study, just as he should cut his hair, make an effort to subdue his senses, and wear white clothes.

There are occasions, however, when *śuci* means *being pure*, an affirmation that a person or thing *is* in a state of purity. When such a static meaning is intended, *śuci* invariably stands in the position of the *predicate* rather than a simple *attribute*[12]—thus, *śvā mṛgagrahaṇe śuciḥ* ('in catching a deer a dog is pure': **B** 1.9.2); *ahataṃ vāsasāṃ śuci* ('new clothes are pure': **B** 1.13.4); *nityam āsyaṃ śuci strīṇām* ('the mouth of a woman is always pure': **M** 5.130). The predicative meaning, however, is comparatively infrequent and occurs mostly with reference to objects rather than to persons.

The multiple meanings and nuances of *śuci* permit the authors sometimes to play with that diversity. A good example is Manu 5.106 (variants in **Vi** 22.89; **Y** 3.32): *sarveṣām eva śaucānām arthaśaucam paraṃ smṛtam / yo 'rthe śucir hi sa śucir na mṛdvāriśuciḥ śuciḥ //* 'Of all forms of purifications [*a*], keeping oneself pure [*b*] in transactions is the best, *smṛtis* say, for a man is pure [*c*] when he makes himself pure [*d*] with respect to transactions (or procuring wealth); he is not pure [*e*] by becoming pure [*f*] using earth and water.' Here [*a*] has the general meaning of purification (see section 2.1), while [*b*] already borders on keeping oneself honest; [*c*] and [*e*] appear to have the static meaning of *being pure* (as predicate), but that state is earned through a dynamic process of purification [*d*] and [*f*], where [*d*] again has the meaning of honesty and integrity, while [*f*] is washing to get rid of stain and smell. As this verse shows, the four meanings I have separated for heuristic purposes are seen by the authors as forming a single spectrum of meanings.

[12] It appears that when *śuci* used adjectivally has a somewhat static meaning, then it refers to moral character ('upright'; meaning # 2) rather than to personal purity.

1.1. ***Śauca*** *Śauca* is what Sanskrit grammarians call 'a *vr̥ddhi* derivative', that is, a word derived from another word by strengthening its first syllable. We get *śauca* from *śuci* with the strengthening of '*u*' to the *vr̥ddhi* grade of the diphthong '*au*'. Words derived in this manner indicate in the most general way a relationship to the meaning expressed by the primary word. When the derived word is a neuter substantive, however, as is the case with *śauca*, it often expresses an abstract concept. Accordingly, we should expect *śauca* to mean 'purity'. Its primary meaning, however, is not the abstract quality of 'purity' but the dynamic process of 'purification'. This may well be due to the specialisation of meaning that *vr̥ddhi* derivatives often undergo; but I think it is more likely that this meaning became attached to *śauca* because, as we saw, the primary meaning of *śuci* is not simply 'being pure' but 'becoming pure'. Thus *śauca* came to mean 'that which is connected with becoming pure', that is, the process by which a person becomes pure.

Just as *śuci* acquired the specialised meaning of 'becoming pure' with reference to persons, so *śauça* is used specifically with reference to the purification of persons (see Figure 1: B.1.a). We saw above that the Dharma literature distinguishes the purification of persons from that of things by using *śauca* for the former and *śuddhi* for the latter. The rules of personal purification are collectively referred to as *śauca*: thus, a teacher is instructed to teach *śauca* to his students (**M** 2.69; **Y** 1.15).

Although *śauca* is used as a general term for purification by bathing, washing, sipping water, purificatory rites, and penances, it is used especially with reference to washing the anus, the penis, and the hands with water and earth (used as a cleansing agent) after voiding urine or excrement. Thus, for example, *kr̥taśaucāvaśiṣṭa* is earth 'left over from a previous purification' after toilet (**Va** 6.17). Manu (4.93) instructs a person to perform *śauca* after he has risen in the morning and answered the call of nature. And when texts refer to the different degrees of *śauca* for students, householders, hermits, and ascetics, they are speaking about the purification after toilet (**Va** 6.19; **M** 5.137).

I have failed to notice a single occurrence of *śauca* as an abstract noun indicating 'purity' in the Dharma literature.[13] The closest we come to such a usage is in passages that list *śauca* among other virtues or habits that a person should cultivate (Figure 1: B.2). The earliest such occurrence is in Gautama: *athāṣṭāv ātmaguṇāḥ / dayā sarvabhūteṣu kṣāntir anasūyā śaucam anāyāso maṅgalam akārpaṇyam aspr̥heti*—'Now, the eight virtues/qualities of the self are: compassion toward all creatures, patience, lack of envy, *śauca*, tranquillity, having an auspicious disposition, generosity, and lack of greed' (**G** 8.22–23). The commentator Haradatta, citing a series of verses that explain each of these virtues, states that *śauca* refers to the *purification* of things, mind, speech, and body. Later, explaining the provision that even Śūdras should cultivate the virtues of truthfulness, not getting angry, and *śauca*, Haradatta gives the same explanation. I

[13] Here I take 'purity' as an abstract concept connected in some ways to the way it is used by Dumont as an objective state inherent in different castes. *Śauca* does refer to 'purity' in the sense of concern with, and the procedures for, 'becoming pure'; such concern is evident in the use of the term for a specific virtue or habit.

think the natural tendency of the native commentator to take *śauca* even within the context of virtues as attention to internal and external purification is correct. Virtues, after all, are not unalterable states, like being white or tall; they are habits to be cultivated. It makes better sense, therefore, to see the virtue of *śauca* as the habit of engaging in activities of purification.[14]

Although *śauca* applies most frequently to persons, it is used occasionally in some texts with reference to the purification of things (see Figure 1: B.1.b). Thus Baudhāyana uses it for the purification of honey and milk (**B** 1.14.16), Vasiṣṭha for the purification of articles made of ropes, bamboo, and leather (**Va** 3.53), and Manu for the purification of metal vessels and grain (**M** 5.118; 6.53).

1.2. Aśuci Even though *aśuci* is the negative of *śuci*, its earliest usage indicates that it had already acquired a technical meaning connected more with *śuci* in the sense of 'upright, honest, innocent' than in the sense of 'pure'.

Āpastamba uses *aśuci* eight times. Certainly in six of these and in all likelihood also in a seventh,[15] *aśuci* is used not as an adjective but as a substantive with reference to a type of sinner. The sins that create this state are called *aśucikara*, 'making someone *aśuci*'. Āpastamba does not know or does not recognise the distinction common in later literature between *mahāpātaka* and *upapātaka*, grievous and secondary sins causing loss of caste. He begins the section on sins by stating that 'social interaction with outcastes (*patita*) is not permitted, as also with degraded (*apapātra*) people (**A** 1.21.5–6). Then he describes one group of sins which he calls *patanīyāni* ('causing loss of caste': **A** 1.21.7–11), and a second group of sins which he calls *aśucikarāṇi* ('causing someone to be *aśuci*': **A** 1.21.12–19). These two groups must correspond to the two categories of people in the introductory statement; an *aśuci*, therefore, is an *apapātra*, a degraded person with whom social interaction is forbidden.

Gautama uses *aśuci* four times (see Figure 1: B.l.a, b). Certainly in three of them, and possibly also in the fourth (**G** 16.46), the term has the same or similar technical meaning. Thus, when someone sees an *aśuci*, he should look at the sun to regain purity (**G** 23.22). An *aśuci* is also listed alongside *mleccha* and *adhārmika* (barbarians and the unrighteous) as people with whom one should not speak (**G** 9.16).

Besides Āpastamba's *patanīyāni* sins, Baudhāyana is the earliest writer to mention the traditional *upapātakāni*, secondary sins causing loss of caste (**B** 2.2.1–14). Nevertheless, he gives as a third class of sins, the *aśucikarāṇi* (**B** 2.2.15). This category of sins disappears from the Dharma vocabulary after Baudhāyana.

[14] The other option in these contexts is to take *śauca* as referring to *śuci* in the sense of upright and honest. If that is the meaning, then the virtue to be cultivated is uprightness or honesty.

[15] The doubtful case is the compound *aśuciśukla* which can mean 'impure semen' or 'the semen of an impure man', meaning the semen of a man who has committed a crime making him an *aśuci*. The sentence reads: *aśuciśuklaṃ yan nirvartate na tena saha saṃprayogo vidyate*—'Likewise, there can be no association with what is produced [i.e., child] by the semen of a sordid man' (**A** 1.29.14). I think here also *aśuci* refers to the class of sinners listed earlier, for otherwise it is difficult to explain how the issue of impure semen would be subject to such serious social disabilities. The same expression occurs in the very same context also in **B** 2.2.24. The eighth case is **A** 1.2.29 discussed later.

An element of this meaning, however, is retained in the use of *aśuci* within moral and criminal contexts (see Figure 1: B.1.c). The king should punish *aśucīn*, 'guilty' or 'immoral' people (**N** 18.41); the word of the king can make an innocent person (*śuci*) guilty (*aśuci:* **N** 18.49); and when cattle are stolen, suspicion falls on a village where there are 'bad people' (*aśucir janāḥ*: **N** 14.24).

In later texts the common meaning of 'impure' both as an adjective and as a substantive emerges. Thus, a menstruating woman is *aśuci* for three days (**Va** 5.6), menstrual blood is *aśuci* (**Va** 4.23), and one is *aśuci* for ten days upon hearing of a relative's death (**M** 5.79). Used substantively with reference to things, *aśuci* means simply filth, especially bodily excretions. Āpastamba (**A** 1.2.29) speaks of limbs 'smeared by *aśuci*' (*aśuciliptāni*), where *aśuci*, as the commentator Haradatta himself acknowledges, refers to filthy substances such as urine and faeces.[16] A lavatory is *aśucisthāna* ('place of *aśuci*': **N** 5.6).

An interesting feature of the negative *aśuci*, a feature shared by its counterpart *aśuddha* (see section 2.3), is that in its diverse senses it frequently exhibits a static meaning, a feature quite different from the generally dynamic meanings of the positives *śuci* and *śuddhi*.

1.3. Āśauca Like *śauca*, the term *āśauca* is a '*vr̥ddhi* derivative' with the negative prefix '*a*'.[17] Even more than *śauca*, however, *āśauca* developed a restricted technical meaning. In the Dharma literature it invariably applies to the period of impurity following a death or a birth (see Figure 1: D). The period of impurity following a birth is sometimes characterised as *sūtaka* ('caused by childbirth'), while the period following a death is sometimes distinguished from the former with the expression *śavāśauca* ('*āśauca* caused by a corpse').[18]

[16] In a very similar context, **Va** (3.48) uses the phrase *amedhyaliptāni*, 'smeared with *amedhya*', a term more closely identified with bodily excreta (see section 6.1).

[17] The grammatical derivation of *āśauca* is somewhat problematic because of the double *vr̥ddhi* of both the initial negative '*a*' and the second vowel. The easiest derivation is the addition of the negative prefix '*a*' to *śauca*. This would give *aśauca* and not *āśauca*, and Pāṇini's rule 7.3.30 is intended to permit the optional strengthening of the initial '*a*' even in such cases. The alternative is to derive it from *aśuci*. Pāṇini 5.1.121 disallows such a derivation if *aśuci* is taken as a Tatpuruṣa compound (i.e., meaning 'not pure'). Even if we take it as a Bahuvrīhi (i.e., 'one who does not possess the quality of pure'), the derivative should be *āśuci* and not *āśauca*. Although grammatically the derivation from *śauca* is easier, semantically the latter appears to make better sense, for then *āśauca* would mean 'a state of being *aśuci* or impure'. As we have seen, *śauca* does not simply mean 'purity' but 'purification'; hence its negative should be 'non-purification' rather than 'non-purity'. Alternatively, we would have to take *āśauca* to mean precisely 'non-purification', that is, a period when purificatory rites are disallowed, as is in fact the case when people are in a period of *āśauca*. The expression *sadhyaḥśauca*, 'immediate purification' (for example, for a king: **M** 5.94; **G** 14.9–12, 44–46), that is contrasted with *āśauca* does support the latter meaning. I want to thank George Cardona and Madhav Deshpande for their valuable insights on this question.

[18] Manu (6.62), for example, clearly distinguishes *śāvam āśaucam* from *sūtakam*. Space does not permit me to discuss here the unresolved question concerning the different periods of *āśauca* for different *varṇas*, the length of time increasing for lower *varṇas*. See Dumont (1980: 70); Mines (1990); Orenstein (1970); Tambiah (1973: 208–18).

The term *āśauca* (or *aśauca*) is a strictly technical term in the Dharma literature. It is never used with a more general meaning of 'impurity'.[19]

2. *Śudhyati*

The verb *śudhyati*[20] in all its verbal forms has the meaning of 'becoming purified' and is used most frequently with reference to a ritual or an act of purification (Figure 2: A). The verb is used indiscriminately with reference to persons and things. Both references are found in the same verse of Vasiṣṭha: *rajasā śudhyate nārī nadī vegena śudhyate*—'A woman is purified by her menstrual flow, and a river by its current' (**Va** 3.58; cf. **M** 5.108). The verb has a wide semantic compass, referring to the purification from bodily stain or ritual impurity, the release from sin, the acquittal from a criminal charge, and the discharge from a crime by paying the penalty.

The verb is used very frequently, and this may be due in part to the fact that the term *śuci* does not have a verbal counterpart with the same meaning.[21] Thus, when an author wants to use a verb for purification, his choices are limited to this and to the less frequently used verb *pūyate* (see section 4).

When the texts want to indicate an act of purification in a transitive sense, the only term they use is the causative *śodhayati* ('make someone/thing pure'). It is totally absent in the vocabulary of the older texts, appearing for the first time in Manu (Figure 2: B). Although used much less frequently, it has about the same semantic range as *śudhyati*. Some exceptional usages include neutralising the effects of poison in food (**M** 7.218), clearing roads of dangers such as robbers (**M** 7.185), and deducting expenses in legal calculations (**Y** 2.122; 2.146).

Śodhana, the nominal derivative from *śodhayati*, appears for the first time in Vasiṣṭha (Figure 2: C) and refers to a means (see *pavitra* and *pāvana*) or the act of purification with the same semantic range as the verb.

2.1. Śuddhi We have seen above that the texts make a clear distinction between the purification of persons and things by using *śauca* for the former and *śuddhi* for the latter.

[19] The only instance when such a meaning appears possible is in Gautama: *na tadupasparśanād āśaucam*—'No impurity is contracted through his (i.e., a child before initiation) touch' (**G** 2.3). Stenzler's edition reads here *āśaucam*, while the commentators Haradatta and Maskarin appear to read *aśaucam*, glossing it with *aśucitvam* ('state of being impure'). Here also my suspicion is that the provision refers to a child a relative of whose has died or who has touched a corpse; even in that condition his touch, unlike that of an adult in a similar condition, does not create *āśauca*. The two forms *āśauca* and *aśauca* (both permitted by Pāṇini 7.3.30) occur in the Dharma texts, although the former is much more frequent; orthographic confusion often makes it difficult to isolate the original reading. But both forms generally have the same meaning. The term *āśaucin* ('a person in a period of *āśauca*') is found only in **Vkh** 2.14.

[20] In the Dharma literature this (the Parasmaipada) is the dominant form. The Ātmanepada form *śudhyate* is much less common: **B** 1.13.19; **Va** 3.67; **M** 5.108.

[21] *Śuci* is, of course, derived from the verbal root *śuc*, but the verb itself did not undergo the semantic development of *śuci* and is never used in the Dharma literature for becoming pure.

Figure 2

A. śudhyati

1. Person:
   a. purification: **G** 14.6; 14.30; 22.6; **B** 1.8.2; 1.11.8 (twice); 1.11.41; 3.1.27; 3.8.12; **Va** 3.58; 3.60; 4.24; 4.30; 18.16; 20.21; 27.12; **M** 3.132; 5.63; 5.64; 5.65; 5.66; 5.72; 5.76; 5.78; 5.83 (twice); 5.85; 5.87; 5.88; 5.99; 5.101; 5.102; 5.103; 5.108 (twice); 5.109 (twice); 11.199; 11.201; 11.202; **Y** 1.21; 3.20; 3.277; **Vi** 22.11; 22.39; 22.58; 22.72; 22.74; 22.77; 22.85; 22.87; 22.91; 22.92; 62.9.
   b. moral/legal: **G** 20.10; 20.15; 23.1; 23.11; 23.19; **B** 1.8.2 (twice); 2.1.40; 3.1.27; 3.3.17; 4.1.4; 4.1.21; 4.2.14; 4.5.14; 4.5.27; 4.5.28 (twice); **Va** 3.60 (twice); 21.12; 25.6; 26.5; 27.14; 27.15; 28.3; 29.16; **M** 5.107; 5.109; 11.46; 11.83; 11.100; 11.103; 11.123; 11.141; 11.146; 11.149; 11.162; 11.193; 11.249; 11.254; 11.257; **Y** 1.72; 3.246; 3.248; 3.249; 3.258; 3.262; 3.263; 3.280; 3.283; 3.287; 3.289; 3.301; 3.311; **Vi** 22.90; 22.91; 22.92; 28.50; 35.6; 36.8; 40.2; 50.47; 54.28.
2. Non-person:
   a. purification: **B** 1.9.7; 1.10.1; 1.13.19; 3.1.27; **Va** 3.57; 3.58 (twice); 3.59; 3.63; **M** 5.108 (twice); 5.112; 5.122; 5.123; 5.124; 5.125; 5.126; **Y** 1.186; 1.194; 1.197; **Vi** 22.91 (twice); 23.2; 23.38; 23.40; 23.41; **Vkh** 3.2.

B. śodhayati (and verbal derivatives)

1. Person:
   a. purification: **Va** 27.13; **M** 11.160; **Vkh** 2.13; 3.3.
   b. moral/legal: **M** 8.202; 11.226 (twice); 11.258; **Y** 2.269; **N** Mā 2.39; 20.37; 20.40.
2. Non-person:
   a. purification: **M** 5.108; 7.218; 9.282; 9.283; **Y** 3.32; **Vi** 22.91; 23.44; **Vkh** 3.3 (thrice).
   b. legal: **M** 7.185; **Y** 2.122; 2.146; **N** Mā 3.5; 1.80; 19.26; 19.27.

C. śodhana

1. Person:
   a. purification: **Va** 25.12; **M** 11.125; 11.143; 11.156; 11.160; 11.165; 11.200; **Y** 3.24; 3.34; **Vi** 41.5 (twice); 50.49.
   b. legal: **M** 1.115; 9.253; **Y** 2.122; 2.146; **Vi** 11.9; **N** Mā 2.39; 12.76; 15–16.6; 20.6; 20.31.
2. Non-person: **N** 5.6; 19.17.

D. śuddhi

1. Person:
   a. purification: **G** 24.4; **B** 1.8.3; **Va** 4.20; 27.10; **M** 5.21; 5.57; 5.61; 5.67 (twice); 5.71; 5.100; 5.105; 5.134 (twice); 5.136; 6.30; 6.69; **Y** 3.14; 3.20; 3.25; 3.31; 3.32; 3.34; 3.62; **Vi** 22.21; 22.35; 22.88; **N** 5.33.
   b. purity: **M** 9.9; 11.160; **Vkh** 1.9; 3.3 (four times).
   c. moral/legal: **B** 1.8.52; 4.3.7; **Va** 25.1; 26.15; **M** 11.53; 11.72; 11.89; 11.117; 11.138; 11.163; 11.164; 11.181; 12.105; **Y** 1.77; 2.94; 2.95; 2.107; 2.109; 2.111; 3.159; 3.220; 3.243; 3.244; 3.248; 3.250 (twice); 3.253; 3.265; 3.268; 3.274; 3.326; **Vi** 11.12; 13.7; **N** Mā 3.6 (twice); 1.102; 1.222; 6.19; 7.2; 7.4; 15–16.7; 15–16.25; 20.7; 20.24.
2. Non-person:
   a. purification: **G** 1.29; **M** 1.113; 5.57; 5.110; 5.111; 5.115; 5.116; 5.117; 5.119 (twice); 5.121; 5.146; **Y** 1.183; 1.188; 1.189; 1.190; 1.191; 3.32; 3.60; **Vi** 22.93; 23.7; 23.39; 23.46; 23.57; 96.8.
   b. legal: **Y** 2.92; **N** Mā 1.3; Mā 2.44; 1.78 (twice); 18.43 (twice).

E. śuddha

1. Person:
   a. purified: **G** 20.10; **B** 1.7.2; 1.11.32; **M** 2.160; 5.77; 11.190; 11.242; **Y** 3.159; **Vi** 22.73; 54.32; 99.18.
   b. pure: **B** 1.9.1; **Va** 27.15; **M** 5.129; 10.76; **Vi** 23.48; **Vkh** 3.6; 3.8; 3.11 (four times); 3.12; 4.3.
   c. moral/legal: **B** 3.6.10; 3.8.27; 3.9.10; 4.2.14; 4.2.16; 4.5.32; 4.7.2; 4.7.4; 4.8.12; **M** 7.219; **Y** 2.102; 2.113; 3.159; **Vi** 10.12; 11.8; 12.6; 13.5; 14.5; **N** Mā 2.39; 1.133; 20.12 (twice); 20.20; 20.26; 20.27; 20.39.

2. Non-Person:
   a. purification: **Vkh** 2.15.
   b. pure: **A** 1.19.7; **Va** 27.15 (white); **M** 5.128; 10.90; 12.27; **Y** 3.72; **Vkh** 2.12; 2.13; 2.14; 3.1; 3.5; 3.8.
   c. moral/legal: **M** 4.11; 8.201; 9.279; **N** Mā 3.6; 1.102; 7.8.

F. aśuddha

1. Person: **Va** 27.15; **M** 5.58; **Vi** 11.8; 12.6; 14.5; 57.4; **Vkh** 3.11 (twice); **N** 17.5.
2. Non-person: **M** 4.127; **Y** 2.266; **N** 7.8.

Śuddhi, the nominal derivative of the verb *śudh*, however, is used more generally with regard to both persons and things, but with rare exceptions it normally has a dynamic meaning, referring to the act or process of purification/cleansing rather than to a state of purity. The dynamic meaning is even more pronounced in *śuddhi* than in *śuci*. Unlike the latter, *śuddhi* is a noun and refers directly to the act of purification, the getting rid of impurities, whereas *śuci* indicates a person 'becoming pure'.

Even in moral contexts *śuddhi* refers to the elimination of immoral or sinful qualities through an appropriate penance rather than to a state of moral purity. Thus, in introducing the chapter on secret penances, Vasiṣṭha (25.1) states: 'I will explain fully the purification (*śuddhi*) of all sinners whose guilt has not been made public'.

In legal contexts *śuddhi* is used with reference to the discharge of a debt (**Y** 2.94; **N** 1.102), the exoneration of an accused man (**Y** 2.95; **N** 1.222; 6.19), the settlement of a dispute (**N** 1.78), and the establishment of the authenticity of a legal document (**Y** 2.92)—all appearing in late texts.

The fact that *śuddhi* always indicates purification rather than purity may be the reason why its negative form, *aśuddhi*, is totally absent in the Dharma vocabulary.[22] It is clear that although it is possible to speak of *impurity*, it makes little sense to speak of *non-purification*.

2.2. **Śuddha** Like *śuddhi*, the past participle *śuddha* is used with regard to both persons and things, both in ritual and moral/legal contexts (see Figure 2: E). Unlike *śuddhi*, however, it is used in the sense of both 'purified' (dynamic) and 'pure' (static). The former is the most common. Thus, for example, Baudhāyana (1.11.32) states: 'When someone accidentally touches the corpse of an outsider, he becomes pure (*śuddha*) immediately after taking a bath with his clothes on'; and Gautama (20.10): 'An excommunicated man may be purified (*śudhyet*) by performing a penance, however, and when he has been so purified (*śuddha*), they should fill a golden pot with water from a very sacred lake or from a river and make the man take a bath with the water from that pot.'

The term, however, often simply means pure or white (Figure 2: E.l.b, 2.b), and in this sense it is used predicatively. Thus, 'almsfood is pure' (*śuddhā bhikṣā*) and may be eaten (**A** 1.19.7); the hand of an artisan is always 'pure' (*śuddhaḥ kāruhastaḥ*, **M** 5.129).

22 The negative occurs only once, in the compound *śuddhyaśuddhi* (**Vkh** 1.9) in the context of holy ascetics (Paramahamsas) who eliminate all binary opposites. This is a unique usage and may be an artificial formulation limited to this context.

2.3. Aśuddha As in the case of *aśuci*, the negative *aśuddha* often has a static meaning, although the dynamic meaning is quite common. The first use of this negative is found in Vasiṣṭha (25.15) and has a dynamic meaning: 'When a man consumes barley grains in accordance with the rules, he becomes visibly pure (*śudhyati*): if he has become pure (lit. if his being has become pure: *viśuddhabhāva*) the grains remain white (*śuddha*), whereas if he has not become pure (*aśuddha*) the grains become discoloured.' When an initiated child dies, the relatives become impure, *aśuddha* (**M** 5.58). Both persons and things are said to be *aśuddha*, in the sense of both ritual impurity and moral/legal culpability (see Figure 2: F).

3. *Prayata*

Prayata is the past participle of the verb *yam* with the prefix *pra* and in the vedic literature meant simply 'outstretched' or 'presented/offered'. This meaning is still present in the expression *prayatāñjali* ('with his cupped hands outstretched': **B** 2.1.35), but even here we see that this gesture is done within a ritual context calling for a proper mental and bodily preparation.[23] In the Dharma texts, however, the term came to mean 'pure' (see Figure 3), although, as Gonda (1961–62) has shown, it has the much wider meaning of proper internal and external preparation for a solemn rite.

Figure 3

A. prayata

1. Person:
   a. purified: **A** 1.11.23; 1.15.2; 1.15.17; 1.15.23; **B** 1.11.40; 2.7.2; 2.7.4; 3.6.7; 4.2.13; **Va** 26.14; **M** 2.222; 4.145; 4.146; 5.86; **Vi** 52.2.
   b. pure: **A** 1.15.3; 1.15.13; 1.16.9; 2.3.1; 2.17.4; **B** 2.7.2; **M** 2.183; 2.185; 3.216; 3.226; 3.228; 3.258; 4.49; 5.145; 8.258; 11.258; **Vi** 66.15.
2. Thing:
   a. purified: **A** 1.17.11.
   b. pure: **B** 2.17.37.

B. aprayata

1. Person: **A** 1.14.18; 1.14.19; 1.14.20; 1.15.8–9; 1.15.13; 1.15.18; 1.16.14; 1.16.21; 1.16.22; 1.31.4; 2.15.19; **B** 1.3.29 (twice); 1.3.30; 2.7.2; **M** 5.142; 11.153; **Vi** 23.54.
2. Thing: **A** 1.16.21; 1.29.14; **B** 2.2.22.

C. prāyatya

1. Person: **A** 1.31.19.
2. Thing: **B** 1.9.11; **Va** 3.56.

D. aprāyatya

1. Person: **A** 1.11.25; **Vkh** 2.9.

The oldest dharmaśāstric writer, Āpastamba, uses *prayata*, as well as the negative *aprayata*, much more frequently than any other term with regard both to persons and things. The term is absent in Gautama, used infrequently by Baudhāyana and Vasiṣṭha, and falls into relative disuse in later literature, except in standard

23 For an extended discussion of the range of meanings of *prayata*, see Gonda (1960–61).

expressions such as *prayatātman* ('with himself ritually prepared or purified': e.g., **Va** 26.14). The use of the term with reference to things is limited to the early texts, especially Āpastamba (see Figure 3: A.2, B.2, C.2).

4. *Pūyate*

Derivatives from the verbal root *pū* are used much less frequently in the Dharma literature than those from the root *śudh*. The active voice *punāti* ('purifies') is never used outside of vedic mantras, except by Vasiṣṭha, who uses it no less than five times, perhaps with an intent to archaise his language.[24] More frequent is the passive *pūyate* ('is purified'), and it is used with the same semantic range as the verb *śudh* with reference to both persons and things, and with regard to both ritual purification and the expiation of sins and crimes (Figure 4: A).

Figure 4

A. pūyate
(including derivatives and negatives)

1. Person: **Va** 23.22; 28.10; **B** 3.7.1; 3.7.18; 3.9.10; 4.2.12; 4.2.16 (twice); 4.7.10; **M** 2.62; 8.257; 8.311.
   punanti: **Va** 6.3; 6.5; 22.10; 26.4; 28.15.
2. Non-person: **B** 2.17.18; 3.1.13; **Va** 3.61; **Vkh** 3.4.

B. pavitra

1. Rite or mantra: **A** 1.2.2 (thrice); 1.26.7; 1.27.2; **G** 25.7; 26.10; **B** 1.2.16; 1.2.17; 2.7.2; 2.7.4; 2.14.5; 4.1.22; 4.2.16 (twice); 4.8.3; 4.8.4; **Va** 22.10; 23.47; 25.3; 25.4; 28.10; **M** 3.256; 11.225; **Vi** 46.25; 56.1; 64.36; 64.40; 72.5 (virtue); 100.2; **Vkh** 3.8.
2. Object: **B** 1.9.9; 1.9.10; 2.4; 2.8.11; 2.11.24; 2.17.11; 2.17.34 (twice); 2.17.37 (twice); 3.2.7; 3.2.17; 3.5.1 (twice); 3.6.5; **Va** 11.35; 14.24; 25.4; 28.4; **M** 2.75; 3.210; 3.223; 3.235; 3.256; 5.127; 6.41; 10.102; 11.85; **Y** 1.240; 3.325; 1.251; **Y** 1.226; 1.230; **Vi** 23.47; 23.57 (cows); 48.6; 48.17; 79.16; **Vkh** 2.6; 2.8 (twice); 3.6 (twice); 3.8.
3. Purity: **B** 3.7.4.

C. pāvana

1. Person: **A** 2.17.22; **G** 15.27; 15.28; **B** 2.14.2; **Va** 3.19; 11.20; **M** 3.183; 3.184; 3.186; **Y** 3.306; **Vi** 1.57; 99.4; 83.1.
2. Non-person: **G** 19.12; **B** 1.2.16; 1.3.43; 3.10.10; 4.5.9; 4.5.25; 4.5.29; **Va** 1.16; 22.9; 25.11; **M** 2.26; 11.85; 11.177; **Y** 1.281; 2.83; **Vi** 8.16.

The past participle *pūta* also has the same broad range of meanings but, unlike its counterpart *śuddha*, always has the dynamic meaning of 'being purified' rather than simply 'pure'. This dynamic meaning is evident also in the rarely used negative *apūta*, which always means something or someone 'not purified' or 'not yet purified' rather than simply 'impure'.[25]

4.1. ***Pavitra*** Of the nominal derivatives of the verb *pū*, the most common is *pavitra* (Figure 4: B). It refers to any agent or instrument of purification. Thus, a water strainer is called *pavitra*, as also the two blades of Kuśa grass between the

[24] **Va** 6.3; 6.5; 22.10; 26.4; 28.15.
[25] **G** 25.6; **M** 2.40; 8.330 (re. unhusked grain).

fingers during rituals, purificatory verses and rites, and penances. Other means of purification, such as a woman's menstrual flow, are also called *pavitra*. Here also we note the focus on regaining lost purity, this time with reference to instruments that impart purification.

4.2. Pāvana The term *pāvana* ('purifying' or 'imparting purity') is derived from the causative of *pū (pāvayati*, 'to make someone/thing pure'). In the Dharma literature it has a somewhat restricted meaning (Figure 4: C). Although it is used a few times with reference to actions and rites that impart purity (in the same ways as *śodhana*: Figure 4: C.2), *pāvana* is used most frequently as a technical term with reference to specially holy/learned Brahmins who are called *paṅktipāvana*, 'purifying those alongside whom they sit' during a meal.[26]

5. *Ucchiṣṭa*

Ucchiṣṭa is the past participle of the verb *śiṣ* with the verbal prefix *ut* and means 'left' or 'left over'. Its most common meaning is with reference to food that is left over after a person has eaten (Figure 5: 2). Such food may be either left on the plate or attached to a person's hands and lips. In general *ucchiṣṭa* is viewed as impure and causes anyone coming into contact with it to become impure. In this sense, *ucchiṣṭa* is most frequently used as a neuter substantive (*ucchiṣṭam*).[27]

Figure 5

ucchiṣṭa

1. Person:
   a. from food: **B** 1.8.28; **M** 2.56; **Vi** 68.36; 70.17.
   b. from bodily discharge: **A** 1.16.11; **G** 1.41; **B** 1.8.27; 1.8.29 (*ucchiṣṭī*); 1.8.51; 1.10.34; **Va** 3.27; 3.42; **M** 4.75; 4.82; 4.109; 4.142; 5.141; 5.143 (both thing and person?); **Vi** 23.53; 23.55; **Y** 1.155; **Vkh** 2.14 (twice); 3.2; 3.3.
   c. unclear source: **G** 1.28; **B** 1.13.26; 1.14.1; 1.14.17.
2. Food: **A** 1.3.27; 1.3.37; 1.4.1; 1.4.2; 1.4.11; 1.4.5; 1.6.36; 1.7.27; 1.7.30; 1.15.23; 1.17.3; 1.21.17; 1.31.22; 2.9.7; 2.18.11; 2.20.2; **G** 2.32; 10.59; 17.17; **B** 1.3.35; 1.3.36; 2.1.26; 2.8.10; 3.6.5; 3.8.10; **Va** 11.10 (twice); 11.21; 11.22; 11.23; 14.20; 14.21 (twice); 18.14; 23.9; 23.11; **M** 2.56; 2.209; 3.245; 3.249; 4.80; 4.211; 4.212; 10.125; 11.26; 11.152; 11.159; **Vi** 21.3; 21.15; 28.11; 28.33; 51.10; 51.46; 51.47; 51.50; 51.51; 51.52; 51.53; 51.54; 51.55; 51.56; 54.19; 71.49; 73.17; 73.25; 81.22; 91.18; **Y** 1.33; 1.154; 1.162; 1.167; 1.168; 1.209; 1.242; 1.257; 3.37; **Vkh** 3.2; 3.4; **N** 5.6.
3. Objects: **B** 1.8.32; 1.13.27; 1.14.2; **Va** 3.43; **M** 11.148; **Vi** 48.20; **Vkh** 3.3; **N** 1.57.

In an adjectival sense, however, the term refers to a person who is rendered impure by coming into contact with *ucchiṣṭa* food. Thus, after a meal a person remains *ucchiṣṭa* until he or she has performed the required purification (*śauca*).

[26] *A* 2.17.22; *G* 15.27–28; *B* 2.14.2; *Va* 3.19; 11.20; *M* 3.183, 184, 186; *Vi* 83.1. The opposite of *paṅktipāvana* is *paṅktidūṣaṇa*, a man who defiles a company (*A* 2.17.21).

[27] For a detailed discussion of this term, see Malamoud (1972). Some types of *ucchiṣṭa* are good and can be eaten. Generally such leftovers belong to a person superior to oneself. Thus, a wife may eat the leftovers of her husband, and a student the leftovers of his teacher (*A* 1.4.1–11; *G* 2.31–32). Leftovers of a sacrifice or an offering to a god is especially holy.

There are, however, other extended meanings of the term. Medhātithi (on **M** 4.80), an early commentator of Manu, isolates four possible meanings of *ucchiṣṭa*: (*a*) because of contact with the inside of mouth while eating, the eater, the eaten food, and the plate from which one eats become *ucchiṣṭa*; (*b*) food left on the plate after someone has eaten off it is *ucchiṣṭa*; (*c*) as also what is left in the dish from which food has been served to someone; (*d*) and food left in the pot after people have been served; and (*e*) a person is *ucchiṣṭa* after voiding urine or excrement and before purification. According to Medhātithi, the primary meaning of the term is the first, (*a*), resulting from food and fingers come into contact with the inside of the mouth.[28]

6. *Medhya*

In its vedic usage the term *medhya* referred to animals and substances suitable for use in a sacrifice. In the Dharma literature, it is used with the wider meaning of 'pure' (Figure 6: A). The old connection with sacrificial substances, however, is evident because the term is used most frequently with reference to food or sources of food. Other items called *medhya* include the bodily parts above the navel, vessels, and soil. Persons are generally not called *medhya*. The only exception, interestingly, is women, who, like food, are to be enjoyed by men.[29]

Figure 6

A. medhya

1. Food sources: **A** 1.17.31; 2.16.28; **B** 1.9.1; 1.9.2; **Va** 14.46; **M** 5.54; 5.129; 6.5; 6.11; 6.13; 11.153; 6.12; **M** 5.133.
2. Non-food items: **B** 1.7.4 (twice); 1.13.19; **M** 5.133; **Vkh** 3.4; **N** 18.41.
3. Parts of human body: **B** 1.10.19; **Va** 28.6; 28.8; 28.9; **M** 1.92; 5.132; **Y** 1.71 (twice); 1.194; 1.195; **Vi** 23.40; 23.51.
4. Actions/rites: **G** 19.13; **B** 3.10.11; **Va** 22.11.

B. amedhya

1. As substantive:
   - a. Bodily substance: **A** 1.16.24; 1.16.25; 1.16.26; **G** 1.42; 9.12; **Va** 3.48; **M** 4.56; 5.126; **Y** 1.191; **Vi** 22.39.
   - b. Filth: **A** 1.16.14; **G** 9.15; **B** 1.9.4; 1.9.10; 1.10.1; 1.14.18; 1.15.31; 2.2.36; 2.8.6; 3.8.18; **M** 2.239; 4.53; 5.5; 5.128; 9.282 (twice); 11.96; 12.71; **Y** 1.148; 2.213; **Vi** 23.43; 43.41; 51.36; 51.41; 71.32.
2. As adjective:
   - a. Re. food/beverage: **G** 20.4; 23.23; **Vi** 22.84.
   - b. Re. body below navel: **B** 1.10.19; **M** 5.132; **Vi** 23.51.
   - c. Re. people/animals: **A** 1.17.5.

28 There is an interesting rule given by Āpastamba (1.31.22): 'He should not give his leftovers to someone who is not a Brahmin. If he does so, he should pick his teeth, place what he has picked from his teeth on the leftovers, and then give it.' Here *ucchiṣṭa* as (*c*) or (*d*) has to be converted to *ucchiṣṭa* as (*b*) if leftover food is to be given to an inferior person.

29 See **Va** 28.6; *Y* 1.71. The verb *bhuj* is used often with regard to both food and women: see, for example, Vijñāneśvara on **Y** 1.71.

6.1. ***Amedhya*** The negative of *medhya*, just as the negative of *śuci*, developed a technical meaning. With rare exceptions *amedhya* is used as a neuter substantive to refer to impure or dirty substances, especially bodily excreta. Baudhāyana (3.8.17–18), for example, says that one should not look at urine and faeces, and immediately adds, 'if he sees *amedhya*', clearly equating the latter with bodily excreta. This specialised meaning is not only documented in the Dharma literature but is also singled out for comment by medieval commentators. Vijñāneśvara, commenting on Yājñavalkya 1.191 (see also on **Y** 2.214), defines *amedhya* as *sarīrajā malāḥ*, 'dirt originating from the body'. Anticipating Mary Douglas's (1966) definition of dirt as substances that violate boundaries of cultural categories (i.e.,'matter out of place'), Vijñāneśvara explains that the impure nature (*amedhyatva*) of *amedhya* substances results from the fact that they have come out of the body; only those substances that have come out of the body are *amedhya*, not those that remain in their respective places (*amedhyatvaṃ caivam eṣāṃ. . .dehacyutānām eva na svasthānāvasthitānām*). So, a substance is not impure in itself but only in so far as it has been displaced and has crossed a boundary.

Vijñāneśvara's astute observation is supported by the usage of the early Dharma texts. Āpastamba (1.16.23–24), for example, says that food 'in which there is a hair or some other *amedhya*' is unfit to be eaten, indicating that *amedhya* must refer to other bodily substances such as hair. This is confirmed by the fact that commentators *instinctively* take *amedhya* to be some bodily substance, as when Sāyaṇa (on Taittirīya Āraṇyaka 10.1.13) glosses the term with *niṣṭhīvanādi*, 'substances such as saliva'.

7. *Mala*

The term *mala* is a noun indicating dirt or impure substance (Figure 7: A). The early Dharma texts use the term only within the technical expression *malavadvāsas*, 'one with dirty clothes', with specific reference to a menstruating woman.[30] The term is used extensively for the first time by Manu. Although it can refer to spiritual 'stains' or sins, in its most common meaning *mala* is a synonym of *amedhya* and refers to bodily excretions. That is the meaning in the well-known statement listing the twelve *malas* of human beings: 'Oily exudations, semen, blood, fat, urine, faeces, snot, ear-wax, phelgm, tears, discharge of eyes, and sweat—these are the twelve *malas* of men' (**M** 5.135; ***Vi*** 22.81). Vijñāneśvara (on **Y** 1.191) cites this list in explaining the meaning of *amedhya*, indicating that he saw the two terms as synonyms.[31]

Mala, however, can also refer to the 'stain' of moral infractions (Fig. 7: A.l.c). Authors sometimes play on this double meaning. Manu (11.94), for example, shows that both liquor and sin are *mala*, 'dirt' and 'sin', respectively: 'Liquor is

[30] **A** 1.9.13; **G** 9.3; **Va** 12.5 (*malinavāsas*); **M** 4.34.

[31] The vedic text Kāṭhaka Saṃhitā (34.12) gives a similar list of twelve impurities of a man and calls them *amedhya*. Sāyaṇa, commenting on Aitareya Brāhmaṇa 7.13.7, explains *mala* as *śukraśoṇita* ('semen and menstrual blood'), seeing in the term a reference to the householder's *āśrama* connected with childbirth.

Figure 7

A. mala

1. As substantive—dirt
   a. bodily filth: **M** 4.220; 5.132; 5.134; 5.135; **Vi** 22.77; 22.81; 23.1; 23.40; 23.51; **Vi** 51.2; 64.18; 96.47; **Y** 1.194.
   b. other impurities: **M** 6.71; 11.93.
   c. moral: **M** 2.102; 11.70; 11.93; 11.101; 11.107; 11.125; **Vi** 33.5; 41.4; 41.5; 43.30; 44.9; 99.18; **N** 15–16.15.
2. As adjective—dirty: **A** 1.9.13; **G** 9.3; **Va** 12.5; **M** 4.34; **Vi** 63.35; 69.11; 69.12; 71.9; 71.24; **Y** 1.70; **Vkh** 3.2; 3.14; 3.15; **N** 9.7; 15–16.15.

B. amala/nirmala

1. Purified re. person (always moral/legal): **Va** 19.45; 26.6; **M** 8.318; 11.250; **N** 19.55.
2. Pure re. person: **Vi** 47.10.
3. Bright/spotless re. thing: **Vi** 99.10 (twice).

the dirt (*mala*) derived from food,[32] and sin is also called dirt (*mala*). Therefore, Brahmins, Kṣatriyas, and Vaiśyas should not drink liquor.'

The negatives *amala* and *nirmala* are used as adjectives to indicate the absence of *mala* especially in a moral sense (Figure 7: B). Thus *nirmala* means a persons who is 'immaculate', free from the taint of sin.

II
Conclusions

I started this investigation with four questions: does a term refer: (*a*) to a person or to a thing; (*b*) to a condition or to a transition; (*c*) to purity or to the areas of morality or criminal law; (*d*) to an individual or to a group?

We are now in a better position to answer these questions. The vocabulary of pure/impure in the Dharma literature makes a clear distinction between persons and things. Although a variety of objects and animals are characterised as impure, the main focus is on bodily discharges, those oozing substances that violate the boundary of the human body.

With respect to persons, the vocabulary clearly indicates that the focus is not on any permanent, or even transitory, condition of purity but rather on the transition from impurity to purity, on the recovery of lost purity. The dynamic meaning dominates the use of *śuci* and *śuddhi*. There is no discussion about how one may remain in a condition of permanent purity, although the texts do talk about avoiding sources of moral and ritual pollution. To remain permanently pure is not only impossible (one has to eat and go to the bathroom), but also undesirable, for it would entail not having sex or children, both sexual activity and childbirth being sources of pollution.

Most of the terms for pure/impure are used both with respect to ritual purity and in the context of moral and criminal law. In the Dharma literature these three areas are not compartmentalised.

32 Liquor is considered dirt possibly because it results from fermentation.

Finally, we see no instance when a term for pure/impure is used with reference to a group of individuals or to a *varṇa* or caste, the only exception being people who have fallen from their caste due to grievous sins; these are often called *aśuci*.[33] Groups outside the established society, especially the Cāṇḍālas, are subsumed under the category of the 'fallen'. In general the Dharma texts place both Cāṇḍālas and grievous sinners in the same group and treat them alike. These people are impure precisely because they have breached the boundary of *varṇa* society; they have been excreted out of the social body and are hence impure, *amedhya*. Social interaction with these people is forbidden, and any contact makes a person within society impure (morally and ritually). But the overwhelming focus of the vocabulary concerns individuals, irrespective of their caste/*varṇa* affiliation, who have become impure and are in need of recovering their lost purity. A person of any *varṇa*, including a Śūdra, can become *aśuci*, impure, and can recover purity (become *śuci*) by employing the appropriate purification (*śauca*).

Dumont is correct in his assessment that the ideology of *varṇa* is not based on purity. If it were we should expect to find at least some comment on the relative purity/impurity of the different *varṇas*. What is even more important is that the ideology of purity/impurity that emerges from the Dharma literature is concerned with the individual and not with groups, with purification and not with purity, and lends little support to a theory which makes relative purity the foundation of social stratification. The mythical legitimisation of the *varṇa* division is, of course, contained in the Puruṣa Hymn of the Ṛg Veda (10.90). Some may think that the connection of the different *varṇas* with different parts of the body, especially the association of the Śūdra with the feet, may support a theory of the relative purity of *varṇas*. But this conclusion is never drawn in the Dharma literature even in contexts when such a conclusion would have buttressed the author's argument. Baudhāyana, for example, appeals to the Puruṣa Hymn to demonstrate that Śūdras should serve the higher *varṇas*, 'for they were created from his feet' (**B** 1.18.5–6). Feet here symbolise service, not impurity.

The evidence of these ancient texts gives greater support to the theory of impurity proposed by Mary Douglas (1966) than to Dumont's theory of caste as based on the gradation of purity.[34] Scholars have connected impurity with hygiene, with morality, with the separation of spirit and matter, and so forth. I think Mary Douglas is right to reject such definitions, as well as the temptation to reify the pure and the impure, to see these as somehow descriptive adjectives like heavy or

[33] At **M** 1.92 there is an oblique reference to the Brahmin coming from the mouth (*mukha*) which is the 'purest' (*medhyatama*) part of the body. But no explicit conclusion is drawn from this fact that the Brahmin is purer than other *varṇas*, only that he is the 'lord of the whole creation' and that gods consume offerings through the medium of the Brahmin's mouth.

[34] Quigley (1993: 45–46) is right in his assessment: 'For Dumont, as we have seen, the opposition of the pure and the impure is the principle of hierarchy in "the caste system". As it stands, this formulation is problematic because the opposition of pure and impure is a universal feature of human societies. The reason for this has been brilliantly explored by Mary Douglas in her book *Purity and danger*, and it is regrettable that she did not exploit her own insight further when she wrote the introduction to the first English-language translation of *Homo hierarchicus*'.

blue, as indicating objective qualities inhering in substances. Pure and impure are relational and evaluative concepts—they are related to an ideology that establishes categories and fixed boundaries and they evaluate actions, objects, persons, and social interactions in relation to those categories. In this sense, with William James (Douglas 1984: 164) and Freud (Kubie 1937: 390), we can define impurity or dirt as 'matter out of place'.

> If we can abstract pathogenicity and hygiene from our notion of dirt, we are left with the old definition of dirt as matter out of place. This is a very suggestive approach. It implies two conditions: a set of ordered relations and a contravention of that order. Dirt then, is never a unique, isolated event. Where there is dirt there is a system. Dirt is the by-product of a systematic ordering and classification of matter (Douglas 1966: 35).

Concern for impurity translates into concern for maintaining the integrity of boundaries, both physical and classificatory, which in turn relates to the concern for maintaining social boundaries. The human body becomes the locus for expressing all these concerns, especially the concern for maintaining purity.

> The body is a model which can stand for any bounded system. Its boundaries can represent any boundaries which are threatened and precarious. . . . We cannot possibly interpret rituals concerning excreta, breast milk, saliva and the rest unless we are prepared to see in the body a symbol of society, and to see the powers and dangers credited to social structure reproduced in small on the human body (Douglas 1966: 115).

The most common examples of breaching boundaries concern the body. When internal substances break the bodily surface and ooze out, then the person becomes *aśuci*, impure. Other persons coming into contact with such *amedhya* or unclean substances also become *aśuci*. This is the type of impurity that has been subject to most scholarly scrutiny.

There are, however, other boundaries, and the impurities associated with their breach provide further insights into the Dharma ideology of impurity. Let me focus on just two: the spatial boundary of the village (although interesting information comes also from the boundary of the house) and the temporal boundaries of day, month, and year. In this context I want to deal with a subject totally ignored by scholars but looming large in the Dharma literature, namely the events causing *anadhyāya*, or the suspension of vedic recitation. Here are some of Āpastamba's (1.9.14–19) prescriptions: there is *anadhyāya* in a village when a corpse is brought or a Cāṇḍāla walks into its boundaries. Likewise when outsiders, even respectable people, come into a village there is *anadhyāya* for the duration of that day. This prescription mirrors another rule (**A** 1.10.11) which forbids collective vedic recitation for a day when a fellow student has gone out of the village. When a newcomer arrives or a member of a group leaves, its boundary is breached and the community disrupted; the two events are comparable to a birth and a death, both of which carry a period of impurity (*āśauca*) and also *anadhyāya* for those within the affected group. I think death causes a period of impurity to the community of which the dead person was a part precisely because the community has been disrupted and has to be reconstituted over a period of time. This is the reason, I believe, why in the *Dharmaśāstras* death impurity and birth impurity are always treated together in spite of the enormous difference between the two events. This is also the reason why the deaths of some individuals, such as infants, outcastes, and ascetics, do not cause *āśauca*, because they are not full and integral parts of the community.

An analysis of the times when recitation is suspended provides even more interesting data. Whenever normalcy is violated, there is *anadhyāya*. So, for example, when there is a solar or lunar eclipse, an earthquake, or a whirlwind, recitation is suspended. Interestingly, lightning, thunder, clouds, and rain cause a suspension only when they appear *out of season*. In the rainy season they are normal and are to be expected; therefore, they do not cause *anadhyāya*. A large number of time-related suspensions happen when one time unit ends and another begins—that is, the time of twilight or *sandhyā* when time boundaries are breached. Thus, there is *anadhyāya* during the morning and evening *sandhyā*, on new- and full-moon days, at the beginning of seasons, at spring and summer festivals, and even on the day that opens and concludes the annual course of study. The boundaries between time zones are marginal and thus ambiguous and inappropriate.

A final comment on boundary and margin: as the margin—the betwixt and between—is a zone where normal activity is suspended, so people temporarily or permanently in such a marginal zone are *not subject to impurity*, showing once again that impurity has to do with structure and thus concerns only those within a structure. So, for example, the death of a family member does not make a *brahmacārin* (student), a *dīkṣita* (a man consecrated for a sacrifice), an officiating priest, or an ascetic impure. Likewise, children before their vedic initiation (*upanayana*) are exempt from all purity rules (**A** 2.15.19–25; **G** 2.1–6). Inversely, the death of a family member who is not fully incorporated into the corporate structure does not cause impurity or causes minimal impurity to its living members—thus there is no impurity when an infant dies.

Another interesting point about marginal people is that they are not permitted to engage in purificatory acts while they are in that state: thus menstruating women are not permitted to bathe or comb their hair before the conclusion of that period; people in mourning cannot bathe; and, according to some, a student is not allowed to bathe or brush his teeth (**A** 1.7.1; **G** 2.13). These are purificatory acts signalling the end of the period of impurity and, hence, are inappropriate during the period of impurity.

What stands out when we examine the Dharma vocabulary on pure/impure is the preoccupation with the body, a preoccupation that borders on scrupulosity and anxiety—*śaṅkā*. Madan (1988: 32, 61) speaks frequently about the *śaṅkā* of his Kashmiri pandits, an anxiety relating primarily to the observance of purity rules. Madhav Deshpande (1993: 41) refers to a suggestive euphemism prevalent in Maharashtra: going to the bathroom is *śaṅkā*, urinating is called *laghuśaṅkā* ('short anxiety') and defecation *dīrghaśaṅkā* ('long anxiety').

Anxiety is connected with intentionality. One recurring problem with scholarly treatments about purity in India is that it is often reified and turned into a self-existing reality. An important component of the Dharma ideology of impurity serves to undermine such a notion—and that is the connection between impurity and intentionality. Intention plays a central role in ethics, and some scholars, including Mary Douglas, contrast ethical and purity rules precisely on this point—intention has a role in ethical rules but not in rules of purity (Douglas 1966: 160). This, I believe, is mistaken. In Dharma discourse not only are terms for impurity and immorality often interchangeable, but intentionality is central also to rules of impurity, although its role there is in many ways different from its role in ethics. Let me cite a few examples in support.

First, it is a rule repeated frequently in the *Dharmaśāstras* that *ignorance makes a thing pure*. Let me repeat—lack of awareness (*adṛṣṭa*) is given as one of the three means that makes a thing pure.[35] If I have not seen that my rice has been licked by a dog, then, as far as I am concerned, my rice is pure. That this is not merely a śāstric fantasy is shown by a story that Dumont (1980: 383) himself relates. At a *śrāddha* a boy from the dead man's family mischievously touches the plate of one of the assembled Brahmins. When the Brahmins are about to abandon the dinner, one of them remarks that there were no witnesses to the touching. So they proceed to eat, and the boy's mother admonishes him never to tell this to anyone. Surely, if purity were an objective reality my ignorance should have nothing to do with its existence. In a similar manner, the death of a relative away from home makes the relatives impure only when they hear about it, and then for a shorter period of time than if he were to die at home.

Second, there is what I would call 'stipulative purity'—that is, rules stipulate that certain people or objects are pure by definition. So, the hand of an artisan or cook, items sold in the market, the mouth of a woman, the beak of a bird that makes a fruit fall, a dog when catching a deer, and the excreta of a child, and so forth—these are all reckoned pure by definition (**Vi** 23.48ff). The earth is also pure by definition; so it cannot carry impurity from one person to another. Thus if a pure man and an impure man are sitting on a seat of straw properly arranged then the pure man contracts impurity because that straw constitutes a 'seat', whereas if the straw is strewn haphazardly he does not contract any impurity (**A** 1.15.13).

And finally, there is a wonderful method of purifying a thing suspected of being impure—you get a Brahmin to declare it to be pure. This method is resorted to also when one is anxious about one's own purity (**B** 2.12.6). This is rather like going to a confessor or psychologist—you want someone in power to say that everything is OK.

[35] 'Gods invented three means of purification for Brahmins: being unaware that something is impure, sprinkling it with water, and getting it verbally declared as suitable.' See **Va** 14.24; **B** 1.8.52; 1.9.9; **M** 5.127; **Vi** 23.47; **Y** 1.191.

The rules and practices relating to impurity in the Dharma texts constitute, I believe, a ritual apparatus rather than a social ideology. These rules do not create social structures but are intended to sustain and reinforce such structures. Within the specifically Indian context, I do not think that purity was the historical cause of the *varṇa* or caste system, nor did it serve as a theodicy to justify that system. As boundaries must precede attempts to sustain and strengthen those boundaries, so the caste system must precede rules concerning the pure and the impure that aim to sustain it. In this sense, Mary Douglas is right in saying that 'dirt' is a by-product of a system.

We can consider impurity rules as a system of socialisation. Individuals within the society must be made to acknowledge and support the social boundaries imposed on them, and this is effected primarily through social rituals. This may be one reason why many of the *Dharmaśāstric* rules on impurity are found in the sections dealing with the vedic student. In any programme of socialisation you have to start young! And it is within the socialising context that what I said about intentionality makes sense. Socialising involves paying attention, involves anxiety—*śaṅkā*. Rules of purity are meant to cause anxiety, for anxiety creates heightened attention to the boundaries that the rules are meant to uphold.

The socialising aspect of these rules also explains another aspect of purity/impurity: the ultimate aim of these rules is not to make people remain constantly pure, which is in principle impossible. Their aim, I believe, is to make people intent on *recovering purity*. Hence most of the terms used for purity, especially *śuddhi* and *śuci*, as we have seen, mean not *being pure* but the act of *becoming pure*. It is purification not purity that is at the heart of the system.

Attention to the socialising aspect of purity also helps us understand the connection between purity and auspiciousness (*śubha*) that has received considerable attention recently (Carman and Marglin 1985; Madan 1988: 48ff). The two have been viewed as both contradictory and complementary. I see the two as dealing with very different aspects of human and social life. *Śubha* deals with the flow of time and life and seeks to direct that flow in benign, fertile, and prosperous directions. *Śubha* is not connected with a programme of socialisation, with the protection of social boundaries and structures. That is the province of purity/impurity. In a totally pure world time would stand still, there will be no change; the world of total purity, ironically, would be a world of death. To be totally and always pure is not only impossible but from a variety of perspectives a highly undesirable condition. But that is pushing the system to its absurd limit. Purity is one among many competing and often contradictory values of human existence and human society. The purpose of rules of impurity is not to ensure permanent purity but to make people anxious about becoming impure and when they become impure, as they must, to make them anxious about recovering their lost purity. This anxiety, finally, is an integral part of the socialising process that sustains and strengthens cultural and social boundaries, including the caste system.

ABBREVIATIONS

A	*Āpastamba Dharmasūtra*
B	*Baudhāyana Dharmasūtra*
G	*Gautama Dharmasūtra*
M	*Manu Smṛti*
N	*Nārada Smṛti*
Va	*Vasiṣṭha Dharmasūtra*
Vi	*Viṣṇu Smṛti*
Vkh	*Vaikhānasa Dharmasūtra*
Y	*Yājñavalkya Smṛti*

REFERENCES

Āpastamba Dharmasūtra. Ed. G. Bühler (3rd edn).: Bombay Sanskrit Series Nos. 44, 50. Poona: Bhandarkar Oriental Research Institute, 1932. Tr. G. Bühler. Sacred Books of the East, vol. 2. Oxford: Clarendon Press, 1879.

BERREMAN, G.D. 1971. The Brahmanical view of caste. *Contributions to Indian sociology* (n.s.) 5: 16–23.

Baudhāyana Dharmasūtra. Ed. E. Hultzsch (2nd edn).: Abhandlungen für die Kunde des Morgenlandes, 16. Leipzig: 1922. Tr. G. Bühler. Sacred Books of the East, vol. 14. Oxford: Clarendon Press, 1882.

CARMAN, J and F.A. MARGLIN, eds. 1985. *Auspiciousness and purity.* Leiden: Brill.

DAS, VEENA and J.S. UBEROI. 1971. The elementary structure of caste. *Contributions to Indian sociology* (n.s.) 5: 33–43.

DESHPANDE, MADHAV. 1993. *Sanskrit and prakrit: Sociolinguistic issues.* Delhi: Motilal Banarsidass.

DIRKS, NICHOLAS B. 1990. The original caste: Power, history and hierarchy in south Asia. *In* McKim Marriott, ed., *India through Hindu categories*, pp. 59–77. New Delhi: Sage Publications.

DOUGLAS, MARY. 1984 [1966]. *Purity and danger: An analysis of the concepts of pollution and taboo.* London: ARK Paperbacks.

DUMONT, LOUIS. 1980 [1966]. *Homo hierarchicus: The caste system and its implications.* Rev. edn. (trans. M. Sainsbury, L. Dumont and B. Gulati). Chicago: University of Chicago Press.

DUNDES, A. 1997. *Two tales of crow and sparrow: A Freudien folkloristic essay on caste and untouchability.* Lanham, Maryland: Rowman & Littlefield.

FÜRER-HAIMENDORF, C. VON. 1971. Tribes and Hindu society. *Contributions to Indian sociology* (n.s.) 5: 24–27.

Gautama Dharmasūtra. Ed. A.F. Stenzler. London: Trübner, 1876. Tr. G. Bühler. Sacred Books of the East, vol. 2. Oxford: Clarendon Press, 1879.

GONDA, J. 1960–61. Prayata. *Bhāratīya vidyā: Munshi indological felicitation volume* 20–21: 45–51.

KANE, P.V. 1968. *History of Dharmaśāstra* vol. 1, part 1 (2nd edn). Poona: Bhandarkar Oriental Research Institute.

KHARE, R.S. 1992. *The eternal food: Gastronomic ideas and experiences of Hindus and Buddhists.* Albany, NT: State University of New York Press.

KUBIE, L.S. 1937. The fantasy of dirt. *The psychoanalytic quarterly* 6: 388–425.

LEACH, E. 1971. 'Esprit' in *Homo hierarchicus. Contributions to Indian sociology* (n.s.) 5: 13–16.

MADAN, T.N. 1971. On the nature of caste in India: A review symposium on Louis Dumont's *Homo hierarchicus. Contributions to Indian sociology* (n.s.) 5: 1–13.

———. 1988. *Non-renunciation: Themes and interpretations of Hindu culture.* Delhi: Oxford University Press.

MADAN, T.N. 1989. Caste and the ordering of Hindu society. *In, The Cambridge encyclopedia of India*, pp. 364–66. Cambridge: Cambridge University Press.

MALAMOUD, C. 1972. Observations sur la notion de 'reste' dans le brāhmanisme. *Wiener Zeitschrift für die Kune Südasiens* 16: 5–16

Manu Smr̥ti. Ed. J. Jolly. London: Trübner, 1887. Tr. G. Bühler. Sacred Books of the East, vol. 25. Oxford: Clarendon Press, 1886.

MARRIOT, McKIM, ed. 1990. *India through Hindu categories*. New Delhi: Sage Publications.

MINES, D.P. 1990. Hindu periods of death 'impurity'. *In* McKim Marriott, ed., *India through Hindu categories*, pp. 103–30. New Delhi: Sage Publications.

Nārada Smr̥ti. Ed. and tr. R. Lariviere. 2 parts. University of Pennsylvania Studies on South Asia, vols. 4–5. Philadelphia: 1989.

OLIVELLE, P. 1995. Food in India. *Journal of Indian philosophy* 23: 367–80.

ORENSTEIN, H. 1970. Death and kinship in Hinduism. *American anthropologist* 72: 1357–77.

RAMANUJAN, A.K. 1990. Is there an Indian way of thinking? An informal essay. *In* McKim Marriot, ed., *India through Hindu categories*, pp. 41–58. New Delhi: Sage Publications.

QUIGLEY, D. 1993. *The interpretation of caste*. Oxford: Clarendon Press.

SMITH, B.K. 1990. Eaters, food and social hierarchy in ancient India: A dietary guide to a revolution in values. *Journal of the American Academy of Religion* 58: 177–205.

TAMBIAH, S.J. 1973. From varna to caste through mixed unions. *In* J. Goody, ed., *The character of kinship*, pp. 191–229. Cambridge: Cambridge University Press.

Vaikhānasa Dharmasūtra. Ed. W. Caland. Bibliotheca Indica, 242. Calcutta: 1927. Tr. W. Caland. Bibliotheca Indica, 251. Calcutta: 1929.

Vasiṣṭha Dharmasūtra. Ed. A.A. Führer. Bombay Sanskrit and Prakrit Series, 23. Poona Bhandarkar Oriental Research Institute, 1930. Tr. G. Bühler. Sacred Books of the East, vol. 14. Oxford: Clarendon Press, 1882.

Viṣṇu Smr̥ti. Ed. V. Krishnamacharya. 2 parts. Madras: Adyar Library and Research Centre, 1964. Tr. J. Jolly. Sacred Books of the East, vol. 7. Oxford: Clarendon Press, 1880.

Yājñavalkya Smr̥ti. Ed. U.C. Pandey. Kashi Sanskrit Series. 178. Varanasi: 1967.

4

Secularism, unicity and diversity: The case of Haracandi's grove

Frédérique Apffel-Marglin

This paper argues that secularism as a concept and practice arose from the need in 16th and 17th century Europe to create a neutral space making possible intra- as well as inter-State discourse. This neutral space was from the beginning part of the emerging scientific revolution; it transposed in a different key the dogmatic unicity of the two warring religious denominations. Secular science created the 'sacred/spiritual' as an other-worldly domain totally separate from this-worldly realms of nature and society. By looking at an important festival in coastal Orissa taking place in a so-called 'sacred grove', the paper argues that the category of sacred thus wielded does violence to a different reality where unicity and the sacred/secular dichotomy, among others, are not found. Rather than essentialist categories, local practice conjures a dynamic, shifting, alternating reality, in which no single principle or reality dominates. The paper argues that unicity is lethal to diversity and that secular nation-states have everywhere adopted science as both a strengthening and legitimising tool, thus endangering diversity. Newly emergent religious 'fundamentalisms' negatively mirror the unicity of the secular nation-state, whereas much of local practice retains its diversity-generating ways of life.

Scientific forestry came to colonial India with the appointment of Sir Dietrich Brandis as the first Inspector General of Forests in 1864 (Sivaramakrishnan 1995: 8). In the 1880's Brandis was already lamenting the destruction of what he, along with others, called 'sacred groves' under the British system of forest management (Gadgil and Guha 1995: 91). The term 'sacred grove' is still in widespread use today to designate a phenomenon outside the secular scientific realm of rational approach to forests. Sacred groves are understood as exemplifying folk conservation practices. Gadgil and Guha view sacred groves as 'entire patches of forests...[that] may be treated as sacred and accorded protection against human exploitation' (ibid.).

Here the sacred is strongly attached to the non-utilitarian. It is also a permanent characteristic, materially embodied in the visibly untouched, uncut grove. A patch of forest is either sacred or profane; if the former, it is left uncut, unexploited; if the latter, it is used for human purposes. The problem with such a classification is that in the practices of peasants and fishermen in the subcontinent the earth and the sea are also sacred in the sense that they are the recipients of offerings and other rituals. Cattle, as well as certain wild animals, tools and utensils, houses, stones, rivers, hills and mountains, the sun, the moon, certain stars and constellations, among other things, are at certain times the recipients of offerings and prayers. In this list one cannot associate the sacred with either what is wild or what is non-utilitarian.

A close observation of the festival held in Haracandi's grove in coastal Orissa at the break of the monsoon in mid-June has led me to see the grove as a spatial transposition of a temporal alternation between fallow (or wild) and cultivated, wet and dry, work and rest. In his latest book, Madan (1997) has argued knowledgeably and elegantly for the indispensability of understanding the emergence of secularism in Europe in order to gain a clear view of present conditions in India. Following his lead, I have found it necessary to revisit the birth of secularism for approaching issues of diversity in India.[1]

I
Secularism and unicity

The essentialist understanding of the sacred as a permanent inherent characteristic is the historical legacy of the creation in 17th century Europe of a secular realm, a realm from which the religious or the sacred has been excluded. The secular realm, carved out of a previous world in which religion pervaded every aspect of life, took its modern particularity with the creation of a space in which religion and politics were out of bounds. Shapin and Schaffer (1985) credit Robert Boyle, the inventor of the air-pump in the 17th century, as the one who first created this space. Thus the secular was from its inception a practice of science as well as a political phenomenon. This new domain separated out the good from the true, as well as from the beautiful. Moral considerations have no place in the pursuit of truth. The secular realm emerged also as a utilitarian domain, opposed to other-worldly matters belonging to a 'supernatural' realm.

The category of the 'supernatural' antedates the emergence of the characteristically modern political, civic and cognitive realm of the secular since it presupposes the corresponding domain covered by 'natural law'. Thomas Aquinas, the great synthesiser of the Aristotelian and the Christian world views in the 13th century, made a careful distinction between phenomena that have natural causes on the one hand and signs on the other hand. The latter could be of two kinds, those sanctioned by the church and those not so sanctioned. The latter were categorised by Aquinas as superstitions (Belmont 1982: 14).

As noted, the particularity of the modern is that it created a special social category to deal with the realm of 'natural causes', separating it from religious as well as political authorities. According to Shapin and Schaffer, Robert Boyle had instituted a practice of public witnessing of 'scientific'[2] experiments by educated and

[1] Although the present essay is about India, this of course holds true for most other places as well.

[2] The term 'scientific' did not become common usage until much later. Robert Boyle and men like him were 'natural philosophers'.

trust-worthy gentlemen who could argue and disagree about what they were seeing only by keeping religious and political matters strictly out of bounds. This new social category was in the 17th century the seed of what was later to become the professions and the academic disciplines. The logic of this winning strategy of Boyle[3] necessitated the separation of the good and the true. Moral concerns for the outcome of experimental activity had to be left out along with all other religious issues. Eventually moral issues became constricted into 'professional ethics', which did little more than counsel one to do the job properly.[4]

The necessity for strictly separating religious and political issues from 'matters of fact' (Shapin and Schaffer 1985) was complex but can be boiled down to two related issues: the issue of unicity and the issue of certainty.

The issue of unicity

In 17th century Europe, it was impossible to have gentlemanly disagreements over religious matters. The very term 'secularization' was coined at the peace of Westphalia (1648) which put an end to the thirty years' war in 17th century Europe (Madan 1997: 13).[5] The thirty years' war was an international religious conflict which was a sequel to a series of eight bloody religious wars in 16th century France. The unity of western Christendom had been rent asunder by the Reformation, plunging Europe into bloody conflicts between two equally dogmatic and intolerant religious factions (Bayrou 1998). Henri IV's attempt to craft a pluri-religious France with the Edit de Nantes eventually failed. His assassination in 1610 marked the beginning of the end for this unique (at the time) experiment in religious tolerance. Assassination attempts had begun as soon as the Edit was signed in 1598; there were seventeen of them. Henri IV, himself the product of a religiously divided marriage, embodied the Renaissance humanist spirit of tolerance so eloquently evident in someone like Montaigne. Although Toulmin (1990) has argued that the 17th century marked a retreat from humanist tolerance, Bayrou's detailed account of the events that led to the Edit de Nantes and its subsequent abrogation makes it clear that in 16th century France, the 'spirit of the age' made it well nigh impossible to have two religions peacefully coexisting. With the Edit, Henri IV, former King of Navarre, made the catholic cult legal in protestant Bearn and Navarre, albeit with the same restrictions as the Edit made for the practice of the protestant cult in catholic France. This provoked spontaneous revolts in these protestant strongholds. Both religions had Inquisitions to try and burn 'heretics' of the other persuasion. Speaking of the 17th century in France,

[3] The rival strategy of Thomas Hobbes refused to separate out the realms of knowledge from those of politics and religion. Hobbes' strategy had enormous weight for over a century but finally was abandoned in favour of Boyle's strategy. See Shapin and Schaffer (1985).

[4] Philosopher Kathryn Pyne Addelson (1998) has remarked that the phenomenon of whistle blowers confirms these facts, since these courageous individuals alert the public to the nefarious consequences of their enterprises or institutions. Such individuals take enormous risks and are often severely punished.

[5] Secularisation referred to the State's takeover of landed property belonging to religious establishments (Madan, ibid.).

Bayrou names this spirit of the age:

> But the unitary exigency, sometimes idealist, sometimes furious, the desire to convert the other, if not banish him, did not extinguish itself in either camp. In this militant faith, it is compassion that is most lacking. Catholic proselytism was to put its imprint on the century, until the abrogation [of the Edit de Nantes] (Bayrou 1998: 233; author's translation).

The manner in which this unitary exigency was articulated at the time was in the saying '*une foi, une loi, un roi*'.[6] It is this unitary vision that started whittling away at the Edit immediately after Henri IV's assassination and gave birth to Louis XIV's infamous '*dragonnades*' and the abrogation of the Edit by him in 1685, less than a century after its promulgation. The 16th century may have witnessed the flowering of tolerant Renaissance humanism in France and elsewhere, but the circumstances attendant upon the effects of the Reformation killed that flower. Since both sides adhered equally to the '*une foi, une loi, un roi*' vision, the protestants made attempts on the king's life (Francois Ier was the first one) and this was retaliated by events such as the killing of Saint Barthelemy. In this context, tolerance, ambiguity, context sensitivity and pluralism eventually died out in spite of such remarkable efforts as those of Montaigne in the realms of ideas, and of those of Henri IV in the political domain.

The issue of certainty

Toulmin has given us the context of Descartes' life from his youth at the Jesuit College of La Fleche founded by Henri IV, where he likely penned his first essay on the occasion of the anniversary of Henri IV's assassination, to his years observing the war at close range first with Maurits of Nassau in Holland and later with the Duke of Bavaria. He died only two years after the end of the thirty years' war (Toulmin 1990: 60–61). Tolerance of ambiguity, uncertainty, and context sensitivity could not withstand the violent effects of unicity. Descartes sought an answer to Montaigne's challenge as to the impossibility of finding 'one certain thing' and he found it in his *cogito*. By contextualising Descartes' life, Toulmin makes visible the debt Descartes' method owes to historical circumstances. By removing the *res cogitans* from everything else, Christian 'other-worldly absolutism'[7] is transposed to men's minds, thus opening the possibility of recovering lost certainty, albeit in a different key. It took the work of Boyle to put Descartes' method into practice and institutionalise it.

Boyle's expert witnesses are the social embodiments of the decontextualising implicit in separating the mind from the body and the world. It was only by making one's religious and political persuasions out of bounds that the certainty of 'matters of facts' could be established.[8] The impasse to which the unitary spirit

[6] One faith, one law, one king.

[7] The phrase is Pouillon's (1982: 8).

[8] The decontextualising was ideological since these educated and trustworthy witnesses had in fact to be of a certain gender and class, something that lasted well into the 20th century.

of the age had brought Europe could only be escaped by inventing a different kind of unicity, one outside of the concrete religious and political realities of the place and time, and thus timeless and universal. This different kind of unicity is located in the transcendental *res cogitans* whose relationship to the *res extensa* parallels the relationship between God and nature. So much so that the word 'idea' was first used by Descartes to refer to men's minds, having previously referred only to God's (Varela et al. 1991: 141). The postulate of objectivity which places the mind outside of all contingency, all context, relates unicity to certainty. The mind is not affected by what it observes; the relationship is unilateral. Certainty is achieved by way of the stability of this observing mind whose position relative to the known is unaffected by shifting contingencies. The certainty that rationality, formal logic and geometry enables is achieved at the price of decontextualising, abstracting and simplifying. It is bound up with unicity by the fact that these procedures require a unitary mind positioned outside and beyond the shifting realities and ambiguous contingencies of the world.

Shapin and Schaffer's work on the debate between Boyle and Hobbes shows that Hobbes' radical unitary solution in which the social, the political, the religious and the cognitive were all to be under one materialist regime eventually lost out because of its dogmatism. Boyle's more flexible approach allowed for disagreements and discussions, in fact required them, as the basis for establishing matters of fact. The crucial point was that such disagreements and discussions could only be had by carving a domain separate from the religious and the political. Dogmatism had brought with it too much violence and was thus rendered suspect. The possibility of gentlemanly disagreement given by Boyle and its positive role in establishing matters of fact were a central selling point in Boyle's programme.

The new practice and method of science enabled the construction of a universal language that by-passed the impossibility of a common discourse, within European states and among them. During the course of the 17th century scientific ideas about the order of nature began to be transposed to ideas about the order of society. This is Toulmin's central thesis of Cosmopolis in which the order of nature and the order of society mirror each other. The following passage captures the gist of his argument:

> Everything in the natural order testifies (or can be made to testify) to God's dominion over Nature. That dominion extends through the entire fabric of the world, natural or human, and is apparent on every level of experience. What God is to Nature, the King is to the State. It is fitting that a Modern Nation should model its State organization on the structures God displays in the world of astronomy: le Roi Soleil, or Solar King, wields authority over successive circles of subjects, all of whom know their places, and keep their proper orbits. What God is to Nature and the King is to the State, a Husband is to his Wife, and Father to his Family [. . .] In all these ways, the order of Nature and the order of Society turn out to be governed by a similar set of laws (Toulmin 1990: 127).

And Toulmin concludes that 'the world-view of modern science—as it actually came into existence—won public support around 1700 for the legitimacy it apparently gave to the political system of nation-states' (ibid.: 128), as much as for its explanatory power as regards the mechanisms of the natural world.

Secularisation was the very specifically European solution to a very specifically European predicament, born out of the 'unitary exigency' that gripped the age. It was both a political and a scientific phenomenon, or, to put it as Shapin and Schaffer do, the scientific practice that Boyle and his associates carved out of religion and politics was itself a political phenomenon. It transposed the old religious unicity into a different and safe key and thus provided the ground for intra- as well as inter-State stability, resolving the explosive stalemate of two equally dogmatic and unitary religious factions.

By 1765, science was becoming an indispensable tool of the State to collect revenue, carry out censuses, do cadastral mapping to know land ownership, and many other things. Scientific forestry emerged first in what is today Germany around that time.

II
Scientific forestry and the state

Scientific forestry was first developed in Prussia and Saxony between 1765 and 1800, and was then extended to other European States as well as to the US. It is one of the many applications of science that were part of the centralised state-making processes of the time (Scott 1998: 14). It also represents the practice of science as the ideology legitimating as well as strengthening the centralised nation-state. It is thus no happenstance that Sir Dietrich Brandis was German; the first scientific forestry departments emerged there. Brandis created the Indian Forest Department and was the first Inspector General of Forests. His work consisted in demarcating and surveying forests, preparing working plans, constructing roads, bridges, drainage, etc. In most provinces, the Forest Department was placed administratively under the Revenue Department. Using a quote from Stebbing to make the point, Sivaramakrishnan remarks that the Forest Service came to be regarded as 'a purely commercial concern–its chief *raison d'être* the production of revenue' (Stebbing 1926: 345 in Sivaramakrishnan 1995: 9–10).

The Indian Forest Act of 1878, which resulted from Brandis' work, is basically still in force today. Scientific forestry is taken by Scott as the paradigm for his argument about 'State simplifications', the abstracting, simplifying, decontextualising requirements for the effective bureaucratic management by the State of its 'resources' for which science was the indispensable tool (Scott 1998: ch. 1). The point Scott makes is that this requirement for efficient management tended to erase the multiplicity of context-sensitive local practices, local weights and measures, local ways of speaking, local ways of living, through its relentless demand for standardisation and 'improvement'. That is, improvement from the point of view of the rationalising managing experts. This ended up by creating a homogenous, geometric, monocultural landscape; it marginalised and in some cases erased many local ways of speaking and living, relentlessly promoting a standardised language and way of life in European countries as in the US. What was initially just an efficient tool for revenue management ended up by reshaping the natural and cultural landscape.

As we saw with the example of scientific forestry, this tight partnership between the State and Science was exported worldwide through colonisation, and so were its effects.

III
'Sacred groves'

For Brandis, and many after him, the phenomenon this label refers to has its reality as much in whatever the locals say and do as in the reality of scientific forestry. A patch of forest dedicated to a local deity or spirit, made up of a variety of local species, left uncut, and the site of ritual offerings, conjures up the opposite of the secular revenue forest, rationally known and managed by a secular State. The notion of the sacred here is profoundly inflected by the secular/scientific, making of it a non-utilitarian entity bearing none of the characteristics of its opposite, except its essential nature. The local grove is sacred like the government forest is a resource; the fact of being a resource or of being sacred are essential characteristics in both.

What I wish to highlight is the kinship between essentialism and unicity/certainty. The certainty that scientific method and practice deliver circumvented 'the theological dogmatists, by arguing in their own idiom—the idiom of certainty' (Toulmin 1990: 70). As discussed earlier, certainty and unicity are indissoluble partners. There is one truth, one measure, in short, one reality. Things can be understood because they are what they are: if a tree or group of trees are seen by some as also a goddess, they are surely seeing or speaking metaphorically or expressing a 'religious belief'.

With the advent of secularisation in Europe, whatever contravened scientific understanding of reality became increasingly relegated to a private domain of religious belief. This has led to a division between perception and knowledge on one side, and belief bearing on a 'supernatural' reality on the other. But as Pouillon has argued in the context of the Dangaleat of Chad, the world for them (and probably for many other people) is not divided between a this-worldly reality and an other-worldly reality. The spirits are experienced rather than 'believed' in and this experience is above all a local one. Such spirits do not necessarily exist everywhere. This leads Pouillon to remark that: '[w]hile the encounter with otherness relativizes Christian belief in an otherworldly absolute, it confirms the Dangaleat experience of the world, which is relative from the beginning and so cannot be disturbed by diversity' (Pouillon 1982: 8).

Science establishes a this-worldly absolute unassailable by others' reality since it relegates this other reality to the safe domain of 'beliefs' held in the privacy of one's mind. This is safe since 'supernatural' reality does not compete with reality *tout court*.

The creation of a secular scientific domain averted the explosive situation of reacting to the presence of a different religion existing in the territory of a catholic French king as a provocation (Bayrou 1998: 176). However this was not accomplished in the manner of the Dangaleat who are 'relative from the beginning' but rather by separating two absolute domains: a this-worldly one whose knowledge is established by a secular community of expert witnesses, and a supernatural one in whose reality one believes in the privacy of one's heart and mind.

By 'relative from the beginning' I understand Pouillon to mean a non-unitary, hence non-essentialist, exigency. The 'sacredness' of groves in the subcontinent, I will argue, cannot be understood as an essential quality. To substantiate this, let us go to the grove at Bali Haracandi, Haracandi of the sand, some 20 km south of the city of Puri in coastal Orissa.

IV
Haracandi's grove

Haracandi's grove is the site of an important yearly festival at the time of the onset of the monsoon in mid-June. The festival is celebrated by all castes including so-called untouchables, except for Brahmins. The local Muslims also play an important role in it. It is a peasant and fisher-folk festival and draws villagers from some sixty villages around the grove. The festival is named Raja Parba, the festival of the menses. Like women's menstrual observances, it lasts four days. The goddess/earth/sea is menstruating during the first three days and on the fourth she/they take a purificatory bath. Men congregate in the grove where all men from one village sleep and eat in the same tent, regardless of caste or touchability. The women celebrate in the villages where they take over all public spaces and where young women play on swings hung in the branches of trees. All agricultural, fishing, and in general all productive activity is suspended and there is an intensification of gift exchanges from husbands and brothers to their wives and sisters. The men in Bali Haracandi's grove have pooled their money and food stores to offer animal (rams and fishes) sacrifice to the goddess and feast several times daily. The Muslims skin and clean the rams, keeping the skins for themselves.

Menses are spoken of as the fallow time of women—who must do no work during their menses and during the festival—and of the earth. During the hot season, the earth lies fallow, hot and dry (in the sense of not giving fruit) like women at their menses. The yearly rhythm of the seasons, of the alternation between dry and wet, synchronises with the rhythms of women's menses, their alternation between fallow times (menses) and productive times. Men as well synchronise their activities with those same rhythms. They abstain from any agricultural/productive activity during the four days of the festival. These seasonal alternations are synchronised in time and place by actions in which the human and the non-human collectivities participate. This participation involves exchanges and reciprocities between the two collectivities. It is this collective action engaged in by both human and non-human collectivities that brings about—if carried out successfully—the continuity and regeneration of both the natural and the cultural world.

This corresponds closely to practices of the Hill Marias, shifting adivasi cultivators of Bastar in Madhya Pradesh. For the Hill Marias the meaning of

> fallowness and of the year of 'no cultivation' is established by the correspondence between the menstrual cycle of a woman, the fallow land and forest regeneration.... The rhythms of the household routines are set with reference to menstruation. This is similar to the way rhythms of cultivation work cycles are set with reference to the fallow periods. Both menstruation and 'fallowness' signify recuperation of fertility.... In a forest the dry seasons are barren and the wet seasons are fertile. However, the dry season is necessary for clearing the forest and for the ripening of the crop, just as menstruation is necessary for the regeneration of fertility (Savyasaachi 1993: 64–65).

Although with permanent rice cultivation (practised in coastal Orissa) there is no cycle of forest regeneration, in both cases we have an articulation between cycles of natural regeneration and cycles of human regeneration. This is also true of fisher folk who do not fish during certain times of the year to allow for the regeneration of the fish. The most surprising realisation for me was that Muslims not only participate in the festival at Bali Haracandi but that Muslim girls undergo the exact same menarche ceremony and menstrual observances as non-Muslim women. In 1992 I spoke with the owner of a paan stall at the mela at Bali Haracandi. Mr Fariduddin lived in a Hindu–Muslim village 2 km from the grove of Bali Haracandi and had created a youth club to help keep law and order at the fair in the grove, along with other non-Muslim youth clubs. He told me the following:

> We try to see that everything goes well at the mela. We join with our Hindu brothers. They also join us at our festivals. We keep good relations with the Hindus, we exchange [gifts] with them.... The Hindus say that their Goddess is at her periods but we do not understand this. We don't ask about this, it may offend them. We observe *raja* by stopping our ploughs. Some of our girls and women play on swings and wear new clothes.

Walking with Mr Fariduddin back to his village we met a Muslim farmer, Sheikh Imabul who told me that during *raja*:

> we give rest to the land, the bullocks, and to men. It is the way people do, it is a custom. We also make *pithas* [special cakes made by all women at *raja*]. The people stop work. If we cultivate at that time, people will surely feel bad, so why should we do it?

Asked whether he thought like the Hindus that the earth menstruates during that time, he replied: 'No, there is no such thing in our book.... But this earth is Mother; only because of that we give rest to her.' In these statements is expressed not only solidarity with Hindu neighbours but the view that the earth is Mother and that she should be given rest. Thus the practices of not ploughing and of stopping work (among others) are engaged in not only to keep harmonious relationships with their Hindu neighbours but also because of their way of viewing the earth as Mother.

V

Is sacred to profane as non-utilitarian is to utilitarian?

The festival of the menses (Raja Parba) is a moment, an articulating moment, within a larger cycle of time; it happens in particular places that are also located in larger places. This articulating moment, which we call a festival or a ritual, is at once separate—in the sense of being emphatically different from daily time and place—as well as part and parcel of the rest of the yearly cycle. The timing of the festival marks the end of the hot and fallow period of the earth and the beginning of the fertile and wet period of planting. The Oriya (and Sanskrit) word *ritu* means both the articulation of the seasons and a woman's menses. The collective actions undertaken by the human collectivity in interaction with the non-human collectivity bring about the regeneration of the human community by synchronising it with the regenerative cycles of the seasons, the earth, the sea, the animals and the plants. In other words, such collective action is efficacious in its impact not only on the human collectivity but on the environment, or more properly on non-human collectivities (the word environment is too anthropocentric in our context). Its efficacy pertains to the fact that it ensures the continuity of life, in other words, the survival of the people and the place, and cannot therefore be separated from a utilitarian outcome.

The regenerative cycles of nature are the collective actions of the beings that make up the non-human world and the local people do not place themselves in a dimension radically separate from these. Both collectivities communicate, exchange, and reciprocate. The ontology of a non-human world made up of many different live beings is no less arbitrary than the mechanistic Cartesian/Newtonian ontology of a non-human world made up of inert particles that are moved solely by external force.

The regenerative cycles of nature have been seen as the guarantors of continuity at least since vedic times, if not well before that. *Ritu* in the vedic literature refers to the articulating activity which creates *rita*, the ordered cosmos (Silburn 1955). The word 'order' is not quite appropriate since it conjures up a static and essentialist reality. I prefer to use the word 'orchestration'. Orchestration is a dynamic rhythm in which the sun articulates by its movements a well orchestrated continuity. It is a dynamic activity that humans do not observe from an outside position, but is one in which humans play an essential role. Without the performance of *ritu-als* (a word appropriately derived etymologically from the Sanskrit *ritu* [Benveniste 1973: 380]), the well-orchestrated movement of the cosmos is threatened. This has tended to be viewed as a ritualistic attitude whose lack of material efficacy is contrasted with the efficacy of rational scientific/technological action. Such a view is predicated on the assumption that the ontology of science is a given rather than a construction. If the ontology shifts to one where both human and non-human collectivities of sentient beings make up the world, the divide between efficacious rational/technological action and ritual action vanishes. Without necessarily positing a continuous historical link between vedic times and contemporary peasants and fisher folk of coastal Orissa, the performance of rituals is seen by them in exactly the same terms as those posited for vedic times.

We moderns see both the cycles of the sun and of the seasons as well as the monthly cycles of women as part of nature, activities that are devoid of mindfulness. This is not the case with the peasants and fisher folk who participate in Raja Parba. The earth and the sea is a woman and she actively bleeds rather than being the passive vehicle of some wholly foreign biology. The word *ritu* refers not only to the bleeding but to the activities that men and women, humans and non-humans, engage in at that time, all consisting in refraining from work and productive activities.[9] Men are as involved in these actions as women; although they do not bleed they must do many things, such as refraining from touching women or ploughing the earth at that time, or making their bullocks work. The body and the place are not separated from what one might call mindfulness or consciousness. To call the personification of various natural phenomena such as mountains, rivers, the sea, rocks, trees, the earth, a religious belief, misses the point.

In an attempt to illustrate the relationship between the human forms of the goddess and her various natural forms as well as to clarify the sacred/non-utilitarian *versus* profane/utilitarian dichotomies, let me cite the words of a peasant, Bhikari Parida, who spoke with me during the festival in the grove:

> The Mother, the earth and women are the same thing in different forms. During the four days of *raja*, the earth, the Mother, is bleeding. We think that women are bleeding too [at that time], not really but symbolically (*sanketika*) and that the Mother bleeds through them. During the menses of the earth women do not work; they play and sing with their friends. The sole reason is for them to rest, just like during their monthly period when they do not work and must not be disturbed, must not be touched, they are untouchable then. When the Goddess is bleeding we also stop all work in the fields, and not only we farmers but all other men, blacksmiths, carpenters, potters, washermen, barbers, fishermen, etc. It is incumbent upon us that we should please the Goddess and women at this time.

The opening phrase could not be clearer. The Mother (*ma*, the goddess here) does not symbolise the earth in the form of a woman. The word for 'symbolically' (*sanketika*) is not used here. It is used later to refer to the fact that women do not actually bleed during the festival, they bleed 'symbolically'. All three are one in different aspects, different forms. For the fishermen, both those who fish in Chilika lake and those who fish in the sea, Goddess Haracandi is their main deity

[9] Sexual intercourse is considered a productive activity and hence proscribed during menstruation as well as during Raja Parba.

and she is the sea. Ramacandra Nayak, a fisherman, told me the following during the festival: 'We fish in the sea. Goddess Haracandi protects us from all sufferings; she is the Lady of the sea and protects us from floods and famine.'

Thus it appears that there is no essential identity for Goddess Haracandi. She can be at once the earth, the sea, the Mother, women in different circumstances. She can also be the trees of the grove, as I learned during one of my visits to the festival and found that one of the trees next to Haracandi's temple was garlanded, encircled with cloth and marked with *sindur*. The priest on duty explained that before the temple was built, the goddess resided in the trees and she still does. Her anthropomorphic image in the temple is only one of her manifestations.

This does not exhaust the list of Haracandi's multiple and fluid identities. During the four days of Raja Parba, Goddess Haracandi is considered to be Draupadi, the heroine of the Mahabharata—specifically, Draupadi separated from her five husbands, whose temples are in five different villages in the area.[10] At other times of the year, some of these husbands visit Haracandi, but they do not do so during Raja Parba. This is because at that time Draupadi is menstruating (Apffel-Marglin 1996). Fishermen as well as farmers and artisans all come to the grove during Raja Parba; all observe this time of rest and do no work.

For farmers and related artisans one important aspect of the Goddess is the earth from which comes their livelihood. As we know, artisans gain their livelihood from a portion of the harvest in the farmers' fields to whom they supply the needed services or implements. (This is known as the jajmani system.) For fishermen, a major aspect of Goddess Haracandi is the sea upon which they depend for their livelihood. For most, during the period of the festival she is Draupadi at her menses, and in general she is also women and the grove itself, that is, the trees that are never cut. For all, including the Muslims, she is the Mother who must now rest. What emerges from this list of some of the most important aspects of Haracandi is that it would be wrong to identify Haracandi solely with the grove or forest preserves. The grove is indeed a sort of forest preserve, a traditional form of forest conservation as Brandis understood it. It would be wrong to say that this grove is sacred because the trees are the Goddess and cannot be cut for use. The trees are indeed the Goddess, but so is the earth and the sea and these are definitely used by farmers and fishermen. The earth and the sea can also be qualified by the word 'sacred' since they are worshipped not only in the form of Goddess Haracandi in her temple, but also directly with offerings in the fields at various moments of the agricultural cycles or offerings to the sea. Thus sacredness cannot be equated with the non-utilitarian, supernatural or other-worldly. This is where lies a profound difference between forest preserves, parks, wild life sanctuaries and other biodiversity preserves on the one hand, and the so-called sacred grove. Although the 'sacred grove' shares with all manner of modern preserves the fact of being set aside and not used for human consumption, what it emphatically does

[10] The villagers are not bothered by being told that the 'real' sites of the great deeds of the Mahabharata are elsewhere. This notion of 'reality' presupposes the kind of absolutism that only a detached, observing and judging mind can achieve.

not share with these is its relation with those parts of the world that are used for human ends.

Thus, rather than sacred/non-utilitarian *versus* profane/utilitarian categorical dichotomies we see a rhythmic alternation and orchestration between rest/fallow and active/productive, both being suffused with rituals and worship, in other words, by what has usually been qualified with the word 'sacred'.

The collective human actions that lead to the preservation of the grove around Haracandi's temple, to the migration of the men from some sixty villages to the grove during the four days of Raja, to their pooling of their resources and making abundant offerings to the Goddess and cooking rich feasts for themselves, in short to the manifold collective actions that constitute this festival, amount to what I have elsewhere called the regeneration of the body, the land and the community (Apffel-Marglin 1993). The salient distinction between the grove and other members of the non-human collectivity is not one of sacred *versus* non-sacred but rather one of active alternating with resting, of fallow alternating with productive, of menstruating alternating with non-menstruating, of being in use alternating with not being in use. These are not categorical oppositions but rhythmic alternations orchestrated by both human and non-human collectivities. The regeneration of life depends on such alternations. There is a period to plough and till and a period to let the land rest; there is a period to fish and a period to let the fish regenerate; there is a period for conception and a period to let the womb regenerate; there are uncut groves and there are cultivated fields. This is of course a rather abstract way of speaking. These actions and arrangements all involve invocations, gifting, other expressions of gratitude for the gifts of the productive season of the earth or the sea. That is, all involve communicating with and exchanging with the non-human collectivity. The rhythm of the seasons, from the daily rising and setting cycles of the sun and moon to the larger cosmic cycles, to animal and plant and human life-cycles, to water cycles, all involve alternations between hot and wet, between fallow and productive, between light and dark, between touching or joining and not touching or separating, between rest and activity.

In other words, orchestrated alternations between states that more often than not are dramatically different and even opposed to each other (such as dry and wet, light and dark, active and inactive) are the actions by the human and non-human collectivities whose outcome—if successfully carried out—is the continuity of life. These alternations are rhythmic and the place and/or moment in time at which one phase or mode articulates with another, opposed phase or mode are marked by special activities which have been called rituals. The grove is a spatially orchestrated alternation with the cultivated field. The grove and the field alternate, like the dry and wet season alternate. The grove is untouched, unused land on which trees are allowed to stand and grow undisturbed. The women who sit and do no work and are untouched during their menses, or who do no work during the festival, the men who set up their tents under the shade of the ancient trees huddled around menstruating Haracandi/Draupadi/grove/earth/sea and all who speak to the Goddess and offer her sacrificed rams and fish and other foods are all acting in ways that are opposed to the phase of activity, of productivity. They engage in intense interactions with the non-human collectivity as well as within the human collectivity, but it is a kind of interaction different from, and in some cases opposed to, the interaction they engage in during the phase of productive activity. The oppositions, even reversals, are obvious. Menstruation is usually carefully kept out of temples and worship. People of different castes do not usually share food or sleep in the same room. Women do not usually take over all the village public spaces. Girls and young women do not usually swing from trees, etc. Many, if not most, of these practices do not follow rules of purity and impurity, and they erase hierarchical distinctions.

VI
Unicity and hierarchy

The fact that Brahmins do not celebrate this festival, which is observed all over rural Orissa, is significant. It is clear that Raja Parba has its existence not in the pure/impure nexus but in the auspicious/inauspicious one; and that one speaks of regenerativity and the continuity of life (Apffel-Marglin 1985; Apffel-Marglin and Carman 1986; Madan 1987; Raheja 1988). The rules of purity are not followed on this occasion, beginning with the fact that it celebrates menses, a well-known source of impurity. With the purificatory bath on the morning of the fourth day, the movable image of Haracandi is taken out of her temple in the grove and processed to a nearby pond where it is bathed. The priest puts red powder in the water and tells the pilgrims that this water is her menstrual blood. The pilgrims receive this water in their hands and drink it. The fact that all castes (except Brahmins), including so-called untouchable groups, sleep and eat together during the festival also does not follow the rules of purity and pollution.

The anthropological literature has offered varied theories to account for this type of practice. Max Gluckman called them 'rituals of rebellion' (1963), in which the stresses and tension in the social structure find a safety valve. Victor Turner sees such rituals as part of the liminal phase of rites of passage characterised by egalitarianism or what he calls communitas (Turner 1966: 96 *passim*). For both Gluckman and Turner 'the social structure' is the pivotal construct that determines their understanding of practices that seem to flaunt it. For example, Turner says that liminality is where 'social structure is not' (1966: 96). Social structure, here, negatively defines the liminal. What is clear in both these authors is that such practices are perceived as in some sense aberrant and needing explanation.

The auspicious/inauspicious axis is central to kingship, to *kshatra* and its concerns with the well-being, generativity and regenerativity of the realm, its people, animals and land.[11] It seems to me that the scholarly discussion of the relationship

[11] Bali Haracandi is the guardian of the southern entrance into Samkhya Kshetra, the holy territory of Jagannatha. The king as the living embodiment of Jagannatha, has special status in that land; indeed he sends three rams to Bali Haracandi at the time of Raja Parba for sacrifice. This information was given to me by the late K.C. Rajguru, *purohita* of the king of Puri, and confirmed by the priests at Bali Haracandi.

between *kshatra* and *brahman* summarised by Madan (1997: 180–88), is weighed down by what we can call the unitary exigency and its attendant essentialism. Is *kshatra* secular or is it not? The question betrays its essentialist perspective. Furthermore, *kshatra* and/or the secular is contrasted to the spiritual embodied in the Brahmin. The secular and the spiritual are wielded as essential qualities in the way that they have functioned in European history. This gives rise to great difficulties in conceptualising the relationship between *kshatra* and *brahman*. Besides the difficulty of using a term such as 'secular' so deeply steeped in the specifics of European history, a difficulty Madan has eloquently written about, there is the deeper difficulty of perceiving contradictory principles. For example the king as wielder of force is impure; however as the preserver of the social order he maintains the caste hierarchy and thus the principle of purity and impurity. This seeming paradox is captured, for example, in Dumont's view of an absolute disjunction between status and power (1980: 71–72). Dumont surmounts the difficulty that such a disjunction presents by his notions of the encompassed and the encompassing that attempt to reunite these seeming opposites under one hierarchical umbrella. Heestermann speaks of kingship as being 'suspended between sacrality and secularity, divinity and mortal humanity' (1985: 111, cited in Madan 1997: 183), whereas Biardeau 'recognizes the secular content of kingship, but hardly allows it any autonomy' (Madan 1997: 182). All these formulations have an implicit essentialist (unitary) character.

Dumont's notions of encompassed and encompassing in particular attempt to house under one regime, one structure, one scaffolding, realities that simply do not pertain to the unitary exigency. Like Turner's and Gluckman's notion of social structure—a notion pervasive to much social science until recently—they are static and unitary.

Dirks points out that British colonial practices, such as census taking and classificatory schemes, as well as the destruction of kingship, have created a rigid, linear and ossified 'caste hierarchy' both in thought and in practice (Dirks 1989, 1990). Raheja (1988) breaks with the heavy legacy of unicity with her notion of shifting positionality in which, according to context, principles which she names centrality, mutuality and hierarchy are at play. In such a perspective, principles or practices that do not follow one single logic cease to become problematic. Ramanujan in his justly famous essay 'Is there an Indian way of thinking?' (1990) saw context sensitivity as pervasive in the Indian subcontinent as well as radically opposed to the demand for consistency characteristic of European thought and action. A single hierarchical principle can no longer be seen as the overriding reality in caste society simply because there is no such thing as an 'overriding reality'. It is one moment, one reality among others. The equivalency and sharing practised during Raja Parba is as real, as important, as the hierarchical relations during other times.

No one truth, no one principle, no one perspective can account for shifting, dynamic, and constantly changing contingencies. The requirement of things being 'true to themselves', being non-contradictory, being what they are and not something else is the legacy of what Bayrou named the 'unitary exigency'. This exigency is lethal to diversity. The notions of context sensitivity, of positionality and of orchestrated alternations are generative of diversity. In the absence of a division between a natural and a supernatural (or other-worldly) realm as well as of a division between a mind (*res cogitans*) and the world (*res extensa*), essentialism, logical consistency and unicity evaporate.

VII
Conclusion: Human and non-human diversity

Maps, cadastral and otherwise, rely on a standardised representation of the world with standardised measures of latitudes and longitudes. By their nature, these representations simplify and summarise. But, as Scott (1998) has made clear, they also transform the world in their image of universal space when they become instruments of the State. Furthermore, simplifications have been used by both the right and the left, from National Socialism to Socialism and Communism (Scott 1998: 89). The same applies to time, which becomes standardised and hence universalised. It also becomes linear. In this modern view of space–time, it matters where exactly Kurukshetra was located and when exactly the great battle and other epic deeds of the Mahabharata took place. In fact such questions become the bread and butter of many professional historians, archaeologists, and other scholars.

By contrast, the places and times[12] in which the events of Raja Parba have their existence are specific to the collective actions of all the participants and are made by them. These participants—both human and non-human—are specific to these places–times. Draupadi and the Pandavas have their existence in the naming and doing collectively engaged in. It makes no sense in this context to look for the 'real' plain of Kurukshetra or the 'actual' time of these various deeds. In other words, diversity is not only not a threat to these place–times; rather it is, as it were, a built-in presupposition.

Diversity characterises not only the human collectivity but also the non-human collectivity. There is no singular, unidimensional frame of reference that would make one species of trees, for example, to be valued above all others, as is the case with scientific forestry. Different trees offer different sorts of gifts for different uses, occasions, contingencies. In agriculture, polyculture rather than monoculture had been the rule until the advent of various developmental packages.

I will end with one more example of religious diversity, in honour of Professor Madan's chosen theme in *Modern myths, locked minds*. I will briefly speak of one of the most important Pir shrines in Orissa. The shrine is that of Bokhari Baba, and it is located in Kaipadar, a village not far from the city of Khurda. This shrine is the most important Muslim shrine in the region. During its most important festival, according to the *khadim* on duty when I visited in 1994, 75 per cent of devotees are Hindus. One of the most remarkable features of this shrine is that the flower garland providers as well as the providers of sweets for the daily offerings

[12] I am thankful to Kathryn Pyne Addelson for introducing me to the notion of 'place–times', and for the many discussions over the years on these and related issues.

are Hindus. The pamphlet which the *khadim* gave me (written by one Trinatha Sricandana) gave a short history of the Pir. Bokhari Baba was born in Bokhara in the 17th century and eventually settled in Kaipadar. There he attracted followers among the local population by his saintly aura and his performance of miracles. King Ramacandra Deva[13] resided in the nearby Varunei Hill. He met the *baba* while hunting in the forest and thus came to know of his saintliness. When the *baba* was covered by an ant-hill, thus becoming a living Pir (*jinda pira*), the Gajapati (title of Orissan dynasty) instituted a cult of the Pir by granting land to a *khadim* family, to a Hindu family of garland-makers and to a Hindu family of sweet-makers for the continued performance of offering at the place. An ornate shrine was built in the last century over the ant-hill. The Hindu families of garland-makers and sweet-makers are still in possession of the land given by Ramacandra Deva, and continue to discharge their duties at the shrine.

What this king institutionalised, namely the worship by two different religious communities at the same shrine, was simply unthinkable in Europe. The most that Henri IV achieved with the Edit de Nantes was to allow the discreet performance of the cult of the minority religion; and that did not last very long. Joint worship by two different religions has been inconceivable in European history.

What is as remarkable as Ramacandra Deva institutionalising joint worship is the fact that this arrangement has lasted till today. Furthermore it is an arrangement that reflects local practice. Hindus flock to Muslim Pirs' shrines and Muslims participate in Hindu festivals such as we have seen with Raja Parba. This is not a medieval practice that has long since disappeared. The furious unitary exigency displayed by different fundamentalist movements today mirrors, in its negative response, the unitary exigency of the modern centralised nation-state and the science that legitimates it.

The simplification practices of the colonial State in India, continued by the Indian State after independence, have tended to transform the diversity of place–times along the lines of the European Cosmopolis. As in Europe, the indispensable tools of the State for achieving this have been the sciences, both social and natural. Some of the results of these simplifying practices have been the rise of what Vandana Shiva has called a 'monoculture of the mind' (1993) that finds its expression in other types of monocultures. In particular, caste hierarchy has taken on a more dominant and relentless reality, marginalising other aspects of caste such as mutuality and centrality, as well as making them more invisible. It is, however, quite another matter to reduce caste to hierarchy even today.[14] The practices narrated in this paper and those referred to are real enough. The ferocious unitary impetus of the last 200 years or so has not managed to erase many of the diversity-generating

[13] He is clearly not the Ramacandra Deva who reconstituted a small Hindu kingdom around Khurda in 1580 and reconsecrated the images in the Jagannatha temple in Puri in 1590 after the conquest by the Afghan Bengal armies (Kulke 1978: 322). The pamphlet gives the date 1734 for the gift of land by this king.

[14] In 'Gender and the unitary self: Looking for the subaltern in coastal Orissa' (1995), I have taken to task Ranajit Guha's unitary (essentialist) view of gender and, by extension, of caste.

practices that continue to make a multiplicity of place–times in the subcontinent. They must be made visible, since they are the ones to turn to when looking for a way out of the impasse created by different types of unitary exigencies, be they in a religious or a scientific secular idiom.

REFERENCES

ADDELSON, KATHRYN PYNE. 1998. Responsibility and collective agency. Working paper from the Center for Mutual Learning at Smith College. K.P. Addelson & F. Apffel-Marglin, eds, Ms. August, 43–58.

APFFEL-MARGLIN, FRÉDÉRIQUE. 1985. *Wives of the God-king: The rituals of the devadasis of Puri.* Delhi: Oxford University Press.

———. 1995. Gender and the unitary self: Looking for the subaltern in Coastal Orissa. *South Asia research* 15, 1: 78–130.

———. 1996. Rationality, the body, and the world: From production to regeneration. *In* F. Apffel-Marglin & S.A. Marglin, eds, *Decolonizing knowledge: From development to dialogue*, pp. 142–81. Oxford: Clarendon Press.

APFFEL-MARGLIN, FRÉDÉRIQUE and JOHN CARMAN, eds. 1986. *Purity and auspiciousness in Indian society.* Leiden: Brill.

APFFEL-MARGLIN, FRÉDÉRIQUE with PURNA CHANDRA MISHRA. 1993. Sacred groves: Regenerating the body, the land, the community. *In* Wolfgang Sachs, ed., *Global ecology: A new arena of political conflict*, pp. 197–207. London: Zed Books.

BAYROU, FRANCOIS. 1998. *Ils portaient l'écharpe blanche: l'aventure des premiers réformés, des guerres de religions à l'Edit de Nantes, de la Révocation à la Révolution.* Paris: Bernard Grasset.

BELMONT, NICOLE. 1982. Superstition and popular religion in western societies. *In* M. Izard and P. Smith, eds, *Between belief and transgression: Structuralist essays in religion, history, and myth*, pp. 9–23. Chicago: University of Chicago Press.

BENVENISTE, EMILE. 1973. *Indo-European language and society.* Coral Gables, Fla.: University of Miami Press.

DIRKS, NICHOLAS. 1989. The invention of caste: Civil society in colonial India. *Social analysis*, Special Issue: 42–52.

———. 1990. The original caste: Power, history and hierarchy in South Asia. *In* McKim Marriott, ed., *India through Hindu categories*, pp. 59–77. New Delhi: Sage Publications.

DUMONT, LOUIS. 1980. *Homo hierarchicus: The caste system and its implications* (revised edn). Chicago: University of Chicago Press.

GADGIL, MADHAV and RAMACHANDRA GUHA. 1995. *Ecology and equity: The use and abuse of nature in contemporary India.* London: Routledge.

GLUCKMAN, MAX. 1963. Rituals of rebellion in South-East Africa. *In* Max Gluckman, *Order and rebellion in tribal Africa*, pp. 110–36. London: Cohen and West.

HEESTERMAN, J.C. 1985. *The inner conflict of tradition.* Chicago: University of Chicago Press.

KULKE, HERMAN. 1978. The struggle between the Rajas of Khurda and the Muslim Subahdars of Cuttack for dominance of the Jagannatha cult. *In* A. Eschmann, H. Kulke & G.C. Tripathi, eds, *The cult of Jagannath and the regional tradition of Orissa*, pp. 321–42. New Delhi: Manohar.

MADAN, T.N. 1987. *Non-renunciation: Themes and interpretations of Hindu culture.* Delhi: Oxford University Press.

———. 1997. *Modern myths, locked minds: Secularism and fundamentalism in India.* Delhi: Oxford University Press.

POUILLON, JEAN. 1982. Remarks on the verb 'to believe'. *In* M. Izard & P. Smith, eds, *Between belief and transgression: Structuralist essays in religion, history and myth*, pp. 1–8. Chicago: University of Chicago Press.

RAHEJA, GLORIA GOODWIN. 1988. *The poison in the gift: Ritual, prestation, and the dominant caste in a north Indian village.* Chicago: University of Chicago Press.

RAMANUJAN, A.K. 1990. Is there an Indian way of thinking? An informal essay. *In* McKim Marriott, ed., *India through Hindu categories*, pp. 41–58. New Delhi: Sage Publications.

SAVYASAACHI. 1993. An alternative system of knowledge: Fields and forests in Abhujhmarh. *In* Tariq Banuri and F. Apffel-Marglin, eds, *Who will save the forests? Knowledge, power, and environmental destruction*, pp. 53–79. London: Zed Books.

SCOTT, JAMES C. 1998. *Seeing like a state: How certain schemes to improve the human condition have failed.* New Haven: Yale University Press.

SHAPIN, STEVEN and SIMON SCHAFFER. 1985. *Leviathan and the air-pump: Hobbes, Boyle, and the experimental life.* Princeton: Princeton University Press.

SHIVA, VANDANA. 1993. *Monocultures of the mind: Biodiversity, biotechnology and the Third World.* Penang: Third World Network.

SILBURN, LILLIAN. 1955. *Instant et cause: Le discontinu dans la pensée philosophique de l'Inde.* Paris: Librairie Philosophique J. Vrin.

SIVARAMAKRISHNAN, K. 1995. Colonialism and forestry in India: Imagining the past in present politics. *Comparative studies in society and history* 37, 1: 3–40.

TOULMIN, STEPHEN. 1990. *Cosmopolis: The hidden agenda of modernity.* New York: The Free Press.

TURNER, VICTOR. 1966. *The ritual process: Structure and anti-structure.* Glenside PA: Aldine.

VARELA, F., E. THOMPSON and E. ROSCH. 1991. *The embodied mind: Cognitive sciences and human experience.* Cambridge, Mass.: MIT Press.

5

The politics of moral practice in psychotherapy and religious healing

Arthur Kleinman and **Don Seeman**

T.N. Madan made the study of comparative moral systems into an important mainstay of Indian sociology. In this essay, we will be using the idea of 'moral practice' to compare notions of efficacy in psychotherapy and various forms of religious healing. We argue that the realm of 'the moral' in ethnographic analysis consists not of abstract rules or ideologies, but of whatever has overwhelming practical relevance in the lives of the people and communities we study. Both psychotherapy and religious healing systems define efficacy in terms of culture-specific understandings of personhood and moral order; these, however, are mediated by the irreducible contingencies of social position, political strategy, and life histories of both sufferers and healers, as well as by large scale economic and political forces. Healing efficacy emerges from this study as a shifting, multi-vocal, and sometimes unattainable value. By turning our attention from the language of moral concepts to that of moral stakes, therefore, we are attempting to accommodate a concern with the concrete experience of suffering and healing as they are embedded in lived worlds of human experience.

Among the many contributions T.N. Madan has made to academic discourse in the social sciences are his writings on the relation of political and religious processes to everyday moral and medical practices. Whether his focus is the non-renunciation practices of the householder, the religious commitment to pluralism and tolerance that undergirded the politics of an earlier generation of Indian modernisers (whom he believes are mistakenly understood as 'secularists'), or the social forces moulding recruitment, training, and the organisation of health professionals, Professor Madan has insisted on the importance of the mediation of moral vision and practice between cultural representation, political activity, and collective experience. For this reason, our contribution to his Festschrift will focus on the politics of moral practice in two distinctive but clearly related domains: psychotherapy and religious healing.

In arguing that both psychotherapy and religious healing are forms of moral practice, we will not be charting altogether new terrain. Categories of illness and wellness, whatever the specific healing practices involved, are famously suffused with local moral and cultural conceptions, including the often implicit question 'how best to live', which Professor Madan has located at the centre of the idea of the moral in anthropological analysis (Madan 1981: 126). In an attempt to 'reaffirm the dialectical nature of anthropological knowledge' (ibid.: 149), he has called upon us to undertake a study of comparative moral systems, by which he means the concepts to which people refer 'when they want to know what is *right* in a certain situation and what one *ought* to do in it', especially, as in illness, where the consequences of particular choices can be extreme. One result of this systematic and intellectualist formulation, however, is that 'calculations of prudence and utility are here ruled out in principle' (ibid.: 126). It is important to note, therefore, that we will be using the term 'moral' in a somewhat different sense than that to which it is typically applied in moral systems analysis.

For one thing, our emphasis is on forms of practice, oriented not just with regard to the elaboration of values for formal decision making, but with defining and responding to whatever is most at stake in local worlds of experience—a consideration from which questions of prudence and utility can never be discounted in principle. The first author has elsewhere defined the realm of the moral as that of 'overbearing practical relevance' (Kleinman and Kleinman 1991) in the varied contexts of daily living. It is a matter not just of systemic concepts but of embodied states, ritual and political transactions, and the construction of selves in accord with culturally specific models. By shifting from the language of moral concepts to that of moral stakes, we are attempting to accommodate a concern with the concrete experience of suffering and healing. As Professor Madan noted some time ago in an essay on anthropological fieldwork, it is only through 'living intimately with strangers' that we can develop anthropological theory in a way that is true to that which really matters in people's lives—and hence avoid being led astray into misunderstanding (Madan 1975). This is the sense of moral practice to which we will be referring in this analysis of psychotherapy and religious healing.

I

The moral, the medical, and the politics of psychotherapy

In an instructive analysis of the French psychotherapeutic tradition, the late Gladys Swain (1994) showed that one could understand the emergence of moral therapy in French medical psychology at the end of the 19th century in terms of the increasing recognition by members of the famous Nancy School of Hypnotherapy that their patients sometimes resisted the influence of hypnotic suggestion. This resistance resulted first in the reemergence of pathology, but allowed later for a psychotherapy of persuasion in which the patient was expected to play an active role, eventually taking responsibility for his or her own healing. Swain shows that this transformation, from passive recipient of care in an authoritative (not to say authoritarian) medical system to active agent of change in one's own self processes, was what Pierre Janet (1925) had in mind as the *moral* basis of psychological healing. It involved a reconstruction of the patient from object of care to moral agent, in terms elaborated by the Western liberal tradition.

This moral movement was initially taken up and advanced in a huge wave of psychoanalysis that swept all other forms of healing before it in the early 20th century. As Ellenberger (1970) and others have shown, however, this was soon replaced (especially, by mid-century, in North America) by a form of psychoanalysis in an almost engineering mode, a psychoanalysis in which psychic processes were diagnosed and manipulated as if the person as a moral agent did not exist. In this form of psychoanalysis, the active engagement of a person, a healer, and a unique, personally specific context of dilemmas and choices, was reduced to a set of presumably universal and inflexible categories.

For all its insight, however, the kind of moral therapy described by Gladys Swain and her colleague Marcel Gauchet (1994) suffers both from being overly Western, and from a certain narrowness of conceptualisation. These two limitations, moreover, intensify each other's effects, so that we are left with an approach that locates the relationship between the moral and the medical spheres almost entirely in the individualisation of the person as moral decision maker. The therapeutic corollary of this construction is an emphasis on techniques of treatment that place control in the hands of the individual patient, or which require the transformation of the patient from a passive recipient of care into an active—hence moral—agent of change.

Closely related, in this Western orientation to the moral, has been an emphasis on what Roger Shattuck (cited in Delbanco 1995: 4) called 'the soul's scruples', by which he meant that 'civilization can exist only if persons think hard about the effects of acting on their wants.' We are thus forced to operate in the world 'between desire and "the soul's scruples"' (ibid.), under a weight of heavy moral responsibility. According to this view, moral experience results from the recognition of limits to knowledge and passion, and from action informed by reflection on the dangerous potentiality of selfishness and evil in human nature. Shadowing this conception has been the fear of a 'loss of the human'—an anxiety that release of human selfishness and evil could lead to a loss of the compassion and sensibility which make us distinctively human in a morally ramified evaluative framework (Kleinman 1997).

It is this understanding which can be most forcefully contrasted with that which emerges from recent medical anthropological studies of social experiences related to suffering and healing. In these studies, 'the moral' is not defined against an implicit model of good—whether secular or religious in orientation—but through 'what is at stake' for social actors in a local world where they are embedded in transpersonal contestations, alliances and networks (Kleinman and Kleinman 1991; Wikan 1995). Some things matter definitively in local worlds, and those values, statuses, choices, and actions, can differ greatly from one local world to another. In some cases there are considerable disjunctures in what is at stake for people across even narrow divides of social position—class, gender, age cohort, religious or ethnic subgroup—within the same complexly interwoven local world (Das 1994; Farmer, Connors and Simmons 1996).

The medical anthropology perspective would seem to indicate, therefore, that psychotherapeutic practice reflects the interplay not only of large scale cultural, institutional, and economic conditions, but is also shaped by the location of the therapeutic encounter in a local moral world. Paris and Nancy, France, at the *fin de siècle* were not the same worlds as Boston or New York, even though psychotherapy in both American and French settings was powerfully constrained by visions of moral practice that emerged from a shared Western intellectual and ethical tradition. It is this disjuncture between local worlds, which still does not indicate their complete incommensurability—linked after all by global social and economic forces, as well as by shared elements of a recognisably human condition—which gives medical anthropology its special epistemological and methodological burden in the analysis of suffering and healing. One area in which this disjuncture of local worlds is especially apparent is in the development of psychotherapy as a healing practice cross-culturally.

Seen from the perspective of East or Southeast Asia, for instance, the moral vision of increasing individualism and liberation of the self (or its Janus-faced opposite, self constraint) which has come to characterise dominant forms of psychotherapy in the West seems remarkably one-sided, even in the globalised terms of contemporary discourse. Psychotherapy has developed hesitantly, by fits and starts, in Japan, Taiwan, Hong Kong, China; but it has not gathered anything like the unifying force it has in the West. Examples can be found of the Western moral vision and associated psychotherapeutic practices taking root in East Asia—Jungian therapy and psychoanalysis have small numbers of devoted followers in Japan, and cognitive psychotherapy in Hong Kong and Taiwan—but by and large these have not been major forces. Rather, what is most impressive is the resistance these societies have continued to offer to Western approaches, as well as the tendency for hybrid practices to develop (like Morita psychotherapy, that combines indigenous Buddhist and Western approaches). Biomedical practice has been adopted—but indigenised—in a variety of widespread forms of day-to-day patient care around the world.

In China, moral practice in psychiatry is much more likely to involve the use of moral exhortations presented in an authoritative fashion by staff to whom patients with psychological problems often represent a threat to the moral order rather than a locus of theoretically inalienable individual rights (which is not to say that those rights have always been accorded primacy in practice by Western liberal states). In Chinese mental health care systems, emphasis is on social control, public safety, and the individual's obligation to society, rather than patient rights. The chronic mentally ill are treated in a way that aims first to control the threats they pose to social order, and only afterwards to address questions of optimum care for an individual person's problems. The family, the work unit, and the institutions of health, welfare, and police figure more centrally in the care of patients with schizophrenia or manic-depressive disorder than does the sick person.

Even these profound societal-level cultural differences, however, are shifting today under the influence of global political economy, the politics of local worlds, and the social history of institutional and professional practices. In the United States, the political economy of health care financing reform under the rubric of managed care is making it much more difficult for patients to receive psychotherapy. When patients do gain access, the psychotherapy they receive emphasises short term control of symptoms over long term, morally relevant treatment of issues relating to the personality or to family and social contexts.

The upshot of such epochal change is a shift in moral vision and emotional reactions. Thus, there is a political economy of inner experience and the modes of treatment applied to this terrain of the soul. The moral, in this medical anthropological perspective, is not reducible to cognitive process and ethical decision making. Rather it is seen as embodied in the connection of public symbols and transpersonal meanings to inner emotional states of fear, grief, rage, and resentment. The emphasis includes awareness of how political processes (say, violence and terror) shape moral-emotional responses (say, resistance or complicity). A person, so viewed, is the result of his or her own individual agency constrained, oriented, or substantially created out of the effects of social structure. It is this dialectic between collective and individual experience which brings together the political, the moral and the medical, as in the health effects of poverty or political violence, as mediated by contestation over resources and power, on bodies and selves (high rates of diarrhoeal deaths in infants, higher rates of heart attacks in lower level civil servants, higher levels of emigration of the richest from the killing fields leaving the poorest to cope with ethnocide). Here resistance to malign structures or betrayal of others under reigns of terror, as in Cambodia under Pol Pot, the former Soviet Union under Stalin or China under Mao, rebalance structure–agency into menacing results that make politics determinative of moral-medical outcomes, and therefore changes in political processes become truly crucial as the focus for 'therapies'.

There is then a politics of moral practice in psychotherapy. Psychotherapy was conducted in both Stalin's political regime of terror and Hitler's. One can only imagine what kinds of therapeutic practice took place in those malevolent settings. But in all settings of psychotherapy, no matter how benign or 'progressivist', political processes represent the usually unarticulated hidden structuring of problems and practices. The psychotherapist in the United States, who treats inner city African American patients diagnosed as sociopaths without taking institutionalised racism and injustice created by the politics of ethnic/class inequality into account, fails to see his or her own participation in the political process. The psychotherapist who labels victims of Sri Lankan or Afghan political violence as patients with posttraumatic stress disorder (PTSD), and treats them for the pathological effects of memory but does not bring the politics of PTSD into the treatment is as much a victim of politics as his or her client. The appropriation of the suffering of those who are bereaved or at end-of-life as major depressive disorder treatable by antidepressant medications and cognitive psychotherapy involves a political and moral transformation of collective and individual experience (especially in a time of high competition between therapists where creating new patients has a financial incentive); it brings into question the purpose of psychotherapy.

The very action of reconstructing collective problems (violence, substance abuse) as individual ones indicates the political and moral processes in psychotherapy which structure agency. But there is more to the politics of the moral in psychotherapy than even this illustration suggests. Elsewhere one of us has shown that epochal shifts in social orders are associated with deep transformations in the moral-emotional foundations of experience to such a degree that one can speak, with historical and cross-cultural justification, of transformations in the existential lineaments of human nature (Kleinman 1997). That is to say, human nature is not fixed, but itself is responsive to political change to such an extent that what we can so easily assume to be the independent and unchanging psychological and moral domains of life are themselves caught up in the politics of societal change. We take this to be what Daniel Jonah Goldhagen (1996) suggests represents what took place in the Holocaust as Nazi political motivations of eliminationist anti-Semitism were translated into collective and individual psychological and moral practices that enabled the industrial scale murder by 'ordinary men' of ordinary Jews. And we assume that a process not very different characterises different examples of genocide and other forms of political violence. Can a psychotherapy of survivors that fails to get at such historical transformation make sense without taking into account the politics of moral and psychological experience (see Kleinman et al. 1997)?

In this sense, two historical processes interact. The appropriation of the voices of victims of social suffering—such as the survivors of the Bhopal disaster—by institutions of the state (law courts, medical clinics, other bureaucratic agencies) includes the appropriation of victims' subjective complaints by psychotherapists. But both patients and practitioners are themselves in the subject positions of moral-emotional aspects of historical change that are undergoing transformation as part of those large scale political, economic and cultural changes that define the passing of an epoch and the emergence of a new age. In our times such a transformation is discernible. In the United States and other societies, the commercialisation of ordinary experience is thinning out compassion, creating voyeurism for suffering at a safe distance, and intensifying the replacement of moral and religious strategies by psychotherapeutic ones so that courage and endurance in the face of pain and misery are converted into manipulatable medical states. The intersection of this historical transformation in social experience (and subjectivity) with historical change in institutions and their political functions is what makes the politics of moral practice in psychotherapy so significant a focus for research and theory.

The following illustration comes from field notes from observation of a medical psychotherapy session between a senior male psychiatrist and a married female patient at a psychiatric clinic in a city in China in 1991.

Psychiatrist: What problem?

Patient: Headaches, pain, the same bad feelings as before.

Psychiatrist: As I told you last time, you must learn to live with your problems, to endure them.

Patient: My husband and my inlaws don't understand. They treat me badly. They don't give me the care I need. I want us (husband and her and their 5-year-old daughter) to move to our own place. I don't care how small or how far. I need rest. I can't do my office work and then return to do all the things around the house. Too much pressure all the time.

Psychiatrist: This is not good. Always you complain. You must obey your husband and his parents. Then all will become harmonious. Now all is chaos; you must do your part to bring harmony and cooperation.

Here we see, quite typically, a Chinese psychotherapist assert traditional paternalistic values as a moral command. He denies this woman's criticisms of oppressive family life and also fails to acknowledge her suffering or requests for change. The politics of moral practice in therapy in this instance instate traditional Confucian values of paternalistic sociocentrism while undercutting any possibility for a feminist alternative.

Another case illustration comes from a telephone call one of us (A.K.) recently received. The call was made by an immigration lawyer in the Western part of the United States whose clients were the parents of an adolescent with a serious mental illness. The lawyer was considering making a case for political asylum based on the fact that China's mentally ill do not have adequate mental health services available and when they are in such care their rights are often abridged. While the latter part of the assertion has some merit (see Pearson 1995), the first part is a much more complex issue. On the one hand, some of the very best rehabilitation programmes for the chronically mentally ill are to be found in China (Xiong et al. 1994). On the other hand, few Chinese have access to such services. Yet, the reality in the United States could hardly be said to be very good. So poor are community services for the mentally ill in the United States that they are a major reason why so many chronically mentally ill becomes homeless during the course of their illness.

But debate over scientific facts was not the issue here. Rather the attorney meant to appeal to a sentiment of moral solidarity in order to manipulate the politics of asylum on behalf of her clients. Becoming a political refugee meant appealing to experts to make a case out of compassion for which there was no convincing evidence. I am sure this happens routinely. It represents another example of the politics of moral experience in psychiatry and in psychiatry's relation to the state.

II

Religious healing, efficacy, and moral practice

> When Rabbi Hiyya bar-Abba became ill, Rabbi Yochanan went in to see him. He said to him, 'Is your suffering dear to you?' He replied, 'Neither the suffering nor its reward!' Then he said, 'Give me your hand.' He gave him his hand, and raised [i.e., healed] him.
>
> Babylonian Talmud, Berachot 5a

The inconstant disjuncture of local worlds is, if anything, more pronounced and obvious with respect to religious healing than it is with respect to globalising psychotherapeutic practice. A few cautionary words are in order, however, as to the meaning of healing and illness in this context. Whether we are discussing the so-called 'world religions' in their classical forms (Bowker 1970; Hick 1977; Kraemer 1995; Levenson 1988; Weber 1993) or the innumerable local traditions which help to shape religious experience around the world (Brodwin 1996; Lewis 1989; Lienhardt 1962; Sullivan 1989), the problem of suffering is everywhere, in one way or another, at the heart of religious experience. For Geertz (1973), who views religion as a system of articulate symbols, the question posed to religion is not 'how to escape suffering, but paradoxically, how to suffer, how to make suffering something as we say, sufferable'. In defending religion as a 'cultural system' against the challenge posed by our society's glorification of technical efficacy, Geertz's comment is certainly well placed. Religion is never simply a failed or premature science, as some writers have claimed (Horton 1967).

On the other hand, it may reasonably be asked whether the problem of meaning which Geertz locates at the centre of religious life can be separated so easily from the search for efficacy in healing, or in more religious terms, for salvation from pain and cosmic disorder. Good (1994) has argued that not even biomedicine, with its highly articulated emphasis on a purely technical construction of efficacy, has been able to escape the soteriological provenance of healing to which it is heir, and it is similarly true that religious systems which have been subject to varying degrees of rationalisation and disenchantment continue to complement, compete with, or simply coexist with global biomedicine in the alleviation of concrete distress on the part of human beings.

In some cases, the persisting importance of religious healing may be related to the inadequate provision of biomedical or psychotherapeutic services along lines of economic deprivation and political disempowerment (Farmer 1992; Lewis 1989; Wikran 1988). At the same time, however, religious healing as the alleviation of concrete forms of distress—even where dominant idioms of distress include a bifurcation between the physical, psychic, and social worlds—continues to flourish in relatively affluent communities in industrialised nations (Csordas 1994; Littlewood and Dein 1995; McGuire 1988), reinforcing the view that efficacy is 'complex, differentially constructed, even contested in experience, and needs to be examined simultaneously on several levels' (Kleinman 1995: 10). Our object in this essay, however, is that aspect of complex efficacy which is related specifically to moral practice, especially as this relates to or can be compared with, psychotherapeutic forms of healing.

The realm of the moral in anthropological analysis, as we have stated, refers to that element of experience wherein is elaborated what overwhelmingly is at stake for social actors in local worlds. As an extension, moral practice can be defined as activity which is not purely instrumental, but has in view the attainment or embodiment of those values which are most at stake in local worlds. We will argue, however, that moral practice also goes beyond this cognitive conception, to embrace the transformation of social experience as embodied in particular instances of suffering and healing—or the failure at such transformation—in a way which is thoroughly contingent, processual, and embedded in complex local worlds, themselves positioned with respect to global forces. This is part of what makes 'efficacy' such a difficult concept to define for comparative use; it does not stand on its own, but is revealed in specific ethnographic cases to be mutually constitutive with the moral practices which are (in a logically prior sense) employed to bring it about.

An example of this difficulty can be detected in the strong claim made by Gananath Obeyesekere (1985:144) some years ago, regarding the incommensurability of 'depression' as conceived in global psychotherapeutic terms with any experience made possible through the discipline of Buddhist religious and moral tradition. As Obeyesekere frames the argument, this incommensurability is rooted in divergent orientations to the moral stakes of experience, and expressed through divergent moral practice. The 'work of culture' among Sri Lankan and other Buddhists, argues Obeyesekere, actively encourages and invokes the affect of '*sokaya*, sadness or sorrow, and *kampanaya* or *kampava*, the shock of loss; another word is *sanvegaya*, pain of mind'. These experiential categories, communicated through popular stories and parables, as well as specific meditative techniques (especially meditation on the worthlessness and transitory nature of the physical body—the body as a bag of faeces in one popular set of images), are associated with larger cosmological conceptions of *dukka* or *kalakirirma*, the necessary suffering which accompanies attachment to the transitory things of the world. These experiences are no more 'enjoyed' by Buddhists than would be the corresponding affective state in a non-Buddhist setting, except that they are correlated for Buddhists with the attainment of liberating knowledge of the self and the universe. They are not 'free floating' affects to be labelled as disease or abnormality, but important and much sought moments in a process of liberation from attachment and suffering.

Obeyesekere makes the relativising claim that persistent feelings of worthlessness, sorrow, and despair that would fit psychotherapeutic diagnostic categories of depressive disorder are given an entirely different reading among Sri Lankan Buddhists and cannot be considered pathological: 'One thing is clear enough: that which may be labelled as depression in the West is given a radically different form of cultural canalization and expression' (Obeyesekere 1985: 145; cf. Reddy 1997). A 'depressive' in one moral and cultural setting may be a 'good Buddhist' in another (ibid.: 135). Commenting on the by now well-worn medical anthropological distinction between 'illness' and 'disease' (Kleinman 1988: 311–74), Obeyesekere argues that with respect to mental illness, at least, the distinction does not hold:

> A determinate biological/genetic mechanism in mental illness is absent or, if present, is superlaid by social-psychological conditions that are products of human experience in different socio-cultural settings. In this situation the manner in which the so-called symptoms are put together and given cultural meaning or symbolization is intrinsic to their nature as illness/disease. The *conception*

of the disease (i.e. illness) *is* the disease. Or to put it differently, there are only illnesses and no diseases (ibid.: 136).

What does this argument mean for the relationship between efficacy in religious healing and moral practice which we have been discussing?

For one thing, it portrays the 'work of culture' as a sovereign endeavour: meaning is constructed, selves are oriented, and value imposed freely, without resistance from the life worlds of those who suffer. This is the sense in which the first author, at an early stage in his writing, made the claim that efficacy in religious healing is definitionally assured (Kleinman 1980)—a claim which now seems in need of serious revision. Obeyesekere himself expresses some doubt, and concludes his essay on a note of disquiet. While this disquiet was largely confined to the possibility that biogenetically overdetermined disease categories might one day be confirmed in the area of mental health, there are other, more ethnographically accessible issues which need to be raised as well.

Obeyesekere himself notes that the institutions and culture of international biomedicine in places like Sri Lanka may have worked to foster and reinforce the appearance of an identifiable 'disease category' (so labelled by both clinicians and by sufferers themselves) of depression. It is important to consider this process as a counterpart or contrast to the process of 'indigenisation' of psychotherapeutic services described in the previous section of this essay. Local and global institutions and conceptions both work, sometimes in opposing ways, to constrain and shape the social experience of suffering, and the force of that constraint can only be traced through the ethnography of specific contexts. At the same time, institutions and moral practices are themselves shaped through their encounter with specific cultural constellations and historical contingencies. These are the processes which help to define the inconstant disjuncture between local worlds, neither homogeneous (as they are still often presumed to be in biomedical discourse) nor as unbridgably incommensurate as anthropologists have sometimes portrayed them.

The complex analysis of efficacy which is mandated by the interplay of different social institutions, explanatory models, and experiential realities must also take into account the fact that efficacy, however defined, is not to be taken for granted. It may, for instance, be compromised or prevented by factors in the life history and experience of the sufferer which confound or exceed the expectations of cultural and religious models (Hollan 1994). We must also begin to make more subtle distinctions in the *directionality* of efficacy, which is really a way of asking 'efficacy for whom?' The integration and coherence of local worlds of meaning may sometimes be purchased at the expense of imposing burdens of blame and victimisation on those who occupy structural positions of vulnerability in the local world—the victimisation of poor women in this way has been documented for both rural India (Das 1994), and the United States (Farmer et al. 1996).

Efficacy is not only directional though. It is also multiple and contested, defying the efforts of wholistic model builders. Particular healing systems and their accompanying models of efficacy may in fact be mobilised in a moral practice directed towards ends other than those explicitly valorised by the healing system itself. The choice of a biomedical or an indigenous Indian healer in the Peruvian Andes may be part of a strategy to shift one's place in a highly articulated ethnic and political hierarchy (Crandon-Malamud 1991); in rural Haiti, the choice of religiously affiliated healing strategies may relate to one's desire to affiliate with powerful foreigners, or to make claims of local religious authenticity (Brodwin 1996). This kind of strategising is part of the moral practice of healing because it forces analysis to confront the most salient stakes of experience in the local setting—what stands most importantly to be gained by healing efficacy, or lost by its failure?

If medical anthropology has shown that efficacy cannot be exclusively associated with the alleviation of symptoms defined by biomedicine, however, it is also true that, contrary to Geertz's confident assertion about the 'religious problem of suffering' over twenty years ago, the quest for alleviation of anguish resurfaces in ethnographic accounts that go beyond the elicitation of reified cultural or religious 'models'. This is what the philosopher Emmanuel Levinas, in an essay entitled 'Useless suffering', identified as 'the originary cry for help', which he not fortuitously associates with the claims of biomedicine to represent a form of moral practice. Indeed, it is at least in part the promise of an efficacious response to the 'originary cry' (together with institutional and economic forces, to be sure), which has contributed to the enormous international prestige of what was once rather too parochially known as 'western medicine'. This is the sense in which Byron Good has referred to biomedicine as inherently 'soteriological', underlining the continuity which exists on some level between biomedical and religious conceptions of healing.

Levinas argues that it is only the cry for relief from radical suffering—which is essentially the cry for help from another person—which retains its moral coherence as an alternative to theodicy in the latter part of the 20th century. The search for meaning, order, and personal transcendence of suffering which informed religious healing and theodicy in times past have simply been rendered irrelevant to human experience by the dislocations of recent history. But while Levinas has called our attention to an important component of the contemporary temper, he has also certainly overgeneralised. Religious healing and theodicy in their classical forms remain important aspects of moral experience even at the heart of communities most demoralised by the 20th century's 'age of catastrophes' (cf. Hobsbawm 1994), and meaning-generating practices have retained their vitality in the face of biotechnology's flattened, technical, definition of efficacy.

It might be more ethnographically useful, therefore, to describe localised forms of efficacy as if they were located along a continuum between Geertz's 'problem of how to suffer', and Levinas' 'orginary cry' for the alleviation of pain. In some cases, these poles are almost indistinguishable: charismatic healing among Ethiopian Pentecostals whom the second author has interviewed tends towards the total identification of meaning-making and technical efficacy, to the point of disavowing any possibility for the failure of religious healing to cure disease. Some American evangelical groups of the 19th century went so far as to deny the possibility of bodily death among the faithful; a claim which has rarely survived its first generation of proponents. In other cases, the two poles are more distantly related. One of the tasks facing medical ethnography today is to trace the connections and discontinuities between these different aspects of healing efficacy in specific cases.

Take the condensed case study of a woman whom we can call Bertukan, an Ethiopian-Israeli whose immigrant family the second author has maintained contact with over most of the last decade. Together with her parents, several siblings, husband and four children, she migrated to Israel from Ethiopia in 1984, after a lengthy stay in a Sudanese refugee camp. Another adult sister and brother were left behind in Ethiopia, able to reach Israel only years later, while a fourth sister died during the long trek from Ethiopia's Gonder province to the Sudanese border. Several members of this family—although not Bertukan herself—had complained over the years of diffuse unwellness and chronic symptoms which their frequent visits to the local health clinic never seemed to relieve. Bertukan's brother, when he finally arrived in Israel, managed to remarry (his first wife had died) and to find a job, but frequently missed work with complaints that 'my whole body is no good. The climate here is not good for me.' Her mother complained more explicitly of headaches 'all the time, for my daughter who is in Ethiopia', while another brother attacked the biomedical doctors who seemed unable to successfully intervene. 'They are doctors, aren't they?' he asked me in exasperation. 'They should be able to help.'

Bertukan herself did not seem to be ill much. She did not give up traditional dress, as her younger sister did, nor did she find a job, as her sister and brothers did. This was not unusual for an Ethiopian immigrant of her age, however, especially as she had young children to care for. At family gatherings, it was possible to miss Bertukan entirely, because of her quiet demeanour, and the lack of favour she and her children seemed to enjoy with the aging family patriarch, her father, who occasionally disparaged them for lack of intelligence or misbehaviour. Because she didn't talk much, the ethnographer too paid less attention to her than to some of the other family members. All of that changed, however, sometime during 1995.

Bertukan became increasingly listless and relinquished all active care for her children—including an infant daughter—to her husband who, like most Ethiopian men, had never assumed that role in the past. She and her husband secretly obtained a divorce without informing her family (who were also their immediate neighbours) in which she ceded to him both the house and full responsibility for the children. She then moved in with her aging parents, claiming that her husband had beaten her, a claim which most of the family did not believe. At family gatherings, like the daily coffee drinking ritual, she showed no interest in her children, whom her ex-husband and mother seemed to have completely accepted responsibility for. A younger brother who still lived with their parents, meanwhile, actively lobbied to have her thrown out of the low rent apartment, in concern that she would come to contest his inheritance rights over it. She also began to wake in the night with screams that someone was trying to do her harm, and once had to have a kitchen knife pried loose from her hand.

After local doctors and Ethiopian spirit healers (*tankway*) proved ineffective, a decision was made by the family to send Bertukan with one of her brothers back to Ethiopia, at considerable expense, in the hopes of consulting a renowned spirit healer there, whom they had heard might be able to help. With relative affluence among Ethiopian-Israelis growing, this type of healing pilgrimage back to Ethiopia has become increasingly popular in recent years, with visits to holy sites, healing springs, and indigenous healers of different types all being employed. Bertukan and her brother were away for a full month in their ancestral province, and returned with an account of her illness that raised as many questions as it answered. The healing springs, they said, had been of little help, but they had met a spirit healer who had predicted their coming, and diagnosed the cause of Bertukan's condition.

Before immigration, according to this account, Bertukan had had a young son (the ethnographer had never been told of this son before, but that does not make this account impossible). One day she gave him a new garment for a present and then, leaving him in the care of a servant, had gone to the market. While she was away, the servant was not paying attention, and the boy's new garment had caught on fire, burning him to death. At that time she became inhabited by a *kolle* spirit, which had (for some reason) only begun troubling her in a serious way more recently. The healer had prepared a series of herbal treatments for her, which the family was to burn each night in such a way that the smoke would be able to rise up through her dress. After an initial improvement, however, her symptoms began to seem worse. Despite the family's initial resistance to seeking psychiatric care, she was eventually referred by physicians for a psychiatric evaluation. She was hospitalised and medicated, and subsequently allowed only short visits to her family on weekends.

Now this episode can be analysed from any number of perspectives, but what interests us here are the multiple perspectives on efficacy as moral practice which it opens for consideration. Bertukan's biomedical and psychiatric caregivers did not elicit any meaningful story from her about the history of her depression and its rootedness in a particular life world. Indeed, it is almost certain that none of them spoke any Amharic, the only language in which she is comfortable. Their greater success in bringing her symptoms under control was appreciated by the family—although she refused to take drugs whenever possible—and their ability to have her physically removed from the home was a powerful benefit from the point of view of her younger brother. Successfully transferring her burden of treatment from the family to the state was in fact one of the most important results of the family's decision to seek biomedical help.

On the other hand, it was the narrative of personal loss and grief, inscribed in a context of collective loss and grief experienced by her whole community, which was adopted by Bertukan's family as a way of making sense of her illness. The making of meaning and the quest for a 'cure' were at first inseparable for them in the act of help seeking. As the intractability of Bertukan's condition imposed itself more and more on the family, however, a certain shift became noticeable. The family began to concern itself with management of the disruption she caused to their own lives on the one hand, and to the elaboration of a narrative with wide communal significance on the other. Who among immigrant women had not lost a child in Ethiopia? Who among them had not felt some burden of guilt, or a desire to revisit the sites of memory in their land of origin, now hidden from view? The efforts of the *kolle* healer were efficacious in this communal sense, but left the suffering of Bertukan—and the problems she posed for her family—largely untouched. Her family brought Bertukan to the hospital, but it is the story of her dead child that they tell amongst themselves and to interested outsiders, or to strangers living intimately among them. What this has meant to Bertukan's own subjective experience of intractable illness and loss remains opaque. Neither the biomedical nor the traditional healing 'system', as such, delivered all that it promised, or all that was asked of it. The moral practice of healing sometimes consists in finding ways—within the infrapolitics of ordinary life—to make do.

III
Conclusion

Psychotherapy and religious healing are each revealed as forms of moral practice in the way that they shape efficacy through attention to what is most at stake in local worlds. The power to define healing in this way does not necessarily ensure that it will be attained in the complicated reality of lived experience. But it does suggest a mode of analysis grounded in ethnographic description rather than reasoning from first principles. Calculations of locally defined utility, constructions of self and cosmology, and the micro-politics of local social life are all central to healing as moral practice, whether it takes an explicitly religious or avowedly cosmopolitan, biomedical form. This is not meant to deny the important differences between forms of healing as diverse as psychotherapy and the charismatic laying on of hands, or Ethiopian *zar* possession rituals. But it does suggest that what these forms of healing have in common is precisely what distinguishes them in particular local worlds, which is their embeddedness in varied contexts of lived experience, where different stakes are held, and differing things are at stake. This is where the uncertainty of healing is always located, and where anthropological analysis properly begins.

REFERENCES

BOWKER, J. 1970. *The problem of suffering for the religions of the world.* Cambridge: Cambridge University Press.

BRODWIN, PAUL. 1996. *Medicine and morality in Haiti.* Cambridge: Cambridge University Press.

CRANDON-MALAMUD, LIBBET. 1991. *From the fat of our souls: Social change, political process, and medical pluralism in Bolivia.* Berkeley: University of California Press.

CSORDAS, THOMAS. 1994. *The sacred self: A cultural phenomenology of charismatic healing.* Berkeley: University of California Press.

DAS, VEENA. 1994. Moral orientations to suffering: Legitimation, power and healing. *In Arthur Kleinman, N. Ware and L.C. Chen, eds, Health and social change in international perspective*, pp. 139–67. Cambridge, Mass.: Harvard University Press.

DELBANCO, ANDREW. 1995. *The death of Satan: How Americans have lost the sense of evil*. New York: Farrar, Strauss and Giroux.

ELLENBERGER, HENRI F. 1970. *The discovery of the unconscious: The history and evolution of dynamic psychiatry*. New York: Basic Books.

FARMER, PAUL. 1992. *AIDS and accusation: Haiti and the geography of blame*. Berkeley: University of California Press.

FARMER, PAUL, MARGARET CONNORS and JANIE SIMMONS, eds. 1996. *Women, poverty and AIDS*. Monroe, Maine: Common Courage Press.

GEERTZ, CLIFFORD. 1973. *The interpretation of cultures*. New York: Basic Books.

GOLDHAGEN, DANIEL JONAH. 1996. *Hitler's willing executioners: Ordinary Germans and the Holocaust*. New York: Vintage Books.

GOOD, BYRON J. 1994. *Medicine, rationality and experience: An anthropological perspective*. The Lewis Henry Morgan Lectures. Cambridge: Cambridge University Press.

HICK, JOHN. 1977. *Evil and the God of love*. San Francisco: Harper.

HOBSBAWM, ERIC. 1994. *The age of extremes: A history of the world, 1914–1991*. New York: Random House.

HOLLAN, DOUGLAS. 1994. Suffering and the work of culture: A case of magical poisoning in Toraja. *American ethnologist* 21: 74–87.

HORTON, ROBIN. 1967. African traditional thought and western science. *Africa* 37: 155–87.

JANET, PIERRE. 1925. *Psychological healing: A historical and clinical study* (trans. Eden and Cedar Paul). London: G. Allen and Unwin.

KLEINMAN, ARTHUR. 1980. *Patients and healers in the context of culture: An exploration of the borderland between anthropology, medicine, and psychiatry*. Berkeley: University of California Press.

———. 1988. *The illness narratives: Suffering, healing, and the human condition*. New York: Basic Books.

———. 1995. *Writing at the margin: Discourse between anthropology and medicine*. Berkeley: University of California Press.

———. 1997. 'Everything that Really Matters': Social suffering, subjectivity, and the remaking of human experience in a disordering world. *Harvard theological review* 90, 3: 315–35.

KLEINMAN, ARTHUR and JOAN KLEINMAN. 1991. Suffering and its professional transformation: Toward an ethnography of interpersonal experience. *Culture, medicine and psychiatry* 5, 3: 275–301.

KLEINMAN, ARTHUR, VEENA DAS and MARGARET LOCK, eds. 1997. *Social suffering*. Berkeley: University of California Press.

KRAEMER, DAVID. 1995. *Responses to suffering in classical rabbinic literature*. Oxford: Oxford University Press.

LEVENSON, JON D. 1988. *Creation and the persistence of evil*. Princeton: Princeton University Press.

LEVINAS, EMMANUEL. 1988. Useless Suffering. *In Robert Bernasconi and David Wood, eds, The provocation of Levinas: Rethinking the other*, pp. 156–67. London: Routledge.

LEWIS, I.M. 1989. *Ecstatic religion: A study of shamanism and spirit possession*. New York: Routledge.

LIENHARDT, GODFREY. 1962. *Divinity and experience: The religion of the Dinka*. New York: Oxford University Press.

LITTLEWOOD, RONALD and SIMON DEIN. 1995. The effectiveness of words: Religion and healing among the Lubavitch of Stamford Hill. *Culture, medicine and psychiatry* 19: 339–83.

MADAN, T.N. 1975. On living intimately with strangers. *In* André Béteille and T.N. Madan, eds, *Encounter and experience: Personal accounts of fieldwork*, pp. 131–56. Honolulu: University of Hawaii Press.

MADAN, T.N. 1981. Moral choices: An essay on the unity of asceticism and eroticism. *In* Adrian C. Mayer, ed., *Culture and morality: Essays in honor of Christoph von Fürer-Haimendorf*, pp. 126–52. Delhi: Oxford University Press.

MCGUIRE, MEREDITH. 1988. *Ritual healing in suburban America.* New Brunswick: Rutgers University Press.

OBEYESEKERE, GANANATH. 1985. Depression, Buddhism, and the work of culture in Sri Lanka. *In* Arthur Kleinman and Byron Good, eds, *Culture and depression*, pp. 134–52. Berkeley: University of California Press.

PEARSON, VERONICA. 1995. *Mental health in China: State policies, professional services and family responsibilities.* London: Gaskell.

REDDY, WILLIAM A. 1997. Against constructionism: The historical ethnography of the emotions. *Current anthropology* 38, 3: 327–40.

SULLIVAN, LAWRENCE E., ed. 1989. *Healing and restoring: Health and medicine in the world's religious traditions.* New York: Macmillan.

SWAIN, GLADYS. 1994. *Dialogue avec l'insense: Essai d'histoire de la psychiatrie.* Paris: Gallimard.

WEBER, MAX. 1993 [1922]. *The sociology of religion* (trans. Ephraim Fischoff). Boston: Beacon Press.

WIKAN, UNI. 1988. Bereavement and loss in two Muslim communities: Egypt and Bali compared. *Social science medicine* 27, 5: 451–60.

———. 1995. *Managing turbulent hearts: A Balinese way of living.* Chicago: University of Chicago Press.

XIONG, W., et al. 1994. Family-based intervention for schizophrenic patients in China. *British journal of psychiatry* 165, 2: 239–47.

6

The issue of 'right to food' among the Hindus: Notes and comments

R.S. Khare

The paper starts with a comparative discussion of food in Hindu religion and law and in Indian democratic polity, examining the general question whether the Hindu system possesses at all a substantive cultural basis of its own for addressing the goal of 'food-accessibility-for-all'. Though democracy demands egalitarian 'public policy' and 'public action programmes' for food for all its citizens, the Hindu system frames the issue within its language of karma, debts and duties, and yields some moral-practical (if socially weak) formulations and four specific 'notions of shared sustenance'. But today, as dharma, history, caste, and modern India entangle with one another, there is no clear social direction, and the issue of 'right to food' also remains correspondingly muddled.

> ***Bhojan*** (eating and giving food to others to eat) is one of the most important subjects treated of in *Dharmasastra works*. . . .
> These directions to give food even to outcasts, dogs and birds were the outcome of the noble sentiment of universal kindliness and charity, the idea that One Spirit pervades and illumines the meanest of creatures and binds all together (Kane 1974: 757, 746).

> A single necessary good, and one that is always necessary—food, for example—carries different meanings in different places. Bread is the staff of life, the body of Christ, the symbol of the Sabbath, the means of hospitality, and so on. If the religious uses of bread were to conflict with its nutritional uses...it is by no

Acknowledgements: This is a slightly rewritten (but not revised) version of a lecture given on the subject of 'Human rights to food: Religious promise and practice', in March 1991, at the Alan Shawn Feinstein World Hunger Program, Brown University. Foremost, I am indebted to my several high and low caste informants/discussants in Lucknow for their cultural insights and practical observations (see note 1). At Brown, I greatly benefited from the discussion that the university students and my colleagues, Professors Morris Morris, Akos Ostor, Lina Fruzzetti, and my gracious host, Ellen Messer, had on the Indian cultural politics of food and the role of Hindu common (*sadharan*) dharma. While I am of course exclusively responsible for the final content and presentation, this paper also distinctly gained by subsequent presentations at Delhi University in 1993 and at Oxford University in 1995, and by Patricia Uberoi's recent editorial commentary.

means clear which use would be primary. How, then, is bread to be incorporated into the universal list? (Walzer 1983: 8).

I
Food in dharma and the state

These epigraphs from Hindu tradition and from modern Western political philosophy point toward a central issue food raises at the end of the 20th century: a necessary and sufficient access to food by all humans, as a moral and a basic human right. As a corollary in democratic societies, it also means that there is equal opportunity and fairness for everyone in securing food, including for the poor, marginal and weak. Similarly, the right to food cannot be limited to the socially dominant and the biologically fittest. A democratic welfare state must ensure a uniformly just and equitable system of rights to production, distribution and consumption of food for all its different constituent groups and communities. But at the end of this modern century, most nations and international organisations still treat these as distant public ideals. The right to food is nowhere near an internationally assured universal political-legal right of peoples. Even some of the richest countries have not been able to wipe out hunger from their midst. Generally, food scarcity and hunger intensify with increasing social dependence, control, inequity and injustice. These conditions globally produce today the half-fed in massive numbers, on the one hand, and the totally starving, on the other.

Human food availability is thus subject to enormous inequalities, more often because of human factors than natural disasters and calamities. Similarly, food is governed by at least two sets of values, one morally ideal or universal, and the other contextual, practical and conditional. Both sets of distinctions are at the heart of Indian—traditional and modern—debates surrounding food and food availability. The issue of the right to food is even more elusive. If the food-security debate in India today rests on a plethora of interdependent political, economic and legal initiatives of the state, then food availability within families rests, as surely, on several concurrent moral, religious and cultural criteria that ordinary Indians enforce.[1] But the question central to this paper is: how do these two distinct cultural

[1] Though my discussion focuses mainly on Hindu ideals, conceptions and social practices, the terms 'Hindu' and 'Indian' will be distinguished by context, accommodating the diverse forces of contemporary and modern India. Any discussion of the right-to-food issue in India now demands that we neither substitute the one for the other, nor separate them at the expense of social reality. This realisation was repeatedly brought home during the several discussions my knowledgeable field informants and discussants (Brahmans, Thakurs, Yadavas and Untouchables or Dalits) had during 1988 in Lucknow. Since their textual interpretations, social observations and practical approaches to issues of hunger, social injustice and poverty form the basis of this paper, they deserve my foremost gratitude. While everybody recognised the continued power of caste separation, dominance and exclusion, they also refused to reduce Hindu social life to caste practices alone. If only tentatively, many insisted on questioning the socially given. Similarly, as I found them interrelating selected strands of tradition *and* democracy in daily life, they thought about much more than narrow caste and religious conflicts within a diversifying Luckhnawi society. They worried if their children would have more social tranquility and justice in their lives.

languages (in simple terms 'traditional'or 'modern') today relate to (or miss or ignore) the right-to-food issues in India? Both often exist and work in India under either mutual denial, separation or obviation. Even when recalled together, the two 'languages' remain separate, confined to their own distinct spheres of concern. If the state dominates economic, political and legal aspects of food production and distribution, then family needs, customs and religious values shape the daily food procurement and consumption. Realising that both sides are now indispensable, open ideological conflicts between the two are either played down or are carefully avoided. But whenever in conflict, Indian politicians, administrators and courts discover, sooner or later, the overriding significance of the people's controlling grass-root ways and values.

Thus, to succeed at the grass-root level, major political, economic and legal initiatives on food distribution by the state must not only have a socially persuasive and acceptable face, but they should also converge (and deal equitably) with local people's actual food needs and their sense of balance and fairness. Before planning any major administrative and legal changes in public food distribution, the state must know (and co-opt, when useful) the non-restrictive ways ordinary people employ to access, share and control food among themselves every day. Despite its tendency to doubt the people's capacity to harness customary behaviour for efficient food acquisition and use, the state must still trust the people's overall sense of social fairness. In tackling hunger, as the country has already successfully shown during the past decades, Indians are hardly passive. In fact, they actively join the government efforts when these are sincere, well-focused, just, equitable and effective in reducing (rather than only staving off) hunger.[2]

In the paper I pursue food as a polyvalent—cultural, economic and legal—arena of traditional duties and modern rights, including claims, complaints and conflicts. In India, if food is well known as a moral, caste-ordered substance, binding the self, body and society together, then it is also about economic status, prosperity, social domination and political control. Considered together, the two domains allow me to explore a basic similarity in the moral quandary that food raises under the traditional caste order on the one hand, and, on the other, for the guiding values and approaches of the modern Indian nation-state for achieving social justice via human rights (e.g., for India-sensitive approaches to human rights issues, see Baxi 1987; Desai 1986; Kothari and Sethi 1989). At the heart of such a dual inquiry are a whole range of operative assumptions that interdigitate contemporary India's traditions with a modern democracy, allowing us to see how people interrelate their food needs, social duties, and practical problems to the state's role and responsibility.

[2] Open-ended and intensive inquiries into the interdependence between the government (or the *sarkar*) and the common or ordinary people are still rare. This is so even where the government might have a success story to tell (as in resolving Indian food shortage). Perhaps as a vestige of the colonial era, the government remains distant from, and distrustful of the capability of, the ordinary masses. Its bureaucracy still orders and directs the people from above and from a distance, rather than routinely trusts and consults its citizens.

The following discussion focuses on a cluster of interrelated Hindu cultural constructs for their interrelationships with contemporary Indian approaches, traditional and modern, to issues of food entitlement, hunger, social justice and human rights. The exercise purposely takes up a less-known aspect of Hindu moral economy and related social practices, juxtaposing them against the modern Indian state's approach to the Indian food problem, expressed in the language of economic individualism and human rights against hunger. This paper aims to show that despite major and continuing caste-engendered social inequalities, the Hindu religious ethic does outline a chain of long-recognised constructions for approaching 'the goal of feeding all creatures'. Second, though its actual social and economic role in the society is still largely unaccounted, a morally and socially inclusive spirit of food remains highly receptive to such a goal. But here caste rank and its debts and duties distinctly constrain such a spirit by establishing rules of ritual exclusion, social dismissal, injustice and hunger. Third, the same cultural grammar, however, takes us to four interdependent concepts of non-restrictive, caste-transcending sustenance, constituting the core of 'common' (*sadharan*) dharma. Fourth, modern social reformers and leaders have often latched on to these principles and their customary provisions, challenging caste by common dharma ethic and, only recently, by placing both within the survival and right-seeking history of independent India. Fifth, though still inconclusive, the struggle shows how India today may work both through its traditions and the state to let people approximate rights and claim social justice with the help of activist social reform and political protest and revolt.

The Indian human rights movement will remain a cultural anathema to ordinary Indians until the Indian traditional and modern worlds devise ways to transcend many internal gaps, anomalies and contradictions between them. It is a historically unavoidable social exercise for India and it must reach socially working solutions, for there are no short cuts here. Until then, one might argue, India will lack a broad-based, active civic culture, the soil necessary to germinate and sustain social justice and human rights. So far, even the most modern (or 'advanced') segments of Indian society fail to meet these criteria uniformly in public *and* private life.

Although Indian social responses to modernity, already spanning two centuries, are far from final, they nevertheless repeatedly show a distinct cultural 'bridge-work', evident more in social life than in conceptual schemes and philosophical ideologies. Food availability and consumption issues also reflect the same pattern. That is, while Indians have upheld many religious and caste rules in domestic food use, they have also pragmatically accepted, during the last fifty years, the Indian government programmes of subsidised food distribution.

But the performance of the Indian state on supporting a grass-root human rights movement has been weak. The subject of human rights is unknown and unfamiliar to the ordinary Indian, until evoked by the elite in a locally critical event or example. It is a subject discussed most often in English-language newspapers, academic seminars, city-based 'people's rights' groups and occasional lectures given by public-spirited judges and legal scholars. International (and now some national civic) oversight groups, often with divergent politics, keep the issues burning before the national government. On the other hand, it is also significant that there is no organised ideological, theological or doctrinal resistance from Hinduism to what the human rights movement generally stands for—survival and social justice for one and all. In principle, this is what Gandhi's Rama Rajya proposed, and what the dharma order, at its best, works for. However, today if dharma faces degeneration, the modern state is too weak to translate the same goals into practice. This renders human rights in India culturally alien and socially rootless (see Kothari 1989: 19–29).

II
Dharma, modernity and anthropology

Under such conditions, an anthropological study might start with a preliminary but substantive exercise in cultural translation and interpretation of some relevant (convergent or divergent) Hindu/Indian cultural ideals, conceptions and practices. While studying them from both within and without, an anthropologist may better ascertain how the two domains (i.e., the traditional Indian ways and modern human rights goals) get differentiated by social contexts, crises and conditions.[3] When considering the Hindu traditional approach to issues of access to food, we encounter two basic questions: First, what *is* its 'internal' moral/cultural language on matters concerning the natural circulation and availability of food, and what are the major forces that limit and constrain justice and fair play in society? Second, how close (or removed) are the religious ideals and ideas from actual local conditions and conflicts on the one hand, and from the modern liberal 'right-to-food' goals and debates, on the other?

Today's Hindus (or India more generally), however culturally self-isolating, cannot insulate themselves from these issues any longer. Rather, they must critically examine their own operating cultural assumptions, attitudes and practices that, besides overlooking the food need of the suffering, may actually deepen and widen social inequities in the name of customary dharma-karma observances and caste practices. Food and hunger issues in India today are seldom so simple that one could squarely blame either the Hindu traditional system or the modern state welfare policies and programmes. Actually, when Indians suffer from a drought or famine today, people tend to blame, by context, both their own efforts and the government. Often, however, government is found to promise more than it can deliver. Simple ideological oppositions between tradition and modernity, the underpinning of many an academic debate, also simplify and distort the overall Indian social and pragmatic sensibilities. Such debates often overlook internal differentiation and underestimate not only the social resilience of Indians, but their eye on fairness as well. They often miss people's capability for social care, resourcefulness, and practical ingenuity while facing adversity and hunger. Indian

[3] As a reading of some recent human rights literature on India might reveal (see Baxi 1987; Kothari and Sethi 1989), we need to have a more culturally differentiated and pragmatic approach to traditional Hindu (and other Indian) moral conceptions and social practices. This way, we may also be able to see more than that all-controlling caste in Indians' lives.

customs, then, show far more give-and-take than a standard sociological view of food control by dominant castes might indicate.

Without denying or minimising the fact of continuing poverty and hunger in India, we may explore this view of traditional reasoning a little further for its actual roles, meanings and limitations. Foremost, although every major Indian religion and community may assert that its distinct ideology disallows social injustice and human hunger in any form, they still fail to deliver in practice. On the other hand, the modern Indian state, along with its ideology of individual rights, is similarly deficient. Anthropologically speaking, both domains examine critically their ideals, assumptions and actual practices, but without any presumed bias for one side or the other. Second, one should not underestimate (much less dismiss) the everyday supplementary role of traditional Hindu, Muslim, Sikh and Christian food-gifting ethics, feeding programmes and charities. While these are quite frequent, they are usually hidden behind festivals and rituals for earning special religious merit.[4] Third, while institutionalised, this food distribution system often cuts across caste and community lines, and stands outside the ledgers of formal economy. It is also known to respond quickly (and often substantively) during famines and disasters.

However, these religious actions are no match for the regionally varied problem of continuing hunger and poverty in India. Nevertheless, it might be sociologically relevant to ask: Why does this system not voluntarily organise itself beyond localities to forge a more responsible, just and equitable system of food entitlement and distribution in India? Similarly, what keeps the traditional Indian food-gifting, charity and philanthropic initiatives isolated from those that the state launches? Without denying that there is a strong general disconnection (even a repulsion) between the government and Indian traditions, could one not keep an open mind toward the whole issue in future, particularly as the modern Indian polity and economy move beyond the Western colonial shadows and invite people's private, voluntary, open-market initiatives to participate in removing social injustice, hunger and poverty?

In a similar frame of social partnership, one might reconceptualise a cultural discussion of food as a human right in India, recognising that in the Hindu world 'dharma' stands at once for law, custom and daily morality. Dharma applies directly to individual persons as well as communities, the natural and the supernatural, and the seen and the unseen. The textual, local and contextual here show their close interdependence. They flow into and come out of each other. Even esoteric textual debates on philosophical principles and conceptions might not be that irrelevant to the problems of the present (for a convergent view from Indian philosophy, see Krishna 1996). Thus, Hindu 'legal' injunctions on food and food

[4] My older educated informants in Lucknow often complained that in modern India the role of traditional Hindu culture and its activities were seen only in a socially negative light by the modern elite. Though they well knew that their religious charity alone could not wipe out hunger and poverty, they found its collective significance to be much more than modern Indians allowed. On every major religious occasion, Indians feed a few hungry people—known or strangers, high or low, or rich or poor—within their community.

availability also produce several situationally differentiated 'internal' positions and interpretations. Here, encountering the language of duties rather than that of rights, the Hindu conception of dharma is found to be more than a narrow conception of the law and its coercive apparatus. In Robert Lingat's words:

> In building up their law the Hindus have not taken as their starting point that element which has served in the West as a foundation for a specific discipline, namely the coercive element, which characterizes a legal rule and distinguishes it from other rules which also control human activity. They have derived it from a more general notion which exceeds the domain of law in many respects...: *duty* (Lingat 1973: xii; my italics).

Given such a conceptual difference,[5] which is closely sustained in practice by the vast Hindu majority, the power of customary law clearly outweighs the formal state law in everyday life, especially where family and community matters are concerned. But Hindu (and Indian) customary law is regionally and locally so varied that it is best approached in our study for its overarching conceptions, rules and practices, rather than specific textual principles and philosophical conundrums. In life, Hindu ideals and practice transform into each other rather than dichotomise, oppose or negate each other. This is also true of India as a whole, where ideals, practices and practicalities must be considered together to bring us closer to people's perceptions of the prevailing social reality and its constraints. These cultural properties must also interest those responsible for shaping a grass-root public policy for improving all Indians' access to food. As Amartya Sen (1987: 7) had observed some time ago in the general context of hunger and food entitlement, research and public policy in India must reach out to, and thrive on, 'grass-root' political and social activities. '[This] is the task of research for action. Even the courage and determination to confront the problem of hunger and famine in the modern world may be influenced by a better understanding of what can be achieved by public action.'[6]

III

Food availability as karmas, debts and duties

The Hindu world is characterised by an elaborate (and cosmically coded) notion of moral order—dharma. It recognises differences between normal and abnormal,

[5] The contrast becomes clearer when juxtaposed to a recent explication of human rights by an Indian scholar. For example, Parekh (1987: 9–12) notes that a right is a claim, an entitlement, and an exclusive access, supported by an established legal authority for legal enforcement, with freedom to act (but in conformity with the conditions of grant). A right also means imposition of certain requirements on others, including their non-interference. Finally, a formal right exists even when the individual in question is physically or mentally unable to exercise it himself or herself.

[6] Sociologically, the core of what Sen calls 'public action' will have to be in India a converging cluster of moral duties, social customs, and the local practical and political interests of the people. Any successful grass-root public policy must link up with this working cultural core, rather than limit itself to only the legislated laws, policies and public welfare programmes.

and ordinary and special conditions, and allows for appropriate modification of one's duties and actions (*kartavya* and karma).[7] One's own karma (actions and efforts) always leaves a moral record of merits and demerits, and the karmic record passes from one life to the next, affecting one's next birth, life experiences, and life span. Aware of the enduring interdependence between one's own actions, life situation and worldly conditions, the Hindu views *all* his rights as obligations (toward himself and others) or duties (*kartavya*), situated within a dharma-ordered cosmos. Together, the dharma-karma of the Hindu thus produces a morally comprehensive but situationally intricate ledger of moral duties and their (direct or indirect) results or 'fruits'.

The dharma-karma configurations, though variable, speak in a culturally different (but not logically unrelated) language of duties than does the modern scheme of publicly agreed and legally binding charter of individual rights and claims. We need to know more about the first system, including its moral, sociological and jural assumptions and interpretations. Briefly, it says that if you want to secure what is due to you, you must first make sure that you give what is due to others. In other terms, you secure your status, identity and presence only by recognising others' and by performing your status-based duties toward them. Short of this, you fail your dharma. Thus, in both learned and popular cultures one finds only the language of duties being repeatedly (and primarily) invoked. The right-to-food movement must not only recognise the presence of this duty-based 'cause–effect' relationship, but it must also read correctly the significance of ordinary people's *reciprocal and interdependent duties*. As some educated Hindu informants repeatedly argued during my fieldwork, the language of modern human rights, based on the self-interest of the modern individual, has an in-built alienation, and it downgrades the social collective. The self suffers, standing exposed and alone. Asserting his/her rights, a modern self must engage in a lifelong competition, protecting his/her own rights against those of all others. Instead of social interdependence, 'each person must become selfish for his or her own good, leaving others to fend for themselves'.[8]

As a next step, the Hindu's web of duties translates into notions of social, moral, and spiritual debts (*rna*), incurred at birth and by everyday living. Instead of a civil contract of individual rights, one encounters in Hindu society an unwritten but persistent social reminder about discharging major moral duties and social debts. The two together still very much constitute the core of ordinary Hindus'

[7] Since the terms are found in most English dictionaries, I do not italicise 'karma' and 'dharma' or 'dharma-karma'. However, when contextually necessary, I will italicise those terms formed of these words that may have some special meanings or uses.

[8] At various places, I quote or summarise relevant interview data collected during the eighties in the north Indian city of Lucknow, capital of Uttar Pradesh. Mostly during the years 1979–80 and 1988, I worked on the subject of food entitlement in the neighbourhoods with several high, middle, low and Untouchable caste groups. I investigated the urban poor and the silently hungry in different castes during the same period. The issue of interpersonal responsibility for feeding the family invariably appeared within these discussions, enabling me to learn how both the poor and the middle-class households exploited different strands of both Hindu traditions and modern state initiatives.

dharma-karma, verily their whole lives. A father provides food to his children because it is his duty; a son feeds his old parents to discharge his debt toward the parents (and ancestors) who raised him. Similarly, he must discharge his debt to the guru (the spiritual preceptor) for imparting spiritual knowledge. Only a proper discharge of one's debts and duties ensures good life in this world and beyond. If one thus earns religious merit (*punya*), social respect and honour, one also gains practical advantage.

To summarise the preceding in general terms, let us note:

(*a*) the Hindu conceives of the self, the body and 'us–them' relationships within a comprehensive and living notion of the moral order (dharma-karma);
(*b*) the Hindu views his everyday life in terms of a host of karmas, duties and debts, arising from his own past, and he directly relates these to his present and future social conditions;
(*c*) the Hindu's notion of the self (or *karta*, the moral agent), in contrast to the Western, is demarcated by caste status and its duties on the one hand, and by inherent as well as spiritually *cultivated* dispositions and inclinations, on the other;
(*d*) the caste-regulated life is a crucial part of social life, but it is not one's whole life, nor is it the only and the ultimate reality; dharma-karma guides both this-worldly and other-worldly existence;
(*e*) irrespective of caste, the operating principle for the duty-based moral agent is: 'others must, with dharma, secure your rights', for the applicable principle is (as quoted from the Mahabharata, Santiparva, 259): 'Whatever a person desires should happen to himself he should desire to happen also to others'; and
(*f*) the ideas and transactions of eating and feeding (i.e., of giving to and sharing food with others) are integral to one's *cosmic* duties, debts, and dharma, to ensure prosperity life-after-life 'in food, cattle and progeny'.

As my Hindu informants repeatedly emphasised, caring for and feeding any and everybody (even creatures) stands at the heart of what is called *sadharna-dharma* (literally, the ordinary or everyday dharma). This dharma *precedes* that more socially restrictive and entrenched—and better known—caste (or *jati-varna*) dharma. While caste rules rank, exclude, control and even render faceless those who are low and distant, everyday dharma includes every living being and ordains the sharing of food irrespective of the condition and status of the recipient. The ethics of everyday dharma still remains socially so open, tolerant and inclusive that it may provide perhaps the best hope, as a modern Hindu reformer like M.K. Gandhi had argued, for Hindus to link up with democratic and egalitarian social forces aimed at the maximum public good. Human rights activists may also find here that much-needed internal social foothold.

The learned texts promote this dharma by calling it 'the implicit social contract' (*samaya*; Rege 1985: 11), in which people, individually and collectively, undertake to honour and protect the rights and interests of others in the society. By doing so, as the texts repeatedly proclaim, a person best secures his or her own interest. The weakening of ordinary dharma, on the other hand, reflects a genuine rise in injustice and a decline in the cosmic moral order. And when the decline is alarming, the Hindu argues, divine avatars intervene to resurrect and reinforce the everyday as well as special dharmas.

In summary, we may thus remark that the Hindu world, being still predominantly based on fulfilling major duties and debts of dharma rather than individual rights, (*a*) renders self-interest as only a complementary (and dependent) domain of serving others' interests; (*b*) treats all persons, irrespective of their caste rank and economic circumstance, as dharma-karma bound *moral agents* (and hence responsible for their own good and bad actions toward others); and (*c*) extends this model of interpersonal duties to social situations far beyond those found in caste groups and inter-caste exchange relations (i.e., as in the traditional *jajmani* model of inter-caste exchange of goods and services). Though now socially weak and atrophied, the *jajmani* model had long structured a generally socially liberal and inclusive access to sustenance. Though one's social and ritual status were seldom unimportant, much social leeway was allowed in polity and daily practice to maintain an 'orderly—and just—social life' (or *lokayatrarthama*, as the Mahabharata says).

IV
Four crucial concepts of sustenance

With some essentials of the Hindu cultural universe in place, let me now briefly discuss some crucial cultural-ethical concepts which guide the living Hindu's everyday moral sensibility, common sense and practical behaviour concerning food and food need. Neither merely philosophical speculations nor ideals, the Hindu may employ these guiding notions for coping with actual food and hunger issues in life. Let us remember that eating and feeding are serious moral and social activities within the Hindu world.[9] Here good customs are constantly identified, adapted and maintained with the help of reputable local elders. Ordinary Hindus also determine in this way what is their just and fair duty under a particular circumstance, with an emphasis on the need to feed others whenever one can. Functionally, they also respond in this way to the modern right-to-food goal.

While examining the Hindu tradition from within, the following four mainstream Hindu conceptions and their cultural applications particularly merit our attention:

[9] 'Eating and feeding' (*khana aur khilana* in Hindustani) refer to a distinct but very general activity of personal *and* social religiosity or dharma. These should not be equated simply with inter-caste commensal relations and their rules. Feeding here refers to gifting of cooked/uncooked food (*annadana*) to any human being, or even to any living creature. To assess its actual social scope, role and economic worth, we need to study in detail (and quantitatively) the Hindu (and Indian) feed-the-hungry impulse among all (high and low, and rich and poor) households. There is at present no calculation of the economic contribution such a food distribution system makes annually in India.

1. *apadharma*
2. *palana-posana*
3. *yogaksema*
4. *annamabrahma*

1. Dharma under normal and abnormal conditions

The Hindu distinguishes between ordinary (*sadharana*) and special (*visesa*) notions of dharma on the one hand, and between dharma under normal and abnormal conditions of life on the other. Dharma is thus *not* an undifferentiated moral pole for the Hindu. It is rather spectral, with some zones open and others closed to contingencies. In situations of drought, famine or tyrannical food control, for example, the notion of *apadharma* (i.e., dharma under conditions of distress) applies, where normal rules are either modified or suspended. As the authoritative sources repeatedly declare, one must save a life at all cost. This is recalled in the popular story of sage Visvamitra, who survived a famine by eating the hind parts of a dog at an Untouchable's house. However, today's Hindu often reinterprets such a traditional provision too liberally, to serve widely different, even conflicting social interests.

Since self-preservation (*atmasamraksana*) is one's paramount duty (*paramkartavya*), we need to examine how such a provision affects food availability for saving the life of those dependent and weak. However, we must recognise that self-preservation is not allowed for its own sake; instead, it is for fulfilling one's duties toward others (Chousalkar 1986: 73, quoting Bhisma from the Mahabharata). This provision continues to guide practical strategies of survival in distress (see Greenough 1982: 254ff, for a discussion of an aspect of this issue during the Bengal Famine of 1943–44). It is particularly so when dependents, especially women and children, are neglected or are pushed aside to save one's own life (ibid.: 11, 264–65, 271). The traditional rules under such circumstances may be significantly modified by local elders. If anything, such a practical approach, over time, has maintained an intricate and conditional, yet flexible, view of dharma. Learned texts devote much space to these discussions, stressing the close relationship of dharma to life and its quandaries. Even dependents, marginal groups, and the subalterns have variously evolved a whole dharma-based protest culture, launched from their own vantage point. Hence, paradoxically, dharma continues to provide the ground for both culture and counterculture. Within such a spectral approach to cosmic morality, dominance and dissent are as natural as anger and despair are alongside faith and hope (cf. Bardhan 1990: 36–41).

2. The conception of *palana-posana*

Within everyday social and domestic contexts, the issues of the accessibility and adequacy of food fall into the comprehensive and crucial notion of nurture (*palana-posana* or the duty to nourish, protect, and support the dependent and the needy). For the Hindu, nurture is natural to all creatures; it is an irreducible part of nature (*prakriti*), rather than opposed to it as culture. The provider–dependent (*bharta–asrita*) relationship may pattern itself after either parents and children, master and servant, god and devotee, or a combination of these. If the mother exemplifies selfless nurture *par excellence*, the father is the provider and protector. The father, in this view, is duty bound to provide first (and before self) to all his dependents.

This notion of the provider-protector, enjoined by dharma, stands at the heart of the Hindu notion of succour and sustenance. However, in the popular Hindu view, people's practices today fall short of the norm, as the prevalent age and gender discrimination in food sharing within Indian families shows. Still, when asked, people assert that as parents (whether by nature or *svabhava*, by emotional attachment or *mamta aur moha*, or by dharma-ordained duties or *kartavya*), they cannot but do 'our best to feed our children'.[10] In the words of an informant, 'Only under dire conditions does a parent fail. And whenever a wife feeds her husband or son better than her daughters, she does so to secure the next meal for the whole family. The survival of a male is more important than that of a female because he is still the bread winner.'[11]

During 1988, my several poor Brahman and Untouchable informants in Lucknow repeatedly asserted that whenever any family in the neighbourhood went without meals, their relatives and neighbours, ever watchful, tried to help them as best as they could.[12] When long unemployed, for example, one's relatives (i.e., parents, uncles, brothers or sisters) or same-caste neighbours fed the family for several days. Sometimes children stayed with relatives for weeks, while the couple tried to live on only one meal a day or even on tea and water. On other occasions, a mother borrowed some edibles from a neighbour 'to feed my children at least'. Whenever despondent, people variously blamed as well as gathered courage from God, destiny, karma, and personal failures. These explanations also gave people the motivation to work harder to see better times.

[10] These three criteria are crucial to the Hindu interpretation, where the instinctive, emotional and cultural motivations converge to ensure a 'just and fair feeding of one's dependents, especially women and children'. P.V. Kane's (1974) epigraph at the beginning of this paper labels the same quality as a 'sentiment'. In contrast, as Greenough's work (1982: 223–24) has shown, families today tend to feed adult males, particularly the bread-winner, first, and with the best and most food. This bias tends to become critical to the lives of women and children, especially in a severe drought or famine.

[11] I am purposely quoting here, without comment, my Hindu informants' responses to the problem of age and gender discrimination in food sharing under adverse conditions. The quoted remark justifies the discrimination as 'natural' but not socially 'normal' any more. Here the people tend to invoke and mingle a whole range of feelings and reasons to defend their practice, ranging from instinctive, emotional, customary, and personally preferred to the practical and practicable.

[12] Critical comments of neighbours and friends continue to be an important social deterrent against parental carelessness. In a close-knit neighbourhood (*mohalla*), where everybody knows everybody else, relatives and friends routinely watch families, especially those going through bad times. Missed daily cooking attracts immediate attention within compact, small-house lanes of poor and low-caste families. Neighbourhood children, visiting different houses everyday for play, work as 'little messengers' among different families. Thus, if the hearth does not get lit for some reason within a neighbouring house, people inquire, and render the help, if needed. Usually, some appropriate foods (cooked or uncooked) are immediately offered.

While Brahmans generally tried to hide their abject poverty by either stressing the spiritual value of an austere life or by claiming some past social honour and glory, the unemployed and poor Untouchables (or Dalits) often expressed anxiety as well as anger. Some educated Dalits blamed the government's failures as well as social discrimination. However, failure to feed one's family was universally painful to admit. During these times, even the poorest families claimed that they fed their children first and foremost, males next and women last (and often the least). Some Untouchable men knew that their bad habits, particularly drinking and gambling, had brought poverty to the family, but they felt anxious and helpless. They could neither give up drinking nor free themselves of the guilt. As they mistreated their family members, they often bitterly blamed outsiders. 'The corrupt social welfare workers and government's sahibs always promise so much but deliver so little,' was the remark of a Dalit.

Such an internally differentiated social picture of the Indian domestic feeding practices is essential to understand (*a*) people's crucial conception of the 'food provider', (*b*) the continuing role of the Indian age and gender discrimination practices, and (*c*) the actual cultural reasoning, practical strategies, and the social-safety net available to people when facing scarcity and hunger.

We thus also know more about how Hindu householders, high and low, and rich and poor, justify themselves as fair and just family providers in good and bad times, while also explicating the notion of a socially honourable nurturer-protector (*palak-poshak*).[13] Despite the recent age and gender politics surrounding food and human nutrition, Hindu householders still remain largely rooted within their hierarchical-yet-socially-liberal rules of food sharing for upholding dharma. The situation nevertheless poses a challenge for the modern human rights movement: how can it reconcile traditional norms of the Hindu householder with the facts of hunger and malnutrition among Indian women and children?

In brief, the Hindu conception of *palana-posana* (and its surrogates found among Indian Muslims, Sikhs, etc.) stands at that moral-practical centre which any serious right-to-food debate in India must confront. Given its crucial cultural significance, we will return to the provider-protector complex again while discussing Indian tradition and democracy in sociological, historical and practical terms.

3. The concept of *yogaksema*

The contemporary Hindu conception of *yogaksema* is particularly complex, since it evokes an amalgam of the notions of protection of the weak by the powerful,

[13] Two important points need to be stressed here. First, the criteria of measuring eating and feeding within the hierarchical Hindu world involve people's sense of what is (or is not) 'appropriate' and 'adequate' qualities and quantities of foods for an eater by his/her age, sex, social status, and health condition. Unlike the West, there is no individual-based uniform and universal 'standard'. To recall an informant's remark, 'Men and women naturally differ in their eating by age and health. How can everybody be the same? It is like our hands; they must have fingers of different length to do their work.'

by giving him/her refuge, understanding, well-being (*razi-khushi*), and protection (*panah* or *saran*). The Hindu devotional (bhakti) movement particularly consolidated and popularised it under its divine-inspired egalitarianism. God became the ultimate refuge and the protector of all. He fed and looked after all those whom society rejected or despised. Literally, the conception of *yogaksema* or protection and sustenance is comprised of two essential components. The first component is *yoga*, or the conjoining of one's mind, body and actions in pursuit of one's chosen worldly, devotional or spiritual goal. The second concerns *ksema* or well-being with security. Traditionally, a king's duty was to ensure his subjects' well-being. As a commentator on the *Arthasastra* (the Hindu treatise on the material and political affairs of the state) noted, a successful ruler (or analogously, the head of a village or a household) must secure his people freedom from fear and want (see Ghoshal 1959). Further,

> [t]he king, we read, should constantly adopt the behavior of a pregnant woman: as the mother disregarding her likes seeks the good of the child in her womb, so should the king behave toward his subjects; the righteous king should constantly behave in such a way as to give up what is dear to him for the sake of what is beneficial to his people (ibid.: 215).

The notion of the 'provider-protector' or *yogaksema* concept (in popular culture variously called the *poshaka-poshya, raja-praja, malik-sevak*, and *mai-baap* relationships) therefore posits a moral, political and jural (*dharmadharma, ucita-anucita*) compact between the provider and the dependent, ruler and the people, master and servant, and the powerful and weak (see section V, for a discussion of historical incorporation of such an element within the pre-British famine relief programmes and its possible extension to some aspects of the Famine Code of British India). Conversely, as so many Hindu mythological and historical stories emphasise, only a cruel and unjust king allows his subjects to go hungry and unprotected, a situation eventually incurring divine wrath on the king. Violent natural forces (storms, floods, earthquake, droughts and pestilence) rock a cruel king's land until he is removed (cf. Greenough 1982: 45–52).

As a part of the strong devotional ethos, the 'provider-protector' (*yogaksema*) concept in India today also has a distinct social and ethical component. When all else fails, the divine, the ruler of all rulers (*adhisthata*), is considered the final refuge of all, providing sustenance, safety and security particularly to the poor, weak, distraught and outcast. Even an illiterate peasant firmly believes that the divine protects and sustains those who are most needy and desperate. The source of such an assurance is the *Bhagvad Gita* (IX, 22), which declares that when worshipped with unflinching faith, 'God takes up all the cares and burdens of His devotees.' The divine becomes an unfailing protector-provider (*palaka-posaka*) of his steadfast devotees, whether high or low, or mighty or weak. Though unfailing, inscrutable and beyond all human reasoning, divine justice remains unpredictable for humans. As a popular Hindi saying goes, 'God's justice may be slow [in response] but there is no injustice [at his place]' (*bhagvan ke ghar der hai par andher nahin*).[14]

In Hindu social practice, however, the multidimensional provider-protector concept (*yogaksema*) has, over time, become a part of what we may call segmentary social dominance. Here the failures and weaknesses of the socially excluded and weak protectors-providers are always expected to be covered by those more hegemonic and powerful. Thus the failures of a family head must be rectified by a relative or a friend of better means, of a caste leader by the village head, of a village head by the regional landlord, ruler or the king, and of a king by the divine or the supreme king. The final appeal for justice is always directed to the divine, the ultimate (and unfailing) provider-protector. Equally importantly, the divine, the ultimate provider-protector, is known to be partial, just like a mother, to the weakest and the most oppressed.

4. *Annamabrahma* and the eater-marked food

The conception of eater-marked food, where food is considered not only a form of the divine but also 'marked' by the divine for every eater in creation, extends the provider-protector (*yogaksema*) notion into everyday food need, eating and feeding. Within the Hindu world, the divine ultimately ensures *all creatures* a dharma-enjoined access (or the natural 'right' and 'entitlement') to food. It is the way of nature (*prakriti*). Since the divine feeds and protects a soul for nine months within a mother's womb, it alone remains the surest, unfailing provider of all those born into this world.[15] Thus, in northern (Hindi-speaking) India, two popular sayings are: 'the one who has given birth will feed us within this world' (*jisne paida kiya hai wohi khane ko bhi dega*); and 'the one who gave us [literally, slit open our] mouth will also [as surely] feed us' (*jisne muh cira hai woh khane ko bhi dega*). These assert the inviolable protector-protected relationship between the creator and creatures.

Put another way, the eater-marked food shows the work of the unseen divine hand, ensuring that the food gets to its eater. Depending on the context, this 'hand' is called either nature (*prakriti*), karma, effort, destiny, or just the divine provision (*daivi vyavastha*). A Bombay (Hindi) movie of the 1970s, for example, pithily conveyed the principle of eater-marked food in a hit film song: 'The eater's name comes stamped on each grain of food...' (*dane dane par likha hai khanewale ka nam*...). Simultaneously, as already noted, an eater's past karmas and the divine hand are superimposed as he/she goes through periods of food abundance,

[14] This Hindu conception thus renders 'divine law' as *the* 'natural law', which applies to humans as well as to all other living creatures. The Hindu divine law (or dharma in its most basic sense) asserts that there is no irremediable lawlessness and no irreversible anarchy feasible within the universe. Viewed comparatively, the roots of Western secular jurisprudence are also not found free of certain religious bases in its conception of 'natural law' (see Bodenheimer 1974).

[15] Put another way, such a moral placement of food also excludes any totally coercive and permanent control of food and nurture by any human agency, ruler or government, however powerful.

scarcity or hunger in life (see Khare 1976). But this is not all, for above it all must also appear the all-benevolent, the always-just-divine, 'who sits in everybody's [a king's as well as a pauper's] heart as a charioteer and guides them all'.[16]

Undoubtedly, a striking distance exists, first, between the caste-ordered and the divine-supervised moral economy of Hindu food (including its promise of unfailing distributive and compensatory justice), and, second, between these and the one that the individual-based modern egalitarian economy, with roots in Judeo-Christian traditions, postulates. However, in practice, a modern Hindu reformer these days often tries to 'marry' (or graft) workable strands of this moral economy with those of modern Western notions of 'human rights', producing that neo-classical Hindu humanism or the 'religion of humanity' (*manavtavada* or *manava dharma*), represented best earlier in this century by M.K. Gandhi.[17] This 'human dharma' is a composition of certain traditions of common social (*sadharan*) dharma on the one hand, and of the principle of yogic 'sameness' (*samata*) on the other, carving out a path for humanistic 'people'/'public' service (*janseva*) in India. This is the moral-religious-public domain from which other major modern reformers like Vinoba Bhave and Jai Prakash Narayan also launched movements to reduce social and economic inequality among Indians, hoping to supersede all particularised dharmas of caste, social position and coercive power. But these bridging movements failed, perhaps because they missed the people's prevailing calculus of pragmatic interests toward both traditional Hinduism and modernity.[18]

In social practice, a similarly less restrictive ethic takes over when food-gifting and public feeding are concerned. The driving idea in this may be that early upanishadic formulation which proclaimed that 'food is god' (*annamabrahma*) and that its essence is found in sharing and circulation. Feeding others (particularly the hungry–*daridra narayan*) is verily to feed God (Narayan). Such an act pleases God like no other, my informants repeatedly emphasised, and the divine, sitting in hearts of the hungry and the poor, sees all those who fail in their duty and neglect the needy and the poor.

Reviewed briefly, food production and its just availability within the Hindu world depends on four interrelated criteria: (*a*) the watchful and unerring divine who is the ultimate provider (*jagadbharta*); (*b*) the cosmic and the immediate

[16] I quote here the words of one of my informants, but the idea comes from the *Bhagvad Gita* (18, 61), where the divine is found immanent in everybody's heart, overseeing his/her—good, bad and indifferent—karmas. One thus cannot unjustly suffer without the knowledge of the divine.

[17] In contrast, as shown later, a radical social reformer like B.R. Ambedkar could hardly interpret the neo-classical Hindu humanism so charitably. He insisted that in practice not only has the Gandhian hope of a tolerant Hinduism failed, but actually the Hindu rules of caste, karma and rebirth have tightened around the poorest and the lowest.

[18] I am grateful to Patricia Uberoi for alerting me to internal contradictions in both Hindu traditional and modern discourses on food, when the issue of 'right' or 'entitlement' to food is concerned. However, the efforts of Jai Prakash Narayan and Vinoba Bhave on land and food distribution require more systematic study in this context. Both closely knew Hindu religious traditions and both tried to marry these to a political and economic modernity that they thought was suitable for independent India. Yet the marriage is known now more for its failures than success.

order of dharma and its observance in nature (*prakriti*) and in daily religious and social duties; (*c*) the personal faith in divine justice and in the ledger of good or bad karmas, as manifest in current life; and (*d*) a just and fair rule of a king or a government (*sarkar*). These four criteria and the cultural conceptions standing behind them give us a blueprint of the moral economy of Hindu food. Considered alongside social context, 'they ensure', as my informants said, 'adequate and appropriate food to all within this creation.' To the Hindu, such a composite formulation of moral economy is *not* merely an ideal but a life-guiding faith. Here moral suggestion, social persuasion, individual conscience, and the fear of punishment in the other world converge to stress the need for the fair and just sharing of food with others.

V

Dharma, caste, history and modern India

However, despite all the moral sanctions against neglecting the hungry (and the bad karmas so earned), people with means continue to act with selfishness and under greed, controlling or denying food to the poor and the needy. How do we explain such a situation? Do we conclude that the dharma-karma morality, though still crucial, is not persuasive enough any more in the matters of food and hunger? Or is it that the Hindus are not religious enough any more? To my many Hindu informants, the answer to both these questions was, 'yes', although they gave different explanations. Some settled for the orthodox Hindu religious cosmology that predicts weakening of all dharma, particularly ordinary dharma, during the Kali Age. Others found fault with 'modern government programmes and promises' while, as my Lucknow informants said, 'cheating and confusing the simple and ordinary people'. Still others (a small group), particularly orthodox Hindus, wanted to revive government-dismantled Hindu traditional institutions (of the *jajmani* system, gifting and charity), replacing the 'fair-price' (but actually corrupt) government ration shops. Grass-root religious charity and the voluntary social protection of the weak have already significantly declined in cities, the same people observed.

All my informants were agreed that no right-to-food inquiry on Hindu India can today ignore these increasingly intolerant social tendencies, although they are hardest to track since they are socially informal, small-scale, morally conditional, and related to daily pressures of life. In cities, those with means, whether Hindus or Muslims, Sikhs, Christians, etc., may increasingly tend to shut off, dismiss or overlook the needy. We must now more directly comment on the matter..

As already noted, attributing all problems of Indian food, hunger and social injustice to caste, religion and community divisions is no longer very productive. We tend to run in circles while explaining caste dharma by history, or vice versa. We need to remember that where food problems are concerned, India has already been working long with selected strands of both traditional and modern institutions. Here, if the Indian caste system's interdependent institutions widely work in daily food acquisition, use and feeding and eating, then the Indian government has developed during the last fifty years food production, storage, transportation and wholesale and local food distribution and its marketing. Considered together, both have their strengths and weaknesses. However, the traditional food-distribution network spread over thousands of villages and cities (with or without the *jajmani* system), involves the overwhelming majority of Indian households in some way everyday. Self-regulated, it has largely survived intact the British Raj as well as the major state-sponsored changes in independent India, but it is now under increasing internal criticism, especially by the urban Indian.[19] In a modern critical view, the same higher (and often the locally dominant) Hindu castes not only perpetuate social inequalities but also institutionalise the exploitation and dependence of the poor. In such a context, the changing logic of the Indian caste–class complex must also be recognised, where the poor of all castes, including, for example, the Brahman–Bania–Kayasth cluster in U.P. must now seek favour from the rich and the politically dominant Yadav–Ahir–Kurmi ruling combine.

The overall system still heavily tilts toward those born in the upper three varnas—Brahman, Kshatriya and Vaishya. By and large, these constitute the privileged social core. Considered another way, women, children, low castes and outcastes (including Untouchables) variously form the dependent 'peripheral' circle, seeking their sustenance and social validation from the upper-caste male core. This is generally true whether one is Hindu, Muslim, Christian or Sikh, all of whom feed the hungry as religious charity (e.g., although distinct from one another in institutional organisation, religious meaning and practice, Hindus do so by *sadavrat*, Muslims by *khairat*, and Sikhs by *langar*). While there is little institutionalised social space available in India for such an egalitarian goal as the individual right to food, still, as I have argued in this paper, Hindu and Indian social food sharing goes far beyond institutionalised caste rules and their restrictive practices. Guided by the four major concepts of sustenance (see section III), people, 'rework' their crucial dharma-karma norms and formulations in such a way that they can cope with widely different social situations. A modern social reformer like M.K. Gandhi amply stressed the adaptability of Hindu dharma so as to incorporate in it his modern notions of egalitarian welfare and care of the poor.[20]

Over all, major weaknesses of the traditional religious reforms are still undeniable, whereas the modern Indian state has played a significant economic and political role in mitigating the Indian food problem, especially by all-India schemes for food production, massive storage, speedy transportation and elaborate subsidised

[19] In modern historical terms, the caste order during this century has shown internally contradictory tendencies where food and hunger issues are concerned. If its ritual rules for sharing different cooked foods have relaxed, especially in cities, the system has not followed up by expanding exchange, gifting and charity food in *bulk* across caste and community divisions. 'Unfortunately, others' hunger is still not our hunger,' was the remark of a Lucknow reformer.

[20] Today, traditional or orthodox Hindus accord increasingly more room to M.K. Gandhi for uplifting the poor and the deprived. He is also credited with not demanding the abolition of the entire caste system, but proposing only selective reform. However, Gandhi is not followed by the same people when it comes to sharing property, privilege and status with those less privileged.

food distribution. On the other hand, this successful government role (and its Green Revolution) has also been economically uneven and not always socially equitable; it reduced the hunger but aggravated some major religious and political conflicts during the 1980s, especially in states like Punjab, Uttar Pradesh and Bihar (between Hindus, Muslims and Sikhs). Though we lack enough research on such issues, the situation clearly demands a *closer* watch, with an appropriate regional rather than a state or community limited perspective on Indian food and hunger issues. One state's surplus (e.g., Punjab and its conspicuous consumption) in a country like India might reduce as well as trigger new or widening pockets of hidden, silenced and voiceless hunger in other neighbouring states, especially as the stagnating traditional food charity, rising caste conflicts and deepening religious differences clash with people's rising social expectations.

Analytically, the questions of food and food accessibility in India are now hardly traditional or modern, or even a simple combination of the two. While ordinary Hindus, like other Indians, now depend on government programmes for food supply in partially regulated markets at a reasonable price, they also eat and feed according to family customs, local caste rules and religious values. Their goal in both domains is to *maximise* the chances their families have to secure a stable, affordable and agreeable food supply. The temperamental local government support, market-price fluctuations, fuzzy caste rules and practicable family adaptations are indispensable to them for survival. In domestic life, they are well aware that the modern individual right to food simply has no standing in practice independent of the duty-based rules, family dispositions and life's practical conditions.

When facing sudden adversity, they know very well that they can depend only on their traditional social security net for avoiding starvation. These are socially far more reliable, dependable and resourceful than the government's programmes. For the vast majority of Indians, however, both relatives in a neighbourhood and the government are necessary for survival. Thus, overall, the Green Revolution, government regulatory institutions and the traditional moral economy and domestic food management are necessary to secure the maximum from all sides.[21] In practice, all these initiatives show a tentativeness, where all sides muddle through to feed 960 million Indians, rather than evolve into a genuinely new ideology, with a strong commitment to individualised food entitlement.

At this point, it might be useful to comment further on this dual control of food in India, and on the sociological relevance of the ration cards for ensuring daily food supply to people and the special relief efforts launched during droughts and famines. As already noted, when we consider these state interventions together, we realise how the British Raj and the modern Indian state have perhaps most

[21] If the government 'ration shops' did make food uniformly accessible to the poorest, the public distribution system still could not eliminate the poor people's dependence on private food markets, grain merchants and moneylenders. Thus, the traditional and the modern have long selectively constrained and thwarted each other in India, both sectors adjusting over time to help improve most people's food procurement.

decisively altered the Indian ways of bulk food production, storage, transportation and marketing of food on the one hand, and of family food consumption, on the other. The Indian food rationing system, resting on *families*, represented one arm of such a change, altering the common Indian's food procurement. Sociologically, however, it also meant the indirect introduction of Western notions of individual food entitlement by quantity (and supposedly caloric and nutritional requirements). The government issued ration cards to families but allotted a government-determined quantity of food to individual family members (distinguished as adults and children) per week. Though such a subsidised food quota system acquires another face under the Nehruvian socialist pattern of society, I will focus on the modern contrast where food distribution based on individual needs is supposedly made more '*rational*' and equitable for the poor and socially deprived. But the cultural rationale of this new system was lost to most people, since there was no education of the public. The government responsibility ultimately rested in the hands of a local ration shopkeeper, who actually sold specified food quantities (of wheat, rice, sugar, etc.) against a family's ration card. In practice, not only bogus ration cards emerged but the local ration-shop owner negotiated 'special deals' with his unscrupulous customers, sometimes at the expense of the needy and the poor.

But the shopkeeper's role in food distribution stopped at the family level. The daily actual food consumption by family members, however, remained totally customary, leaving actual feeding and eating with all the major Indian moral economies (Hindu, Islamic, Sikh, etc.; see also Khare 1986: 277–96). In practice, not only did the traditional and modern economic regimens of food procurement and entitlement exist in their own domains, but the locally dominant families and caste groups influenced (or bought off, as some would say) the ration shopkeeper and the weak and the poor. For example, the rich often bought the food allocated to poor families, defeating the socialism-inspired role of the Indian ration card.[22]

My second example comes from India's approach to famine relief in recent historical times. (For a range of comments on the state's development of a famine relief code in Indian history, see Bhatia 1967; Greenough 1982; Sen 1982; Smith 1958; K. Suresh Singh 1975.)[23] The overall cultural message of the famine experience in India remains rather similar to that of the previous case. The government development programmes in India still have to learn to recognise, accommodate and coexist with an ambiguous but tenacious—sometimes helpful and sometimes

[22] For example, besides swindlers, the urban middle class also devised ways to subvert the ration card system to augment its food availability at less cost. Bogus and multiple ration cards, for example, were usually obtained in the name of domestic servants and other consenting low-caste, poor families.

[23] Besides the insider–outsider difference in such studies in analysing the conditions of hunger and famine in India, several writers, during the 1970s, focused on the necessity of 'structural' realignments of modern political and economic institutions for solving the problem of hunger. Since these authors often underestimated the crucial role of people's motivations for or against such a structural change, they sought 'final' solutions only in a top-down government-controlled programme of food distribution and marketing. Greenough's study is, however, distinct for the way it perceptively interweaves historical and cultural forces in accounting for Indian famine and famine relief efforts.

hindering—traditional order. In practice, Indian traditions are found to selectively impose controls on, and accept controls from, the modern state. Greenough (1982: 266–72), for example, examined the presence of both forces in the Bengal Famine of 1943–44, with comments on their strengths and weaknesses. His historical approach, critical yet balanced, allowed him to present an economically realistic account of what a famine meant to Bengalis (and Hindus more generally), along with a perceptive analysis of the Bengali notions of prosperity and misery (ibid.: 52–61, 10, 12–14).

We may now summarise the preceding discussion of the Hindu moral economy of food in contemporary India in the following general points:

(*a*) Though traditional rules and practices are increasingly unevenly followed within rural and urban surroundings of Hindu society, they still significantly pattern everyday domestic food availability and its consumption.

(*b*) Despite a generally inclusive, all-Indian government approach to food availability (or scarcity) issues, Hindus continue to treat food distribution under predominantly local sectarian, caste, kinship and ritual rules.[24] This dual—officially inclusive but customarily restrictive—approach to food acquisition and use in India suggests social adaptability as well as major internal gaps, conflicts and ambiguities. For some critics, however, such a duality only weakens both traditional and modern schemes. In general, if people now readily accept the state's measures regulating bulk food production, marketing, storage and transportation, they still reject (or keep at bay) modern egalitarian ideas when intra- and inter-family food handling is concerned.

(*c*) Nonetheless, the role of the modern government (*sarkar*) in attacking the food problem of independent India remains distinct and significant, introducing a national political, economic and *legal* framework that removed most food production and distribution out of restrictive local, political, religious, and caste considerations. Instead, food became a culturally unrestricted (but state-regulated) national economic commodity throughout the entire country. In cultural terms, however, since the government still largely played the traditionally expected provider-protector role, people quickly noticed and protested against government failures even while state initiatives were accepted on food supply in customary terms.

(*d*) Accordingly, any grass-root movement for right-to-food in India is bound to show this multiple cultural strategy of Indians which continues to seek feasible cooperation from the traditional forces even as it tries to modify or confront some restrictive caste rules and practices and accepts the role of state policies and programmes.

[24] This dual Hindu approach to food has its own costs, strains and burdens that cannot be historically or sociologically denied. Its roots run deep in the classical culture, where one's sectarian and caste status determined one's actual relationship to food. (For the classical system based on differences between householders and renouncers, see Heesterman 1985.) While the householder regulated circulation of food to all creatures, the renouncer, taking to begging, adopted a hands-off approach in this domain.

VI
Approximating rights with social reform and justice

Though modern India, not unlike other developing countries, aimed early to wipe out hunger and social deprivation by promoting social justice (e.g., in Mahatma Gandhi's language, Rama Rajya, a combination of the best of both Indian traditions and modern values [see Bondurant 1971: 151]), the task is still largely unachieved. Ordinary Indians, for example, still lack the required motivation to link their survival concerns, interests and priorities with those that the modern state favours for promoting social justice with equality. In the absence of any significant (and sustained) public education programme, even educated urban Indians are obliged to improvise. To grapple with issues of civil or human rights in everyday life, one needs appropriate (and sustained) socialisation within both private and public life. Instead, what we most often have are political leaders' and reformers' occasional pro forma public exhortations and official statements on the subject, framed with a routine homage to leaders like M.K. Gandhi and Jawaharlal Nehru, who yoked two horses of very different breed—traditional and democratic—to pull India into modern times. As some now argue, the last fifty years have taught Indians how to initiate tentative practical bridges between the traditional and modern social domains, often learning by trial and error to negotiate through opposing ideologies, exploitative social practices and rising conflicts. (For recent appraisals of the human rights debate in India, see Smitu Kothari and Harsh Sethi 1989; for a similarly critical legal and juridical discussion, see Baxi 1987; Iyer 1987.)

Though such a situation may be analytically ambiguous and confusing, it has actually produced a distinctly Indian way of managing multiple regional, caste, economic and political differences. The same Indian way also throws up those eclectic and moderate political leaders and reformers who disapprove extremism and prefer accommodation over confrontation between democratic and traditional forces. They seek to find a working—or a workable—position rather than wait for either tradition or modernity to annihilate each other ideologically. Even a modern radical Dalit leader like B.R. Ambedkar rejected an extremist political or cultural stance. Finding it against the Indian temper, he subscribed to Buddhism to take a long-term civilisational view of the upper-caste Hindu and Dalit value conflicts, but without softening his political stand on annihilating the Indian caste system, the root of continuing social injustice (e.g., see Ambedkar 1944, 1946).[25] He saw hunger and helplessness of the dependent as a form of slavery, and he exhorted Untouchables to action by saying, as my Dalit informants often recalled, 'Tell the

[25] Viewed historically, Ambedkar alone, among modern Indian leaders, writers and reformers, provided a genuinely radical critique of the traditional Hindu scheme of caste and its dharma-karma. He saw the necessity of annihilating caste, root and branch. For a discussion of the subject by local Indian academics in Lucknow, who regarded Ambedkar as a revolutionary leader, see Bharill (1977); Jatava (1965).

slave he is a slave and he will revolt.'[26] To get their share of dignity and equality, he wanted Dalits to inculcate values of self-confidence and political assertion:

> You had better die and relieve this world if you cannot rise to new life and if you cannot rejuvenate yourselves. As a matter of fact it is your birthright to get food, shelter and clothing in this land in equal proportion with every individual, high or low (quoted in Keer 1962: 60–61).

Ambedkar's call actually encodes an issue more fundamental to the poor and the dispossessed than that promoted by the United Nations' definition of global universal human rights. It is 'the right to be human', to use Upendra Baxi's perceptive phrase, where people's basic survival needs are met by ensuring to them social justice and dignity. 'The right to be human' must thus precede any other fundamental rights (Baxi 1987: 185–200). In India, it means providing its different communities a socially just and equitable right to acquire food, clothing, shelter and security. And it is only these rights that can render the West-inspired modern human rights eventually sensible and substantive for Indians. Today, the people's need for food and freedom globally interrelate. Both are necessary, but freedom movements without ensuring people's survival needs result in a bigger tragedy. On the interrelationships between bread and freedom, Baxi (ibid.: 186) remarks:

> The issues are not really 'bread' and/or 'freedom' in the abstract, but rather who has how *much* of each, for how *long*, at *what* cost to others, and *why*. Some people have both 'bread' and 'freedom'; others have 'freedom' but little 'bread' or none at all; yet others have half a loaf (which is better than none surely!) with or without freedom; and still others have a precarious mix where 'bread' is assured if certain (not all) freedoms are bartered.

Baxi's argument also cautions us against reifying and reducing the deprived people's world to just a variable in an abstract philosophical debate. Though still without the necessary political voice and social representation, the poor and the exploited nevertheless pose the most crucial test to liberal democratic thought, especially now, at the end of the 20th century, when it is viewed as the only globally workable and viable political system. In the world of the weak and the oppressed, questions of human 'dignity', 'rights', and 'basic rights' or 'minimum rights' are *seldom* conceivable independent of the ever-present need of daily survival. In India, it means, as already shown, working through *several* participating moral economies that conceive survival only through overlapping networks of religious debts, provider-protector economic locations and social duties (*rna, palana-posana* and *kartavya*). Changes and modifications are here regularly tried and often incorporated.[27]

[26] My informants in Lucknow mentioned it first to me in the early eighties. See also Jatava (1965: 12).

[27] This includes hundreds of thousands of ordinary Untouchables (or Dalits) that Ambedkar converted into Buddhism. In a recent random survey in a Lucknow locality, where I studied reform-minded Untouchables (Chamars) for their changing cultural outlook, nine out of ten still subscribed to the Hindu (or 'Hindu-style') dharma-karma complex. However, since modern democratic politics, state

While studying how most Indians are engaged in securing 'a right to be human' (as a step toward securing other human rights) in contemporary India, one must actually focus on the other side of the Indian cultural coin. We must know how major Indian traditions have responded since independence by neutralising, modifying, accommodating, obstructing or dismissing modern initiatives. If Indian traditions have often played during this period an ambiguous, even self-contradictory role, they have been seldom merely socially passive or destructive. If they have been stout cultural gate-keepers against open-ended and blind modernisation, they have also selectively accepted, admitted and even encouraged modern ideas to reach and influence ordinary people. Any simpler view, where the moral economy of traditional India either exposes only weaknesses and failures of the modern state and its public culture or accepts them unquestioned, is both sociologically and historically untenable.

Today's India is fast becoming ever more socially complicated. This is evident as the recent major religious conflicts, the rise of Hindutva and social protest movements against both traditions and the state appear alongside an activist, pro-public judiciary and an opening and privatising Indian economy. Here people selectively dissemble and recombine the forces of both tradition and modernity in such a way that both could help people reassert and reposition them for the next round of major social change in India.

Overall, though increasingly socially conflicted and uneven, these developments remain generally averse to extremist positions and options. Even a radical Dalit leader like Ambedkar recognised the limits of an extremist religious, social or political struggle for India. Given the people's diverse social bases and cultural attitudes, extremism generally loses steam and disperses. Under such conditions, the modern Indian human rights movement cannot hope to have any other social trajectory. One of its best cultural linkages might be with people's view of hunger, food, food charity and feeding the stranger. Here the right to food appears as an approximation of the just economic and social entitlement to food under dharma, and by the inexorable divine plan. But for the larger social goals of human rights, both sides (Indian traditions and the modern state), after suitable translations, must learn to negotiate, where situational moral, social and practical compromises and cooperation take precedence over ideological battles, leaving little room for a clear victory for either side. Congruently, an anthropological study of right-to-food issues in India must contribute by regionally explicating and evaluating the multiple cultural—moral, political, economic and situational—languages and forces over time, from the classical to the colonial, to that of modern independent India. Only in this way do we also learn more about how different Indian groups today constrain and control food, disallowing its just social distribution among the needy and the poor.

Since the culture, the people and the modern Indian state are already actively engaged in an exercise on food entitlement, anthropology can perhaps best help

---

programmes and urbanisation have indeed relaxed and modified some caste inequalities during the last fifty years, Ambedkar's Dalits might claim to be winning one battle at a time rather than the whole war.

by deciphering how the traditionally obvious, hidden and anomalous forces now actually work (with or without the state's programmes) to impede or help achieve the goal of a hunger-free society. And while doing so, anthropology must scrupulously avoid the mistake of siding with modern ideology. Also, it must neither import into India unexamined modern Western theories apportioning blame on underdeveloped people, nor absolve the modern state and its government of responsibility, without sufficiently examining the evidence, whether good, bad or indifferent. In India, neither its traditions nor the government can be underestimated (much less discounted) for creating or prolonging the Indian food problem. Actually, in any major socially sustained Indian impetus toward seeking the right-to-food for all Indians, both Indian traditions and democracy, though horses of different breed, must stay yoked together until they learn to pull as a team.

REFERENCES

AMBEDKAR, B.R. 1944. *Annihilation of caste* (Ambedkar school of thought). Amritsar: Katra Jaman Singh.

———. 1946. *Who were the Shudras?* Bombay: Thacker & Co.

BARDHAN, KALPANA (trans., ed.). 1990. *Of women, outcastes, peasants, and rebels: A selection of Bengali short stories.* Berkeley: University of California Press.

BAXI, UPENDRA. 1987. From human rights to the right to be human. *In* Upendra Baxi, Geeti Sen and Jeanette Fernandes, eds, *The right to be human*, pp. 185–200. New Delhi: Lancer International.

Bhagvad Gita. 1969. Trans. R.C. Zaehner, with a commentary on original sources. Oxford: Oxford University Press.

BHARILL, CHANDRA. 1977. *Social and political ideas of B.R. Ambedkar.* Jaipur: Aalekh Publishers.

BHATIA, B.M. 1967. *Famines in India (1860–1965)* (2nd edn). Bombay: Asia Publishing House.

BODENHEIMER, EDGAR. 1974. *Jurisprudence: The philosophy and method of law.* Cambridge: Harvard University Press.

BONDURANT, JOAN V. 1971. *Conquest of violence: The Gandhian philosophy of conflict.* Berkeley: University of California Press.

CHOUSALKAR, ASHOK S. 1986. *Social and political implications of concepts of justice and dharma.* Delhi: Mittal Publications.

DESAI, A.R., ed. 1986. *Violations of democratic rights in India.* Bombay: Popular Prakashan.

GHOSHAL, U.N. 1959. *A history of Indian political ideas.* Delhi: Oxford University Press.

GREENOUGH, PAUL R. 1982. *Prosperity and misery in modern Bengal: The famine of 1943–1944.* New York: Oxford University Press.

HEESTERMAN, J.C. 1985. *The inner conflict of tradition.* Chicago: University of Chicago Press.

IYER, KRISHNA V.R. 1987. *Social justice—sunset or dawn* (2nd edn). Lucknow: Eastern Book Company.

JATAVA, D.R. 1965. *The political philosophy of B.R. Ambedkar.* Agra: Phoenix Publishing Co.

KANE, P.V. 1974. *History of dharmaśāstra* (vol. II, pt. 2) (2nd edn). Poona: Bhandarkar Oriental Research Institute.

KEER, DHANANJAY. 1962. *Dr. Ambedkar: Life and mission* (2nd edn). Bombay: Popular Prakashan.

KHARE, R.S. 1976. *The Hindu hearth and home.* Delhi: Vikas Publishers.

KHARE, R.S. and M.S.A. RAO, eds. 1986. Hospitality, charity and rationing: Three channels of food distribution in India. *In* R.S. Khare and M.S.A. Rao, eds, *Aspects of South Asian food systems: Food, society and culture*, pp. 277–96. Durham: Carolina Academic Press.

KOTHARI, RAJNI. 1989. Human rights—a movement in search of a theory. *In* Smitu Kothari and Harsh Sethi, eds, *Rethinking human rights: Challenges for theory and action*, pp. 19–29. New York: New Horizons Press.

KOTHARI, SMITU and HARSH SETHI, eds. 1989. *Rethinking human rights: Challenges for theory and action.* New York: New Horizons Press.

KRISHNA, DAYA. 1996. *The problematic and conceptual structure of classical Indian thought about man, society and polity.* Delhi: Oxford University Press.

LINGAT, R. 1973. *The classical law of India* (translated from French by J. Duncan Derrett). Berkeley: University of California Press.

Mahabharata. 1988. Santiparva, vol. 6. Translated from the original sanskrit text by M.N. Dutt. Delhi: Parimal Publications.

PAREKH, BHIKHU. 1987. The modern conception of right and its Marxist critique. *In* Upendra Baxi et al., eds, *The right to be human*, pp. 1–22. New Delhi: Lancer Publications.

REGE, M.P. 1985. Concepts of justice and equality in the Indian tradition. R.R. Memorial Lecture. Pune: Gokhale Institute of Politics and Economics.

SEN, AMARTYA. 1982. *Poverty and famines: An essay on entitlement and deprivation.* Oxford: Clarendon Press.

———. 1987. *Research for action: Hunger and entitlements.* Helsinki: World Institute for Development Economics Research.

SINGH, K.S. 1975. *The Indian famine, 1967: A study in crisis and change.* New Delhi: People's Publishing House.

SMITH, VINCENT. 1958. *The Oxford history of India* (3rd edn, ed. Percival Spear). Oxford: Clarendon Press.

WALZER, MICHAEL. 1983. *Spheres of justice: A defense of pluralism and equality.* New York: Basic Books.

7

The female family core explored ethnosociologically

McKim Marriott

Extended family households of South Asia distinguish their core female personnel as sexually active or inactive, junior or senior, and own or other. (i) Noting similar variables in the region's classical theories and elsewhere in its ethnography, and constructing from these a paradigm to assist further questioning, this paper finds (ii) eight major societal qualities generated by the same paradigm, (iii) eight corresponding domestic role-types, (iv) a common female life-course through those role-types, (v) characteristic relations of worship complementing that female life-course, and (vi) diverse related perspectives on male–female differences. So many results from questioning with this one paradigm make the common and congruent female family core a likely source of the civilisation's diversity as well as of its underlying assumptions.

Extended family households of South Asia are being newly examined today from feminine perspectives. Long discussed as patrilineal[1] groupings of males and their dependents by male ethnographers (e.g., Madan 1965), comparative sociologists (e.g., Shah 1974), and critics (e.g., Kakar 1989), such households are now being observed, principally by female ethnographers, as having at their domestic cores groups of females. What makes observations of these groups most interesting is what makes them instantly recognisable as South Asian—their finding of an (at least) threefold internal differentiation by sexual activity, relative seniority, and variable belonging. That even these small, ubiquitous groups exhibit multi-dimensional logics that are peculiar to South Asia suggests again the need for an indigenous social science—an ethnosociology that can deal systematically (as conventional Western social science cannot) with the distinctive culture of the region.[2]

[1] Male landholding and patrilocality, virilocal marriage, and the consequent dependence of females upon males (Menon 1995; Reynolds 1980; Wadley 1995: 100) are all fundamental to the kinds of families discussed here, but typifying families as 'patrilineal' models only part of their structures (Uberoi 1995). Using the alternative common androcentric term 'patriarchal' would further ignore the separation of males, especially senior males, from the female domains of daily life (e.g., Lamb 1997; Papanek and Minault 1982).

[2] With editor Madan's encouragement, an outline of such an ethnosociology with specimens of its uses was first presented as vol. 23, no. 1 of *Contributions to Indian sociology*, then republished as a book (Marriott, ed. 1990); it was discussed critically in vols. 24, 25, and 26, and is further developed here.

I

The general paradigm and its six components

The three kinds of distinctions that women make in domestic groups are similar, respectively, to the distinctions of 'hot' and 'cold', 'high' and 'low', and 'near' and 'distant' that are repeated elsewhere throughout South Asian customary practice. They are, for example, much like the distinctions made within the best-known classical analytic sets of three or more variable properties—(a) *bhūta* 'elements' (ether, air, fire, water, and earth), (b) *doṣa* 'humours' (phlegm, bile, and wind), (c) *guṇa* 'strands' (goodness, passion, and darkness), and (d) *artha* 'aims' (coherence, advantage, attachment, and release) (Table 1). These sets are paradigmatic in the literatures of *sāṃkhya, āyurveda, dharmaśāstra*, and *jyotiśāstra;* in equivalent vernacular terms, their components and properties have been popularly understood as operative in most spheres of human life. Since the components are often treated by South Asians as mutually homologous, the sets are arranged here in parallel columns.[3]

Shared by all the classical sets (aligned with them in column [e] of the table) is an impartible set of three antiequivalent relational logics—nonReflexivity, nonSymmetry, and nonTransitivity.[4] The continuous variance expressed by each of these negatively prefixed terms fits well with the Hindu[5] assumption that all the ultimate components of the world are kinds of 'liquid substance' (*dravya*). Noting how this and other verbal, conceptual, and practical usages endow these components with motile tendencies as well as materiality (E. Daniel 1984; Larson 1987: 65–73; Marriott 1992: 270–73; Zimmermann 1983), I describe them (in column [f] as 'substantial processes', naming the top three (R̸) 'mixing–unmixing', (S̸) 'unmarking–being marked', and (T) 'unmatching–matching'.[6] In their definitions I attempt to summarise the kinds of actions that are commonly attributed to and shared by the terms in their rows.

[3] Exactly the alignments made here of sets (a), (b), and (c) have been reported independently from Nepal by Kondos (1982). My alignment of set (d) is supported by much ethnography and other indology, although it differs from the one stated in Manu 12.38 (Doniger and Smith 1991: 282), which is most often cited by today's scholars. Urdu equivalents for the Sanskrit terms of (a) and (b) are given by Pugh (1984).

[4] In contrast to the dichotomous assertion or denial conveyed by terms like 'symmetry' or 'asymmetry', whose use is preferred by most logicians, 'non-' terms like 'nonsymmetry' allow that both properties may exist within the same universe (Carnap 1958: 117–20). Such equivocal, or 'antiequivalent' axioms allow for South Asian diversity and better approximate the apparent (and from a Western perspective pessimistic, if realistic) assumption that all relations are more or less irreflexive, asymmetrical, and intransitive.

[5] 'Hindu' in this essay refers to people and institutions operating with the properties defined in columns (a) to (d) of Table 1.

[6] To facilitate cross-reference among the figures, the slashed letters (R) for nonReflexivity and mixing, (S̸) for nonSymmetery and marking, and (T̸) for nonTransitivity and unmatching are inscribed along their corresponding dimensions. Like the prefix 'non-', the slashes indicate that these terms are contraries of the standard 'logics of relations' concepts. The same initials happen to alliterate with the similar Sanskrit 'strand' terms *sattva, rajas, tamas,* except that the slashed S̸ indicates more markedness and thus less, rather than more of *sattva* 'goodness'.

Table 1

Derivations and definitions for a South Asian ethnosociology

Distinctions in families among females	*Classical analytic sets*				*Relational logics*	VARIABLE PROPERTIES *(defined as substantial processes)*
	Elements (bhūtas) (a)	*Humours (doṣas)* (b)	*Strands (guṇas)* (c)	*Aims (arthas)* (d)	(e)	(f)
Active, erotic, hot	3. Fire (*agni*)	2. Bile (*pitta*)	2. Passion (*rajas*) (R̸)	3. Attachment (*kāma*)	1. NonReflexivity	MIXING... (opening, intersecting expanding)
Less active, cold	less fire	less bile	passionless [*tapas*]	nonattachment (*niṣkāma*)	// reflexivity	...UNMIXING (closing, isolating, condensing)
Senior, ascendant, high	4. Water (*āp*)	3. Phlegm (*kapha*)	1. Goodness (*sattva*)	2. Advantage (*artha*)	2. NonSymmetry	UNMARKING... (outranking, neutralising pervading)
Junior, descendant, low	less water	less phlegm	less goodness (*asattva*) (S̸)	disadvantage (*anartha*)	// symmetry	...BEING MARKED (outranked, differentiated, pervaded)
Other, distant	2. Air (*vāyu*)	1. Wind (*vāta*)	3. Darkness (*tamas*) (T̸)	incoherence (*adharma*)	3. NonTransitivity	UNMATCHING... (reversing, negating, separating)
Own, near	less air	less wind	less darkness [*tejas*]	1. Coherence (*dharma*)	// transitivity	...MATCHING (continuing, affirming, uniting)
House, womb, connection	5. Earth (*pṛthvi*)	[body, tissue, channel]	[entity, group, person]	[heaven, *svarga*]	[example]	PLACING (reifying, limiting, contextualising)
Name, deity, force (*śakti*)	1. Ether (*ākāśa*)	[emptiness, *śūnya*, pores]	[life force, *jīva*]	[dissolution, *pralaya*]	[definition]	SPACING (communicating, dispersing, decontextualising)
Self	O. None of the above (*puruṣa*)	[soul, *ātman*]	[strandless, *nirguṇa*]	4. Release (*moksa*)	[none]	CONSCIOUSNESS (invariance, nonrelationality, transcendence)

For the table's construction, see Marriott (1989: 6–9). Set components are numbered as conventionally recited. Square brackets indicate interpolations.

(Ɍ) 'Mixing' is an intersective, irReflexive process that increases entities' kinetic 'heat' (or energy) and size by opening them and increasing their external exchanges of markable properties; 'unmixing' works against mixing to promote reflexive 'coolness' by reducing entities' external exchanges, closing and condensing them, internalising their resources, potentialising their energies. (Ꞩ) 'Unmarking' and 'being marked' are aSymmetric processes by which entities rise or fall in relative ranking as they move less marked (i.e., more 'neutral' [Waugh 1982]), more penetrating or pervasive properties in a 'higher' direction, and more marked and differentiated, less penetrating properties in a contrary, 'lower' direction. (Ŧ) 'Unmatching' processes are inTransitive changes or differences—actions considered to be alien or inappropriate to entities' own properties, whether actual, past, imagined, or desired. Unmatching processes reverse or negate properties and separate one entity from another, while the contrary, transitive 'matching' processes continue or affirm actual or desired properties and move entities toward merger or unity.

All the variables Ɍ, Ꞩ, and Ŧ are assumed to compose every action and entity in some measure, so that while each is distinguishable and can vary in its incidence, each is found only in combination with the others. Thus the top three components in each column of Table 1 require common places where they can intersect as well as spaces where they can vary. These two background requirements, respectively satisfied in column (a) by the next pair of elements known as 'earth' and 'ether', are seen in such analogues as appear in those rows of the other columns. They are interpreted in the summary column (f) as processes of 'placing' and 'spacing', which raise the number of components to five. Placing is represented in the figures by the cubic outlines, spacing by the paper on which the diagrams are printed. In social life, the 'earth' process of placing is exemplified by collocations of the first three variables in such entities as worlds, regions, groups, households, families, persons, etc., and by the channels that connect such entities with each other. The spacing process (supplied by ether's property of emptiness) is evidenced socially by openings for communication and other action—notably for hearing, speaking, and the electronic media; these are vacuous but penetrating forces that move like *śakti*s (Wadley 1975: 53–58) within, among, and beyond all entities and places. 'Consciousness' or 'soul' (*puruṣa, ātman*) (Larson 1987: 73–83), a sixth, also intangible, variously named, but generally presupposed component, resides in and beyond all present and past lives; it may witness this page while simultaneously experiencing any or everything else, contingent on the other components.[7]

The reappearance of from three to six similar components in each of the sets and the three-dimensional 'property-space' (Barton 1955) which each set requires for its operation—these common features suggest that a construct like Figure 1 might fairly serve as the general paradigm of a comprehensive South Asian social

[7] This second trio of components facilitates the South Asian phenomenon that Ramanujan (1989) calls 'contextual sensitivity' and that Raheja illuminates ethnographically as 'shifting perspectives' (Raheja and Gold 1994: ch. 3).

Figure 1
The general paradigm

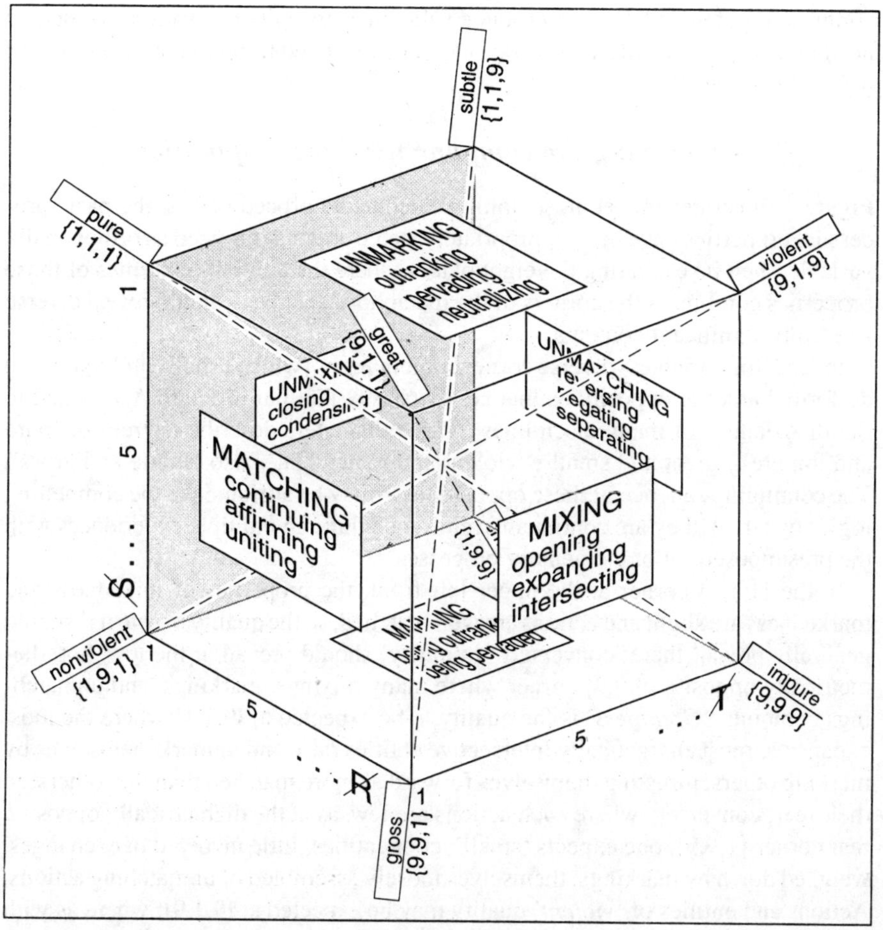

science (Marriott 1989).[8] It is offered as a device with which further empirical inquiry may proceed, generating questions that may be appropriate ones, and thus helping to perceive and describe much that has been real for 20th century people

[8] Algebraic, chromatic, kinetic, or hydraulic representations might all be appropriate for what is verbalised and tabulated above, but geometric diagrams are probably more easily grasped and published. To provide a system of coordinates (which should be understood as relative measures only), I use cubes calibrated from one (meaning 'less' of a property) to nine (meaning 'more') on each of their three dimensions. Each cube can be read like a book, first (R) from left to right across the line, then (S) from the top to the bottom of the page, then (T) from the (left) front to the (right) back. The bracketed address of any place contains three numerals in the same order of R (mixing), S (marking) and T (unmatching), so that an address such as '{9,1,1}' means $r = 9$, $s = 1$, and $t = 1$, and refers to the corner labelled 'great' in the cartouche attached to that address in each figure.

Following assertions that none of these analytics is ever completely absent from a given set and that no one ever completely displaces the others, also that the whole of anything cannot be known,

of South Asian culture. Like any other scientific tool, it needs critical testing: can the foregoing assumptions as to its form, properties, and applicability be either confirmed or denied? Does it produce valid answers and observations, or does it need to be reformulated? If it works, can it be extended to serve the next round of inductive studies?[9]

II

Combining the components: Corner qualities

Figure 1 illustrates this ethnosociology's deductive procedures: if the basic processual properties have been appropriately stated and diagrammed as orthogonally variable, then investigating the eight places where the contrary extremes of those properties combine—the corners of the metaphorical cube—should reveal diverse and triply significant contents.

Indeed, the variables' diverse corner combinations (which I shall call 'qualities') do form diametric oppositions that are extremely familiar to South Asians and to South Asianists of many disciplines. These diameters describe degrees of 'pure and impure', 'great and small', 'violent and nonviolent', also 'subtle and gross'. The continuing salience of these oppositions[10] may be attributed to the compelling logics by which they are continually reinforced through multiple experiences with the presupposed set of elementary processes.

In the {1,1,1} corner at the upper left front, the properties of mixedness and markedness are slight and actions are well matched, so the quality of '*purity*' should generally prevail there; conversely 'impurity' should prevail at the low, hot, diametrically opposite {9,9,9} corner where many mixings, markings, and unmatchings combine. '*Greatness*' is the quality to be expected at {9,1,1} where the most expansive, most energetically intersective entities raise and unmark themselves by marking others, thrusting themselves forward as more matched than the 'others' to their rear; conversely where such actions are few, as at the diametrically opposite, rear corner {1,9,9}, one expects 'small', cool entities, little involved in exchanges, weighed down by markings, themselves loosely assembled of unmatching actions. Actions and entities of '*violent*' quality may be expected at {9,1,9}, where as with greatness, the heat and strength of mixing may be used to mark others beneath it, but

---

the figures eliminate the zero base-points that are conventional in graphing and extend their numerals only as far as 9—not to the decimal wholes implied by numbers such as 10 or 100. (The diagrams herein were executed by Catherine Sexton.)

[9] Readers of previous publications on this paradigm (Marriott 1989, 1991) should note some changes: elaborations of the corners where the first three components combine (Figures 1 and 2), kinetic treatments of relations among them (Figures 3 to 5), revised definitions and greater use of the earth and ether components *passim*, also mutually offset variants of the whole property-space (Figure 6). The form and presumed universal applicability of the paradigm have not so far had to be revised.

[10] In our time, 'purity' and 'impurity' continue to divide persons—vegetarians from carnivores, teetotalers from alcoholics, caste from caste. People of 'great' wealth, privilege, and numbers dominate 'small' followers, weaker minorities, and the poor. Tactics of 'violence' and 'nonviolence' are deployed on many scales. Religious and secular definitions of the nation, astrology and astronomy, faith and science, continue to exemplify numerous contentions between 'subtle' and 'gross'.

in disorganising—negative, separative, reversing—ways; at the opposite {1,9,1} corner, the lower and lesser entities that could be victimised (marked) by violence may prefer to shrink into unmixing cool in order to maintain matched, 'nonviolent' qualities. Whatever is at {1,1,9} shares a similar unmixing coolness and diminutive stature, but may also claim superiority through its unmarkedness and its distance from ordinary affairs—in effect its qualitatively '*subtle*' power; its 'gross' opposite, at {9,9,1}, is made large, warm, and familiar by open mixing, and is marked by many superiors, yet remains well matched within the centrally established order.

Notice that each of these eight qualities has three components, as may be illustrated by common talk about the 'purity' of things at the {1,1,1} corner such as ghee (clarified butter)—a quintessentially pure substance. Ghee is commonly praised for (R̸) its 'cool', self-sufficient, resistant (i.e., unmixing nature), (S̸) its refined, penetrating, unctuous (i.e., self-unmarking) capacities, and (T̸) its lasting, incorruptible freshness (i.e., matchedness). Of this purity definition that fits ghee so well, one third—the unmixing component—may be extended to cool substances such as refined white sugar in the adjacent 'subtle' corner at {1,1,9}, although sugar's easy fermentation proves its corruptibility. The unmixing component of ghee's purity may on the other hand be attributed to gentle ('nonviolent') comestibles like rice water at {1,9,1}—a substance which is cool and not so easily fermented, but which as a residue of cooking lacks ghee's refinement—its unmarkedness. At a third angle, a purity of just the refined, superior kind may be attributed to a substance like unclarified butter, which is strengthening and costly ('great'), but also 'heating'. As each of the three components of ghee's 'purity' thus extends to adjacent corners, so the adjacent corners' partly similar qualities—subtlety, nonviolence, and great power—are commonly attributed to ghee itself (e.g., Alter 1992: 120, 126, 129).[11] Such qualities and their overlappings—all results of this world's (at least) three-dimensionality—systematically generate differences of perspective and perception, differences that should be conspicuous also among female role-types, according to the paradigm's logics.

III
Female roles and activities in the domestic core

If questions about the eight qualities generated above are transposed to the domestic realm, they are readily answered by the eight corresponding female role-types in the corners of Figure 2.[12] Reading those corners in the order in which one reads a book, I attempt here to fill them with what I learn from the ethnographies.

[11] Conflation with adjacent loci also occurs with ghee as a dietary item. Being considered an appropriate food for priests and teachers whose role-types may be placed at {1,1,1} (Lynch 1990: 104), it is thought suitable in lesser amounts also for gods, children, and rulers, whose roles are at adjacent corners; but it is unsuitable for others who are more distant—servants, slaves, criminals, junglis.

[12] The brief labels invented here for the corner clusters of components that I call 'role-types', like those previously attached to the corners' qualities, follow some actual verbal usages, but are not intended fully to describe the corners, qualities, or roles, much less to represent as uniform what is in fact terminologically varied.

Figure 2
Family role-types

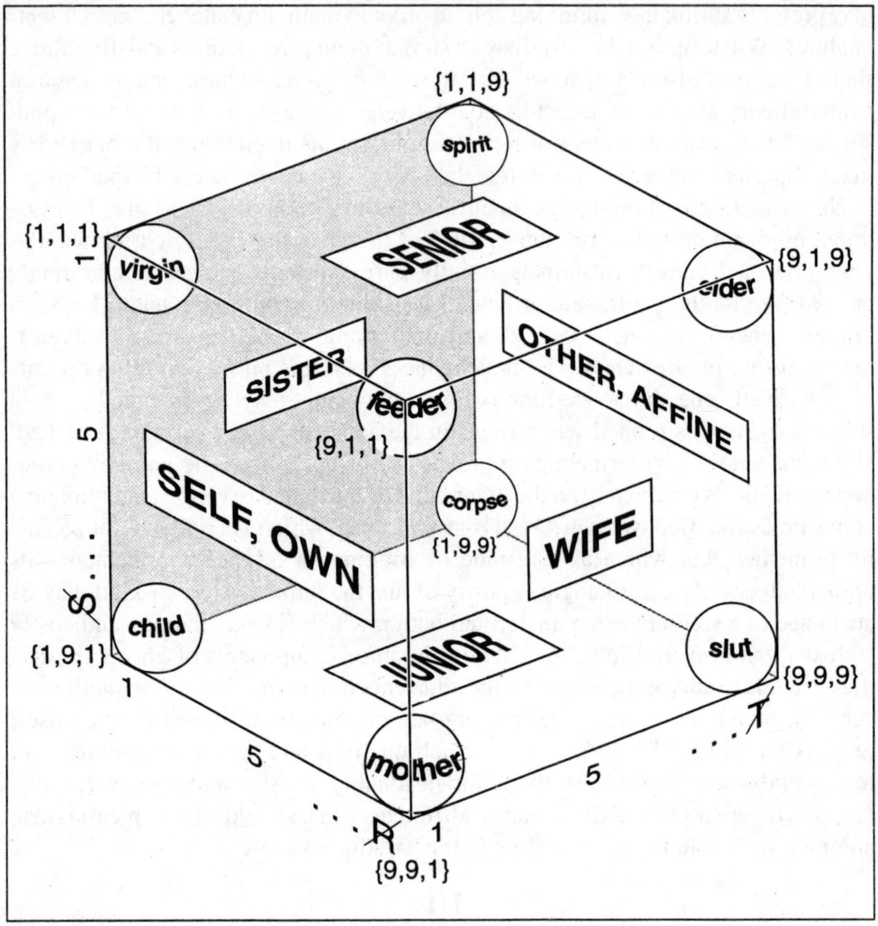

Beyond the initially subtle, theandric {1,1,9} state of infancy that some envisage (Minturn & Hitchcock 1963: 105; Misri 1986: 128–29, 131), the female who is 'purest' in all three senses is surely the nubile *virgin* at {1,1,1} (Wadley 1976: 155).[13] She is preserved as far as possible in a matching state, shielded from social mixing (Das 1979: 93; David 1980: 100–104; Jacobson and Wadley 1977: 37), often bathed and perhaps nourished on cooling foods, she is also kept relatively neutral, receiving fewer markings from her seniors than her brothers do through their outside work and additional samskara rites (M. Davis 1983: 96; Inden and

[13] The intense efforts by Rajputs to maintain what they call the 'honour' (*izzat*) of their virgin daughters (Minturn 1993)—efforts which might suggest actions more like those of the 'great' feeder at {9,1,1}—appear in fact to differ only verbally from what others call 'purity'.

Nicholas 1977: 57–62; Jacobson and Wadley 1977: 35; Lamb 1997: 290–91; Menon 1995: 143, 166, 238–44). 'Greatest' in domestic influence is the *feeder* at the house and storeroom door {9,1,1} who commands the cooking and distribution of food to most others, notably including the domestic deities (David 1980: 113–21; Khare 1976: 70–93, 224, 253–54; Menon 1995: 261–68).

'Nonviolent' is a descriptor that is perhaps most applicable to the girl *child*, whose place is logically at {1,9,1}, below her senior, the nubile virgin. Her adjacent, earthbound *mother* at {9,9,1}, an icon of nourishment if she is pregnant or nursing, socially expanded if she is attending to youngsters, would have the strongest claim on the epithet 'gross'.

Moving now to the rear of the property-space, the 'subtlest' females of the household at {1,1,9} are undoubtedly the deceased, now invisible wives whose cool *spirits* have been absorbed namelessly into the collectivity of lineage ancestors (Lamb 1992: 290–303, 357–61). Among close contenders for accommodation in the subtle corner, however, may be those living wives who have secretly outwitted their husbands in money or love at {1,1,9} (Bonner 1991; Doniger 1994; Raheja and Gold 1994: 39–72).

Most likely to be 'violent' in her feelings—angry, aggressive, possibly suicidal—is the living, but peripheralised *elder* at {9,1,9} who sometimes aims hot, disordered criticism toward her juniors or the neighbours (Lamb 1997: 286–89; Menon 1995: 279–86).

Of 'small' social merit, at least in those classes where she is counted as the corrupt half-body of her deceased husband, is the *corpse*-like widow, also the sick or barren woman, all relegated to the {1,9,9} corner (Dhruvarajan 1989: 31, 92; Kolenda 1982b: 240–42; Lamb 1997: 292–95; Wadley 1995).

However essential to the family's continuance, the junior wife (or '*slut*', as some mothers-in-law designate her) performs sexual, reproductive, and infant care duties—all hot, low, unmatching tasks that tie her to the 'impure' site of {9,9,9} (Menon 1995: 148–49, 244–61; Raheja 1995: 49–50). Menstruating women may join her there periodically (Das 1979: 91; Egnor 1980: 28; Moore 1989: 173, 178, 196).

Daily activities in the household also readily respond to questions derived from the general paradigm and its qualities. 'Greatness' at {9,1,1} comes from the feeding of others, 'grossness' from being fed at {9,9,1}. 'Violence' occurs in quarrelling or working at rough tasks near {9,1,9}, 'subtlety' in play at {1,1,9}. 'Small' activity occurs during idleness or sleep at {1,9,9}, 'impure' activity in coupling, excreting, or carousing at {9,9,9}. Temporary 'purity' at {1,1,1} may be regained by an unmarking, heat-reducing, orderly bath which one may receive at {1,9,1}. For each of these activities women commonly develop routine procedures and places, thus reifying parts of the above paradigm (e.g., Moore 1989). Such recurrent activities and loci, together with the common role-types inventoried above, work as ever-present sources of awareness and concern with the paradigm's qualities. They are reinforced further by the corresponding principal sentiments and emotions[14] of Indian dramatic and devotional theory (Rangacharya 1996: 53–67; Sinha 1961: 307–13, 432–35) and by the similarly patterned genres of women's stories, songs, and dances—blessing, celebrating, praising, begging, joking, insulting, cursing, crying, lusting, etc., reported by Trawick (1986) and by Raheja and Gold (1994: 39–67, 125–48).

So much apparent replication of the general paradigm among persons in the family core may suggest that a single outlook is being imposed. As shown in the example of ghee, however, three-dimensionality multiplies overlappings and perspectives and offers many different possibilities of interpretation. The contraries that are paired in the diagrams and table, the differing orders of recitation for the elements, humours, strands, aims, and sentiments all deny any one hierarchy. No single value, no one or two points of view or lines of analysis, however accurately depicted, can fully or definitively describe action within such a property-space—not the difference between wives and sisters highlighted by Bennett (1983), nor the tyranny over young wives by their marital kin stressed by many critics, nor any single quality, such as purity (Yalman 1963), even if assisted by a shifting, ego-relative value such as auspiciousness (Harlan and Courtright 1995: 5–8). Multiple contextualised views and larger syntheses are needed (Ramanujan 1989) and are richly supplied by Gold (1995), Raheja (1995,1998), Raheja and Gold (1994: 3–13), and Trawick (1986, 1988).

More than most males', a female's mixings may be seen as variable through time and space (S. Daniel 1980: 63; Jacobson 1977; Kemper 1980: 751; Lamb 1997: 290–92, 295). Since her markings depend more on others' markings, and since evaluations of her matchings differ with the perspectives of those evaluating her, each of these interpersonal contexts must be specified before her action at any moment can be stated or fully interpreted. Raheja shows how within either her natal or her marital house, a married woman may be defined by rapid ritual turns as some residents' 'own' daughter, sister, or mother, then as 'alien' to those same residents, even if she is a current resident, because she is at some time also an affine—a wife, daughter-in-law, sister-in-law, or mother-in-law. Raheja interprets such shifts among overlapping categories as evidence of North Indian women's 'double' kinship perspective (Raheja and Gold 1994: 73–120), a perspective which expands to triple or more when affiliation with a mother's natal family is also invoked (Madan 1965: 209–13).[15] Married women themselves may interpret their multiple but attenuated ties negatively–as proof that a wife fully belongs nowhere (Raheja 1995: 37, 1998; Trawick 1991: 236–45). Intensely overlapping

[14] The corners (in book order) should give rise to the following eight classical sentiments: {1,1,1} pity, {9,1,1} pride, {1,9,1} tranquility, {9,9,1} surprise, {1,1,9} laughter, {9,1,9} anger, {1,9,1} fear, and {9,9,9} disgust. *Śṛngāra* 'interest', a ninth sentiment that is arguably the source of all the others, might be located medially at about {5,5,5}.

[15] The marriage diagrammed in the centre of Figure 4 makes the bride an affiliate of two families, A and B. The marriages shown at the left and right margins of the same figure suggest how brides may at times calculate their affiliations with as many as four families.

and contending calculations of female kinship are even more elaborated in the two- and three-dimensional South Indian networks presented by Trawick (1988, 1990: 117–86). These alternative perspectives enhance at an intimate level the multivocality for which India is justly famed.

IV

Life-courses: Syntactics of the property-space

Since the extremities and ambiguities of female roles thus typify a general paradigm for South Asia, should not movements among such role-types similarly reveal the diverse syntactics of that world? The evidences reviewed below indicate that they can.

As mapped in Figure 3, females' lives appear to develop mostly by short, orthogonal shifts up, down, and around the cube, usually along just one edge at a

Figure 3

Female life-course

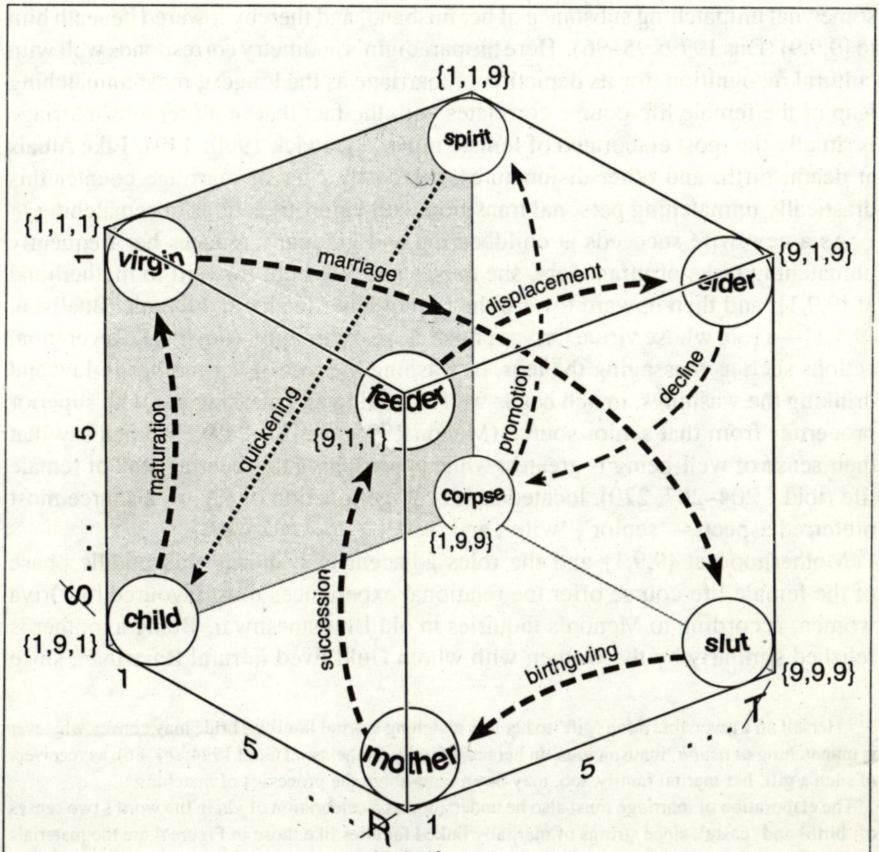

time, stopping at an adjacent corner. While each of these eight common moves involves changes and is thus somewhat unmatching, five out of the eight moves are minimal, reversing only one of the three role- or quality-components. Two moves reverse two components by longer, diagonal paths—the transmission of a subtle life-force from a spirit source to a foetus or neonate (from {1,1,9} to {1,9,1}) (Gold 1987: 79, 201, 260; Misri 1986: 127; Trawick 1990: 274) and the decline of an elder from {9,1,9} toward death at {1,9,9}.

A major exception to the shortness of female moves is marriage. Although begun early in the South by the celebration of a virgin's 'flowering' (Good 1990; Kolenda 1984), and not followed there by such remote journeying as in the North, marriage everywhere effects a female's displacement from her natal household and her diametric, three-dimensional qualitative transition from virgin to slut, albeit joining a husband who is senior to her in another household that may be unmarked as 'higher' (Figure 4). The former virgin of {1,1,1} may be briefly celebrated as such in her marital household, even as its regnant goddess at {9,1,1} or {1,1,9} (a moment omitted from Figs. 3 and 4), but she is soon mixed and marked with the somewhat unmatching substance of her husband, and thereby lowered beneath him to {9,9,9} (Das 1979: 95–96). Here the paradigm's geometry corresponds well with cultural recognition, for its depiction of marriage as the longest, most unmatching leap of the female life-course correlates with the fact that in all regions marriage is ritually the most elaborated of female moves (Trawick 1990: 149). Like rituals at death, birth, and other disjunctures, the costly rites of marriage counter this drastically unmatching personal transition with vigorous actions of rematching.[16]

As a new wife succeeds at childbearing and gradually reduces her frequently unmatching tasks of infant care, she makes her way both forward to motherhood at {9,9,1}, and then upward toward the role of chief feeder and female ritualist at {9,1,1}—a role whose virtue Oriyas praise as 'distributivity' (*dāyitva*). Reverential actions such as massaging the legs, or washing the feet of her mother-in-law and drinking the washings, match her as well as mixing and marking her with superior properties from that senior source (Menon 1995: 26–27, 249). Women say that their sense of well-being is greatest while approaching this central peak of female life (ibid.: 204–207, 220), located as it is at the junction of Figure 2's three most preferred aspects—'senior', 'wife', and 'self'.

Motherhood at {9,9,1} and the roles adjacent to it during this middle phase of the female life-course offer the relational experiences most favoured by Oriya women, according to Menon's inquiries in old Bhubaneshwar. Being a mother is relished similarly by the women with whom Gold lived in rural Rajasthan, since

[16] Herself an irreversible *dāna* 'gift' to her less matching marital family, a bride may convey whatever is unmatching or *aśubh* 'inauspicious' in her natal family (Raheja and Gold 1994: 74–86); as receivers of such a gift, her marital family, too, may be anxious about the processes of matching.

The elaboration of marriage must also be understood as a celebration of *jāti* in the word's two senses of 'birth' and 'caste', since strings of maritally linked families like those in Figure 4 are the materials from which such cautiously mixing, marking, and matching communities of South Asia are continually reborn.

Figure 4
Marriage and life-course

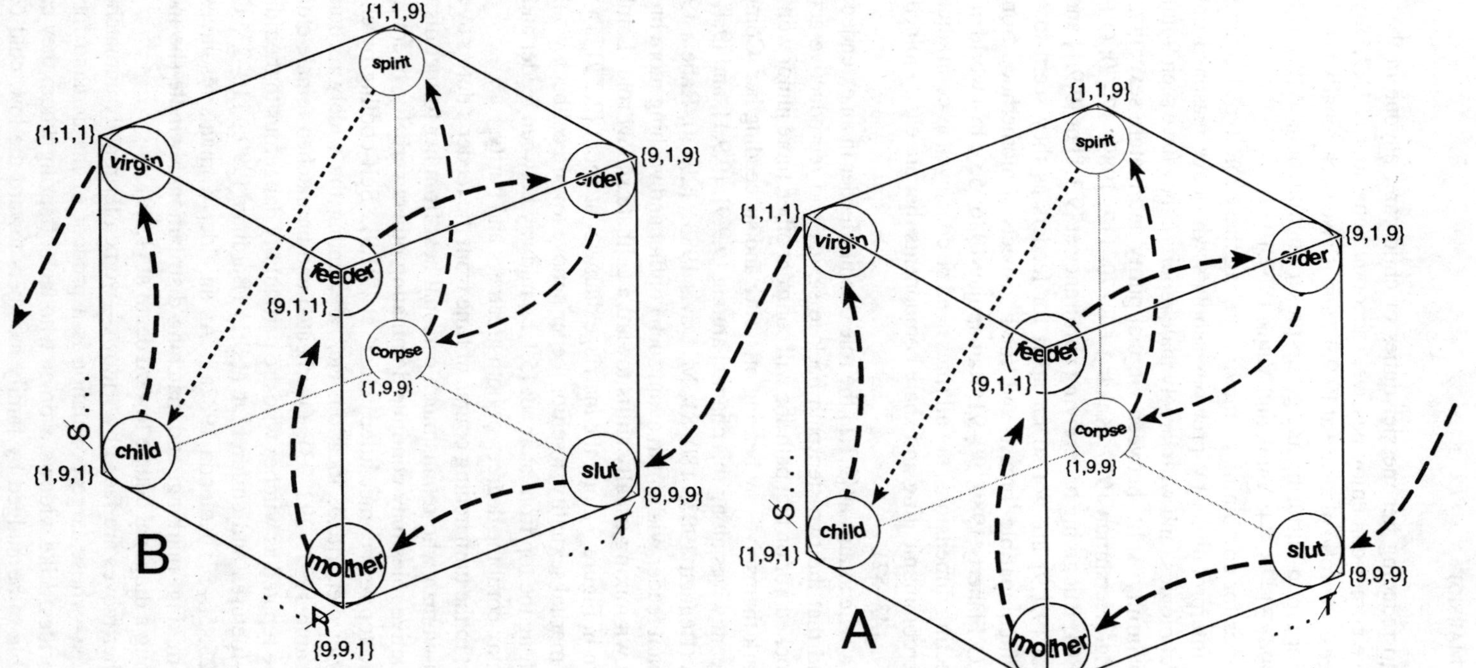

in addition to reducing her messier duties of child care, anyone in that central and expansive corner can enjoy passive, succorant behaviour at {1,9,1}, yet may still have access to erotic pleasure at {9,9,9}, and is also occasionally privileged to perform senior group-nurturing and group-preserving functions at {9,1,1} (Raheja and Gold 1994: 31–38, 44; Vatuk and Vatuk 1967,1979).

Opportunities for combining or moving among these role-typed activities cast doubt upon interpretations by previous scholars who have reasoned only with Western psychologics (and with largely male reports); they have seen South Asian women as painfully 'split' between virginal purity and mature sexuality, {1,1,1} vs {9,9,9} (e.g., Hershman 1977; Kakar 1978: 79–112; 1989: 17–20; O'Flaherty 1980: 239–80). But giving or receiving nurturance at {9,1,1} or {9,9,1} and acting with anger at {9,1,9} are not so far apart for feeders as they seem to analysts who project incompatible 'breast' and 'tooth' aspects of motherhood from infant experience (O'Flaherty 1980: 90–91; Ramanujan 1986: 55). In a world of at least three intersecting dimensions, not all roles need be conceived as contradictory, for they are intercommunicating and share components that are easily joined (Kurtz 1992: 55–89, 143–52).

But once a wife attains at {9,1,1} the role of chief feeder in an extended family, she may find that the two-step path back to sexual and reproductive activity at {9,9,9} is blocked, for on that path she will confront other, more junior women who aim to unmark themselves by bearing offspring and succeeding her. Competition among adjacent wives along this channel among {9,9,9}, {9,9,1}, and {9,1,1}, is in fact parlous (Bennett 1983: 180–81; M. Davis 1983: 129–30; Raheja 1998). A once-dominant feeder wishing to avoid such conflict and wishing more broadly to reduce her own mixing usually shifts toward a celibate *sādhvī* role (Lamb 1997: 288). Shown in Figure 5 along the marriage diameter at about {2,2,2} is a virgin's rejection of marital sexuality; a senior feeder's move toward celibacy would place her rather along the top front at about {5,1,1}, midway between feeder and virgin, where she may combine degrees of both greatness and purity.

Displaced in the unmatching course of time from the feeder's duties by a junior successor, a woman who retains much personal heat from her former distributive and reproductive roles may continue dominating others verbally, operating from the agonistic top rear corner titled 'elder' at {9,1,9}. Self-cooling by change of clothing style, diet, ritual, location, etc., are among the widely recommended remedies (Lamb 1997: 292–93). Overheated and unmatched female elders may otherwise be reputed as witches who are particularly dangerous to their diametric opposites—foetuses and children at {1,9,1} (Bardhan 1990: 110–27; Carstairs 1983: 14–25, 56–57; Kolenda 1982a). As an elder woman's resources shrink and as her mixing, marking, and matching distributions dwindle she inevitably declines along a diagonal course toward death at {1,9,9}.

Still further moves are faced by widows—women terminally unmatched from their spouses—whose large population is a product of the demand for young, unmarked brides. Like widows, women who lack offspring whom they can mark are also liable to be nudged by family members toward the low, cold corner of {1,9,9}. There the homonymy between words for 'widow' and 'prostitute' tells that a woman's search for a new partner could bring additional markings to her family from outside males (Das 1979: 97–98; Lamb 1997: 293; Minturn 1993: 235–36). Her recoupling within, or extrusion from her deceased husband's family are alternatives (Dhruvarajan 1989: 95; Wadley 1995), but her remaining there in active dedication to some superior deity or spirit offers a third exit from the widow's corner–one that can be matching for all concerned without her remating (Minturn 1993: 236–38). Courtright (1995) and Gupta (n.d.) report that such devotion can shift a widow back toward the properties of a child or virgin, bringing her peace and virtually completing a living cycle of the domestic property-space. Oldenburg (1991) describes prostitutes who, similarly lacking husbands, themselves elicit such unmarking devotion from their clientele that they may be raised to occupy spirit-like {1,1,9} roles.

Unmarked and unmixed after her death by the rematching ritual efforts of her survivors, a decedent married woman's soul may be merged with her husband's ancestral spirits at {1,1,9}. From that collectivity, if it is benevolent, new life-forces are expected to descend to quicken embryos in the family's wombs (Gold 1987: 66, 91, 96, 255–60; Harlan 1992: 140, 156; Mines 1989; Steed 1955: 140; Vatuk 1990). Marking processes operating thus through a family's ultimately circular life-course channel may be conceived as sustaining it through time, as an organic growth.

Striving through this channel from role to role, females circumscribe the core of the family and in so doing help to propel those ahead of and behind them. By providing the nurturant routines or samskaras that remark and advance their juniors, seniors of both sexes also make self-unmarking, downward transfers of properties that deplete their own capacities for further economic and reproductive expansion; while thus exhausting themselves and vacating their former roles, they may ask the juniors whom they are leading to reciprocate with later care. By such transactions members construct the interpersonal 'network of attachments' (*māyājāl*) (Lamb 1997: 283–86; Vatuk 1990) which supports the life-course channel.

Certain backward moves, or failures to move, may be counted as unmatching for the family because they block the progress of others ahead of and behind them in this main channel. Thus the failed marriages of Mira Bai (Harlan 1995: 214) and Balasatimata (Courtright 1995: 195) (represented by the *sādhvī* in Figure 5), who both devoted themselves fervently to gods or spirits at {1,1,9} and thus became exemplars to some women, also prevented their parents' repose and might have delayed any younger sisters' marriages. Similarly a wife's childlessness, absence, or early death may deprive senior females of a follower who could advance them in their life-cycles by helping to unmark and unmix them, and ultimately to unmatch them from this world (Vatuk 1990; Wadley 1995). So also untimely deaths, particularly those of mothers or children, or of others who have not detached themselves from life, produce ghosts that linger nearby and can obstruct a variety of other moves (Gold 1987: 63–79; Lamb 1997: 280, 286).

Most unmatching of all may be the death or widowing (which some women regard as equivalent to death) of a chief feeder in midlife: she falls from a warm optimal {9,1,1} to a cold, corpse-like, pessimal {1,9,9} position (Lamb 1997: 288,

294), and in so doing traces a diameter as long as that of marriage. The rituals attempting to heal such traumata are often large. Traversing this path in spectacular reverse is the Rajput *satī*, who rises from the threat of a corpse-like existence to regain in some outer sphere the vital role of royal wife (Weinberger 1996: 141) (Figure 5). Those who would maximise greatness over all other aims may see the upward course of a *satī* seeking final apotheosis with a fierce goddess at {9,1,9} as approximating the path of a warrior who rises through self-sacrifice in battle from ignoble death at {1,9,9} to heroic triumph at {9,1,5} or {9,1,1} (Harlan 1992: 118–33; Weinberger 1996: 78–79, 82).

V
Family life and worship—complementary planes

The above review of female coursings through eight extreme role-types has displayed the outer limits more than the interior of the domestic property-space. Inspection of the four transecting diameters should tell more, as along those diameters are encountered many other, intermediate female role-types.

Two of the diameters, both vital to family life, appear in Figure 3, but may be seen more clearly from the matching front. The smaller cube at the lower left of Figure 5 simplifies and shows these diameters as two descending and intersecting arcs, one from adolescence at {1,1,1} to birthing at {9,9,9}, the other from seniority at {9,1,1} to demise at {1,9,9}. Together they define a plane that slopes from the figure's upper front to its lower rear, connecting four issues that are critical for families—fertility and sustenance above, death and birth below. They are congruent with the intersecting diameters of the general paradigm that connect the corners 'pure' with 'impure' and 'great' with 'small'.

Shown in the larger diagram of Figure 5 are *devadāsīs* like those of Jagannatha at Puri, who dance over this family-life plane at about {5,5,5}, as if suspended between virginity and mature sexuality; they mark humans with a fertility which they owe to their deathless coupling with a deity both subtle {1,1,9} and royal {9,1,1} (Marglin 1985: 46, 169) who may be figured to reside above them at about {5,1,5}. Nearby, holding steady along the other family diameter that connects sustenance with death is the 'husband-devoted' *pativratā* widow, who neither dies with her spouse nor dishonourably recouples with another, but remains devoted to his memory in neutral celibacy (Harlan 1992: 118–19; Lamb 1992: 371–77; Leslie 1989: 298–304).

Physically less often travelled by females in the ordinary course of life is the other, orthogonally placed plane—that of worship.[17] Shown in the small cube at the lower right of Figure 5, this plane is defined by the other two main diameters, which are identical with the 'gross–subtle' and 'nonviolent–violent' diameters

[17] The ancestral grant of fertility (dramatised in the Brahmanic rite of *sapiṇḍīkāraṇa* (Knipe 1977) and in the Ganga pilgrimage from rural Rajasthan reported by Gold (1987: 241–60), as in Fig. 3), and also the gradual descent of a divinised neonate into childhood—all downward movements along the unmixing edge of Fig. 5's plane of worship—are liminally human exceptions to this claim of rarity. Blessings and boons, threats and attacks are the more usual downward traffic on this plane.

Figure 5
Family life and worship roles

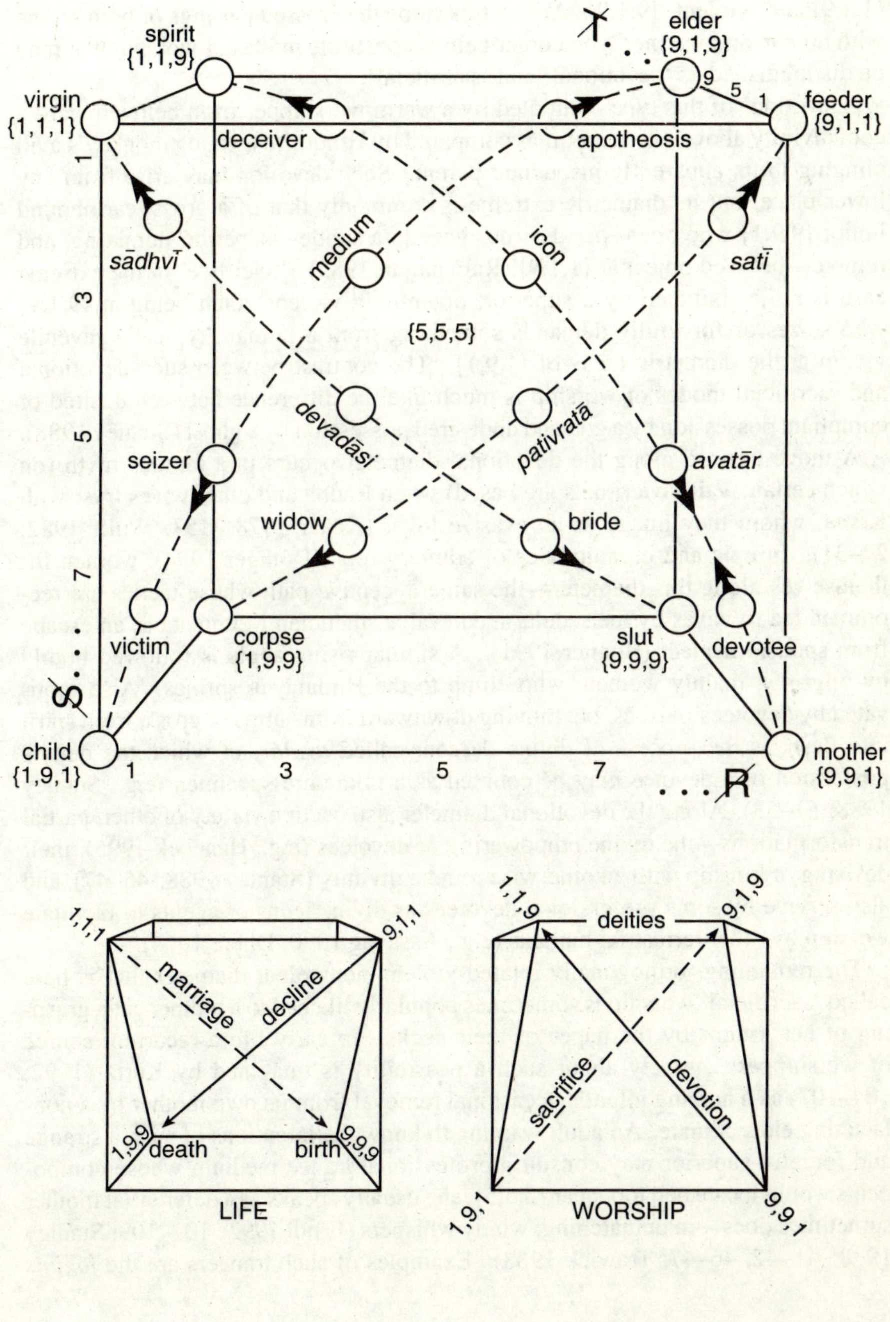

of the general paradigm. This plane reaches up from the potentially most marked and matched domestic juniors (children and mothers at {1,9,1} and {9,9,1} respectively) to the least marked, least matched seniors—ancestral spirits and elders (who are often male) and their divine or demonic analogues who reside between 'subtle' {1,1,9} and 'violent' {9,1,9}. Across this slope the crossed pairings of both divine with human and warmer with cooler beings constitute modes of worship that may be distinguished as 'devotional' and 'sacrificial'.

'Devotion' of this type—initiated by a warm worshipper from below toward a cool divinity above—is sometimes compared by Hindus to a young monkey's avid clinging to its apparently insouciant parent. Such devotion may arise from any lower place, but its diametric extreme is commonly that of a gross, earthbound junior {9,9,1} who opens her desirous gaze to a subtle—superior, unmixing, and remote—beloved object at {1,1,9} (Ramanujan 1982). 'Sacrifice' in the extreme case is rather initiated by a superior, potentially violent, alien being at {9,1,9} who seizes or forcefully demands something from a human, typically juvenile victim at the diametric locus of {1,9,1}. The contrast between such devotional and sacrificial modes of worship is much like the difference between desired or compliant possession by a god and undesired possession by a ghost (Stanley 1988).

A move upward along the devotional diameter occurs in a famous myth (on which certain Vaiśnava rituals are based) when Radha and other wives tryst with Krsna, whom they image as an evasive lover (Kakar 1978: 153; Wulff 1982: 27–31). In epic and puranic tales of adultery (e.g., Doniger 1994), women lift themselves along this diameter—the same deceptive path whose tactics are recommended to wives by the secular medieval aesthetician Mammata as an escape from spousal neglect (Bonner 1991). A similar rising angle is followed bodily by pilgrims, mainly women, who climb to the Himalayan shrines. Also motivated by devotees' wishes, but moving downward from subtle to gross, from spirit into flesh, is the process of divine descent called *avatār*, of which the deity's possession of a devotee may be counted as a miniature specimen (e.g., Stanley 1988: 51–53). Along the devotional diameter also occur a variety of other, partial transformations—the divine empowering of devotees (e.g., Hancock 1995), their devising of kinship with an otherwise remote divinity (Stanley 1988: 46–47), and also service by some professional devotees as divine icons or agents to facilitate worship by other terrestrial humans (e.g., Assayag 1990; Dhere 1964).

The remaining, orthogonally related violent–nonviolent diameter that is here called 'sacrificial' worship is sometimes popularly likened to a mother cat's grasping of her kittens by the napes of their necks. In early life a recurrent source of worshippers' anxiety about such a possibility is imagined by Kurtz (1992: 104–107) as a nursing infant's occasional removal from its own mother by a nonlactating elder female. An adult wanting to know the intentions of such a strange and forceful superior may consult a professional trance medium whose components would locate her, too, near {5,5,5}; she usually speaks as a deferential mother sometimes does—in unmatching, windy whispers (Erndl 1993: 107–109; Stanley 1988: 41–42, 46–47; Trawick 1988). Examples of such trancers are the *joginīs* of Karnataka–daughters whom suffering families have dedicated to a threatening female divinity both as trance mediums and as icons (Assayag 1990). After heavy marking with the properties of such a divinity, many a victimised female elsewhere in villages of South India is said to have merged with the attacker, founding by her apotheosis a new local goddess cult (e.g., Beck 1981; Egnor 1984; Trawick 1991). Thus at least four intermediate types of females, each combining contrary corner qualities, cluster near where the planes and most active diametric paths of family and worship intersect—at {5,5,5}. Precisely at this junction, the princess Mira Bai's devotion to the god Krsna blocks her self-sacrificial yielding to the angry demands of her late husband's surviving kin (Harlan 1995: 209–11).

While distinct from and complementing the usual moves of the female life-course, these relations of worship are congruent with quotidian affects among human seniors and juniors of either sex, affects which may sometimes take simian, sometimes feline, and sometimes other forms. Between, beyond and combining them also are many other varied pairs, both familial and worshipful, that are situated in diagonal or adjacent relations of respectful love or fear, compliance or defiance (e.g., Chandola 1991; Moreno 1985; Moreno and Marriott 1989).

Figure 5's resemblance to a horoscope or map of astral movements is enhanced when one notices that the gravities of the persons or qualities at the corners seem to bend the trajectories of the passing personnel. Subtlety appears to pull upon potential sluts, celibates, *devadāsīs*, and spirit mediums, as it does upon the fabled 'Jungli Rani' (Gold 1995), who without her devotion to Surya would have been unable to move from wild child or witch to queen. Violence also may attract passing *satīs*, junior wives, and apotheoses (Raheja and Gold 1994: 149–63), although it has been known to deflect the marches of satyagrahis between small and great roles. Greatness and impurity seem variously to lure certain *avatārs*, widows, and others. Such lateral forces invite systematic inquiry, adding a realistic note of multivalence to all internal moves.

VI

Conclusions: Females, males, and civilisation

The recent female-focused, extended family ethnographies examined here have responded clearly to questions posed by a South Asian ethnosocial paradigm, one that had been constructed both from other ethnography and from the civilisation's classical elements, humours, strands, and aims. Eight recognised female family role-types have been found to correspond closely to the composite qualities previously generated from that general paradigm. Movements through these roles in the usual course of female lives have also been found to demonstrate, often in explicit detail, the paradigm's core processes of mixing–unmixing, marking–unmarking, and matching–unmatching. Both personal experiences and ritual usages have confirmed the shifting perspectives on social reality that develop in the female core's multidimensional property-space. These evidences suggest that practice in the female domestic core is and may long have been a powerful source of what appears to be a South Asian ethnosocial paradigm of general and continuing import—one as relevant to medieval and modern politics and religion[18] as it is to today's extended family households.

Figure 6
Males and females?

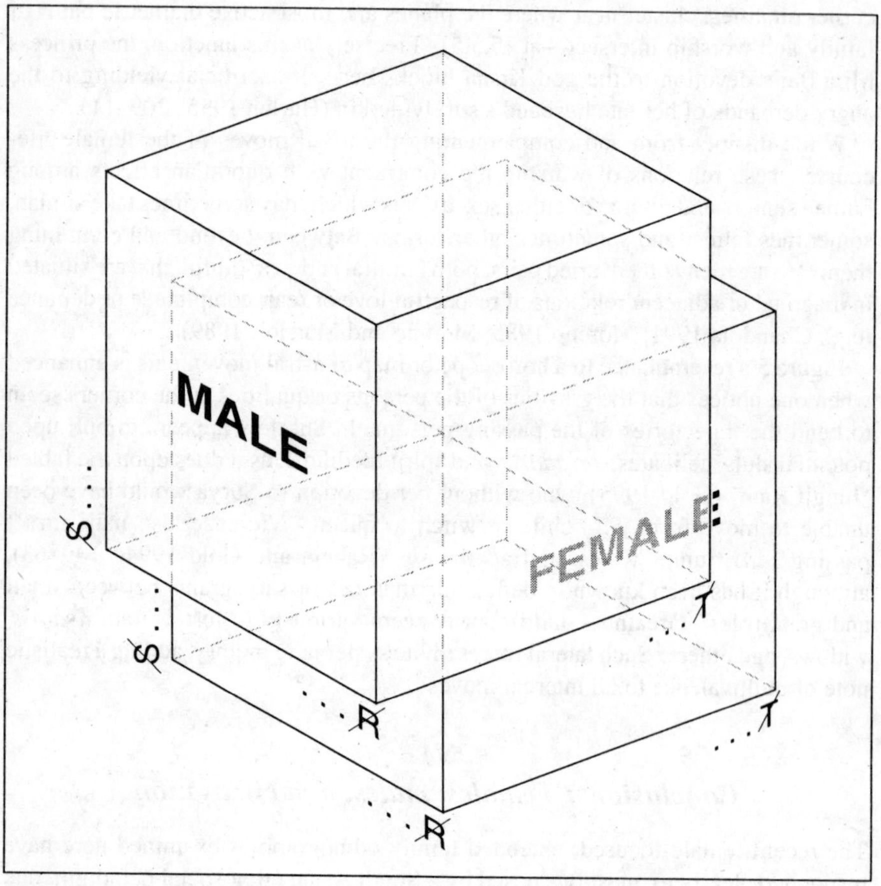

That this may be true is further supported by the fact that females have been widely regarded as archetypic and iconic of the region's civilisation. The archetypy of females (noted again recently by Kakar 1989: 129–40, 143; Marriott 1992: 266–67, and Menon 1995: 367–79) appears to be more enduring and significant than either the negative colonial stereotypes or the positive nationalist responses noted by historians such as Chatterjee (1993: 116–34). Females are exemplary of the postulated paradigm because as a class they are more participant in mixing flows than males, and also more subject to fluid markings and unmatching

[18] See footnote 10.

flux (S. Daniel 1980; Das 1979; Dhruvarajan 1989: 27–34; Lamb 1997: 290; Ramanujan 1982).

But females' greater liquidity and internality are also understood as making them potentially more skilled at contrary strategies—at closing to potentialise their inner heat (Menon 1995: 399), at matching with others to promote their interests (Raheja 1998), or at concealing their evasions of male controls (David 1980; Narayana Rao 1991; Narayana Rao and Ramanujan 1994: 14–16; Raheja and Gold 1994; Ramanujan 1991). Their greater inner-bodily space, if firmly contained by their greater earth component, is felt by some to give them greater *śakti* (Egnor 1980); they may apply such a force even to the self-sacrificial shaming of insufficiently aggressive husbands (Harlan 1992: 158–66). Otherwise males' putatively harder, cooler, less open natures are felt as permitting or encouraging them to mix in wider, more alien worlds, although not without unmatching effects (Reynolds 1980); and the kinetic energy males may develop outside the household enables them also to mark females and to represent themselves as restraining and domesticating what some see as females' generically greater tendencies toward mixing, being marked, and unmatching (Inden and Nicholas 1977: 23, 30–31).

The differences between females and males that are thought by some to cause and/or to result from these contrary processes are summarised in Figure 6, which shows males in their usual public posture—as more inclined to mixing, as less marked, and as more matched than females. A more defensible modelling of male–female ethnodialectics will require more two-sexed ethnographies than now exist, and so must be left to future research. Special complexities loom in this comparative task as partisans of both sexes accept, contest, and/or attempt to counteract any such configuration as the one diagrammed here (S. Daniel 1980; Derné 1995; Jacobson and Wadley 1977: 59–69; Raheja and Gold 1994; Menon 1995: 157–72, 367–79). Some would reverse the relative placing of the cubes, others would merge the two. Both those who would affirm and those who would deny these placings agree, however, that the issues of their argument are the same as those posed by the variables of the present paradigm.

Much more is reported in the recent gynocentric ethnographies than has been examined here. While processes of mixing, unmarking, and unmatching (analogues of fire, water, and air) have been traced, less explicit attention has been given to the background processes of placing, spacing (analogues of earth and ether), and consciousness. Only about half of the sixty-two possible moves between the property-space's corners have been noticed here, mostly shifts between adjacent or diametrically related roles. Recurrent patterns of female and female–male alliance and rivalry (such as those reported by Raheja and Gold 1994: 73–148 and by Raheja 1998), for example, have yet to be generally incorporated into an ethnosociology of the female family core. But even the present limited beginnings could not have been made without the questions generated from the postulated paradigm. By systematic deduction, testing of hypotheses, and discoveries of gaps in knowledge as well as by eliciting new findings, an indigenous South Asian ethnosociology itself continues to develop.

REFERENCES

ALTER, JOSEPH S. 1992. *The wrestler's body: Identity and ideology in North India.* Berkeley and Los Angeles: University of California Press.

ASSAYAG, JACKIE. 1990. Modern devadasis. *In* G. Eichinger Ferro-Luzzi, ed., *Rites and beliefs in modern India,* pp. 53–65. New Delhi: Manohar.

BARDHAN, KALPANA, ed., trans. 1990. *Women, outcastes, peasants, and rebels: A selection of Bengali short stories.* Berkeley and Los Angeles: University of California Press.

BARTON, ALLEN H. 1955. The concept of property-space in social research. *In* P.F. Lazarsfeld and M. Rosenberg, eds, *The language of social research,* pp. 40–53. Glencoe: Free Press of Glencoe.

BECK, BRENDA E.F. 1981. The goddess and the demon. *Purusartha* 5: 83–186.

BENNETT, LYNN. 1983. *Dangerous wives and sacred sisters: Social and symbolic roles of high-caste women in Nepal.* New York: Columbia University Press.

BONNER, RAHUL. 1991. Sexual dynamics in the Amaruśataka. Ph.D. dissertation, University of Chicago.

CARNAP, RUDOLF. 1958. *Introduction to symbolic logic and its applications.* New York: Dover.

CARSTAIRS, G. MORRIS. 1983. *Death of a witch: A village in North India, 1950–1981.* London: Hutchinson.

CHANDOLA, ANOOP. 1991. *The way to true worship: A popular story of Hinduism.* Lanham: University Press of America.

CHATTERJEE, PARTHA. 1993. *The nation and its fragments.* Princeton: Princeton University Press.

COURTRIGHT, PAUL B. 1995. *Satī*, sacrifice, and marriage: The modernity of tradition. *In* Lindsey Harlan and P.B. Courtright, eds, *From the margins of Hindu marriage,* pp. 184–203. New York: Oxford University Press.

DANIEL, E. VALENTINE. 1984. *Fluid signs: Being a person the Tamil way.* Berkeley and Los Angeles: University of California Press.

DANIEL, SHERYL B. 1980. Marriage in Tamil culture: The problem of conflicting models. *In* Susan S. Wadley, ed., *The powers of Tamil women,* pp. 61–92. Syracuse: Maxwell School, Syracuse University.

DAS, VEENA. 1979. Reflections on the social construction of adulthood. *In* Sudhir Kakar, ed., *Identity and adulthood,* pp. 89–104. Delhi: Oxford University Press.

DAVID, KENNETH A. 1980. Hidden powers: Cultural and socio-economic accounts of Jaffna women. *In* Susan S. Wadley, ed., *The powers of Tamil women,* pp. 93–136. Syracuse: Maxwell School, Syracuse University.

DAVIS, MARVIN G. 1983. *Rank and rivalry: The politics of inequality in rural West Bengal.* Cambridge: Cambridge University Press.

DERNÉ, STEVE. 1995. *Culture in action: Family life, emotion, and male dominance in Banaras, India.* Albany: SUNY Press.

DHERE, RAMCHANDRA CHINTAMANI. 1964. *Marāṭhī lokasaṃskṛtīce upāsaka.* Pune: Jnanaraja Prakashan.

DHRUVARAJAN, VANAJA. 1989. *Hindu women and the power of ideology.* Granby: Bergin and Garvey.

DONIGER, WENDY. 1994. Playing the field: Adultery as claim-jumping. *In* Ariel Glucklich, *The sense of adharma,* pp. 169–88. New York: Oxford University Press.

DONIGER, WENDY and BRIAN K. SMITH, trans. 1991. *The laws of Manu.* Harmondsworth: Penguin.

EGNOR, MARGARET TRAWICK. 1980. On the meaning of śakti to women in Tamil Nadu. *In* Susan S. Wadley, ed., *The powers of Tamil women,* pp. 1–34. Syracuse: Maxwell School, Syracuse University.

———. 1984. The changed mother or what the smallpox goddess did when there was no more smallpox. *Contributions to Asian studies* 18: 24–45.

ERNDL, KATHLEEN M. 1993. *Victory to the Mother: The Hindu goddess of Northwest India in myth, ritual, and symbol.* New York: Oxford University Press.

GOLD, ANN GRODZINS. 1987. *Fruitful journeys: The ways of Rajasthani pilgrims.* Berkeley and Los Angeles: University of California Press.

———. 1995. The 'Jungli Rani' and other troubled wives in Rajasthani oral traditions. *In* L. Harlan and P.B. Courtright, eds, *From the margins of Hindu marriage*, pp. 119–36. New York: Oxford University Press.

GOOD, ANTHONY. 1990. *The female bridegroom: A comparative study of life-crisis rituals in South India and Sri Lanka.* Oxford: Clarendon.

GUPTA, SANJUKTA. n.d. Hindu woman, the ritualist. Paper presented at the European Conference on Modern South Asian Studies, Toulouse, 1994.

HANCOCK, MARY. 1995. The dilemmas of domesticity: Possession and devotional experience among urban Smārta women. *In* L. Harlan and P.B. Courtright, eds, *From the margins of Hindu marriage*, pp. 60–91. New York: Oxford University Press.

HARLAN, LINDSEY. 1992. *Religion and Rajput women: The ethic of protection in contemporary narratives.* Berkeley and Los Angeles: University of California Press.

———. 1995. Abandoning shame: Mīrā and the margins of marriage. *In* L. Harlan and P.B. Courtright, eds, *From the margins of Hindu marriage*, pp. 204–27. New York: Oxford University Press.

HARLAN, LINDSEY and P.B. COURTRIGHT. 1995. Introduction: On Hindu marriage and its margins. *In* L. Harlan and P.B. Courtright, eds, *From the margins of Hindu marriage*, pp. 3–18. New York: Oxford University Press.

HERSHMAN, PAUL. 1977. Virgin and mother. *In* I.M. Lewis, ed., *Symbols and sentiments*, pp. 269–92. London: Academic Press.

INDEN, RONALD B and RALPH W. NICHOLAS. 1997. *Kinship in Bengali culture.* Chicago: University of Chicago Press.

JACOBSON, DORANNE. 1977. Flexibility in Central Indian kinship and residence. *In* K. David, ed., *The new wind*, pp. 263–83. The Hague: Mouton.

JACOBSON, DORANNE and SUSAN SNOW WADLEY. 1977. *Women in India: Two perspectives.* New Delhi: Manohar.

KAKAR, SUDHIR. 1978. *The inner world: A psychoanalytic study of childhood and society in India.* Delhi: Oxford University Press.

———. 1989. *Intimate relations: Exploring Indian sexuality.* Chicago: University of Chicago Press and Penguin/ India.

KEMPER, STEVEN E.G. 1980. Time, person, and gender in Sinhalese astrology. *American ethnologist* 7: 744–58.

KHARE, RAVINDRA SAHAI. 1976. *The Hindu hearth and home.* New Delhi: Vikas.

KNIPE, DAVID M. 1977. *Sapiṇḍīkāraṇa*: The Hindu rite of entry into heaven. *In* Frank E. Reynolds and E.H. Waugh, eds, *Religious encounters with death: Insights from the history and anthropology of religion*, pp. 111–24. University Park: Pennsylvania State University Press.

KOLENDA, PAULINE M. 1982a. Pox and the terror of childlessness. *In* J. J. Preston, ed., *Mother worship*, pp. 192–209. Chapel Hill: University of North Carolina Press.

———. 1982b. Widowhood among 'untouchable' Churhas. *In* A. Ostor et al., eds, *Concepts of person*, pp. 172–220. Cambridge: Harvard University Press.

———. 1984. Woman as tribute, woman as flower: Images of "woman" in north and south India. *American ethnologist* 11: 98–117.

KONDOS, VIVIENNE. 1982. The triple goddess and the processual approach to the world. *In* M.R. Allen and S.N. Mukherjee, eds, *Women in India and Nepal*, pp. 211–49. Canberra: Australian National University.

KURTZ, STANLEY N. 1992. *All the mothers are one.* New York: Columbia University Press.

LAMB, SARAH ELIZABETH. 1992. Growing in the net of maya: Persons, gender and life processes in a Bengali society. Ph.D. dissertation, University of Chicago.

———. 1997. The making and unmaking of persons: Notes on aging and gender in North India. *Ethos* 25: 279–302.

Larson, Gerald James. 1987. Introduction to the philosophy of *Sāṃkhya. In* G.J. Larson and R.S. Bhattacharya, eds, *Sāṃkhya, a dualist tradition in Indian philosophy*, pp. 3–103. Princeton: Princeton University Press.

Leslie, I. Julia. 1989. *The perfect wife: The orthodox Hindu woman according to the Strīdharmapaddhati of Tryambakayajvan.* Delhi: Oxford University Press.

Lynch, Owen M. 1990. The mastrām: Emotion and person among Mathura's Chaubes. *In* O.M. Lynch, ed., *Divine passions*, pp. 91–115. Berkeley and Los Angeles: University of California Press.

Madan, Triloki Nath. 1965. *Family and kinship: A study of the pandits of rural Kashmir.* Bombay: Asia Publishing House.

Marglin, Frederique Apffel. 1985. *Wives of the God-King.* Delhi: Oxford University Press.

Marriott, McKim. 1989. Constructing an Indian ethnosociology. *Contributions to Indian sociology* (n.s.) 23: 1–39.

———. 1991. On 'Constructing an Indian ethnosociology'. *Contributions to Indian sociology* (n.s.) 25: 295–308.

———. 1992. Alternative social sciences. *In* John MacAloon, ed., *General education in the social sciences*, pp. 262–78. Chicago: University of Chicago Press.

Marriott, McKim, ed. 1990. *India through Hindu categories.* New Delhi: Sage Publications.

Menon, Usha. 1995. Giving and receiving: Distributivity as the source of women's well-being. Ph.D. dissertation, University of Chicago.

Mines, Diane Paull. 1989. Hindu periods of death 'impurity'. *Contributions to Indian sociology* (n.s.) 23: 103–30.

Minturn, Leigh. 1993. *Sita's daughters: Coming out of purdah.* New York: Oxford University Press.

Minturn, Leigh and John T. Hitchcock. 1963. *The Rājpūts of Khalapur, India.* New York: John Wiley.

Misri, Urvashi. 1986. Child and childhood: A conceptual construction. *Contributions to Indian sociology* (n.s.) 19: 115–32.

Moore, Melinda Ann. 1989. The Kerala house as a Hindu cosmos. *In* M. Marriott, ed, *India through Hindu categories*, pp. 169–202. New Delhi: Sage Publications.

Moreno, Manuel. 1985. God's forceful call: Possession as a divine strategy. *In* J.P. Waghorne and N. Cutler, eds, *Gods of flesh, gods of stone: The embodiment of divinity in India*, pp. 103–20. Chambersberg: Anima.

Moreno, Manuel and McKim Marriott. 1989. Humoral transactions in two South Indian cults: Murukan and Mariyamman. *Contributions to Indian sociology* (n.s.) 23: 149–67.

Narayana Rao, Velcheru. 1991. A Rāmāyaṇa of their own: Women's oral tradition in Telugu. *In* P. Richman, ed., *Many Rāmāyaṇas*, pp. 114–36. Berkeley and Los Angeles: University of California Press.

Narayana Rao, Velcheru and A.K. Ramanujan. 1994. *When God is a customer.* Berkeley and Los Angeles: University of California Press.

O'Flaherty, Wendy Doniger. 1980. *Women, androgynes, and other mythical beasts.* Chicago: University of Chicago Press.

Oldenburg, Veena Talwar. 1991. Lifestyle as resistance: The case of the courtesans of Lucknow. *In* Douglas Haynes and Gyan Prakash, eds, *Contesting power: Resistance and everyday social relations in South Asia.* pp. 23–61. Delhi: Oxford University Press.

Papanek, Hanna and Gail Minault, eds, 1982. *Separate worlds: Studies of purdah in South Asia.* Delhi: Chanakya.

Pugh, Judy Fayrene. 1984. Concepts of person and situation in North Indian counseling: The case of astrology. *In* South Asian systems of healing. *Contributions to Asian studies* 18: 85–105. Leiden: E.J. Brill.

Raheja, Gloria Goodwin. 1995. 'Crying when she's born and crying when she goes away': Marriage and the idiom of the gift in Pahansu song performance. *In* L. Harlan and P.B. Courtright, eds, *From the margins of Hindu marriage*, pp. 19–59. New York: Oxford University Press.

RAHEJA, GLORIA GOODWIN. 1998. Negotiated solidarities: Gendered representations of disruption and desire in North Indian oral traditions and popular culture. *Oral traditions* 12. Cambridge: Cambridge University Press (forthcoming).

RAHEJA, GLORIA GOODWIN and ANN GRODZINS GOLD. 1994. *Listen to the heron's words: Reimagining gender and kinship in North India.* Berkeley and Los Angeles: University of California Press.

RAMANUJAN, A.K. 1982. On woman saints. *In* J.S. Hawley and M. Wulff, eds, *The divine consort*, pp. 316–24. Berkeley: Graduate Theological Union.

———. 1986. Two realms of Kannada folklore. *In* Stuart H. Blackburn and A.K. Ramanujan, eds, *Another harmony*, pp. 41–75. Berkeley and Los Angeles: University of California Press.

———. 1989. Is there an Indian way of thinking? *Contributions to Indian sociology* (n.s.) 23: 41–58.

———. 1991. Toward a counter-system: Women's tales. *In* Arjun Appadurai et al., eds, *Gender, genre, and power*, pp. 33–55. Philadelphia: University of Pennsylvania Press.

RANGACHARYA, ADYA, trans. 1996. *The nāṭyaśāstra: English translation with critical notes.* New Delhi: Munshiram Manoharlal.

REYNOLDS, HOLLY BAKER. 1980. The auspicious married woman. *In* Susan S. Wadley, ed., *The powers of Tamil women*, pp. 35–60. Syracuse: Maxwell School, Syracuse University.

SHAH, ARVIND M. 1974. *The household dimension of the family in India.* Berkeley and Los Angeles: University of California Press.

SINHA, JADUNATH. 1961. *Indian psychology*, vol. 2. *Emotion and will.* Delhi: Motilal Banarsidass.

STANLEY, JOHN M. 1988. Gods, ghosts, and possession. *In* Eleanor Zelliot and Maxine Berntsen, eds, *The experience of Hinduism: Essays on religion in Maharashtra*, pp. 26–59. Albany: SUNY Press.

STEED, GITEL POZNANSKI. 1955. Notes on an approach to a study of personality in a Hindu village in Gujarat. *In* M. Marriott, ed., *Village India*, pp. 102–44. Chicago: University of Chicago Press.

TRAWICK, MARGARET. 1986. Internal iconicity in Paraiyar 'crying songs'. *In* Stuart H. Blackburn and A.K. Ramanujan, eds, *Another harmony*, pp. 294–344. Berkeley and Los Angeles: University of California Press.

———. 1988. Spirits and voices in Tamil songs. *American ethnologist* 15: 193–215.

———. 1990. *Notes on love in a Tamil family.* Berkeley and Los Angeles: University of California Press.

———. 1991. Wandering lost: A landless laborer's sense of place and self. *In* A. Appadurai et al., eds, *Gender, genre, and power in South Asian expressive traditions*, pp. 224–66. Philadelphia: University of Pennsylvania Press.

UBEROI, PATRICIA. 1995. Problems with patriarchy: Conceptual issues in anthropology and feminism. *Sociological bulletin* 44: 195–221.

VATUK, SYLVIA J. 1990. 'To be a burden on others': Dependency anxiety among the elderly in India. *In* O.M. Lynch, ed., *Divine passions*, pp. 64–88. Berkeley and Los Angeles: University of California Press.

VATUK, VED PRAKASH and SYLVIA VATUK. 1967. Chatorpan: A culturally defined form of addiction in North India. *International journal of the addictions* 2: 103–13.

———. 1979. The lustful stepmother in the folklore of northwestern India. *In* Ved P. Vatuk, ed., *Studies in Indian folk traditions*, pp. 190–221. Delhi: Manohar.

WADLEY, SUSAN SNOW. 1975. *Shakti: Power in the conceptual structure of Karimpur religion.* Chicago: Department of Anthropology, University of Chicago.

———. 1976. Brothers, husbands and sometimes sons: Kinsmen in North Indian ritual. *Eastern anthropologist* 29: 149–70.

———. 1995. No longer a wife: Widows in rural North India. *In* L. Harlan and P.B. Courtright, eds, *From the margins of Hindu marriage*, pp. 92–118. New York: Oxford University Press.

WAUGH, LINDA. 1982. Marked and unmarked: A choice between equals in semiotic structure. *Semiotica* 38: 299–318.

WEINBERGER-THOMAS, CATHERINE. 1996. *Cendres d'immortalité; la crémation des veuves en Inde.* Paris: Éditions du Seuil.

Wulff, Donna Marie. 1982. A Sanskrit portrait: Rādhā in the plays of Rūpa Goswāmī. *In* J.S. Hawley and D.M. Wulff, eds, *The divine consort: Rādhā and the goddesses of India*, pp. 27–41. Berkeley: Graduate Theological Union.

Yalman, Nur Osman. 1963. On the purity of women in the castes of Ceylon and Malabar. *Journal of the Royal Anthropological Institute* 93: 25–58.

Zimmermann, Francis B. 1983. Remarks on the conception of the body in ayurvedic medicine. *South Asian digest of regional writing* 8: 10–26.

8

The diaspora comes home: Disciplining desire in *DDLJ*

Patricia Uberoi

A significant new development in the field of Indian family and kinship, and one which has so far barely been addressed in the sociology of India, is the internationalisation of the middle-class family. This paper analyses two popular Hindi films of the mid-1990s, Dilwale dulhania le jayenge (DDLJ) *and* Pardes, *that thematise the problems of transnational location in respect of courtship and marriage. The two films share a conservative agenda on the family, but differ in their assessment of the possibility of retaining Indian identity in diaspora.* DDLJ *proposes that Indian family values are portable assets, while* Pardes *suggests that the loss of cultural identity can be postponed but ultimately not avoided. These discrepant solutions mark out Indian popular cinema as an important site for engagement with the problems resulting from middle-class diaspora, and for articulation of Indian identity in a globalised world.*

I
Prologue

This paper presents an analysis of two exceedingly popular commercial Hindi films of the mid-1990s: *Dilwale dulhania le jayenge* (Those with the heart win the bride), familiarly known by its acronym, *DDLJ* (Director Aditya Chopra, 1995), and *Pardes* (Foreign Land, Director Subhash Ghai, 1997). The two films have much in common; so much, in fact, that the second is often deemed a mere 'clone' of the former. Both are love stories, involving Indians settled abroad. And both identify a specific set of 'family values' with the essence of being Indian. Or, to put it the other way around, both define Indianness with reference to specificities of family life, the institutions of courtship and marriage in particular.

Sociologists and social anthropologists tend to be a little embarrassed, if not actually apologetic, when using fiction or other products of the imagination as their

Acknowledgements: Earlier versions of this paper were presented at the Seminar on 'Translatings: Ideas about India since Independence' (Art Gallery of New South Wales, Sydney, 4–7 July 1997), and at the Department of Sociology, University of Poona (January 1998). I am especially grateful to Rachel Dwyer, Shohini Ghosh and Nandini Sundar, to my companions at several viewings of the films analysed here and, as always, to Aradhya Bhardwaj for her very generous assistance.

primary source material, and there are very good reasons for this (see Berger 1977: esp. ch. 8). But while it is important to be self-conscious of the conceptual and methodological pitfalls involved in such exercises, it is also the case that address to new types of data, such as literature, the arts, and forms of popular and mass culture can open up dimensions of human experience that are otherwise relatively inaccessible to sociological scrutiny. The point was made by T.N. Madan while introducing the two essays of his anthology, *Non-renunciation* (1987), that base themselves on modern Indian novels. 'Anticipating scepticism on the part of some colleagues', Madan contended that the novelists might be likened to 'highly motivated informants', and the novels themselves conceived as 'first or second order interpretations of socio-cultural reality which provide invaluable insights into the moral perplexities that a people experience' (1987: 5). In a similar vein, writers on Indian popular cinema have proposed that these films tap into, play on, and ultimately resolve through a variety of narratival strategies the concerns, anxieties and moral dilemmas of the everyday life of Indian citizens (e.g., Chakravarty 1996: 16, 99, 132, 210; Dickey 1993: ch. 8, 1996; Kakar 1981, 1989: ch. 3; Nandy 1995; Prasad 1998: 97, 163; Thomas 1996, etc.). Focussed particularly on the relations of the sexes, relations within the family, and the relations between social classes, popular cinema constructs an 'ideal moral universe' that is intrinsically—if not always *explicitly*—connected with ideas about tradition and nation (Thomas 1996: 160).

The two popular films taken up for discussion here, *DDLJ* and *Pardes*, elaborate certain dilemmas of moral choice that resonate profoundly in contemporary Indian society. These dilemmas are of two kinds, interwoven in and through the cinematic narrative. The first is the conflict between individual desire and social norms and expectations in respect of marriage choice; one could call it the animating logic of south Asian romance (cf. Uberoi 1997). Its felicitous solution in both these films is the contemporary ideal of 'arranged love marriage',[1] that is, a style of matchmaking whereby a romantic choice already made is endorsed, *post facto*, by parental approval and treated thereafter like an 'arranged marriage'. The second is the contradiction between transnational location and the retention of Indian identity. To this latter problem, as I will show here, the two films provide contrasting solutions, notwithstanding their superficial resemblances.

In their address to these two moral dilemmas, *DDLJ* and *Pardes* touch upon practical questions which have been of some interest to sociologists of Indian family and kinship. On the one hand, many sociologists had expected that the modernisation of Indian society would undermine the practice of 'arranged marriage', both by encouraging an individualistic ethos and by subverting the rules of endogamy that have sustained both communal separatism and the hierarchical

[1] I have elaborated elsewhere on the concept of 'arranged love marriage' (see Uberoi n.d. [a] and n.d. [b]), the ideal solution to the conflict of 'arranged' *versus* 'love' marriage, obedience to social norms *versus* individual freedom of choice. In the latter paper (n.d. [b]), I have specified two different forms of 'arranged love marriage': (i) where a romantic choice is subsequently endorsed by parental approval (as in the case of *DDLJ*); and (ii) where a couple proceed to 'fall in love' *after* the parentally arranged match (a variation on 'post-marital romance' [see Singh and Uberoi 1994]).

system of caste in south Asia (see, e.g., Shah 1998: ch. 8). (This, needless to say, has not happened—or, at least, not to the extent once expected.) On the other hand, being set among Indians living abroad, the films register and comment on an important development in Indian family and kinship in the final decades of the 20th century: the phenomenon of the internationalisation of the middle-class family and the consequent problem of the cultural reproduction of Indian identity in transnational locations. Indeed, foregrounding the social and psychological effects of diaspora, these two romantic 'Bollywood' hits have engaged with issues that professional sociologists and anthropologists of the family have only just begun to confront (see Appadurai 1997: esp. 43ff; Nadarajah n.d.).[2] For this reason, if for no other, such films should command our urgent—and unapologetic—attention.

II
Indianness: At home and abroad

Indians 'at home' have had quite contradictory attitudes to their own diaspora.[3] So long as the diaspora was constituted largely of the descendants of indentured labour in the ex-colonies, of farmers and lumberjacks in Canada, or—by the '60s—of working-class immigrants in Britain, the diaspora could be both out of sight and, mostly, out of mind. But with professional middle-class emigration in the '70s and '80s, and the Indian community's attainment of a 'model minority' status in the North American context, the diaspora could no longer be ignored. Simultaneously, a new role was discovered for emigrant Indians as patriotic investors in their country's future.

The less-than-satisfactory outcome of the investment incentives for Non-Resident Indians (NRIs) has by now somewhat impugned their patriotism, which was in any case compromised by the decision to emigrate to greener pastures rather than serving the homeland, as well as by the association of some of them

[2] There is a rapidly growing literature on aspects of the family life of emigré Indians in UK and North America and other diasporic destinations, particularly from feminist and social work perspectives (see, e.g., Bhattacharjee 1992; and references in Bharat and Desai 1995: 65–72). However, studies of the family *in India* have barely registered this development. This asymmetry may be seen as an aspect of a larger phenomenon. That is, while much attention has been focussed on the 'nostalgia' of diasporic peoples for the imagined homeland (see, e.g., Appadurai 1997), the complementary opposite, that is, the longing for translocation/transnationality and the visualising of family dispersion, have received little attention. An exception here is Leela Gulati's book (1993) on the effects on families of working-class male out-migration to the Gulf. Indian migration to the Gulf represents a peculiar case, however. Since only certain classes of workers have been permitted to take their families along with them, this migration is unlikely to result in permanent settlement. The sense of 'Indianness' of the Indian diasporic community in the Gulf might also be inflected by the fact that a large proportion of such workers have been Muslims. See also Naveed-I-Rahat 1990.

[3] I am aware that there is a 'politics' involved in the use of the term 'diaspora' for persons of Indian origin settled abroad (see, e.g., Nadarajah n.d.; Rayaprol 1997: 4; also Jain, this volume). The term represents an effort to construct as a unified 'community' peoples with very different histories and class backgrounds. For a recent summary of the changing connotations of the terms 'Non-Resident Indian' (NRI), 'People of Indian Origin' (PIO) and 'Indian Diaspora' with reference to changing official policies, see Sidharth Bhatia, 'Cashing in on the "Indian" in the NRIs' (*Pioneer* 30/06/1998).

with Indian separatist movements on foreign soil. On their part, the NRIs tend to resent being treated like Kamdhenu, the wish-fulfilling cow, ever in milk. They also begrudge Indian citizenship and taxation laws which, notwithstanding policies of economic liberalisation, appear to them to match every incentive to invest in the home country's development with bureaucratic obstacles, infrastructural snags and generalised mistrust.

At the level of the imaginative, the emigré or foreign returned Indian, or the excessively westernised one, has been defined as the moral antithesis of the one who stays behind, the one whose values remain steadfast. This projection of the anxieties of modernisation and identity loss, typically focussed on women's sexuality, has been a fairly consistent theme in Indian commercial cinema and other media of popular culture over the last half century or so (see, e.g., Chakravarty 1996: esp. ch. 8; Prasad 1998: esp. ch. 4; Rangoonwalla 1979: 47; Thomas 1985, 1996; Vasudevan 1995). And, one must emphasise, it certainly remains so. But *DDLJ* challenged this polarisation. In this film, contemporary Indian identity is constructed not *in antithesis to*, but rather *through*, the romantic engagement, emotional travails and psychological conflicts of protagonists who are *both* NRIs.

As in real life for the NRI community, the crisis of identity in *DDLJ* (and in *Pardes* as well, as we shall see) condenses around the marriage choices of the children of first generation immigrants. Marriage advertisements in Indian newspapers at home and abroad bear ample witness to this dilemma of continuity as parents seek to channel and discipline the romantic aspirations of their children and to ensure the perpetuation of Indian 'culture', 'tradition' and 'values' into the next generation even as they continue to enjoy the material and professional advantages of expatriate living.

While the sexual behaviour and marriage choices of first and second generation Indian emigrants are a matter of major concern for the NRI community, both in real life and in diasporic fiction, drama and cinema, these are not questions that have hitherto specially concerned the *home* community. But with *DDLJ, their* problems of being Indian in a foreign setting are projected as *our* problems of identity as well. Conversely, *our* problems of constituting a 'moral universe' of family relations are seen to be *their* problems as well. That is, the challenge of being (and, more importantly, *remaining*) Indian in a globalised world is one that must be met equally by those who stay at home and those who live abroad, by the 'yuppy'/ 'puppy'[4] as much as by the NRI. Secondly, whether at home or abroad, it is the *Indian family system* that is recognised as the social institution that quintessentially defines being 'Indian' (cf. Thomas 1996).[5] It is an institution that is now projected as portable. And it can remain firm—or so it is fervently hoped—even when all else changes. Whether in accounting for the superior academic achievements of second

[4] Slang for the Punjabi *nouveau riche* 'yuppy'.

[5] This is, if you like, a *secular* solution to the challenge of transnationality. In practice, the other social institution that functions to represent Indianness is the Hindu religion (see Rayaprol 1997), a connection that feeds back, materially and ideologically, into Indian communal politics (see also Appadurai 1997: ch. 1).

generation Indians, or for the fortunes that have propelled some of the emigrants into the roll-call of the richest Britons today,[6] Indian 'family values' are proposed as the crucial markers of Indianness. (Happily, and enviably, they are also believed to correlate positively with the achievement of worldy success in competitive foreign settings.) The dissident minority within the expatriate community which questions these values from a feminist standpoint is branded as shamelessly anti-national (Bhattacharjee 1992).

At home, the iconic status of the Indian family as an institution representative of the nation was already evident in the rhetoric surrounding *Hum aapke hain koun....!* (Who am I to you! Director Sooraj Barjatya, 1994; see Uberoi n.d. [a], 1996a). According to Aditya Chopra, *DDLJ*'s director, the earlier superhit had demonstrated that 'the public . . . reacted overwhelmingly to the fact that the lovers . . . were willing *to sacrifice their own feelings for their families*' (Mohamed 1996a, emphasis added). *DDLJ* reiterates the *HAHK* formula quite self-consciously, but now links it *explicitly* to the question of defining Indian identity.[7] Thus, at every turning point in the film narrative, and with every existential crisis, the protagonists pause to remind themselves and each other of what it means to be 'Indian' (usually rendered as '*Hindustani*'). In fact, the gesture is so conspicuous that it is just short of comical.

I begin this paper by looking closely at the several dramatic situations in the cinematic narrative of *DDLJ* in which specific features of Indian family, kinship and marriage are identified—and, one should add, *valorised*—as being especially Indian. Substantively speaking, what *are* these features, and what are the circumstances and modalities through which they are manifested? However, as with every complex cultural text, one also finds in the narrative structure and ideological edifice of *DDLJ* some untied ends and discrepant notes which commend special attention. That is, along with the insistent valorisation of the Indianness of the Indian family at home and abroad one finds also a muted and inconclusive critique of the Indian 'tradition' (*parampara*). The opposition thus posited between 'culture' (with positive connotations) and 'tradition' (negative) echoes the sort of distinction that some articulate members of the NRI community themselves seek to make when defining their Indian identity in multicultural settings.[8] What are the

6 'Britain's "Tandoori Fortune 500"'. *Pioneer* (New Delhi), 9/03/1997.

7 Rosie Thomas has argued that in Indian popular cinema 'ideas about kinship and sexuality feed directly into ideas about national identity' (1996: 160; cf. Chakravarty 1996: esp. ch. 1). In my study of the reception of *HAHK* (Uberoi n.d. [a]), I found Delhi cinema audiences consistently affirming that the film concerned Indian 'culture' and 'tradition', though Indianness was not a theme that was explicitly invoked in the cinematic narrative of *HAHK* in the way it is in *DDLJ* or, even more saliently, in the subsequent *Pardes*.

8 For instance, actress and writer, Meera Syal, told an interviewer that her generation of British-born Indians constructed their identity, whether consciously or unconsciously, by drawing a distinction between 'culture'—'the core, the fundamental essence, of a way of life and beliefs'—and 'tradition'—'a series of habits and practices which can safely be jettisoned without affecting essential identities'. See Ranjana Sengupta, 'Warm beer and chicken tikka masala', *Times of India*, 12/04/1998.

repressive features of this 'tradition', and how are they manifested through family dynamics? And what is the line that separates the positive quality of Indianness from the impugned features of 'tradition'?

I then take up, though in rather less detail, a successor NRI-focussed romance, *Pardes*. As already noted, this latter film bears close resemblance to *DDLJ*,[9] but it arrives at a different, and indeed more pessimistic, assessment of the possibility of maintaining Indian identity in diaspora. That is, where *DDLJ* proposes that Indian identity can survive translocation, albeit requiring renewal and replenishment through periodic return to the homeland, *Pardes* discloses a deep ambivalence with respect to diaspora—glamourising its material benefits and enabling possibilities, while condemning its moral consequences. The dilemma was rather neatly summed up in the review of *Pardes* published in the conservative English-language women's magazine, *Woman's era*:

> The dilemma of the Indian people who migrated to the land of promises, the USA, in the 1960s and the 1970s to strike it rich there is that they cannot detach themselves from India, where their emotional roots are planted deep into the earth, and they cannot leave America either for all the material well-being it offers them.
>
> .... So they look for excuses which would enable them to stay in America and remain Indians at the same time.[10]

In its narrative closure, *Pardes* would appear to suggest that it *is* indeed possible to preserve Indian family values in diasporic settings. But other voices insist there can be at best postponement, but ultimately not avoidance, of the loss of cultural identity; that, in the end, national identity must be territorialised.

Taken together, the dissonant voices within the cinematic narratives of *DDLJ* and *Pardes* and the discrepant solutions they propose, indicate that contemporary popular cinema has emerged as an important site for engagement with the problems resulting from Indian middle-class diaspora, and for the articulation of Indian identity in a globalised world (see Appadurai 1997: ch.1). They also suggest that the issue is a deeply *contested* one: a true dilemma to which there can be no easy solution, in the world of the imaginary, as also—presumably—in real life.

As a cautionary note at this point, before proceeding with the analysis, one should be reminded that the Indian screen also offered through these years (as it has subsequently) quite a range of issues, besides romance and the family, through

[9] Subhash Ghai has had to continually defend himself against charges of 'copying' *DDLJ*, the more so because *Pardes* appears rather different from the action films with larger-than-life villains that are regarded as Ghai's usual stock-in-trade. See Subhash Ghai, 'Straight answers', *Times of India* 19/11/1997.

[10] *Woman's era*, September 1997, no. 2, p. 141. Interestingly, a number of fictional short stories in this magazine have recently focussed on the problematics of diasporic romance, while numerous articles simultaneously introduce readers to the pleasures of foreign travel and the advantages and tribulations of expatriate living. With economic liberalisation, foreign tourism has become an increasingly affordable luxury (and status symbol) for the Indian middle classes. A considerable measure of this international travel and tourism is presumably funded by diasporic relatives.

which to construct and assert Indianness: the restoration of the pristine values of the freedom movement in the face of social and political degeneration (*Hindustani*); the undeclared war against terrorism and secessionism (*Roja, Maachis*); and the re-enacted battles to secure the country's territorial integrity (*Border*). It also offered some contrasting, and more deeply *conflictual*, images of family relations (*Dil*).[11] But the assertion and endorsement of Indian 'family values' in an uncertain and globalising world has become a conspicuous and insistent theme in popular culture in the 1990s. It is this that I seek to address here.

III
Dilwale dulhania le jayenge

DDLJ was the first directorial venture of a very young and still media-shy director, Aditya Chopra, made under the 'Yashraj' banner of his father, the formidable and long-established Bollywood director, Yash Chopra.[12] Aditya Chopra had himself devised the plot and scripted the screenplay for the film,[13] and ultimately also directed it himself, since his father was not especially fired by the idea or—alternatively—since the latter had thought this film a suitable vehicle through which to 'launch' his son as a full-fledged director.[14] The primary aim of *DDLJ*, according to the younger Chopra, was simply 'to make a very honest love story... a love story that would make it at the box office.... A wholesome film which I wouldn't mind seeing again and again' (Mohamed 1996a). Interestingly, he also wanted 'to show the international audience that India isn't a country of snake-charmers..., to acquaint them with how we Indians live, love, think and react

[11] I am grateful to Shohini Ghosh (personal communication) for this observation, and for raising the larger issue on which this bears: How, sociologically speaking, does one account for contemporary Hindi cinema's neo-conservative agenda in respect of family values, especially as compared to the more radical solutions of earlier eras?

[12] *DDLJ* lays claim to this lineage in an intertextual allusion of the sort that delights connoisseurs of popular cinema. This is the moment when Amrish Puri joins in the singing of marriage songs with '*Ai meri zohra jabeen*', an exceedingly popular number from the opening scenes of the film *Waqt* (1965), directed by Yash Chopra. As in the earlier film, the song was addressed to Achala Sachdeva, who in *DDLJ* plays the role of the grandmother (Shohini Ghosh [personal communication]).

Rajadhyaksha and Willemen have described the senior Chopra's films as 'plushy, soft-focus, upper-class love stories (*Kabhie Kabhie*), battles over family honour (embodied by the mother: *Deewar, Trishul*), and the conflict between the laws of kinship and those of the state' (1995: 75). See also Prasad (1998: 79–80) who notes in Chopra's films both the 'promotion of middle-class consumerism in the course of narratives of love, betrayal, sacrifice and reunion', and also 'an attempt to represent the woman's point of view or to centre the narrative on a woman caught between desire and an oppressive tradition'. Others of Yash Chopra's well-known films include *Kala Pathar, Silsila, Chandni, Lamhe*, and the Shah Rukh Khan starrer, *Darr*. Chopra is the younger brother of B.R. Chopra, a senior figure of the Bombay film industry and maker of the TV *Mahabharata*.

[13] There has, however, been a somewhat unseemly dispute with Honey Irani over the credit for the script. See 'Best director, best screenplay, best dialogue—Aditya Chopra', *Filmfare* 43, 4 (April 1996).

[14] The younger Chopra had already assisted his father with several films, including *Aaima* and *Chandni*, and was intimately involved with the production of the critically acclaimed but commercially unsuccessful *Lamhe* (1991).

today' (ibid.), a rather curious ambition considering how few foreigners (excluding NRIs, with whom the film was reportedly exceedingly popular[15]) would be likely to volunteer to see the movie. To these Chopra added two further, if somewhat more abstract, considerations:

> I was also trying to get something out of my system. I'd be quite troubled by watching those love stories in which the boy and the girl elope. I'd wonder how can they just cut themselves off from their parents who've done so much for them? How can they be so callous? They have no right to break the hearts of their parents. I wanted to say that if your love is strong enough, your parents will be convinced about your love ultimately.
>
> I also wanted to comment on the position of the girl in Indian households. In fact I'm especially proud of the scene between the girl and her mother.[16] I think it describes the situation that Indian women are caught in very clearly. We may be in the 1990s, but there are certain things about the Indian family structure that haven't changed at all.

In this statement, one finds both *endorsement* of the normative order of Indian kinship, and *resistance* to it from the perspective of women (cf. Prasad 1998: 80). This dissonance, as it reveals itself in the film narrative, will be the subject of discussion in due course.

The plot of *DDLJ* is an exceedingly simple one: indeed, it is so simple that the hero, Shah Rukh Khan, described the film as merely 'made up of so many beautiful moments', with 'no story' to it at all![17] Chopra himself claims to have deliberately restrained himself from developing intricate subplots in the profligate style of so many Bollywood movies, or from unnecessarily elaborating on the character of the (quasi)-'villain' (the heroine's jilted fiancé), the better to concentrate on the central romance (Mohamed 1996a). I give the gist of the plot, such as it is, below: typical Bollywood.

> Raj (Shah Rukh Khan), the exuberant son of a very successful self-made NRI businessman, Dharam Vir Malhotra (Anupam Kher), living in London, has just failed his degree examination. Before joining his father in business, he plans a holiday in Europe with his college friends. Coincidentally, Simran (Kajol), the elder daughter of an NRI shopkeeper, Baldev Singh Chowdhury (Amrish Puri),

[15] See 'Des pardes'. *Times of India* (New Delhi), 22/11/1997. A number of commentators have noted the important role that Indian popular cinema plays in constituting the NRI 'community'. See e.g., Chakravarty 1996: 3–4; also Appadurai 1997.

[16] This problematic scene is analysed in greater detail below.

[17] 'Best actor, Shah Rukh Khan'. *Filmfare* 43, 4 (April 1996). Compare the similar comment of Madhuri Dixit on the plot of *HAHK*, a film which she described as constructed of just 'little-little scenes' (see Uberoi n.d. [a]). The lack of a strong story-line is not peculiar to these films, however, but is a characteristic and defining feature of Bombay commercial cinema, and one which some critics see as intrinsically linked to the fragmented mode of production of Indian commercial cinema (that is, the specific division of labour between directors–producers–financiers–distributors–exhibitors) and the indigenous aesthetic traditions and genres on which it draws. See Prasad 1998: esp. ch. 2; also Thomas 1985: 122ff.

has persuaded her conservative and authoritarian father to allow her to go on a European holiday with her girl-friends, before returning to Punjab for an arranged marriage with Kuljeet (Parmeet Sethi), son of her father's old friend, Ajit (Satish Shah). Temporarily separated from their friends in Switzerland, Raj and Simran spend time together and fall in love, despite the shadow of Simran's impending arranged marriage to Kuljeet hanging over them.

On return to London, Simran confides in her mother (Farida Jalal). Her mother is sympathetic, but her father, when he comes to know of it, is furious at her betrayal of his trust. The family leave immediately for the Punjab for Simran's wedding.

Sensing his son's disappointment, Raj's father persuades him not to give up the quest for Simran. Raj thereupon pursues Simran to Punjab, where preparations are already in motion for her marriage. Simran is not attracted to the uncouth Kuljeet, and continues to dream of Raj. Raj and Simran are reunited in the golden mustard fields, but Raj refuses to consider elopement.

Raj insinuates himself into Kuljeet's household (where he is incidentally identified as a suitable husband for Kuljeet's pretty younger sister, Preeti), and thence into Baldev Singh's household, where he tries to win the approval of Simran's father. On her part, meanwhile, Simran contrives to avoid ritually pledging herself to Kuljeet, secretly breaking the Karva Chauth fast with Raj. Meanwhile, the senior Malhotra arrives on the scene to fetch his son and bride back to London.

In a sudden turn of events, the marriage date is advanced in deference to the wishes of Simran's elderly grandmother, and a state of crisis is reached. Simran's mother, who has come to know of Raj's true identity, urges the two to elope, but Raj insists that he would marry Simran only the 'right' way, that is, with her father's approval.

However, when Baldev Singh discovers that Raj is the boy with whom Simran had romanced in Europe, and also recognises him as one of a group of Indian boys who had once taken advantage of him in London, he orders Raj out of the house.

A defeated Raj and his father are waiting at the railway station when Kuljeet and his friends arrive there, armed with guns and sticks and seeking revenge for Kuljeet's humiliation. A bloody fight ensues, stopped only by the arrival on the scene of Baldev Singh and Kuljeet's father, along with Simran and her mother.

As Raj and his father get into the train to depart, Simran pleads with her father to let her go with Raj. At the very last moment, as the train is pulling out, her father relents. Acknowledging the sincerity of Raj's love and his willingness to sacrifice that love for the wider interests of the family, he finally lets go of his daughter. Simran flies into Raj's outstretched arms.

There has been little public comment on *DDLJ*, apart from the regular fare of film magazines. Perhaps film critics, feminists and public conscience-keepers of the

Left and the Right had already spent themselves in commenting on the commercial success, unprecedented popularity and ideologically conservative agenda of the rather similar *HAHK* in the previous year. Understandably under the circumstances, such comment as there has been on *DDLJ* has focussed on the extent to which the film resembles (in general) or differs (in detail) from *HAHK*. It is almost impossible to avoid doing likewise.

Like *HAHK*, which Aditya Chopra has confessed to greatly admiring, *DDLJ* was a stupendous success, outdoing *HAHK*'s takings within the year and confirming that the commercial success of such movies was no mere 'flash in the pan' but evidence of a decisive turn in public taste. Yashraj Productions followed, more or less, the canny publicity and distribution strategies developed by the Barjatyas: withholding the release of video rights and policing video piracy, thereby continuing to draw the middle classes back to the cinema for wholesome entertainment (Chatterjee 1996). Close observers have noted some minor differences in the producers' promotional strategies, reflecting on the slightly different (home-grown or cosmopolitan) audiences they were presumed to be aiming at; but this may be making rather a fine point of things (see Doraiswamy 1996). In terms of content, both *HAHK* and *DDLJ* provide what is regarded as clean, non-violent, 'family' entertainment, in contrast to the violence and revenge fare that had dominated Bollywood films of the 1980s and that still continues as a major idiom in Hindi popular cinema.[18] And in either case they do so by foregrounding marriage rituals and festivities, a strategy which, as I have pointed out in the case of *HAHK*, has the additional function of 'naturalising' the song–dance items and making them seem less artificial to sophisticated and westernised tastes (Uberoi n.d. [a]; see also Gupta 1996). That is, the songs and dances that are an almost obligatory ingredient in commercial Hindi cinema appear to blend more 'naturally' into the film narrative.

On a more critical note, it is obvious that both films endorse glamorous lifestyles, and effortless and guiltless consumption (see Bharucha 1995; also Dickey 1996: 147).[19] Unlike *HAHK*, where Lord Krishna himself (assisted by Tuffy the dog) joins the action at crucial moments and where religiosity is very much in the air, religion *per se* does not play much of a role in *DDLJ*.[20] But in terms of its *communal*

[18] See Prasad (1998: esp. ch. 6) for a linking of the establishment of this trend, what he terms 'the cinema of mobilization', with the wider political economy of the 1970s. Films such as *HAHK* and *DDLJ* could be said to mark the revival, or consolidation, of 'middle class cinema', a second significant trend of the 1970s (ibid.), though these films have also proved immensely popular with the 'front-benchers'.

[19] Rachel Dwyer (personal communication) sees the absence of poverty and of servants as characteristic of Yash Chopra's recent movies where, as she says, 'everyone is rich, usually way beyond any possible earned income, although their jobs are often mentioned (doctors, architects, TV presenters, etc.)'. The foreign setting of *DDLJ* functions to naturalise this affluence.

[20] However, one might note two instances in *DDLJ* where the principle of what one might call 'metaphysical bonding' is conspicuous. Both are moments of dramatic tension. In the first, in the course of an engagement ceremony, Simran contrives to avoid Kuljeet's putting a ring on the ring finger of her left hand by producing a bandaged finger. (She receives the ring on *another* finger,

cast, the superficially more secular and cosmopolitan *DDLJ* may well appear more sinister. For here we have contemporary Punjab fervently eulogised ('*mera desh, mera Panjab*!') and soundly caricatured (the golden fields of mustard flowers, *makki di roti* and *sarson da sag*, a lot of eating, drinking, camaradarie and jollity, machismo and male bonding, hunting and horse-riding[21]), with no mention whatsoever of the undeclared civil war that had driven a wedge between Hindus and Sikhs in the region, in the nation and in the diasporic communities as well. *HAHK* may have had a 'token' Sikh decorating the front line of the boys' chorus; *Raja Hindustani* (Indian King, 1997) may have rehabilitated the comic figure of the erstwhile '*sardarji*' jokes; *Maachis* (Matches, 1996) may have confronted the problem of terrorist violence head-on. . .; but *DDLJ* returns to the villages and mustard fields of Punjab without a single Sikh, or for that matter AK–47 rifle, in sight![22]

Assuming a 'mimeticist' point of view, *DDLJ*'s erasure of the harsh fact of communal conflict (along with caste and class differences) would appear to impair the film's authenticity as a social document. On the other hand, such gestures of systematic erasure are themselves significant 'social facts', contributing importantly to the construction of a utopian vision of social order. That is, they are significant pointers to the film's broader *ideological* agenda (see Prasad 1998). In practical terms, they also allow the director to focus centrally and without unnecessary

---

however, and gives a ring to Kuljeet, too.) The situation is repeated, but with enhanced tension, shortly afterwards. As the married women of the assembled families break the Karva Chauth fast with water offered by their husbands, Simran fakes a swoon, and is opportunely revived by a sip of water administered by Raj. Simran and Raj subsequently consummate this ritual bonding in the moonlight on the terrace by the exchange of food with each other.

These two instances of avoided and consummated ritual bonding are sociologically interesting in themselves. The former is something of a hybrid custom, melding the Christian practice of the exchange of rings and vows and the dedication of the 'ring finger' with Hindu custom. Though Karva Chauth has long been an important Hindu festival, it is one of the domestic rituals which, like Bhai Duj, appears to have gained massive ground in recent years through the castes and classes of north Indian society (Madhu Kishwar, personal communication).

21 A jarring note for Punjabi viewers: 'Where is the *shikar* these days?', they complained to me.

22 Aditya Chopra's mother, Pamela, is from a Sikh family, and the family are said to follow some Sikh rituals. Several of Yash Chopra's movies have had Sikhs in major roles, and Hindus are shown participating in Sikh ceremonies in *Silsila*. The conspicuous avoidance of Sikhs and Sikhism in *DDLJ* would thus seem to indicate the deliberate avoidance of a politically sensitive issue (Rachel Dwyer, personal communication).

Sumita Chakravarty notes that, in general, 'the Bombay film treads its ground gingerly, not willing or capable of upsetting the two major divisions in Indian society: those of religion and language. (Intercommunal or interlinguistic love-affairs or attachments have been taboo on the Indian screen.) Class, the other major division in Indian society, on the other hand, is seen as a less crucial barrier to peaceful co-existence and citizenry and is routinely transcended through "magical" upward mobility' (1996: 312; cf. Rangoonwalla 1979: 46–47). It is interesting to the sociologist that 'caste' as a divisive factor in society is not mentioned by Chakravarty in respect to postcolonial Indian cinema, though issues of caste and untouchability were prominent in the social films of the pre-Independence period and, post-'Mandal', continue to wrack the social fabric.

The general reluctance of popular cinema to portray or confront the problems of inter-communal relations makes films like Mani Ratnam's *Roja* and *Bombay*, or Gulzar's *Maachis*, appear most unusual.

diversion on the *elementary aspects of romance*, the transference of a woman from one man (and one family) to another, and on the exploration, through this romance, of the existential dilemmas of being Indian. It is to these that we now turn.

IV
Romance, Indian-style

As already remarked, throughout the film narrative of *DDLJ*, the chief protagonists are constantly reminded of the moral responsibility of being 'Indian'. Significantly, these reminders constitute major sign-posts and crisis-points in the unfolding of the film narrative. I set them out here in their order of occurrence:

1. In the opening scene of the film, providing the background for the titles and credits, Baldev Singh Chowdhury is shown walking through Trafalgar Square en route to his shop and, as is obviously his wont, feeding the pigeons. Talking to himself, he reflects:

> This is London, the biggest city in the world.
> I've been here now for 22 years.
> Every day I pass down this road and it asks me: 'Who is Chowdhury Baldev Singh? Where has he come from? What is he doing here?'
> What can I reply? I have spent so many years of my life here, and still this land is alien to me.
> Nobody knows me here, except these pigeons.
> Like me, they don't have a country; they go to the place where they get food.
> Now necessity has enchained me.
> But one day, definitely, I will return to my country!

The scene cuts briefly to golden mustard fields, icon of the Punjab, a colourful Punjabi folk dance, and Baldev Singh in the mustard fields, feeding his pigeons.

As is shortly evident by a metonymic juxtapositioning, the question, 'Who am I?', 'Why am I here?', has clearly been provoked not only by the crisis of Baldev Singh's middle age: it also coincides with the coming into maturity of his elder daughter, Simran.

Our first glimpse of Simran at her home, hair blown across her face, conveys an impression of barely controlled sensuality. She has been writing love poems—to no-one in particular, she assures her mother in confidence—but the film shortly interleaves cameos of her life with Raj's to establish their destiny with each other against the background of the very sensually rendered song, '*Mere khvabon men jo aye*' ('Someone has come to tease me in my dreams; ask him to come before me'). The connection of Baldev Singh's identity crisis with Simran's budding sensuality is further underlined by his joyful reaction to the coincidental arrival that very evening of Ajit's letter, redolent with the flavours of Punjab (the famous *makki di roti* and *sarson da sag*!), renewing the proposal for Simran's marriage to his son, Kuljeet.

2. Simran, reading out Ajit's letter to her father, suddenly breaks off and runs to her room. Her mother intuitively realises that news of the proposal has upset her daughter, though Simran has been aware of the possibility of marriage to Kuljeet since she was a little girl. But her father interprets her moodiness as the 'shyness' appropriate to a modest young girl facing the prospect of marriage and, of course, mature sexuality:

B.S. See, Lajo, she is feeling shy.
This is our culture. . . . Indian culture.
Even today a daughter feels shy in front of her father.
You see, I haven't failed. I have kept India alive here in the heart of London.

In the privacy of her room, Simran tears up her love poems, the record of her unspecified longing.

3. Raj and his friends on a night out together, pull up to buy some beer from Baldev Singh's shop just as he is closing for the day. Baldev Singh refuses one of the boys, but Raj tries another tack. Pleading a migraine, for which he needs medicine, Raj appeals to their shared identity as 'Indians' ('*Hindustani*'). Baldev Singh relents and obliges him, but when Raj then tries to buy some beer, Chowdhury realises that he has been taken advantage of. He is furious, and demands to know how such ruffians can dare to call themselves Indian. Raj makes off with the beer anyhow, tossing the payment on to the counter. Chowdhury is still fuming over the incident when he reaches home.

Clearly, boyish exuberance is a challenge to the deadly serious role of being an emigré Indian. It is also an index of a liminal stage in the male life cycle—the 'boys will be boys', male-bonding, 'I hate girls' phase of flirtatious and teasing relations with the opposite sex, prior to acceptance of the responsibilities of adult heterosexuality. As will be seen, the attainment of mature adulthood, scripted as acceptance of Indian identity, is exemplified in the first instance in the exercise of sexual *self-control* (cf. Uberoi 1996b: xx).

4. As their paths cross in Europe, Simran and Raj establish a teasing, attraction/hostility relation with each other. Thanks to Raj's pranks, Simran misses her train to Zurich, and attempts to hitch a ride there. The Swiss police are questioning her, when Raj comes by in his car and claims her as his wife. She petulantly accepts a lift from him under the circumstances, but they gradually open out with each other and confirm that they are both Indian.

5. This confirmation of shared Indian origins is only the beginning of a major test which is, arguably, the most dramatic episode in the first half of the film. Their car having broken down, Raj and Simran are forced to spend the night together in a small hotel where only a single room is available. Mindful of the compromising situation she had got into, Simran stalks off to the barn. Raj joins her there. He tries to persuade her to eat something or share some rum with him, but she instead berates him for daring to drink in front of an *Indian* girl. He appears to drop off to sleep. As the snow falls through the roof and she shivers with cold and hunger, she eyes the rum bottle and fantasises an intimately romantic relationship with Raj (the song, '*Jara sa jhum lun main*').

In the morning, to her consternation, Simran wakes up back in the hotel room, dressed in Raj's pyjamas. Raj, bringing her tea, comments that she looks even more beautiful in the morning, adding for good measure that this must have been her 'first time'. Greatly perturbed, she demands to know what had happened in the night, and he teasingly leads her to believe the worst—'What happened last night is what is meant to happen'—, he declares, revealing a cluster of lipstick 'love-bites' on his bare chest. She becomes quite hysterical. Suddenly, Raj stops joking and becomes serious. Looking into her eyes he swears that, rogue though he may appear to be, he is after all '*Hindustani*', and is well aware of what an Indian girl's 'honour' (*izzat*) means to her: 'Nothing happened last night to make us ashamed; I was only joking with you'. She concludes with relief that she has not lost her virginity after all, while Raj for his part promises not to make such upsetting jokes again.

6. Something changes between Raj and Simran after the episode in the hotel, though Simran's disclosure that she is engaged to be married casts a pall over the developing relationship. Learning of it, Raj expresses surprise that Simran could think of commending her whole life to someone she had never met:[23]

> **S.** I don't feel the need [to meet him]. My father has seen him. He's my father's friend's son.
>
> ....
>
> In our society [India], that's what happens.

Nonetheless, before they rejoin their friends, Raj discloses his love for Simran.

7. Back in Punjab, where marriage preparations are well under way, Simran and Raj are reunited. Simran begs Raj to take her away, but Raj declares:

> No, I have not come here to steal you.
> True, I was born in London. But I am an Indian.
> I will persevere till I marry you, and your father himself will put your hand in mine.

8. At a gathering at the Chowdhury's, Raj's father meets Baldev Singh. The senior Malhotra identifies himself as '*Hindustani*':

> My country, my land! Everything is available [over there], but not this culture.... Everywhere I go, I have India in my heart.

He announces that he has come to India to fetch Raj's bride.

9. Simran contrives to avoid drinking water and taking food from Kuljeet at the breaking of the Karva Chauth fast. She is discovered by her mother as she completes the ritual bonding with Raj on the terrace. At the sight of them together, her mother urges Simran not to sacrifice herself for 'tradition' (as she herself had

[23] NRIs are well aware that the institution of arranged marriage—marriage to a person they have never courted and often never met—appears particularly bizarre in the cultural settings in which they now live. They are sometimes quite defensive on this score, arguing that Indian-style arranged marriage is demonstrably more stable than so-called 'love marriage'. Experientially, the institution of arranged marriage is a major point of contention between first and second generation emigré Indians, the latter often sharing the cultural presuppositions of their western peers.

done) and, handing over a bundle of jewels, she advises the two of them to elope. Again, Raj refuses:

> **R.** Mother ... I lost my own mother when I was very young. But I remember one thing she said to me: 'There are two paths in life. One is right and one is wrong. Maybe one has to suffer a lot in choosing the right path, but there is success in the end. That doesn't happen with the wrong path.'
>
> ....
>
> I want my Simran with her father's consent. Now don't you worry. She's my responsibility.

'You don't know my husband', the mother warns. 'But your husband doesn't know me,' replies Raj. The stage is now set for the denouement.

10. Raj seeks to win Baldev Singh's affection by sharing with him his early morning communion with the pigeons in the mustard fields. In one of these encounters, Baldev Singh confides how he has loved to feed pigeons ever since he was a small boy. This gives Raj an opening, and he asks if there is any difference between the pigeons of Punjab and those of London. Baldev Singh replies: 'I know the pigeons here, and they know me. We are of the same soil. The London ones are foreign to me.' Raj replies: 'Maybe you haven't got to know them [i.e., the London ones] properly yet.'

That Raj is the metaphorical 'London' pigeon, seeking recognition for his true self in contrast to the local pigeon is immediately made clear. A shot rings out. Kuljeet gallops by with his rifle in his hand and a wounded pigeon flutters to the earth. Raj picks it up and dresses its wounds with the healing powers of the soil of Punjab, disclosing his identity as the boy of the London episode and asking Baldev Singh's forgiveness.

11. In the final showdown between Baldev Singh and Raj, Baldev Singh recalls this conversation, and accuses Raj of insinuating himself into the household to steal both his daughter and his honour. In a grand soliloquy, which fortunately did not make the cinema audiences either hoot or titter (indeed, it was touch-and-go, according to the director [Mohamed 1996a]), Raj renounces his claim over Simran, and returns her to her father's care. Once again, his sentiments echo those that he had earlier characterised as being quintessentially 'Indian':

> Our mother and father gave us life and love.
> We have no right to disobey them.
> [to Simran] I've got no right over you.
> Your father was right. I'm a nobody (*awara*).
> I should have known love can't fix everything.
> [to Baldev Singh] Here, she's yours.

It was this simultaneous assertion of love and of the willingness to renounce it for the sake of honouring parental authority that ultimately persuades Baldev Singh to relent of his stand and forfeit his personal bond of honour with his friend Ajit. He commends Simran into Raj's outstretched arms.

Comment

As already noted, Baldev Singh's anxiety as an Indian takes an acute form at the moment when his elder daughter is sexually mature and ripe for marriage. This makes it encumbent on him to arrange her marriage without delay. The arrangement takes the form of the revival of a 'deal' made between two friends when their children were infants. Baldev Singh's honour (*izzat*) is now implicated not only in fulfilling his commitment to his friend, but in ensuring that his daughter's virtue is untainted. He is most reluctant to allow her to go on a holiday with her friends in Europe, and relents only when Simran promises that she will give him no cause for complaint.

The discovery of Simran's European romance with Raj threatens Baldev Singh's honour as an Indian in several ways. Firstly, it challenges his authority as a patriarch; his daughter has been disobedient to his will, and must be corrected. Secondly, it threatens his sacred duty as a Hindu father to *gift* his daughter in marriage, for the troth involves only the young couple, Simran and Raj. Thirdly, it challenges the principle of 'alliance', whereby marriage is construed as a union between two *families* through the 'exchange' of women, rather than just an arrangement between two individuals setting up a new conjugal family together. Fourthly, by compromising Simran's virtue, her purity as a gift-object is depreciated, and his own honour therewith.

The whole effort of the film thereafter is to provide reassurance on all these counts such that Raj succeeds in winning Simran not by eliminating or displacing her father but by becoming Indian himself in his commitment to the crucial principles of the Indian 'culture' of kinship. Thus, Raj refuses to defy Simran's father, but works to bring him round. More importantly, he does not contest the father's authority to bestow her. Twice given the chance to elope, he refuses to do so and vows that he will marry Simran only the 'right' way, the '*Indian*' way, that is, with the father's active consent. This tribute to paternal authority is rationalised as 'gratitude' to the parents who gave her life and brought her up. It is Raj's stubborn stand on this principle that almost spells personal disaster, while at the same time constructing him as a true Indian, respectful of parental authority to the point of self-denial. (Ultimately, of course, his willingness to make this 'sacrifice' stands to his credit.)

Director Aditya Chopra's commitment to the authority of parental will over individual freedom of choice and youthful desire has already been quoted—in words that are in fact almost identical to those mouthed by Raj in his statements first to Simran and then, more elaborately, to her mother, as justification for his refusal to elope (see below). The final, and even more elaborate statement, eyeball to eyeball with the enraged Baldev Singh, was also to the same effect. Reading backwards one recalls that Raj had earlier identified these sentiments as springing from his *Indian* heritage.

Apart from the director, the film's hero Shah Rukh Khan also echoed the point that gratitude to parents should take precedence over individual self-gratification.

Interviewed after receiving the *Filmfare* best actor award for his role, Shah Rukh Khan, in an interesting conflation of his off-screen and on-screen roles, stressed his personal experience of the same moral dilemmas (as were faced by Raj in *DDLJ*) in the course of his inter-communal courtship of his wife-to-be, Gauri. It may be significant here that the script was supposedly written with Shah Rukh Khan in mind for the role of Raj.

Q. How close did you feel to Raj?

SRK I'm like Raj in the film. I live recklessly like him.
Like Raj who was so confident about winning over Simran's parents, I knew I could win over her parents and Gauri would be mine.

Q. You had to go through all those troubles even in real life?

SRK Sort of. Gauri's parents were dead against the marriage. Her mother threatened to commit suicide. Her father called me over and said it wouldn't work out. . . .
. . .
They're a typical Punjabi family. Just like Simran's. . . . I managed to *patao* [butter up] all her relatives one by one. . . .

Q. What about the trying times?

SRK Ya, things weren't working out. Gauri was locked up at home. . . . Like Simran in *Dilwale* . . . she would keep telling me, 'Shah Rukh, you don't know my parents . . . . You take things so lightly', and I would tell her that things would be alright.[24]

Q. You never thought of eloping?

SRK No, like Raj and Simran we never wanted to go against the wishes of our parents. The thought of running away from home never crossed our minds. But we knew we'd get married for sure.
When I met Gauri's parents, I just couldn't get myself to say that I loved their daughter. That, I thought, was a stupid thing to say . . . because *I could never love their daughter as much as they loved her. They had given birth to and brought up Gauri. . . . My love would never be a substitute for their love* (emphasis added).[25]

Initially it appears that Raj's success in marrying Simran would subvert the principle of marriage as alliance between two *families* (rather than between two individuals). After all, the (chaste) consummation of young love takes place in a setting—neither his home nor hers, neither London nor Punjab—where the protagonists have temporarily shed both their families and their respective peer groups: it is just between themselves. And God, of course.

[24] Again, these are almost the exact words of the film script used on two occasions: (*i*) in Raj's conversation with Simran when she begs him to take her away; and (*ii*) in conversation with her mother, when the latter advises Raj and Simran to elope.

[25] 'Best actor, Shah Rukh Khan', *Filmfare* 43, 4 (April 1996). Shah Rukh's final comment here echoes the words used by Raj in his penultimate and most dramatic confrontation with Baldev Singh.

But the satisfactory conclusion of the romance in marriage requires the active participation of the parents. Raj is in fact as quick to involve his father as Simran is to involve her mother, and it is Raj's father, identifying with his son, who urges him not to give up his quest just because Simran is promised to someone else. The senior Malhotra doesn't leave matters there. He shortly proceeds to Punjab, announcing that he has come to fetch Raj's bride home and lending a hand in various ways (including showing up Kuljeet as a rather nasty piece of work). When he finally meets the lovely Simran, who spontaneously drops at his feet,[26] he actively gives his approval: 'Terrific, fantastic, done, *challo* [let's go].' True, Baldev Singh's good friend Ajit is displaced as the affine of first choice, but the principle of '*affinity as a value*' (to use Louis Dumont's apt term [1983]) shows every sign of robust renewal.

Finally, when it comes to the point and Raj has Simran alone and drunk, desirous and very desirable, he recalls that he is after all an Indian and that he understands what an Indian girl's 'honour' means to her. It may be remarked here that Simran's 'honour' resides in her virginity understood in the narrowest physiological sense, for Raj has already undressed and ravished her. Similarly, what passed between them in a subsequent night together in the mustard fields is left to the imagination, but the assumption is of continued chastity: at least in its most literal figuration.[27]

This is all consistent with the 'blushing' reply of Aditya Chopra to an interviewer's question about the 'sexual permissiveness' of the '90s: 'Sex is there...', he conceded. 'It's on everyone's mind. You just have to know when to exercise *self-control* and not take advantage of the other person' (Mohamed 1996a, emphasis added). The remark is interesting for its valorisation of *male self*-control[28] whereas, at least going by the text of *DDLJ, female* sexuality requires either control, or else self-denial, by the male 'other'.

V
The tyranny of 'tradition'

Let us now retrace our steps to chart the undertow of resentment and critique that lies beneath the normative culture of Indian kinship. I single out four episodes in particular. Significantly, in each case the perspective is that of *female* characters.

[26] A gesture so nicely rendered that Aditya Chopra describes it as 'brilliant' acting on Kajol's part (Mohamed 1996a).

[27] While the heroine's chastity must be maintained, the definition of chastity is pushed to its narrowest. This is consistent with a point made by Rosie Thomas (1996), namely that popular cinema must perforce operate within the moral code acceptable to viewers, but that it is always negotiating (and transforming) its limits. A similar literalness in respect of virginity is often invoked in judicial discourse in rape cases (see Veena Das n.d.; Uberoi 1996c: 199–200, n.d. [b]).

[28] See Alter 1997; also Uberoi 1995b and 1996b: xx, for the valorisation of chastity and the linking of individual *brahmacharya* with national regeneration. See also Anuja Agrawal's discussion (1998) of popular Hindi magazine short stories on the theme of the encounter of a male protagonist with a prostitute. Agrawal makes the important point that the male exercise of sexual self-restraint is what marks out the object woman as one of *his own community*: paradoxically, both marriageable, and requiring control. The women of 'other' communities are, as it were, 'fair game' for a man's sexual impulses.

1. Simran is trying to win her father over to allow her to go to Europe with her friends. She first impresses him with her piety (he discovers her, early morning, bathed and dressed in a sari, praying at the family shrine), confirming in his mind his success in instilling Indian values in children raised in a foreign land (see above). Simran then pleads with her father in the following terms: She is about to leave for Punjab, in deference to her father's wishes, to marry a man she has never met. And she may never come back. Before she does so, she would like to visit Europe, to have just one month of her own life for *herself*, to fulfil her own desires. She promises that she will do nothing to embarrass her father.

The suggestion here is, firstly, that a girl's desires are of little account when it comes to arranging her marriage. Though *we* (i.e., the audience) now know, and her mother knows, of Simran's longing for a still unspecified object of desire, the father sees only the modesty (*sharam*, 'shame') proper to a well–brought up Indian girl discussing the prospect of her marriage with her father. Nor is there space for her exercise of free will in the matter of mate selection: the choice of groom is entirely her father's, and her abiding by that choice a question of his personal honour. It is in this context of the negation of both desire and agency that she begs for just one month of her life to be herself, between her present role as daughter and her impending role as daughter-in-law.

2. Following the intimate incident in the Swiss hotel, already described at some length for its crucial importance in defining male Indianness, Raj confides to Simran that he is still waiting for the girl of his dreams who will one day materialise before him. He seeks to know if Simran has a similar longing. Implicitly critiquing her own lack of agency (for she has, after all, been brought up in the same foreign setting as Raj), she replies matter-of-factly:

S. There is no place for any unknown, unseen person in my dreams. I'm already engaged to someone in India.
R. Oh. What's he like? He must be very handsome.
S. I don't know. I have never seen him.
R. You haven't seen the person you are going to marry?
S. I don't feel the need to. My father has seen him.
He's my father's friend's son.
R. How can you think of spending your life with a person you don't know, whom you've never seen. Can you commit your whole life to him?
S. In our society, that's what happens.

3. Simran's grandmother observes to her father that Simran does not seem as happy as she should be at the prospect of her marriage. Her father assures his mother that there is no problem—that Simran is merely unfamiliar with the place, the people and the food, etc. But, recalling Simran's European romance, he tells his wife in no uncertain terms that Simran had better forget the European affair: *or else*. . . .! Meanwhile, Simran's mother takes her daughter aside and cautions her:

M. When I was a little girl, my grandfather used to tell me that there is no difference between a man and a woman. Both have the same rights. But once I grew up I understood that it was not the case. My education was stopped so that my brothers' education could be continued; their education was more important than mine. After that, I sacrificed my life; first as a daughter and then as a daughter-in-law.

But when you were born I took a vow that you would never have to make the same sacrifices as I did. I wanted you to live your own life. But Simran, I was wrong. I forgot that a woman has no right to make such a pledge. Women are born to make sacrifices for men, but not the other way round. I beg you, give up your happiness and forget him [the boy]. Your father will never allow it.

S. You're right, mother. I was being foolish. I don't even know whether he [Raj] loves me or not. My father has done so much for my happiness. Can't I make a little sacrifice for his happiness?

This scene, which was regarded by the director and by the actors involved as a crucial and challenging one, is interesting in two respects. Firstly, though it is not *explicitly* so stated, the mother's instinctive identification with her daughter's longings and with her present dilemma (being married to someone against her will) suggests that she has a similar and never forgotten desire in her own life, though she has been a dutiful and loving wife and mother for many years. (There is just a *hint* of transgression here.) Secondly, the condemnation of the injustice of 'tradition' (*parampara*) is paradoxically the *very* ground on which the mother asks Simran to *give up* her own aspirations and 'sacrifice' her personal happiness. Simran is asked to be obedient to a tradition which they both recognise to be unjust—for the simple reason that, realistically speaking, in this society women have no other option. The result is that Simran tells her mother to convey to her father her willingness to go ahead with the marriage to Kuljeet.

Actress Kajol identified with this defeatism; maybe not personally, but on behalf of many girls she had known.

> I will never forget that scene where Simran tells Faridaji [her mother] that she's ready to get married. And there was that scene where I break down [as Raj leaves her house]. I don't get hysterical or anything. . . . I just seem to *give up. It was almost as if I don't care what happens to me anymore. I just give up, like many girls do in real life when they don't have an option.*
>
> . . . .
>
> I must have met 120 girls like Simran, girls who have fallen in love. . . . But they have not always seen a happy ending like the characters in the film.
>
> I think *Dulhania* . . . also made thousands of parents think about what happens to their children when they try to force them into marriage with someone they don't know. . ., let alone love (emphasis added).[29]

[29] 'Best actress, Kajol'. *Filmfare* 43, 4 (April 1996), emphasis added.

4. Simran's mother has discovered her on the terrace in the moonlight, breaking the Karva Chauth fast with Raj, and she realises that this must be the boy that Simran had fallen in love with. She now repeats her condemnation of Indian tradition, but with a different conclusion this time: defiance, not submission.

> I won't let what happened to me happen to my daughter. She will not be just a daughter or a daughter-in-law. She will live her own life. . . .
> . . . .
> You need not sacrifice your love.
> [to Raj] My blessings. She will be happy with you. Take her away. I'll take care of the rest.

But, as already noted, Raj declines to run away with Simran and insists he must win her father's approval. In so doing, he identifies with patriarchal authority, with the 'law' of the father, and distances himself from the socially subversive and sentimental complicity of mother and daughter.

Comment

In the subtext of *DDLJ*, when women *speak*, it is to criticise a culture of kinship in which there is no space or time when they can legitimately be the subjects of their own desire and destiny: they are first daughters, then daughters-in-law, the objects of exchange between men. At the same time, when they sacrifice their personal desires, it is not seen as an assertion of individual *agency*, but simply as recognition of the fact that they have 'no option' in a situation which is inherently unjust.

The position is different for men. When faced with a conflict between individual desire and conformity to social values, they may *choose* to sacrifice the former, but this exercise of agency is ultimately ennobling, not diminishing. The happy ending that can result from the resolution of this conflict—parental endorsement of a romantic relationship—is for them at once an affirmation of individual agency and a consummation of desire. For women, the resolution of the crisis is just 'good luck'. As Kajol acknowledged, Simran was simply luckier than most other girls, than Indian girls in real life: She gave in to the system, yet she was happily able to achieve the object of her desire.

VI

Pardes: *Reinstituting the contradiction of India and the West*

DDLJ belongs not only in a genealogy of immensely successful 'clean' and 'simple' romantic dramas, with gorgeous backdrops, catchy music and old-fashioned 'family values'. It was also, as subsequent releases have demonstrated, one of a new series of popular movies in which the NRI is positioned as hero. This *in itself* seems to be a social trend worth watching and reflecting on—a testimony at once to the enabling opportunities of the liberalised economy of the 1990s, and to the emergence of a new transnational Indian elite class as the reference group for the upwardly mobile Indian middle classes (Arvind Das 1997; also Appadurai 1997: ch. 1; Prasad 1998: esp. 81–88).

Now, exotic foreign locales are nothing new in Indian popular cinema, and there have been times when they have seemed positively *de rigueur* for enhancing the visual pleasures of a film, and its song–dance items in particular.[30] But *DDLJ* had introduced an element of novelty in this practice by its attempt to define Indian identity for Indians both at home and abroad through the emotional travails of a young NRI couple in love, rather than through the more conventional confrontation of Eastern versus Western cultures and values. Following soon after *DDLJ*, however, Subhash Ghai's *Pardes* (1997) reverted once again to the old formula. Before commenting further on this film by way of both comparison and contrast with *DDLJ*, one must perforce, and with the usual disclaimers, try to provide a brief summary of the plot:

> Kishori Lal (Amrish Puri), an NRI millionaire, has returned from America to find a bride for his son, Rajiv (Apoorva Agnihotri), brought up in the U.S. He selects Kusum Ganga (Mahima Chaudhary), the young and lovely daughter of his old friend, Suraj Dev, whom he meets by chance.
>
> Back in the States, Kishori Lal asks Arjun (Shah Rukh Khan), his adopted son, to escort Rajiv back to India to meet the girl and persuade him to marry her. Rajiv, a bit of a playboy, is reluctant, but when he meets Ganga he agrees to the marriage on the condition that Ganga first try out living in the States for a month to see if she can adjust to the change. Suraj Dev's family members are initially disapproving, but relent when Kishori Lal assures them that Ganga and Rajiv can get formally engaged first, and that an aunt can chaperone Ganga to the States.
>
> In the States, Ganga is dismayed to discover Rajiv's weakness for cigarettes, drink and women, and to learn of his earlier physical involvement with a long-term girl friend. She comes to rely increasingly on Arjun who, despite his unacknowleged feelings for her, continues to try to smoothen things over between Rajiv and Ganga in deference to his foster-father's commission. Their closeness is noted by Arjun's friend, who urges him to declare his love; and by a malicious aunt, who sows suspicion in Kishori Lal's mind.
>
> At the malicious aunt's insistence, Kishori Lal sends Arjun away, and Rajiv and Ganga go on a trip together to Las Vegas. Here Rajiv attempts to rape Ganga. She knocks him unconscious and runs away, but is located by Arjun who escorts her back to India.

[30] See, e.g., Chakravarty 1996: 202–203, 210. The famous examples of an earlier era, combining the attractions of consumption and an ultimately moralising voyeurism, were *Sangam* (1964), *Love in Tokyo* (1966), *An evening in Paris* (1967) and *Purab aur Paschim* (1970), but the trend continues up to the recent *Jeans* (1997), the most expensive popular movie ever made, in which beauty queen Aishwarya Rai dances in front of seven wonders of the world. Some observers link the present fondness for foreign locales with the unavailability of Kashmir for film shooting. Incidentally, Yash Chopra is well-known for setting scenes of his movies abroad—Rekha dancing in the Dutch tulip fields in *Silsila* is a well-remembered example—and he has been actively wooed by British tourism authorities for more of the same (see Mohamed 1996b).

Incensed, Rajiv and Kishori Lal pursue the couple to India. Ganga's father attempts to kill Arjun for compromising his honour. Arjun draws his own blood on the sword, and leaves, declaring his and Ganga's innocence.

At a Sufi shrine, while qawalis sing of divine love, a fight takes place between the rival 'brothers'. Kishori Lal and Ganga's father arrive to intervene. Though Arjun concedes that he has fallen in love with Ganga, he denies betraying his foster-father's faith and maintains that he has never laid hands on Ganga. Ganga displays the signs of Rajiv's brutal attempted rape.

Recognising the truth and purity of Arjun's love for Ganga, Kishori Lal proposes that she should marry not Rajiv, who has proved himself unworthy, but Arjun. Father and foster-son, and father and daughter, are then happily reconciled.

Like *DDLJ, Pardes* has been exceedingly popular with NRI audiences,[31] though its commercial performance in India was somewhat uneven through different circuits of the movie distribution network, and different constituencies of the viewing public. This unevenness of response may represent a degree of public saturation with the 'clean' NRI-as-hero formula (at least, that is what the critics and distributors seem to think), but it may also express popular discomfort with the rather unsatisfactory narrative closure that *Pardes* ultimately arrives at: the story-line hinges on just too many 'unbelievable' details, a disappointed viewer assured me.[32]

Detailing all the instances in *Pardes* where Indianness is directly invoked, as was just done in the case of *DDLJ*, would be a thoroughly tedious and nearly impossible exercise, for the contradiction of India and the West permeates and structures the whole text. This was not quite the case with *DDLJ*: Though set in the NRI community and show-casing the scenic attractions of England and the Continent, Aditya Chopra had used this exotic background, as he put it, simply 'to create the character of a rigid father',[33] that is, someone whose patriarchal 'rigidity' in the context of a romantic drama is given plausibility by his situational alienation from his roots:

[31] The film reportedly celebrated a 100-day run in fourteen of the sixteen centres in the UK, USA and Canada where it was being shown. See 'Des pardes'. *Times of India*, 22/11/1997.

[32] She was referring to the 'unlikely' events (*i*) that a father would arrange his daughter's marriage with an NRI without checking adequately on the boy's character; and (*ii*) that a girl would be allowed to go and live with her fiancé's family *before* actually getting married. Though ethnography suggests that the second is indeed unlikely to happen, it is sadly true that parents over-eager to arrange advantageous matches for their daughters with NRI grooms often fail to make adequate inquiries about the prospective mates. However, as Rosie Thomas has pointed out (1985: 128), viewers' criteria of verisimilitude 'refer primarily to a film's skill in manipulating the rules of the film's moral universe. Thus one is more likely to hear accusations of "unbelievability" if the codes of, for example, ideal kinship are ineptly transgressed . . . than if a hero is a superman who single-handedly knocks out a dozen burly henchman and then bursts into song.'

[33] Typically, the mainspring of a Bollywood romance is provided by the factor of parental opposition (e.g., Rangoonwalla 1979: 36, 39), often justified by differences in socio-economic status or by long-term feuding relations between the young couple's families.

> I felt that the character of Amrishji [i.e., played by Amrish Puri] could be shown to be far away from his roots. In a sense he is a displaced person and yet his outlook is very stubborn. Without intending to, I touched upon the issue of the major generation gap that exists between Indian immigrants and their children (Mohamed 1996a).

Pardes, on the contrary, explicitly *problematises* the opposition of India and the West in its narrative structure which unfolds through a series of situations of conflict between characters marked by their different degrees of Indianness. Thus, there is the aptly named heroine, Ganga, a girl so innocent of the larger world that she has never been out of her village. There is the foreign-born and bred Rajiv, who smokes, drinks and womanises, and despises everything about India and Indians. There is the 'Little Master', Arjun, Rajiv's foster-brother, whose roots are still in India and whose dream girl conforms to the ideal picture of the Indian woman (the picturisation of the song, '*Meri mehbooba*', evoking the ambience of 'calendar art'). There is the millionaire Kishori Lal, thirty-five years resident in the States, for whom every visit to India feels like return to the love and security of the mother's lap. A caricature of the nostalgic NRI, his 'long-distance patriotism' (Arvind Das [1997]) is now focussed in his self-deceiving search for an Indian bride for his son Rajiv; he needs Ganga to remove the accumulated toxins of life in America. As a villain (of the comic more than the menacing variety), there is even a *phoney* NRI, Amir Chand, whose claim to the prestigious status of NRI is compromised by the fact that his stint abroad was merely in Sri Lanka.

As will have been evident in the plot summary, there are two major crises in the story-line of *Pardes*, both of which are privileged moments for reflection on the problematics of transnational Indian identity. The first critical point is reached when Rajiv tries to force his fiancé, Ganga, to make love to him. After all, he remonstrates with her, they are going to get married in a few days in any case. And besides, his American friends all have sex with their girl-friends and see nothing wrong in it. Rebuffed by Ganga, who insists that they should wait for the consecration of their relationship through the sacrament of marriage (the 'seven *pheras*'), Rajiv gives voice to his contempt for India as a land of shit, of hypocrisy and of sexual double standards; a land where people mouth sanctimonious platitudes about chastity but where the population goes on increasing anyhow.[34] 'It stinks', he adds for good measure. 'How dare you insult my India!', Ganga screams at him as she sends him flying. A furious Rajiv then forces himself on her until she manages to knock him out and flee.

The second crisis is the film's denouement. Following a bloody fight between Rajiv and Arjun, Rajiv is exposed for his assault on Ganga's chastity as a person morally unworthy to call himself an 'Indian' ('*Hindustani*'): 'Go back to America',

[34] This last statement, a forthright condemnation of Indian sexual hypocrisy, drew massive applause from the 'front-benchers' in cinema halls in Delhi. Seemingly contradictorily, there was also spontaneous applause for Ganga's riposte—perhaps not so much for her indignant verbal defense of national dignity as for her spirited assault on the unattractive Rajiv.

he is told, 'that's where you belong'. For his part, too, Kishori Lal is exposed as someone living a lie, vainly trying to stem the process of Americanisation in his family by marrying his playboy son to an innocent Indian girl. And Arjun is revealed as the true hero, his love for the heroine expressed in, and ennobled by, his exercise of sexual self-restraint. Though his heart registers his love almost independently of his will (the song, '*Yeh dil, diwana*'), he restrains himself from declaring his love, firstly out of loyalty to his foster-father's commission to bring about the marriage of Rajiv and Ganga, and secondly—even when he has the opportunity—because he is a true Indian in his respect for the sacred institution of Indian (Hindu) marriage.

Initially a mediator between Rajiv and Ganga, Arjun's ultimate victory in the love-triangle is testimony to his mediating position between India and the West.[35] He can translate each for the other, and combines in himself the best of both worlds. Though his future will presumably lie in America, he remains emotionally and morally an Indian, as his dedication to building a music school in India in his father's memory and his spontaneous choice of a pure Indian girl as love-object both indicate.

Arjun's true affinity with the motherland contrasts with that of his foster-father. 'In America', Kishori Lal expansively informs his astonished foreign friends as they wonder at the perfection of the Taj Mahal, 'love is give and take. But in India, love means give and give'. But Kishori Lal's Indianness has been irrevocably corrupted by his wealth and power. His arrogant self-deception leads him to believe that he can re-Indianise his spoiled son by marrying him to an Indian girl. The women in his family know better, however. Whether kindly, like the *bua* Krishna, or nasty, like the peevish *caci* (paternal aunt), Neeta, they can see that preserving Indian family values through the challenges of diaspora is ultimately an unsustainable ambition. One can only 'adjust' to this fact as best one can, while enjoying the compensatory material benefits of living in the West. Even the pure Ganga, they warn, will sooner or later have to become one of 'them'.

VII

'American dreams, Indian soul'[36]

The voices of women are not the only interrogative notes that are first registered, and then repressed, as *Pardes* proceeds towards narrative closure, for the film explores not only the problematics of love and sexual desire in the context of diaspora, but the problematic desire for diaspora *in itself.*

On the one hand, in matters big and small, *Pardes* is manifestly an exhibition of Indian patriotism even as it is an affirmation of Indian familism.[37] Released to

[35] On the function of the characteristically 'mediating' role of the hero/heroine figure of popular Hindi films, see Thomas 1996.

[36] From the publicity posters for Subhash Ghai's *Pardes* (1997).

[37] It was presumably owing to this combination of virtues that the film was exempted from entertainment tax in some circuits.

coincide with the celebration of fifty years of Indian Independence, it begins and ends with the banner tribute, 'Long Live India: Celebrating 50 Years of Independence'; it prominently displays the tricolour logo of the anniversary celebrations; it even, rather implausibly, endorses the national carrier, Air India!

The mood is captured in one of the film's most popular songs, 'I love India'[38]:

I've seen London,
I've seen Paris,
I've seen Japan.
I've seen Michael,
I've seen Elvis,
I've seen them all, beloved.
But in the whole universe, there's none like Hindustan.
In this world
India is like the jewel on the forehead of the bride. . . .
I love my India,
I love my India.

The song is initially sung, very early on in the film, by Kishori Lal, remonstrating with the America-worshipping children of Suraj Dev's family. Its background (of mountains, rivers, palaces, forts, Hardwar and Rishikesh, an idol of Lord Krishna, verdant fields, a beautiful young girl ripe for love, cute children, a large happy family bursting with patriotic joy) recalls national television's promotional imagery of India as both a charming tourist destination and as the embodiment of patriotic sentiments transcending regional and communal differences. But the familiar sights and nostalgic sentiments of 'I love India' are subverted by the seductive visual splendour of America that unfolds in the second half of the film. As Ganga looks down in awe at the lights of New York, we hear in the background the exultant beat of a pop-song, 'My first day in the USA' (sung in English by Hema Sardesai), which tells a different story and indexes a different desire: the new immigrant's desire for freedom, for opportunity, for the living out of fantasies—in AMERICA:

On my way to a new place
A whole new world and new ways.
So many questions on my mind
I'll find answers here though every time.
America, America.

[38] This song is often compared both to pop-star Alisha's saucy Music Video, 'Made in India', and also to the famous song in Raj Kapoor's *Shri 420* (The Gentleman Cheat, 1955), whose chorus line goes:

These shoes are made in Japan.
My trousers are fashioned in England.
The red cap on my head is Russian.
But my heart is 'Hindustani'.

See also Chakravarti 1996: 203–204.

There's a fascination of things to come
And no doubt now can be done.
I feel a sense of freedom up above
I know this is where I'll find love.
America, America.

I'm finally here in America
It's where I want to be.
I'm finally here, with my fantasies
This is where I'll find my destiny.
Destiny, destiny.
. . . .

Improbably, as though to neutralise the seductive spell of America, this triumphant paean to the promised land is framed at either end by a chanted invocation to the Hindu trinity, Brahma–Vishnu–Shiva (an extraordinary instancing of musical fusion in the age of globalisation), and followed shortly afterwards by Ganga's rendering of 'I love India' for an Indian embassy function. But the splendour of *Pardes*'s visual imagery of America ensures that the truth of America as the land of desire and the desired land cannot be entirely suppressed.

In sum, the narrative structure of *Pardes* is semiotically dependent on the contradiction of India and West, a contradiction which is resolved through the agency of a hero who embodies the best of both worlds and exemplifies the possibility, howsoever utopian, of the retention of Indianness in diaspora. But other voices—and they are, once again, *women*'s voices—warn that such a solution is unrealistic, unstable, and ultimately unsustainable into the next generation, notwithstanding the hero's marriage to a heroine who is Indian to the core. These voices, contrariwise, foretell the depletion and alienation that must inevitably attend the process of dislocation; or else, even more subversively, they celebrate without inhibition the liberation of fantasies come true—in America. . . .

VIII
Indian dream, transnational location

In this essay, I have pointed to both similarities and differences between *DDLJ* and *Pardes* as two contemporary popular films that link the institutions of family, courtship and marriage to the articulation of Indian identity in the context of diaspora. It remains now to detail these continuities and discontinuities and to comment on their wider sociological import.

In the first place, it will have been obvious that there are many points of superficial and substantive resemblance between *DDLJ* and *Pardes*, confirming popular opinion in this regard. Apart from the commonality of two principal actors (Shah Rukh Khan and Amrish Puri), and the use of foreign locales, there is the shared focus on the NRI nostalgia for India, the return to India for the denouement, the emphasis on family values as the core of Indianness, the attempt to discipline the younger generation by marriage with Indian partners, the voyeuristic preoccupation with feminine virtue in general and virginity in particular, the role of women characters in critiquing patriarchal authority, and so on. There is even a bizarre coincidence which a committed structuralist would recognise as a perfect example of symbolic inversion: the fake love-bites that index Simran's fantasised but chaste desire for Raj in *DDLJ*, and the brutal teeth marks of Rajiv's real assault on Ganga in *Pardes*!

More importantly, as 'formula' romances set in an *Indian* culture of kinship, the romantic happy ending in both *DDLJ* and *Pardes* requires the reconciliation of paternal authority and individual desire. In either case, the objective is achieved not by the young couple's *defiance* of the normative order of Indian kinship, but by their demonstration of *adherence* to this order. In particular, the hero is required to exercise self-restraint in two crucial respects. First, he should not contest paternal authority, but should concede its rightfulness even at the cost of forfeiting the object of his desire. Second, he must not allow himself to 'sexualise' the love relationship[39] in advance of its sacramental consecration, an act of self-denial that incidentally enables the heroine to maintain her purity as an object worthy of bestowal. On her part, similarly, the heroine is required to submit to an arrangement that is man-to-man and family-to-family before it is the consummation of her own desires. Interestingly, in both films, women (especially older women) and children are able to recognise and articulate the injustice of 'tradition' and the constrictiveness of 'society' from the woman's point of view, though such misgivings are discounted in the final resolution.[40]

Taken together, these common features can be read as pointers to a shared ideology of family and kinship which has three important and characteristic constituents. The first, albeit relatively muted in this case (as compared, e.g., to *HAHK* [cf. Uberoi n.d. (a)]), is the idealisation and naturalisation of the institution of the *patrilineal joint family*. Thus, for instance, both films assume that the pattern of recruitment to household membership will automatically follow the principle of patrivirilocal residence. That is how the senior Malhotra in *DDLJ* and Kishori Lal in *Pardes* both return to India to 'fetch' their sons' wives, and stand around to supervise at the melodramatic denouements.

Secondly, and relatedly, the family is construed as a *patriarchal* institution,[41] the father having the authority and responsibility to arrange his children's marriages, or to endorse or reject the choices they have independently made. For the father of a daughter, this authority is scripted as the right and duty to *gift* his daughter in

[39] The useful term from Veena Das (n.d.).

[40] Some critics might like to connect this acknowledgement of women's subjectivity with the history and characteristics of 'melodrama' as a genre (see, e.g., Prasad 1998).

[41] The term 'patriarchal', despite its importance and ubiquity in feminist discourse, is a troublesome one, for reasons I have discussed in another context (see Uberoi 1995a). Here I use the term in its originary and literal sense, pertaining to the authority of the male head of family over *both* females *and* junior males.

marriage, and on the purity of this gift and the solemnity of his pledge is staked his personal honour as a patriarch (see Prabhu 1995: ch. 5). When this honour is compromised, he can be expected to take drastic action—to insist on the girl's marriage to the person of his choice . . . ., '*or else*' (as in *DDLJ*); or to attempt to kill her and her suspected lover to assuage family honour (as in *Pardes*).

Thirdly, there is the principle of marriage as alliance—family to family—rather than just an arrangement between a young couple in love. For those unfamiliar with the wider Indian culture of Indian kinship, *Pardes* would seem to have a rather curious ending—for a *love* story. Here we do not find the young couple embracing each other, or even uniting with each other with parental blessings. On the contrary, the final scene shows father and (foster-) son on the one hand, and father and daughter on the other, embracing. The happy young couple merely eye each other over the respective shoulders of their fathers as the tricolour tribute to fifty years of Indian Independence comes on to the screen. This reconciliation of parents and children, of the conflict of parental authority and youthful desire, allows the two fathers to reaffirm their troth as affines. Indeed, at this moment Kishori Lal reminds his *samdhi*-to-be that they had simply pledged to transfer Ganga from the home of Suraj Dev to that of Kishori Lal. In the final dispensation, this troth would remain intact, with only the minor difference that Ganga would marry another—and more worthy because more 'Indian'—son![42]

In both *DDLJ* and *Pardes*, all three elementary principles of the Indian culture of kinship (i.e., the institution of the joint family; the patriarchal authority to dispose; and marriage as interfamily alliance) are challenged in the context of diaspora—and finally reaffirmed. In both films, the heroes refuse to elope with the heroines, but chastely await paternal blessing. This not only indexes their Indianness, but also facilitates the bride's eventual patrilocal incorporation into her husband's household. It endorses the parents' authority to arrange the marriages of their wards. And it confirms that marriage is foremostly an arrangement family to family *via* the gifting of a daughter. Women realise that they are thereby the objects of these transactions between men, that the system denies them their subjectivity; but they know that they can only 'adjust' to it all and hope for a happy outcome.

However, while *DDLJ* and *Pardes* are both agreed in their constitution of the moral economy of Indian family relations, with just a hint of dissatisfaction from the viewpoint of women, the two films are at variance on the question of whether or not Indian identity can survive deterritorialisation. *DDLJ* proposes that Indian family values are portable assets, which may be replenished through periodic visits to the source. But *Pardes*'s answer is ambiguous. Reinstituting the well-tried opposition of India and the West, it at one level endorses the hope that Indian culture can survive deterritorialisation, while at another level it suggests that westernisation/Americanisation can at best be delayed. For while the hero,

[42] Note the similar solution to a conflict between desire and social obligation in *HAHK*: the young woman simply marries *another* brother—without, that is, disturbing the original affinal contract (see Uberoi n.d. [a]).

Arjun, is able to combine in himself the best of India and the West, this is not the case with Kishori Lal, thirty-five years resident in the US, and his American-born son, Rajiv. Insistently, women's voices foretell the depletion that must eventually overtake the long-term immigrant, though he may sing ever so robustly to the tune of 'I love India'.

It may appear from the organisation of this essay and from my taking *DDLJ* as my point of departure, that I regard *DDLJ* as registering an epistemic break with certain established representational idioms of Indian popular cinema, and *Pardes*, conversely, as a retreat from that position. To some extent I do, but whether the one or the other represents a definitive 'trend' of the 1990s is still premature to say. For the moment I would simply propose that, *read together*, the two films register an important site of ideological transformation and contestation as populár culture comes to terms with the new reality of middle-class diaspora and its challenges to national identity—for those at home, for many of whom the West is now the desired destination, as well as for those in '*pardes*', nostalgically recalling the imagined homeland.

The consistently conservative agenda for the Indian family that the two films share—almost a parodic instantiation of the normative order of Indian kinship—is not merely an independent phenomenon in the realm of kinship, expressing the complacency and cynicism of the post-Independence generation for whom political idealism and the compulsion to defy family pressures and societal conventions no longer hold much attraction. Nor is it merely an index of the self-indulgent mood of the '90s, which sees no need to choose between 'arranged' and 'love' marriage, the traditional and the modern, the Indian and the Western, when one can enjoy the social and material benefits of an 'arranged love marriage'. Metonymically linked in the cinematic narrative of both *DDLJ* and *Pardes*, this conservative construction of family values is also a reflection of the anxieties regarding national identity that have been provoked by the Indian middle-class diaspora of the last two or three decades.

The new social contract that Indian Independence brought into being a half-century ago has now to be renegotiated in a globalised environment.

REFERENCES

AGRAWAL, ANUJA. 1998. Addressing the male psyche: Some observations on the representations of prostitution in a Hindi popular magazine. *Thamyris: Mythmaking from past to present* 5, 1: 59–78.

ALTER, JOSEPH S. 1997. Seminal truth: A modern science of male celibacy in north India. *Medical anthropology quarterly* 11, 3: 275–98.

APPADURAI, ARJUN. 1997 [1996]. *Modernity at large: Cultural dimensions of globalization.* Delhi: Oxford University Press.

BERGER, MORROE. 1977. *Real and imagined worlds: The novel and social science.* Cambridge, Mass.: Harvard University Press.

BHARAT, SHALINI and MURLI DESAI, compilers. 1995. *Indian bibliographies on the family.* Mumbai: Tata Institute of Social Sciences.

BHARUCHA, R. 1995. Utopia in Bollywood: 'Hum aapke hain koun...!' *Economic and political weekly* 30, 15: 801–804.

BHATTACHARJEE, ANANNYA. 1992. The habit of ex-nomination: Nation, women and the Indian immigrant bourgeoisie. *Public culture* 5, 1: 19–43.

CHAKRAVARTY, SUMITA S. 1996 [1993]. *National identity in Indian popular cinema, 1947–1987.* Delhi: Oxford University Press.

CHATTERJEE, SAIBAL. 1996. Back to the movies. *Outlook*, 17 January 1996: 58–63.

DAS, ARVIND. 1997. India's expanding universe. *Pioneer*, 27 September 1997.

DAS, VEENA. n.d. Sexual violence, discursive formations and the state. Paper presented at the seminar on 'Violence, political agency and the construction of the self', Rajiv Gandhi Institute for Contemporary Studies, New Delhi, and SSRC, New York, 1995.

DICKEY, SARA. 1993. *Cinema and the urban poor in south India.* Cambridge: Cambridge University Press.

———. 1996 [1995]. Consuming utopia: Film watching in Tamil Nadu. *In* Carol A. Breckenridge, ed., *Consuming modernity: Public culture in contemporary India*, pp. 131–56. Delhi: Oxford University Press.

DORAISWAMY, RASHMI. 1996. The home and the world. Images of self-perception. *India International Centre quarterly: Signs of our times.* Summer: 123–29.

DUMONT, LOUIS. 1983. *Affinity as a value: Marriage alliance in south India, with comparative essays on Australia.* Chicago: University of Chicago Press.

GULATI, LEELA. 1993. *In the absence of their men: The impact of male migration on women.* New Delhi: Sage Publications.

GUPTA, DIPANKAR. 1996. Ritualism and fantasy in Hindi cinema. *Times of India*, 28 August 1996.

JAIN, RAVINDRA K. 1998. Indian diaspora, globalisation and multiculturalism: A cultural analysis (this volume).

KAKAR, SUDHIR. 1981. The ties that bind: Family relationships in the mythology of Hindi cinema. *India International Centre quarterly* 8, 1: 11–21.

———. 1989. *Intimate relations: Exploring Indian sexuality.* New York: Penguin.

MADAN, T.N. 1987. *Non-renunciation: Themes and interpretations of Hindu culture.* Delhi: Oxford University Press.

MOHAMED, KHALID. 1996a. Best director, best screenplay, best dialogue: Aditya Chopra. *Filmfare* 43, 4, April 1996.

———. 1996b. Dilwale London le jayenge. *Times of India, Sunday Review*, 16 June 1996.

NADARAJAH, M. n.d. Diaspora and nostalgia: Towards a semiotic theory of the Indian diaspora. (Unpublished m.s.)

NANDY, ASHIS. 1995. An intelligent critic's guide to Indian cinema. *In* Ashis Nandy, *The savage Freud and other essays on possible and retrievable selves*, pp. 196–236. Delhi: Oxford University Press.

NAVEED-I-RAHAT. 1990. *Male outmigration and matri-weighted households: A case study of a Punjabi village in Pakistan.* Delhi: Hindustan Publishing Corporation.

PRABHU, PANDHARINATH H. 1995 [1954]. *Hindu social organization: A study in socio-psychological and ideological foundations* (2nd edn). Bombay: Popular Prakashan.

PRASAD, M. MADHAVA. 1998. *Ideology of the Hindi film: A historical construction.* Delhi: Oxford University Press.

RAJADHYAKSHA, ASHISH and PAUL WILLEMEN. 1995. *Encyclopaedia of Indian cinema.* Delhi: Oxford University Press.

RANGOONWALLA, FIROZE. 1979. *A pictorial history of Indian cinema.* London: Hamlyn.

RAYAPROL, APARNA. 1997. *Negotiating identities: Women in the Indian diaspora.* Delhi: Oxford University Press.

SHAH, A.M. 1998. *The family in India: Critical essays.* New Delhi: Orient Longman.

SINGH, AMITA TYAGI and PATRICIA UBEROI. 1994. Learning to 'adjust': Conjugal relations in Indian popular fiction. *Indian journal of gender studies* 1, 1: 93–120.

THOMAS, ROSIE. 1985. Indian cinema: Pleasures and popularity. *Screen* 26, 3 & 4: 116–31.

THOMAS, ROSIE. 1996 [1995]. Melodrama and the negotiation of morality in mainstream Hindi film. *In* Carol A. Breckenridge, ed., *Consuming modernity: Public culture in contemporary India*, pp. 157–82. Delhi: Oxford University Press.

UBEROI, PATRICIA. 1995a. Problems with patriarchy: Conceptual issues in anthropology and feminism. *Sociological bulletin* 44, 2: 195–222.

———. 1995b. Body, state and cosmos: Mao Zedong's 'Study of physical education' (1917). *China report* 31, 1: 109–33.

———. 1996a. The family in official discourse. *India International Centre quarterly: Second nature: Women and the family.* Winter: 134–55.

———. 1996b. Problematising social reform, engaging sexuality, interrogating the state. *In* Patricia Uberoi, ed., *Social reform, sexuality and the state*, pp. ix–xxvi. New Delhi: Sage Publications.

———. 1996c. Hindu marriage law and the judicial construction of sexuality. *In* Ratna Kapur, ed., *Feminist terrains in legal domains: Interdisciplinary essays on women and law in India*, pp. 184–209. New Delhi: Kali for Women.

———. 1997. Dharma and desire, freedom and destiny: Rescripting the man–woman relationship in popular Hindi cinema. *In* Meenakshi Thapan, ed., *Embodiment: Essays in gender and identity*, pp. 147–73. Delhi: Oxford University Press.

———. n.d. (a). Imagining the family: An ethnography of viewing '*Hum aapke hain koun. . . .!*'. *In* Rachel Dwyer and Chris Pinney, eds, *Pleasure and the nation: The history and politics of popular culture in India* (forthcoming).

———. n.d. (b). A suitable romance? Trajectories of courtship in Indian popular fiction. Paper presented at the Seminar on 'Images of women in media', IIAS, Leiden, November 1995.

VASUDEVAN, RAVI S. 1995. 'You cannot live in society—and ignore it': Nationhood and female modernity in *Andaz*. *Contributions to Indian sociology* 29, 1 & 2: 83–108.

9

Indian diaspora, globalisation and multiculturalism: A cultural analysis

Ravindra K. Jain

The paper focuses on Indian diaspora as a case study of globalisation and multiculturalism. It raises the question of a structural and historical distinction between the socio-cultural pluralism of societies like India and the ones overseas where Indian populations migrated and settled, and answers it in terms of dialectically related civilisations and settlement societies. A cultural analysis, using the comparative and theoretical approach of socio-cultural anthropology, leads to the positing of a 'field of forces' paradigm to orientate and position empirical instances of Indian diaspora globally. Three major issues affecting the overseas Indian communities are explored, namely, difference and translation, hybridity and creolisation, and policies of multiculturalism. The conclusion underscores factors such as the locationality of the analyst, the general pacifist orientation of diaspora communities and slippage between the imaginary and the imagined in relation to India that characterise Indian diaspora and influence its sociological study.

I
Introduction

This paper looks at the facts of Indian diaspora globally and raises certain theoretical issues entailed by the comparison of particular cases . In what follows, I shall skirt around issues of the nation, of activism and even of identities. My reason for not dealing centrally with the nation is that this aspect is considered in detail in other specialised writings. Activism of the kind advocated by the anti-racist movement, the human rights movement, the minority discourse movement, the 'new' left or right movements, etc., has not been part of my own experience. Finally, the question of identities, though germane to any discussion about multiculturalism and globalisation, has been treated either too loosely in the extant literature or entails complex expertise in social psychological/psychoanalytical theories which in my present discourse I can only touch upon.

Paradoxically enough, while I do not deal with the question of the nation and nationality in this paper, this issue forms the starting point of my discussion. Very recently, Partha Chatterjee (1997: 30–34) has suggested 'civil society–modernity' versus 'political society–democracy' as the overall framework for examining the debate about 'beyond the nation or within' India. Chatterjee veers basically towards a nationalist rather than a 'beyond the nation' point of view for Indian socio-political development. Methodologically, the point of both departure and arrival in this debate is the nation-state. The three points with which Chatterjee begins are highly relevant for tracing the contemporary cartographies of globalisation: (*a*) the greater disciplinary powers of the nation-state; (*b*) the dissociation of collective social movements and identities from territory; and (*c*) the erosion of the relations between spatial and virtual neighbourhoods through the powers of the electronic media. These, according to Chatterjee, are the three major precipitating causes for putting a question mark against the hegemony of the nation-state in the era of globalisation. As I shall try to show later in this paper in my 'field of forces' paradigm, these causes have culminated in the 'deterritorialisation' thesis of Arjun Appadurai (1990) and others.

If a cultural rather than a nation-state framework is kept in mind, however, the fact of diaspora assumes analytical significance. We shall take that as our point of departure and further confine our discussion largely to the Indian diaspora as a case study of globalisation. At the outset, a few words should be said about the way that the notion of culture is being deployed in this paper. We take a continuous rather than a discontinuous or 'billiard ball' view of culture, assuming the permeability of culture and shifting the emphasis from cultural persistence to multiculturalism as an aspect of cultural flux and dynamics. (For the notion of interweaving of cultures, see Lechte and Bottomley 1993: 22–37.) This is quite apart from this concept (multiculturalism) being a policy imperative (which I discuss later). However, boundaries are drawn and redrawn across space and time around particular cultures wherever 'difference' between cultures is emphasised in the everyday life of communities in all countries. Defining the 'difference' is at the heart of the problematique of diasporic culture in the era of globalisation. The view of culture as continuous and permeable does not mean the abandonment of emphasis on the reinforcing and reproductive aspects of culture. Another way of expressing this would be to say that an 'essentialist core' of culture is thereby retained amidst all the flux and change, or to put it in Fredrik Barth's words, 'central and culturally valued institutions and activities in an ethnic group may be deeply involved in its boundary maintenance by setting internal processes of convergence into motion. . . .' (Barth 1994: 18).

II

The study of Indian diaspora

Indian diaspora can be seen in three sequential phases in global historical terms. Firstly, the ancient and mediaeval Indian monarchs and traders, from the east and west coasts of India, tried to reach out and established contacts with the Middle East, eastern and northern Africa and with Southeast Asia. The expansion during the ancient period has given rise to the historical imaginary called 'Greater India' which was a staple of our post-independence history books as school children in

India, and an appellation we hastily dropped after encounter as adults with the new nationalistic countries of Southeast Asia. The mediaeval period of Indian diaspora was mainly connected with trade. This phase has been very well documented historically, but the anthropologist would find more meat and a more sensitive delineation in novels like *In an antique land* by Amitav Ghosh and Salman Rushdie's *The Moor's last sigh*. In these fictional works, the magic of hybridisation that cast a spell over mediaeval Indian diaspora is brilliantly evoked. The second period belongs to the 19th century emigration, often based on forced recruitment or deceit, of the labouring population to plantation territories of the colonial world. This emigration from India also included traders and white-collar workers to the British, Dutch and French colonies. The scholarly depiction of this phase of the Indian diaspora is redolent with the deafening music of colonialism. In fact, as we shall see, it has been argued with some plausibility that the third phase of Indian diaspora, the emigration from India in the present century to industrially developed and oil-rich countries of the west, forms an organic linkage with the colonial diaspora. It seems reasonable to point out this connection now, because in what follows we shall be concerned mainly with putting the contemporary Indian diaspora in a post-colonial context.

Needless to say, there are diverse angles from which to view the Indian diaspora. The one angle that has attracted the attention of the general public in India itself is concerned with the investment capacity of the NRIs (Non-Resident Indians) in the wake of liberalisation and the structural changes in the Indian economy ushered in since 1991. It has been pointed out that, compared to the overseas Chinese investments in mainland China, the overseas Indians are five times behind in their investments in India. Observations such as these have led to the economists' interest in migration, remittances and capital flows (Nayyar 1994). Similarly, in a rare positive evaluation of ethnicity, NRIs settled in the USA have been viewed as entrepreneurs, and their entrepreneurial gifts compared with the similar gifts of the Chinese, the Japanese and the Jews in the United States (Kotkin 1993). In the transnational framework, the economists are viewing the Indian exodus to the affluent countries of the west as 'brain-banks' rather than 'brain-drain'.

An academically influential and forcefully articulated point of view on the Indian diaspora emanates from the writings of literary critics and creative writers belonging to the Indian diaspora, for instance, Salman Rushdie and V.S. Naipaul. Let me cite the views of Tejaswini Niranjana, because her statement is as representative as any of the literary genre, although she herself does not belong to the diaspora:

> At a time when both in India and in many overseas communities the stakes in defining oneself as 'Indian' are being re-examined, at a time when the terrain of identity has become a crucial location for engaging in cultural politics, it seems increasingly important to analyse the many complex ways in which different groups of people claim 'Indianness' and the different kinds of significance attached to this claim. For this kind of analysis, I would argue, the construction of 'Indian' identities in Trinidad, Guyana, Surinam, Fiji, Mauritius, Tanzania

> or South Africa (or even, to mention a different kind of a context, in the Gulf countries, for example) is as relevant as the NRI identities being shaped in the metropolitan, post-colonial diaspora. An interesting problem that remains by and large untheorised is the one about what slippages occur, and what their significance is, when a notion like 'Indian culture', shaped within the social imaginary in India, is deployed in a context where 'Indians' are not culturally hegemonic (Niranjana 1994: 3–4).

A couple of comments on this perspective on the Indian diaspora may be made here. Firstly, though the question of identity is inescapable and recurs in many contexts, it is a question better dealt with outside our present universe of discourse by the discipline of social psychology. Secondly, not only the Indian diasporics in metropolitan countries, but even those of the 19th century diasporas, are part of a larger politico-economic framework that shows a great deal of continuity from the colonial to the post-colonial period. The kind of distinction which Niranjana makes between the NRIs and what have sometimes been called the People of Indian Origin (PIOs; cf. Motwani 1993: 3) is not tenable since both these diasporic streams are caught up in the same contemporary currents of post-coloniality, globalisation and transnationality.

Demographers have shed light on some of the basic parameters of Indian diaspora: the numbers involved, fertility rates (Muthiah and Jones 1983), the role of linguistic and religious variables in the immigrant population, marital trends, etc. The quantum of South Asian diaspora globally is evident from the fact that about 8.6 million South Asians live outside Pakistan, India, Bangladesh, Nepal and Sri Lanka. The largest population of overseas Indians is in UK, followed by Malaysia and South Africa. In countries like Guyana, Surinam, Trinidad & Tobago, Mauritius and Fiji, Indians constitute nearly half of the total population (Clarke et al. 1991).

Some of the demographic data on migrants in Australia (as a case in point) suggest sociologically interesting issues for Asian, as also the South Asian, diaspora to industrially advanced countries (Report 1995). In 1991 nearly 7 million Australians or 42 per cent of the population were born overseas or had one or both parents born overseas. The Asia born constituted 4.6 per cent of the total population (British and Irish born 7 per cent; European born 6.5 per cent; Middle East born 1.2 per cent). The percentage of Asians in the population as a whole (including local born) had increased to 7.4 per cent by mid-1995. Up to two-thirds of all second-generation migrants were marrying outside their ethnic group, so that by the year 2000, 40 per cent of the Australian population will be ethnically mixed. These projections certainly include South Asians, though the exact quantum of South Asian ethnics in this melting pot (the Australian population being characterised as consisting of 'melts rather than Celts' as someone put it) is not easily ascertained. However, the general point of interest here is that the so-called 'untranslatability' of Indian culture abroad (cf. Niranajana 1994) is a very relative matter, subject to the history and socio-economic background of the migrants and the policies of the host society. Again, building on the demographic profile of the South Asian population, it is interesting to note that Hindi-speakers and Hindus predominate among Fiji Indian migrants to Australia (the so-called 'twice migrants'), rather than among immigrants from India. Another issue that merits investigation is the manner in which the Hindu religious category cuts across nationality of birth (Malaysian, Sri Lankan, Fijian, Indian). A sub-set of the above: what is the interaction and complex of attitudes among and between Tamilian Hindus from Malaysia, Sri Lanka, India and Fiji? This comes as close as one could wish to being an experimental situation for a comparative study of Tamil nationalism. Similarly, it would be sociologically rewarding to study the implications and consequences of the fact that Anglo-Indians from India and Ceylon Burghers from Sri Lanka were permitted to enter Australia earlier than the bulk of other South Asians. How are they placed—status-wise and in terms of ethnic distance—relative to other Indians and Sri Lankans, as well as to the white society?

Coming to another viewpoint, that of the geographers, the spatial provenance of the Indian diaspora is seen as divided into six zones: Africa and Mauritius, West and Southeast Asia, the Pacific, the Caribbean, North America, and Europe. Perhaps in a more eco-geopolitical sense, the Indian Ocean zone and the Asia–Pacific zone have been delineated. One of the earliest comparative surveys by an anthropologist of Indian communities abroad was an article published by the late Chandra Jayawardena in the *Geographical review* (Jayawardena 1968: 426–49). From geopolitics to politics and international relations would seem to be a logical and easy step. The questions of cultural minorities, ethnic movements and their interface with nationality and national movements, the role of the nation-state in transnational ethnicity and the deterritorialisation thesis in the context of global non-governmental organisations, etc. have been at the forefront of contemporary social science thinking. And for those who still see some value in making a nuanced distinction between social anthropology and sociology, the latter discipline subsumes discussions of the Indian diaspora under the rubrics of race relations, plural society and multiculturalism. We shall return to some of these concerns shortly.

Anthropological concerns today typically cut across and challenge disciplinary boundaries such as those presented above. Sample, for instance, the discussion of ethnicity and the nation-state linkage in a recent anthropology text on ethnicity (Vermeulen and Govers 1994). Contra Weber, who was inclined to put the rise of ethnicity and the nation-state in an evolutionary order, the anthropologist Verdery (one of the contributors to the volume) says: 'It is not from ethnic identities that national identities develop; rather the latter creates the frame that generates the former—the frame within which ethnicity qua difference, in its broadest sense, acquires social significance' (ibid.: 47). This process of ethnicity emerging from nation-building finds its extreme in the present 'transnational' world in which people bearing preconstituted national identities migrate elsewhere and 'become' ethnic groups whose home nations remain durable in their self-conception and political behaviour. Benedict Anderson calls this the 'ethnicization of existing nationalities' practising 'long distance nationalism'. Some 'purist' politicians have advocated the applying of what they call the 'cricket test', namely, which international team do the immigrant ethnics support? On the final day of a cricket test match between the West Indies and Pakistan in Port-of-Spain, Trinidad & Tobago, the Pakistani victory was celebrated by Indian Trinidadians by waving the Indian tri-colour flag in jubilation. Ethnicity has cut across nationality in a double manner: not only were the Indian Trinidadians (West Indians by nationality) cheering the Pakistani team but it did not matter that the flag they were waving was not the Pakistan national flag (green with the crescent moon and the star) but the Indian one (tri-colour with a wheel in the middle)!

There now exists also a fairly coherent tradition of primarily anthropological studies dealing with the Indian diaspora (Jain 1993: 52–57). Without pretending to review the literature as a whole, let me take up three studies, one each for the decades of the 1960s, 1970s and the 1980s. The first study I have in mind is Morton Klass's monograph, '*East Indians in Trinidad: A study in cultural persistence*' (1961). This is a community study, emphasising (as its subtitle indicates) the continuities in the cultural patterns and institutional structures of the second- and third-generation population of East Indians in the village Felicity of central Trinidad, with the culture and social structure of eastern India (states of eastern Uttar Pradesh and western Bihar) whence their progenitors came. The macro-framework for this study is provided not by a detailed look at the formation of the particular community in historical terms, but through a sketch of the history of East Indian migration to Trinidad. Institutional areas of East Indian life, such as family and kinship, caste and religion, are viewed in terms of cultural persistence. As has been observed in later studies of the Indian diaspora, the approach of the 1960s failed to connect the Indian community's adaptation with the wider socio-economic and political dynamics of the host society.

An approach of the 1970s period may be illustrated with reference to my own monograph (Jain 1970) on the Tamilian rubber estate workers of South Indian origin on a plantation called 'Pal Melayu' (a pseudonym) on the west coast of Malaysia (then The Federation of Malaya). This was conceived as a study of socio-cultural adaptation. However, the theoretical framework belonged to the structural-functional paradigm, tempered with the situational approach for the study of ongoing social processes exemplified in the studies of the so-called Manchester School of social anthropology. In this book, I sought to study the adaptational social processes on Pal Melayu in terms of an interaction, over time, between analytically separable 'industrial' (i.e., 'on work') and 'community' (i.e., 'off-work') sub-systems of social relationships in a 'total institution' (Goffman). The macro-structure was delineated both in terms of the historical formation of the community in question and a notion of the changing plural society of Malaya.

A good example of the study of the 1980s is the monograph *London Patidars: A case study in urban ethnicity* (Tambs-Lyche 1980). Here a structural-functional closure of the sort attempted in the community studies mentioned above was not possible because of the different range, magnitude and variations in the diasporic population. Set firmly in the empirical tradition of Fredrik Barth's transactional analysis, this monograph chooses to adopt a theoretical (nomothetic) rather than an historical (ideographic) framework. The emphasis throughout is on the choices which London Patidars make within the homogeneous value-set which, as a caste, they adopt in their adaptations to life and opportunities in London. Tambs-Lyche is helped in delineating a consistent framework of analysis by the emic fact of the Patidars behaving as a caste with a homogeneous value-set. However, within the terms of these constraining factors, his adoption of the games theory framework enables him to delineate effectively the contours of an encompassing/encompassed niche for these entrepreneurial diasporics from Gujarat in the city of London. The macro-structure, too, is handled within the framework of a transactional theory. Tambs-Lyche makes the important point that, seen from a local perspective, immigrants form an 'encompassed society' within the wider British society. Seen, however, in terms of their international kin and friendship networks, Britain is the encompassed society. Their assessment of it as an environment to be 'exploited' depends on the range of economic opportunities available to them in different countries. From this point of view the London Patidar study should also be treated as a forerunner of studies of 'twice' or 'thrice' migrants in the Indian diaspora.

A comment may be added here on the approach to ethnicity in Tambs-Lyche's work and beyond. Following the lead of Barth and associates, ethnicity is defined as the social organisation of culture difference. Barth has recently written (Barth 1994) that his concept of culture, right from the time of the publication of *Ethnic groups and boundaries* (1969), would appear to have been a postmodernist one, for he had consistently characterised culture as continuous rather than discontinuous, wrought by variation and flux, and contested rather than homogeneous. Finally, though culture was seen mainly as a boundary-making mechanism, its content was not altogether unimportant. Such a statement of the relationship between ethnicity and culture will be a subject of our synthesis in what follows.

III

Indian and diasporic pluralism: Civilisations and settlement societies

In order to pose a basic question regarding Indian diaspora and multiculturalism, I may mention briefly some of my other researches subsequent to the Malaysian study. In the early 1970s I undertook a field study of status and power structure in the eastern Bundelkhand region of northern Madhya Pradesh in central India. This research was closely related to my job as Lecturer in Indian Sociology at the University of Oxford. From 1984 to 1987 in Trinidad & Tobago, and during 1993–94 in Durban, South Africa, I found the opportunity to resume research on the Indian diaspora. It was the juxtaposition of the Indian and overseas Indian researches which led me personally to ask the comparative question as to the similarities and, more particularly, the differences between socio-cultural 'pluralism' in India and in the countries where Indian immigrants had settled. As a preliminary step, I published a paper delineating a broad contrast between civilisations and settlement societies (Jain 1994: 1–14). In what follows, I shall spell out the building-blocks of the more elaborated framework for comparison and dialectical interaction between civilisations and settlement societies, but let me first say a few words about this initial contrast.

I shall speak of civilisations a little later, with India as my focussed example (cf. Cohn 1971), but the starting-point in my notion of settlement societies comes from J.S. Furnivall's celebrated discussion of the plural society in Burma and the Dutch East Indies (Furnivall 1948). In his terms, a plural society exists when a country under colonial rule shows the following broad cultural, economic and political characteristics: (*a*) Culturally, it comprises groups which are institutionally disparate and do not share the same basic values and way of life; (*b*) Economically, these separate social entities have interaction mainly in the marketplace, in buying-and-selling types of relationships; (*c*) Politically, these disparate but economically interacting segments are held together by a superordinate authority—that is, the colonial rulers. To paraphrase Furnivall broadly, these plural societies do not have a common social 'will'. The segments may mix (as in the marketplace) but they do not blend.

I build the concept of settlement societies basically after Furnivall's characterisation, augmented by the theorists of plantations in the New World who have contrasted plantation societies, as 'settlement institutions', with rural societies (E.T. Thompson 1959). Settlement society is a polythetic category in the sense that not all instances of such societies have every characteristic which can be conceived as belonging to this type. In other words, in actual instances, there may be some characteristics present in one case but not in another. Among the characteristics of settlement societies are: (*a*) a short history (basically post–1492) marked by recent massive immigration; (*b*) presence of native populations, variable in numbers; (*c*) colonialism or dependent status of one kind or another; (*d*) a correlation between the economy and ethnic relations in such a way that if the economy is buoyant, interethnic relations are better, and vice versa; (*e*) the settlement society is also a geopolitical entity in the sense that in the New World, for instance, Mexico and Latin America can be contrasted with the Caribbean, the USA and Canada. The former provide examples of civilisations, and the latter of settlement societies. In the Old World, India, China, much of Europe and parts of Africa can be contrasted with island societies, the former being seats of civilisation while the latter are settlement societies.

In regard to our notion of civilisations, we should like to make a clarification at the outset. Since our take-off point in a civilisational theory of Indian diaspora (Jain 1997) is the Indian or Indic civilisation, the generalisations attempted here apply, in the first instance, to what Louis Dumont has called the 'non-modern civilisations' (Dumont 1975). European civilisations in much of their pre-Renaissance history are part of that conceptualisation. For us the proposed dialogue or dialectic between settlement societies and civilisations has primarily a heuristic value. Empirically, the past history of civilisations would be marked by a settlement society configuration and the future of settlement societies would lend itself to a civilisational design. Furthermore, as in the case of European and North American or so-called 'western' nations, there is the development of a technologically advanced civilisation. The present analysis focuses on the symbolic rather than political or technological frontiers of civilisations (e.g., Durkheim and Mauss 1913), but in this respect we do not deal with what Frederick Jameson (1984) has called 'nostalgia for the present' in modern western civilisations.

In relation to civilisations which, as we shall presently suggest, may be conceptualised as sustained by an interaction between a great tradition and several little traditions, the settlement societies form a dialectical relationship. We can see, for instance, this dialectical relationship in time, as in South Africa, and metonymically, as in UK. According to Professor R. Thornton of the University of Witwatersrand (personal communication), multiculturalism in South Africa lends itself historically to a civilisational conceptualisation, around a model of three city-states (Durban, Capetown and Johannesburg) and their hinterlands. This is in contrast to the modern European and North American conceptualisation of a network of urban–industrial centres and rural–agricultural areas. From our point of view, Thornton's position is a valid and useful point of departure for examining conquest states such as the collection of three city-states in South Africa. The point of arrival, on the other hand, especially throughout the 19th and 20th centuries (and more particularly in the present-day Republic of South Africa), is a conceptualisation of multiculturalism as a consequence of settlement societies dynamics. The crucial population element in this dynamics is the Indian South African community. Unlike both the whites and the blacks who contest autochthonous versus settler statuses in South Africa, the Indians have regarded themselves as belonging to South Africa in the sense of citizenship and political status in general, and yet not based their claims on any other than the 'settler' status. (The small numbers of Indians in the population is, of course, a crucial variable but not the dominating one.) The example of multiculturalism in UK suggests a metonymic relationship between a civilisation (in this instance a long-established centralised state and a cohesive nation-state) and a settlement society (the large numbers of Asian and African diasporic elements). Here, firstly, the settlement society is not coterminous with the nation-state, but is a part thereof. Secondly, the notion of diaspora itself may refer either to a place or a people, depending on the context of the discourse.

The dialectical rather than oppositional relationship between civilisations and settlement societies has a definite historical effect. As the example of late capitalism at the end of the 20th century and the ushering in of the 21st century clearly shows, there is high probability of a feedback such that the dynamics of settlement societies can energise/refurbish civilisation. The civilisational teleology of development and cultural evolution throughout 20th century thought seems to have been a mirror-image of 19th century social evolutionism. The dialectical relationship such as advocated here between civilisations and settlement societies has the potential of reversing the hallowed centre–periphery relationship paradigm, in cultural terms, of the world-system theorists.

In this discussion it is not possible to outline in detail the theoretical parameters of settlement societies, but it may be useful to bear in mind that one can postulate a distinction between the elementary structure of such societies and their complex forms. Most of the island societies of the 19th century Indian diaspora, viz., Mauritius, Fiji, Trinidad & Tobago, etc. belong to the elementary type, while societies like the USA, Canada, South Africa and Australia, the kind of societies that have been written about as 'New Societies' (Hartz 1964), represent the complex structures.

The point of origin for the Indian diaspora has been the Indian civilisation. The civilisational side of the dialectic has so far, in this paper, been assumed and not spelt out. It would seem valid to say that during a process of interaction between the great tradition and several little traditions over the millennia, a civilisation like India cannot be said to lack a common will. The self-same religious, architectural, anthropomorphic and social structural patterns and symbols recur in India as a palimpsest (Lannoy 1971) that may be predominantly 'Hindu' in origin but which effectively cuts across religious, communal, ethnic and caste groups. As such, what Cohn (1971) characterises as the study of cultural communication in understanding the Indian civilisations has been much helped by the concepts of great tradition and little traditions, and of universalisation and parochialisation (cf. Marriott 1955; Singer 1972). The *longue durée* of civilisation distinguishes it from the short time-span of the settlement societies. Besides, the former having a sort of common cultural will, it also enables a synthesis of various disparate cultural elements which is a 'blend' rather than a mere 'mixture'. The symbiosis between Muslim and non-Muslim cultures in India is an evidence of this process. Nevertheless, there are two main criticisms of the particular way in which the process of cultural communication in Indian civilisation has been conceptualised by the anthropologists of the Chicago School. Firstly, though lip-service is paid to the mutual interaction between the great tradition and little traditions, in fact, the former is treated as hegemonic over the latter. The difficulty seems to be that in this civilisational teleology, acculturation, which is an asymmetrical and hegemonic process has been emphasised over and above 'interculturation', which is perhaps a much more prevalent and powerful process over time (Jain 1986). A critique of the 'sanskritisation' process of cultural change in India reveals that a number of protest movements were simultaneously active, perhaps more active, during the last 100 years of Indian history than the movements of change imitating the cultural practices of the higher castes. The second big gap in the culturally asymmetric paradigm of cultural change in India is that the politico-economic factors of change, viz., those involved in building the Indian nation (in the last 200 years) and the Indian state (in the last fifty years), are completely marginalised. In sum, the prevailing anthropological models of the process of Indian civilisation would revert to the paradigm of a cultural persistence type of analysis if employed in the context of diaspora. We believe that the dialectic between civilisation and settlement society, the one complementing the other, and the one feeding back into the other as a process in real time, provides a dynamic frame in the study of Indian diaspora.

Before concluding this section of our presentation, let us note that one salient contrast between studies and frameworks for the study of settlement societies and of civilisations has been the accent on political economy in the former, and culture in the latter. As our earlier remarks would imply, there is a need for each perspective to be augmented by the other. In the settlement societies framework, the researches by anthropologists like M.G. Smith on pluralism and ideas of plural society have sought to blend the Furnivallian politico-economic framework with reflections on culture and society. M.G. Smith's post-colonial paradigm of pluralism (Smith 1969) distinguishes between structural, social and cultural pluralisms. In structural pluralism there is differential incorporation of the various segments in the nation. This is the kind of situation which existed in South Africa during the apartheid era. Social pluralism is based on consociation, a condition of formal equivalence among the segments. Illustrations are nations such as Switzerland and Belgium. Cultural pluralism refers to universalistic, uniform incorporation, the kind of situation which should ideally exist in a country like the USA.

Conversely, sociologists like John Rex (Rex 1982) assimilate a politico-economic viewpoint in their analyses of race relations in plural societies. Relevant to the study of the Indian diaspora is Rex's postulation of a continuum between the 19th century and the 20th century emigration and settlement of people from India in territories overseas. This follows from Rex's argument that in the modern world migratory movements take place according to the need of different economies for labour, a major movement of this kind being the migration of men and women from post-colonial to metropolitan societies. Where this happens, metropolitan labour movements and metropolitan political parties seek to establish barriers of a racist kind to such movements. In so far as these are effective, what one sees is racial discrimination on a world-wide scale, designed to ensure that the hard-won freedoms of the metropolitan workers will not be shared, even if this means a permanent division of the world into rich and poor nations. As post-colonial societies get control of their own destinies, and either eliminate racism or direct it against new targets, this division between rich white and poor coloured and black nations may come to be the most important form of racism in the modern world. What is true of the working classes is true also, if to a lesser degree, of white-collar workers and professionals of the post-colonial countries migrating to metropolitan centres. The general point, of course, is that there is an organic linkage between the immigration and settlement of Indians abroad in the 19th century, and those who have migrated to the industrially advanced countries in the present century. Furthermore, this diaspora bears the marks of colonialism and racism.

IV

The universe of discourse: A framework

I have already spelled out, briefly, the distinction between civilisations and settlement societies. I now locate this distinction in a wider field of forces which is comprised not only of empirical cases that contextualise the Indian diaspora but also the intellectual/analytical currents which flow in this field. This combination of descriptive and analytical perspectives is suggested by the fact that there now

Table 1
Field of forces

	A	*B*
Societal correlate	Settlement societies	Civilisations
Historical conjuncture	Late capitalism	Early capitalism
Evolutionary thrust	Models *of* development	Models *for* development
Intellectual current	Post-modernism	Modernism
	Reverse orientalism	Valorisation of tradition
	Fragmentation and deconstruction	Holism (Gandhian & Marxist approaches)
	Deterritorialisation	Multiple territorialisation
Subliminal currents	New Age religions	Economic liberalisation & 'consumption of modernity'

exist, in the study of the Indian diaspora, not only anthropologists and sociologists of metropolitan (western) countries and the 'Indianists' (so-called) of Indian and western vintage, but also diasporic scholars themselves who bring to bear—in the changed circumstances of the admissibility of a subjective or agent-oriented viewpoint in the social sciences—an experiential and creatively articulated dimension. I present this field of forces, with its magnetic polarities, in Table 1.

To explain this table briefly, the polarity between civilisations and settlement societies has already been discussed. That between late and early capitalism is largely self-evident. The distinction between models *of* and *for* development can be explained by the fact that while in A there has been satiation with high-tech and concern now for sustainable development and environmental preservation, in B there is still a shortfall, not only real and material, but also perceived and felt, between the technological progress actually attained and that sought to be attained. In that sense, even where a question mark is raised over the adoption and import of western technology, there is continuing and deep concern with models for development, rather than a distant and somewhat dispassionate interest in what kinds of developmental models are available and need to be implemented. In other words, in A the interest in developmental models may not be for urgent implementation but as knowledge-packages. In the third set of polarities, viz., those referring to intellectual currents, the distinction between the postmodernism of A and the continuing modernism of B is noteworthy. It means in effect that while the traditional/modern or the modernity of tradition/modernisation of tradition theses still define the terms of discourse in B, in A on the other hand the idioms of collage and surrealism are adopted at even more popular levels than was the case in late modernism (Jameson 1984). In postmodernity the dead-hand of globalisation has replaced the affect-prone particularities. As such, the holistic notion of 'tradition' (whether in the unconsciously imperialistic redaction of Raymond Williams or the moral philosophy rendition of Alisdair MacIntyre [MacIntyre 1981; Williams 1961, 1983]) continues to haunt B. In A, on the other hand, the critique of Orientalism has not only managed to throw the baby of tradition out with the bathwater of colonialism and imperialism, but a kind of 'reverse-Orientalism' has taken its place. Let me give two examples in the context of studies of diaspora. Firstly, in the description and analysis of the formation of settlement societies, there is virtually no consideration of what in the older literature would be called the 'pioneering spirit', that is, the adventure and entrepreneurial skills of the founding fathers. The besetting sin of these founding fathers was the fact that they happen to have been largely of the Nordic races. Thus, in the literature on plural societies, multiculturalism, and diaspora generally, the inadmissibility of notions such as that of 'New Societies'(cf. Hartz 1964) has become patent; it has become a postmodernist blasphemy to dilate on the contribution of the whites. (A good example of this tendency is Appadurai [1993] especially his diatribe against the 'heart of whiteness'.) A second example comes from multicultural Australia. Let me cite the observations of a demographer who is uniformly respected for his fair and balanced views on immigration and settlement of the Australian population:

> The Executive Committee of the New South Wales Ethnic Communities Council . . . has some 57 members, one of whom is a Scot and the other 56 first- or second-generation persons of continental European or Asian origin. Similarly, the Prime Minister's new Multi-Cultural Council has 22 members, one the President of the Australian Council of Trade Unions, one a leading industrialist, one academic with much experience in ethnic matters, one leading academic of Australian Aboriginal descent, and 18 persons of continental European or Asian origin. In short, while multiculturalism claims to be a policy for all Australians, it is very much in the hands of first- and second-generation persons of non Anglo-Celtic origin (Price 1987).

In a table accompanying this statement Price shows how in three generations of Australians, Anglo-Celts only, Non-Anglo Celts only, and Mixture, constitute 47.3 per cent, 23.2 per cent and 29.5 per cent respectively of the total population in the late 80s.

Another element of the postmodernist ambience in A is reflected in the carryover from the social science discourse of deconstruction and fragmentation to diasporic studies. The crisis of representation in ethnography has been projected on to the studies of migration and settlement. These currents stand in contrast to the holisms of B, prominent among these being the Marxist notion of totality (cf. Jay 1984) and, in the context of Indian civilisation, Gandhian views of swaraj (self-government) and self-sufficiency. The deterritorialisation thesis enunciated and elaborated by diasporic Indian intellectuals in the USA (Appadurai 1990, 1991, 1993; Gupta 1992; and Gupta and Ferguson 1992) and in Australia (Mishra 1995), is a particularly acute manifestation of the pains and dilemmas of the diasporic intellectual/academic in settlement societies. They emphasise transnationality, hyphenated identities and the diasporic deterritorialisation of immigrant populations. The argument is sustained by the examples of displaced peoples and refugees all over the world, and the importance of global and transnational organisations, such as the Red Cross, Amnesty International, etc. is cited as proof that the identities and loyalties of diasporics, including of Indians in the 'complex' settlement societies (read USA or even Australia), have become fragmented and deterritorialised.

At the beginning of this paper I had stated that the subject of identities—a matter mostly of social psychology in the context of diaspora—is largely outside our present concern. But when anthropologists like those cited above take up this theme and begin theorising on a global scale, it becomes necessary to reappraise the situation from the Indian angle. Stated somewhat bluntly, the deterritorialisation thesis seems to have unmistakably psychological roots, as the many personal interludes, at least in the writings of Arjun Appadurai cited above, would seem to bear out. In this genre of anthropological or literary writing, there are symptoms of an intellectual or academic disease wherein a splintered (rather than a split) identity of the intellectual/academic is projected on to the nation-state or 'country' of adoption, viz., the US or Australia. In his article, 'Patriotism and its futures'(1993), Appadurai draws a contrast between 'belonging to' or 'loyalty for' on the one hand, United States of America, and on the other, America. The former (USA) is portrayed as the persecutor (preserver of whiteness and of the contrast between the WASP and the others). It has the 'land of the immigrants' ideology, and it consciously or unconsciously panders to the image of the 'tribalism' of the non-white groups. The latter (America) is the 'ethnoscape' of real freedom; it is just a node in diaspora and the epitome of deterritorialisation without the fetters. In this scenario the former is all bad and the latter good to utopian perfection.

I do not wish to contest here the subjective preferences of these authors. But let me say that depending on the vantage point of the 'intellectual' concerned, if USA or Australia based (our Pole A), the glass looks half empty, and if India or counter-diaspora based (our Pole B), the glass looks half full. For instance, from the vantage point of an Indian academic, an equally plausible case can be made for multiple territorialisation rather than deterritorialisation. The advantage of a multiterritorial perspective would be: (*a*) that the economic dimension of immigration and settlement, e.g., the class background and investments in India of the diasporics, would be studied; (*b*) that the policies of the host society and the nation-state dimensions of the statuses of the diasporics would become clearer (thus in Australia, for example, multiculturalism, immigration quotas, English versus non-English speaking backgrounds and steps being taken to remedy the latter would be the object of one's study); and (*c*) the distinctive politics of the settlement society diasporics, e.g., their ethnic politics, their perceptions, of the 'niche' of opportunity, etc., would become clearer.

In my Field of Forces table, the last set of contrasts between A and B is in terms of subliminal currents. This is an especially useful index because it shows how the elements of each sub-field are present in the other. Thus, while tradition and holism are largely unrepresented in A, the existence of New Age religions, e.g., the marginalised current of movements like the Hare Krishna, complementary to economism in general, play a role in settlement societies. On the other hand, if one took a realistic view of the currents of globalisation and economic liberalisation which are moving civilisational sites like India, China and Mexico, the burgeoning middle classes and consumption of modernity by them (Breckenridge

1995) belong to the twilight zone between early and late capitalism. Any particular instance of Indian diaspora will then be placed at different points in relation to this field of forces, but with an area where the interpenetration between the sub-fields would be present.

V
Implications

Difference and translation

I now wish to draw out three major implications in operating with the above field-of-forces paradigm in the study of the Indian diaspora. The first of these pertains to the issues involved in translation and translatability. The problems of cultural translation in this area are twofold in nature. In the first place, as Niranjana (1994) has argued for the plural society of Trinidad & Tobago, it is ironical that while the Indian identity is already translated (see the section on creolisation), there is a defiant refusal by sections of the Indian (or better, Hindu) population to be seen to be translated. Niranjana's example is the *chutney soca,* a form of hybrid Trinidadian Indian calypsonian song-form which drew loud protests from sections of the Indian population as being non-Indian, if not a downright corruption, and hence a disgrace to Indian arts. This is one form of 'untranslatability' of Indian culture in an arena where interculturation (as in the cultural interchange between the East Indians and the Creoles) rather than acculturation is the operative dynamics. (A more sociological example, according to Niranjana, would be the rarity and criticism of inter-racial marriages among Indians.) The second kind of problem in cultural translation refers to problems of translatability when social relations are set in a matrix of hierarchy. This is not peculiar to a multicultural or plural society, but is a phenomenon wherever socio-cultural stratification is pronounced.

In terms of our paradigm of the field of forces, this second kind of untranslatability seems to have been largely glossed over in the postmodernist sub-field A. A critique of the dialogical strategy of the postmodernist ethnographer, in contrast to the dialectical one of the materialist/Marxist, is this observation by Nicole Polier and William Roseberry:

> However experimental the format, however 'democratic' the process by which dialogues are selected for presentation, presentation still involves a process of translation and encounters problems with translation that [Talal] Asad (1986) analyzes with care. He cites Rudolf Pannwitz: 'Our translations ... proceed from a wrong premise. They want to turn Hindi, Greek, English into German instead of turning German into Hindi, Greek, English'. Noting the inequality of languages, the resistance of the 'stronger' languages—and structures of academic discourse—to the sensitive kind of translation called for by Pannwitz, Asad contends that there is a powerful tendency for dominated cultures to accommodate their language to the dominant culture. In the act of translation, anthropologists are often of the belief, or else simply assume, that their native tongue and conceptual equipment have the metaphors adequate to interpret 'Europe's others' (Polier and Roseberry 1989: 253).

However, we believe that not all is lost in the process of translation even when, or precisely when, in the words of Polier and Roseberry, 'the post-modern anthropologists encounter the other and discover themselves'. This is the attainment of a view of the 'us as others', or as Geertz has pointed out, 'an imaginative entry into. . .an alien turn of mind' (Geertz 1986). It is this attainment which seems to lie behind Clifford's defence of 'collage' in ethnography. He says:

> Collage brings to the work (here the ethnographic text) elements that continually proclaim their foreignness to the context of presentation. . . . The ethnography as collage would leave manifest the constructivist procedures of ethnographic knowledge; it would be an assemblage containing voices other than the ethnographer's, as well as examples of 'found' evidence, data not fully integrated within the work's governing interpretation. Finally, it would not explain away those elements in the foreign culture which render the investigator's own culture newly comprehensible (Clifford 1981: 563–64.).

While being impressed by the experimental mode indicated by Clifford, let us join Polier and Roseberry in stating the last word: 'The collage is accountable to its own anti-social, disembodied logic. What we get from the surrealistic assemblage is a view of the interior universe. Unconscious, may be; dialectical, no' (1989: 262).

Despite such critique, the anthropological value of cultural translation—and not only through surrealist ethnography as emphasised by Clifford—is apparent whenever the last step, viz., viewing ourselves as others, has been taken. Let me quote Rhoda Reddock, an African Trinidadian feminist scholar who has been studying for the last fifteen years the vicissitudes experienced by East Indian women in the Caribbean diaspora:

> It was my experience, for example, that in my society, African and Indian women were constantly being defined in opposition to each other, Indian women were/are what African women were not and vice versa. This within the racial contestations of the society, served to narrow the options and spaces to manoeuvre for the women concerned. It was for this reason that in my own historical research (Reddock 1994), my effort to understanding of the experiences of Indian women was as important to me as was my understanding of that of African women. . . . I felt that our differences had in some way contributed to what we had now been constructed to be. In other words, it was impossible to know myself if I did not know my other/s (Reddock 1996).

Elsewhere in the same article, Reddock writes about the importance in her work of understanding 'the other within ourselves'.

Hybridity and creolisation

The hybridity thesis is compatible with the collage view presented above. The debate about hybridity and creolisation, too, focuses on the contestations between the dialogical and dialectical points of view. Celebrating hybridity as a dynamic cultural phenomenon in its own right and critiquing identifiable bounded cultures are some radical authors and cultural critics like Gilroy (of West Indian origin) and Bhabha (born in India). Let me cite their views in relation to the prize example: British culture and identity. Culture, Gilroy insists, 'is not a fixed and impermeable feature of social relations. Its forms change, develop, combine and are dispersed in historical processes. The syncretist cultures of black Britain exemplify this. They have been able to detach cultural practices from their origins and use them to found and extend new patterns of metacommunication which give their community substance and collective identity' (Gilroy 1987). That is to say, a fluid, syncretic black culture defines the possibility of a continuously reconstructed British identity. Bhabha takes up a similar position. *The Satanic verses*, he thinks, has changed the vocabulary of our cultural debate:

> It has achieved this by suggesting that there is no such whole as the nation, the culture, or even the self. Such holism is a version of reality that is most often used to assert cultural or political supremacy and seeks to obliterate the relations of difference that constitute the languages of history and culture.... Salman Rushdie sees the emergence of doubt, questioning and even confusion as being part of that cultural 'excess' that facilitates the formation of new social identities that do not appeal to a pure and settled past, or to a unicultural present, in order to authenticate themselves. Their authority lies in the attempt to articulate emergent, hybrid forms of cultural identity'(Bhabha 1989).

In other words, social identities need to be authenticated, but Rushdie has taught us—so Bhabha claims—that their authentication derives from our ability to continuously reinvent ourselves out of our confused cultural conditions.

Talal Asad has challenged the hybridity thesis both on conceptual and political grounds (Asad 1990). Conceptually, he shows that 'culture' does after all have boundaries and in this connection he refers to the moral philosopher Alisdair MacIntyre's concept of tradition in the latter's *After virtue*. Politically, his criticism is that 'it is a notorious tactic of dominating power to deny a distinct unity to populations it seeks to manipulate, to assume for itself the status of universal reason while attributing to others a singular contingency' (ibid.). This brings me to an elementary structure of hybridity, namely creolisation, which has occupied the attention of anthropologists in societies of the 19th century Indian diaspora.

One of the best examples of the creolisation debate is an exchange between Lee Drummond and Chandra Jayawardena in the pages of the journal *Man* during the early 1980s. Based on the advances in Creole linguistics, Drummond had suggested that cultures, like languages in plural society (the specific example was Guyana), constituted a continuum from, say, pure English to Creole and that the speakers were familiar, unevenly, with the whole range and could adjust their speech according to the interlocutor or the person spoken to. This implied, somewhat paradoxically, a standardised hybridisation. Jayawardena's objection to this thesis was basically on grounds of an implied assumption in the theory, of the neutralisation of the variables of status, class and power. Comparing Guyana with Fiji, he illustrated how creolisation in the former country had developed due to the relatively free intermixture between the East Indians and the Africans, whereas creolisation had not developed in Fiji because of the British policy of divide and rule between the Indians and the Fijians. Even in Guyana, however, culture had became the springboard for politically charged 'ethnicity' because, despite interculturation, stratification had resulted in conflict between the dominants and the subordinate (cf. Drummond 1980; Jayawardena 1980).

In this debate one gets a view of what I would call (based on the examples of Indian diaspora in Trinidad, Guyana, Mauritius and South Africa) the role of the dominance base in creolisation. The dominance base in creolisation refers to the continuing and pervasive presence of linguistic and other forms of cultural expression derived from the former colonial ruling power—whether English, French, Dutch or Portugese—in the hybrid speech and culture of certain settlement societies. It also alerts us to the fact that the factor of colonialism has to be introduced in a nuanced and non-monocausal manner in the comparative study of the Indian diaspora. It is our contention that, unlike the situation in Fiji, in countries where creolisation has taken place (this includes the Indian population despite the existence of a category distinction in overt speech between the 'coolies' and the '*kirwals*', as in Trinidad), overt conflict between the ethnic segments has a tendency to become covert. To uncover the underlying conflict, one has to probe the process of the empowerment/disempowerment of the minorities (minorities not only numerically, but also culturally). As soon as such a probe is mounted, the creolisation base—British, French, Dutch or Portuguese—becomes important. The continuing hegemony of European and North American culture in Trinidad & Tobago, and of French culture in Mauritius, needs 'uncovering', lying as it does beneath the overt rhetoric and posturings in these territories. To take the example of Mauritius, the Hindi nationalism of the Indian 'minority' camouflages the multi-national hegemony of the French in the economic sphere. My evidence is a set of speeches by a Mauritian Indian writer who addressed audiences in India in Hindi. The major brunt of his argument in these speeches was to extol the patriotism of the French in sponsoring and propagating the French language in Mauritius. Why couldn't the Indian government, he asked rhetorically, do the same for Hindi in Mauritius? It was evident, if one deconstructed these speeches, that the Hindi language and the Indian government were being used as proxies to express the real secondary economic status which the Indians enjoy in Mauritius. Hindi nationalism is a sop to assuage the secondary status of the Indians whose economic inferiority is covered and displaced by bolstering Hindi in an otherwise functionally effective creolised universe of discourse, with French at its base.

Also in contemporary Guyana, Brackette F. Williams has shown how the creolisation of cultural practiçes, through interculturation, does not simply slip over into an ideology of 'live and let live'. In her analysis of the celebration of Rum Tadjeh (known as *tazia* in Mohorrum in India) in Guyana, she brings out the coexistence of homogeneity (creolisation) and heterogeneity (the Muslim character of the celebration). In respect to the latter aspect and the dynamics of conflict, one has to go to the colonial roots of the creolisation process (Williams 1990). Similarly, for the East Indians in Trinidad, a recent historical study has shown how the sting of colonial stereotypes of the inferiority and backwardness of Indian culture remained, despite the overt veneer of creolisation. It is this continuing thorn in the Indians' side that made their culture 'distinctive' and untranslatable (Kale 1995). Similarly, the passing on of the fragmented Indian identities in present-day South Africa into ethnic and sub-ethnic components has to be related to the regime of racist segregation during apartheid, a fall-out of a 'pigmentocratic order' (L.M. Thompson 1964) that resisted creolisation on account of the dual presence of the British and the Dutch. Hence, we argue, there was no unitary dominance base for creolisation in South Africa.

Multiculturalism

A recent article (Dhalla 1993) about Indian ethnic politics and the competing moral discourses of non-racialism and multi-racialism in South Africa, presents a wholly emic view of Indian politics in South Africa, employing racial categories like the Whites, Africans, Coloureds and Indians in the discourse on multi-racialism and on their erasure in non-racialism. The former is the government policy, and the latter the view of the African radicals; the Indians are caught somewhere in between. It seems possible to argue that a way out of the dilemma for the Indians—a light at the end of the tunnel—would have been if they as well as the author had set the discourse in terms of multiculturalism rather than multi-racialism or non-racialism. However, the problem with multiculturalism is the same as in discourses of translation and hybridisation/creolisation discussed earlier. If multiculturalism is not culturally relativist, then the 'universal values' have to be of a certain cultural cast (western, European, English, indigenous or whatever), i.e., governed by the dominant strand in the modern history of a particular society. Apropos Australian society, for example, James Jupp (1996) supports the adoption of the American position that multiculturalism must be rejected if it is based on pure cultural relativism. Jupp further points out that the core of Australian life and institutions is still essentially of British origin and that ethnic minorities are small and rather peripheral. We are told that practices such as polygyny and female circumcision, though permitted by the community codes of certain cultures represented in the Australian multiculturalism, will not be tolerated in Australian national society.

The sociologist, John Rex, came face to face with such a difficulty in analysing multiculturalism in Britain. In his earlier writing (Rex 1987), he had spoken of what has come to be known as the 'two domains thesis', which boiled down to equality of opportunity and the shared public culture of the public domain, and cultural diversity in the private and communal domain. As Rex puts it later on (Rex 1991):

> Those who took this [the two domains thesis] view, therefore, seemed able to get the best of both the worlds. Embarrassingly for them, it was also taken up by some of those who did not accept the claims of minority cultures to equal esteem. For them, however, what the two domains thesis means is that, though the diverse cultures of the minorities may be inferior or even noxious, they

> may be tolerated so long as the public domain is insulated from them. Moreover, for them, the culture of the public domain is usually represented, not simply as the shared political culture. . .but an all inclusive British national culture.

Rex goes on to dub the two domains thesis as 'naive and simplistic'. Not only did this thesis seek to encompass diversity within a monolithic concept of British national culture but also, from a theoretical perspective, the broadly functionalist strand in sociological theory-building on the interrelationship of institutions in society would militate against the concept of segregated public and communal domains. In practical terms, it might be shown, for example, that schools in modern societies could not be simply located in either of the two domains. Apart from education, the political culture of the public domain was disputed, as was religion in the public domain (viz., the famous dispute over blasphemy laws being applied to Christian contexts and not to the Muslim ones as in the Rushdie episode). Also involved were the questions of individual human rights, which could not be neatly parcelled out into those of the public domain and of the communal domain. Moreover, the model of the multicultural society based upon the two domains does not encounter difficulties only from the British side. For the minority religions of some minority groups, particularly Islam, the division between public and private domains appears unacceptable, Islam being defined as a whole way of life.

Faced with such serious difficulties in the multicultural model, some commentators have come to the conclusion that in this frame minorities are 'excluded'; that multiculturalism degenerates into 'cultural racialism'; and that culturalism as such should be shunned (Vertovec 1996). In this view, rather than split hairs about the meaning of culture, there should be discussion of policy for the public incorporation of minorities. As John Rex has said: 'The important point to be made in a democratic critique of multiculturalism is not merely to assert that malevolent governments and ruling classes create ascribed ethnicity for their own purposes, but to consider whether those who see themselves as members of ethnic groups should and can attain their objectives within society' (John Rex cited in Vertovec 1996).

VI
Conclusion

It seems clear that there are dialectical, dialogical and reformist implications of the paradigm for the study of the spread and settlement of Indian minorities in the post-colonial context. It is apparent that analyses in terms of imperialism and colonialism, (cf. Hugh Tinker's masterly review of the 19th century Indian diaspora under the title 'A new system of slavery' [1974]), which produced much heat in the 1960s through the 1980s, now need to be re-framed in the context of transnationality and globalisation, processes which affect equally Indian populations in the former colonies and in the metropolitan centres.

While there is no doubt that the historical and spatial aspects of particular diasporas should be taken into account, it is doubtful whether a broad distinction between the PIOs and NRIs is a useful tool in the cultural analysis of the horizontal or lateral dimensions of the Indian diaspora in a post-colonial context. In a certain sense, the *longue durée* perspective inherent in our heuristic distinction between civilisations and settlement societies subsumes, at an analytical plane, the distinctions between the past, the present and the future of Indian diasporas. However, another kind of relativity gets built into this theoretical perspective as a result of the location of the analyst. (We have already had occasion to refer to this in respect of the deterritorialisation and multiple territorialisation theses.) This duality should be transcended in terms of the multipositionality view of the Indian diaspora. In writing about diaspora in general, one of the six characteristics mentioned by Safran is that '[the diasporics] continue to relate, personally or vicariously, to the homeland in one way or another, and their ethnocommunal consciousness and solidarity are importantly defined by the existence of such a relationship' (Safran 1991: 84). This 'homing instinct' is viewed by different, though complementary, perspectives of the 'imaginary' and the 'imagined' by the diasporic Indians and the Indians respectively. The empiricism of the latter and the emotional/mythic attitude of the former are both grist to the mill of the Indian politics of globalisation. If the Indian Indians try and take a 'realistic view' of the economic opportunities and networks of the diaspora, the diasporic Indians display a dogged attachment to the religious, linguistic, culinary and performative aspects of Indianness. Although there are resistance movements against racist and gender discrimination by the Indian diasporics (see Brah 1996 for UK; and Niranjana 1994 for Trinidad & Tobago), there is overwhelming evidence of a largely pacifist orientation of 'settler citizenship' among the diasporic Indians the world over. It is interesting to note that this 'culturalisation of politics' rather than 'politicisation of culture' in the Indian diaspora extends both territorially and extra-territorially. Examples of the former are the politics of societies where Indians are at the helm of public affairs (Mauritius, Trinidad and Guyana). The latter can be seen in relation to the support for the Khalistan movement by diasporic Sikhs and for the Hindutva fundamentalism of the Vishwa Hindu Parishad by diasporic Hindus. The perception of this kind of 'culturally political' support is to my mind the analytically valuable aspect of the deterritorialisation thesis advanced by diasporic Indian intellectuals/social scientists (Appadurai, Vijay Mishra, Akhil Gupta et al.) and literary authors (Rushdie and Naipaul). This slippage between the imaginary and the imagined with regard to India has grown not only among the intelligentsia—teachers and writers—but also among the second or third generation diaspora born recent immigrants and descendants of older immigrants who are equally touched by the forces of globalisation.

REFERENCES

APPADURAI, ARJUN. 1990. Disjuncture and difference in the global cultural economy. *Theory, culture and society* 7: 295–310.

———. 1991. Global ethnoscapes: Notes and queries for a transnational anthropology. *In* R.G. Fox, ed., *Recapturing anthropology*, pp. 191–210. Santa Fe: School of American Research Press.

———. 1993. Patriotism and its futures. *Public culture* 5: 411–29.

ASAD, TALAL. 1986. The concept of cultural translation in British social anthropology. *In* James Clifford and George E. Marcus, eds, *Writing culture: The poetics and politics of ethnography*, pp. 141–64. Berkeley: University of California Press.

———. 1990. Multiculturalism and British identity in the wake of the Rushdie affair. *Politics and society* 18, 4: 455–80.

BARTH, FREDRIK. 1969. *Ethnic groups and boundaries*. Boston: Little, Brown and Company.

———. 1994. Enduring and emerging issues in the analysis of ethnicity. *In* Hans Vermeulen and Cora Govers, eds, *The anthropology of ethnicity*, pp. 11–32. Amsterdam: Het Spinhuis.

BHABHA, HOMI. 1989. Down among the writers. *The New Statesman and Society*, 28 July.

BRAH, AVTAR. 1996. *Cartographies of diaspora. Contesting identities*. London & New York: Routledge.

BRECKENRIDGE, CAROL A., ed. 1995. *Consuming modernity: Public culture in a south Asian world*. Minneapolis: University of Minnesota Press.

CHATTERJEE, PARTHA. 1997. Beyond the nation? or within. *Economic and political weekly* 32, 1 & 2: 30–34.

CLARKE, C., C. PEACH and S. VERTOVEC, eds. 1991. *South Asians overseas: Migration and ethnicity*. Cambridge: Cambridge University Press.

CLIFFORD, JAMES. 1981. On ethnographic surrealism. *Comparative studies in society and history* 23, 4: 539–64.

COHN, BERNARD S. 1971. *India: The social anthropology of a civilization*. New Jersey: Prentice-Hall Inc.

DHALLA, PAUL E.H. 1993. Contesting the future: Indian ethnic politics and the competing moral discourses of nonracialism and multiracialism in South Africa. *In* Sally Falk Moore, ed., *Moralizing states and the ethnography of the present*, pp. 17–54. Arlington: American Anthropological Association.

DRUMMOND, LEE. 1980. The cultural continuum: A theory of intersystems. *Man* 15: 352–74.

DUMONT, LOUIS. 1975. On the comparative understanding of non-modern civilizations. *Daedalus*, Spring: 53–72.

DURKHEIM, E, and M. MAUSS. 1913 [1971]. Note on the notion of civilization. *Social research* 38: 808–13.

FURNIVALL, J.S. 1948. *Colonial policy and practice: A comparative study of Burma and Netherlands India*. New York: New York University Press.

GEERTZ, C. 1986. The uses of diversity. *Michigan quarterly review*, Winter: 105–23.

GILROY, PAUL. 1987. *There ain't no black in the union Jack*, London: Hutchinson.

GUPTA, AKHIL. 1992. The song of the non-aligned world: Transnational identities and the reinscription of space in late capitalism. *Cultural anthropology* 7: 63–79.

GUPTA, AKHIL and JAMES FERGUSON. 1992. Beyond 'culture': Space, identity, and the politics of difference. *Cultural anthropology* 7: 6–23.

HARTZ, LOUIS. 1964. *The founding of new societies: Studies in the history of the United States, Latin America, S. Africa, Canada and Australia*. London: Harcourt Brace Jovanovich Publishers.

JAIN, RAVINDRA K. 1970. *South Indians on the plantation frontier in Malaya*. New Haven: Yale University Press.

———. 1986. The east Indian culture in a Caribbean context: Crisis and creativity. *India International Centre quarterly* 13, 2: 153–64.

———. 1993. *Indian communities abroad: Themes and literature*. New Delhi: Manohar.

———. 1994. Civilisations and settlement societies. *The eastern anthropologist* 47, 1: 1–14.

———. 1997. A civilizational theory of Indian diaspora and its global implications. *The Eastern anthropologist* 50, 3 & 4: 347–55.

JAMESON, FREDERICK. 1984. Postmodernism, or the cultural logic of late capitalism. *New left review*. 146: 53–92.

JAY, MARTIN. 1984. *Marxism and totality: The adventures of a concept from Lukacs to Habermas*. Berkeley & Los Angeles: University of California Press.

JAYAWARDENA, C. 1968. Migration & social change: A survey of Indian communities overseas. *Geographical review* 58, 3: 426–49.

———. 1980. Culture and ethnicity in Guyana and Fiji. *Man* 15, 3: 430–50.

JUPP, JAMES. 1996. Multiculturalism and social cohesion. Paper presented to the workshop on 'Dealing with diversity: Citizenship and cultural change in Australia & Japan', A.N.U., Canberra, 29–30 March (mimeographed).

KALE, MADHAVI. 1995. Projecting identities: Empire and indentured labour migration from India to Trinidad & British Guiana, 1836–1885. *In* Peter van der Veer, ed., *Nation & migration: The politics of space in the south Asian diaspora*, pp. 73–92. Philadelphia: University of Pennsylvania Press.

KLASS, MORTON. 1961. *East Indians in Trinidad: A study of cultural persistence.* New York: Columbia University Press.

KOTKIN, JOEL. 1993. *Tribes: How race, religion, and identity determine success in the new global economy.* New York: Random House.

LANNOY, R. 1971. *The speaking tree: A study of Indian culture and society.* London: Oxford University Press.

LECHTE, JOHN and G. BOTTOMLEY. 1993. Difference, postmodernity and image in multicultural Australia. *In* Gordon L. Clark et al., eds, *Multiculturalism, difference and postmodernism*, pp. 22–37. Melbourne: Longman Cheshire.

MACINTYRE, ALISDAIR. 1981. *After virtue.* London: Duckworth.

MARRIOTT, MCKIM. 1955. Little communities in an indigenous civilization. *In* McKim Marriott, ed., *Village India: Studies in the little community*, pp. 171–222. Chicago: University of Chicago Press.

MISHRA, VIJAY. 1995. The diasporic imaginary: Theorizing the (Indian) diaspora. Paper presented to the workshop on 'Indian Diaspora', Humanities Research Council, A.N.U., Canberra (mimeographed).

MOTWANI, JAGAT K. et al., eds. 1993. *Global Indian diaspora: Yesterday, today and tomorrow.* New York: Global Organization of People of Indian Origin.

MUTHIAH, A. and G.W. JONES. 1983. Fertility trends among overseas Indian populations. *Population studies* 37, 2: 273–99.

NAYYAR, DEEPAK. 1994. *Migration, remittances and capital flows.* Delhi: Oxford University Press.

NIRANJANA, TEJASWINI. 1994. 'The Indian in me': Studying the culture of the Indian diaspora. Paper presented at the International Conference on 'Indian Diaspora', Hyderabad (mimeographed).

POLIER, NICOLE and WILLIAM ROSEBERRY. 1989. Tristes tropes: Postmodern anthropologists encounter the other and discover themselves. *Economy & society* 18, 2: 245–64.

PRICE, CHARLES S. 1987. Australia: Multicultural and non-racist. *New community* 14, 1/2.

REDDOCK, RHODA. 1994. *Women, labour and politics in Trinidad & Tobago: A history.* London: Zed Books.

———. 1996. Conceptualizing 'difference' in Caribbean feminist theory: A preliminary exploration. Paper presented at the sixth International Congress on Women, Adelaide, 22–26 April (mimeographed).

REPORT. 1995. *Multicultural Australia, the next steps: Towards and beyond 2000*, vols 1 & 2. Canberra: A report of the National Multicultural Advisory Council, Commonwealth of Australia.

REX, JOHN. 1982. Racism and the structure of colonial societies. *In* R. Ross, ed., *Racism and colonialism*, pp. 199–218. The Hague: Martins Nijhoff.

———. 1987. The concept of a multicultural society. *New community* 14, 1/2.

———. 1991. The political sociology of a multicultural society. *European journal of intercultural studies* 2, 1: 7–19.

SAFRAN, WILLIAM. 1991. Diaspora in modern societies: Myths of homeland and return. *Diaspora* 1: 83–99.

SINGER, MILTON. 1972. *When a great tradition modernizes.* London: The Pall Mall Press.

SMITH, M.G. 1969. Some developments in the analytical framework of pluralism. *In* Leo Kuper and M.G. Smith, eds, *Pluralism in Africa*, pp. 415–58. Berkeley & Los Angeles: University of California Press.

Tambs-Lyche, Harald. 1980. *London Patidars: A case study in urban ethnicity.* London: Routledge & Kegan Paul.

Thompson, E.T. 1959. The plantation as a social system. *In, Plantation systems of the New World*, pp. 26–37. Washington: Pan American Union.

Thompson, Leonard M. 1964. The South African dilemma. *In* Louis Hartz, ed., *The founding of new societies*, pp. 178–218. London: Harcourt Brace Jovanovich.

Tinker, Hugh. 1974. *A new system of slavery: The export of Indian labour overseas, 1830–1920.* London: Oxford University Press.

Verdery, Katherine. 1994. Ethnicity, nationalism and state-making. *In* Hans Vermeulen and Cora Govers, eds, *The anthropology of ethnicity*, pp. 33–58. Amsterdam: Het Spinhuis.

Vermeulen, Hans and Cora Govers, eds. 1994. *The anthropology of ethnicity.* Amsterdam: Het Spinhuis.

Vertovec, Steven. 1996. Multiculturalism, culturalism and public incorporation. *Ethnic and racial studies* 19, 1: 49–69.

Williams, Brackette F. 1990. Nationalism, traditionalism, and the problem of cultural inauthenticity. *In* R.G. Fox, ed., *Nationalist ideologies and the production of national cultures*, pp. 112–29. Washington: American Anthropological Association.

Williams, Raymond. 1961. *Culture and society, 1780–1950.* Harmondsworth: Penguin Books.

———. 1983. *Key words: A vocabulary of culture and society.* London: Fontana.

10

What did Bernier actually say? Profiling the Mughal empire

Stanley J. Tambiah

Bernier's text Travels in the Mughal Empire; A.D. 1656–1708 *was a primary source for certain European writers from Montesquieu to Marx for their representation and characterisation of oriental despotism. The distinctive features of oriental despotism in their eyes were absolutist and tyrannical monarchs who ruled over polities that lacked a hereditary nobility and private property in land. In this paper I have attempted to demonstrate that, when read closely, Bernier's text discloses particulars that can be shown to yield a quite different patterning. The Mughal Empire of the 17th and 18th centuries, the period I am discussing, was characterised by a devolutionary distribution of authority among multiple lesser sovereignties, by a complex hierarchy of land tenure and appropriation of product, by a developed system of commerce, and by a tolerance and coexistence of pluralistic subcultures. The contours of the Empire seem to conform to a model of what I have previously conceptualised in my writings as the 'galactic polity'.*

The current trend in theorising about post-colonial societies is that the representation of pre-colonial societies at the time of contact as oriental despotisms was a proto-colonial and colonial construction which served as a reason and justification for political intervention, conquest and exploitation. That was so. But I want to emphasise that the stereotypical image of oriental despotism also importantly served as a polemic for an internal *political debate and advocacy in France as a warning against and attack on the alleged absolutist ambitions of French monarchy and a defense of feudal nobility as a break on such tendencies. Montesquieu in particular exemplifies this posture.*

Bernier's formulaic gloss on the Mughal Empire, despite what he actually reports, is one kind of tendentious representation. My own reading of Bernier's text is no doubt informed by my present day intellectual and political concerns.

I
Reading Bernier

Francois Bernier's account of his travels in Asia (Bernier 1914), particularly of his extended stay in India, which lasted some nine years, has been a standard source for European writers on oriental despotism. It is said that he was a precursor of the *philosophes*, and that his works, which portray scepticism, faith in Reason, and a commitment to private property as a basis for good government and prosperity, were essential reading for 18th century thinkers. Montesquieu had read him and used him as a source in *L'Esprit des lois* (1749); and so also later had Marx and Engels, just prior to Marx's writing of his *New York Daily Tribune* articles on India in 1853. Born in 1620 of a leaseholding farmer in Anjou, Bernier took his licentiate in medicine, and began his grand tour in 1654 when he visited Palestine and Syria. Bernier then spent two years in Egypt and, abandoning his plan to visit Abyssinia, sailed for India and entered the port of Surat in late 1658 or early 1659. Finding himself in straitened circumstances and faced with penury, he took employment for a short time with Prince Dara who was engaged in an unsuccessful war for the throne with Aurangzeb. Thereafter he fell in with the mughal *amir*, Dhanishmand Khan, a scholar and diplomat, who was also accorded the status of a commander of 3000 men and paymaster of the army, and who employed Bernier as a physician.

Bernier travelled widely in India: he spent some time in Delhi, and Agra and Lahore, visited Kashmir, and set out on a voyage to Bengal with Tavernier[1] in 1666; from there he travelled to Masulipatam and Golconda. He departed from India in 1667 and, visiting Persia on the way, returned to Paris. But Bernier's characterisation of India and its neighbours was no innocent 'objective account', and like many, if not all, pieces of reporting it contained axioms that he had inherited from his predecessors' accounts of the Orient which he employed in a typically European political discourse.

Bernier's unforgettable pronouncements were that Asiatic states lacked private property in land, or a hereditary nobility, and the personalistic monarchs ruled tyrannically and arbitrarily. Consequently the people were ground down into a state of servile 'equality', and they were all alike in their common subjection to the caprices of the despot. Government by fear was the strategy of rule. We recognise that these are precisely the features which Montesquieu later attributed to despotism (though he, in turn, added some notions to the tradition he had inherited). It therefore should not surprise us—though I confess I was surprised when I discovered it—that Bernier himself, despite his authentic travels and his reporting of events he had lived through, was reading the Indian scene almost verbatim in terms of the account of earlier travellers to India, particularly Sir Thomas Roe, who led an English embassy to the court of Emperor Jahangir during the years 1615–19, some forty years earlier (see Foster 1926).

A letter Thomas Roe wrote to Prince Charles dated 30 October 1616 (ibid.: 270–71) had this to say about the 'Great Mogull', emperor of India. (The emperor in question was Shah Jahan.) The contents of this letter are later echoed by both Bernier and Montesquieu: 'The present emperor is descended from Temarlane the Great.' His vast territories lie on both sides of the Indus and beyond the Ganges: 'The border westward is Persia, east the Gulph of Bengala, north the mountaynes of

[1] Jean-Baptiste Tavernier's *Travels in India* (1925 [1676]) was another famous source for information on India, and may also have been consulted by Montesquieu. Although Tavernier made some six voyages to Asia and travelled a great deal in the Mughal Empire, buying and selling diamonds and precious stones, his book does not compare with Bernier's as regards political and administrative information. Indeed his description of Mughal politics seems to have been largely derived from Bernier.

Tarus (that divide him from the Tatars), south the kingdom of Deccan and the Bay of Cambaya'. He is plentiful in wealth and the commodities of trade, with revenue far above any eastern monarch known; in jewels he is the 'treasury of the world'.

'And yet all this greatness, compared and weighted judiciously, is like a play, that serves more for delight and to entertayne the vulgar than for any use. For noe man enters his house but eunucks; his weomen are never seene; his nobilitye are like counters, placed high and low at his pleasure; his servants base and barbarous; and all his life as regular as a clock that stricks at sett howers.' His time is spent in routine audiences, in attendances at the fights of elephants and wild beasts, and in nightly drinking with much affability. 'The rest of his motion is inward among women, of which sort, though hee keepe a thousand, yet one governs him, and wynds him up at her pleasure.' He claims to be as great a prophet as Mahomett and confesseth not 'that they are both impostures in that kind.'

Of the Mughal emperor's Hindu subjects, Roe wrote: 'The naturalls are Gentils, following sundry idolatryes and worshiping the creatures of heaven and earth promiscuously. . . . The severest of these are Pythagorians for the opinion of the soules transmigration, and will not kyll any living creature, no, not the virmine that bites them, for fear of disseising the speiritt of some friend departed. . . .all sorts of religions are wellcome and free, for the King is of none. . . .'

'They are governed by noe constant lawe, which in all new occasions is received from the Kings mouth, and, farr distant, from his vizeroyes. No man hath proprietye in land nor goods, if he please to take it; soe that all are slaves. . . .'

Roe's letter of 30 October 1616 to the Lord Bishop of Canterbury (ibid.: 272) referred to court factionalism and intrigues: 'the ambitions and divisions in the present state, that like impostumes lye now hidd, but threaten to break out into the rending and ruine of the whole by bloody warr; the practises, subtiltyes and carnages of factions and court-secretts, falsely called wisdome. . . .'

The foregoing excerpts refer to the territorial spread of the Mughal empire, the fantastic wealth of the emperor and his decadent court life, the lack of an independent nobility and private property in land, the servile condition of the populace wallowing in a lush heathenism and presided over by an ungodly emperor. A cluster of such stereotyped signs constituted oriental despotism in the European mentality.

Having shown Bernier's antecedents in Roe, I could go on to demonstrate that Roe himself was in part anticipated by the observations of some other Englishmen who travelled in northern and western India, such as Ralph Fitch (1583–91), John Mildenhall (1599–1606), William Hawkins (1603–13), William Finch (1608–11), Nicholas Withington (1612–16) and Thomas Coryat (1612–17).[2] All these English gentlemen, including Roe, had a common task which was to establish their right to conduct trade in India, notwithstanding the opposition of the Portuguese who had preceded them. I could then show that some of these travellers in turn plagiarised

[2] Aside from Sir Thomas Roe, who has left us a lengthy account of his embassy, these other travellers left records and letters which were published in various places. Relevant portions of their records, plus a selection from Edward Terry (1616–19) who was in India at the time of Roe, are to be found in Foster (1968).

from others before them,[3] but I will spare you this trail of regress, and also the speculation it raises in my mind concerning the constraining influence in my own subject of anthropology of earlier ethnographers upon later ones who, whether in imitation or in rebellion, inevitably must grapple with the blinders placed on their vision by their predecessors.

Instead, I have another argument to make here about Bernier, which is that while he conspicuously affirmed the traditional western stereotype of oriental despotism he also reported in detail the colourful facts of the political scene of his time in India which, if patiently read and arranged, compose a pattern quite different from that proclaimed by him.

Our text shall be his Letter to Monseigneur Colbert, who was finance minister to Louis XIV of France: the subtitle of this letter is 'concerning the Extent of Hindoustan, the currency towards, and final absorption of gold and silver in that country; its Resources, Armies, the administration of Justice, and the principal Cause of the Decline of the States of Asia'.

First we have to place our text in its context. Bernier's arrival in India coincided with the installation of Aurangzeb as emperor, whose rule (1658–1707) was marked by an indulgence in excesses—particularly the persecution of Hindus on a wide scale and the extension of the empire by expensive and ultimately ruinous wars. In fact Bernier's deservedly most famous piece in the Travels is called 'The History of the Late Rebellion in the States of the Great Mogol' in which he reported the tortuous intrigues and gory battles surrounding the competition among the previous emperor Shah Jahan's four sons ('the great contending belligerents') for the throne and the final triumph of Aurangzeb.[4]

Now, the Mughal empire itself was founded by Babur in 1525, and many would hold that it attained its greatest stature under Akbar, who as a youth succeeded to a

[3] Thus Ralph Fitch, apparently distrusting his literary skills, closely copied the narrative of Cesar Federico, the Venetian merchant who, starting in 1563, travelled by way of Basra and Ormuz to Goa, and paid visits to Gujarat and Vijayanagar, and most of the Portuguese settlements. Fitch copied from Frederico whenever routes taken by him overlapped with Frederico's journeys.

Quite the opposite took place with William Finch's accounts: Johannes de Laet availed himself freely of the materials provided by Finch in his *De Imperio Magni Mogolis* (1631); and Thomas Herbert in turn copied de Laet in the second edition (1638) of his own travels in India which in fact were confined to the immediate vicinity of Surat only (Foster 1968: 122)!

[4] Bernier's account of the fratricidal war of succession fought by Shah Jahan's four turbulent sons forewarns us of the potentiality for the fragmentation of power at the very centre of the empire. Here is a sample passage:

> He [Shah Jahan] was indeed in perpetual apprehension of their having recourse to arms, and either erecting independent principalities, or converting the seat of government into a bloody arena, in which to settle their personal differences. To save himself, therefore, from some impending and overwhelming calamity, Chah-Jehan resolved to bestow upon his sons the government of four distant provinces. Sultan Sujah was appointed to Bengale; Aureng-Zeb to the Decan; Morad-Bakche to Guzarate; and Dara to Caboul and Moultan. The three first-mentioned Princes repaired to their respective provinces without delay, and soon betrayed the spirit by which they were animated. They acted in every respect as independent sovereigns, appropriated the revenues to their own use, and levied formidable armies under pretence of maintaining tranquility at home, and commanding respect abroad (Bernier 1914: 15).

precarious dominion over territories which were represented by parts of the Punjab and the United Provinces of Agra and Oudh.[5] By 1584 Akbar had vastly extended his domains, partly by diplomacy and partly by conquest. He had become master of Gujarat, Malwa and the bulk of Rajputana; in the east he had subdued, but not entirely assimilated, the provinces of Bihar and Bengal. Later in his reign he recovered control of Kabul and added to his empire Kashmir, Sind, Kandahar, Khandesh, and parts of Ahmadnagar. Akbar was followed by Jahangir (1605–1627) who consolidated the empire and followed a policy of conciliation toward the Hindus; then came Shah Jahan (1627–1658) whose magnificence reached its climax with the building of the Taj Mahal.

Bernier's letter to Colbert will be more comprehensible if we note that during Akbar's time and later, south of the Mughal dominions lay the Muslim kingdoms of Ahmadnagar on the western and Golconda on the eastern sides of the peninsula. South of Ahmadnagar was still a third Muslim kingdom, that of Bijapur. The rest of the peninsula was ruled by petty Hindu princes, the chief of whom was the Raja of Chandragiri (referred to in contemporary records as 'King of the Carnatic').

There is no doubt that Bernier's letter is written with a view to siding with the French monarch in the polemics about French absolutism. Bernier makes no bones of the fact that it was in 'Hindoustan' that he came to appreciate by comparison the happiness of France, and that the Mughal despotism was quite different from the regions of 'our great Monarch'. Towards the end of the letter, Bernier drives home the differences he sees thus:

> Those three countries, Turkey, Persia, and Hindoustan have no idea of the principle of meum and tuum, relatively to land or other real possessions; and having lost that respect for the right of property, which is the basis of all that is useful and good in this world, necessarily resemble each other in essential points: they. . .sooner or later, experience the natural consequences of those errors—tyranny, ruin and misery.
>
> How happy and thankful should we feel, My Lord, that in our quarter of the globe, Kings are not the sole proprietors of the soil! Were they so, we should seek in vain for countries well cultivated and populous, for well-built and opulent cities, for a polite, contented, and flourishing people.[6]

[5] The following are the regnal years of the Mughal Emperors from 1556–1748: Akbar 1556–1605; Jahangir 1605–1627; Shah Jahan 1627–1658; Aurangzeb 1658–1707; Bahadur Shah 1707–1712; Farrukhsiyar 1712–1719, and Muhammad Shah (1719–1748).

[6] Elsewhere, Bernier describes the naming customs such that the eldest son of the Great Mughal is called Darius, the second Sultan Sujah (the valiant prince), the third Aurangzeb (the throne's ornament):

> The reason why such names are given to the great, instead of titles derived from domains or seigniories, as usual in Europe, is this: as the land throughout the whole empire is considered the property of the sovereign, there can be no earldoms, marquisates, or duchies. The royal grants consist only of pensions, either in land or money, which the king gives, augments, retrenches, or takes away at his pleasure (Bernier 1914: 5).

> . . .If the same system of government as that of Asia existed with us, where, I must ask again, should we find Princes, Prelates, Nobles, opulent Citizens, and thriving Tradesmen, ingenious Artisans and Manufacturers? Where should we look for such cities as Paris, Lyons, Toulouse, Rouen, or, if you will, London, and so many others? (Bernier 1914: 232–33).

Thus the lesson, which the European political philosophers had accepted as axiomatic, is driven home: 'there can be no analogy between a kingdom whose monarch is proprietor of a few domains, and a kingdom where the monarch possesses, in his own right, every acre of the soil.' To this is added the presence or absence of a system of laws and the rule of law: 'In France the laws are reasonable, that the King is the first to obey them: his domains are held without the violation of any right; his farmers or stewards may be sued at law, and the aggrieved artisan or peasant is sure to find redress against injustice and oppression. But in eastern countries. . .the only law that decides all controversies is the care and the caprice of a governor' (ibid.: 236). In sum, 'take away the right of private property in land, and you introduce, as a sure and necessary consequence, tyranny, slavery, injustice, beggary and barbarism' (ibid.: 238).

If such are the conclusions Bernier rhetorically proclaimed as the results of his comparison of Europe and Asia, let us now review the facts he reported, and see whether his conclusions are logically derived from them. My submission is that Bernier's description of the Mughal empire shows it to be a vast 'galactic' assembly with a complicated replication of authority, of administrative structures, and of rights over the management and produce of the soil, and that therefore its characterisation as an absolutist oriental despotism is a bizarre distortion.

Bernier gives an idea of the spatial vastness of 'the Great Mogol's empire' of Hindoustan at the time of emperor Aurangzeb by comparison with France. At the ordinary rate of travel at that time it would take a journey of three months to the frontier of the kingdom of Golconda (in the south) and to Ghazni or beyond it, near to the Persian border town of Kandahar (in the northwest). He surmises that the distance could not be less than five hundred French leagues, or five times as far as from Paris to Lyons.

Bernier comments on the fertility of this empire, the articles of commerce it manufactures and exports, its imports, and the flow of gold and silver into it. A large portion of the tract is fertile, the large kingdom of Bengal for instance surpassing Egypt itself, not only in the production of foodstuffs but also in articles of commerce such as silks, cotton and indigo 'which are not cultivated in Egypt'. There are many other parts of the country famous for manufacture, not only of silk and cotton goods but also carpets, brocades, embroideries, gold and silver cloths.

Bernier informs that gold and silver come from every quarter of the globe to Hindoustan to be swallowed up and in large measure to remain permanently there. From Europe and America, gold goes to Turkey in payment for goods imported from it; from Turkey by further trade with Persia and Yemen, it passes to Hindoustan in exchange for the latter's goods, at the three celebrated ports of trade,

Moka on the Red Sea, Bassora on the Persian Gulf and Gomeron near Ormuz. On the Southeast Asian side, Indian vessels, whether they belonged to Indians or to the Dutch, English or the Portuguese, carried merchandise from Hindoustan to Pegu, Tenasserim, Siam, Ceylon, or Acheen (in Sumatra), from which countries it received a quantity of precious materials. Moreover a part of the gold and silver which the Dutch draw from Japan also finds its way to Hindoustan.

Although Hindoustan imported goods from all over the world—she obtained copper, cloves and nutmegs from the Moluccas and Ceylon, broadcloths from France, lead from England, more than 25,000 horses from Usbec, Arabia and Persia, musk and porcelain from China, pearls from El-Bahrein and Ceylon, rhinoceros horns and slaves from Ethiopia, and an immense quantity of fresh fruit from Samarkand, Bokhara and Persia—nevertheless she paid for these imports with her own products, hence had no need to export her stock of gold and silver.

Although Bernier is immensely impressed with the incalculable wealth of the Great Mughal, the gold, silver and varied goods that were imported, and the equally varied goods that were exported in turn, he says little about the institutions, arrangements and specialists, both indigenous and foreign, who must have made possible Hindoustan's array of manufactures and complex trade flows. But he does tell us much about those many circumstances which form a 'counterpoise' to the Mughal emperor's riches and his sovereignty of ownership. It is these antithetical factors that we should look at closely, for he enumerates under this guise the centrifugal components and the satellite powers that revolve around the centrepiece of the Mughal court.

The first circumstance need not detain us for long, for it is pretty standard evidence of 'despotism' whose import can actually be read in the opposite way. Bernier says that many of the poor peasantry, driven to despair by the tyranny and demands of rapacious lords, abandon the country, and seek an existence in the towns or camps, or fly to the territories of a less oppressive raja. Some modern scholars read this as evidence of peasant resistance and why monarchs could not afford to be despots.[7]

The second circumstance is all-important. The empire of the Moghul, Bernier tells us, 'comprehends several nations, over which he is not absolute master'. Most of these polities 'still retain their own peculiar chiefs or sovereigns' who obey the Mughal or pay him tribute 'only by compulsion'. In many instances the tribute is of trifling amount, in others none is paid, and in certain other cases, they themselves 'receive tribute' or subsidies instead of paying out.

(1) The petty sovereignties bordering the Persian frontiers seldom pay tribute either to the Mughal empire or the Shah of Persia. Nor does the Mughal emperor receive anything considerable from the Baluchi, Afghan and Pathan tribes. Indeed the Baluchis once arrested the march of the Mughal forces on their way to Kabul and

[7] Others, however, including Moreland and Barrington Moore, cite Bernier as providing important evidence of heavy extortions by the officials leading to agrarian instability and peasant rebellions. I shall refer to this later.

solicited presents before they could proceed further. The Pathans were intractable, and therefore mortally hated the Mughals; previously their sultans had reigned at Delhi (between 1200–1550), many of their neighbouring rajas being then their tributaries.

(2) If the north-west border tribes were virtually independent, the king of Bijapur in the region south of Ahmadnagar, engaged in perpetual warfare with Mughals, from whose control he strove to keep his dominions. The king of Bijapur's preservation was owed mostly to the fact that his kingdom was at a great distance from Agra and Delhi, the usual places of residence of the Mughal. Bernier reports that several other rajas joined Bijapur for the sake of their mutual security when attacked by the Mughals, and that in one such encounter they even plundered and burnt the rich seaport of Surat.

(3) Even more deflationary of the Mughal emperor's despotism was the existence of more than a hundred rajas of considerable strength, dispersed over the whole empire, some near and some at a distance from Agra and Delhi. Fifteen or sixteen of these rajas were rich and formidable, particularly the ruler of Chitor or Udaipur, 'formerly considered emperor of the Rajas'. Bernier is in fact referring here to the Rajput kingdoms, and admits that if the three rajput kings of Udaipur, Jesseingue and Jessomseigngue chose to enter into an offensive league, they would prove dangerous to the Mughal because each of them could muster twenty thousand cavalry.

(4) Bernier next proceeds to explain the complex problem of why the Great Mughal emperor, a foreigner in the midst of his courtiers, was forced to rely so much upon the military prowess of his Rajput tributaries.

The Mughal emperor was of the Sunni sect, while the majority of his courtiers, being Persians, were Shias. He was moreover a foreigner in Hindustan because he was a descendent of Tamerlane who overran India about 1401, and the proportion of Mughals to the gentile or Hindu population was insignificant. The court itself did not at this time consist of real Mughals, but was 'a medley of Usbecs, Persians, Arabs, and Turks, or descendants of these people'. But amongst all these, loosely called Mughals, the third and fourth generation descendants sank in the social scale, having the brown complexion and languid manner of their country, and were seldom employed in official positions, and were fortunate and happy if allowed to serve as private soldiers in the infantry or cavalry. This implied then a dilution of court society, and not an exclusive rule by the ruling circles, let alone a tight hold on power.

Thus to maintain himself in the midst of domestic and powerful enemies, and always in danger of hostile movements on the side of Persia and Usbec, the emperor was under the necessity of keeping numerous armies, even in the time of peace. These armies were composed of Rajputs, Pathans and of Mughals, both genuine and spurious. And they involved the emperor in a vast expenditure of his effective means and resources.

To the Rajput rajas, the Mughal emperor granted large sums for the service of a certain number of their soldiers 'to be kept always ready at his disposal'. These rajas enjoyed an equal rank with the foreign and Muslim Omrahs, [Amirs] whether they were present in the emperor's capital or stationed in the provinces.

There were many good reasons why the Mughal emperor was obliged to retain the rajas in his service, and why he found the rajas essential in order to hold on to his empire. The rajas were not only excellent soldiers, they could mobilise and bring to the field in any one day twenty thousand men. They were necessary to keep in check kingdoms outside the Mughal control and to bring to submission those who refused to pay tribute or give military assistance. 'Whenever the King of Golkonda [Golconda] withholds his tribute or evinces an inclination to defend the King of Visapour [Bijapur] or any neighbouring Raja whom the Mogol wishes to despoil or render tributary, Rajas are sent against him in preference to the Omrahs, who being for the most part Persians, were Shias and therefore of the same Islamic sect as the Kings of Persia and Golconda, and different from that of the Mughal emperor.' Thus the Mughal emperor never found the Rajas more useful than when he was engaged in hostility with the Persians. Finally the rajas were always at hand to be employed against the rebellious Pathans or against any rebellious Omrah or governor.

The Mughal emperor found equally good reasons for engaging Pathan soldiers in his operations against internal and external enemies. And the well-known strategies of divide and rule, of fomenting jealousy, and of dispensing invidious favouritism, were employed to keep the rajas in check or to kindle warfare amongst them.

Despite the partial reliance on such local military assets, the principal armed forces of the emperor were composed of the Mughals themselves and maintained at great expense. A part of these troops, both cavalry and infantry, were always near the emperor's person in his capital or residence at any point of time, while the remainder was dispersed in the several provinces.

Bernier described the ranks of these troops, the principles of their recruitment and the manner in which they were maintained and remunerated. His assertions that the nobility were precarious and servile creatures of the emperor apply to this segment of the Mughal court, and not at all to the rajas, petty sovereigns and chiefs plentifully found outside the central region of direct imperial control.

The cavalry kept near the person of the emperor were the elite force and Bernier divides them into four categories—the omrahs [amirs] at the top, followed by the mansebdars [mansabdars], then the rouzindars, and finally the common troops at the bottom.

The amirs, the 'lords of the court', are not, Bernier stresses, 'members of ancient families, as our nobility in France'. 'The King being proprietor of all the lands in the empire, there can exist neither Dukedoms nor Marquisates; nor can any family be found possessed of wealth arising from a domain, and living upon its own patrimony' (Bernier 1914: 211). The courtiers are not even descendants of amirs, because the Mughal emperor, being heir to the possessions of his Amir lords, systematically dispossessed their sons and grandsons, and reduced the latter at any rate to beggary or the status of mere troopers. Of course the amirs did seek to advance their sons' careers while they were alive, but advancement through royal favour was slow from inferior offices to positions of trust. Hence, Bernier concluded, the amirs 'mostly consist of adventurers from different nations who entice one another to the court'; they were sons of low descent, and destitute of education, and the emperor 'raises them to dignities, or degrades them to obscurity, according to his own pleasure and caprice'.

The ranked military titles of the amirs were associated with the number of horses normally in their control. A hazari was a lord of a thousand horses; the superior hazari successfully controlled two, five, seven, ten and twelve thousand horses, the last being the position held by the emperor's eldest son. A trooper was assigned to look after two horses, and from this formula the number of troopers in the control of each hazari could be calculated. Bernier remarked that the body of horses and men assigned to the titles was inflated and fictional, and that the emperor controlled their effective number.

Most of the amirs received large cash payments from the treasury according to the horses and men under their direct management, but some fortunate ones received jagirs of land (i.e., office tenures of land) from which to receive a part of their income. The amirs ran large establishments of their own consisting of wives, servants, camels and horses, lived extravagantly, and were obliged to give costly presents to the emperor at annual festivals. The lesser cavalry officers—the mansabdars and rouzindars etc.—were paid salaries on a similar basis, and their lifestyles varied according to their incomes.

Bernier acknowledges that he could not ascertain the number of amirs who must have been numerous in the armies, provinces and at court. He never saw fewer than twenty-five to thirty at court. It is these amirs who were 'the pillars of the empire', and attained to the highest honours and positions at court, in the provinces and in the armies. They moved mounted on elephant or horseback, or were carried in palanquins, and they were attended by their retinue of cavalry and servants on foot. They in turn attended on the king twice a day, and kept guard in the fortress once a week. And whenever the king went on an excursion, they were bound to accompany him on horseback.

The army stationed in the provinces did not differ from that about the king's person, except in its greater number. In every district were posted amirs, mansabdars and rouzindars, cannon troops, infantry and artillery. In the Deccan alone the cavalry numbered some twenty to twenty-five, even up to thirty, thousand, and such numbers were necessary to overcome the powerful king of Golconda, and to maintain war against the King of Bijapur, and the Rajas who joined their forces with his. No less than twelve to fifteen thousand were stationed in the kingdom of Kabul to guard against hostile movements on the part of the Afghans, Baluchis and the Persians. In Bengal, so frequently the seat of war, the number was much greater. And since in fact no province could dispense with a military force, the total number of troops in Hindoustan was almost incredible. Bernier calculates that the combined effective cavalry—composed of those about the emperor's person, those in the control of the indigenous rajas and Pathans, and those in the provinces—formed a total of 200,000 horses.[8]

In the light of these military deployments and commitments, we can readily appreciate Bernier's assertion that although the Mughal emperor's revenue was great—indeed greater than the joint revenues of the Grand Seignieur of France and of the King of Persia—yet his expenditures and redistribution of wealth being equally great, he was in real effective terms hard-pressed, frequently in difficulties, as regards paying and supplying his armies. Moreover, the emperor's vast treasure of jewels and precious stones, being considered the sole property of the crown, could not readily be converted to money or be used as security for raising cash, in times of crisis.

What we need to decipher in Bernier's voluble and gossipy account of the exotic extravagances of the court is the nature of the king's devolution of the land of Hindoustan, for on this rests Bernier's major allegation of tyranny, slavery and lack of private property.

He informs us that the emperor 'as proprietor of the land' made over a certain quantity of it as jagir grants to military men. (Jagir he glosses as 'the spot from which to draw, or the place of salary.') 'Similar grants are made to governors, in lieu of their salary, and also for the support of their troops, on condition that they pay a certain sum annually to the King out of any surplus that the land may yield.' Bernier does not tell us what proportion of the Empire is in the emperor's direct gift: he surely cannot be including the domain in the control of the Hindoustan rajas—whether of Golconda or Udaipur or other Rajput little kingdoms; nor can the border tribal territories under the control of Baluchi, Afghan and Pathan tribes have been the emperor's to alienate. The jagirs he refers to were situated in the secure provinces and were alienated as office tenures to amir lords and provincial governors.

The rest of the lands in the emperor's control, Bernier tells us, were given out to contractors (fermiers), royal agents, and officials to administer and pay him annual rents. It is Bernier's accusation—on what direct evidence this is based we are not told, since Bernier's direct knowledge is confined to the courtiers surrounding the Emperor's person—that these royal officials exercised 'an authority almost

[8] The mansabdars or 'petty amirs' acknowledged no other chief but the king and directly served him. They apparently controlled from two to six horses bearing the king's mark and they received incomes ranging from 150 to 700 rupees. There were never less than 200–300 attached to the court.

The rouzindars received daily pay, and though their total salary may not have been inferior to that of the mansabdars, they had inferior court privileges. They filled the inferior offices, many being clerks and under-clerks and such like.

The common horsemen who served under the amirs, carried their amir's mark on the thigh, and were paid variably according to the generosity of their lord. Bernier also gives some interesting information about the footsoldiers and the artillery. The infantry proper Bernier thinks was not large—not more than 15,000 immediately about the King. Though the numbers swelled when the king was on the move if we add the porters, the servants, those in charge of tents and kitchens, not to mention the accompanying women.

absolute over the peasantry, and nearly as much over the artisans and merchants of the towns and villages'. The point behind this tendentious assertion is revealed when Bernier comments that the injured peasant or trader had no redress because 'no great lords, parliaments, or judges of local courts, exist as in France, to restrain the wickedness of the merciless oppressors, and the Kadis, or judges, are not invested with sufficient power to redress the wrongs. . .' (Bernier 1914: 224). This sad abuse of the royal authority, Bernier conceded, may not be felt in the same degree near capital cities such as Delhi and Agra or in the vicinity of large towns and seaports.

In a somewhat less condemnatory paragraph a few pages later, he admitted that the eastern states 'are not altogether destitute of good laws, which if properly administered, would render Asia as eligible a residence as any other part of the world'. But he countered that the existence of such laws was of little advantage when the power to redress wrongs rested with the grand vizier or Kings who appointed the self-same provincial tyrants. Indeed the very sale of offices to officials ensured that extorting tyrants would be appointed. This practice prevailed at all times, but especially at the outbreak of a war, the sale of governorships for immense sums of money was intensified. Naturally it became the principal object of the individual thus appointed to obtain repayments of the purchase-money, which he had borrowed at a ruinous rate of interest.

This 'debasing state of slavery' obstructed the progress of trade, and influenced the mode of life of every individual. When wealth is acquired, great care is taken by the possessor to hide it and to appear indigent; he dare not invest his wealth on dress, lodging or furniture, nor indulge in the pleasures of the table. Both agriculture and commerce decline under this tyranny, and 'the arts in the Indies would long ago have lost their beauty and delicacy, if the Monarch and the Omrahs did not keep in their pay a number of artists who work in their houses', and if powerful patrons did not afford protection to rich merchants and tradesmen who pay workmen rather higher wages (ibid.: 225).

These were the facts and arguments that Bernier adduced to drive home the lesson that compared with the monarchy of France, which had limited dominion over the land, which ruled according to the law, and which supported the social ranks and institutions that mediated between monarch and populace, Hindoustan, and by extension, all Asiatic states were despotic tyrannies which on every point of comparison proved to be the absolute opposite.

That Bernier's dramatic assertions had become standard lore, even among circles not devoted to the French monarchy, can be confirmed by their grave academic repetition by no less a person than Barrington Moore in his well-known liberal treatise on the social origins of dictatorship and democracy (Moore 1967).[9]

Moore made much of the alleged concentration of powers in the hands of Akbar, and his absolutist relation to the imperial political elect, the nobility and their

[9] Moore's chief authority for the Mughal period was W.H. Moreland's *India at the death of Akbar* (1920), and *The agrarian system of Moslem India* (1929).

military followers, especially the mansabdars and amirs. Moore's own 'despotic reading' looks on these imperial commanders and administrators negatively as examples of 'no landed aristocracy of national scope independent of the crown'. Indices of this condition are that 'Land was held theoretically, and to a great extent in practice, at the pleasure of the ruler', the imperial officers being assigned the imperial revenue over an area according to the dignity of his office; that there was no such thing as the inheritance of office and that on the death of the holder his wealth reverted to the treasury; and that there was prevention of 'the growth of property rights in office'. All these signify an Asian version of 'agrarian bureaucracy' and 'royal absolutism'. Moore however recognised that the implication of the assignment of the royal share to officials was that 'During the Moghul period, sometimes as much as seven-eights of its area, was in the hands of such assignees.' And when we consider that this arrangement served as a method of recruiting troops to the army by the mansabdars we see the immense opening toward a galactic parcelling out of the revenue rights. Moore moreover concedes that despite the rules prohibiting the inheritance of office among the nobles a number of noble families endured and persisted in the regimes of the emperors, and that the Hindu chiefs, local rulers whom the Mughals conquered, were left in authority and exempted from interference as the price paid for their loyalty. In any case, this structure of 'an agrarian bureaucracy imposed on top of a heterogeneous collection of native chieftains' reverted to looser forms as the Mughal authority weakened in the 18th century.

Barrington Moore with his Eurocentric liberal socialist perspective stands in a direct line of descent from Montesquieu and Locke when he stresses that in Mughal India there was no independent national nobility and no coalition between landed interests and local merchants and traders which are preconditions for the indigenous development of capitalism and parliamentary democracy. Indeed, in what amounts to a reversed Whig reading of history, the contours and trajectory of Mughal India are discussed as if they were perversely designed so as not to achieve cumulatively Western-type democracy and industry:

> The dynamics of the Mughal system were unfavourable to the development of either political democracy or economic growth in anything resembling the Western pattern. There was no landed aristocracy that had succeeded in achieving independence and privilege against the monarch while retaining political unity. Instead their independence, if it can be called that, had brought anarchy in its train. What there was of bureaucracy likewise lacked an independent base. Both features are connected with a predatory bureaucracy, driven to become ever more grasping as its power weakened, and which by crushing the peasants and driving them into rebellion returned the subcontinent to what it had often been before, a series of fragmented units fighting with one another, ready prey for another foreign conqueror (Moore 1967: 330).

So, according to this account, when the despotic bubble bursts, India fragments into its atomistic village communities whose organisation of labour in terms of caste was a cause for poor cultivation, and whose organisation of authority in the local community, again in terms of caste, inhibited political unity. 'By its very flexibility Indian society seems to have rendered fundamental change very difficult' (ibid.: 341).

II

Property rights under the Mughals

An effective dissolvent of the myth of the absolute property rights of the Mughal emperor has been the authoritative work of Irfan Habib (1963) based on the revenue records of the imperial administration. In fact his exegesis of the status and powers of the zamindar is a crucial falsification of the Bernier–Montesquieu thesis of there being 'no private property in land' and no fragmentation of political power, and the non-existence of 'intermediate powers' in the oriental polities.

Habib divides the category zamindar into two types, those who were situated within the territories under direct imperial administration, and those who were outside it in the status of vassal chiefs and tributary petty rulers. Let us deal with each type in turn. The alleged Mughal administrative ideal of controlling the assessment and collection of revenue from the centre through its officials was never achieved—except perhaps in relatively small areas and for brief periods—because its implementation would have required a large body of salaried officials under the emperor's direct control. This was beyond his capacities and resources.

Apart from the system of assigning the royal revenue of stipulated areas to offices (watans), the Mughals found it necessary to rule and tax through those native intermediaries who have come to be known as zamindars, a label which has, as we all know today, no uniform signification, especially as regards the degree of independence enjoyed by them from the control of the central authority, and the character of their rights over the cultivating peasantry they dominated.

Now, the important point is that the Mughal revenue scheme recognised the powers of the local dominant castes or other elites which, through various processes from invasion and conquest to local expansion and manipulation, had established their own ruling rights to collect revenue and taxes over the peasant in the regions they dominated. The rights of the zamindars were thus anterior to the Mughal assumption of power, which had therefore to come to terms with them. After their incorporation into the imperial administration they frequently collected their dues and taxes as before, being now called upon to pay a certain portion of their takings to the imperial treasury, a demand not always successfully enforced. It is quite clear that zamindari rights could be subdivided, transferred by inheritance, and sold, and that if the Mughal authorities strained to press the zamindars of the most populous and affluent areas into imperial service, the zamindars, in turn, resisted the assimilation. Habib trenchantly sums up the situation thus. In Mughal India there was no one integral single 'private property' right, whether it be claimed by ruler or independent gentry. There were various rights over the land, to its occupancy and to varying shares in its produce, which were 'individually salable'. Of these the most important non-peasant right was that of zamindari. 'Sixteenth and seventeenth century records show beyond doubt that zamindari right was completely an article of property: it was fully inherited and it was sold without any kind of caste or other restriction.' The zamindars spread all over the country were a class 'quite apart from the "bureaucracy" of the State'; they 'were treated by the nobility (jagirdars) as basically and potentially antagonistic to the State'; they were in no sense like the 'bureaucratic gentry' of China (Habib 1963: ch. 5).

The zamindars outside the range of direct imperial administration were in fact autonomous chiefs. The line between a zamindar and a raja was in practice frequently difficult to draw. Although a zamindar in the imperial territories was subordinate to the administration which frequently strove to convert him into a tax gatherer, he shared certain features with men of greater power, with chiefs and petty kings called rajas, ranas, raos. These were traditional titles generally confirmed by the Mughal emperors upon the submission of these personages.

> Like them he [the zamindar] held some territory which he could call his own; like them he was no creature, normally, of the imperial government; and like them he had warriors to defend his possessions. Sometimes the lines between the two could not be rigidly drawn. We may find a person calling himself a raja selling his right to a village like any other zamindar. And in the Dakhim, a deshmukh (equivalent to the north Indian chaudhuri) could grow into a chief, while the descendants of a powerful chief might shrink into deshmukhs (ibid.: 183).

But of course these similarities should not obscure important differences. Not only did the chiefs control greater military power and greater territory, they also, more importantly, enjoyed greater autonomy vis-à-vis the imperial government. The relations between the chiefs and the Mughals were not uniform (ibid.: 184), but once the imperial government had exacted military service or money from the chiefs, it left them free to manage their internal affairs, such as holding their own courts of justice, levying cesses and duties on trade passing through their territories at rates fixed by themselves, and collecting their own revenues. Some Rajput states, the kingdom of Jodhpur for example, seem to have been influenced by the general pattern of Mughal administration: the Raja held a few villages in each pargana for his own treasury, while he assigned the rest in pattus, equivalent to jagirs, to his officers in lieu of pay.

Irfan Habib gives an emphatic confirmation of what we discerned from Bernier's account as the pattern of relationships between the central regions under control, and the surrounding satellite, border and peripheral regions. In the 17th century the Mughal Empire's area of direct control was the great belt of the Zabti provinces from Lahore to Bihar. A series of petty kingdoms stretched along the Himalayas from Jammu to Kumaun, and more sporadically in the Tarai further eastwards. West of the Chenab, in Multan province, the Baluchi chiefs held sway, while on the southern fringe of the plains, part of Haryana was controlled by Rajput chiefs. The southern parts of Agra, Allahabad and Bihar which merged with the spurs of the Vindhya mountains were outside imperial control and, at the eastern end, large areas of the province of Bengal were covered by petty kingdoms.

The bulk of the Ajmer province comprised the dominions of the great Rajput princes, and in Gujarat and Malwa, the entire sarkars of Mandsur and Kathiawar respectively were given over to tributary states. The imperial territories in Gujarat were themselves ringed by a belt of tributary states, which terminated with the kingdom of Baglan. There was finally a large block of states in Central India extending from Garh to Telingana.

It seems then that while one must not underrate the size and power of the Mughal administration in its richest and most populous lands of the Indo-Gangetic plain, even there the imperial officialdom was supplemented by zamindars and important princes whose incorporation into the official scheme frequently left them with much of their previous autonomy. But beyond this, the territory ruled by chiefs and rajas was impressive, and a commonality of aspirations to rule, and past memories of affinity, joined these satellite regions with the numerous zamindars whom the imperial government had tamed. As Habib has put it, in a language not altogether emancipated from the myth of despotism: 'from the view-point of the Mughal Government there was a chain of local despotisms, covering the whole Empire, here semi-independent, there fairly subdued, here represented by chiefs, there by ordinary zamindars' (1963: 184).[10]

Although Bernier's interpretation of land tenure and property rights were unduly exaggerated on the side of absolutism, it is clear that he had a less clouded comprehension of the organisation of the imperial court as such, and the special rules of etiquette and ties of patronage that bound the Mughal emperor and his immediate circle of superior mansabdar nobles. Recent scholars, both Western and Indian, have painted in rich colours the contours of court life, and the images of personages, both emperor and courtier. These accounts enable us to appreciate that the most distinctive feature of the Mughal empire, as compared with Indian polities that preceded and succeeded it, lay in the special charisma of the emperor's person and the 'personalistic' bonds that magnetised courtiers to him, rather than in the pattern of devolution of office tenures of land (jagir) from centre to periphery.

III
Mughal administration and imperial court

J.F. Richards, for example, has given a positive account of how Akbar has 'built upon his personal appeal to establish an image of the emperor's person as an embodiment of the Empire' (Richards 1975: 253). Akbar was a charismatic leader who successfully bound his amirs and mansabdars of diverse social origins to

[10] Some, like the great Rajput chiefs entered imperial service and obtained mansab ranks, their ancestral domains being considered a special type of untransferable and hereditary jagir known in official records as Watan. The usual practice was to assess the total revenue of a territory at some figure, and assign that sum as the salary or pay of the holder and the rank corresponding to it. From some of these mansabdars, and from almost all of the chiefs not so absorbed into imperial service, a fixed annual tribute called peshkash was commonly extracted, its payment being the hallmark of submission. Peshkash was paid into the imperial treasury. Many chiefs also additionally paid an annual assessment called jama to whomsoever their territory was assigned in jagir.

himself. The glue of 'tolerance', and the ritual of receiving 'the honor robe' that had been brushed against the body of the emperor were as integral to the relationship as was the rhetoric that the officials were 'slaves' of the emperor. Moreover Akbar strove in a creative manner to synthesise the Sunni and Sufi religious strands, and his close relationship to Saint Sheik Selim enabled him to assimilate some of the Saint's sanctity to his own political authority, and to fuse religion and politics in a special way at the highest level.[11]

Stephen Blake (1979) has taken the A'in-i Akbari (Regulations of Akbar) of Abu al-Fazd as his major text for expounding the formal structure of Akbar's imperial administration—a structure which apparently survived in its basic form down to the early 18th century. Having disposed of the question of the relations of satellite and tributary principalities to the Mughal Empire proper, let us now dissect the anatomy of the latter.

The A'in-i Akbari states that the art of governing comprises three topics, the (imperial) household (manzil), the army (sipah) and the empire (mulk).

The Mughal imperial household was centred on Akbar, the emperor, a man touched by god, whose received divine illumination enabled him to rule with virtue and efficacy. The text says that 'Royalty is a light from god'. The imperial household had a central position in the organisation of the empire, and Blake refers to its organisation as 'the mixing of household and states' in that what appeared to be the domestic arrangements and functions of the emperor's court—the harem, the wardrobe, the kitchen, the perfumery, were interlocked with departments—like the imperial mint, the treasury and the state arsenal—that had wider politico-economic ramifications.

The army was essentially divided into four classes: mansabdars and their men, ahadis, other soldiers, and infantry. Of course the mansabdars were the elite segment whose composition and direct relations with the emperor gave that distinctive stamp, both military and face to face, to the court whether it was located in the capital or in a mobile camp. The mansabdars received their ranks and their assignments only after interview with the emperor. A remarkable piece of evidence, that Bernier read as absolutist control and others might construe as personalistic bonds, is that 'all mansabdars related directly to the ruler and not to other men of greater rank; no chain of command separated emperor and officer. Mansabdars had to spend a good deal of time in the presence of the emperor. They were called to court on change of assignment and for promotion, and they had to stand three separate guard duties in the Imperial household' (Blake 1979: 86).

In a realm that was by and large ruled 'indirectly' in that, as Pearson says, 'most of the subjects of the Mughal emperor handled their own affairs by themselves, within their own group, or groups, and had nothing to do with any official' (Pearson 1976a), the core clients surrounding the ruler stood out in contrast by virtue of their direct face-to-face ties with him. Pearson calculates that those holding the

[11] The 'fusion' referred to here is not meant to minimise the important fact that Islam does not give any ruler the right to make alterations in laws codified under its aegis.

mansab rank bestowed by the emperor numbered at most 8,000 men in an empire of sixty or seventy million people. Attuned to military exertions and to conquest as their primary ethic of action, these 8,000 men 'were the empire, the only people linked to the emperor by direct patronage ties'. And among these in turn the inner core nobility, with ranks of 1,000 or more, could not have numbered more than a thousand men. And, as Bernier himself remarked, since these mansabdars were heterogenous by racial origin or religion or place of birth, it was the direct tie of patronage to the person of the emperor that was alleged to activate and seal their loyalty—a dogma that in good times encouraged fierce love and in bad times, callous desertion to another leader who had been more successful in intrigue or war.[12] Pearson goes as far as to argue that since only the mansabdars were the direct clients of the Emperor, and since their promotions depended primarily on military success, the mansabdars alone amongst a vast mosaic of populations were loyal to the empire.

By and large the main core of the Mughal army functioned in two parts—one of which was quartered in the imperial household and the other stationed in posts around the realm or fighting a campaign.

The imperial administration, as set out in the A'in-i Akbari, enumerates diverse officials with their competences, which defies understanding especially in terms of a 'rational bureaucratic' blueprint, because its departments and ministries were not informed by a clear division of labour; or by a hierarchy of offices, pertaining to different levels from village to region to state, and within each department by a graded system of offices assigned differentiated duties and responsibilities.

Thus, for example, under the aspect of imperial administration seven kinds of officials are named: the army commander, and his military subordinate, whose duties in the subdivisions (parganas) of the province included not only the command of the cavalry but also restraining the greed of local revenue collectors and jagir holders; the provincial judicial officers; the chief official of the towns, who maintained order, regulated artisans, merchants and markets; the chief tax collector at the subprovincial level who dealt directly with village officials and mediated between them and provincial and imperial officers; the accountant, assisting the tax collector; and finally, also the treasurer assisting the same personage.

It is clear that in this charter of administration as proposed by the centre and looking towards the periphery, land revenue was, as Irfan Habib has emphasised, of utmost importance. And here the first cut of critical importance, especially in the central Indo-Gangetic provinces, was the proportion that was to be reserved as the 'household lands' of the imperial domain, and the proportion that was conceded as assignable lands, given as jagirs or office tenures to mansabdars, who could thereby

[12] According to Pearson 'in the period 1658–1678 of Aurangzeb's top mansabdars (with mansabs of 5000 or more) 49% were born Hindu or born outside India, while 82% were Hindu or of foreign extraction. The foreign born came not only from Persia and Central Asia, but also from other places' (Pearson 1976a: 224). The point Pearson is making in this somewhat unclear statement is that the nobles surrounding Aurangzeb were not connected to him by birthplace, religion or 'racial origin': these were not the bonds of loyalty to him.

claim for themselves the states' tax on the lands so assigned. Blake asserts that the lands assigned mansabdars 'ranged from a minimum of 75 percent of the empire during the reign of Akbar to a maximum of 95 percent during the reign of his son Jahangir'. It was inevitable that the seven kinds of imperial officers enumerated above could scarcely be expected to oversee with any degree of stringency the activities of the mansabdars' agents who managed the jagirs in the provinces.

Indeed, these seven kinds of imperial officers present two kinds of problems for political theory. On the one hand, at least some of them are assigned duties which cut across levels from province through district to village, while others suggest some sort of chain linking these levels. On the other hand, it is not clear how they interlocked with the chief officers of the imperial court, especially in the face of the dogma that they reported directly to the emperor. The highest officers of the imperial household described in the A'in-i Akbari are, besides those who waited upon the emperor and his family in a domestic capacity, the most eminent persons heading the different groupings of the mansabdars. They are the vakil (prime minister), who was most concerned with the army commanders, the diwan, whose chief interest was the collection and disbursement of state funds, and the sadr who headed the men of learning and religion, especially the jurists, and to whom provincial officials responsible for law and justice reported.

Given this pattern of devolution of authority and distribution of office that showed 'no clear-cut lines of authority, no separate departments at successive levels of administration, and no tables of organization', scholars have tended to interpret certain calendrical features of imperial court life, and certain court administrative practices, as being strategies evolved by the centre for controlling officials and for securing imperial interests. Blake, for example, enumerated the following as the strategies of control: requiring attendance at court, establishing overlapping spheres of authority, transferring officials frequently, using intelligence gatherers, and travelling regularly' (1979: 80).

Many of these features are not unique to the Mughal polity alone,[13] but two of them deserve special comment because the Mughal administration developed them to an unusual degree. One was the frequent transfers of far-flung provincial governors and high level officials to prevent them from stabilising their local power base, to curb their independence, and to scotch any ambitious move towards rebellion or secession. The other was the spectacular reliance on 'royal progress', that is, on frequent travels across the countryside by the Emperor, his harem, his household, indeed his entire court together with armed forces, artisans and artificers, the treasury, the mint, the crown jewels, artists and musicians. It was spectacular enough that the Mughal emperors shifted their monumental capital cities many times—Agra was the capital city from 1564–71, Fatehpur Sikri from 1571–85, Lahore from 1585–98, Agra again from 1598–1648, and Shahjahanabad from 1648–1858. But the even more remarkable addiction was the royal travels, undertaken to a degree

[13] For instance, the overlapping, cross-cutting, and parallel areas of authority and responsibility between departments or occupants of office is a hallmark of 'galactic polities', to which family all Indian polities have belonged.

that surpassed the normal travels of kings elsewhere. Whatever the special motivations of the Mughal travels—such as the pure pleasure of movement traceable to their Mongol nomadic origins—the royal progress and the royal hunts were also a way of controlling the regions of a far-flung empire, through the displaying of the king's charisma, and the renewing or forming of the special ties of loyalty between emperor and subordinate. These constituted the special glue of the Mughal superstructure. The splendid mobile camps of the emperors—indeed they were moving cities of urban populaces and palatial tent-residences—enacted the special Mughal cosmology that the person of the Emperor himself, daily exposed at audiences as a radiant presence, was the centre of the cosmos on whom shone the light of God.

We are now in a position after our own reading of Bernier, handsomely supplemented by some selected modern historical scholarship on the Mughal empire, to embark on the positive task of labelling it as a political formation such that its distinctive features are foregrounded and seen in a way that is in accord with indigenous conceptions of political norms and practice.

We might say that the Mughal empire was more a 'galactic confederacy' than an absolutist empire,[14] ringed on the north-west by independent tribal polities, in the south by independent kingdoms, and much of its internal territory in the indirect rule of rajas, whose military capacity was indispensable to contain competitive challenges. Whatever large parts of the empire were directly controlled by the Mughals, were in fact either alienated as jagirs, much of the revenue of which accrued to the superior lords, or entrusted to governors as administrative provinces and districts as their principalities, or controlled by zamindars who were dominant local elites already in place and of whom a varying portion of the revenue they collected was expected to be delivered up. It was precisely this complexity in the ranges of control and jurisdiction that a modern scholar conveys to us, when he tried to make sense of the political pattern and organisation of the Benares region in the 18th century. Bernard Cohn (1962) disaggregates four levels in his analysis of a major region within the larger empire: (*a*) Imperial: The Mughal Empire represented this level, and its local elements and polities, even the

[14] The Mughal Empire, as indeed other instances of polities ranging from empire to little kingdom, presents us with the problem of 'labelling'. Stephen Blake, in the essay which I have cited (1979), is vocal that it be called, following a usage coined by Max Weber, as a 'patrimonial-bureaucratic' empire. I find this usage problematic and cumbersome. In this hyphenated label, the empire is seen as some kind of in-between, neither truly patrimonial (in that the realm in question is more than a projection on the model of a huge household directly dominated and ruled by a master) nor truly bureaucratic (in the sense of Weber's own ideal type description of rational bureaucracy). Moreover Blake takes for granted that Weber's notion of patrimonial as a projection upon the model of a 'patriarchal family' is self-explanatory. The word 'household' in its minimal signification implies a co-residential, commensal unit whose core is some kind of 'family' surrounded by other dependents. An imperial establishment, or a royal court, which includes multiple queens and concubines, officers such as stewards of the royal bath, wardrobe etc., plus officers of a military and civil nature in charge of the capital, and the larger realm—such a constellation of personages with their retinues is not an extension on a national level of a 'minimal household', or of the 'patriarchal authority' of a joint family. In other words the Mughal term manzil, translated as the 'household', has to be glossed in terms of its metaphorical and cosmological dimensions of expanded meaning.

rebellious ones, sought accreditation by the imperial power to justify their power seizure; (*b*) Secondary: This realm exercised rule over a major cultural or historical region such as Oudh or Bengal; (*c*) Regional: This level of political organisation consisted of appointees having local jurisdiction; they owed their positions to the imperial or secondary authority. They were frequently autonomous, and only loosely linked to national power; (*d*) Local: The local political level comprised lineages, tax officials, adventurers, and indigenous chiefs.[15]

I think our understanding of pre-British political structure can be taken a little further if we can study closely realms at what Cohn has labelled the 'secondary' level of a region. Let us take as our example the sultanate of Gujarat, which after it was incorporated into the Mughal Empire became a secondary level region within it.[16]

IV

The sultanate of Gujarat in the 17th century[17]

Much of what we have said about the relation between ruler and his nobility, between Muslim ruler and Muslim and Hindu local rajas and chiefs, the structure of the domains over which noble and raja presided, and the pluralism of subcultures—all this can be illustrated with even greater clarity for the sultanate of Gujarat in the 17th century, before (and even after) it was conquered by Akbar in 1572–73 and incorporated into the Mughal Empire.

The sultanate of Gujarat achieved its widest limits during the rule of Mahmud 1 (1458–1511) and Bahadur (1526–37): the westernmost boundary was somewhere on the Gulf of Kutch beyond which stretched Sind, and the southern boundary was the sultanate of Ahmadnagar.

Gujarat was the haven of textile manufacturing centres like Ahmadabad, Pattan, Baroda, Broach, Surat, and Cambray; the next product of importance was indigo. In this essay I shall not deal with the organisation and activities of Gujarat's merchants, and with the patterns of devolutionary relations between the political authority and commerce, i.e., between the ruling kshatriya and the trading vaisya (or bania). Here we are concerned only with its political layout, in the study of which, first of all, a separation has to be made between the nobility which was the court circle[18] and which received jagir revenue grants, and the hereditary Hindu

[15] Also see A.M. Shah (1964).

[16] Another example relating to a much later period than that under scrutiny might be Henri Stern's 'Power in traditional India: Territory, caste and kinship in Rajasthan' (1977). Stern describes the totality of some twenty-odd Rajput states during the 19th and early 20th centuries on both their cohesive and divisive manifestations. During Moghul times this collection of Rajput states was a power bloc with which the Mughal emperor tried to cement an alliance. Stern is reminded, in the course of describing the political dynamics of these Rajput states, of the discussion in the Arthashastra of the mandala strategy of forming circles of allies to contain enemies. Stern might find Bernier's description of Mughal imperial alliances to contain rebellion and subversion relevant to this discussion.

[17] This account is based on M.N. Pearson *Merchants and rulers in Gujarat* (1976b).

[18] Following Pearson (1976b), the word nobility will hereafter only refer to this segment.

aristocracies which controlled larger areas of Gujarat and which were expected to pay tribute.

The aim of any strong ruler in Gujarat was horizontal territorial expansion, while the vertical integration of the component territories must necessarily appear 'loose' from the standpoint of 'centralisation' or 'patrimonial domination' in the Weberian sense. For in considerable parts of the sultanate, the Rajputs and Kolis, the pre-Muslim local rulers, remained in power. These, as well as local Muslim chiefs, paid tribute only when they were compelled to. It seems that even the strong sultans recognised their right as being limited to one quarter of the land revenue. Pearson describes the mosaic of differential revenue and tribute payments as follows:

> In the three-eighths of Gujarat which, under the Mughals, were meant to pay tribute, the rulers were satisfied if tribute was paid occasionally. Precise sums, regularly paid, were never forthcoming. In the other five-eighths, where land revenue was collected, the ruler's control was greater but far from complete. . . . More important, many smaller divisions within these ten revenue-paying sarkars in fact did not pay revenue. Like the six tribute-paying sarkars, these smaller divisions were controlled by zamindars who paid tribute. Thus in a majority of the area of Gujarat there was in the sixteenth century no regular collection of land revenue, but only the payment of tribute, and this only 'when it [could] be enforced' (Pearson 1976b: 62).

The nobles were encouraged to develop local bases of power, and one of Gujarat's strongest sultans, Mahmud Bigarh, laid down that when a jagirdar died, his son was to inherit his jagir. If he had no sons his daughter was to be given half of it. Many of Mahmud Bigarh's nobles built towns or villages, which served as their permanent base.

> Thus Ahmadabad had 360 or 380 puras (suburbs; quarters), each of which was focused on the palace of the founding noble. Each pura had a mosque and was a city in itself, with all classes of inhabitants there. The sultans apparently seldom tried to move these nobles from one jagir to another (ibid.).

The basis of power of the nobility, as indeed the sultans, was control over resources, most notably land and people. A noble could attain power and wealth either through personal favour and influence with the sultan or through control of a specific area in Gujarat. In the latter case, distance from the sultan would be crucial. A base in the environs of Ahmadabad would mean greater supervision from the sultan. 'Optimal power would be attained by a noble who could control a large distant local base while retaining influence at court' (Pearson 1976b: 63). It is also to be noted that very often the gift of a jagir by a sultan to a noble meant that the gift covered an area infested by enemies and robbers, a frontier region to be domesticated, so that a jagir of this sort may aptly be translated as 'a place to be subjugated'.

Another feature that drives home to us the 'galactic' nature of the Gujarat sultanate was that the whole Gujarati army consisted of troops raised by the nobles. Thus, often in a clash between sultan and noble, the troops frequently sided with their immediate superior, the noble.

In the context of such replicating autonomies, what could an ambitious sultan do to tighten his control over the nobles? As his hold strengthened, he would try to eliminate the established nobles and install ones of his own creation; he would balance one faction against another and maintain or increase his control; he had at his disposal a number of honours and titles to distribute. Even when we take all these strategies available to the sultan into account, it is yet impressive that in both the 16th and 17th centuries, an overwhelming number (Pearson [ibid.] gives the percentage of 74.6) of the subhadars were close relatives of previous or existing nobles—as confirmation of the entrenched position of the nobles in the towns and villages of their jagirs.

The scope of the legal system in Gujarat reflected both the limited aims of the sultans and the impediments to extending judicial control over a people who formed a mosaic of groups with their special customs. Serious criminal cases may have come before the judicial officers called the gazis who were represented at the court, at the provinces and in the districts. Muslim civil law itself did not apply to non-Muslims, among whom civil cases were virtually settled within the community concerned, whether it be caste, occupational group, religious seet, or local community, according to their customary law.

A medieval sultanate such as that of Gujarat clearly poses for us the challenge of finding the right paradigm for describing its structure, which was predicated on certain positive understandings such as the following: that the ruler at the centre and his court nobility radially associated with him as his clients, and the nobles distributed in the rural provinces as jagirdars, themselves centres of similar leader–retainer constellations, exercised authority and force only in certain delimited contexts. Much of the outlying provinces of the sultanate were ruled by local Hindu or Muslim aristocracies whose relationship to the sultanate was at best tributary. The mass of the inhabitants belonged to a mosaic of more or less 'autonomous' groups and associations, whether these be merchant guilds (mahajans), trade or caste panchayats, religious sects and the like, which managed most of their ordinary affairs. Indeed the political authority regarded many matters concerning religious, social, and economic practices and customs as outside its political cognisance.

The historical phenomena we have been looking at are situated in Muslim-dominated *late medieval* India. They possess many special features that are distinctively Mughal. However, there are certain features that show some affinity with classical Indian society, and its understanding of the relationship between *dharma* (morality), *artha* (instrumental political action) and *varta* (economy), between ruler and subject, and other allied questions. Moreover, political theory and practice in India had from early times recognised a variety of political constellations and assemblages, and we might further inquire how the examples we have cited relate to them. Another separate inquiry outside the scope of this essay might relevantly relate the foregoing profile of the Mughal Empire to a dynamic sketch centred on the Rajput states, but also contrasting them with the Maratha and Mughal formations, by a British officer, James Tod, who served in India *much later in time*, in the early decades of the 19th century.

James Tod served the British Resident at the Maratha court of Daulat Rao Sindhia from 1805 until his appointment as Political Agent to the Western Rajput States from 1818 to 1822. His texts on Rajasthan (1829, 1832)[19] have recently been discussed with nuanced subtlety by Norbert Peabody (1996), who remarks that although they were ostensibly about 'feudal' Rajputs, they articulate 'a number of distinctions between different indigenous social and political types' (ibid.: 188). Tod situated his discussion of Rajput feudalism within 'debates about the nature of various European states' (ibid.: 197), and had especially English feudalism in mind as a comparative referent. Within India 'Tod favourably contrasted the Rajput feudal polity with two other types, Mughal "despotism" and Maratha "predation"' (ibid.: 200). His discourse was, it seems, informed by a favoured conception of Romantic nationalism which he attributed to the Rajputs in particular, although he treated the denigrated Marathas and Mughals as also distinct nations.

V
Concluding comments

Alterity, a theme which Triloki Madan has thoughtfully probed, is based on the recognition of difference in others. Moreover, the practice of toleration presupposes the recognition and accommodation of differences between groups and individuals, and this in turn leads to an enrichment of collective life and civilisational choices. As Michael Walzer has remarked: 'Toleration makes difference possible; difference makes toleration possible' (1997: xii).

Multinational and multicultural imperial formations, such as the one we have examined, though usually authoritarian and hierarchical, have also incorporated to a significant degree communitarian difference. They administratively attempted to provide for a peaceful coexistence of groups by virtue of tributary and devolutionary arrangements and by enabling groups to occupy specialised niches. Though certainly non-democratic and oriented towards groups rather than individuals, such formations in the sense stated above were precursors of what today's theorists of democracy in plural societies identify as 'consociationalism'(for example, Lijphardt 1984).

Imperial formations such as the Mughal empire, and others such as the Asokan, Ottoman and Austro–Hungarian empires (and on a small scale the pre-colonial galactic kingdoms of South and Southeast Asia) were capable of violent wars of expansion and repression of rebellions and popular protests, but they did sustain to a notable degree the coexistence of, and transactions between, groups and communities with different historical traditions, religions and languages, and socio-cultural practices.[20]

[19] For a discussion of the spatial divisions at various levels of territorial organisations, illustrating a devolutionary pattern of replicated units of smaller scale see Wills (1919).

[20] For example, see my treatment of the Asokan empire and the Thai kingdom of Ayuttheya in *World conqueror and world renouncer* (1976: chs 5 and 8 respectively).

In our time, the nation-state project espoused by the post-colonial and post-independence countries of South and Southeast Asia (and others similarly liberated) has all too frequently in the course of pursuing policies of administrative centralisation, intrusive development engineered from the centre, and homogenisation in the name of common citizenship, provided space for majority populations to dominate and discriminate against minorities. Democratic politics in these countries of plural societies has in fact provided the opportunities and mechanisms for punitive dominance that has in turn spawned ethnonationalist resistance and conflict. Historically, and generally, a crucial feature of nation-state making (with some rare exceptions like Switzerland) has been for a state's majority population to secure its enduring dominance by organising political life in terms of its own language and culture, and by determining the character and substance of public education and state rituals.

Nation-states committed to democracy while advocating the equality of citizens as individuals, tend to be suspicious of and to resist the toleration of groups and communities attempting to organise on their own to foster their separate religions and social practices and 'personal laws'. Towards the end of the 20th century it is surely problematic that India, previously celebrated for its diversity, pluralism and lack of homogenising religious and cultural orthodoxy, has generated a movement called 'Hindu nationalism' intolerant of its massive Muslim minority. But there is a good chance that out of India's powerful experience of, and precedents for, diversity and tolerance of difference, there will arise consociational arrangements giving space to cultural, social and legal pluralism above a minimum baseline of necessary human rights applicable to all citizens.

REFERENCES

BERNIER, FRANCOIS. 1914. *Travels in the Moghul empire:* A.D. *1656–1708.* (Translated and annotated by Archibald Constable [1891], revised by Vincent A. Smith). Oxford: Oxford University Press.

BLAKE, STEPHEN P. 1979. The patrimonial–bureaucratic empire of the Mughals. *Journal of Asian studies* 39, 1: 77–94.

COHN, BERNARD. 1962. Political systems in eighteenth century India: The Benares region. *Journal of the American Oriental Society* 82: 312–20.

FOSTER, SIR WILLIAM, ed. 1926. *The embassy of Sir Thomas Roe to India 1616–1619.* London: Oxford University Press.

———, ed. 1968. *Early travels in India, 1583–1619.* New Delhi: S. Chand & Co.

HABIB, IRFAN. 1963. *The agrarian system of Mughal India, 1556–1707.* Bombay: Asia Publishing House.

LIJPHARDT, AREND. 1984. *Democracy in plural societies: A comparative exploration.* New Haven: Yale University Press.

MOORE, BARRINGTON, JR. 1967 [1966]. *Social origins of dictatorship and democracy: Lord and peasant in the making of the modern world.* Boston: Beacon Press.

MORELAND, W.H. 1920. *India at the death of Akbar.* London: Macmillan and Co.

———. 1929. *The agrarian system of Moslem India.* Cambridge: W. Heffner and Sons.

PEABODY, NORBERT. 1996. Tod's *Rajasthan* and the boundaries of imperial rule in nineteenth century India. *Modern Asian studies* 30, 1: 186–220.

PEARSON, M.N. 1976a. Shivaji and the decline of the Mughal empire. *Journal of Asian studies* 35, 2: 221–35.

———. 1976b. *Merchants and rulers in Gujarat.* Berkeley: University of California Press.

RICHARDS, J.F. 1975. The formulation of imperial authority under Akbar and Jahangir. *In* J.F. Richards, ed., *Kingship and authority in South Asia*, pp. 252–85. Madison: University of Wisconsin, South Asia Studies Series 3.

SHAH, A.M. 1964. Political system in eighteenth century Gujarat. *Enquiry* 1, 1: 83–95.

STERN, HENRI. 1977. Power in traditional India: Territory, caste and kinship in Rajasthan. *In* Richard G. Fox, ed., *Realm and region in traditional India*, pp. 52–78. Durham: Duke University.

TAMBIAH, STANLEY J. 1976. *World conqueror and world renouncer.* Cambridge: Cambridge University Press.

TAVERNIER, JEAN-BAPTISTE. 1925 [1676]. (trans. V. Ball). *Travels in India.* London: Oxford University Press.

TOD, (Lt. Col.) JAMES. 1829. *The Annals and antiquities of Rajasthan or, the Central and Western Rajpoot states of India*, vol. I. London.

———. 1832. *The Annals and antiquities of Rajasthan or, the Central and Western Rajpoot states of India*, vol. II. London.

WALZER, MICHAEL. 1997. *On toleration.* New Haven: Yale University Press.

WILLS, C.U. 1919. The territorial systems of the Rajput kingdoms of medieval Chhattisgarh. *Journal and proceedings of the Asiatic society of Bengal* (n.s.) 15, 5: 197–262.

11

Rejecting violence: Sacrifice and the social identity of trading communities

Lawrence A. Babb

In recent decades Agravāl leaders have been promoting a centre for caste pilgrimage at Agroha, the supposed place of Agravāl origin, and an associated Agravāl origin myth. Analysis reveals that this origin myth belongs to a class of similar origin myths found among North Indian trading castes. The central element in these myths is the ancient rite of sacrifice. The origin myths of the Khaṇḍelvāl Vaiśyas, Māheśvarīs, and Khaṇḍelvāl Jains all attempt to show how the caste in question acquired its current identity and social persona because of an alienation from the sacrifice, followed by a restoration to the rite on a new basis (or in the case of the Jains, a shift to an alternative ritual order). Variants of the Agravāl origin myth being publicised currently are often presented in a context suggesting social and scientific modernity, but underlying contemporary retellings we find the same sacrificial symbolism seen in the myths of other trading castes.

In May of 1997 the Akhil Bhāratiya Agravāl Sammelan, an organisation claiming to represent the entire Agravāl community, sponsored its sixteenth annual national meeting at Talkatora Indoor Stadium in New Delhi. Although their actual number is uncertain, the Agravāls are a large trading caste, a rich and powerful group of great importance in modern India's economic and political life. The event was announced with much fanfare in full-page advertisements in Delhi's major newspapers, and the advertisement was itself a culturally significant text. The version appearing in *The Indian Express* (17 May), an English daily, contained an article entitled 'The twenty two years of awakening', which was an account of the Sammelan's efforts to 'give identity to Agrawal society'. As the context made clear, by 'identity' was meant a sense of caste membership and unity among Agravāls. The article mentioned the Sammelan's support of educational institutions and efforts to combat 'social evils' such as dowry, but it mainly emphasised its promotion of a place called Agroha (Agrohā) 'as a religious shrine'. The importance of

Acknowledgements: The research on which this paper is based took place mainly in Jaipur from August 1996 to June 1997, and was supported by a senior research fellowship from the American Institute of Indian Studies. I am very grateful to the Department of Anthropology, University of Rajasthan, for allowing me an affiliation during my stay in Jaipur. Special thanks are due to John Cort for a very helpful reading of an earlier draft.

Agroha—located about 190 km from Delhi near Hissar in Haryana—is that it figures centrally in the Agravāls' origin myths. These myths assert that it was once the capital city of an ancient king named Agrasen, whom Agravāls consider to be the creator of their caste.

This paper is about the origin myths of certain North Indian trading castes with special emphasis on the Agravāls. The Agravāls have a claim on our attention because of the intensity and public conspicuousness of their current efforts to foster caste consciousness and unity. This paper will show that these efforts cannot be fully understood without considering a wider cultural context. The Agravāls belong to the same social milieu as other North Indian trading castes, especially those of Rajasthan.[1] Though differing in some ways, these castes are very similar in outlook and manner of life; they tend to be strongly vegetarian and committed to nonviolence as a core value (see esp. Ellis 1991). They also have very similar myths of origin. The importance of these narratives lies in the fact that they project and ratify images of group character and identity. My object in this paper is to demonstrate the existence of common themes in these origin myths, and to show how the Agravāls utilise and give their own twist to these themes. Among other things our materials vindicate T.N. Madan's astute observations on the tenaciousness with which religious symbols, albeit sometimes in modernistic guise, continue to occupy societal space in India (Madan 1997: esp. ch. 6).

Let us return to the Agravāls. For over twenty years Agroha has been the focus of a vast publicity and development effort undertaken by two Agravāl organisations, the Sammelan and a sister organisation, the Agroha Vikas Trust. These groups have supported archaeological research at Agroha, and have also published much literature about Agrasen, Agroha, and Agravāl origins. They have sponsored the installation of images of Agrasen at various public places, promoted the use of his name for schools and other institutions, and have successfully lobbied for the issuance of an Agrasen commemorative postage stamp.

The Trust, moreover, has built an enormous pilgrimage centre at Agroha that embodies and glorifies the basic symbols of Agravāl origin mythology. Its centrepiece is a vast religious complex consisting of three temples and a hall large enough to seat 5,000 persons. The temples contain images of King Agrasen and the goddesses Mahālaksmī and Sarasvatī. Behind this complex is a large bathing tank and a home for the elderly. Partially excavated ruins, said to be the remains of Agrasen's ancient capital, are a short walk away. Also nearby are a recently renovated temple for Śīlā Mātā (a *satī* venerated by many Agravāls)[2] and an

[1] On the Rajasthani traders in particular (known generally and somewhat erroneously as 'Marwaris'), see Timberg 1978.

[2] Temple authorities are downplaying the fact that she was a *satī*. A book given to me by one of the temple priests (Garg n.d.) alters the manner of her death appropriately, but for an unexpurgated version see Temple (1977, I: 243–366). Sīlā Mātā was the daughter of the legendary Seṭh Harbhajśāh, a vastly rich Agravāl who is said to have restored Agroha after one of its many destructions. His story is vigorously promoted by the Trust because it serves as a myth-model for current efforts to restore Agroha.

Agravāl-sponsored medical college. The entire complex is billed as '*agrohā dhām*', the Agroha 'abode'. This is a manner of speaking usually reserved for a holy place of pilgrimage, and its use here implies that Agroha is such a sacred place. Agrasen is represented as a deity among deities, enshrined on land sanctified by the origin of the Agravāl caste.

Nor is the display of these symbols confined to Agroha. In the Rajasthani city of Jaipur—the locale of most of my research on this topic—Agrasen Jayantī is celebrated by local Agravāls on a massive scale.[3] This occasion belongs almost entirely to the realm of public culture. In essence, it is a form of outdoor theatre designed to display the caste's wealth and power, and its venue is the streets, not private houses. When I saw it in 1996, the main event was a gigantic evening procession that wound its way through some of the city's main streets. Three brass bands, four mobile tableaus with children serving as actors, marching dignitaries, and a moving temple containing an image of Agrasen passed slowly under 18 arches stationed along the route. Each arch was named for one of the 18 Agravāl *gotra*s (exogamous patriclans). Agrasen's image was worshipped at the procession's outset and from time to time as it moved through the city.

The tableaus juxtaposed two separate but complementary themes. Two of the displays were concerned with social reform, one portraying the low-expense group marriages currently being promoted by the caste's leadership, and the other depicting the evils of dowry murder. The remaining two dealt with caste origin, which is our main concern in this paper. One portrayed Agrasen and his 18 sons, who are (according to some versions of Agravāl origin) progenitors of the 18 Agravāl *gotra*s; 18 young boys were dressed as princes, each carrying a shield on which was written the name of one of the *gotra*s. In the other, 18 children were each sitting before a diminutive sacrificial altar while a bearded Agrasen looked on from his throne. This scene portrayed 18 sacrifices that, as we shall see, played a crucial role in the creation of the Agravāl caste. The overall message conveyed by the procession was that the Agravāls are second to none in their up-to-date responsiveness to important social issues, but that they are also an ancient community with a royal pedigree and deep roots in Indic religious culture.

Central to this message is the rite of sacrifice. Its inclusion in the procession was in no way incidental, for sacrifice is deeply linked with concepts of group-creation in the cultural world in which Agravāls are trying to project an identity, and is the basis for what follows in this paper. We first turn to the origin mythology of non-Agravāl trading castes. Here we find a pattern common to all these myths: a group's alienation from the sacrifice followed by its restoration to the rite (or, in one case, to an alternate religiosocial order) with a new identity and social persona. We then return to the Agravāls where we see this same pattern embedded in both older Agravāl origin myths and in contemporary retellings.

[3] On Āśvin s. 1

I
Sacrifice and group-creation

We must begin by recalling that from ancient times the rite known as 'sacrifice' (*yajña*) has been associated with creative power in India. Vedic ritualists believed that the order and unity of the cosmos were produced by a primordial sacrifice, and that every earthly performance of the rite was a recapitulation of this creative process (Smith 1989). The social order itself was a product of the sacrifice. In one of the most famous Ṛg Vedic hymns (10: 90), the creation emanates from the sacrificial dismemberment of the Puruṣa, the Cosmic Man, and the four *varṇa*s emerge from parts of his body: Brahmins from his mouth, Kṣatriyas from his arms, Vaiśyas from his thighs, and Śūdras from his feet. The association between the sacrifice and the creation of social groups appears in more recent materials as well. A well known example from Rajasthan is the fire-lineage (*agni-kul*) Rājpūts, who were created—legend proclaims—from a sacrificial fire at Mount Abu. It seems highly likely that sacrificial imagery is a part of the origin legends of many other groups. It is certainly a very important theme in the mythologies of the trading castes of Rajasthan.

I now present brief summaries of the origin myths of three of these castes: the Khaṇḍelvāl Vaiśyas, the Māheśvarīs, and the Khaṇḍelvāl Jains. Each is a well known group, both within and outside Rajasthan. These materials show two things. First, they reveal common themes in the origin myths of the groups in question. Second, they also demonstrate a range of variation in the way the myths treat the relationship of groups to the sacrifice. Later we will locate Agravāl origin myths within this range of variation.

Khaṇḍelvāl Vaiśyas

Contrary to common usage, there exists no such entity as the 'Khandelvāl' caste. Rather, two quite distinct castes bear the Khaṇḍelvāl label: the Khaṇḍelvāl Vaiśyas, who are entirely Hindu, and the Khaṇḍelvāl Jains. It is possible that these two groups share a common past, but nowadays there is no intermarriage between them, or any other connection of which I am aware.[4] The Khaṇḍelvāl Vaiśyas have probably added the term 'Vaiśya' to their name to avoid being confused with the Khaṇḍelvāl Jains.

The origin mythology of the Khaṇḍelvāl Vaiśyas is preserved and transmitted by traditional caste genealogists known as Jāgās. Most of the other trading castes of the region have lost their genealogists to other professions, but the institution still displays some signs of life in this community. In 1996 I had the opportunity

[4] Historian Rāmballabh Somānī says that it 'is said' that Jain and non-Jain Khaṇḍelvāls once intermarried just as Jain and non-Jain Agravāls do today (1997: 3/3). He gives no source for this assertion. My own comparison of published lists of *gotra*s for each caste (from Pāṭodiyā 1986 and Kāslīvāl 1989) reveals hardly any overlap, but for another view, see M. Gupta (n.d.: 25–29). The phenomenon of multiple castes bearing similar names based on putative origin in the same place is common in western India. The Śrīmālī Brahmins, Vaiśyas and Sonīs are well known examples.

to interview some genealogists of this caste who live near Dausa (west of Jaipur). Their books (constructed like old-style account books, and wrapped in characteristic red cloth) appeared to be in good order. There exists no canonical version of Khaṇḍelvāl Vaiśya origin mythology. By this I mean that there are various myths, or versions of myths (one writer [Pāṭodiyā 1986] has summarised a total of seven), but there is no consensus within the caste about which one is correct, nor have caste organisations promoted any single version. A variant closely linked to the origin mythology of the Khaṇḍelvāl Brahmins (properly, Khāṇḍal Vipras) has been published in a book (M. Gupta n.d.) written by a Khaṇḍelvāl Vaiśya academic, but it has not, as far as am aware, received much acceptance. The version presented here was told to a Jaipur resident (and acquaintance of mine) by his family Jāgā (Śrī Suvālāljī Jāgā) some years ago, and was then published in a caste journal (Khaṇḍelvāl 1984).

According to this story, in an 'ancient period' the city of Khandela (Khaṇḍelā) was ruled by a king named Khargal.[5] Khandela is a small town located in north-eastern Rajasthan about 100 km north–north-west of Jaipur, and the term 'Khaṇḍelvāl' means 'of Khandela'.[6] One time this king sponsored a sacrifice that was performed by the great sage, Durvāsā. Sages from many different places had been invited, and among them was the famous Jamadagni Ṛṣi, who came with his two disciples from Lohargal (Lohārgal). Lohargal, located about 20 km north–north-west of Khandela, is an ancient pilgrimage spot and one of the most important holy places in this part of Rajasthan. On the way, Jamadagni killed a deer, and he unwisely brought the dead deer into the place of the sacrifice. Durvāsā became extremely angry when he saw the body in this holy place, and he cursed Jamadagni and his disciples, turning them into stone.

When news of the curse reached Jamadagni's wife in Lohargal, she rushed to the place of sacrifice where she threatened a counter-curse if her husband were not restored to life. King Khargal, fearing that the sacrifice might not be completed, then became very uneasy. He pleaded with her not to curse Durvāsā, but she was adamant. So the king then begged Durvāsā to return Jamadagni and his disciples to their former state. Durvāsā agreed, but only under the condition that Jamadagni would no longer be a Brahmin. He would be allowed to live on the earth, but as a Vaiśya, and his descendants would be called Khaṇḍelvāl Vaiśyas. Durvāsā also commanded that the descendants of one of Jamadagni's disciples would become the Khaṇḍelvāl Brahmins, who would serve the Khaṇḍelvāl Vaiśyas as priests.[7] The other disciple's descendants would become the Khaṇḍelvāl Vaiśyas' Jāgās. Ultimately—the story concludes—different *gotra*s within the caste developed and separated from each other, acquiring their names on the basis of locality and the names of individual ancestors.

[5] No actual date or period is indicated.

[6] Although the town is quite unprepossessing today, it is believed to have been a great city in ancient times. Whether it was ever a sizable city remains to be shown archaeologically, but it is certainly a very old settlement. Its earliest inscription dates from the third century B.C.E., and it was once an important Śaiva centre (Jain 1972: 261–66).

[7] As far as I am aware, this is not a tradition among the Khāṇḍal Vipras ('Khaṇḍelvāl Brahmins').

The story contains two central assertions. The first is that the Khaṇḍelvāl Vaiśyas were originally Brahmins, not Vaiśyas.[8] The second is that their transformation from Brahminhood to Vaiśya status was connected with the rite of sacrifice, and more specifically, a change in their relationship to the sacrifice. What began as Jamadagni's positive relationship with the rite—his invitation to participate—turns negative: he pollutes it with an act of violence. Because of the resulting curse, he and his disciples then enter an interim condition of stone-like non-interactivity. After an interval, they are restored to life, but Jamadagni (and thus his descendants) then acquires a completely transformed relationship with the sacrifice. He and his descendants are no longer Brahmins, and thus no longer officiants of the sacrifice. They will, however, be served by other Brahmins, thus becoming patrons of the sacrifice. We must also note that a female figure—Jamadagni's wife—plays an important role in this transformation.

The story has four key elements: the to-be-transformed group (in the person of Jamadagni), the sacrifice, the rejection of violence, and a catalytic female figure. These same elements are present in our next myth, that of the origin of the Māheśvarīs.

Māheśvarīs

The Māheśvarīs, like the Khaṇḍelvāl Vaiśyas, are Hindus. The name of the caste, 'Māheśvarī', is also a name of Pārvatī, who is the wife of Śiva, a major figure in the Hindu pantheon. Images of Śiva are displayed at caste functions, and his picture is often displayed on the covers of caste publications. From these facts one might suppose that the Māheśvarīs are Śaivas. But although this might once have been the case, and although Śiva is an important current symbol of caste identity and a major figure in the caste's origin myth, contemporary Māheśvarīs are almost entirely Vaiṣṇavas of one sort or another.

Unlike the Khaṇḍelvāl Vaiśyas, the Māheśvarīs do indeed possess a canonical version of their caste's origin story, one that serves as a charter for their annual festival of Māheś Navmī, celebrated on the day on which the caste is said to have been created.[9] The dominance of a single origin story is largely a result of the efforts of one man, Śivkaraṇ Darak, usually referred to as 'Darakjī'. He was a Māheśvarī who became interested in the history and organisation of his own caste, and in the end became a self-taught ethnographer. During the second half of the 19th century he collected a massive amount of material on the Māheśvarīs and some other castes, mostly from traditional genealogists (here also called Jāgās). He published the results in a book (Darak 1923) that first appeared in 1893 and subsequently went through at least three more editions.[10] Although some caste

[8] In other versions they are said to be descended from Rājpūts.

[9] Jeṣṭh s. 9.

[10] This work is a good example of a type of local history that became quite prominent during the late 19th century. Bhāratendu Hariścandra's work, cited later in this paper, also belongs to this category. These were works that foregrounded the history and common traditions of parochial groups, including castes, on the basis of which such groups could define and publically project corporate identies. On this subject, see Pandey (1990).

Jāgās still exist, they are very few nowadays.[11] By default, therefore, Darakjī's book has served as the basis for most recent published accounts of Māheśvarī origins, and is the source of the summary presented here (ibid.: 27–31).

This myth returns us to Khandela, which—according to this story—was once ruled by a Cauhān (Rājpūt) king named Khargalsen.[12] He was an able ruler, and his kingdom flourished, but he had no son. When he consulted learned Brahmins about his problem, they told him that Lord Śiva would give him a son as a boon, but only under certain conditions. First, under no circumstances should the boy be allowed to travel northward before the age of sixteen. Second, the boy should never bathe in the Sūrya Kuṇḍ (the main bathing tank at Lohargal). Third, the boy should always honour Brahmins. Unless these conditions were met, the Brahmins said, the prince would undergo a 'rebirth' *(punarjanam)* in his own body.

The prince was born. He was given the name Sujjānkunvar (spelled variously in different versions) and educated as a ruler. For a time all went well, but when the prince became older, though not yet sixteen, he became a Jain. As a result, he began replacing Śiva temples with Jain temples, and developed a deep hostility to Brahmins. He also began travelling around the kingdom to promote his new religion. At first he avoided the north, but eventually word reached him that Brahmins were performing sacrifices at Lohargal (to the north of Khandela), and he journeyed there with his 72 Rājpūt henchmen. There six Vedic sages were indeed performing a sacrifice. The enraged prince ordered his men to disrupt it, which they did. The equally enraged sages responded with a curse that turned the prince and all of his men to stone.

When news of this calamity reached the city, the king died of shock, and 16 of his wives became *satī*s. Neighbouring kings then took over the rulerless kingdom. On the advice of the Brahmins, the wives of the frozen prince and chieftains went to a particular cave where they practised severe austerities and prayed to Śiva and Pārvatī. After a time, the two deities appeared on the spot, and as a result of Pārvatī's intervention, Śiva returned the men to life. Because the kingdom was lost, Śiva said they would all have to give up the Kṣatriya way of life (*kṣatriya dharm*) and take up the ways of Vaiśyas (*vaiśya dharm*). But their hands were still stiff, and they could not relinquish their weapons. So Śiva then commanded them to bathe in Sūrya Kuṇḍ. When they obeyed, their swords became pens and their spears and shields became scales, the tools of the trade of businessmen.[13] The descendants of the 72 chieftains are the 72 Māheśvarī *khāmp*s (patriclans) existing today.[14] The prince was a special case. He made the mistake of looking at Pārvatī with lust. She then cursed him, with the result that his descendants became the Māheśvarīs' Jāgās.

But there remained an important piece of unfinished business. The sages pointed out that the king and his henchmen had been released from the curse and transformed

[11] At the time of my research (1996–97) there was only one Jāgā of the Māheśvarīs remaining in the Jaipur area.

[12] Darakjī does not indicate the period.

[13] Darakjī gives us no date for this occurrence.

[14] Five have been added to the original list of 72.

into Vaiśyas, and this despite the fact that they had destroyed the sacrifice. Yet the sacrifice itself had not yet been completed. Śiva then replied that the now kingdomless erstwhile Rājpūts had nothing to give the sages at that time, but that in the future the new Vaiśyas would give them things whenever auspicious ceremonies occurred in their houses. In turn, they—the sages—should 'desire' that the new Vaiśyas abide by their proper (that is, Vaiśya) way of life. The descendants of the six sages later became gurus of the 72 Māheśvarī *khāmps*. In turn, the new Vaiśyas came to be called *yajmān* (sacrificial sponsor). They had possessed this status previously as Rājpūts; now they had returned to it on the basis of wealth rather than martial valour.

While Darakjī's version of the Māheśvarī myth appears in print more than any other, there exists a slightly different telling that deserves brief mention (Bihani 1985: 7–26). In this version, instead of going forth to propagate Jainism, the prince and his followers are hunting, and by chance they wash their bloody weapons in a pool (presumably Sūrya Kuṇḍ) being used by nearby sages as a source of water for their sacrifice. The sages cursed them in retaliation, with essentially the same results as before.

The Māheśvarī myths are thematically similar to our Khaṇḍelvāl Vaiśya legend, but add significant variations. The most obvious similarity is that in both cases Vaiśya castes are held to have been created from groups of an entirely different sort: the Khaṇḍelvāl Vaiśyas from Brahmins, the Māheśvarīs from Rājpūts. In each case, too, the rite of sacrifice is implicated in the transformation. The key issue is violence, which is hardly surprising in light of the fact that an aversion to violence (as manifested in diet and in other ways) is probably the strongest behavioural marker of trading-caste status (Hindu or Jain) in this region. When violence enters the situation, it gives rise to a negative relationship between the sacrificial rite and those who are about to be transformed. In the Khaṇḍelvāl Vaiśya myth and in one of the Māheśvarī myths the violence affects the sacrifice through the medium of third-party animal victims. In Darakjī's Māheśvarī myth, the violence is directed at the sacrifice itself. But whatever the particulars, in all instances the offence leads to the same sequestration in an inanimate state, which is followed by a re-emergence of the ancestor/group with a completely new social persona. As in the Khaṇḍelvāl Vaiśya myth, a feminine intervention—in this case from the wives and the goddess Pārvatī—helps to resolve the situation. For the Māheśvarīs, the bath in the Sūrya Kuṇḍ serves as a clear marker of the final transition.

Changing relations with the sacrifice and with those who officiate at sacrifices, the Brahmins, are at the heart of the transformation. The Khaṇḍelvāl Vaiśyas remain alienated from the sage Durvāsā and lose their own Brahmin status; no longer sacrificial officiants, they become patrons of newly-created Brahmins in accord with their new Vaiśya status. In Darakjī's Māheśvarī myth, Rājpūt aristocrats are stripped of a kingdom, and without it they must become Vaiśyas. These newly-made Vaiśyas then once again become *yajmān*, sacrificial sponsors, as they presumably were before initial separation from the rite. Now, however, they will do so as Vaiśyas, not as Rājpūts; that is, as traders instead of ruler/warriors. And as sacrificial sponsors, they will become the patrons of the descendants of the Brahmin sages they had formerly offended.

Readers will note that the structure of these narratives is quite reminiscent of the underlying logic of rites of passage (Van Gennep 1960): there is a decisive separation from a previous status, a period of betwixt-and-between liminality, and then a social reincorporation on a new basis. But the reincorporation need not always occur, as we learn from our next example, the Khaṇḍelvāl Jains.

Khaṇḍelvāl Jains

The Khaṇḍelvāl Jains, belonging entirely to the Digambar sect of Jainism, are the largest Jain caste in the city of Jaipur. They are often called 'Sarāvgīs', a word derived from the term *śrāvak*, which means 'Jain layman'.

A single basic story of the Khaṇḍelvāl Jains' origin has been in circulation for centuries, and is well known to members of the caste. It has been particularly salient of late, for it was the basis for a recent effort by influential members of the caste to heighten caste-consciousness by organising a renovation of a Digambar temple in Khandela, the caste's alleged birthplace.[15] A detailed version of the myth is presented in Kastūrcand Kāslīvāl's Khaṇḍelvāl Jain caste history (Kāslīvāl 1989). His account is partly drawn from manuscripts available in temple repositories, and of these the earliest cited is dated C.E. 1573. Another early source is Bakhatrām Śāh's *Buddhi Vilās* (1964) dated 1770, which contains (among much else) an account of the origin of the Khaṇḍelvāl Jains.[16]

This story (summarised here from Kāslīvāl 1989: 64–69)[17] requires us to return to Khandela yet again. The period is the 1st century of the Vikram era. According to the story, Khandela, then prosperous and at the height of its glory, was ruled by a king named Khaṇḍelgiri. At that time the city was a major centre for Digambar Jains, and the king was himself a Jain,[18] but he was also inclined toward Śaivism. All his ministers and priests (Brahmins) were Śaivas, and he had great faith in the rite of sacrifice.

Now, a time came when the city was suddenly struck by a terrible plague; people were dying and fleeing from the city in great numbers. The desperate king turned to his ministers and Brahmin priests for advice. The Brahmins insisted that only a sacrifice with a human offering could save the city. At first the king rejected this outrageous suggestion, but the Brahmins were not deterred. As mischance would have it, a group of 500 Jain monks arrived at Khandela at precisely this time, and in the evening they retired to a garden outside the city where they became absorbed in meditation. The Brahmins went to the garden in the night, caught some

[15] The consecration took place in May 1997.

[16] A Khaṇḍelvāl Jain himself, Bakhatrām Śāh was a ferocious polemicist whose best known work is *Mithyātva khaṇḍan nāṭak* (1763), a critique of the reformist Adhyatma movement. For details concerning him, see Padmadhar Pāthak's introduction to the 1964 edition of *Buddhi Vilās* and Lath 1981: xxviii, lix–lx.

[17] See also Barjātyā (1910).

[18] Not in all versions of the story.

meditating monks, and fed them into a sacrificial fire. As a direct consequence, the plague attacked the city even more furiously, and the people gave up all hope of deliverance.

In time, news of the human sacrifice reached Ācārya Aparājit Muni (a famous Digambar ascetic of those days, also known as Yaśobhadrācārya), and he immediately dispatched an *ācārya* named Jinsen to Khandela. When Jinsen arrived with his fellow monks, he first called the city's lay Jains to a retreat outside the city. He then prayed to the goddess Cakreśvarī Devī, and when she manifested before him, he asked her to protect all those living in the retreat. She agreed, and all who were outside the city (i.e., the Jains) were saved from the plague.

In the meantime, King Khaṇḍelgiri himself was stricken. When all other remedies failed, he went to meet Jinsen at the retreat. He greeted the monk with respect, sat at his feet, and received his blessing. When the king told the story of his plight, Jinsen assured him that all would turn out well if he would stay at the retreat for a week, pray to the Tīrthankara, and lead a life completely pure in behaviour and diet. Jinsen added that, as a Jain monk, he possessed only his broom and waterpot, and thus had no medicine to give, but by means of meditation on the Tīrthankara, the king could free himself of his disease. The king completely changed his mode of life, and Jinsen prayed to Cakreśvarī. At the end of the seven days, the king's health was restored. When the king praised Jinsen as a miracle-worker, the monk demurred, insisting that the king was saved only because of his worship of the Tīrthankara and the good will of the goddess Cakreśvarī. The monk then declared that from that time forward the king would be under the protection of the Tīrthankara, and that he would have to accept Jainism publicly.

The scene now shifts back to Khandela and the king's *darbār* hall. Here, in the year C.E. 44 (in other versions, 55 B.C.E), and in the presence of Jinsen and other monks from his party, King Khaṇḍelgiri and 13 of his Cauhān (i.e., Rājpūt) feudatory lords became initiated Jain laymen. Their descendants became 14 of the 84 *gotra*s of the Khaṇḍelvāl Jain caste.[19]

Despite the fact that Jainism has been added to the mix, the myth of the Khaṇḍelvāl Jains is strikingly similar to the others we have seen. Here, as before, the sacrifice plays a crucial role in a group's fundamental change in character, but with some differences. As previously, the group (represented by the king and his henchmen) first enters a negative relationship with the rite; here, however, the negativity is, in comparison to our other cases, greatly accentuated by the murder of saintly ascetics. The sin of that act mainly stains the Brahmin instigator/perpetrators, with the clear implication that a break with them, and with the sacrifice over which they preside, cannot be repaired.[20] Thus, instead of culminating in a renewed and readjusted relationship with the social and religious order represented by the sacrifice, this myth propels the Jains-to-be outside that order altogether.

[19] For accounts of the origin of the 84 *gotra*s see Kāslīvāl (1989: esp. 85–92).

[20] In other versions the king does know and even participates, but as far as I am aware the Brahmins are always the motive force behind the act.

After a betwixt-and-between sojourn in the retreat outside the city, the king returns to his palace: his brief separation from the social order is now over. What occurs, however, is not a reincorporation, but a neoincorporation, for the king does not return to an old order on a new basis, but to a completely new order. In this case, too, a female figure—the Jain goddess Cakreśvarī—plays a key role in the narrative. This time, however, there is no re-establishment of relations with Brahmins, which would signify a return (albeit in a different role) to the Hindu social order of which Brahmins are both the apex and emblem. Instead, Jain ascetics replace Brahmins as the defining 'others' in the situation, thus transforming Rājpūts into a Jain caste.

As do the Māheśvarīs, the Khaṇḍelvāl Jains claim to be descended from Rājpūts. Most Vaiśya groups make similar assertions, although the Agravāls are a partial exception, as will be seen. Quite possibly the reason for this is the immense prestige of the Rājpūt aristocracy in the Rajasthan region. For the Khaṇḍelvāl Jains, moreover, the assertion of Kṣatriya ancestry is not only consistent with the general trend, but fits well into the martial (though nonviolent) tenor of Jain tradition (see Babb 1996). The Khaṇḍelvāl Vaiśyas' claim (in the particular version of their origin myth we have examined) to Brahmin ancestry is possibly unique among Rajasthani trading castes. It seems possible that, by emphasising their 'Hinduness', the claim of Brahmin descent highlights the distinction between Khaṇḍelvāl Vaiśyas and Khaṇḍelvāl Jains, groups that are otherwise easily confused.[21]

The myths we have seen provide us with a general paradigm for conceptions, in this part of India, of how trading castes come into existence. They also indicate points of variation within the paradigm. It seems that Vaiśya castes are created from other kinds of groups, mostly Kṣatriya/Rājpūts. Crucial to the transformation is a change in the group's relationship with the sacrifice, and thus with the social order represented by this axial rite. The group (through its ancestor/s) must first undergo a break of some kind in its relations with the rite. In all cases the basic issue is violence; the breach results from its misuse or misdirection. After a period of liminal separation from any normal social status, the group (again through its ancestor/s) returns to social visibility. But whether this return is to the old social order on a new basis, or an entirely new kind of social order, depends on the severity of the original break. It will be noted that, with the exception of the Māheśvarīs, the life of trade is not at the centre of these myths. The main issue is the rejection of sacrificial violence.

These points provide a context for examining the Agravāl myth of origin, to which we now turn.

II
Agroha

Agravāl origin mythology has multiple sources and has been retold, and modified in the retelling, many times over. Currently, moreover, the Agroha Vikas Trust is

[21] Against this, however, I must record that there is little resistance to the idea of a past relationship with Khaṇḍelvāl Jains among Khaṇḍelvāl Vaiśyas.

promoting a version that can be said to be acquiring canonical status. Here we focus first on an older but highly influential version. It is drawn from a brief essay entitled 'Origin of the Agravāls' (*Agravālõ kī utpatti*) that was written in 1871 by the famous Hindi author and poet, Bhāratendu Hariścandra, who was an Agravāl himself.[22] Bhāratendu tells us that he compiled his version from 'tradition' and 'ancient writings', and especially from a text called 'Sri Mahālakṣmī vrat kī kathā' that he found in a later part of the *Bhaviṣya Purāṇa*.[23] There seems little doubt that this variant is a good reflection of a myth of Agravāl origin that was in general circulation in the last century, and it later became the basis for many other written retellings, including recent Trust versions.

Agrasen and Agroha

According to Bhāratendu's version (here paraphrased from Śarmā 1989: 583–87), Agrasen—also called Agra or Agranāth—was born in the house of King Vallabh of Pratāpnagar (location uncertain, but said to be in the 'south').[24] Vallabh, in turn, was a descendant of Dhanpāl, the first Vaiśya on earth, whom Brahmins put on the throne of Pratāpnagar.

Agrasen's kingly glory was so great that even Indra (the King of the Gods) had to make friends with him; this indeed is a major theme of the myth. It so happened that Kumud, the King of the Nāgas (snake-deities), brought his daughter Mādhvī from the abode of the Nāgas to earth. Indra was attracted to her, and asked her father for her hand in marriage, but Kumud gave her to Agrasen instead. (Interrupting the thread of his narrative at this point, Bhāratendu observes that Mādhvī is therefore the mother of all Agravāls, and for this reason Agravāls call snakes 'maternal uncle'.) Indra was furious with Agrasen, and retaliated by ceasing to send rain to his capital. But Brahmā was able to stop the conflict temporarily.

Agrasen then turned over his kingdom to Mādhvī and went on pilgrimage. When he came to the holy city of Banaras, he visited the Kapildhārā *tīrth*,[25] and there he performed a sacrifice for Śiva and gave lots of charitable gifts. In response, Śiva appeared on the spot and offered Agrasen a boon. Agrasen said that all he wanted was victory over Indra, to which Śiva replied that if he worshipped the goddess Mahālakṣmī, all his wishes would be granted. Agrasen then resumed his pilgrimage, and with the help of a ghost (about which we are told nothing), he arrived at Hardwar. In the company of Garg Muni (a famous sage), he then visited all the nearby holy spots, and after his return to Hardwar, he worshipped Mahālakṣmī. She was pleased, and made the following promises: that he would be victorious over Indra, that his descendants would be spared all unhappiness,

22 For a close look at Bhāratendu and his work, see Chandra (1992).

23 Others (including this author) have looked for this text in various editions of the *Bhaviṣya Purāṇa* without success, but this Purāṇa is a highly malleable document. Historian Vidyālankar has reproduced the copy of the text he found in Bhāratendu's personal library (1976: 156–95).

24 Bhāratendu does not give a date for these events. Other sources commonly put Agrasen's birth at the end of the *dvāpar yug*, eighty-five years before the beginning of the *kali yug* (cf. Ṭāṇṭiyā 1996: 9).

25 A famous temple site, the fifth and last stop on the Pañckrośī pilgrimage (see Eck 1982: 353).

and that after his death he and his wife would dwell together near the North Star.

Mahālakṣmī also instructed Agrasen to go to a place called Kolāpur where the *svayamvar* of the daughters of Mahidhar (described as the '*avtār*' [incarnation] of 'Nāgrāj')[26] was taking place. Marry them, the goddess said, and produce descendants. So he went there, married the daughters (their names and number are not mentioned in this version), and then came to the Delhi region. He established his rule and spread his descendants from the northern part of Punjab to Agra. In the meantime, Indra had become fearful when he heard about Mahālakṣmī's boon, and he decided to make final peace with Agrasen. He sent Nārad as his ambassador, gave an *apsarā* named Madhuśālinī as a peace offering, and in this way hostilities came to an end. After this, Agrasen went to the banks of the Jumna river where he performed severe austerities for Mahālakṣmī. Again she was pleased, and she bestowed these boons: that from that day onward Agrasen's descendants would bear his name, and that she would be the protectress and *kuldevī* (lineage goddess) of his descendants, who in turn would celebrate her special festival of *divālī*.

At this point in the text, Bhāratendu shifts to a description of Agrasen's kingdom. It extended from the Himalayas and rivers of the Punjab in the north to the Ganges in the east and south, and the western boundary ran from Agra to the countries adjacent to Marwar (which are all areas in which Agravāls are in fact found). The main area in which the Agravāls settled was from Punjab to Meerut and Agra. Bhāratendu also lists the names of the main cities of the Agravāls—Agra, Delhi, Gurgaon and several others—which, he says, were all in Agrasen's kingdom. Agrasen's capital, where he built a great temple for Mahālakṣmī, was called Agranagar, and is now known as Agroha. Agra, says Bhāratendu, was also named for him.

King Agrasen sponsored seventeen-and-a-half sacrifices (for which no reason is given in this version). The half sacrifice came about in the following manner: After Agrasen had begun the eighteenth sacrifice, he experienced great remorse for the violence perpetrated in such rites. Nobody in his lineage ate meat, he said, but nonetheless '*devī hiṃsā*' (here apparently meaning animal sacrifice to the goddess) was taking place. He then vowed that animal sacrifice would no longer take place in his line. Thus, the eighteenth sacrifice was never completed.

Agrasen had seventeen queens and one subqueen. Each had three sons and one daughter. To this information Bhāratendu then adds that from 'seventeen and one-half sacrifices came seventeen and one-half *gotra*s' (Śarmā 1989: 586). This is a somewhat confusing point, because Bhāratendu has not previously indicated any connection between the sacrifices and the *gotra*s, but it is clear that the sacrifices had something to do with their formation. Agrasen named his own *gotra* (Garg) after Garg Muni, who was his 'helper' (presumably referring to help in ritual matters). The other *gotra*s were also named 'on the basis of' the sacrifices (a point

[26] There thus seem to be two Nāgā kings in the story. These may be two variants of one story that arrived in Bhāratendu's tale by different routes.

to which we shall return). King Agrasen appointed the Gauṛ Brahmins as his lineage priests, and at that time they were preceptors and priests for all Agravāls.

When Agrasen became old he left the throne in order to perform austerities, and his son, Vibhu, took over the kingdom. Jainism came to the Agravāls when Agrasen's descendant, King Divākar, was converted. Agroha was finally destroyed utterly by the invasion of Shihab-ud-din, after which the Agravāls scattered to the west (in Marwar) and to the east of their ancient kingdom. Many left their religion and broke their sacred threads. The Agravāls recovered after the Mughals came to power, and two of them became Akbar's vizirs.

Modifications

The Bhāratendu version of Agravāl origin became the main source—or at least a source—for many subsequent retellings of the Agravāl myth, but later versions have also drawn on sources other than Bhāratendu. The issue of how the Bhāratendu version relates to others is thus extremely complex, and it is not possible to explore all of its ramifications here. It needs to be stressed, however, that the Bhāratendu version has powerfully influenced the Trust's tellings of Agravāl origin, probably because of the prestige of the author as a literary figure belonging to the Agravāl caste. It is reprinted in Trust publications, and is a principal source for Campālāl Gupta's semi-official book (1993, 1996) on the history of Agroha and the Agravāls.

The Trust/Bhāratendu retellings, moreover, have attained far more currency among Agravāls than any previously-existing narrative of Agravāl origins, a result of the Trust's intense promotion efforts. Unquestionably one of the most effective of the Trust's many projects was a *rath yātrā* that began 1995. This was a roadshow that included a mobile Agrasen temple travelling with a vehicle filled with literature, pictures and other Agroha-related paraphernalia. The convoy wound its way through cities and villages in several states of northern India, spreading the word about Agroha and Agrasen, and also collecting donations. In 1997 I interviewed several Agravāl small businessmen in a village just north of Sikar in Rajasthan. From what they told me, it is clear that, at least in this rural area, little was known about Agrasen and Agroha prior to the arrival of the convoy. Since then, awareness of these matters has grown enormously, and a few Agravāls from this village have actually visited Agroha. In other words, as a result of the efforts of the Sammelan and Trust an increasingly standardised narrative of Agravāl origins is emerging as a foundation for efforts to mobilise and unify the caste.

In comparing this narrative with others considered in this paper, three issues stand out as requiring special discussion: the question of Vaiśya descent, the relationship between the sacrifice and the origin of the caste and its *gotra*s, and the adjustments current tellings bring to the basic Agravāl origin myth. Let us examine each of these in turn.

On the issue of Vaiśya descent, we note that the Bhāratendu version accepts Vaiśya ancestry for the Agravāls, and this is also the line currently being pushed by the Trust (see, for example, C. Gupta 1996: 63–66). This view is not shared by all Agravāls. Various written accounts of Agravāl origin claim Rājpūt/Kṣatriya descent,[27] and many Agravāls with whom I have discussed these matters are convinced that Agrasen was a Rājpūt or Kṣatriya. Nonetheless, the Bhāratendu/Trust version emphasises Vaiśya descent, and this is clearly a departure from the pattern we have seen in the origin mythology of other trading castes.

Was Bhāratendu himself pursuing some special agenda having to do with Vaiśya identity? Possibly, but I know of no actual evidence that he was. We may thus have to assume that in stressing a Vaiśya heritage for the Agravāls he was merely following the lead of one of his principal sources, the 'Mahālakṣmī vrat kathā', which refers to Agrasen with such expressions as 'Lord of the Viś' (87–88, in Vidyālankār 1976: 157). Why this text—or any other of its sort—should assume a Vaiśya origin for Agravāls is another question. A possible answer is that the regional milieu from which it emerged was one in which Vaiśya identity was more salient, and Kṣatriya identity perhaps less so, than in the Rajasthani cultural zone, which is the primary regional context of this paper.

The Trust's much later commitment to a Vaiśya origin for the Agravāls is a more complex matter. It might, of course, simply be a reflex of Bhāratendu's support for the idea. It seems likely, however, that it also arises from a desire to reach out socially and politically to other trading castes by using the Vaiśya *varṇa* as a unifying category. This idea seems to have been part of the mix from the inception of the Sammelan in 1975 (on which see Akhil Bhāratīya Agravāl Sammelan 1983 and Rāmeśvardās Gupta 1995). One of its founding figures (and a person of great importance in Agravāl affairs today) told me that he was originally propelled into Agravāl-related activities by his deep anger at hearing the 'business community' continually maligned in Parliament. This same individual strongly believes in the importance of Vaiśya identity and its potential as a framework for organising India's trading castes. He suggested to me that other trading castes—he mentioned the Osvāls, Khaṇḍelvāls (of which sort he did not say), and Māheśvarīs in particular—could well have also been descended from Agrasen. Although these views were presented to me as those of only one individual, and although they would certainly find little support among the other castes in question, I suspect they reflect the general drift of at least some recent conversation and debate within the Agravāls' political elite.

But leaving aside the contemporary politics of Vaiśya identity, the Agravāl claim to Vaiśya ancestry is probably less of a departure from our other cases than first appearances would suggest. Although the Bhāratendu/Trust version identifies Agrasen as a Vaiśya, it also characterises him as a king who belonged to a lineage of kings. He was the founder of a kingdom, a ruler, and so valorous that he even challenged mighty Indra. He was also, as befits a Ksatriya ruler, a sponsor of blood sacrifices. So heroic was he that he even challenged mighty Indra. In other words, if Agrasen was a Vaiśya, he behaved a lot like a Ksatriya. This suggests

[27] For example, Rāmcandra Guptā (1926: 63–64); Cunnīlāl Agravāl (1915: 11); Bālcandjī Modī (n.d.). In the Cunnīlāl version, Agrasen had been cursed by Parasurām to remain issueless; he became Vaiśya in order to undo the curse (1915: 10).

that although the Bhāratendu/Trust narrative makes a claim of Vaiśya origin for the Agravāls, that claim is coloured by our by-now familiar myth-pattern of Kṣatriya heritage for a Vaiśya caste. Whether it arises from sensitivity about negative stereotypes of traders as physically weak or cowardly or for some other reason, there seems to be a reluctance to accept an undiluted Vaiśya ancestry

This is consistent with the fact that, whatever one is to make of Agrasen's *varṇa* status, the Trust places great emphasis on the contention that martial valour has always been a part of Agravāl character. The Trust, for example, has published an entire book entitled (in translation) *Legacy of heroism: A brief introduction to the valour, sacrifice, and devotion to duty of Agravāl (Vaiśya) heroes* (Bansal 1992). This book celebrates the heroism of Vaiśya kings and warriors of the past, as well as modern military men from the Agravāl caste. Its tone and the spirit in which it has been published are deeply resonant with the claim of Kṣatriya/Rājpūt lineage so often made in the origin legends of other trading castes. The implicit claim is that, although they are Vaiśyas in lineage and diet, the Agravāls are in a significant way Kṣatriyalike in character.

Our materials thus suggest that a *purely* Vaiśya heritage is never quite acceptable, or at least not without some modulation. These groups usually claim some other pedigree. The Khaṇḍelvāl Vaiśyas (in the myth cited in this paper) claim Brahmin ancestry; most other trading castes claim to have been Kṣatriyas originally. Although some (but not all) Agravāl myths of origin assert a Vaiśya pedigree, it seems to be a hedged claim, linked with suggestions of quasi-Ksatriya group character. It can therefore be said that there is, in the cases we have seen, an apparent instability in Vaiśya identity, by which I mean a tendency to decompose into claims that reach toward other *varna* categories, especially the Kṣatriya category.

As in all our other cases, the sacrifice is central to the actual creation of the Agravāls as a caste. If the group persona projected by the Bhāratendu/Trust legend is one of heroic Vaiśyahood, the precise moment at which that identity crystallises is when King Agrasen gives up the ritual shedding of blood in the last of a sequence of 18 sacrifices.[28] Ritual violence is the crucial consideration, and also the vegetarianism with which it is linked in the story. This is because, as we know, the manner of one's participation in the sacrifice is emblematic of the manner of one's participation in the social order it represents. Agravāls are members of this order, but not as meat-eaters or shedders of blood.

We thus see that the Bhāratendu/Trust legend of Agravāl origin falls within a pattern common to all the trading castes we have considered. In every instance, the ancestor/s of the caste undergo an identity transition that involves a change in the group's relation to the sacrifice. First, there is a break of some kind with the sacrifice. The issue is always violence, which is logical when one considers the centrality of nonviolence to the cultural personae of trading groups. The intensity of the break varies. Among the groups considered here, the break is most radical in the case of the Khaṇḍelvāl Jains, who leave the social order symbolised by the sacrifice, never to return. The Khaṇḍelvāl Vaiśyas and the Māheśvarīs reject less

[28] Not all versions of the legend refer to a sacrifice (such as Agravāl 1915). Most do.

radically; they then re-enter the order they rejected, albeit on a new basis. The Agravāls represent the most minimal break with the sacrifice, a rejection of a mere one-half sacrifice from a total of 18—i.e., 1/36 of the whole. So microscopic is the breach that there is apparently little scope or need for the rite-of-passage symbolisms we have noted for the other groups. But the separation does indeed occur, symbolising a small but decisive alteration in the Agravāls' relationship to ritual violence, and thus to the sacrifice itself.

We must also note that in the Agravāl legend, as in all others we have considered, a female figure plays a key role in the group's transition from its old to its new status, in this case the goddess Mahālakṣmī. This phenomenon is quite striking, and merits more consideration than is possible here. It should be pointed out, however, that it falls within a paradigm, described by Harlan for Rājpūt lineage goddesses (1992: 52–64), in which female figures are associated with the founding and protection of groups with which they develop permanent links. Two of the cases considered in this paper manifest this permanent connection. Cakreśvarī remains an important goddess to the Khaṇḍelvāl Jains (and apparently a clan goddess to some). And of course Mahālakṣmī, goddess of prosperity, has a special relationship with the destiny of the Agravāls, an idea embodied in the gigantic temple the Trust has erected for her at Agroha.

The relation between the sacrifice and the creation of Agravāl *gotras* is somewhat unclear in the materials I have seen. Of those accounts that link Agravāl origin to sacrifices, one (Modi n.d.: 8) maintains that Agrasen performed 17 1/2 sacrifices because he had no sons. As a result of these prenatal rites, his 17 queens and one subqueen bore sons; these became the apical ancestors of 17 1/2 *gotras*, each *gotra* deriving its name from the vedic sage (*ṛṣi*) who presided over the sacrifice (with the half *gotra* inferior to the others). In other accounts, the sacrifices generate the *gotras* but have nothing to do with the birth of sons. Bhāratendu, as we know, links the 17 1/2 *gotras* to 17 1/2 sacrifices, and he says that just as Agrasen's *gotra* was named for Garg Muni, the other *gotras* were also named on the basis of the sacrifices (presumably from the names of participating sages, though this is not spelled out). In a version in which no sacrifices are mentioned at all (Rāmcandra Guptā 1926: 44–49), the *gotras* are created when 17 sages educate and initiate Agrasen's 18 sons; the sons become apical ancestors of 17 1/2 *gotras*, each taking its name from one of the sages. Each sage's descendants, in turn, become the family priests of members of the *gotra* he created.[29]

It seems to me that in these various accounts of *gotra* origin the most important theme is that of the linkage between *gotras* and sages. Bringing the sages into the foreground places emphasis on the crucial fact that, whatever the nature of the transformation that created the Agravāls (i.e., a leap from Kṣatriyahood or a small step from one kind of Vaiśyahood to another), the caste is firmly reintegrated into the ritual-social order over which Brahmin sages preside. As in the Māheśvarī myth, the post-transformation Agravāls are shown to be *yajmāns*—that

[29] There were in fact only 17 sages, so that one sage had to educate and initiate (i.e., give *dīkṣā* to) two sons. One of those sons became the apical ancestor of the half *gotra*. According to the author, the system of family priests was long ago defunct (and I know of no traces of such a system).

is, sacrificial sponsors—but crucially different in character from *yajmāns* who preside over lethal sacrifices.

The sacrifice remains central to the most recent officially-sponsored expressions of Agravāl origin mythology. As we noted at the start of this paper, a tableau portraying 18 sacrifices was a prominent feature of Jaipur's 1996 celebration of Agrasen Jayanti, and I suspect such scenes play a similar role in celebrations elsewhere. A framing picture distributed by the Trust and sold at the temple at Agroha depicts 18 sacrifices presided over by a regal-looking Agrasen. At each of 18 fire altars a man and his wife are shown performing the rite with the assistance of two ritual officiants, and each pair is labelled with the name of an Agravāl *gotra*. The picture is entitled (in translation) 'King Agrasen and 18 *gotras*'. Here are all the important elements together: the caste's apical ancestor (Agrasen), the *gotras*' apical ancestors (18 sons), the sacrificial rite, the Brahmin officiants. This is the moment of creation of the Agravāl caste.

III
Old and new

But if the sacrifice continues to be the foundation for even the most contemporary expressions of the Agravāl origin legend, we also find evidence of efforts to update and modernise the legend in certain respects. This tendency is manifested with particular clarity in the writings of Campālāl Gupta, whose two books (1993 and a successor volume, 1996) have been published and extensively distributed by the Trust.

One important recent modification is the denial of the idea that all Agravāls are actually descended from Agrasen. Author Gupta (1996: 93–95; also Badlu Ram Gupta 1975) states that the Agravāl *gotras* could not be descended from 18 sons of Agrasen, arguing that intracaste marriage would be incestuous if it were true. The *gotras*, he says, are actually remnants of the political organisation of Agrasen's ancient kingdom. The kingdom was divided into 18 *śreṇis* or *kuls* (by which he means leading families); each of these sent a representative to a council where they assisted Agrasen in matters of governance. Agrasen did indeed sponsor 18 sacrifices, and a representative of each of these groups served as *yajmān* for each sacrifice. The descendants of these families became the 18 Agravāl *gotras*, named according to the sages who officiated at the sacrifices. This is how the Agravāl *jāti* emerged as an independent *jāti*—as Gupta puts it—from within the pre-existing 'Vaiśya *samāj*'. Agrasen loved his subjects with fatherly affection, and it is because of this that the idea arose that the eighteen *gotras* are his progeny. He promoted the exogamy of these families/*gotras* in the interest of *rakt śuddhi* (blood purity, which I take to mean avoidance of allegedly harmful inbreeding).[30]

[30] The names of Agravāl *gotras* were fixed and the number set at 18 by the Sammelan at its first annual meeting in April 1975 (Akhil Bhāratīya Agravāl Sammelan 1983: 17; see Crooke (1896) for differences between past lists). How the list was derived is unclear, but it is now deeply entrenched in the caste's affairs, a result of the sheer weight of literary, iconic and ceremonial reiteration. By my reckoning, five or six of the listed *gotras* are of doubtful existence.

The same author (ibid.: 55–56) has also propounded a theory of the sacrifice that departs dramatically from older notions. It is, in effect, a quasi social-scientific recasting of the theory of the sacrifice and group creation. In those days, Gupta says, kings sponsored *aśvamedh* sacrifices as a measure of their fame and standing, and also as a way of fostering unity within their kingdoms. The whole kingdom would take part in such ceremonies, and the 'mental outlook' of both ruler and subjects would be purified by doing so. This inevitably led to virtuous conduct within the kingdom. It is for these reasons that Agrasen sponsored his 18 sacrifices. They bound the people of his kingdom together, and because they were linked with the 18 subdivisions of the kingdom, they played a role in creating the 18 Agravāl *gotra*s.[31]

These highly modernistic and scientistic rerenderings of the origin of the Agravāls support an image of Agrasen, and thus the Agravāls as a community, as enlightened and anti-obscurantist. Agrasen emerges as a social engineer who even incorporated knowledge of genetics in the organisation of his kingdom. His kingdom was a republic, run on democratic principles. This latter assertion is consonant with values embedded in the wider political culture in which the Agravāl community and its leaders must continue to find a niche for themselves. The implication is that the Agravāls take a back seat to none in their commitment to progressive values, an idea reinforced by the great stress given to the public display of reformist themes on such occasions (as we have seen) as Agrasen Jayantī. I suspect that the future will bring more efforts to modify the Agrasen legend along these lines.

It is far from clear, however, that these revisions have yet achieved much currency within the Agravāl community itself. While I have no survey data, it is evident that large numbers of those Agravāls who know anything about these matters believe that they are actually, not metaphorically, descended from King Agrasen. The designers of the Jayantī float portraying Agrasen's 18 sons had obviously not gotten the new message yet, because the sons are labelled with the separate names of the *gotra*s. And a framing picture that I purchased at Agroha, one that bears the imprimatur of the Trust, shows Agrasen with his 18 'sons', labelled as such, along with a list of the 18 *gotra*s. I suspect, moreover, that few Agravāls have come to think of the sacrifice in the manner of functionalist sociologists. Even Campālāl Gupta, apparently forgetting himself, returns to older ritual images in the end—a testimony to their extraordinary power. As in other versions, the crux of his telling of the narrative is reached when Agrasen halts the proceedings at the 18th sacrifice. The work of Vaiśyas, Agrasen says, is the protection of creatures, not their slaughter—this is why God made the 'Vaiśya *Jāti*'. It is precisely at the moment when he prohibits the further slaughter of animals that the participating Vaiśyas become, at last, Agravāls.

[31] At another point in the book (1996: 68–69) Gupta proposes a somewhat different motive. At that time the Vaiśyas' rights to Vedic study and the sacrifice were being threatened. Agrasen sponsored his sacrifices in order to protect the rights of the Vaiśyas; the resulting organisation of the Agravāl caste was so sound that it lasted for centuries.

We find, therefore, that the sacrifice remains central to images of group formation and identity in all of the materials we have surveyed. It apparently hardly matters whether it is rationalised as a source of progeny, prosperity, or (in a newer mode) of social cohesion. Whatever is said of it, the association between the sacrifice and creative power—including the power to create social groups—remains as a presupposition, seemingly beyond the reach of doubt. In the particular case of the Agravāls, we find that continuity with the past is far greater than first appearances might suggest. The glitzy promotional efforts of the present day are, finally, rooted in old symbols of lasting validity.

REFERENCES

AGRAVĀL, CUNNĪLĀL. 1915. *Agravāl itihās.* Calcutta: Lalit Press.

AKHIL BHĀRATĪYA AGRAVĀL SAMMELAN. 1983. *Akhil Bhāratīya Agravāl Sammelan ke āth vars* (*Sammelan ke āth vars kā jīvan aur kārya*). Published on the occasion of the 7th annual meeting convened in Vārāṇasī, 22–23 January 1983. New Delhi: Rāmeśvardās Gupta.

BABB, LAWRENCE A. 1996. *Absent Lord: Ascetics and kings in a Jain ritual culture.* Berkeley: University of California Press.

BANSAL, CAPTAIN KAMAL KIŚOR. 1992. *Vīrtā kī vīrāsat: Agravāl (Vaiśya) vitrõ ke śaurya, tyāg evam karttavyaparāyaṇtāū kā sankṣipt paricay.* Agroha: Agroha Vikas Trust.

BARJĀTYĀ, RĀJMAL. 1910. *Khaṇḍelvāl Jain—itihās.* Bombay: S.V. Press.

BĪHAṆĪ, RĀMCANDRA. 1985. *Māheśvarī vamśotpatti.* Bīkāner: Māheśvarī Sevak.

CHANDRA, SUDHIR. 1992. *The oppressive present: Literature and social consciousness in colonial India.* Delhi: Oxford University Press.

CROOKE, W. 1896. *The tribes and castes of the North-Western Provinces and Oudh* (4 vols). Calcutta: Office of the Superintendent of Government Printing.

DARAK, ŚIVKARAṆ RĀMRATAN. 1923. *Vaiśyakulbhūṣaṇ va itihāskalpdrum Māheśvarīkulśuddhdarpaṇ aur sāṛhī bārah va caurāsī nyātkā varṇan* (4th edn; original v. 1950). Mumbaī: Gangaviṣṇu Śrīkṛṣṇdās.

ECK, DIANA L. 1982. *Banaras: City of light.* New York: Alfred A. Knopf.

ELLIS, CHRISTINE M. COTTAM. 1991. The Jain merchant castes of Rajasthan: Some aspects of the management of social identity in a market town. *In* M. Carrithers and C. Humphrey, eds, *The assembly of listeners: Jains in society*, pp. 75–107. Cambridge: Cambridge University Press.

GARG, ŚIVŚANKAR (of SIKAR, RAJ.) n.d. *Śīlā Mātā kā jīvan paricay.* Agrohā Vikās Sansthān.

GUPTA, BADLU RAM. 1975. *The Aggarwals: A socio-economic study.* New Delhi: S. Chand & Co.

GUPTA, CAMPĀLĀL. 1993. *Agrohā: Ek aitihāsik paricay.* Agroha: Agroha Vikas Trust.

———. 1996. *Agrohā: Ek aitihāsik dharohar.* Agroha: Agroha Vikas Trust.

GUPTA, MOTĪLĀL. n.d. *Khaṇḍelvāl jāti kā prārambhik itihās.* Jaipur: Śrī Khaṇḍelvāl Vaiśya Mahāsabhā.

GUPTĀ, RĀMCANDRA. 1926. *Agravamś arthāt Agravāl jātī kā itihās.* Sekhā, Rājya Paṭiyālā, Panjāb: Śobhārām Smārak Granthmālā Kāryālay.

GUPTA, RĀMEŚVARDĀS, ed. 1995. *Agrohādhām ke nirmāṇ ki kahānī citrõ kī zabānī.* New Delhi: Agroha Vikas Ṭrust.

HARLAN, LINDSEY. 1992. *Religion and Rajput women: The ethic of protection in contemporary narratives.* Berkeley: University of California Press.

JAIN, KAILASH CHAND. 1972. *Ancient cities and towns of Rajasthan: A study of culture and civilization.* Delhi: Motilal Banarsidass.

KĀSLĪVĀL, KASTŪRCAND. 1989. *Khaṇḍelvāl Jain Samāj kā vrhad itihās.* Jaipur: Jain Itihās Prakāśan Sansthān.

KHAṆḌELVĀL, M.C. 1984. Khaṇḍelvālõ kī utpatti. *Khaṇḍelvāl Mahāsabhā Patrikā* 23, 1–2 (July–August 1984), unnumbered pages.

LATH, MUKUND. 1981. *Half a tale: A study in the interrelationship between autobiography and history.* (*The Ardhakathanaka* translated, introduced and annotated by Mukund Lath). Jaipur: Rajasthan Prakrit Bharati Sansthan.

MADAN, T.N. 1997. *Modern myths, locked minds: Secularism and fundamentalism in India.* Delhi: Oxford University Press.

MODĪ, BĀLCAND. n.d. *Śrī Mahārāj Agrasen: Saṅkṣipt jivan caritra.* Calcutta: Akhil Bharatvarṣiya Agravāl Mahāsabha. Date not given, but bound with other booklets dating from the 1930s.

PANDEY, GYANENDRA. 1990. *The construction of communalism in colonial North India.* Delhi: Oxford University Press.

PĀṬODIYĀ, RĀMKIŚOR. 1986. Khaṇḍelvāl Vaiśya jāti kī utpatti. *In, Sambhāv: A. Bh. Khaṇḍelvāl Vaiśa Mahāsabhā 27th Adhiveśan, Alvar (Rājasthān).* (26–28 December 1986). Unnumbered pages.

ŚĀH, BAKHATRĀM. 1964. *Buddhi-vilās.* Ed. Padmadhar Pāṭhak. Jodhpur: Rajasthan Oriental Research Institute.

ŚARMĀ, HEMANT, ed. 1989. *Bhāratendu Samgra.* Vārāṇasī: Hindi Pracārak Sansthān.

SMITH, BRIAN K. 1989. *Reflections on resemblance, ritual, and religion.* Oxford and New York: Oxford University Press.

SOMĀNĪ, RĀMBALLABH. 1997. Khāṇḍelvāl sarāvgiyõ ke prācīn śilālekh. *In, Mahāvīr Jayantī Smārikā, 1997.* Jaipur: Rājasthān Jain Sabhā, 3/3–5.

ṬĀṆṬIYĀ, HARPATRĀY. 1996. *Agrohā-darśan.* Agroha: Agroha Vikas Trust.

TEMPLE, RICHARD CARNAC. 1977. *The legends of the Panjāb* (3 vols). Reprint of 1884–1900 edn. New York: Arno Press.

TIMBERG, THOMAS A. 1978. *The Marwaris: From traders to industrialists.* New Delhi: Vikas.

VAN GENNEP, ARNOLD. 1960. *The rites of passage.* Translated by M.B. Vizedom and G.L. Caffee. Chicago: University of Chicago Press.

VIDYĀLANKĀR, SATYAKETU. 1976. *Agravāl jāti kā prācīn itihās.* Masūrī: Śrī Sarasvatī Sadan.

12

Caste and politics: The presumption of numbers

Dipankar Gupta

The belief that caste loyalties determine electoral outcomes is usually not subjected to a close factual scrutiny. The paper argues that there is no systematic relationship between caste numbers and election results. If, in spite of this, certain castes tend to dominate in the political arena, then it is probably because they have access to better organisational resources. Census and election figures from Uttar Pradesh, Bihar and Maharashtra form the primary data base for this presentation.

In short there is no systematic formula through which a candidate in his constituency, or a party in the state, can employ caste loyalties to win elections… (Bailey 1960: 129).

I

The limits of caste arithmetic

It is commonplace in the analysis of caste politics to give in to the presumption of numbers. Thus it is often argued that political outcomes can be determined to a fair degree by the caste composition of electoral constituencies. This falls quite in line with the overall assumption that Hindus are generally bound by their caste loyalties, so why should politics be any different? There are periods when the domination of politics by caste seems like a near truism (as during the 1996 elections), but then again there are times when caste does not seem to play that influential a role. Even so, in many considered works on the subject of caste and politics it is assumed that political fortunes depend primarily on the caste composition of individual constituencies (Frankel 1989: 82–83, 100–101, 1990: 512–13).[1]

There are indeed several problems with such a perspective. A scrutiny of election results reveals quite easily that political parties are rarely able to hold on to

[1] Francine Frankel acknowledges the fact that castes occupy different economic locations within society (Frankel 1989: 87), yet she chooses to privilege caste above all else in analysing politics in India. This is quite in keeping with her overall view that India is basically a religious society (Frankel 1990: 484, 514). Contrast this style of scholarship with the essays compiled by Srinivas (1996) where the emphasis is not so much on how castes spontaneously form political units as on how caste affiliations are stoked by vested political interests.

their seats over successive elections. A Bharatiya Janata Party (BJP) stronghold today might well be stormed by the Congress or by the Samajwadi Party (SP) in the next election. This is also true of parties that are supposedly based on caste loyalties in a more overt fashion. The Samajwadi Party is said to be the vehicle of newly emergent peasant castes such as the Ahirs or Yadavas, yet it is not easy to predict its electoral fortunes. All this should not have been the case if caste and political preference were so closely tied together. For example, the Janata Dal (out of which the Rashtriya Janata Dal, or RJD, was born) won in 1991 in Kodarma, Chhapra and Bettiah constituencies in Bihar, only to lose them to the BJP in both the 1996 and 1998 elections. Similarly, the BJP won in 1991 in Jaunpur, Saidpur, Ghatimpur and Ghazipur constituencies in Uttar Pradesh (UP) but lost them in 1998 to the Janata Dal.

Likewise in Maharashtra the Shiv Sena (SS) won from Amravati in 1991 but lost this seat to the Republican Party of India (RPI) in 1996. In 1998 the same seat was won by the Congress. In Bhid, again in Maharashtra, the BJP won in 1991 and 1996 but lost to Congress in 1998. These illustrations demonstrate that electoral outcomes in India cannot be pre-determined, and therefore the role of caste in politics should also be cautiously understated.

In this paper examples will be drawn from Maharashtra, Bihar and Uttar Pradesh in order to estimate the extent to which caste influenced electoral verdicts in the last three elections. As the Indian political situation has changed considerably over the past five decades it would be more pertinent to focus on recent elections. It is for this reason that the parliamentary elections of 1991, 1996 and 1998 have been taken into account. In these years the Mandal commission recommendations helped consolidate the politics of the so-called Backward Castes. The Bahujan Samaj Party (BSP) and the caste support to Maulayam Singh Yadav and Laloo Yadav have also been much written about during this period.

It needs to be admitted at the outset that it is difficult to match population by caste and election results. This is for two reasons. In the first place, the last caste census was published as far back as 1931. Second, caste enumeration is provided district-wise and these districts do not always coincide with parliamentary electoral constituencies. Nevertheless, with the help of Singh's painstaking efforts (Singh 1996), an attempt has been made to match one with the other. The result is an approximation, no doubt, but a close approximation (see *Census of India, 1931*, Part II tables, for Bombay, for United Province of Agra and Oudh, and for Bihar and Orissa). For obvious reasons attempts to superimpose census areas over the smaller state legislative assembly constituencies would be victim to much greater inaccuracies. At the level of parliamentary constituencies, however, it is worth taking the risk. There is a fair chance that census information can be a reliable indication of a parliamentary constituency's caste profile. The examination of the relationship between caste numbers and electoral results would not only help us add another dimension to our understanding of caste and politics, but can also be a useful scaffolding for revisiting conceptual discussions on the caste system. Let us now turn to the cases that we have selected for our study.

Maharashtra

The situation in Maharashtra is certainly not conducive to advancing the conception of caste based politics. This is primarily because Marathas constitute such an overwhelming proportion of the population of this province that all the other castes are reduced to a kind of minority status. The Marathas alone constitute about 31 per cent of the population. In the Konkan region of Maharashtra they account for nearly 40 per cent of the population. After this there is a huge drop. The Mehras are the second most numerous caste in Maharashtra, constituting only 4.7 per cent of the population. Brahmans come next, comprising a mere 3.9 per cent of the population. The other castes usually fall below 1 per cent (see Lele 1990: 117–18). The political contest in this state over the last three elections has really been between the Congress and the BJP–SS alliance. Occasionally the Republican Party of India appears but without any consistency. In fact, barring a few constituencies, there is hardly any consistency whatsoever in the electoral profile of Maharashtra. Bombay North Central was won by SS in 1996, by RPI in 1998 and by the Congress in 1991. The latest RPI victory is, in all likelihood, an outcome of its alliance with the Congress. It is interesting to note that the RPI won in Akola, Amravati and Chimur as well, but only in 1998 when it came to an electoral understanding with the Congress.

Maharashtra is really a two-party state. It is either the Congress or the BJP–SS that has won seesaw battles in the last three elections. In general a high Maratha presence can be correlated somewhat with the Congress. This would be particularly true of south-west-Maharashtra constituencies such as Khed, Baramati, Karad, Sangli, Icchalkaranji and Kolhapur. In all these areas the Congress won consistently between 1991 and 1998. In Kopargaon and Sholapur which belong to the same region and have the same caste profile, the Congress has yielded occasionally to the BJP. Ramtak and Bhandara tell a somewhat different story. Though these constituencies are somewhat atypical, as the Marathas constitute less than 30 per cent of their total population, they nevertheless voted for the Congress in the last three elections, just as the Maratha dominated areas

Table 1

High Maratha presence (over 30%) and electoral results

Constituency	*Elections*		
	1998	*1996*	*1991*
Bombay South	Congress	BJP	Congress
Bombay South Central	Shiv Sena	Shiv Sena	Shiv Sena
Ahmednagar	Shiv Sena	Congress	Congress
Kopargaon	Congress	BJP	Congress

Source: H.D. Singh, 1996, *543 faces of India*, New Delhi: Newsman Publishers; Unpublished Lok Sabha election results, 1998; and *Census of India, 1931, Bombay* (Part II tables), Bombay: Government Central Press.

mentioned above did. So the easy identification between the Congress and the Marathas does not always hold. Marathas are known to reject the Congress just as much as the other castes are known to vote it to power.

The situation is the same with the BJP–SS alliance. This combine does particularly well in parts of urban Bombay. Bombay South Central, Bombay North West and Bombay North have been strongholds of the BJP–SS alliance from the 1991 election onwards. These constituencies share roughly the same caste profile as Bombay North Central and Bombay North East, but here the Congress fared better during this period. In general, the BJP–SS and the Congress share the electoral booty in and around Bombay. In areas with the same caste profile political allegiances have changed, and at the same time different caste combinations have often brought about the same political results.

If we enter the Muslim factor the picture does not change in any significant way. Take Bombay for instance. A relatively high Muslim population of between 15 and 20 per cent in Bombay South Central could not prevent the BJP–SS from winning successive elections during 1991–98. Aurangabad which also has a Muslim population of 15–20 per cent returned Shiv Sena candidates in 1996 and 1991.

Without taking into account the presence of the Scheduled Castes (SCs) the picture would not be complete. In constituencies around Marathwada where the SC population is quite high the Congress seems to do better than the BJP–SS alliance. In Latur, Nanded and Osmanabad the Congress is by and large better placed than its rivals. In all these constituencies the SC population is quite high, constituting roughly 20–25 per cent of the population. Akola is the only other place in Maharashtra that has such a high proportion of Scheduled Castes. But it does not conform to the pattern just suggested. In 1991 and 1996 the BJP or the BJP–SS alliance won the elections. In 1998, however, the RPI won at the hustings, but this, as we said earlier, was probably because of Congress support.

It is apparent that caste loyalties are quite fickle when it comes to electoral choices. Obviously there is a lot more than just caste that matters. But Maharashtra may well be made out to be a special case as the Marathas numerically preponderate over all other castes by a long way in the entire state. In practically every

Table 2

Strong Scheduled Caste presence (over 20%) and election results in Maharashtra

Constituency	*Elections*		
	1998	*1996*	*1991*
Latur	Congress	Congress	Congress
Nanded	Congress	Congress	Congress
Osmanabad	Congress	Shiv Sena	Congress
Akola	RPI	BJP	Shiv Sena

Source: *Census of India, 1991*; H.D. Singh, 1996, *543 faces of India*, New Delhi: Newsman Publishers; Unpublished Lok Sabha election results, 1998; Sanjeeb K. Behera, 1999, *Data base on Scheduled Caste literacy in India* (*based on Census 1991*), New Delhi: Indian Social Institute.

region of Maharashtra the elites are drawn from this caste (see Lele 1981: 56–57). With the kind of overwhelming majority the Maratha caste enjoys it can probably afford the indulgence of internal differentiation. At least this could be a possible explanation. As the Marathas are not threatened by any other caste there is little compulsion for the Marathas to consolidate and present a united front to the outside world. But in Bihar and Uttar Pradesh no single caste numerically predominates like the Marathas do in Maharashtra. The facts from UP and Bihar should therefore help to fill out the picture a little more comprehensively.

Uttar Pradesh

The information that the census figures provide about UP are indeed very striking. In only a handful of districts do castes such as the Brahmans, Rajputs, Ahirs or Kurmis barely make up between 15 and 20 per cent of the population. In Kanpur and Gonda Brahmans constitute between 15 and 20 per cent of the population; in Robertsganj and nowhere else are Kurmis somewhere between 15 and 20 per cent of the population; in Saidpur, Azamgarh and Jaunpur Ahirs comprise between 15 and 20 per cent of the population; and, finally, Rajputs are roughly 15–20 per cent of the population of Garhwal, Tehri Garhwal and Nainital. In only nine out of a total of sixty-three districts do the so-called upper castes and dominant agrarian castes have some kind of a presence. In the famous Jat districts of Muzaffarnagar, Meerut, Agra and Saharanpur, Jats hardly make up even 10 per cent of the population. In Muzaffarnagar, which is widely claimed to be a Jat lair, only 8.44 per cent of the population belongs to that community. The same trend holds for districts such as Bijnor, Bulandshahr, Agra and Meerut, and yet they are famously associated with the Jat leader Chaudhari Charan Singh (see *Census of India, 1931, United Province*, Part II tables). Obviously, the identification of certain dominant agrarian castes with a region cannot be based on numbers alone. Why then is it believed that Jats, or Ahirs, or Kurmis, control the politics of certain constituencies? The answer surely does not rest on numbers alone.

Interestingly, only the Scheduled Castes constitute above 25 per cent, and in some cases even above 30 per cent, of the population in practically every district of UP. Yet, there is no area in UP that is known to be controlled by Scheduled Castes. If numbers and caste loyalty were all that important, then surely the SCs should be ruling UP. In Muzaffarnagar the Jats number only about 8.5 per cent of the population, but are able to contain the SCs who make up over 20 per cent of the population. One answer to this conundrum could easily be that the dominant landowning Jats terrorise the SCs into submission, not letting them organise politically, and perhaps even disallowing them from casting their votes. Such an explanation sounds very compelling once caste populations are factored into the analysis.

It is, therefore, not just numbers, but something more that makes for the power of certain castes over other castes. In contemporary times, however, an explanation that rests on sheer power appears a little less convincing than it would have in the past. This is because SCs are now increasingly able to free themselves from rural subordination. More and more rural SCs are looking outside the village for employment; and if they seek employment within the village, then it is not as agricultural labourers. To a great extent this situation has arisen because there are not enough jobs in the villages. The green revolution and sub-division of holdings have converted most farms into either family plots or capitalist enterprises. Lack of agricultural jobs in the villages has had at least one salutary effect. Now that SCs are relatively free of Jat, Gujar, Ahir or Rajput domination they have greater political manoeuvrability.

This loosening of ties with the landed castes has not always led to successful urbanisation of SCs. In a large number of cases they continue to live in the village and work in neighbouring cities and townships. Even so, the fact that they are no longer dependent on the agricultural sector for jobs in the way they used to be in the past, has enabled, and emboldened, them to join alternative political formations. It is not at all surprising that it is only in the last ten to fifteen years that the politics of the Bahujan Samaj Party is becoming credible in UP. As long as the SCs were fettered as agricultural labourers without any opportunities outside the village, a party like the BSP could hardly be expected to be an active political option for them.

In Maharashtra something quite similar happened that allowed the SCs, particularly the Mahars, to become politically active. The literacy rate and urbanisation of the Mahar community is the highest among the Scheduled Castes of Maharashtra. This process of secular literacy and employment was also aided by the formation of a Mahar regiment in the British Indian Army. It was from such stirrings that the Republican Party of India under B.R. Ambedkar was born. Scheduled Castes in UP have not yet undergone the same kind of cultural upliftment as the Mahars of Maharashtra have accomplished. Even so, the general secularisation of economic opportunities outside the village has certainly played an important role in consolidating the BSP in UP. The Harijans (or the Chamars) are the most advanced of all the SCs in UP and it would be safe to surmise that many of them play a leading role in the SC politics of their respective constituencies.

Judging from the figures of caste population and electoral outcome, it appears that the BJP and Congress tend to do well when the Brahman population is higher than average, i.e., around 10–15 per cent. This seems to hold in constituencies like Garhwal, Tehri Garhwal, Nainital, Almora, Amethi and Sultanpur. But before

Table 3
BSP's progress in UP Lok Sabha elections

Year	*Percentage of Votes*
1985	2.6
1989	9.5
1991	11.0
1996	20.6
1998	22.0

we set off to draw conclusions from this we ought to note that Sultanpur and Akbarpur share roughly the same kind of caste profile, but with vastly different electoral outcomes. In both these constituencies Brahmans and Ahirs comprise 10–15 per cent of the population, Rajputs and Kurmis roughly 5–10 per cent, and the Scheduled Castes over 25 per cent of the population. Yet in Sultanpur the BJP has consistently won the last three elections, while in Akbarpur the BSP won in 1996 and 1998. So an explanation based on caste numbers does not do too well beyond a point.

The BJP prospers in a variety of caste configurations. It has also been successful in areas where the population of the more affluent and powerful castes is quite low. For instance, the BJP won in Kheri, Hardoi and Shahabad where Ahirs, Brahmans and Rajputs each comprise between 5 and 10 per cent of the population while the SCs make up more than 25 per cent of the population. The BJP has also done well in areas such as Etah and Bareilly in the last three elections. Ahirs make up about

Table 4

Higher than average Brahman population and election results

Constituency	*Brahman (%)*	*Elections*		
		1998	*1996*	*1991*
Garhwal	5–10	BJP	Congress	Congress
Tehri Garhwal	-do-	BJP	BJP	Congress
Nainital	-do-	BJP	Congress	Congress
Almora	-do-	BJP	BJP	Congress
Amethi	10–15	BJP	Congress	–
Sultanpur	-do-	BJP	BJP	BJP
Akbarpur	-do-	BSP	BSP	JD

Source: H.D. Singh, 1996, *543 faces of India*, New Delhi: Newsman Publishers; *Census of India, 1931, United Province of Agra and Oudh* (Part II tables), Allahabad: SPS; Unpublished Lok Sabha election results, 1998.

Table 5

BJP strongholds and caste composition of constituencies

Constituency	*Castes and their Percentage*				
	Ahirs	*Brahmans*	*Rajputs*	*Kurmis*	*Scheduled Castes*
Kheri	5–10	5–10	5–10	5–10	Over 25
Hardoi	-do-	-do-	-do-	-do-	-do-
Shahabad	-do-	-do-	-do-	-do-	-do-
Etah	10–15	-do-	-do-	-do-	15–20
Bareilly	5–10	-do-	-do-	-do-	-do-
Gorakhpur	10–15	10–15	-do-	10–15	-do-
Saidpur	15–20	5–10	-do-	5–10	Over 25

Source: H.D. Singh, 1996, *543 faces of India*, New Delhi: Newsman Publishers; *Census of India, 1931, United Province of Agra and Oudh* (Part II tables), Allahabad: SPS.

Table 6
Ahir population percentage and Janata Dal (JD)/Samajwadi Party (SP) results

Constituency	*Percentage of Ahirs*	*Election Result*		
		1998	*1996*	*1991*
Azamgarh	15–20	BSP	SP	JD
Jaunpur	-do-	SP	BJP	JD
Ghazipur	-do-	SP	BJP	Other

Source: H.D. Singh, 1996, *543 faces of India*, New Delhi: Newsman Publishers; *Census of India, 1931, United Province of Agra and Oudh* (Part II tables), Allahabad: SPS; Unpublished Lok Sabha election results, 1998.

Table 7
Caste composition and election outcome

Constituency	*Caste Composition (%)*					*Elections*		
	Ahirs	*Brahmans*	*Rajputs*	*Kurmis*	*SCs*	*1998*	*1996*	*1991*
Moradabad	5–10	5–10	5–10	5–10	15–20	SP	SP	JD
Kheri	-do-	-do-	-do-	-do-	-do-	BJP	SP	BJP
Hardoi	-do-	-do-	-do-	-do-	Over 25	BJP	SP	BJP
Shahabad	-do-	-do	-do	-do-	-do-	BSP	BJP	BJP
Misrich	-do-	-do-	-do-	-do-	-do-	BJP	BSP	–

Source: H.D. Singh, 1996, *543 faces of India*, New Delhi: Newsman Publishers; *Census of India, 1931, United Province of Agra and Oudh* (Part II tables), Allahabad: SPS; Unpublished Lok Sabha election results, 1998.

11.7 per cent of the population of Etah, and in Bareilly the Kurmis constitute approximately 10.2 per cent of the population. The same could be said about Gorakhpur as well. The trend is expressed more strongly in Saidpur. The population of Ahirs is quite high here, standing at between 15 and 20 per cent of the population.

Elsewhere, however, where castes such as Ahirs and Kurmis account for between 15 and 20 per cent of the population, the Samajwadi Party of Maulayam Singh Yadav appears to fare well. This is certainly true of Azamgarh, Jaunpur and Ghazipur. However, it is not as if the SP or JD have these constituencies in their pockets. The BJP, and even the BSP, have done equally well in the same areas. Judging from constituencies where the JD or SP have won, it is quite clear that no straight correlation can be drawn between these victories and caste numbers.

It would be worthwhile to reiterate in this connection that with the same kind of caste composition a variety of electoral results are possible. Take for instance the case of Moradabad, Kheri, Hardoi, Shahabad and Misrich. In these constituencies Ahir, Brahman, Kurmi, Rajput and SC proportions are roughly the same. Yet the election outcomes differ widely between constituencies, and within the same constituency over different elections.

The relationship between the Bahujan Samaj Party and Scheduled Caste population figures is also rather tenuous. As we have noted earlier, SCs dominate the population of UP in terms of sheer numbers. On an average they make up about 21 per cent of the population of UP. In several constituencies they comprise more than 25 per cent of the population. Yet the BSP does not always do well in places where the proportion of SCs is very high. For example, the BSP has failed to make a significant impact in constituencies such as Unnao, Rae Bareilly, Amethi, Sultanpur, Faizabad, Bansgaon and Chail, where the SC population is quite high, i.e., above 25 per cent. In Misrich, however, BSP victory could be linked to the fact that the SCs constitute more than 25 per cent of the population there. But Misrich is also a reserved constituency, so it is hard to be sure if caste numbers alone made the difference. On the other hand, Bahraich has a lower-than-average percentage of SC population and yet the BSP won the last elections there. Interestingly, the BJP won the Bahraich seat in both 1991 and 1996.

Neither can we relate literacy among the SCs with the BSP's success at the polls. Though in 1998 the BSP actually won only four seats in Uttar Pradesh, it won the second largest number of votes in as many as fourteen constituencies. If we take all these eighteen constituencies together we find that we cannot correlate the BSP's positive performance with either SC population or literacy. With lower-than-average SC population and literacy rate the BSP won in Pilibhit and Bahraich. But in Saharanpur and Mathura the literacy rate among the SCs is higher than the average for UP and the BSP stood second in both these places. This conclusion, like the others, is only an approximation as we do not have constituency-wise literacy or caste population figures. In the case of electoral constituencies like Misrich, Akbarpur, Hathras and Khurja I have not been able to make an assessment of SC population ratio or literacy rate with any degree of satisfaction. In such cases only a field study can help.

Table 8

Scheduled Caste population percentage, literacy rate and BSP performance in some constituencies of UP

Constituency	*Literacy*			*Population*			*BSP Position in 1998 Elections*
	High	*Average*	*Low*	*High*	*Average*	*Low*	
Pilibhit			✓			✓	2nd Position
Sitapur			✓	✓			2nd Position
Bahraich			✓			✓	1st Position
Ghosi		✓		✓			2nd Position
Azamgarh		✓			✓		1st Position
Fatehpur		✓			✓		2nd Position
Jalaun	✓			✓			2nd Position
Mathura	✓					✓	2nd Position

Source: *Census of India 1991*; Unpublished Lok Sabha election results, 1998, Sanjeeb K. Behera, 1999, Data base on Scheduled Caste literacy in India (based on Census 1991), New Delhi: Indian Social Institute.

When mapping the areas where the BSP is quite strong it is interesting to note that they seem to be clustered in four strips that are geographically quite disparate. The first is the north-central region comprising Pilibhit, Shahabad, Sitapur and Misrich. The next is the eastern strip of UP where Salempur, Ghosi, Azamgarh, Lalganj and Saidpur are situated. The third area of BSP influence is in south-east UP in constituencies like Banda, Fatehpur, Bilhaur and Jalaun. Finally, BSP presence is also quite significant in constituencies such as Mathura, Hathras and Khurja in south-west UP. There is nothing in terms of either population or literacy that unites these four zones of BSP prominence. Nevertheless, the fact that the BSP is strong in four lots of contiguous constituencies would encourage the interpretation that it draws political strength from the synergies of proximity. Collectively, across constituencies, numbers help to shore up SC confidence, which enables them to support the BSP somewhat consistently. This fact also points to the relative weakness of the organisational capacities of the Scheduled Castes and of the BSP. What they lack in terms of organisational resources and capacities they make up for by geographical aggregation.

Bihar

In Bihar the Congress did not feature in any significant way in the last three Lok Sabha elections. The fight in Bihar is really between the Janata Dal, or its 1998 incarnation, the RJD, and the BJP. The RJD certainly got the better of the BJP in the last parliamentary election in 1998. The relationship between caste and politics is a little clearer here than it is in either UP or Maharashtra. But in this case too there is no constituency where a dominant agrarian caste like the Yadavas or Ahirs enjoys a numerical majority. In a handful of constituencies such as Madhepura, Chhapra, Arrah, Khagriya, Patna and Navadah the Yadavas form between 15 and 20 per cent of the population. Nowhere in Bihar do the Yadavas account for anything more than this in terms of their share in the population. In Bihar, too, quite contrary to the general impression, caste arithmetic cannot explain too much.

Nevertheless, certain patterns can be dimly discerned. In Ranchi, Kodarma Jamshedpur and Giridih there is a high concentration of Muslims, SCs and Scheduled Tribes (STs). The Yadava proportions are quite low in these areas. In Giridih and Kodarma Yadavas are about 10–15 per cent of the population, while in Ranchi they are below 5 per cent. In all these three constituencies the BJP is quite strong. In Ranchi it has won every time in the last three elections, while in Kodarma, Jamshedpur and Giridih it has won two out of three times. From this the following conclusion can be drawn. When the number of Yadavas is not very high, but the proportions of SCs, STs and Muslims together account for about 50 per cent of the population, the chances are that the JD or RJD of Laloo Prasad Yadav will face a stiff challenge from the BJP. This conclusion can be extended to other constituencies like Khunti, Purnea, Rajmahal, Dumka, Godda and Singhbhum. They all seem to fit this pattern. Low Yadava population, i.e., between 5 and 10 per cent of total population, generally leads to BJP victory. In

Table 9
Low (below 10%) Ahir population and election results
(Table shows other caste percentages as well)

Constituency	*Muslims (%)*	*SCs (%)*	*STs (%)*	*Ahirs (%)*	*Brahmans (%)*	*Rajputs (%)*	*Elections*		
							1998	*1996*	*1991*
Jamshedpur	5–10	10–15	20–25	5–10	5–10	Below 5	BJP	BJP	JD
Khunti	-do-	-do-	-do-	Below 5	Below 5	-do-	BJP	BJP	BJP
Purnea	20–25	15–20	10–15	5–10	-do-	-do-	BJP	Samata	–
Rajmahal	-do-	10–15	20–25	-do-	-do-	-do-	BJP	Congress	Others
Dumka	10–15	-do-	-do-	-do-	-do-	-do-	BJP	JMM	Others
Godda	-do-	-do-	15–20	-do-	-do-	-do-	BJP	BJP	Others
Singhbhum	5–10	-do-	20–25	Below 5	-do-	-do-	Congress	BJP	JD
Ranchi	10–15	-do-	-do-	-do-	-do-	-do-	BJP	BJP	BJP

Source: H.D. Singh, 1996, *543 faces of India*, New Delhi: Newsman Publishers; *Census of India, 1931, Bihar and Orissa* (Part II tables), Patna: SPS; Unpublished Lok Sabha election results, 1998.

some instances such a caste configuration has also helped the Congress and the Jharkhand Mukti Morcha (JMM).

Even as we arrive at this conclusion we cannot ignore the instances of places like Kishanganj and Araria which are strongholds of the JD or RJD even though the Yadavas constitute only between 5 and 10 per cent of the population. It is not easy to explain this in terms of population figures, for in Araria the Muslims, STs and SCs constitute well above 50 per cent of the population and yet the JD won in both 1991 and 1996. The BJP however wrested this seat away from the JD in 1998. In Kishanganj, on the other hand, with a Yadava population of between 5 and 10 per cent, the JD and RJD have won all the three elections of 1991, 1996 and 1998. To add another wrinkle to this, it is quite likely that the JD or RJD do well in spite of low Yadava numbers because this shortfall is made up by the high proportion of Muslims. As it may be reasonably assumed that Muslims would not vote for the BJP, it is very likely that they voted for the JD or RJD instead. This may account for why the JD or RJD did well in spite of low Yadava numbers. This combination however did not work in Rajmahal and Purnea where the BJP has done much better than its competitors.

I would still like to consider Rajmahal and Purnea anomalous cases that need further investigation. Generally, a high proportion of Muslims tends to offset low Yadava numbers to keep out the BJP. Sometimes it is the Congress and on other occasions it is the JD or RJD that win in these constituencies. This explains to a great extent why Laloo Yadav's RJD is demonstrably 'secular' at least on its position on Muslim minorities.

If one takes into account the cases where the JD/RJD has won with between 10 and 15 per cent Yadava population, it is difficult to explain how the castes lined up. The same holds true in constituencies where the JD/RJD has had mixed results. With 10–15 per cent Yadava population the JD/RJD has done well in places like Gopalganj, Hajipur, Vaishali, Muzaffarpur and Jhanjharpur. However, in constituencies like Ballia, Motihari or Bettiah where the Yadavas again form between 10 and 15 per cent of the population, the JD/RJD has had mixed results. As this is the case in most instances it is hard to interpret electoral results through the optic of caste numbers.

The major correlation in the Bihar scenario is between a middle sized representation of Yadavas and JD or RJD victory. Except for constituencies like Jehanabad, Sitamarhi and Navadah, the JD/RJD has won in the last three elections in those areas where the Yadavas constitute between 15 and 20 per cent of the population. This is true of Madhepura, Chhapra, Arrah, Monghyr, Patna, Barka and Khagriya. While the correlation between Yadavas constituting between 15 and 20 per cent of the population and JD/RJD victories is quite impressive, it still does not explain how the JD/RJD won. It cannot be assumed that the Rajputs,

Table 10

Yadava population between 10 and 15% in some constituencies and mixed election results

Constituency	Elections		
	1998	*1996*	*1991*
Gopalganj	Samata	JD	JD
Hajipur			
Vaishali	RJD	JD	JD
Muzaffarnagar	RJD	JD	JD
Jhanjharpur	RJD	JD	JD
Ballia	RJD	CPI	Others
Motihari	RJD	BJP	Others
Bettiah	BJP	BJP	JD
Madhuban	Congress	CPI	Others

Source: H.D. Singh, 1996, *543 faces of India*, New Delhi: Newsman Publishers; *Census of India, 1931* (Part II tables); Unpublished Lok Sabha election results, 1998.

Table 11

Ahir population between 15 and 20% and JD/RJD performance

Constituency	Elections		
	1998	*1996*	*1991*
Madhepura	RJD	JD	JD
Arrah	SAP	JD	JD
Monghyr	RJD	JD	Others
Barka	Samata	JD	JD
Khagriya	Samata	JD	JD
Patna	–	JD	–
Navadah	RJD	BJP	Others
Chhapra	RJD	BJP	JD
Jehanabad	RJD	CPI	Others

Source: H.D. Singh, 1996, *543 faces of India*, New Delhi: Newsman Publishers; *Census of India, 1931, Bihar and Orissa*, Patna: SPS; Unpublished Lok Sabha election results, 1998.

Bhumihars or Koeris would vote for an ostensible Yadava party out of sheer caste compulsions. There is a great degree of hostility and rivalry between these castes, particularly in rural Bihar. Therefore, in terms of pure caste arithmetic, the JD or RJD need help from other quarters to add to the Yadava numbers. This is of course assuming that the Yadavas vote *en bloc* for the JD/RJD.

The connection between Yadava numbers and JD/RJD victory is thus not at all a clear one. To begin with, as mentioned earlier, nowhere do the Yadavas dominate in terms of sheer numerical strength. At best they constitute approximately 15–20 per cent of the population. If one takes into account the Kurmis, the other agrarian caste, the picture does not become any clearer. The Kurmis are to be found largely in Patna and in south Bihar constituencies such as Hazaribagh, and in the Chhota Nagpur areas. In Patna the JD/RJD does well, but this is also a Yadava area. In Hazaribagh, Ranchi and Singhbhum where there is some Kurmi presence, the JD/RJD position is perhaps the weakest in the state of Bihar.

II
Caste arithmetic or caste chemistry

In all the cases studied in this paper there has been no clear indication of caste arithmetic determining electoral results. That we are accustomed to talk in terms of Jat or Yadava strongholds cannot be attributed to sheer caste numbers. In fact the Yadavas, or Gujars, or Jats or Kurmis, fall way short of numerically preponderating in any electoral constituency. The fact however remains that politicians calculate along caste lines, and candidates too are chosen on this basis. This only means that the choices before the electorates are sought to be placed in caste terms, but it is not as if the votes are always cast according to this logic.

It is quite understandable why politicians should attempt a caste calculus. Most of them would obviously like members of their caste and people they can trust and depend upon to carry the mantle for them. From the electorate's point of view, however, the matter is quite different. Voters can only vote for whoever is actually contesting. The point then is to ask why certain castes Wgure more prominently as candidates than other castes. Concurrently, one must also ask why the SCs do not do as well as they should though they have a fair population representation in many constituencies.

The reason why we easily equate caste numbers with politics has probably to do with the organisational capacities of castes. The poorer SCs and STs may have numbers on their side but lack organisational capacity. Politics is not only about numbers; it is also about the ability to exercise power in a concerted and organised fashion. It is here that economic capacity and relative Wnancial security play a sig-niWcant role. This was recognised even by Mahender Singh Tikait, the Jat leader of the Bharatiya Kisan Union. After a trip to the poor districts of Bihar he said that he quite understood why the poverty-ridden peasants there could not agitate for their demands in the way the Jats and Gujars of west UP could. To quote Tikait:

> We spent forty days agitating in Bhopa, but the wretched kisans of Palamau, Kalahandi or Giridih are so poor that there is no way they can put up such a

> resistance for so long. I really feel soory for them and grateful to god that we are comparatively better off (in Gupta 1997: 94).

To be able to participate in a sustained political fashion it is not numbers alone that matter. The ability to be organisationally effective demands a certain degree of economic security which poorer castes are, more often than not, unable to muster (see also Bose 1992: 379).

The fact that caste numbers and election results do not go hand in hand should caution those who are quick to succumb to the temptations of caste arithmetic. Every time an election is round the corner it is readily assumed that as caste loyalties dominate both the candidates and the public, it is really a question of fine-tuning the numbers game. Whoever does a better job at calculations of this sort wins the day.

This species of reasoning not only ignores the fact that no caste has the adequate numbers to win an election on its own, but it does not in fact understand the caste system itself: neither its characteristics nor its logic. It is not as if all agrarian castes come together spontaneously and unproblematically because the Brahmanic ranking places them close to one another. To begin with it must be remembered that one of the important features of the Hindu system of stratification is the profound mutual repulsion that exists between different castes (Bouglé 1992). This is true for all castes, even those that appear to be close or contiguous to the outside observer. The Jats and Gujars of UP, for example, are constantly undermining each other, though on the face of it they should, as owner-cultivators, be natural allies. Such examples abound everywhere—between the Srivastavas and Patwari Kayasthas of UP, or between the *meccho* and *helo* Koibartas of Bengal, or between the Mangs, Matangs, Chamars and Mahars of Marathwada.

Inter-caste solidarities, therefore, cannot emerge full-blown from the logic of the caste system itself. If one were to add to this the fact that no caste can on its own swing an election unambiguously in its favour it is easy to understand why caste based predictions have invariably come to grief. In states like Maharashtra where the Marathas can claim overall numerical supremacy, their votes are fragmented between different parties such as the Congress, BJP and the Shiv Sena.

It needs to be underlined in this connection that one's loyalty is not towards an untidy and amorphous category called Kshatriya, Sudra or Brahman. A caste Hindu's affiliation is strongest to his or her *jati*. The various Brahman *jatis*, for example, quarrel ceaselessly among themselves to establish who is superior to whom. In the meantime, the Saraswat Brahmans and the Chitpavan Brahmans keep their mutual repulsion alive, as indeed they must, for such is the logic on which the caste system operates.

A brief examination of the two most talked about caste alliances in recent times, viz., the AJGAR and KHAM coalitions, can be quite instructive. The AJGAR has Ahirs, Jats, Gujars and Rajputs, while the KHAM is composed of Kshatriyas, Harijans, Adivasis and Muslims. Such a front can hardly emerge from within the logic of the caste system. For Kshatriyas and Harijans to align with each other is unthinkable by any tenet of caste ideology. The fact that Muslims are partners in this alliance denies the relevance of the Hindu hierarchy altogether. Where in the caste system or in caste ideology can one find a justification for an alliance between Kshatriyas and Muslims? Or between Jats and Gujars? In west UP the rivalry between the Jats and Gujars is intense. They accuse each other of cowardice, of moral impropriety and worse. They have physically clashed with each other on several occasions. Moreover, how is it possible that in Gujarat the peasant Kolis can team up with Bareyas and Rajputs to oppose the newly ascendent agrarian Patidar caste? How could the Kurmis in Bishrampur have a common cause with the other castes to attack the Yadavas who are also peasants like them?

Caste alliances thus appear to emanate from secular and political factors and do not spring full-blown from primordial loyalties. The All India Kurmi Sabha is made up of disparate castes such as the Ayodhyas, Dhanuks, Mahatos, Koeris and Kurmis. These castes not only do not intermarry but in many cases there might even be problems of inter-dining as well. In the Oudh peasant movement of the 1920s, the Kurmis, Pasis and Muslims came together against landlordism, but throughout their struggle they ate in separate kitchens (see Siddiqi 1978: 117). What brings about such horizontal solidarity between castes, then, is the extent to which their secular interests coincide, which in turn depends on their structural location in the society.

Peasant castes often come together against non-peasant castes. Sometimes, as with the Gujarat example, one section of the peasant community aligns with the enemy's enemy in order to assert its economic aspirations. And as secular and political interests vary, caste alliances too undergo significant changes. This explains why Madhavsinh Solanki in Gujarat was voted out of power after he powered his way to the top with KHAM support. It is not as if Kshatriyas, Harijans, Adivasis and Muslims have disappeared. This alliance could no longer sustain a shift in secular interests, which is why what seemed like a good idea some time ago does not resonate any longer. Likewise, Maulayam Singh Yadav lost a chunk of his Backward Caste base when many of his supporters joined the Hindu wave that climaxed with the Babri Masjid episode.

The popular assumption that caste loyalties contribute to caste alliances, which in turn determine voting behaviour, is clearly in error. If anything, caste alliances are shorthand ways of signalling a coalescence of secular interests. What needs to be appreciated is that these interests must really be powerful enough for castes to overcome their natural repulsion from each other and form united fronts. It is therefore caste chemistry and not caste arithmetic that one should pay attention to.

The fact that SCs, in spite of their numerical strength, do not have a proportional strength in the electoral system indicates quite strongly that they are held back by their weak organisational abilities. In rural India it is still very difficult for poor SCs or STs to politically form independent blocs without arousing the wrath of the more affluent communities. For this reason the political ambitions of the SCs rarely get off the ground. That the BSP's influence is also to be found in certain narrow geographic strips of UP may also be on account of the fact that in these regions the SCs have somehow been able to wrest some initiative for themselves. Unfortunately, without further empirical research it is hard to say why this should be the case, for the gross figures, whether of population, literacy rate or urbanisation, provide us with no substantial leads.

More research also needs to be done to ascertain why certain areas are considered to be Jat, or Gujar or Yadava terrain when numerically none of these castes can even remotely claim majority status. In some cases, for instance the Jats, Gujars, or Koeris, their proportions rarely rise above 10 per cent of the population. We also need to know more as to why in certain constituencies in Bihar where the Yadavas number around 20 per cent, the RJD candidates tend to get elected. Obviously, other castes are also voting for them. Assuming that there is a strong relationship between Yadavas and the RJD, the point to enquire into is why members of other castes are voting in the same direction. These questions can be asked, and answers to them will resonate once we realise that in caste arithmetic numbers just do not add up.

REFERENCES

BAILEY, F.G. 1960. Traditional society and representation: A case study in Orissa. *Archives Européennes de sociologie* 1: 121–41.

BEHERA, SANJEEB K. 1999. *Data base on Scheduled Caste literacy in India (based on Census 1991)*. New Delhi: Indian Social Institute.

BOSE, PRADIP KUMAR. 1992. Mobility and conflict: Social roots of caste violence in Bihar. *In* Dipankar Gupta, ed., *Social stratification*, pp. 369–86. Delhi: Oxford University Press.

BOUGLÉ, C. 1992. The essence and reality of the caste system. *In* Dipankar Gupta, ed., *Social stratification*, pp. 64–73. Delhi: Oxford University Press.

Census of India, 1931, Bombay. 1933. Bombay: Government Central Press.

Census of India, 1931, Bihar and Orissa. 1933. Patna: Superintendent Printing and Stationery.

Census of India, 1931, United Province of Agra and Oudh. 1933. Allahabad: Superintendent Printing and Stationery.

Census of India, 1991.

FRANKEL, FRANCINE R. 1989. Caste, land and dominance in Bihar: Breakdown of the Brahmanical social order. *In* Francine R. Frankel and M.S.A. Rao, eds., *Dominance and state power in modern India: Decline of a social order*, vol. I, pp. 46–132. Delhi: Oxford University Press.

——. 1990. Conclusion. *In* Francine R. Frankel and M.S.A. Rao, eds., *Dominance and state power in modern India: Decline of a social order*, vol. II, pp. 482–517. Delhi: Oxford University Press.

GUPTA, DIPANKAR. 1997. *Rivalry and brotherhood: Politics in the life of farmers in northern India*. Delhi: Oxford University Press.

LELE, JAYANT. 1981. *Elite pluralism and class rule: Political development in Maharashtra, India*. Toronto: University of Toronto Press.

——. 1990. Caste, class and dominance: Political mobilization in Maharashtra. *In* Francine R. Frankel and M.S.A. Rao, eds., *Dominance and state power in modern India: Decline of a social order*, vol. II, pp. 115–211. Delhi: Oxford University Press.

SIDDIQI, MAJID H. 1978. *Agrarian unrest in northern India: The United Provinces, 1919–22*. Delhi: Vikas Publishing House.

SINGH, H.D. 1996. *543 faces of India*. New Delhi: Newsman Publishers.

SRINIVAS, M.N., ed. 1996. *Caste: Its twentieth century avatar*. New Delhi: Viking/Penguin.

13

Gifting and receiving: Anglo-Indian charity and its beneficiaries in Madras

Lionel Caplan

This article attempts to further the study of gifting in India by examining both the donors and recipients of charity in a contemporary urban context. Considering the case of Anglo-Indians in Madras, many of whom have been the objects of philanthropy since the colonial period, it explores various dimensions of this activity today. For one thing, it notes the highly personalised character of charity, which contributes to the definition and realisation of a moral community of benefactors and their beneficiaries. For another, it seeks to demonstrate how the relief of poverty is a vital ingredient in the definition of Anglo-Indian leadership—as of leadership in India generally—and occupies a significant place in the discourse of community politics. Finally, it seeks to take account of the recipients of philanthropy, exploring some of the ways in which the ideologies and practices surrounding almsgiving both fragment and unite the poor in their distress, and asks how those in a relationship of almost total economic subjection attempt to assert some control over the conditions of their dependency.

I
Introduction

During the past several decades the topic of gifting in India has generated a good deal of thoughtful and thought-provoking literature. T.N. Madan, in his now classic study of family and kinship in rural Kashmir (1965), was among the first anthropologists to draw attention to the significance of gifts as symbolic markers of affinal relationships, expressing parental affection for a married daughter, signifying the hope that she will be well treated by her in-laws, and enhancing the givers' reputation in their own as well as their daughter's marital village. Later writers have seen gifts as a means to gain spiritual merit or to purge their givers of

Acknowledgements: I owe thanks to the British Academy for an award which supported fieldwork in Madras during January–February 1996, and to the Nuffield Foundation which sponsored a research visit from November 1991–February 1992. Thanks are also due to members of the seminar at the Institute of Social and Cultural Anthropology, University of Oxford, for comments on an earlier rendition of this paper, and to Pat Caplan and this journal's anonymous reader for helpful criticisms of the present version.

sins or inauspiciousness, and examined the moral implications for both donor and recipient of such bestowments (Parry 1986; Raheja 1988). Others have pointed to the significance of temple endowments in the religious, political and economic life of precolonial India (Appadurai and Breckenridge 1976; Bayly 1989; Rudner 1987). Still others have focused on the fundamental link between acts of generosity and 'traditional' political leadership. Thus, Shulman tells us that an 'enormous corpus of South Indian inscriptions bears eloquent testimony to [the] persistent need of the ruler to divest himself of resources' (1980: 306), while for Price, a model of precolonial political organisation would include relationships between rulers and followers based on conferral and acceptance of benefits in return for loyalty and service (Price 1989; see also Dirks 1987).

Indeed, gifting is sometimes seen as the link between medieval Indian monarchy and contemporary leadership, in as much as the individual in a position of political responsibility today continues to have a 'premier role as altruistic benefactor and donor of charity' (Mines and Gourishankar 1990: 764; also Mines 1994: 11). Dickey has also stressed the continuity and deep-seated significance in Tamil culture of gift-giving, and demonstrates how this is manifested in the current politics of Tamil film and film stars (1993: 351–52; also Dickey 1995).

In the course of the 18th and 19th centuries new kinds of gifting, in the shape of philanthropy, emerged, and apart from helping to alleviate distress, introduced new ways of displaying wealth and gaining public recognition. But despite their increasing importance and ubiquity, the latter have hardly been examined by students of India. Obvious exceptions are the work of Hinnells (1985), White (1991) and others on Parsi benevolence. This has expanded as many members of the community have risen to wealth and prominence, so much so that according to Hinnells people in Bombay have a saying 'charity thy name is Parsi' (1985: 262).

A second exception is Haynes's historical account of how Surat merchants came to incorporate philanthropic activities in their wider 'portfolio' of gift-giving during the colonial period, as a way of securing their influence with both members of their own community and the European rulers (1987: 340). Another is Pat Caplan's anthropological study of philanthropic organisations in Madras which are dominated by high caste, elite women who, through their charitable activities, can be seen to reproduce ideologies of class (1985).

In this article I consider the case of Anglo-Indians in the same city, whose poor were the beneficiaries of various charities established by Europeans during colonial times, and who continue to receive support from their successor organisations now run by Anglo-Indians, as well as from a variety of philanthropic agencies introduced by Anglo-Indians themselves since Independence. While no precise figures are available, community leaders estimate that, of Madras city's current Anglo-Indian population of 10–15 thousand, between 50 and 70 per cent live below the poverty line. While these estimates, like all those which seek to quantify poverty in India, are questionable (see Brass 1994: 291), they do give some indication of how Anglo-Indians themselves perceive the extent of hardship and the need for alms within the community. This article focuses on three principal aspects of these contemporary philanthropic activities. Firstly, it explores the highly personalised character of Anglo-Indian charity, which contributes to the definition and realisation of a moral community of donors and recipients. Secondly, it examines the manner in which Anglo-Indians holding or aspiring to positions of leadership fuse two quite different traditions of gifting—'indigenous' and Western—in their charitable works. Finally, it seeks to take account of those who are the beneficiaries of philanthropy, a neglected category in the existing literature on modern forms of almsgiving. It explores how the receipt of charity both fragments and unites the poor in their distress, and goes on to ask how those in a relationship of almost total economic subjection attempt to assert some measure of control over the conditions of their own dependency—how agency is guarded and expressed. This article is thus an attempt to develop the study of gifting in contemporary India in as yet little explored directions.

II

A brief history of Anglo-Indian charity

The people about whom I am writing, the Anglo-Indians, emerged during the colonial period as a consequence of the liaisons—formal and informal—between European males (colonial officials, traders, soldiers, etc.) and local women. Like that in other cities, the Anglo-Indian population of Madras is a medley of different ethnic and racial strains, Indian and European, the latter including Portuguese, Dutch, French, Armenian and, of course, British.

Towards the end of the 18th century the arrival of large numbers of ordinary soldiers from the poorest sectors of British society to swell the ranks of the existing garrison meant that thereafter a large proportion of Eurasians were fathered by 'poor whites' (Hawes 1993: 44).[1] As these soldiers were transferred to distant parts of the country or returned to England, succumbed to various diseases or died in military actions, many of the native women with whom they had formed liaisons, and their Eurasian children, were abandoned and left to fend for themselves. Moreover, official policies towards this 'hybrid' population changed in the same period. Whereas the colonial rulers had previously encouraged the emergence and accepted (if not welcomed) the existence of a Eurasian community, in the last decades of the 18th century a series of regulations debarred its members from access to educational opportunities and most public and military appointments.[2] The upshot was a significant increase in levels of hardship within the Anglo-Indian population.

The growth of poverty was reflected in the raising and expansion of charitable institutions, many of which were directed at Anglo-Indian children in penury.

[1] 'Anglo-Indian' became the official designation of the community in 1911. Previously, they were referred to as East Indians, Indo-Britons, and Eurasians.

[2] The reasons for these proscriptive measures have been much debated. The most frequent explanations are that: *(a)* the British were concerned to limit the economic and political influence of mixed-race populations; and *(b)* they were becoming aware of the fortunes to be made in India, and determined to exclude Eurasians from this patrimony.

The first school in Madras was established for Portuguese Eurasians by a French Capuchin, and in the 17th century was to become a Poor School for Roman Catholic Anglo-Indians (Barlow 1921: 88). In 1715 the St Mary's Charity School, a Free School for small numbers of Protestant Eurasian children, was opened in Fort St George, site of the English factory in Madras, while not long after the missionaries opened a school for Eurasians at Vepery near the Fort (Penny 1904: 168, 352, 506). In the course of the 18th and early 19th centuries, other poor schools as well as a series of orphanages and boarding institutions were established in various parts of Madras and in outlying hill stations to cater for the growing numbers of impoverished Eurasian (and European) children (see Arnold 1979: 106–108; D'Souza 1976: 60; Love 1913: III, 352–55; Penny 1904).[3]

While most philanthropic activity was concentrated in the field of education, other kinds of charitable institution were established as well. The Friend-in-Need Society (FINS) was founded in 1806 'for the relief of the deserving poor and the suppression of mendicity' among Anglo-Indians and Domiciled Europeans.[4] By the latter part of the century the FINS had established a home for the aged, infirm and destitute, and eight local committees in various parts of Madras city dealt with the investigation of hardship and the allocation of relief among members of the indigent population.[5]

Churches were another important source of charity for the Anglo-Indian poor, since by and large Anglo-Indians attended 'European' churches where the language of worship was English. By the latter half of the 17th century there was a Vestry Fund at St Mary's Church in the Fort which supported the poor school and gave assistance to widows. From the beginning of the 19th century, St Mary's inaugurated a Charitable Committee which provided help of various kinds to Eurasian women and children, among others. Penny states that this Committee was 'the parent of the Friend-in-Need Society' (1904: 351, 429). In course of time, other 'European' churches sought to alleviate distress among indigent members of their congregations, and many of the latter were Anglo-Indians. The parish records of St Andrews, for example, built in 1816 for Scottish Presbyterians in Madras city, suggest that a substantial proportion of the 'church poor' were Anglo-Indians. They were the main beneficiaries of the Kirk's various educational projects, its Dorcas society's largesse, and the annual Christmas day dinner for and distribution of clothing to the poor of the congregation.

[3] According to Major Bevan, by the early years of the 19th century the great majority of children in these 'asylums' were Anglo-Indians (1839: 211). By 1829 the total number of children educated in the Madras Civil and Military Orphan Asylums alone had reached over 800 (*Madras Mail* 1886: 2).

[4] Domiciled Europeans were people of European parentage on both sides who were born and lived in India. There were numerous marriages between members of the two communities, and they were organisationally united in 1928 in the Anglo-Indian and Domiciled European Association of Southern India, still the official name of the Anglo-Indian Association based in Madras.

[5] See FINS Report, 1884. The FINS was one of only two institutions in Madras city dispensing indoor charity during the 19th century; the other was the Monegar Choultry, set up in 1809 for the public at large (see Srinivasachari 1939: 149). A municipal Poor House was opened in 1927 (Ranson 1938: 150–51).

In addition, for a period of some thirty years from 1850, there was a Magdalene Asylum in Madras which served as a refuge and temporary home for 'fallen women' of European and Eurasian parentage,[6] and a Gordon Refuge for Anglo-Indian girls too old to be accommodated in the city's orphanages but felt to require protection and training (see Higginbotham 1881: 89–90; Penny 1922: 262).

Victorians, according to Harrison, 'saw philanthropy as an arena in which Protestantism could test itself against Catholicism' (Harrison 1966: 357), and, in colonial contexts, presumably against other religious traditions as well. Philanthropic societies and their activities were thus 'subjects for national pride' (ibid.), and the prosperous mid-Victorian years were a 'philanthropic golden age', according to Prochaska (1988: 41). While charity was certainly not unknown in precolonial times (see Hinnells 1985: 262), British administrators and their wives were instrumental in establishing numerous voluntary organisations in India to undertake philanthropic work (Midgely 1981: 4; see also Haynes 1987: 339). While, as we have seen, various educational and other kinds of charitable institution were well established in Madras by the beginning of the 19th century, Penny regards the period after 1835 as one of great philanthropic activity in the city, with the formation of various societies which 'charged themselves with the obligations of the rich towards the poor' (1922: viii). Much of this activity, moreover, continued to be directed at the alleviation of Anglo-Indian poverty: '. . .the care of the Eurasian poor, the upkeep of the Eurasian school. . .involved committees and meetings. It was much to the credit of the [European] gentlemen and ladies of Madras. . . that these committees never failed for want of members' (ibid.: 275). They raised funds and used their powerful networks to advance their favourite charities. Thus, for example, in 1936 Lady Wright, then president of the FINS, was able to obtain for the Society a grant of Rs 12,000 from the Indian Red Cross branch in Madras (president Lady Erskine) out of its Silver Jubilee Fund allocation, to build a new wing to house Anglo-Indian destitute incurable cases. The activities of these influential Europeans thus accorded very well with the philanthropic values and mood of the time.[7]

The British influence in such enterprises was also evident in the attitudes they brought to the provision of charity, which on the whole aped those in the metropolitan country. For one thing, there was widespread institutionalisation of the poor. In India this policy was applied especially to indigent Europeans, for fear of the negative impression which the appearance of large numbers of them might have on the local population (see Arnold 1979). But it gradually came to include as well many impecunious Anglo-Indians, who were thereby banished from the sight of both the ruling circles and their native subjects. Thus many Anglo-Indian children

[6] The Dorcas Societies attached to various congregations and the Magdalene Homes were extensions of similar institutions in Britain established for the same purposes (see Prochaska 1988: 23, 37).

[7] Macrae's survey of charity directed at Anglo-Indians in Calcutta at the beginning of this century suggests that nearly one in four 'were partially or wholly in receipt of relief' (1913: 85). He lists a large number of agencies (probably many more than were operating in Madras in the same period) and concludes that there is in this community 'a field for charitable work perhaps greater in intensity than in any other community in the world' (ibid.: 86).

were removed to 'orphanages' from what were regarded as the unhealthy cultural influences of their neighbourhood environments and their families (see Hawes 1993: 105–6; Minto 1974: 54, 57). At the FINS, 'inmates' were prohibited from leaving the premises without the permission of the Home's Master or Matron, and they were, on pain of expulsion, prevented from begging or soliciting alms from the public when they were allowed out.[8]

For another thing, underlying the provision of charity was a Victorian ideology which distinguished the deserving from the undeserving poor (Midgely 1981: 18–19; Prochaska 1988: 35). For this purpose the FINS issued 'mendicity tickets' which attested to an individual's entitlement to receive help from the Society and was meant to prevent relief reaching those not so qualified. Potential benefactors were urged to desist from giving to what they might suppose were worthy individuals without first obtaining mendicity tickets which were available from the FINS free of charge. In 1894, the FINS Annual Report noted that of the 246 mendicants referred to the Society for relief the great majority were assisted in some way, but twenty-four were 'not helped' because of 'refus[al] to work', while another fifteen were 'found undeserving of help'. The system of the 'Labour Yard' (where men were given casual physical labour to perform) was established to 'test their willingness' to work, but apparently the Yard continued for years to be a 'source of trouble' as the men assigned there were described in several Reports as 'unskilled ne'er-do-wells' who did not remain in the Yard long enough to learn an occupation (or establish their credentials as deserving poor).

Finally, there was a strong emphasis in virtually all these orphanages, schools and homes providing 'indoor relief' on discipline and control, of the kind Foucault has identified in 'panoptic' European institutions during the same period (Foucault 1982 [1977]: 195–228). Their regimes were spartan, and every aspect of institutional life was planned for the 'inmates': what they would wear, what and when they would eat, when they would sleep and wake, and how they would occupy themselves (see Bell 1812; Minto 1974: 67).[9] At the FINS an elaborate code of rules controlled every aspect of people's lives. Each inmate was supplied annually with two suits of clothes 'of the material, pattern and colour prescribed by the Home Committee'. Everyone was required to 'rise at 5 A.M. from 1st April to 1st October and at 6 A.M. from 1st October to 1st April; and go to bed at 9 P.M. from 1st April to 1st October and at 8:30 P.M. from 1st October to 1st April'. They were mustered morning and evening, their names called, and

[8] A more extreme form of removal occurred briefly in the mid-19th century when, on discovery of gold in Australia, some 250 poor and destitute Anglo-Indian boys were sent out to replace domestics who had left their employ to go prospecting (Clarke 1878: 30). Minto also notes how Graham's aim in the St Andrew's Colonial Homes at Kalimpong (for Anglo-Indian children) was to send many of his 'best products' to Australia and New Zealand, but this was eventually foiled by the 'Whites Only' immigration policies of these countries (Minto 1974: 74–75).

[9] At the Lawrence Military Asylum in the Himalayas 'the children were divided into companies… paraded… taught the duty of prompt obedience'. After being awakened by a bugle call, and private prayer, 'they proceed to the Lavatory. When all are washed and dressed, they are inspected…' (Lawrence 1858: 11, 27).

inspected for cleanliness; males were not allowed to enter female quarters and vice versa; no wine, beer or spirituous or fermented liquors were allowed, etc. The Master and Matron were required to 'enforce industry, order, punctuality and observance of the rules by the inmates'. Even the Gate-keeper's duties were clearly spelled out, and included the task of assisting in preserving order and 'in enforcing obedience and due subordination'.[10] The recipients of charity, as Hawes points out, 'learned. . .the lessons of conformity and their proper place [in society]' (1993: 127).

Although there is every reason to believe that individual acts of almsgiving characterised the relations between well-to-do Anglo-Indians and particular poor throughout the colonial period, it was only with the creation in the late 1870s of the two main community associations that prominent Anglo-Indians began to play a more organised part in the provision of help to poorer members of the community. The efforts of the Anglo-Indian Association of Southern India (the 'Madras Association') and of the All-India Anglo-Indian Association[11] were concentrated mainly on the provision of educational assistance and loans to enable children to continue their schooling. The Madras Association also organised an annual gala on the anniversary of its foundation for the Anglo-Indian children of poor schools and orphanages in the city. By the early part of the 20th century over a thousand children were being entertained on these occasions, a considerable number considering the Anglo-Indian population of Madras at the time was perhaps 15–20 thousand. Income was generated through membership fees, bequests by a few wealthy members of the community, and by holding fund-raising events such as fetes or dances.

For the most part, however, the charities in Madras serving Anglo-Indians during the colonial period were created, run and funded almost entirely by Europeans, a fact sometimes noted with consternation by articulate members of the Anglo-Indian community. In April 1917, the magazine of the Madras Association printed a report of a meeting of the FINS in which the correspondent noted that while the Society 'ministers mainly to the poor of [the Anglo-Indian] community', it 'receives the bulk of its funds. . .from the European community'.

III
Contemporary charitable activities

Since Independence, certain aspects of the charitable work of organisations established during the colonial period have persisted and in some cases expanded, while other aspects have declined. Thus, institutionalisation of the poor is much less in

[10] See Friend-in-Need Society, Rules and Regulations, 1884.

[11] What was to become the All-India Anglo-Indian Association was formed in Calcutta in 1876. Its headquarters is now in Delhi, although it has branches all over the country, including seven in Madras city. The Anglo-Indian Association of Southern India (later the Anglo-Indian and Domiciled European Association of Southern India) was founded in 1879, and has its headquarters and most of its membership in Madras.

evidence. The FINS now has only some forty people in its Home, as compared to between four and five times that number a century ago, although the drop is attributable as much to inadequate resources as to any change of policy on indoor relief. Similarly, the numbers of Anglo-Indian schools which still operate boarding sections has probably halved since Independence, owing mainly to the spiralling costs of providing comprehensive board, accommodation and care for many hundreds of children from the poorest families. Moreover, most boarding schools catering for Anglo-Indian children now have to rely for a major part of their funding on 'sponsorships' by international organisations (e.g., World Vision). Boarding institutions are no longer regarded with favour in global education and development circles, so this support is gradually being withdrawn. While Anglo-Indian philanthropic circles are to some extent aware of contemporary ideological objections in the West to such forms of indoor relief, there is still a strong conviction that institutionalisation is an effective way to deal with the problems raised by indigence. When discussing the projects for which they are seeking funds, or would wish to see come to fruition, philanthropists would most often refer to homes for the aged and destitute children. According to one:

> We're planning a home for poor children, orphans. We'll have a matron [who will] train them, educate them, make good citizens out of them. Anglo-Indians we can be proud of. We want 100 per cent results. If we have only five children, we want to send them all to college, give them good food, make them the best-dressed. We want [to produce] five professionals.

But while their rhetoric may have changed, and their regimes become considerably more relaxed than in the past, such institutions as still exist continue to stress control and submission. The FINS's latest Rules and Regulations, for example, are little changed since Independence. There are still rigid timetables of activity, and detailed prescriptions for (and proscriptions on) many aspects of behaviour. Residents who exceed their outside leave entitlements are required to write letters of apology and include promises to refrain from such breaches of the rules in future.

I have to say, however, that while these institutions undoubtedly help to perpetuate both existing social inequalities and ideologies of deference, they are seen by the beneficiaries as an avenue, perhaps the only avenue, out of dire circumstances. I cannot recall any of the residents of the FINS ever complaining about the constraints of the regime; several, however, quite spontaneously, characterised their present lives in the Home as 'paradise', when compared to the hardship and uncertainty of having to feed, clothe and house themselves on the 'outside'.[12] I also remember the frantic efforts of some impoverished Anglo-Indian parents to arrange introductions to governors or other influential persons who might be

[12] '[M]any of the people who wound up in institutions [in Victorian Britain] previously lived precarious lives outside.... For all the disadvantages, a charitable society looked more promising to them...' (Prochaska 1988: 37).

able to help them obtain scarce boarding school places for their children, regarded as the only chance the latter might have to receive some measure of schooling and the possibility of employment in the future. (The school authorities, for their part, sometimes accuse poor families of seeing the boarding school 'as a way of avoiding the burden of supporting children'.)

Most philanthropic agencies today, however, even organisations created during colonial times, concentrate on 'outdoor relief'. The two Anglo-Indian Associations, for example, provide, in addition to 'scholarships' for schoolchildren,[13] monthly 'pensions' for the elderly and handicapped, while churches with significant numbers of Anglo-Indian congregants (who tend to be well represented on Parish committees) continue to offer assistance of varying kinds. Most give cash to the elderly on a monthly basis, while others have established a more extensive system of assistance—including regular food relief ('rations'), free health clinics and basic medicines, special handouts at Christmas, etc. Several churches also run schools, which are part of the Anglo-Indian School system.[14] Their congregations may fund free school lunches for pupils from the poorest families—almost invariably Anglo-Indian children. A few Anglo-Indian schools, run and funded independently of any church, also provide such help for their impecunious Anglo-Indian pupils.

Since Independence there has been a proliferation of new philanthropic agencies run for and mainly by Anglo-Indians. A few, which are overseas mission and church-sponsored, engage in charity as part of their evangelising programmes. They tend to concentrate on a limited number of recipients but to offer more comprehensive assistance than do other agencies—including help with 'rations' and rent. For the most part, however, they are modest organisations established by prominent families or individuals in the Madras Anglo-Indian community. While some concentrate their efforts on helping poor Anglo-Indians in particular neighbourhoods, others spread their charitable net more widely. Some have been operating for a number of years, others are relatively recent ventures; few are able to survive for very long, and certainly not beyond the lifetimes of their principals.

In selecting candidates for assistance by and large they apply the Victorian notion that only specific categories of poor deserve charitable help.[15] Thus, people with 'bad habits'—who drink, take drugs, or go into prostitution—are definitely undeserving, as are males and females of working age (whether or not they

[13] Although, since 1978, Anglo-Indian children in Tamil Nadu are not charged fees in Anglo-Indian Schools, they are still required to pay special fees (e.g., for access to computers) as well as for books and uniforms.

[14] European schools—where the language of instruction was English, and the curriculum based largely on a British model—were established in the 1880s for the benefit of European and Eurasian children. They were renamed Anglo-Indian schools in 1932. In Tamil Nadu today there are over forty such schools, and while the medium of teaching is still English, the curriculum is now more in line with that taught in other schools in the state, and approved by state educational authorities.

[15] In Victorian Britain, charity was meant to assist deserving cases, while the poor law 'could cope with undeserving paupers' (Prochaska 1988: 35). In the Indian context there is no such protection for the latter.

are employed), unless they are handicapped or otherwise chronically unwell. The elderly and young children merit help, while women in their middle years are a more ambiguous category: they could be working and so are not deserving but, should they be widows or abandoned wives, they probably have sole responsibility for elderly parents and young children, and on that account are deserving—sometimes labelled the 'really poor' or the 'genuine poor'. Thus, most agencies tend to focus on a limited range of charitable activities. One sponsors 'soup kitchens' attended mainly by the elderly and handicapped in two areas of the city where there are concentrations of impoverished Anglo-Indians, while most others give regular cash handouts to the elderly and infirm, assistance for school children, and the provision of meals, hampers and special cash bonuses to a variety of the deserving poor during the Christmas season.

IV
The personalisation of charity

With the exception of those organisations which are supported by mission or church sources abroad, charitable groups and institutions in Madras need to rely on their principals—whether elected committee members of major community organisations or founder-officials of what are in effect private philanthropic associations—to provide funds.

Since most agencies from which poor Anglo-Indians benefit are 'non-secular' in nature, i.e., they are intended to serve only or mainly Anglo-Indians, they are not usually eligible for funding which targets the poor irrespective of community. Parochial foundations are therefore at a disadvantage in raising funds from (central or state) welfare bodies, the general public, major charitable organisations like the Lions and Rotary, and most international aid organisations. All agencies for Anglo-Indian charity, even those major community organisations which have a regular income from trusts, fixed deposits, membership dues and government subventions, must therefore solicit donations or seek additional funds in other ways.

The image of the philanthropist is of someone who gifts to others from his own wealth. Rudner, referring especially to religious gifting in south India, has noted that 'generosity. . .is the moral obligation of any wealthy man' (1987: 375; see also Berry 1987: 305), while Haynes makes plain that in Surat it was the 'commercial magnates' who were the main philanthropists (1987). While the notion of 'philanthropy' thus connotes personal generosity, there are very few Anglo-Indian philanthropists of this kind. Principals of charitable agencies do utilise some of their own funds, to be sure, but the great majority have relatively few resources to distribute, since there are hardly a handful of very wealthy Anglo-Indians in the city. Indeed, those who do involve themselves in charitable work are not noticeably wealthier than most moderately successful Anglo-Indians. Even where an agency is the creation of and focused entirely on an individual, and its largesse seen as emanating entirely from that person, its finances will be drawn from a range of external sources. Individuals who would seek to sustain or enhance a reputation in the community as philanthropists must therefore depend on their ability to raise funds for their activities.

These funds are raised mainly from and through close personal ties—relatives, friends, neighbours, ex-schoolmates and business acquaintances (some of them from outside the Anglo-Indian community). With the emigration to the West of large numbers of Anglo-Indians over the past forty years (see Caplan 1995a), philanthropists and their organisations turn increasingly for assistance to family members and friends settled abroad, and to overseas associations—especially in Australia—formed on the basis of former neighbourhoods, schools or churches in Madras. While letters entreating help often produce results, personal visits abroad, when direct contacts can be made, are said to be the most effective form of appeal. The utilisation of personal links guarantees the bona fides of the organisations and individuals seeking funds, and satisfies the donors that the moneys will reach the designated beneficiaries.

Anglo-Indian charity is highly personalised not only in its style of raising funds, but also in the manner of their disbursement. There are few formal procedures for identifying the needy, or for verifying their claims of distress.[16] Rather, benefactors usually insist that they are personally acquainted with those on whom they confer benefits, and that there is no need for the systematic investigation of pleas for assistance, as might be undertaken by professional agencies. As one philanthropist told me, 'I have known these people for years; I know all about their families.' Another pointed out that he was a 'local boy' and knew 'the full history of all our people', while a third, responsible for helping to bring the Anglo-Indian poor of her church to the attention of the Parish committee, insisted that I had only to mention the name of any person in her 'zone' and she could tell me 'everything about them'. Indeed, in a small community like the Anglo-Indian in Madras, most persons do know one another, or about one another, and can readily locate others in a network of relations, friends or acquaintances.[17] Moreover, since not a few Anglo-Indian philanthropists have themselves come from backgrounds of hardship, if not penury, they can usually trace personal connections to the families they help: through early neighbourhood, school or orphanage ties, sporting links and even, in some cases, distant bonds of kinship, affinity or godparenthood.

Most appeals for help from the poor involve direct approaches to charitable organisations and their principals. Letters of application for assistance—where these are demanded by the donor—often omit the detailed reasons for seeking help, assuming the principal's knowledge of the writer's circumstances. They are, moreover, written mainly by women: 'I am in a very poor state, my husband earns very little, and the days are hard. So please help me, uncle, for which I will be very thankful.' Requests for assistance, however, are generally made in person, although the mediation of an influential person will undoubtedly improve

[16] C.S. Loch, in his classic 'reference book for almoners, almsgivers and others', noted how important it was to inquire into the circumstances of the poor before offering charity (1883: 10).

[17] White similarly points out how in the relatively small Parsi community of 18th-century Bombay 'donors and recipients probably knew each other personally' (1991: 318).

the petitioner's chances of success, especially if the request is for a significant boon, such as a place in a boarding school or old-age home. Where the appeal is for more everyday forms of charity, the result may depend crucially on convincing a watchman, receptionist or office peon to allow the petitioner access to the benefactor, and even on the latter being in a favourable frame of mind. On more than one occasion I heard it said about certain well-known philanthropists, that if s/he was in a 'bad mood' s/he would be 'less likely to give, or will give less'.

From the perspective of the recipients, therefore, such a personalised system can mean unpredictable outcomes, but it does provide an opportunity to present their very singular appeals for charitable assistance without bureaucratic intervention. Thus, individuals informally categorised as undeserving of help (e.g., a young man deemed capable of working) or formally ineligible for charity (e.g., someone not officially designated an Anglo-Indian by virtue of not being descended from a European in the male line) can still make a plea for assistance, and have a greater chance of success if they petition a philanthropist personally than if they have to approach an organisation applying bureaucratic rules 'impartially'. This has occurred in the case of one organisation which has recently begun to move from procedures focused entirely on a single philanthropist to one in which a greater reliance is being placed on 'professional' (social worker) advice. The result has been a chorus of criticism by existing and former beneficiaries against the organisation's principal. ('She listens to the social workers; whatever they say she listens'.) The possibility that the organisation may have limited funds to distribute among a greater number of claimants is not readily acknowledged. Complaints are voiced about the precipitate withdrawal of benefits or their transfer to different recipients, and the impersonal methods of assessment being used to determine individual need by personnel without adequate knowledge of those whose lives they are beginning to affect adversely. Their erstwhile benefactor is now accused of losing touch with the circumstances and needs of the beneficiaries.

Alms conferred in the context of a personalised relationship are, however, often difficult to withdraw. Once committed to assisting particular individuals, there is an ineluctable process of being drawn further into the relationship as demands continue and multiply, and the conditions of poverty giving rise to the initial gift are not alleviated. The outcome is that each philanthropic agency tends to develop a particular (though not mutually exclusive) constituency of dependent beneficiaries who consume the greater part of its resources, and effectively exclude others from its charitable favours. Several organisations have recently announced that they are unable to consider appeals for help from new clients.

Charity procedures which are highly individualised do, of course, invite various kinds of abuse by the poor—the principals of one organisation funded by churches overseas often pray for 'discernment', the ability to detect what Victorians used to call 'imposture' (see below). But for most Anglo-Indian philanthropists a personalised system not only ensures their control over every facet of the organisation's charitable activity, but guarantees the continuance of a close relationship between themselves and their beneficiaries. Whatever the origins of the gifts they bestow—whether their own resources or those of others—the recipients tend to acknowledge the generosity of those who actually confer benefits directly on them. The charitable relationship here as elsewhere in India is thus a highly personalised one, and even the more bureaucratic organisations are usually identified with their leaders who, as Kakar has suggested, 'are believed to be the sole repository of the virtues and vices of the institutions' (quoted in Mines and Gourishankar 1990: 765). In the Anglo-Indian context, individual beneficiaries of charity almost invariably identify the donor organisation by its principal, so that it is the latter ('Uncle A' or 'Auntie B') who provides, rather than the organisation s/he represents.

The symbiotic relationship between the Anglo-Indian poor and their guardians suggests that public gifting operates within and serves to define the boundaries of an Anglo-Indian ethnic universe. These philanthropists often attribute their involvement in charity and almsgiving to 'a concern for poor Anglo-Indians'. This kind of statement is meant to indicate that theirs is not an inclusive regard for all those in poverty, but one confined exclusively to members of a particular population and, as we have seen, Anglo-Indian giving is on the whole confined within the community. Willingness to give expresses personal commitment stemming from a shared identity (Werbner 1990). The obverse of this is that the Anglo-Indian poor, while benefiting to some extent from charity proffered by agencies external to the community (the church is the most obvious example),[18] expect to be the sole beneficiaries of the gifts of Anglo-Indian charities, and to acknowledge the generosity of their principals. Donors and recipients of relief are thus dependent on one another (see van Leeuwen 1994: 607; Seabrook 1985: 5). In this way both acknowledge and constitute what Werbner calls the 'recognized limits of trust' and subscribe to 'membership in a circle composed of mutually trusting others' (1990: 306). This is especially significant in the context of a population whose origins are diverse and whose boundaries are extremely porous (see Caplan 1995b). Involvement in philanthropic activities may therefore be regarded as a way of both declaring a commitment to community—an expression of 'cultural loyalty' in the words of one Anglo-Indian intellectual—and of establishing the boundaries of such a moral universe.

V

The politics of philanthropy

Philanthropists claim to be prompted by different motives. For many, and especially those associated with agencies affiliated to churches or missions, an important inducement for giving is their Christian commitment. In the words of one, it is 'service in the name of Christ. A service of love', and similar sentiments are widely voiced, since virtually all Anglo-Indians would regard themselves as committed

[18] One of the self-defining features of Anglo-Indianness is adherence to Christianity, the majority in Madras being Roman Catholics. There are a number of congregations in the city which were at one time predominantly composed of Anglo-Indian members, and there are still a few in which they form a substantial element. In such congregations, Anglo-Indians tend to play an important part in committees which allocate funds to the poor.

Christians. Others stress their own former poverty—a not uncommon experience, as I have already noted—and how this gives them both important insights into the plight of the poor, and a desire to alleviate their condition. 'We remember hard times, so we want to share now.' Still others, who have lost dear ones, are prompted to memorialise their names through charitable works, and several important agencies in Madras today grew out of such commemorative gestures. In all such declarations, charity appears to be offered without expectation of return.

Those outside the small circle of philanthropists, however, sometimes point to the less than altrustic motives of some Anglo-Indian benefactors. They see much philanthropic effort as an expression of the urge for recognition and influence in the community: 'Feed the poor, get a name' was how one woman phrased it, and numerous people made similar remarks about individuals who are in the forefront of Anglo-Indian charity. I have even heard philanthropists compared to medieval European squires—'helping the poor at the gate'—and to more contemporary mafia 'dons'.[19]

Such comments draw attention to the point that Anglo-Indian leaders or those aspiring to leadership must exercise control of an organisation which engages in charitable activities on behalf of the Anglo-Indian poor. Some do this by seeking office in one or more of the well-established institutions, such as the FINS, the Southern India or All-India Anglo-Indian Associations, the Home Missionary Society of India, or via the governing body of an Anglo-Indian school or the Parish committee of a church with a large Anglo-Indian membership in the city. Those who, for one reason or another, choose or are compelled to remain outside these institutions, will usually attempt to establish an organisation of their own. As one prominent Anglo-Indian figure pointed out, 'Every leader needs a group, something to back him up, to enable him to give'. All such organisations provide a base from which to build or maintain a reputation in the community. Thus, while not all philanthropists engage in community politics, all those with political ambitions must engage in philanthropy.

In this respect, both Anglo-Indian politics and philanthropy must be situated in local political culture, in as much as 'having a duty to care for the material interests of [their] followers' is a crucial ingredient in the definition of modern (and 'traditional') Indian leadership (Brass 1990: 96). In south India, moreover, the 'bestowal and acceptance of gifts have long formed a definitive feature of formal leadership–follower relationships...'(Dickey 1995: 13). Similarly, Mines draws attention to the politics of contemporary philanthropy in Madras, pointing out that when a man acts generously, 'his reputation as a leader grows' (1994: 184). Newspapers regularly (and especially as elections approach) feature reports of politicians distributing free saris or dhotis, toys, cash, ration cards, even land to the poor.

Within the Anglo-Indian community, leadership also establishes itself very largely by charitable acts. The community, I was often told, expects service to the

[19] Mayer (1981) was, of course, among the first to note the discrepancy between an ideal of selfless service, and its rhetorical use by the politically ambitious.

group from its leaders, and this is usually glossed as 'helping the poor'. Struggles for public offices are therefore often competed for in terms of how contestants have succeeded or failed in this mission. Challengers accuse the incumbents of having achieved little; the latter, in turn, dismiss those seeking office as having themselves 'done nothing for the poor of the community', and therefore of being undeserving of support. One leader or set of leaders may also portray opponents as caring only for the well-to-do, whereas genuine leaders should be concerned for the less fortunate (Caplan 1996). Much competitive giving tends to focus on the Christmas season, when many Anglo-Indian organisations organise treats, parties and special meals for children, old people and other 'deserving' poor in their constituency. At such events, gifts of toys, clothing and cash may be distributed, and a number of donor institutions with adequate funds distribute hampers containing various ingredients—one organisation boasted of including fifty different items—to enable the recipients to enjoy what one described as a 'traditional Christmas dinner'. Poverty and its alleviation through philanthropy is therefore an important terrain on which contests for influence and reputation within the Anglo-Indian community are waged.

VI
Accents of the poor

The pursuit of charitable gifts is an important ingredient in the survival strategies of most Anglo-Indians in serious financial straits. There has been an increase since Independence in welfare provision by the state, targeted mainly at 'weaker' sections of society (viz. women and children in poverty), though it has been given low priority and received sparse funding (P. Caplan 1985: 125). Programmes like the allocation of ration cards (which guarantee certain essential commodities at fair prices) are experienced as inefficient and their administration as corrupt by the great majority of Anglo-Indians (and probably others) who have sought their benefits.[20] Other schemes, such as monthly pensions for the elderly, are not widely publicised and so hardly known about by the majority of Anglo-Indians technically eligible for them. The overall view among the poor is therefore that even minimal state social welfare provisions are either inaccessible without influence or bribery, or not meant for Anglo-Indians. (Anglo-Indians would sometimes insist that state pensions, for example, are only meant for Backward Classes or Scheduled Castes.[21]) Thus, while they utilise public hospitals which are free, and have access to free schooling

[20] A substantial minority of Anglo-Indians do not possess ration cards, generally because they have found the process of obtaining one too daunting. Those who have them retail stories of being kept endlessly waiting when collecting their rations, or told that stocks have run out, or given inedible food, etc. In any case, a basic amount of cash is required to purchase bi-monthly rations, which is virtually impossible for the very poor to raise; they tend to shop on a daily basis if money is available, and cannot accumulate the sums required (see also De Wit 1993: 158).

[21] Harriss, in a study of the 'Noon Meal' scheme in Tamil Nadu, estimates that while approximately one in thirty of the population are over 60 (and so entitled to a free noon meal), probably one in 200 and possibly as few as one in 1000 are registered pensioners receiving such a meal (1986: 29).

in both Anglo-Indian and municipal—'Corporation'—schools, direct state benefits have an insignificant impact on the lives of most Anglo-Indian poor, whereas charity is relied on by them to a greater or lesser extent.[22] Indeed, such relief can provide a relatively certain (if limited) source of income in a very uncertain economic climate (see Leeuwen 1994: 606).

The personalised character of Anglo-Indian charity tends to exacerbate the fragmentation of the poor. For one thing, as I have already noted, access to benefactions depends on a variety of particular circumstances surrounding the relationship between donor and recipient and not on any notion of the latter's legal entitlements. In consequence, there are considerable disparities in the extent and kinds of help received from the same and different agencies by persons experiencing similar degrees of hardship. A competitive, zero-sum atmosphere is therefore generated in which some recipients are vexed to see others favoured over themselves. A widow who has to support several dependent children may be outraged at the assistance received by a neighbour whose husband is still alive. According to one: 'She is having her husband large as life, and she is getting this help. We are widows, we don't have a husband to support us...'.

Those in receipt of charity can be scathing, too, when assistance is given to those whom they regard as undeserving or at least as less deserving than themselves. An elderly man, waiting in a queue for his monthly 'pension', had this to say:

> That [name of benefactor] gives lots of people help. But he does not know [their] ins and outs.... I'm not envying.... But give to deserving people. You know that dark girl, the young girl? I've heard that he is giving her Rs [...] a month. How he's giving that big amount? She can go to work.

Many claim to know of someone 'with plenty to eat and a place to live' who has managed nonetheless to obtain a place on a charity's lists by 'dodging' (deceiving) the person responsible for making such decisions; they blame the deviousness of the recipient and the gullibility of the giver. Clients of several agencies which provide basic foodstuffs (rice, pulses, cooking oil) are sometimes accused by those excluded from such gifts of selling them in local markets.

The poor are fragmented as well by their differential access to information about the availability of charity. Those who live outside Anglo-Indian population centres are less likely to be aware of philanthropic activities which tend to take place where community members are concentrated, but even within these locations, some people are much less informed than others. On one occasion a lively discussion took place in my presence about whether a particular 'soup kitchen' was still operating not half a mile from where the disputants lived, and only a few days after I had spent a morning visiting it. In some cases the explanation for this disparity may lie in age and degree of isolation, since elderly people on their own are more likely than most to be less acquainted with the range of charitable agencies

22 Midgely notes how the corruption and inefficiency of Poor Law officials in 19th-century Britain had the effect of encouraging charitable activities (1981: 19).

which they could approach. But just as often the people who claim ignorance of these institutions, or of changes in their practices (e.g., in the amount or kinds of help offered), are neither old nor solitary, but live alongside others who know about and benefit from them. One woman commented: 'Our people, they'll never tell anything where-all they go to [get help].' Then, inclining her head in the direction of a neighbour's house, remarked: 'That one goes to all places and won't tell where she gets; she'll never tell me. Unless you get news how will you know?' What seems clear is that the information networks which work to distribute knowledge about sources of charitable help, while generally efficient and reliable where they operate, are at the same time discontinuous. People share intelligence only within close circles.

While charity tends to individualise experiences of poverty, it serves at the same time to unite those in adversity. There is, for one thing, a coalescence imposed by common dependency on assistance and shared deference on the occasions of almsgiving. In a variety of settings throughout the city, the recurrent distribution of 'pensions' and other forms of charity involves an encounter between recipient and donor. While the dispositions of personnel may be different on each occasion, the hierarchical message is similar. During the Christmas season, for example, there are numerous festive presentations of clothing, cash and food hampers, and the spatial structure and tone of these events invariably underline status disparities. The principals and their special guests are usually arrayed in spaces set aside for donors (e.g., on a stage), while the recipients are invited one by one to receive their gifts and adopt the appropriate demeanour of subservience. At one such occasion during the Christmas season of 1995–96, there was a momentary confusion of categories when one of the stalwarts of the donor organisation, dressed casually and so not very differently from the generality of beneficiaries, unthinkingly seated himself among the latter, and as proceedings neared their conclusion was asked by the person sitting next to him, concerned that he might possibly have been omitted from the list of beneficiaries, if his name had yet been called. The story was later retailed with considerable amusement to fellow principals of the organisation and received with much hilarity.

Moreover, the occasions on which relief is distributed seem invariably to involve long delays, so that the poor are compelled to sit and wait, sometimes for hours at a time, before receiving whatever form of benefit is on offer. During such intervals, there is ample time for talk, and people tell one another about their daily struggles against hunger, illness and all manner of distress. They exchange stories of children unable to find regular employment, desertion by husbands, disabling injuries at work, callous landlords and sub-standard housing, and corrupt state officials who seem invariably to prey on the most vulnerable. Through bartering such accounts of pain and hardship, the poor convert individual into social suffering (Kleinman 1995).

Common bonds of poverty are also acknowledged in the tendency of the poor to help others in need. In the general assumption that philanthropy is a middle class phenomenon, what can go unrecognised is the considerable amount of assistance given by the poor themselves to other poor (Harrison 1966: 368; Leeuwen 1994: 602; Prochaska 1988: xiv). In the Madras Anglo-Indian context this is evident in the way those in receipt of help (as deserving poor) share what little they obtain with others—usually with members of the same household, but often with neighbours and friends as well, some of whom would be categorised as 'undeserving'. Most of the elderly women who attend the daily soup kitchens, for example, take their meals home in containers to apportion in this way. A woman who receives a jar of Horlicks from one agency, meant to provide extra nourishment because she has TB, recognised that she cannot help but share it with others: 'When I'm drinking the grandchildren won't be quiet. I got to give them.'

Finally, attention should be drawn to how those who rely crucially on charity attempt to assert some measure of control over the terms of their own dependency. Despite regimes which seek to impose conformity and deference, it is important, as Mendelsohn and Baxi argue, not to assume 'that the weak are always acquiescent in their own subordination' (1994: 4). There are various ways in which agency is guarded and expressed. One is to resist any diminution of self-respect implied in the idea of accepting charity. According to Khare, some studies in India have found that free kitchens and other forms of benefaction weaken people's sense of self-respect and degrade their social status and honour (1986: 291). Such ideas are not current among the Anglo-Indian poor. According to articulate members of the community's middle class, receiving alms does not affront the poor because, for one thing, 'it is just a part of Anglo-Indian history' or, for another, 'the poor believe it is their right'. The recipients of such gifts themselves often speak of experiencing humiliation, not because they are compelled to seek charity, nor in the process of accepting it, but when it is offered (or refused) without due consideration for their sensitivities. People report feeling degraded when they are 'insulted in front of others' by a philanthropist, or when the latter is 'rude' to them in public. I have occasionally observed such behaviour towards supplicants by their benefactors and wondered at the hurt this can cause. Some poor seek to avoid such assaults on their dignity by avoiding, if they can, certain philanthropists or philanthropic occasions, or accepting help only from particular trusted individuals they have known for a considerable time. Others adopt more subversive strategies towards those who would ignore their sensibilities.

This might involve a refusal to obey the behavioural conventions associated with the receipt of charitable assistance. For years, annual Reports of the FINS included lists of inmates who had 'passed through' the Society's Home, and in some years the figure could be as high as a quarter of the total population of residents. The reasons for their departure were also noted, and it is interesting to see that apart from death, most of those who passed through were reported to have 'left of their own accord', while a goodly number were recorded as dismissed for 'disobedience' or for otherwise being 'troublesome'.

Charitable institutions in Madras—following the lead of those in 19th-century Britain—also made great efforts to prevent what they saw as abuses by those seeking assistance, many of whom were believed to be engaged in 'imposture', the

Victorian equivalent of contemporary 'scrounging' (Midgely 1981: 19; Prochaska 1988: 52). There are undoubtedly still a number of the not-so-poor taking advantage of the fact that most charitable agencies in Madras now offering assistance to Anglo-Indians have neither the resources nor the inclination to investigate with any thoroughness the circumstances of those applying for aid. In addition, many of the 'genuine' poor seek assistance from several sources, partly because no single agency is able to provide more than small amounts of help to any individual, and partly because there is little or no coordination of effort among the donors, making such exploits relatively easy (see also Brennan 1979: 123). Certain faces would reappear time and again at numerous almsgiving events around the city which I attended, and on several occasions I was asked by individuals not to mention to one agency that I had seen them obtaining help from another.[23] One philanthropist providing a Sunday 'fellowship' followed by lunch for poor Anglo-Indians in the neighbourhood abandoned it after concluding that people were not serious about their religious commitment but 'came only for the lunch—they go wherever there is charity'.

Complaining and carping are other ways in which the poor confront the subjection demanded by the charitable relationship. Among the most common grievances are those directed at prominent members of Anglo-Indian school boards and committees who are responsible for admissions and fee waivers, and whose decisions crucially affect the lives of children in poverty. Supplicants are also not slow to criticise agencies (and more especially their principals) for, among other things, the meagreness of their assistance or—as already noted—for refusing the very benefits conferred on others. Since the extent of need far outstrips resources many requests for help cannot be met, or certainly cannot be met in full, so the potential for dissatisfaction and adverse comment is always there. Those excluded from charity might accuse benefactors of 'having their own clique' (i.e., of giving only to their existing clients) or of 'helping only the rich' (i.e., those less deserving than themselves). People in receipt of aid sometimes complain of having to spend more on bus fares to get it than the amount actually received. Criticism might also be directed by Anglo-Indians of one religious persuasion at certain charities which appear to favour Anglo-Indians of another. Several agencies which are supported from abroad and aligned with evangelical causes are also sometimes censured for expecting their beneficiaries to attend their religious 'meetings', and disaffected Catholics, in particular, might accuse these agencies of seeking to 'convert' them ('They want us to come over to their side'.)

Recipients of charity regularly evaluate the gifts they are given by different agencies. Around Christmas, as I have already noted, there are a number of special 'treats' for the poor organised by various philanthropic agencies in the city—e.g.,

[23] Hinnells notes that one feature of Parsi charitable activity has been the lack of coordination among donor agencies (1985: 279). Luhrmann makes a similar comment about contemporary Parsi giving, so that in the words of one of her informants, 'people sometimes get funded from more than one trust' (1996: 151). Nineteenth century European charities were often accused of 'failing to determine whether a beneficiary of charitable aid was receiving help from another source as well' (Midgely 1981: 19).

special meals or teas, toys for children, Christmas food hampers. There is ample opportunity for comparison and criticism, especially since many individuals attend more than one of these occasions. They comment on the quality of the food and other goods they have received, and compare the generosity of different donors.

Finally, humour also disrupts, even if it cannot alter, the hierarchy of donor and recipient. On one occasion people awaiting the distribution of alms at the offices of one philanthropic agency were convulsed with laughter at the miming by one woman of the way in which rupee notes were slowly and carefully counted and handed out by the agency's principal. On another, when I was sitting with a group of women in the grounds of the FINS, someone came along with a tray of curry puffs, donated to the Home by a nearby bakery. The women each took one, and, after the first bite, several threw theirs away. One woman commented: 'these puffs are probably too old to sell, so they send them to the poor. I'll give mine to the birds—if they'll have it.'

By the adoption of these different practices Anglo-Indian recipients of gifts and alms seek to recover some degree of agency where poverty and dependency appear to allow so little.

VII
Conclusion

In presenting an ethnography of Anglo-Indian charity, this article has argued that an anthropological study of gifting must encompass both donors and beneficiaries in its purview. Philanthropy in Madras, modelled on practices in Europe, can be traced to the early colonial period. With growing numbers of poor Eurasians (and Europeans), charitable institutions were created to screen and control what were regarded as the unacceptable products of 'colonial desire' (Young 1995). For colonial elites, as for their counterparts in Britain, charitable work was a matter of *noblesse oblige.* Since Independence, philanthropic work has been taken over principally by Anglo-Indians themselves who have, moreover, expanded its scope. In Anglo-India, charity is not being displaced by state assistance; the inadequacies of the latter ensure that those in need continue to turn to charitable rather than welfare agencies.

Philanthropic activity among Anglo-Indians is highly personalised, in terms of fund-raising, the disbursement of resources, and the absence of bureaucracy. This creates ties of interdependence between donors and recipients of gifts in a mutually reinforcing system. Since the relief of hardship is also a vital ingredient of Anglo-Indian leadership (as of leadership in India generally), philanthropy constitutes a key legitimating activity for those holding or aspiring to prominent positions in the community. It also occupies a significant place in the discourse of Anglo-Indian politics, as 'helping the poor' becomes the focus of debate and contention, while the political economy of poverty receives little consideration—as was the case in the European world of charity until relatively recently (Midgely 1981: 3).

White's argument (1991: 318) that a narrow 'catchment area' for Parsi gifting—its confinement to the Parsi community alone—helped to define group boundaries applies to Anglo-Indian charity in Madras as well. The highly personal character of charity and its vital part in the politics of the group ensure that public gifting and receiving play an important role in defining the boundaries of the moral community, within which benefactors and beneficiaries recognise limits of mutual trust and shared identity. Thus, 'ethnic charity' may imply quite different logics, motives and outcomes than other kinds of aid to the poor.

In India, as in many capitalist societies, the poor must assume individual responsibility for their plight, and Anglo-Indian philanthropy, as we have seen, compounds this isolation by compelling those in penury to seek aid in the context of personal relationships. Ideologies of charity, some borrowed largely from European antecedents, contribute to this fragmentation by distinguishing the deserving from the undeserving, favouring persons of one religion over those of another, or granting help to long-standing clients even though others may be in greater need of assistance. Competition for the limited resources of charities thus creates discontinuous information networks among potential beneficiaries, contributing further to the fragmentation of the poor.

In spite of their isolation, and the constraints of dependency, it is important to note the ways in which the recipients of aid attempt to preserve some measure of autonomy and agency. Those who feel themselves excluded or otherwise ill-favoured—almost by definition the great majority of those in need of aid—adopt a variety of practices contesting the policies, procedures and personnel felt to be responsible for their situation. By disobeying institutional rules, exploiting the absence of coordination among agencies, and engaging in imposture, complaint, criticism, humour and other resistant behaviours they challenge, even if they cannot change, the system of gifting and receiving in which they are enveloped and ultimately the structures of inequality in which charity thrives.

An exclusive analytical focus on individual agency, however, ignores the ways in which the poor translate individual experiences into social knowledge. More significantly, it reproduces the tendency in society—whether Indian or European—to individualise distress, and to blame the poor for their own predicament, rather than view it in the context of the wider political economy of poverty and charity.

REFERENCES

APPADURAI, A. and C.A. BRECKENRIDGE. 1976. The South Indian temple: Authority, honour, and redistribution. *Contributions to Indian sociology* 10: 187–211.

ARNOLD, D. 1979. European orphans and vagrants in India in the nineteenth century. *Journal of imperial and commonwealth history* 7: 104–27.

BARLOW, G. 1921. *The story of Madras.* London: Humphrey Milford, Oxford University Press.

BAYLY, S. 1989. *Saints, goddesses and kings: Muslims and Christians in south Indian society, 1700–1900.* Cambridge: Cambridge University Press.

BELL, REV. A. 1812. *The report of the military Male Orphan Asylum at Madras.* London: John Murray.

BERRY, M.E. 1987. Introduction: Giving in Asia—a symposium. *Journal of Asian studies* 46: 305–8.

BEVAN, MAJOR H. 1838. *Thirty years in India: Or, a soldier's reminiscences of Native and European life in the Presidencies, from 1808 to 1838.* London: Pelham Richardson, Cornhill.

BRASS, P.R. 1994 [1990]. *The politics of India since independence. The new Cambridge history of India* IV. (I) (2nd edn). Cambridge: Cambridge University Press.

BRENNAN, NANCY L. 1979. *The Anglo-Indians of Madras:* An ethnic minority in transition. Ph.D. thesis, University of Syracuse.

CAPLAN, L. 1995a. 'Life is only abroad, not here': The culture of emigration among Anglo-Indians in Madras. *Immigrants and minorities* 14: 26–46.

———. 1995b. Creole world, purist rhetoric: Anglo-Indian cultural debates in colonial and contemporary Madras. *Journal of the Royal Anthropological Institute* 1: 743–62.

———. 1996. Dimensions of urban poverty: Anglo-Indian poor and their guardians in Madras. *Urban anthropology and studies of cultural systems and world economic development* 25, 4: 1–39.

CAPLAN, P. 1985. *Class and gender in India: Women and their organizations in a south Indian city.* London: Tavistock.

CLARKE, T.G. 1878. *The fortunes of the Anglo-Indian race: Considered retrospectively and prospectively by one of fifty years knowledge and experience* (2nd edn). Madras: Higginbotham.

DE WIT, J.W. 1993. *Poverty, policy and politics in Madras slums: Dynamics of survival, gender and leadership.* Academisch Proefschrift. Amsterdam: Vrije Universiteit.

DICKEY, S. 1993. The politics of adulation: Cinema and the production of politicians in south India. *Journal of Asian studies* 52: 340–72.

———. 1995. Opposing faces: Film star fan clubs and the construction of class identities in south India. Paper presented at a workshop on 'The consumption of popular culture in India', School of Oriental and African Studies, London, 19–21 June.

DIRKS, N.B. 1987. *The hollow crown: Ethnography of an Indian kingdom.* Cambridge: Cambridge University Press.

D'SOUZA, A.A. 1976. *Anglo-Indian education: A study of its origins and growth in Bengal up to 1960.* Delhi: Oxford University Press.

FOUCAULT, M. 1982 [1977]. *Discipline and punish: The birth of the prison.* Harmondsworth: Penguin.

HARRISON, B. 1966. Philanthropy and the Victorians. *Victorian studies* 9: 353–74.

HARRISS, B. 1986. *Meals and noon meals in south India: Food and nutrition policy in the rural food economy of Tamil Nadu state.* London: London School of Hygiene and Tropical Medicine.

HAWES, C.J. 1993. Eurasians in British India, 1773–1833: The making of a reluctant community. Ph.D. thesis, School of Oriental and Africa Studies, London.

HAYNES, D.E. 1987. From tribute to philanthropy: The politics of gift giving in a western Indian city. *Journal of Asian studies* 46: 339–60.

HIGGINBOTHAM INC. 1881. *Higginbotham's guide to the city of Madras and its suburbs.* Madras: Higginbotham.

HINNELLS, J. 1985. The flowering of Zoroastrian benevolence. *In* H. Bailey, A.D.H. Bivar, J. Duchesne-Guillemin and J. Hinnells, eds, *Papers in honour of Professor Mary Boyce: Hommages et opera minora*, vol. X, pp. 261–326. Leiden: E.J. Brill.

KHARE, R.S. 1986. Hospitality, charity and rationing: Three channels of food distribution in India. *In* R.S. Khare and M.S.A. Rao, eds, *Aspects of South Asian food systems: Food, society and culture*, pp. 277–96. Durham: Carolina University Press.

KLEINMAN, A. 1995. Social suffering. *Items: Social Science Research Council* 49, 1: 13–16.

LAWRENCE, SIR H.M. 1858. *The Lawrence Military Asylum: Being a brief account of the past ten years of the existence and progress of the institution established in the Himalayas by the late Sir H.M. Lawrence for the orphan and other children of European soldiers serving or having served in India.* Sanawur: Lawrence Military Asylum Press.

LEEUWEN, MARCO H.D. VAN. 1994. Logic of charity: Poor relief in preindustrial Europe. *Journal of interdisciplinary history* 24: 589–613.

LOCH, C.S. 1883. *How to help cases of distress: A handy reference book for almoners, almsgivers, and others.* London: Longmans, Green & Co.

LOVE, H.D. 1913. *Vestiges of old Madras* (3 vols). London: John Murray.

LUHRMANN, T.M. 1996. *The good Parsi: The fate of a colonial elite in a postcolonial society.* Cambridge, Mass.: Harvard University Press.

MACRAE, J. 1913. Social conditions in Calcutta: The problem for charity among the Anglo-Indian community. *Calcutta review* (n.s.) 1: 84–94; 351–71.

MADAN, T.N. 1965. *Family and kinship: A study of the Pandits of rural Kashmir*. Bombay: Asia Publishing House.

Madras Mail. 1886. *References to Madras in* 'The Asiatic journal', *1829 to 1840*. Reprinted from *The Madras Mail*.

MAYER, A.C. 1981. Public service and individual merit in a town of central India. *In* A. Mayer, ed., *Culture and morality: Essays in honour of Christoph von Fürer-Haimendorf*, pp. 153–73. Delhi: Oxford University Press.

MENDELSOHN, O. and U. BAXI, eds. 1994. *The rights of subordinated peoples*. Delhi: Oxford University Press.

MIDGELY, J. 1981. *Professional imperialism: Social work in the Third World*. London: Heinemann.

MINES, M. 1994. *Public faces, private voices: Community and individuality in south India*. Berkeley: University of California Press.

MINES, M. and V. GOURISHANKAR. 1990. Leadership and individuality in south Asia: The case of the south Indian big-man. *Journal of Asian studies* 49: 761–86.

MINTO, J.R. 1974. *Graham of Kalimpong*. Edinburgh: William Blackwood.

PARRY, J. 1986. The gift, the Indian gift and the 'Indian gift'. *Man* 21: 453–73.

PENNY, F. 1904. *The church in Madras: Being the history of the ecclesiastical and missionary action of the East India Company in the Presidency of Madras in the seventeenth and eighteenth centuries*, vol. I. London: Smith, Elder & Co.

———. 1922. *The church in Madras: Being the history of the ecclesiastical and missionary action of the East India Company in the Presidency of Madras from 1835 to 1861*, vol. III. London: John Murray.

PRICE, P.G. 1989. Kingly models in Indian political behavior. *Asian survey* 29: 559–72.

PROCHASKA, F. 1988. *The voluntary impulse: Philanthropy in modern Britain*. London: Faber and Faber.

RAHEJA, G. 1988. *The poison in the gift: Ritual, prestation and the dominant caste in a north Indian village*. Chicago: University of Chicago Press.

RANSON, C.W. 1938. *A city in transition: Studies in the social life of Madras*. Madras: Christian Literature Society.

RUDNER, D.W. 1987. Religious gifting and inland commerce in seventeenth-century south India. *Journal of Asian studies* 46: 361–79.

SEABROOK, J. 1985. *Landscapes of poverty*. Oxford: Basil Blackwell.

SHULMAN, D. 1980. On south Indian bandits and kings. *The Indian economic and social history review* 17: 283–306.

SRINIVASACHARI, C.S. 1939. *History of the city of Madras: Written for the Tercentenary Celebration Committee*. Madras: P. Varadachary & Co.

WERBNER, P. 1990. *The migration process: Capital, gifts and offerings among British Pakistanis*. Oxford: Berg.

WHITE, D.L. 1991. From crisis to community definition: The dynamics of eighteenth-century Parsi philanthropy. *Modern Asian studies* 25: 303–20.

YOUNG, R.J.C. 1995. *Colonial desire: Hybridity in theory, culture and race*. London: Routledge.

14

Arabs, Moors and Muslims: Sri Lankan Muslim ethnicity in regional perspective

Dennis B. McGilvray

In the context of Sri Lanka's inter-ethnic conflict between the Tamils and the Sinhalese, the Tamil-speaking Muslims or Moors occupy a unique position. Unlike the historically insurrectionist Māppiḷas of Kerala or the assimilationist Marakkāyars of coastal Tamilnadu, the Sri Lankan Muslim urban elite has fostered an Arab Islamic identity in the 20th century which has severed them from the Dravidian separatist campaign of the Hindu and Christian Tamils. This has placed the Muslim farmers in the Tamil-speaking north-eastern region in an awkward and dangerous situation, because they would be geographically central to any future Tamil homeland. The first part of this essay traces the historical construction of contemporary Muslim ethnicity and surveys their position in contemporary Sri Lankan politics. The second half of the essay provides an ethnographic portrait of a local-level Muslim community closely juxtaposed with their Hindu Tamil neighbours in the agricultural town of Akkaraipattu in the eastern Batticaloa region of the island.

Nearly 8 per cent of Sri Lanka's people are Muslims, as compared with 18 per cent who are Tamils, but these simple-sounding minority labels actually conceal more than they reveal of the island's ethnic complexity. For the past 100 years the urban leaders and political spokesmen of the Muslim community have strongly denied any suggestion that they could be seen as 'Tamil Muslims' or 'Muslim Tamils', even though they speak Tamil at home, share many Tamil kinship and domestic practices, and have even composed Muslim commentaries and devotional works in Tamil, some of them written in Arabic–Tamil script (Uwise 1986, 1990). The bewildering list of terms for the Sri Lankan Muslims is symptomatic of the identity issues which they have faced over the centuries in differing colonial European, Tamil and Sinhalese contexts.

Acknowledgements: The fieldwork upon which this paper is based was carried out in 1969–71, 1975, 1978, 1993, and 1995 with support from an NIMH fellowship, the British SSRC, the Smuts Memorial Fund and Travelling Expenses Fund of Cambridge University, the Committee on Research and Creative Work, and the Graduate Committee on Arts and Humanities at the University of Colorado. Library research and writing was supported by a University of Colorado Faculty Fellowship and by the Social Science Research Council. I am extremely grateful to the following individuals for their detailed and constructive feedback on earlier versions of this essay: Susan Bayly, Chandra De Silva, Steve Kemper, Sankaran Krishna, Charles Piot, Michael Roberts, John Rogers, Paul Shankman and Margaret Trawick.

From the beginning of the colonial period in the early 16th century, members of the predominant Tamil-speaking Muslim community in Sri Lanka were designated by the term 'Moor' (*Mouro*, 'Moroccan') which the Portuguese applied to Muslims throughout their African and Asian empire, as well as by such familiar European terms as 'Mohammedan' or 'Mussalman'. In the early 1970s, when I began my fieldwork among the Moors of eastern Sri Lanka, I found that 'Muslim' was the most common term they used when speaking in their own native Tamil, although strictly speaking, the religious term 'Muslim' should encompass the ethnically distinct Malays and the small Gujarati trading groups as well.[1] The term *Cōṉakar* (Sonagar, Jonagar), an older Tamil and Malayalam word which originally denoted West Asians, especially Arabs or Greeks, seems to be falling out of fashion, although 'Lanka Yonaka' was still used as an ethnonym for the Sri Lankan Moors in the 1971 Census.[2] In common English parlance, both 'Moor' and 'Muslim' are used interchangeably today to refer to indigenous Tamil-speaking Muslim Sri Lankans, 93 per cent of all followers of Islam in the island, most of whom are orthodox (Sunni) members of the Shāfi'ī school of Muslim jurisprudence.[3]

Figure 1
Sri Lankan population by ethnicity and religion (estimated)

Population of Sri Lanka (1997 estimated)		18.7 million
Sinhalese	74%	13.8 million
Sri Lankan Tamils	12.7%	2.4 million
Indian Tamils	5.5%	1.0 million
Moors	7%	1.3 million
Others (Malays, Burghers, Veddahs, etc.)	1%	.2 million
Buddhists	69%	12.9 million
Hindus	15%	2.8 million
Muslims (including Moors and Malays)	8%	1.5 million
Christians	8%	1.5 million

Sources: CIA World Factbook 1997 and Embassy of Sri Lanka website (http://www.slembassy.org). The most recent Sri Lankan census was conducted in 1981.

[1] The Sri Lankan Malays, so termed by the British because of their Indonesian Malay lingua franca, are Sunni Muslims. Their ancestors were exiled Javanese princes as well as a medley of banished criminals and Dutch Company soldiers of diverse Indonesian origin dispatched from Batavia during the 18th century (Hussainmiya 1986; Mahroof 1994). There are also some small groups of Bombay and Gujarati traders who have businesses in Colombo: Bohras and Khojas (both Ismailis), and Memons (who are Sunnis). Some schismatic Qādiyāṇis (Ahmadiyyas) are said to be found in the Gampola region, remnants of a group once influential in Colombo as well (Abdul Majeed 1971).

[2] Denham (1912: 232n.) observed a half-century ago that *Cōṉi* ('Sōni' or 'Chōni', short for *Cōṉakar*) was commonly used as a term for Muslims in the Batticaloa region, although the nickname has derogatory overtones today. Two other negative slang terms are *Nānāmār* and *Kākkā*, regionally variant Moorish kin-terms for 'elder brother', the latter unfortunately also a colloquial homonym for 'crow' in Tamil. Additional Sri Lankan terms for the so-called 'Coast Moors', expatriate Muslim traders from the South Indian coast, include *Marakkala Minissu* (Sinh. 'boat-people'), *Hambaya* or *Hambankāraya* (Sinh.) and *Cammankārar* (Tam.), both either from Malay *sampan* 'skiff' or from Tamil *cāmān* 'goods', and Tambey (Tam. *tampi*, younger brother), a British colonial term for itinerant trader. See Ameer Ali (1980: 99ff, 1981a) for a general discussion.

[3] I use both terms in this essay, with no intended implications about the basis of contemporary group identity.

The fact that Sri Lankan Muslims would prefer an ethnic label which is European or Islamic rather than Dravidian in origin points to one of the major cleavages within Sri Lanka's Tamil-speaking minority. Recently, a few historians and spokesmen for the Muslim community have even asserted that 'Muslims have no commitment to any particular language', citing the willingness of Moors living in Sinhala-majority districts to enroll their children in Sinhala-medium schools (Shukri 1986b: 70; see also K.M. de Silva 1988: 202). One author contends that the Muslims are becoming 'a linguistically divided community' because young Muslims in Sinhalese districts are learning Sinhalese instead of Tamil (Ali 1986–87: 167). Whether this process will soon result in the loss of Tamil, and the widespread substitution of Sinhala, as the language of the Moorish home seems to me dubious, not least because of the chronic shortage of Muslim teachers qualified in Sinhala (Mohan 1987: 107; Uwise 1986).[4]

The ethnic identity and political stance of the Sri Lankan Muslim community, like that of many culturally-defined groups contesting for a secure place in the world today, have undergone change over the past century in response to colonial and post-colonial pressures and from the internal dynamics of the Muslim community itself. The Moors played a pivotal role in post-Independence Sri Lankan politics, but this became especially true after 1983, when the armed conflict over Tamil Eelam suddenly placed many of them in an extremely tight position, caught between the Sri Lankan security forces and the Tamil rebels of the LTTE.[5] In order to reveal the roots of the dilemma which the Sri Lankan Muslims currently face, I will first trace the historical development of the Moorish ethnic identity in Sri Lanka in comparison with two South Indian Muslim groups to whom the Moors are closely related, the Māppiḷas of Kerala and the Marakkāyars of Tamilnadu. Then, with this historical background in mind, I will ethnographically explore the tense relations between Tamils and Muslims living in Sri Lanka's eastern region where the future outcome—either ethnic accommodation or ethnic division—still hangs in the balance.

I
Early history of Sri Lanka's Moorish community

Although the earliest evidence from the Islamic period is limited to fragmentary travellers' accounts, early Islamic coinage, some tombstones here and a few lithic inscriptions there, the origins of the Muslim community of Sri Lanka are plainly continuous with the pre-Islamic seaborne trade between South and Southeast Asia and the Middle East. Not only Arabs, but Persians too, were frequent early visitors to the island (Ali 1981a: 71–76; Effendi 1965; Kiribamune 1986). With the advent

[4] Colombo is the *only* place in the island where I have ever met a Moor who could not speak Tamil. Multilingualism is, however, gaining among middle-class Colombo Muslims, some of whom prefer to send their children to Sinhala or English medium schools to hedge their bets about the future of the country. The sermons in some Colombo mosques are also delivered in Sinhala or English on certain days (Nilam Hamead, personal communication).

[5] For an up-to-date overview of the Sri Lankan ethnic conflict see Nissan (1996). For more background on the failure of democratic institutions, see Tambiah (1986).

of Islam in the Arabian peninsula in the first half of the 7th century, and the subsequent conquest of Persia, trade across the Indian Ocean was increasingly dominated from the 8th century onward by Arab Muslim merchants from ports on the Red Sea and the Gulf. Unlike the Persian and Turkic invasions of North India which established major states and empires, the Muslim impact upon the coasts of South India and Sri Lanka from the 8th century onward was predominantly Arabic in culture and mercantile in motivation, part of the same historical stream which resulted in the Islamisation of insular Southeast Asia (Wink 1990: ch. 3).

The medieval Hindu and Buddhist kingdoms of Kerala and Sri Lanka, eager for revenues from overseas commerce, allowed Arab merchants—many of whom acquired local wives by whom they fathered Indo-Muslim progeny—to establish a dominant economic position in port settlements such as Calicut and Colombo (Arasaratnam 1964; Dale 1980; Kiribamune 1986).[6] The Tamil-speaking Coromandel Coast of south-eastern India, which was then still linguistically unified with Kerala, also attracted Arab Muslim traders who established an enclave at Kayalpattinam at the mouth of the Tambrapani River—as well as at Kilakkarai, Adirampattinam, Nagapattinam, and other coastal settlements farther north—to which they imported, among other things, Arabian horses for the armies of Tamil Hindu kings and from which they exported Indian textiles (Bayly 1989). When in 1498 Vasco da Gama launched his Portuguese naval crusade against the well-established 'Moors' of Calicut, most of the remaining Arab traders began to depart from the Malabar Coast, leaving locally intermarried Māppiḷa Muslims to carry on the fight, in one form or another, during 450 years of European colonial domination (Bouchon 1973; Dale 1980: 47). At about the same time, the Portuguese encountered 'Moors' in Sri Lanka who spoke Tamil, who had on-going links with the Muslims of the Malabar and Coromandel Coasts of South India, and who had been given royal permission to collect customs duties and regulate shipping in the major south-western port settlements under the suzerainty of the local Sinhalese Kings of Kotte (Ali 1980; Indrapala 1986; Abeyasinghe 1986).

While the period of Portuguese and Dutch colonial rule was onerous to all Sri Lankans, it was especially harsh for the Moors, who were subjected to special penalties and restrictions because of their Islamic faith and the threat they posed to the European monopoly of overseas trade. Ultimately, the effect of Portuguese policies was to encourage (and by an official edict of 1626, to require) migration of many coastal Moors inland to the Kandyan Kingdom, where they engaged in *tāvaḷam* bullock transport and a diverse range of other occupations (Ali 1980: 337ff; C.R. de Silva 1968; Dewaraja 1986). In 1626, King Senerat of Kandy is said to have resettled 4,000 Moors in the Batticaloa region of the east coast to protect his eastern flank from the Portuguese fortification of Puliyantivu which occurred soon thereafter, in 1627. If true, this is the only historically noted Moorish migration to that area (C.R. de Silva 1972: 88; M.I.M. Mohideen

[6] The maritime trading monopoly given to Muslims, Jews, Christians, and Zoroastrians was particularly marked in Kerala, where Brahmanical influence among high-caste Hindus placed a strong ritual taboo on sea voyaging (Wink 1990: 72–73).

Figure 2

Map of Sri Lanka and South India, showing locations of three major Muslim groups referred to in the text: Māppiḷas, Marakkāyars, and Moors.

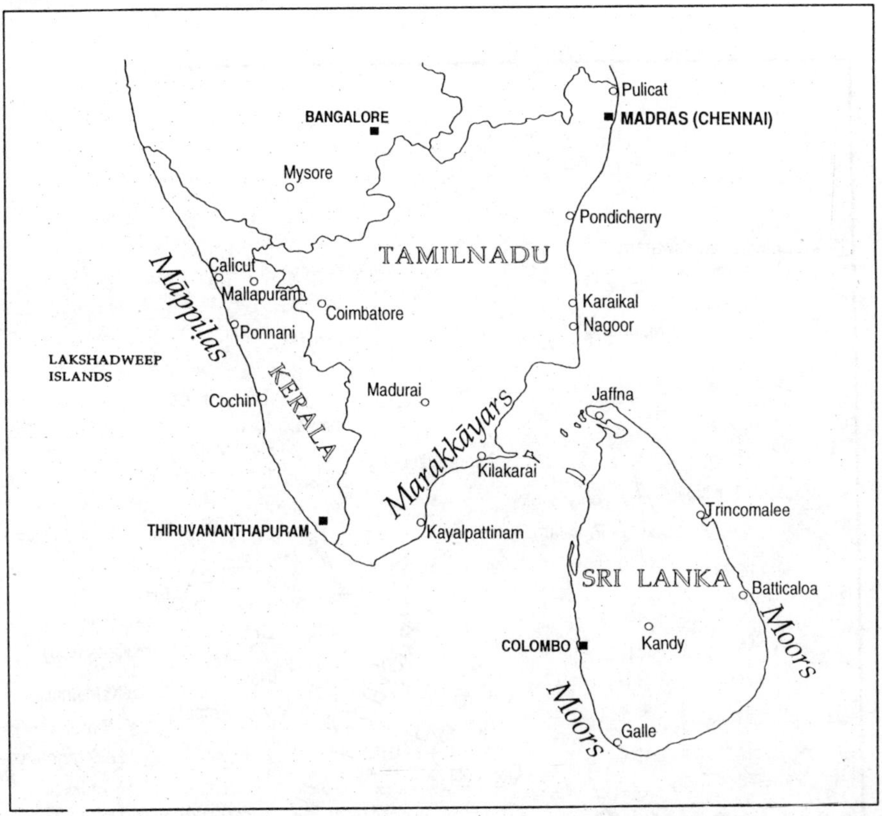

1986: 7–8; Queyroz 1930: 745). Senerat's resettlement is not corroborated in any local sources, but as early as the 15th century, and certainly by the 17th century, large numbers of Moorish farmers were well-established on the east coast.[7] This is the area with the highest proportion of Muslims in the local population today, and also the region where I have done my own fieldwork.

[7] One historian claims that hard evidence for King Senerat's resettlement of the Moors in Batticaloa is lacking in the work of the early Portuguese chroniclers such as Queyroz, upon whom all later historians have depended. Abeyasinghe (1986: 145 fn 46) suggests that Queyroz misinterpreted 16th century letters between Goa and Lisbon which simply report that 4,000 Moors were *already* living in Kandy and Batticaloa at that time. The *Nāṭu Kāṭu Paravaṇi Kalveṭṭu*, a document possibly from the 16th century, clearly indicates that Moors (*Cōṉakar*) were living in the Akkaraipattu-Irakkamam area of present-day Amparai District (Neville 1887; Pathmanathan 1976). A memorandum of 1676 written by Pieter de Graeuwe, the Dutch East India Company chief for Batticaloa, also makes reference to the Moors in this region of the island (De Graeuwe 1676).

Figure 3
Map of Sri Lanka, showing locations of some of the major Moorish (Muslim) settlements referred to in the text.

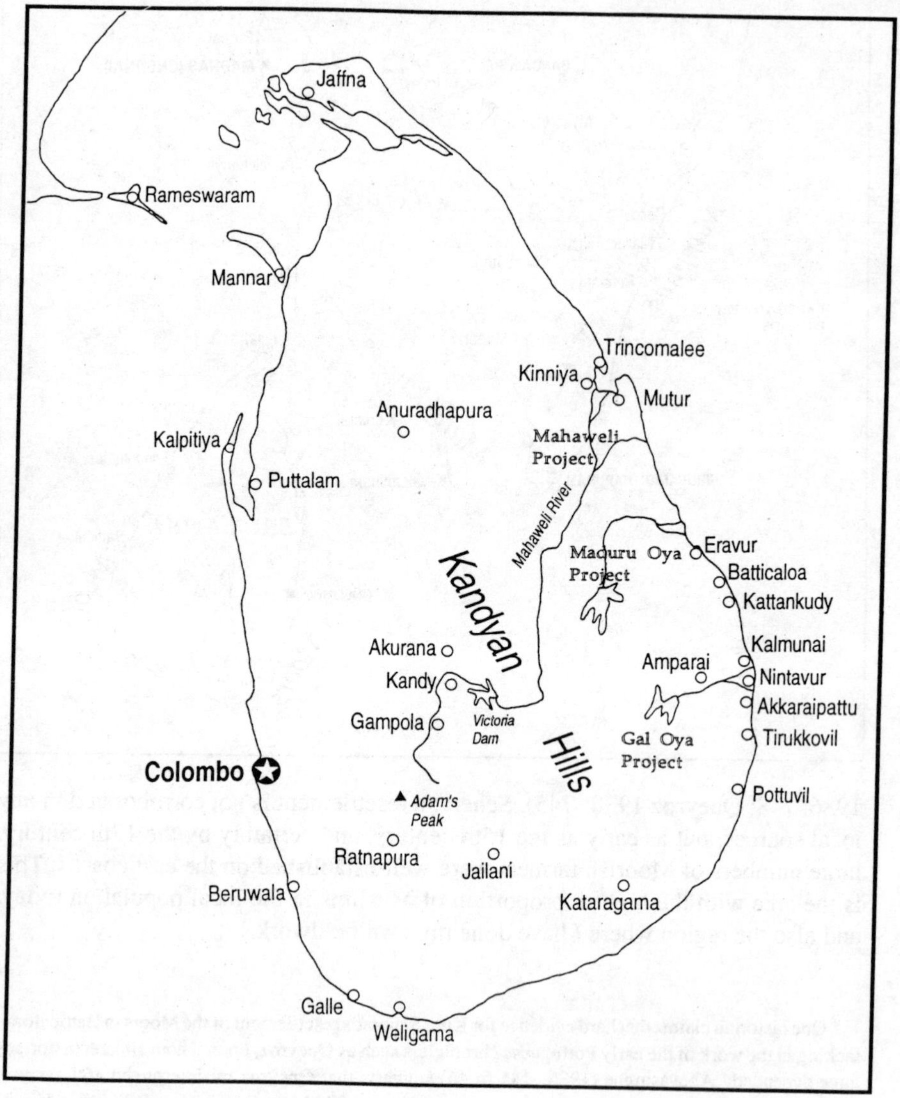

II
Divergent development of Muslim ethnicity in Kerala, Tamilnadu, and Sri Lanka

Both in Sri Lanka and in Tamilnadu, Christians whose native tongue is Tamil generally think of themselves as Tamil Christians, but among Sri Lankan Muslims such a parallel does not hold. In their aversion to identifying themselves as Tamils who happen to follow the Muslim faith,[8] the Moors of Sri Lanka stand in striking contrast to the Marakkāyar Muslims of Tamilnadu who, apart from their Islamic theology, have regarded themselves as fully contributing members of the Tamil literary and cultural tradition. If we include one more Muslim group, the historically militant and rebellious Māppiḷas of Kerala, we have the opportunity to conduct an interesting three-way comparison of Muslim ethnicity in South India and Sri Lanka. All three Muslim communities preserve elements of matrilineal and/or matrilocal social structure which suggest close connections (involving both intermarriage and conversion) with the matrilineal Hindu castes of the Malabar coast, and possibly also with the matrilineal Hindu Maravars of Ramnad. Malayalam, the language of Kerala today, was 'effectively a dialect of Tamil until the fourteenth century'—700 years *after* the advent of Islam and the expansion of Arab trade in the Indian Ocean (Shackle 1989: 405). Communication and social interaction between Muslims of Calicut, Kayalpattinam, and Colombo were once a great deal freer than they are today, part of a more widespread 'traffic in commodities, bodies, and myths' from South India into Sri Lanka over the last 700 years (Roberts 1980).

As a world systems or macro-economic history approach might predict (Bose 1990; Wallerstein 1976; Wolf 1982), there is a striking similarity in the historical circumstances under which these three Muslim communities came into existence. They were all largely founded by Arab and Persian traders who supplied the Mediterranean market for spices and Indian textiles. From the late 15th century onward, all three Muslim communities experienced similar conquest and repression by the colonial Portuguese, Dutch, and British empires, which were then expanding from the European core to exploit the resources of the African and Asian periphery. Yet despite these initial similarities, a comparison of Muslims in Kerala, Tamilnadu and Sri Lanka reveals some striking divergences in the way modern Muslim ethnic identities developed in these three geographically adjacent regions.

The Māppiḷas of Kerala

The Muslims of Kerala, known as Māppiḷas (Mappilla, Moplah)[9] were originally the mixed descendants and religious converts of Arab Muslim spice traders who had been actively patronised by the Hindu rulers of the Malabar coast, especially

[8] Ismail discerns a 'terror' of being viewed as Tamils in elite Muslim discourses (1995: 66 fn 26).

[9] Miller (1976: 30–32) reviews eight etymologies for the term, settling upon 'bridegroom, or new husband' (Tamil *māppiḷḷai*) as the most plausible, given the historical pattern of marriage between Arab traders and local Kerala women. The term was once also used for Christian and Jewish settlers in Malabar (Thurston and Rangachari 1909, v. 4: 460).

the Zamorins of Calicut. They constitute 23 per cent of the population of the state (Hasan 1997: 2–3), making them a much more substantial political bloc than Muslims in Sri Lanka or Tamilnadu. Today the Māppiḷas are not only traders and coastal fishermen, but they also form a large segment (25–60 per cent) of the impoverished rural agrarian tenant class in some of the inland districts of northern Kerala, especially in the south Malabar region (Gabriel 1996; Miller 1976). As with local Hindu castes, some Māppiḷas are matrilineal and some patrilineal in tracing their lineage ancestry, but the pattern of residence after marriage for all Māppiḷas is matrilocal. There are also several clearly ranked, endogamous, caste-like subsections within the Māppiḷa community, ranging downwards from *Thangals* (or *Taṉṉals*, descendants of the Prophet), to *Arabis* (who claim 'pure Arab' descent), to *Malabaris* (the bulk of ordinary Māppiḷas), to *Pusalars* ('new Muslims' who are more recent converts from lower Hindu castes, especially Mukkuvar fishermen), to *Ossans* (hereditary barber/circumcisers and midwives) (D'Souza 1959, 1973; Ibrahim Kunju 1989: 178–80).[10]

In coastal centres of Māppiḷa power such as Cannanore and Ponnani, Muslim rajas and naval pirates enjoyed a semi-autonomous, if brittle, position under Hindu rulers until the Portuguese upset the balance. Under the Mysorean invasions of Hyder Ali and Tippu Sultan in the late 18th century, the Māppiḷas were briefly allied to fiercely anti-Hindu rulers who carried out temple desecrations and forced circumcisions of Hindus on a vast scale (Gabriel 1996). Of all the coastal Muslim groups in South India and Sri Lanka, the Māppiḷas were by far the most militant and rebellious during the British colonial period, sustaining a tradition of Islamic martyrdom through violent, suicidal outbreaks (*jihād*) against colonial authorities and dominant high-caste Hindu landlords, the last of which, in 1922, vainly sought to establish an Islamic theocratic sultanate in south Malabar. A few charismatic Sufi holy men actively encouraged these suicidal attacks against the infidel authorities, and annual *nērcca* mosque festivals today still commemorate slain Māppiḷa martyrs (Dale and Menon 1978). After a vain effort to forge a separate state of 'Mappilastan' at the time of Indian Independence, the Māppiḷas effectively focused their political power through the Muslim League and offered grassroots support for Kerala's successful land reform movement (Gabriel 1996; Herring 1991). Since then, Māppiḷa political tactics have been brilliantly pragmatic, switching coalition partnerships between Congress and Communist parties at various times (Miller 1976: 158–72; Wright 1966). A major achievement of the modern era was the creation of Mallapuram District in 1969, the first Māppiḷa-majority electorate in Kerala (Dale 1980: 225–26).

The Marakkāyars and Labbais of Tamilnadu

Unlike Kerala, where many coastal Māppiḷas spread directly inland and created a large population of tenant farmers, the Muslim community of Tamilnadu has two

[10] The Muslims of the Lakshadweep Islands 200 km west of the Kerala coast are similarly caste-stratified, with *Taṉṉals* at the top, followed in descending order by *Koyas, Malmis, Melacheris*, and *Ossans* (Gabriel 1989; Kutty 1972).

points of origin, and two major internal subdivisions corresponding to the Shāfi'ī versus Hanafī legal schools (Fanselow 1989). The earliest Arab settlements developed into tightly-knit Muslim trading enclaves on the Coromandel coast, while later Muslim armies from the Deccan established a Mughal-style court under the Nawābs of Arcot in the 17th and 18th centuries, who patronised a small Urdu-speaking Deccani Muslim administrative and trading elite (MacPherson 1969; Vatuk 1989). The prosperous Muslims of Kayalpattinam, Kilakarai, Karaikal and other early Indo-Arab port settlements along the coast of Tamilnadu call themselves *Marakkāyars* (var. Maraikkāyar, Maraikkār, probably from the Tamil word *marakkalam*, boat or 'wooden vessel'),[11] insist upon endogamous marriages, and claim the highest status among all Tamil Muslims (More 1991). A lower status group, the Kāyalārs, have been allied with the Marakkāyars but occupy their own streets (Mines 1972: 28; Thurston and Rangachari 1909). The numerically larger population of Tamil-speaking Muslim artisans, weavers, tanners, and merchants of the inland districts of Tamilnadu have been loosely termed Labbais, to which must be added a smattering of 'martial' lines such as Navāyats, Rāvuttars, and Pathāns (Bayly 1989: 71–103; Fanselow 1989; Mines 1973).[12] Overall, Muslims represent 5.5 per cent of Tamilnadu's population (Hasan 1997: 2–3). While the Labbais constitute the bulk of Tamil Muslims today, it has been the elite Marakkāyar traders who seem to have had the earliest historical connection with the Moors of Sri Lanka.

The Marakkāyars of Kayalpattinam have some shallow matrilineages but no formally organised matrilineal clans as in Kerala or eastern Sri Lanka. Postmarital residence is matrilocal for at least a year or so after the wedding, with the married couple eventually living either with the bride's parents in her natal home or in a newly built dowry house in the same *mohulla*, or corporate neighbourhood. Either way, every daughter receives a house at marriage, in addition to jewelry and other movable goods (personal fieldwork in 1983; Bayly 1986: 42; More 1991; 'Kayalar' in Thurston and Rangachari 1909, v.3: 267). Unlike the Labbais who generally follow Hanafī law, members of the Marakkāyar commercial and gem-trading elite, like the Māppiḷas of Kerala and the Sri Lankan Moors, all belong to the Shāfi'ī legal school. Like the Māppiḷas, too, the Marakkāyars have a long history of seafaring, but instead of a warrior tradition they cultivated a reputation for religious, philanthropic and literary pursuits. Marakkāyar towns are noted

[11] There is an enduring etymological debate about the origin of this word. Proponents of Arab ethnic identity prefer to derive the term from *markāb* (Arabic, boat). Others derive it from *mārkkam* (Tamil and Malayalam, religion). More (1997: 22) reports that Marakkāyars today favour an etymology derived from *marakkalarāyar* ('ruler of the boats'). Besides being a Sinhalese term for Indian 'Coast Moors', the term *Marakkala* is similar to a caste title found among the Moger coastal fishermen in South Kanara. See D'Souza (1955: 41–47) and Ameer Ali (1981a: 68–70) for exhaustive discussions.

[12] The Labbai/Marakkāyar distinction is not uniformly observed within Tamilnadu, nor is it more than three centuries old. The contrast dissolves among the Muslims of Pulicat north of Madras, where even the exclusive endogamous Arab-descended coastal traders are called 'Labbay' (Pandian 1987: 128–33). Rao et al. (1992: 265) assign the term Labbai to 'coastal fishermen, divers, weavers, artisans and husbandmen' who were not clearly differentiated from the Marakkāyars in the 17th century. J.B.P. More (1997: 21–25) notes that in the 15th and 16th centuries most Tamil Muslims were referred to as 'Turks' (*tulukkar*), a term which I also occasionally heard in Sri Lanka in the 1970s.

for their profusion of mosques and tombs of Sufi scholar-mystics, some of which were also patronised by Tamil Hindu kings, as well as being famed for their wealth and smuggling activities (Bayly 1986; Fanselow 1989: 276). In the 17th and 18th centuries, a line of Marakkāyar regents wielded great power under the Sētupatis, the Hindu Maravar kings of Ramnad. The most famous of these, Cītakkāti (Abd al-Qādir, also known by the royal title Vijaya Raghunātha Periya Tambi Marakkāyar), patronised Tamil poets and typified the mature cultural idiom of Tamilised Islam (Rao et al. 1992: 264–304).

Marakkāyars take pride in having authored many commentaries and religious works in Arabic–Tamil, including the *Cīrāppurāṇam*, an epic poem on the life of the Prophet commissioned by Cītakkāti and modelled on the Tamil version of the Hindu Ramayana (Casie Chitty 1853–55; Mahroof 1986a: 87; Mauroof 1972: 67–68; Richman 1993; Shulman 1984; Uwise 1990). The most renowned regional pilgrimage centre for Muslims in Tamilnadu and Sri Lanka, the *dargāh* (tomb-shrine) of the Sufi mystic Abdul Qādir Shāhul Hamīd at Nagoor, is a Marakkāyar foundation (Bayly 1986, 1989: chs 2–3). Although some urban 'Islamisation' is now occurring, over the centuries most Muslims in Tamilnadu have identified strongly with, and have been recognised as contributing to, the Tamil literary and cultural tradition (Cutler 1983: 280, 286; Uwise 1990). The leadership challenge from a vocal Urdu-speaking Deccani Muslim faction, and an odd alliance between Tamil Muslims and the atheistic non-Brahmin Self-Respect Movement in the 1920s and 1930s to oppose mandatory schooling in Hindustani, appears to have reinforced this Tamilising tendency (MacPherson 1969; Mines 1983: 112; More 1993a, 1997). Their politics, quite unlike that of the Māppiḷas in Kerala, has not been conspicuously communal or confrontational. They have often supported the Dravidian nationalist parties (DMK, ADMK) or the Congress and have not shown great loyalty to the Muslim League (MacPherson 1969; Mines 1981: 72–74; Wright 1966). Overseas Muslims from Tamilnadu who migrated to Singapore over the last 150 years likewise identify strongly with Tamil culture and ethnicity there, even contributing on occasion to Tamil Hindu temples (Mani 1992). A recent outbreak of Hindu and Muslim fundamentalist violence in 1997–98 in Coimbatore may signal a breakdown in the Dravidian solidarity of the Muslims of Tamilnadu (Gopalan 1998), but it is worth noting that Hindu–Muslim violence has so far not spread from the inland centres of the Labbai and Deccani population to the coastal towns of the Marakkāyars.[13]

The Moors of Sri Lanka

There are many cultural similarities between the Māppiḷas of Kerala, the Marakkāyars of Tamilnadu, and the Moors of Sri Lanka which point to common origins. All three groups are Sunni Muslims of the Shāfi'ī legal school, a shared legacy of their earliest south Arabian forefathers (Fanselow 1989). All

[13] My sources are the South Indian newsmagazines *The Week* (1 March 1998) and *Frontline* (20 March 1998).

three groups began as Indian Ocean trading communities patronised by local Hindu and Buddhist kings, and commerce remains one of their chief occupations today. The influence of Sufi saints and scholars has been quite strong, first linking the Malabar and Coromandel coasts, then spreading to Sri Lanka (Ali 1980: ch. 4; Bayly 1989; Ibrahim Kunju 1995; Mauroof 1972; Shukri 1986c). In fact, two of the most widespread devotional cults of Sufi saints among Sri Lankan Muslims have clear connections both with Kerala and with Tamilnadu. The first is that of Shaykh Muhiyadeen Abdul Qādir Jīlānī (d. A.D. 1166), popularly known in Tamil as Mohideen *Āṇṭavar* ('Lord Mohideen'), Persian-born founder of the Qādiriyya Order whose popularity extends throughout the South Asian Muslim world (Sanyal 1994: 48). He is the subject of the earliest (A.D. 1607) and most highly regarded Muslim *malappatt* or saintly praise-poem in the Arabic–Malayalam literature of Kerala (Ibrahim Kunju 1989: 198–200), and his *dargāh* shrines are the most widespread in Tamilnadu (Mines 1981: 69). He is believed to have visited the popular cave-mosque of Daftar Jailani at Kuragala near Balangoda, Sri Lanka, while on a pilgrimage to Adam's Peak (Aboosally 1975).

A second devotional cult popular with Sri Lankan Moors is that of 16th century saint Shāhul Hamīd, sometimes referred to in Sri Lanka as Mīrān Sāhib, whose impressively-endowed tomb-shrine on the Coromandel coast at Nagoor attracts Muslim pilgrims from both South India and Sri Lanka to witness the death anniversary festival (*kantūri*) at which the saint's tomb is ritually anointed with cooling sandalwood paste from a special container (*cantanakkūṭu*) which is brought in a grand procession (Bayly 1986; Nambiar and Narayana Kurup 1968). The Nagoor saint is believed to have traced the footsteps of Abdul Qādir Jīlānī to Bagdad and to Balangoda, visiting the Maldive Islands and Southeast Asia as well (Shaik Hasan Sahib 1980). Several physically empty but spiritually filled 'branch office' tomb-shrines in Sri Lanka and Singapore celebrate Shāhul Hamīd's death anniversary with flag-raising and *kantūri* celebrations timed to coincide with those at Nagoor (McGilvray 1988b; Shams-ud-di'n 1881). The saint is renowned for his magical power to plug leaks in sinking ships at sea, precisely the sort of boon which would prove useful to his major patrons and devotees, the Marakkāyar sea-traders of Kayalpattinam and Colombo (Sharif 1921: 199; Van Sanden 1926: 31).

All three groups under discussion—Māppiḷas, Marakkāyars, and Moors—as well, in fact, as the coastal Navāyat Muslims of Bhatkal in North Kanara (D'Souza 1955), follow, or at least prefer, some form of matrilocal marriage and household pattern, and many of them also recognise some type of matrilineal descent. The nature of the Sri Lankan Moorish matrilineal system is best documented for the east coast Moors of the Batticaloa and Amparai Districts, where a system of exogamous ranked matriclans, matrilocal residence, and *de facto* pre-mortem matrilineal transmission of houses and lands to daughters through dowry is followed by the Tamil Hindus as well (McGilvray 1989; Yalman 1967). Published research on Moorish kinship in central and western Sri Lanka is still meager, but matrilocal residence has been reported in a Moorish village in Wellassa (de Munck 1993, 1996; Yalman 1967: ch. 13), among the upper class Moors of late 19th century

Galle (Bawa 1888), as well as in eight out of twelve Moorish households in modern Colombo studied linguistically by Raheem (1975: 59).[14] On trips to Colombo and Galle in 1993 I found matrilocal residence in almost all of the middle-class Moorish families I visited. Some Moors were also well aware that other Muslims, such as the Gujarati-speaking Bohras, follow a contrary patrilocal rule.

The title of *Marakkār* or *Marakkāyar* is found among Muslim maritime trading groups from the *Navāyats* of the Kanara coast (D'Souza 1955: 43ff) to the Moors of Sri Lanka. It was borne by the daring Muslim Kunjali admirals of the Zamorin's fleet as well as by more humble Hindu Mukkuvar boatmen of Kerala (Gabriel 1996: 121 ff; Narayan 1995: 94; Thurston and Rangachari 1909 v.5: 112). In Sri Lanka, the term is often rendered as *Maraikkār* (Marikar, Marcar, etc.); it appears both in leading Moorish family names as well as in the customary title of the office of mosque trustee, a leader of the local Moorish community (Ali 1981a; Mahroof 1986a; McGilvray 1974). Commercial, cultural, and even migrational links between the Marakkāyar towns of southern Tamilnadu and Sri Lankan Moorish settlements are attested in the historical traditions of Beruwela, Kalpitiya, Jaffna, and other coastal settlements where some Muslims have lived for centuries (Ali 1981a; Casie Chitty 1834: 254 ff; Denham 1912: 234). Such connections may continue even today: during my early fieldwork in Akkaraipattu (Amparai District) in 1969–71 my Moorish landlord mentioned that he had spent several years as a youth apprenticed to a Marakkāyar merchant in Kayalpattinam, a fact I personally verified on a visit to South India in 1983. Evidence of long-term migration and presumed intermarriage between the Marakkāyars (and Kāyalārs) of Tamilnadu, the Māppiḷas of Kerala, and the Moors of Sri Lanka is also found in the fact that all three groups share a set of distinctive Tamil kinship terms for parents and elder siblings which are not found among the Labbais or other Tamil-speaking Muslim groups in Tamilnadu (Mines 1972: 26–27).[15]

The traditional institution of Moorish community decision-making on the west coast of Sri Lanka was a sort of village or neighbourhood assembly (*ūr kūṭṭam*) under the leadership of the chief mosque trustee, who bore the title of *Maraikkār, Matticam*, or *Nāṭṭāṇmaikkārar* (Mahroof 1986a).[16] Such a pattern of local assemblies was also characteristic of medieval Kerala, where they formed a hierarchy of increasing political authority from the village *(tārā kūṭṭam)*, to the district (*nāṭṭu kūṭṭam*), to even broader territorial units (Padmanabha Menon 1924: 250–69).

[14] Formal matrilineal descent units (matrilineages, matriclans) have not been documented among Moors outside of the east coast. One author briefly alludes to patrilineal kinship among the Moors of Kalutara and Mannar (M.Z. Mohideen 1965: 25).

[15] Father, *vāppā*; Mother, *ummā*; Elder Brother, *kākkā*; Elder Sister, *rāttā* or *tāttā*. For the Māppiḷa kin-terms see Gough (1961: 439–42) and Puthenkalam (1977: 228–32). In the absence of a full list of Marakkāyar kin-terms, I do not know what other kin-terms they may share with the Moors of Sri Lanka. Muslims in Colombo and south-western Sri Lanka recognise as a substitute for *kākkā* (Elder Brother) the term *nānā*, which is also a Singaporean term for the wealthier Tamil Muslims who come from coastal *Marakkāyar* towns such as Karaikal and Nagapattinam (Mani 1992: 341).

[16] Mattisam is derived from the Tamil word *mattiyam* or *mattiyastam*, adjudication or mediation. *Nāṭṭāṇmaikkārar* is a term for certain regional caste headmen in Tamilnadu.

Even today, the oral tradition of district assemblies (*nāṭṭu kūṭṭam*) is still recalled by the matrilineal Tamils of the eastern coast of Sri Lanka, part of a pre-colonial political legacy which they apparently share with the west coast Moors. The likelihood that a prior 'Kerala connection' accounts for many of these matrilineal and maritime Muslim traits among both the Marakkāyars of Tamilnadu and the Moors of Sri Lanka—as well as among the matrilineal Hindu Tamils of the east coast, and even the 'Malabar inhabitants' of Jaffna—seems quite strong (Raghavan 1971: 199–217).[17]

However, there are other respects in which the Moors of Sri Lanka are historically and sociologically distinct from their closest Muslim neighbours in India. In terms of ascriptive status, the Sri Lankan Muslim community as whole is more egalitarian and homogenous than its South Indian counterparts. Although the wealth and class structure descends steeply from elite gem-trading millionaires, to urban entrepreneurs, to rural farmers and boutique keepers (Mauroof 1972), there do not appear to be the sorts of hereditary, endogamous, caste-like divisions among the Sri Lankan Moors which have been documented among the Māppiḷas and between the Marakkāyars and Labbais in South India.[18] Also, as Fanselow (1989) has pointed out, the Māppiḷas, Marakkāyars, and Deccani Muslims of South India either supplied local Hindu kings with strategic military technologies (naval squadrons, cavalry horses) or were themselves part of the Urdu-speaking political elite under the Nawābs of Arcot.[19] The Moors never played such a strategic military or political role in the history of Sri Lanka (Ali 1981a; Dewaraja 1986), and as a result they did not become identified with the state nor did they develop their own political or military ideology of sovereignty.

One must consider, too, the distinctive features of Sri Lankan Moorish geography and demography. In the districts of northern Malabar, the Māppiḷas form a single Muslim population stretching from the urban coastal cities well into the agricultural hinterlands, whereas in Tamilnadu the coastal urban Marakkāyar trading elite has erected endogamous barriers separating them from the inland Labbai population. Neither of these Tamilnadu Muslim groups incorporates a large rural

[17] According to a Māppiḷa tradition, the Marakkāyars themselves were originally a merchant group in Cochin (Nambiar 1963: 59). Some Sinhalese cultural patterns, too, are historically of Kerala origin (Obeyesekere 1984: 425–552; Roberts 1980).

[18] Mines (1973) reports relatively open and egalitarian relations between different Labbai subdivisions in a suburb of Madras, and other writers have pointed to important ways in which Muslim social divisions are *unlike* Hindu castes (Fanselow 1996; Mauroof 1986; Mujahid 1989). Still, the evidence of endogamous status barriers between Marakkāyars and other Tamil Muslim groups remains quite strong (Bayly 1989; More 1991; Pandian 1987; chs 6–8; my own fieldwork in Kayalpattinam 1983). Both the Māppiḷas and the Sri Lankan Moors have traditionally assigned the task of circumcision to a hereditary low-status group of Muslim barbers called *Ossan* in northern Kerala, *Ostā* in Travancore and in Sri Lanka (McGilvray 1974: 306–12). The existence of smaller endogamous marriage circles—possibly even the perpetuation of Marakkāyar pedigrees from Kayalpattinam—among the wealthy Muslim gem-trading families of Colombo, Beruwela, and Galle has been asserted by Mauroof (1972: 69–80), but without supporting data.

[19] For a brief period in the mid-18th century a coastal Navāyat dynasty held the Nawābship (Fanselow 1989: 273).

peasantry. Among the Sri Lankan Muslims, in contrast, there is both an urban Muslim elite and a rural Muslim agrarian population, but each is found on opposite sides of the island, separated by the Kandyan Hills. The numerous Moorish farmers on the northern and eastern coast are not only distanced geographically, but separated socio-economically and culturally as well, from the more affluent and cosmopolitan centres of Muslim trade and political influence in the central and western parts of the island (Figures 3 and 4). The west coast and up-country Muslims are a widely dispersed minority except in certain well-known enclaves (Beruwela, Akurana, Puttalam/Kalpitiya, Mannar, some neighbourhoods of Colombo and Galle, for example).[20] The east coast Moorish paddy farming towns, on the other hand, which are more substantial and concentrated—but also more agrarian-based and integrated into a distinctive regional subculture—represent nearly one-third of all Sri Lankan Muslims (Figure 5). At Mutur and Kinniya south of Trincomalee and in some of the major towns and paddy-growing areas of Batticaloa and Amparai Districts (e.g., Eravur, Kattankudy, Kalmunai, Sammanturai, Nindavur, Akkaraipattu, Pottuvil), half to three-quarters of the population are Moors, making this eastern region the only demographically feasible site in the entire island for a Muslim-dominated electorate (Kurukulasuriya et al. 1988: 94–102).

III
Moorish political ethnicity in the 20th century

In the modern era, the Muslims of Kerala and Tamilnadu—despite their cultural diversity and internal social divisions—have felt reasonably secure about 'who' they are. In contrast, the leading spokesmen for the Moors of Sri Lanka from the late 19th century onwards seem to have been perennially vexed by questions of their biological and cultural origins and the most advantageous formulation of their ethnic identity within an increasingly communalised political arena. Cut off from major South Indian Muslim centres of learning to some extent during 300 years of Portuguese and Dutch colonial repression, the Moors were grateful to be emancipated from feudal obligations in the Sinhalese areas of the island in reward for their loyalty to the British crown during the Kandyan Rebellion of 1817–18. In the first half of the 19th century they took advantage of gradually liberalised British policies permitting freedom of commerce, urban property rights, purchase of Crown land, and the appointment of local Moorish headmen. However, the degree to which the Sri Lankan Moors in the late 18th and early 19th centuries constituted a self-conscious and internally organised minority community is difficult to judge. It is only clear that the Moors formed a visible and distinct census category for British colonial administrators and the compilers of local gazetteers such as Simon Casie Chitty (1834).

Ironically, according to Ameer Ali, whose unpublished Ph.D. thesis offers the most insightful and detailed interpretation of the Muslims in 19th and early 20th

[20] The largest single urban concentration of Sri Lankan Muslims (18 per cent of the total Muslim population) is within the municipal district of Colombo (Phadnis 1979: 29–32).

Figure 4
Ultramodern mosque in Beruwala, and affluent Muslim coastal settlement south of Colombo which is a centre for Sri Lanka's gem trade. Photo taken in 1993.

Figure 5

A Muslim man performs ablutions at the older style Small Mosque (Cinnappaḷḷi) in Akkaraipattu. The drum, possibly unique in Sri Lanka, helps summon the faithful to prayers. Photo taken in 1971.

century Ceylon, the indigenous Moors seized upon these new colonial opportunities to become even more aloof and inward-looking as a community.[21] He observes that they remained absorbed in their customary modes of livelihood and mosque-based institutions, influenced by Sufi disciples and ritualistic *ālims* and pious Indian Muslim trader/missionaries from Kayalpattinam and Kilakarai, and strongly averse to mass-literacy, the printing press, and English-medium education, which was then available only through Christian mission schools (Ali 1980; Shukri 1986c: 348ff). The British-imposed exile to Sri Lanka in 1883 of a charismatic Egyptian revolutionary, Arabi Pasha, finally served to catalyse an Islamic revival and a movement to establish Muslim schools offering a secular western curriculum (Mahroof 1986b, 1986c), but this still placed them far behind the Sinhalese, and even farther behind the Tamils, who had begun to enroll in Christian mission schools in Jaffna sixty years earlier. In any case, the Muslim educational movement was religiously exclusionary and aimed solely at the west coast urban elite;

[21] Another author, M.M.M. Mahroof, has called it the 'Kasbah mentality' (1990: 91).

not a single Muslim school was founded for the children of the Moorish farmers of the east coast (Samaraweera 1978: 471).[22]

The mid-to-late-19th century Tamil Hindu and Sinhala Buddhist cultural revivals spurred by Arumuga Navalar, Anagarika Dharmapala, and the European Theosophists were well under way before the Muslims had even begun to organise. By the end of the century, however, the west coast urban Muslim elite had begun to promote their unique identity as 'Ceylon Moors' in response to several factors. In the first place, being 'Ceylon Moors' established their legitimate claim for seats in the formal system of communal representation which the British instituted and maintained for 100 years (Nissan and Stirrat 1990: 28–29). Muslim representatives (some elected, some appointed) had begun to serve on local Municipal Councils as early as 1866 (Asad 1993: 82), but until 1889 the Moors had been tacitly represented on the all-island Legislative Council by a government-appointed Tamil member, the last of whom was (later Sir) Ponnambalam Ramanathan, a highly influential figure among both Sinhala and Tamil nationalists. By the 1880s, however, the Moors as well as the Sinhala Buddhists had begun to press for separate representation so as to forestall the appointment of better educated or more influential Hindus and Christians to represent them (Wagner 1990: 67).

The underlying colonial discourse in the 19th century assumed 'race' as the criterion for political representation (Rogers 1995). In a strategically calculated speech to the Legislative Council in 1885, Ramanathan marshalled linguistic and ethnographic evidence to argue that, apart from religion, the Moors and Tamils shared a great many cultural and linguistic traits resulting from conversion and intermarriage over the centuries. When he published it three years later as an academic essay on 'The ethnology of the "Moors" of Ceylon' in the *Journal of the Royal Asiatic Society, Ceylon Branch*, Ramanathan's views might have appeared to gain the imprimatur of the British colonial establishment (Ramanathan 1888). His well-argued but politically motivated conclusion, that the Moors were simply Muslim members of the Tamil 'race', was immediately perceived by Moorish leaders as 'planned sabotage' of their hopes for the appointment of a separate Muslim Member of the Legislative Council and as an academic excuse for the continued domination of the Moors by the Tamil leadership (Ali 1980: 102n). Ironically enough, Ramanathan was promulgating a more inclusive definition of 'Tamilness' than many high-caste Hindus of Jaffna and Batticaloa would have liked, given their aristocratic reluctance to recognise members of the lowest castes as 'Tamils'.[23]

Ramanathan's strategy abruptly failed when the British Governor appointed a Moor to the Council a year later. However his essay seemed to embody the

[22] A similar picture emerges with respect to the older, more traditional madrasas or Arabic Muslim seminaries, which were primarily founded in the southernmost Galle-Weligama region (Asad 1994).

[23] I found in the 1970s that high-ranking Vēḷāḷars and Mukkuvars in the Batticaloa region still generally referred to members of low castes such as Washermen (*Vaṇṇāṉ*) and Drummers (*Paṟaiyaṉ*) by their specific caste names, reserving the collective term 'Tamil' (*Tamiḻaṉ*) solely for the highest castes. I am grateful to John Rogers for reminding me that this was true in Jaffna as well.

patronising Tamil outlook found in many rural areas of the island, where even today high-caste Hindus look down upon the Moors as their inferior and uneducated neighbours. In the narrow rhetorical space of colonial politics, the logic of Ramanathan's aggrandising ethnological thesis forced the Moors to further repudiate their Tamilness and to claim they were 'an entirely different race of Arab origin'. Indeed, from that point onward, the Ceylon Muslim leadership embraced the label of 'Ceylon Moor' with great tenacity (Ali 1980: 102). Twenty years later, in 1907, the Moorish editor I.L.M. Abdul Azeez finally published a lengthy rebuttal acknowledging that the Moors' Dravidian traits had resulted from conversion and intermarriage with Tamil women, but insisting that the very earliest forefathers of the Ceylon Moorish 'race'—who may have numbered 'not much more than 100'—had certainly not come from Kayalpattinam in South India and were 'purely Arabs in blood' (Azeez 1907: 22, 46).

Qadri Ismail has provided an insightful deconstruction of Azeez's strategically composed text, with its portrayal of the Moors as peaceful Arab traders (not warlike Tamil invaders) of high religious rank (members of the Prophet's own Hashemite tribe) who thought of themselves virtually as natives (because Adam had fallen from Paradise to earth in Ceylon),[24] tracing exclusively patrilineal descent from Arab males (thereby ignoring all affinal and maternal connections with their Tamil wives and mothers), and conversing in Tamil only as a 'borrowed' language of mercantile convenience (Ismail 1995: 69–70). To keep the story simple, no mention was made of the Persian traders and pilgrims in Sri Lanka reported by Ibn Batuta in the 14th century, much less the vestigial evidence of 19th century Persian influence or Shi'ite Muharram festivals in Puttalam (Ali 1981a: 74–76; Macready 1888–89). The essential subtext of Azeez's historical treatise was that the Ceylon Moors would refuse to be patronised or subsumed as 'Muslim Tamils' in the 20th century. Thus, a hypostatised Arab 'racial' pedigree was promoted to separate the Moorish from the Sinhala and Tamil 'races'.[25] The claim of a shared Tamil ethnic identity for both Tamils and Muslims has continued to be rejected by Moorish leaders throughout the 20th century, notes K.M. de Silva, 'because of its implications of a subordinate role for them vis-á-vis the Tamils, and the assumption of a Tamil tutelage over them' (1994: 43). As we shall see, Muslim/Tamil acrimony over Ramanathan's 'ethnological' thesis has been festering for over a century now, coming visibly to the surface several times in the post-Independence era.

In their determination to foster a unique Ceylonese–Arab identity, however, the Moorish leadership ignored a growing public resentment of their 'extra-territorial allegiance'. As Ameer Ali has noted, the Ceylon Moorish elite at the turn of the century—miming the theatrical loyalism of that exiled dissident, Arabi Pasha,

[24] Although it is not widely recounted in Sri Lanka, there is an extra-Quranic tradition that Adam, having rejoined his wife Eve at Arafat near Mecca, returned with her to Sri Lanka where they gave birth to the human race (Wadood 1976). Any acknowledgement of the many alternative legends which place Adam's fall in India (al-Ṭabarī 1989) would have been awkward from Azeez's point of view.

[25] For critical examination of the Sinhalese and Tamil 'racial' constructions, see Gunawardena (1990); Hellman-Rajanayagam (1995), and Rogers (1995).

who was yearning to return to Egypt (Asad 1993: 42–43)—was so conspicuously devoted to the British monarch, so flattered by the attentions of the Ottoman Caliph, and so proud of their financial donations to build the Hejaz Railway from Damascus to Medina, that their credibility with Ceylonese nationalist leaders was deeply compromised. Even the celebrated 'fight for the fez', in which a prominent Moorish lawyer secured before the Privy Council his right to plead in court wearing a Turkish fez instead of a barrister's horsehair wig, was defined as an exclusively Muslim issue, not as a Ceylonese nationalist cause around which Sinhalese and Tamils could also rally (Ali 1980: ch. 7).

Like the Ceylon Moors, both the Marakkāyar Muslims of Tamilnadu and the highest-status Māppiḷas of Kerala boasted of their primordial Indo-Arab ancestry, but the Moors were reluctant to amalgamate with such a South Indian 'race', fearing it could undermine their rights as fully enfranchised natives of Ceylon. Reinforcing this aversion was the Moors' resentment of the immigrant South Indian Muslims (the so-called 'Coast Moors') who had effectively displaced the Ceylon Muslim traders from the export/import sector, and from other local markets as well, during the expansion of the plantation economy in the second half of the 19th century. The Ceylon Moors showed marked ambivalence toward the Coast Moors, looking to these successful Indian Muslim 'brothers' for a model of wealth and piety, sometimes even defending them in the Colombo press,[26] but resenting at the same time their exclusionary trading practices, their ascetic overhead expenditures, and their sharp business dealings (Ali 1980: chs 6–7,1981b: 14). Echoes of this rivalry can be found in references to jealous quarrels over the congregational rights of the Coast Moors and the Malays in Colombo mosques in the early 20th century.[27]

At the beginning of the 20th century other Ceylon ethnic groups were likewise crafting their identities in terms of 'race' and patrilineal 'blood', two familiar European colonial discourses of the period. I.L.M. Azeez himself pointed to the Parsees of Bombay as an economically and politically successful ethnic-cum-racial minority to emulate (Azeez 1907: 15). In the final analysis, the Ceylon Moors pursued a strategy very similar to that of the Burghers (Eurasians) of Ceylon, who emphasised distant patrilineal Dutch 'racial' pedigrees while downplaying their much stronger maternal Luso-Ceylonese ancestry, extolled a moribund linguistic patrimony (Dutch) while speaking and singing a much livelier vernacular (Portuguese Creole) at home, and all the while lobbied for favourable political treatment through an ethnic association which published historical footnotes and

[26] Indeed, only three years prior to publishing his racially exclusivist rebuttal of Ramanathan, I.L.M. Abdul Azeez had defended the Coast Moors in his Tamil newspaper, the *Muslim Guardian*, arguing that, in addition to their shared bonds as loyal British subjects, 'the Northern Coast [Indian] Moors and the Ceylon Moors are related in terms of their religion and to an extent in terms of their race'. His Tamil word for race was *cāti*, which could also mean caste. 'Northern Coast Moor' is my translation of the phrase *vaṭakarai cōṉakar* (cf. Ameer Ali 1981b: 14, 20n).

[27] *Ceylon Legislative Council Debates*, 21 August 1924, pp. 277–301. 'History of the Maradana Mosque' (anonymous), 38 pp. typescript. Catalogue #297.3595493/1187 in the library of the Moors Islamic Cultural Home, Bristol Street, Colombo. For the Malays see also Asad (1993: 80, 90); Ossman (1990).

northern European family trees. Eventually the Moors Islamic Cultural Home, founded in 1944 by Senator A.R.A. Razik (later Sir Razik Fareed), began to publish the same sorts of historical articles and genealogical pedigrees for the Moorish community as the Dutch Burgher Union had been publishing for the Burghers since 1908 (Jackson 1990; Marikar et al., eds. 1976; McGilvray 1982a; Moors' Islamic Cultural Home 1965, 1970, 1978, 1983, 1994; Roberts et al. 1989).

In the 20th century, however, the social construction of the 'Ceylon Moor' identity has not gone unchallenged, nor has it remained stable (Ismail 1995). Despite the Moors' obviously complex and plural origins, a simplistic dichotomous racial debate over 'Arab' versus 'Tamil' was sustained for many years, with more or less the same political subtext of ethnic estrangement and rivalry. However, by mid-century a long-standing quarrel had intensified within the community itself as to whether 'Moor' or 'Muslim' was preferable as a group designation, nativistic 'Moor' partisans incorrectly asserting that the Portuguese applied this term only to racially pure Arabs (Azeez 1907: 4; Mohan 1987: 27–31, 117; Yule and Burnell 1903: 502), and 'Muslim' adherents emphasising a broader pan-Islamic religious identity which would ignore race and language, and incidentally make room for the Malays and Coast Moors. This discursive debate was reflected in the names of rival 'Moor' versus 'Muslim' political and cultural associations which from the turn of the century served as political fronts for two rival west coast gem-trading dynasties, both of recent Kerala origin, that of M. Macan Markar (Ceylon Moors' Association) and that of Abdul Caffoor (Ceylon Muslim League).[28] Leaders of these two wealthy families also vied jealously for British knighthoods, litigated over control of the Colombo Maradana mosque, and cultivated rival Sufi brotherhoods, with Macan Markar heading the Sri Lankan Shazuliya order and Abdul Caffoor leading the Qādiriyya order (de Jong 1986; Mauroof: personal communication; Samaraweera 1979: 252; Wagner 1990: 84–117, and personal communication).[29] At one point in 1945 the leaders of the Muslim League threatened to pronounce a *fatwa* expelling anyone who called himself a 'Moor' from the Muslim faith, a political ploy clearly intended to discredit the rival Moors' Association under the leadership of Razik Fareed (Wagner 1990: 143). Perhaps one of Fareed's cleverest strokes is seen in the omnibus name he chose for the Moors' Islamic Cultural Home, a title which proclaims at once a domesticated, racial, religious, and ethnic identity for the Moors.[30]

In the period between World War I and Sri Lankan Independence in 1948 the Moors fluctuated in their political stance, a consequence of the most terrifying episode of their pre-Independence history, the 1915 Sinhala–Muslim Riots.[31] The

[28] Michael Roberts asserts that 'the Macan Markars and the Abdul Cafoors' migrated to Sri Lanka in the 18th or 19th centuries from Kerala (1980: 38, 46 fn).

[29] The possibility of something like a dynastic moiety system within the west coast Muslim elite remains strong, as evidenced by the nearly simultaneous publication of two independently sponsored scholarly collections of essays on the history and culture of the Sri Lankan Muslims. One of these volumes enjoys the patronage of a third and newer Moorish gem-trading dynasty, that of Naleem Hadjiar (Mahroof et al. 1986; Mauroof 1972: 69; Shukri 1986a).

[30] Fareed's Tamil name for the MICH is *Cōṉaka Islāmiya Kalācāra Nilaiyam.*

[31] Six papers in the Ceylon Studies Seminar 1969/70 Series are devoted to this event, four of them

multiple causes of this island-wide outbreak of Sinhalese violence against Muslim shopkeepers and workers are still hotly debated. Whether conditioned by Sinhala Buddhist revivalism and anti-British sentiment (Roberts 1994a), or fuelled by resentment against Muslim business practices and triggered by confrontational Islamic zealotry on the part of Coast Moors from Kayalpattinam (Ali 1980, 1981b), the rioting was staunchly repressed by the British, giving Moors good reason to be grateful for British protection and muting their support for the anti-British Khilāfat movement to restore the Sultan of Turkey as the Caliph, or leader, of all the world's Muslims. Indeed, given the Moorish leadership's fawning display of loyalty to the British Raj—a pattern seen in other Sri Lankan communities as well—it is difficult to imagine that the most violent and bloody of the anti-British, anti-Hindu 'Māppiḷa rebellions' was occurring only 400 miles away in Kerala in roughly the same period (1922). The 1915 violence also embittered the Moors against the Tamil elite, still led by Ponnambalam Ramanathan, who sought to retain his prominence in the Ceylonese nationalist movement by rising to defend the Sinhalese rioters against harsh British justice. In Muslim eyes, Ramanathan's stance revealed the hypocrisy of 'Tamil-speaking' solidarity, and this event was later recalled bitterly by Moorish politicians at crucial moments in the 1950s and 1960s (Hassan 1968: 101; Sivathamby 1987: 204).

In the 1920s and 1930s the Moors—divided between the two rival dynastic political organisations, the All-Ceylon Muslim League and the All-Ceylon Moors' Association, and unable to rally behind the leadership of both a Malay (T.B. Jayah) and a Moor (Razik Fareed)—initially followed the Ceylon Tamil leadership in vainly seeking guaranteed '50–50' minority representation under new constitutional reforms (Russell 1982: ch. 12). However, after the disastrous defeat of all their candidates in the 1936 election, which they correctly interpreted as an omen of Sinhalese majoritarian domination on the horizon, the Moorish leadership strategically transferred their support to the Sinhalese-majority parties, explicitly denying any necessary link between Moorish ethnicity and the Tamil language.[32] This accommodating gesture guaranteed both senior Muslim leaders (T.B. Jayah and Razik Fareed) their charter memberships in the leading Sinhala-dominated party at the time of Independence in 1948, the United National Party (K.M. de Silva 1986a, 1986b).[33] Just as most leading Sri Lankan Tamil MPs in the newly established parliament, hoping to salvage some goodwill from the Sinhalese majority in parliament, eventually broke ranks and voted with the UNP MPs to disenfranchise the 780,000 Indian Estate Tamils working on upcountry tea plantations, so the Muslim MPs voted to disenfranchise the 35,000 Indian Muslims still doing

also published in the *Journal of Asian studies* 29, 2 (1970). See also Ameer Ali (1981b), and Roberts (1994a).

32 Note, however, that as late as 1930 there was a daily Colombo newspaper for Muslims, *Tina Tapāl* (Daily Post), published in Tamil (Mahroof 1990: 94).

33 At the very same time, an Indian Muslim radical who had agitated for an independent 'Mappilastan' in Kerala was proposing to create 'Nasaristan' for the Moors in eastern Sri Lanka and 'Safiistan' for west coast Moors. Because of their strategic decision to work within the Sinhalese nationalist parties, the Moorish leadership paid no attention to his efforts (Gabriel 1996: 294 ff; Rahmat Ali 1943).

business in Sri Lanka. Both measures testified to the success of D.S. Senanayake in fostering divisions between the Tamil-speaking communities of the island and thus increasing Sinhala electoral dominance in the post-Independence era (Ali 1986–87: 155–56; Ismail 1995: 71–72, 84–85; and especially Shastri 1998).

Apart from an ephemeral east coast Tamil–Moor Federal Party alliance in the 1956 elections, the Moors from Independence up to the mid-1980s consistently opted for a strategy of coalition politics within the two major Sinhalese nationalist parties, the UNP and the SLFP, in the course of which certain Moorish politicians earned a legendary reputation for switching tickets and crossing the floor to join whichever party had come to power (Mohan 1987: 47; Phadnis 1979). Sir Razik Fareed, who emerged as the leading Moorish spokesman in the early decades of Independence, conspicuously endorsed the Sinhala Only national language policy in 1956 and railed against what he called 'political genocide' of the Moors under 'the Tamil yoke'. His speeches accused the Tamils of discrimination against the Moors in education and in local administrative appointments, as well as apathy and indifference wherever Moorish voters were politically underrepresented. During the Official Language debate in 1956, a Tamil MP sarcastically accused him of being a Sinhala defector. Fareed rhetorically turned the tables by asserting that he and the Moorish community could never be considered 'Tamil converts'. A heated replay of the old Ramanathan–Azeez 'ethnological' argument of 1888–1907 immediately ensued on the floor of Parliament (Hassan 1968: 96–106).

As Kingsley de Silva forthrightly notes, 'Tamil–Muslim rivalry in Sri Lanka is a political reality, and the Muslims themselves have responded with alacrity to Sinhalese overtures to back them against the Tamils' (K.M. de Silva 1986a: 449). In this sense, Moorish politics in independent Sri Lanka coupled the mainstream majority party strategy of the Tamilnadu Muslims with the shrewd communal opportunism of the Kerala Māppiḷas, but all under the rubric of a carefully constructed 'non-Tamil' Moorish ethnicity which was orchestrated from Colombo. De Silva and others have approvingly viewed the Muslims' cultural assimilation into Sinhalese society, and their pragmatic accommodationist politics, as the mark of a 'good' minority, implicitly contrasting them with the troublesome and uncooperative Tamils (K.M. de Silva 1986a, 1988; Dewaraja 1995). A tangible reward for this pliant behaviour, and a token of the government's desire to maintain strong economic ties with the Muslim countries of the Middle East (Ali 1984), was the establishment of a separate system of government schools for Muslim students in the 1970s and the training of a corps of Muslim teachers to staff them. Apart from standard academic subjects, the curriculum in the Muslim schools includes Islam and optional Arabic language, and in recent years a distinctive Muslim school uniform has been introduced (Figure 6). This has improved Muslim educational success (Ali 1986–87, 1992a), but has arguably worsened ethnic tensions by restricting direct face-to-face contact between students and faculty from different ethnic communities. It also represents a unique political concession to the Muslim community which 'vitiates the principle of non-sectarian state education which has been the declared policy of all governments since 1960' (K.M. de Silva 1997: 33).

Figure 6

Boys wear white embroidered caps and girls wear 'purdah' (partā) head coverings at a Muslim government school in Akkaraipattu. Photo taken in 1993.

As Christian Wagner has documented in detail, this effort to extract rewards from the Sinhala-majority parties for a geographically divided and class-stratified Muslim minority depended upon rural east coast Moorish farmers and fishermen electing back-bench Moorish MPs, while a few rich, well-connected west coast Moorish politicians—whose private interests did not often coincide with those of the rural east coast Moors—received influential cabinet appointments. This continued even while Muslim shops, shrines, and paddy fields were periodically threatened by local Sinhalese mobs (M.I.M. Mohideen 1986: 42–44; Roberts 1994b: 283; Wagner 1990: 136–84, 1991).[34] As an educated Muslim middle-class began to emerge in the 1970s and 1980s, its demands for practical socio-economic concessions (university admissions and job quotas, for example) were placated with a broad array of Islamic religious and cultural self-esteem programmes, some of them funded by rival Sunni and Shia regimes in the Middle East, which cost the government nothing (O'Sullivan 1997).

This imperfect arrangement, which privileged the western Moorish elite politically just as it disempowered the eastern Moorish peasantry socio-economically, might have continued indefinitely, if not for the fact that after 1983 the government could no longer guarantee the lives and property of Moors in the east coast Tamil guerrilla combat zone. In the mid-1980s, when President Jayawardene's UNP government employed Israeli military advisors and proposed submerging the key Moorish parliamentary constituencies of Amparai District within an enlarged Sinhalese-dominated Province of Uva, the Moors, led by east coast sentiment, finally broke with the UNP and SLFP, organising the first distinct Muslim political parties in independent Sri Lanka. These included the East Sri Lanka Muslim Front (ESLMF), which later became the Muslim United Liberation Front (MULF), and the Sri Lanka Muslim Congress (SLMC). When in 1989 the SLMC won four parliamentary seats, the political initiative within the Moorish community had been seized for the first time by leaders self-consciously representing the Eastern Province (Ali 1992b; Hennayake n.d.; Wagner 1990, 1991). More recently, however, the success of UNP Muslim candidates from central and western districts in the 1994 elections may signal a growing political cleavage between the assertive policies of the SLMC defending the territorial interests of agricultural Muslims concentrated in the north-east region and the non-confrontational desires of a prosperous and vulnerable Muslim middle class living interspersed with Sinhalese in the island's Wet Zone (O'Sullivan 1997).

IV

A crucial test: Moors and Tamils in the eastern region

Today, in response to the cues of their political leaders and in reaction against the neglect and disrespect they have suffered from the Tamils, the Moors of Sri Lanka

34 In recent decades the Muslim cave-shrine at Daftar Jailani referred to in section II above has been the scene of volatile confrontations between Muslim devotees and Sinhalese monks and politicians who wish to reclaim it as an ancient Buddhist site (Hon. M.L.M. Aboosally, M.P., Chief Trustee of the shrine, personal communication 27 Aug. 1993).

have acquired a clearer image of themselves as a distinct ethnic and religious group. Since the outbreak of the Eelam conflict in the early 1980s, communal interests represented by the Sinhalese majority parties have sought to deepen this schism by deliberately provoking and exacerbating local violence between the Moors and Tamils in order to prevent the formation of a unified Tamil-speaking front comprised of both groups (Ali 1986–87: 164; UTHR Report 7, 1991; personal fieldwork data 1993 and 1995). From 1990 onward, the LTTE guerrillas themselves have committed massacres of Muslims at prayer as well as the forced expulsion of the entire Muslim population from Jaffna and the north of the island (Hasbullah 1996; Sivaram 1992). All of this has drawn attention away from the historically-rooted commonalities of language, social organisation and cultural practices which the eastern Moors and Tamils continue to share at the village level. It is especially in the Trincomalee, Batticaloa, and Amparai Districts of the east coast that large numbers of Muslims and Tamils live as paddy-farming neighbours, competing strongly for the same economic and political resources, testing the limits of their shared cultural heritage. It is here that one of the pivotal issues of the Tamil separatist movement must be decided: will the east coast Moors eventually agree to join the Tamil-led movement for a Tamil-speaking homeland, perhaps with a constitutional provision for Muslim-majority subregions to safeguard their minority rights? Or will they prefer to remain an even smaller and more submerged minority within the Sinhalese-dominated districts?

Based upon my fieldwork (1969–71, 1975, 1978, 1993, 1995) among Tamils and Moors in Akkaraipattu, a large Muslim and Hindu farming town east of Amparai (pop. 37,000 in 1981), as well as shorter fieldwork in other parts of Batticaloa and Amparai Districts, I can sketch some of the cultural background to Tamil–Muslim relations in this suddenly strategic region of the island. Although written in the 'ethnographic present', the description I offer is largely based upon fieldwork I carried out in the 1970s. On two short research trips to the region in 1993 and 1995, I was able to verify that, despite more than a decade of war and strife, the major patterns of Tamil and Moorish matrilineal social organisation and popular religiosity are still honoured wherever possible. However, economic hardships, deaths, disappearances, militant recruitments, and diasporic emigrations abroad have all significantly disrupted normal marriage patterns and public acts of worship. More detailed fieldwork will be necessary to determine what long-term social and cultural changes may emerge as a result of the Eelam Wars. In any case, my baseline ethnographic data from the 1970s can help us to understand the tense but relatively stable pattern of Tamil–Moor relations that existed prior to the radical and bitter communal polarisation of the late 1980s.

History, economy and settlement of the eastern Moors

Apart from King Senerat's poorly documented 1626 resettlement of exiled Moors to Batticaloa, there are no firm dates for the earliest Moorish communities on the east coast—although the preponderance of Muslims in medieval coastal trade leads me to assume they long predate the Portuguese arrival—and very little Sri Lankan scholarship on the subject.[35] I heard about direct Arab origins here mainly from miraculous tales of Muslim holy men who 'floated ashore on a plank (*palakai*)' directly from the Middle East. There is also a widespread folk tradition, known to both Tamils and Moors, which recounts a caste war between the Tamil Mukkuvars and their rivals, the Timilars, for regional dominance, in which the Mukkuvars are said to have enlisted the aid of the local Muslims. As their reward for victory, it is said, the Muslims shrewdly chose Tamil wives, knowing that under the local system of matrilineal inheritance, their spouses would bring land with them as well (Kadramer 1934).

Although its historicity is problematic, this popular legend does tacitly acknowledge that, in the past, there had been a good deal of intermarriage between local Tamils (especially the dominant caste Mukkuvars) and Muslims. Certainly the fact that the marriage and descent systems of the Tamils and Moors today are identically matrilocal and matrilineal—even to the point of some identical matriclan (*kuṭi*) names—lends popularly-agreed support to this view (Saleem 1990: 29). There is also the possibility that some Hindu Tamils converted to Islam, especially the more impoverished and oppressed members of the Mukkuvar community. Although I have no historical proof of this, a tendency toward Muslim and Catholic conversion has been noted among the Mukkuvar fishing caste in Kerala and Tamilnadu (More 1993b: 78; Ram 1991). Under the pre-colonial Mukkuvar chiefdoms of the Batticaloa region, the Moors appear to have occupied a subordinate, or at least somewhat circumscribed, social position. Although mercantile trade, bullock transport, handloom weaving, carpentry, and coastal fishing appear to have been successful Moorish specialties from an early date, their overall rank and influence within the Tamil-dominated social system was below that of the high-caste Vēḷāḷar and Mukkuvar landowners (*pōṭiyārs*). Vestiges of the hereditary incorporation of Moors into the hierarchical caste and matriclan-based rituals of major Hindu temples continued well into the 20th century in some areas (e.g., Kokkatticcolai, Tirukkovil), before the awakening of Moorish religious and ethnic consciousness led to a renunciation of these duties. From the high-caste Tamil Hindu point of view, of course, such Moorish 'shares' (*paṅku*) in temple ritual should be seen as a privilege and honour rather than as a burdensome or degrading service obligation.

Along the east coast, the present-day pattern is one of alternating Tamil and Moorish towns and villages, as well as some internally divided Tamil/Moorish settlements, with the bulk of the population living within a mile or two of the beach. The mainstay of the economy is irrigated rice cultivation, with many Tamil and Moorish farmers commuting daily to their fields from homes in the coastal towns. The east coast Tamils and Moors cultivate adjacent tracts of paddy land, but their houses are located in ethnically segregated residential neighbourhoods. Tamils and Moors may sometimes live on opposite sides of the street, but their houses

[35] An exception is the recent local history of Akkaraipattu by Saleem (1990). See also Kandiah (1964).

are almost never interspersed one beside the other. This ethnic partitioning generally coincides with electoral wards or local Headmen's Divisions, sometimes separated by no more than a narrow sandy lane. Among the Tamils, a pattern of Hindu caste segregation is found as well, with certain streets, wards, and even separate outlying hamlets, reserved for specific hereditary professions such as the Untouchable Paraiyar Drummers (McGilvray 1983). However, apart from a small, endogamous, low-status group of hereditary Muslim barber-circumcisers (*Ostā*, from Arabic *ustād*, master), the Moors have not created a parallel caste hierarchy of their own. The only religious elites are some *Maulānā* families (Sayyids, patrilineal descendants of the Prophet) and some local *Bāwās*, who are members of ecstatic Sufi orders (Aniff 1990; Mahroof 1991; McGilvray 1988b). Fieldwork in 1993 and 1995 revealed that Sufism itself is growing in popularity among middle-class Moors, with itinerant sheikhs from Kerala and the Lakshadweep Islands teaching the distinctive *dhikr* of the Rifā'ī order, among others, to Muslims in Kattankudy, Kalmunai, Akkaraipattu and elsewhere in the island (McGilvray 1997a).

To the west, once largely a Dry Zone jungle thinly inhabited by Veddah hunters and poor Sinhalese chena cultivators (Pieris 1965), there are now well over 150,000 Sinhalese peasants who have been resettled onto lands adjacent to the ancient Digavapi Buddhist stupa watered by the Gal Oya project, Sri Lanka's first post-Independence peasant colonisation scheme. Here, as in all the ethnic frontier districts farther north, the government's use of internationally-funded irrigation projects (see Figure 3) to resettle major Sinhalese populations in immediate proximity to well-established Tamil-speaking districts has been 'successful' but highly incendiary from the standpoint of both Tamils and Moors (Manogaran 1987; M.I.M. Mohideen 1986; Peebles 1990; Shastri 1990; UTHR Report 3, 1990). Profound demographic shifts have occurred in parts of Amparai and Trincomalee Districts, where the Tamils and the Moors have lost their majority status to the Sinhalese (Kearney 1987). This also means the Tamil-majority districts on the east coast are no longer geographically contiguous, so some kind of Tamil–Moor political accommodation will be necessary if a territorially unified Tamil Eelam or north-eastern provincial homeland is to be created.

Tamils and Moors: Similarities and differences

Residential neighbourhoods of Tamils and Moors often look quite similar to the eye. They are laid out along a gridwork of sandy lanes, each household lot guarded by perimeter walls or formidable barbed-wire fences and lushly planted with hibiscus, coconut, arecanut and mango trees. Ordinary Tamil houses tend to follow a traditional floor-plan oriented toward a carefully raked sandy yard to the east and incorporating a windowless interior Hindu shrine-room at the middle of the western wall. Moorish houses show more variation from this basic floor-plan. For example, Moorish families usually allocate the windowless centre room to the husband and wife as their bedroom, and they generally make some provision for female seclusion, such as a high masonry wall extending from the house into the front garden and interior walls or curtains to block the view of male visitors. (For more details and floor-plan drawings see McGilvray 1989: 195–98.) Newer Moorish houses also display more external ornamentation and use of colour than Tamil homes. This tendency is even more strongly marked in the way Moors decorate their bullock carts and fishing boats with colourfully painted floral designs and protective '786' numerology (Figure 7).[36] For reasons no one could explain to me, Tamil carts and boats are devoid of ornamentation of any kind.

As with the popularly alleged 'racial' differences between Sinhalese and Tamils, outward physical differences between Tamils and Moors are often difficult for an outside observer to detect. Local people would occasionally point out Moors with lighter skin and aquiline features as evidence of their Arab ancestry. However, the most reliable marks of Tamil versus Moorish identity 'on the street' are the cultural ones: dress, occupation, and to some degree vocabulary and dialect.[37] Although western-style shirts are nearly universal, Moorish men tend more often to wear as a lower garment a tubular stitched cotton sarong (*cāram*), typically in a plaid or check pattern, sometimes with a wide black belt, while Tamil men more often wear a plain white unstitched cotton *vēṭṭi* and never a belt. Both Tamil and Moorish women wear a sari and blouse, but Islamic modesty requires Moorish women to cover the head and part of the face with the end of their saris in public, a practice locally known as *mukkāṭu* (Figures 8 and 9). Hindu Saivite face and body markings (sacred ash, sandalwood paste, vermilion powder, male earrings) are unmistakably Tamil. Simple white kerchiefs, embroidered skullcaps, or the rare fez may be worn by Moorish men, especially as the hours of prayer approach (Figure 10). However, ambiguity and disguise are always possible: during anti-Tamil riots in Sinhalese areas, Moorish men have sometimes escaped mistaken slaughter only by displaying anatomical proof of circumcision.

Within their ethnically homogeneous wards and neighbourhoods, the Tamils and the Moors maintain places of worship, which are usually managed on a matrilineal basis. Both temples and mosques are governed by boards of male trustees (called *vaṇṇakkars* by the Tamils and *maraikkārs* by the Moors), each trustee representing one of the major matrilineal clans (*kuṭi*) found among the local temple or mosque congregation, and each seeking to preserve the honour and status of his matriclan at annual rituals, whether Hindu temple festivals or Muslim *kantūri* feasts (Figure 11). In the course of fieldwork, I was struck by the difference in religious styles between the Tamils and the Moors. Most of the Tamils I knew enjoyed ritual, and they often encouraged me to enter temples and attend pujas without any doctrinal commitment, whereas the Moors were sometimes more

[36] The number 786, frequently painted on sea-going fishing craft, is numerological short-hand for the Islamic invocation *Bismillāhi 'l-Rahmān 'l-Rahīm* ('In the Name of God, the Beneficent, the Merciful').

[37] The Tamil spoken by the Moors of the Batticaloa region contains a number of Islamic and Arabic-derived words as well as alternative Tamil expressions and kin-terms which are distinctive to Muslim usage. Their pronunciation, however, is broadly similar to the Tamils of the eastern region, as compared, for example, with the notably different Muslim Tamil speech patterns around Galle and the southern coast.

Figure 7
A Muslim bullock cart in eastern Sri Lanka is decorated with yellow and green floral motifs and a crescent moon. Photo taken in 1970.

Figure 8

Akkaraipattu Muslim school teacher K.M. Najumudeen standing in a checked sarong with his daughter, who is modelling a new Indian-inspired Muslim clothing style. Photo taken in 1993.

Figure 9

A Muslim woman with her daughter in Akkaraipattu uses the end of her sari to partially cover her face in public. Photo taken in 1970.

protective of their sacred spaces and more eager to engage in theological debates concerning my personal religious beliefs. As a first approximation, the distinction between Hindu 'orthopraxy' and Muslim 'orthodoxy' does seem to work pretty well, although the east coast Tamil Hindus tend to be less Sanskritic in their rituals

Figure 10

Mr Kaleel, a Batticaloa Muslim merchant who lives in Kattankudy, wears the embroidered cap and white shirt which is common among younger generation Moorish traders. Photo taken in 1993.

Figure 11

Matrilineal clan trustees* (maraikkārs) *of the Grand Mosque* (Periyappaḷḷi) *in Akkaraipattu illustrate some of the older styles for Moorish men in the east coast region. Several men in the centre have shaven heads, and two at the right are wearing the fez. Photo taken in 1970.

than one would find in the agamic temples of Jaffna (McGilvray 1988a). In the sphere of public worship, there is now very little crossover or joint participation by Hindus and Muslims. The only exceptions I noted were some Tamil Hindus who made vows and offerings at the tombs of Muslim saints (*auliyā*) located in mosques (*paḷḷi*) and small chapels (*taikkiyā*).

Moors and Tamils share very similar cultural understandings of sexuality and the body, of heating and cooling foods and substances, and of folk medicine derived from the Siddha and Ayurvedic traditions (McGilvray 1998). Local specialists in both communities are called 'curers' (*parikāri*; colloq. *paricāri*); no one in Akkaraipattu uses the title of *hakīm* or identifies with the Arabic Ūnāni medical system. At the level of ghosts and malevolent spirits (*pēy, picāsu*, Muslim *jinn*), the Tamils and the Moors have a similar construction of the supernatural. There are both Tamil and Muslim *mantiravātis* (experts in the use of mantras to control demonic forces), and there is a propitiatory cult of local female spirits (*tāymār*, 'the mothers') conducted by Moorish women. Until venturing outside of one's own ethnic neighbourhood became a dangerous undertaking as the Eelam 'problems' progressively worsened, some Moors would consult Tamil astrologers concerning marriage, career, and other personal problems. Similar guidance remains available from Moorish numerologists and ink-readers.

Young Muslim children of both sexes continue to attend traditional neighbourhood Quranic 'recitation schools' (*ōtuppaḷḷikkūṭam*) to memorise Arabic scripture, but the agents of modern pan-Islamism are nowadays more visible, particularly young ālims and maulavis, college and seminary-trained teachers of Islam in the Muslim government schools. Their efforts to suppress local traditions and practices as 'non-Islamic' have met with mixed success, and it is sometimes difficult to differentiate the pro-Islamic from the anti-Tamil motives which may lie behind such actions. For example, many Moorish women continue to publicly attend a regional festival celebrating the South Indian saint Shāhul Hamīd of Nagoor at the 'Beach Mosque' (*kaṭaṟkaraip paḷḷi*) near Kalmunai, despite efforts to impose purdah restrictions. For practical reasons, poorer Moorish women still work as members of female weeding and threshing teams in the fields, bringing home cash or a share of the paddy harvest for their families. At the same time, Moors in many areas have stopped employing Hindu caste musicians at local ceremonies and circumcisions because this Islamic 'purification' also enables an anti-Tamil economic boycott. During my visits to Akkaraipattu in 1993 and 1995, many Moors still employed Tamil Washermen for domestic laundry services, and Tamil Blacksmiths still forged agricultural tools and bullock cart wheels for Moorish farmers, despite the heightened ethnic tensions of Eelam War III.

Despite the lifeways they have in common, there are barriers to direct social interaction between the Tamils and the Moors, such as the bifurcated school system. There seem to be virtually no Tamil–Moorish intermarriages today, although they must have occurred widely in the distant past. Similarly, contemporary Tamil converts to Islam are rare; I came across only one or two in my entire fieldwork, always by Tamil women who married Moorish men. I observed very few Tamil–Moor inter-household visitations, gift-giving relationships, or food exchanges except those associated with landlord/tenant obligations or with hereditary low-caste Tamil service to Moorish landowners. Women are generally shielded from contact with the opposite community more than men, and Moorish women are shielded most of all.

The remaining opportunities for direct Tamil–Moor social interaction are largely vocational and economic. In the 1970s, before the escalation of the Eelam conflict, Tamils and Moors might cultivate paddy on adjacent tracts of land, in which case they would also participate together on irrigation committees. Tamil and Moorish landowners would also recruit tenant cultivators and field labourers from the opposite community. As a result of violence starting in the 1980s, paddy cultivation and land tenure patterns have been severely disrupted, and farmers in some areas have lost control of their fields to members of other ethnic communities, or to the LTTE itself. I do not know whether joint Tamil–Muslim irrigation committees continue to function today, but many Tamil labourers are still reported to be employed by Muslim landowners in Akkaraipattu (UTHR Bulletin 11, 1996). In the 1970s, shoppers could choose to patronise Tamil or Moorish or Low Country Sinhalese merchants in Akkaraipattu, depending upon a complex set of considerations (price, selection, convenience, credit, and personal trust). However, ethnic resentment and suspicion was often noted, particularly among the Tamils, because the majority of retail establishments in a town such as Akkaraipattu were owned by Moors or Sinhalese or 'Jaffnese' Tamils. Public markets and shops are culturally defined as a male domain into which respectable women should not venture without a chaperone. Tamil women may shop together or with a male relative, but Moorish women must dispatch men or boys to fetch merchandise samples to view at home. Nowadays the purchasing power of Tamils in a town such as Akkaraipattu has been drastically reduced by the Eelam conflict, while the Muslims are visibly more prosperous (UTHR Bulletin 11, 1996).

At the level of popular culture and day-to-day problem-solving, the Tamils and Moors still have a great deal in common, although they rarely stop to reflect upon it. In addition to a common language, their farming practices, matrilocal marriage and household patterns, matrilineal kinship rules, rites of passage, dietary and medical lore, and magical beliefs are identical or closely related in many cases (McGilvray 1982c, 1989). These are the sorts of everyday patterns which, from an anthropological perspective, give the whole Batticaloa region its distinctive cultural identity in contrast to Jaffna or Tamilnadu, and frankly my own bias would be to read these data optimistically as evidence of consensus rather than conflict. Unfortunately, as the examples of Lebanon, Bosnia, and Northern Ireland prove, in a politically-charged situation these elements of shared regional culture are not necessarily enough to forestall bitter political schism legitimated by history and other markers of cultural difference.

Ethnic stereotypes and self-perceptions

The high-caste Tamils with whom I became acquainted expressed at least a vague awareness of being heirs to a Tamil cultural tradition, a Dravidian civilisation with plausible claims to linguistic roots going back to the pre-Vedic Indus Valley culture—and therefore much older than either Buddhism or Islam (Fairservis and Southworth 1989). Yet, although the linguistic and cultural chauvinism which has characterised Tamil politics in the 20th century has clearly been felt on the east coast, there is also a tinge of ambivalence about the arrogance and presumed cultural authority of the Jaffna Tamils who have led this movement. My Tamil friends were not outspoken on these issues, but they prided themselves on adhering to a coherent and time-tested set of rules for living, including standards for Tamil food and attire, Tamil family patterns, Tamil religiosity, Tamil language and manners. They did not expect me, as a *veḷḷaikkāran* ('whiteman'), to follow the same regimen, but they were appalled when I seemed to have no systematic rules of my own. My blatant dietary promiscuity and my groggy morning regimen seemed particularly lax to them, and the American kinship system struck both the Tamils and Moors as appallingly flaccid. When the postman brought a wedding invitation from my mother's brother's daughter in California, I was admonished for not having closely scrutinised her fiancé, obviously a rival for my cross-cousin's hand.

Many of the very same elements are found in Moorish self-perceptions, especially the concern to evince a well-ordered cultural system for living. However, the Moors have the option of drawing upon both the Islamic and the Tamil traditions, and sometimes there can be debate over which one to emphasise. From the religious point of view, the Moors enjoy a robust, unequivocal self-definition as orthodox Muslims; indeed some of my friends urgently referred me to locally respected treatises on *sunnā* and *hadīth*, especially the 19th century Arabic–Tamil work of 'Māppiḷḷai Ālim' (Ahmad Lebbai 1873/1963). Among some of the young educated Moorish men who became my close friends during fieldwork in the 1970s there was some concern about their own 'hybrid' cultural traits, which they sometimes humourously caricatured as consisting of an Arabic religion, together with a South Indian language, and a mixed programme of clothing and cuisine. Shouldn't the Moors have their own unique 'national dress', some of them asked, instead of just borrowing a Sinhala–Malay sarong and a Tamil sari? A further complication in the 1970s was the official adoption of a Pakistani school uniform, the 'Punjabi costume' of *salwar kameez*, for Moorish high school girls, more recently augmented with an Iraqi-inspired white hooded head-covering (referred to as *partā*, purdah, see Figure 6). With grudging admiration, a Moorish friend of mine remarked that, regardless of where in the world she might live, a Tamil woman would unhesitatingly prefer to wear a traditional Kanchipuram sari and tie the customary jasmine blossoms in her hair. Lacking such a strong cultural identity, a Muslim woman, he felt, would be more inclined to adopt local, or more western, dress.

In agriculture and business, however, the Moorish identity is strong and unequivocal: they see themselves as—and are acknowledged by the Tamils to be—shrewd, hardworking and successful. In the 1970s, east coast Moors readily admitted to me that their MPs would 'reverse hats' (*toppi tiruppuvān*), i.e., switch party affiliations, to ally themselves with the party in power, a manoeuver perfected by the late Gate Mudaliyar M.S. Karaiyapper of Kalmunai, his son-in-law M.M. Mustapha, and his nephew M.C. Ahmed (Mohan 1987: 47; Phadnis 1979: 45–46; Wagner 1990: 157). It should be noted, however, that several east coast Tamil MPs also learned to emulate this tactic quite well (UTHR Report 7, 1991: 45–46).

There are many different perceptions and opinions of Tamil/Moor cultural difference, but some basic themes emerged in offhand remarks I heard from members of each group. Tamils generally concede that the Moors are extremely energetic and hardworking, a fact visibly reflected in their improved houses and growing material wealth. In fact, the increasing prosperity of the Moors is of acute concern to many high-caste Tamils, because it challenges their traditionally dominant position in society. Not only are the Moors getting richer, they are also accused of having too many children. It is true that the Moors have maintained the highest birthrate of any ethnic community in the country over the past fifty years (Kurukulasuriya et al. 1988: 191), a trend which is also true among Muslims in India. With demographic and electoral trends in mind, many Tamils and Moors—and nowadays some Sinhalese as well (Schrijvers 1998: 12)—view such persistent fecundity as a political act.

I also encountered a more covert level of ethnic stereotyping which was constructed from private beliefs and suspicions, a more concealed discourse among younger men with whom I spent time which reflected both their curiosity and anxiety about matters of the body. Whether these ideas have had any real impact at all upon Tamil–Muslim communal politics is impossible for me to say, but at some level they form part of the symbolic web of cultural images which separates the two groups. I found that the more intimate domains of Muslim diet, sexuality and hygiene, because they are blocked from public view, typically generated the most Tamil gossip. Some Tamils theorise that the Moors' vigour and fertility come from their consumption of beef, in Hindu eyes a polluting and highly 'heating' meat that energises the body and the libido. Indeed, according to Māppiḷḷai Ālim's influential 19th century Arabic–Tamil treatise on Islamic teachings, Muslims are encouraged to consume meat and flesh for this purpose (Ahmad Lebbai 1873/1963: 255–67). One inventive Tamil informant hypothesised that Moorish circumcision dulls male sensitivity, prolongs intercourse and allows more Moorish women to achieve orgasm, thereby promoting conception (McGilvray 1982b). I once also heard some Tamil youths jokingly refer to the Moors as 'three-quarters' (*mukkāl*), revealing their muddled fantasies of what was actually severed during male circumcision, an operation which in Akkaraipattu is usually conducted around the age of 9 or 10 with considerable domestic celebration and formal hospitality. The Moorish male circumcision ritual itself is colloquially referred to as a 'circumcision wedding' (*cunattu kaliyāṇam*), and it parallels in interesting ways the Tamil and Moorish female puberty ceremony, which is also referred to as a 'wedding', i.e., an auspicious rite of passage (McGilvray 1982b). The Moorish practice of female circumcision was, however, completely unknown to the Tamils with whom I spoke in Akkaraipattu. This mandatory (*wājib*) operation (Ahmad Lebbai 1873/1963: 479) conducted by the circumciser's wife (*ostā māmi*) within forty days of birth was described by my male friends—who had to turn to their wives and elder sisters for specific information on the topic—as a symbolic cutting of the skin over the baby's clitoris sufficient to draw a drop of blood, but not as full scale genital excision or clitoridectomy.[38]

There are some other grooming and adornment practices as well which serve to distinguish the Moors from the Tamils. It is considered good (*sunnat*) for Moorish men and women to shave or clip their armpit and pubic hair every forty days in order to ensure that all parts of the body are moistened during bathing to remove

[38] The *Fat-Hud-Dayyān* instructs:

> What is necessary to be done in the case of a male is to have the entire foreskin cut off. What is necessary to be done in the case of a female is to cut off a small bit of the flesh of the cock's-comb-like clitoris that lies above the urinary duct. It is *sunnat* to have the circumcision of a male known, and the circumcision of a female kept secret (Ahmad Lebbai 1873/1963: 479).

A recent wire service story (IPS, 19 Aug. 1997) claims that radical female genital mutilation (clitoridectomy) is practised on forty-day old Muslim girls by *ostā māmis* in the Colombo neighbourhoods of Dematagoda, Maskade, and Maradana, but my information from Colombo Muslim sources does not corroborate this report.

ritual pollution (*mulukku*).[39] Some informants also told me there was a *hadīth* against body hair long enough to grasp. I knew a number of older, more traditional Moorish men in the 1970s (e.g., see Figure 11) who had their heads and armpits shaven monthly by a Moorish barber (*ostā*), while there was no corresponding tonsorial practice among the Tamils apart from shaving the head to fulfil personal Hindu vows. While women of both communities wear pierced earrings, and Tamil women wear nose ornaments, it is *harām* (forbidden in Islam) for Moorish women to pierce the septum. Similarly, unlike traditional Hindu Tamils, Moorish men must not pierce their ears or wear earrings (Ahmad Lebbai 1873/1963: 480).

In the sort of intimate observation which only a few of my closest male Moorish and Tamil friends ventured to offer, it was suggested that the substantive focus of everyday pollution anxiety is somewhat different among the Tamils and Moors. While both communities share an aversion to contact with blood, semen, menstrual and childbirth substances, the Tamils have a marked aversion to saliva (*eccil*) which is not reciprocated as strongly among the Moors. Indeed, some ecstatic Sufi rituals conducted by local Bawas involve the transfer of sacred power to implements of self-mortification from the breath and saliva of the presiding *kalifā* (Bayly 1989: 127–28; McGilvray 1988b). The Moors, on the other hand, seem to have stronger taboos on contact with excreta, especially urine and sexual fluids. Moorish men are taught to take special precautions when they squat to urinate so that no urine touches their sarong or other clothing, a form of contamination which would bar them from the mosque and from Muslim prayers. Some male friends of mine said they would use a porous piece of brick to absorb the last drops of urine. Islamic rules also require a full head-bath not only after, but *between*, all acts of sexual intercourse, a fact which can make it something of an embarrassment when the sound of the well-sweep is heard late at night in Moorish neighbourhoods.

The most frequent complaints I heard from Tamils concerning the Moors as a group were that they were politically unreliable, that they were relatively less educated (which was true earlier in the century, but not now), that they lived in unhealthily overcrowded houses and neighbourhoods (for example, in Kattankudy, the most densely-inhabited town in Sri Lanka), that they ate beef (a source of Hindu regret but not anger), and—admittedly a minor point—that they had a fondness for asphyxiating scents and perfumes (*attar*). The latter is obviously a case of selective criticism, for the Tamils burn strongly aromatic camphor and apply sweet-smelling sandalwood paste in all their Hindu rituals. Māppiḷḷai Ālim's treatise on Muslim practices commends the use of perfume before attending Friday prayers (Ahmad Lebbai 1873/1963: 274), and I found that long-lasting, concentrated *attar* scent was also routinely applied to guests and participants at many other Moorish events in order to enhance the sense of ritual occasion.

[39] *Mulukku* (a Tamil word which also means 'immersion') is the Moorish equivalent of *tutakku*, the common Tamil term for ritual pollution in the Batticaloa region. Arabic Islamic terms such as *najīs* (filth), *janāba* (sexual pollution), and *nifās* (childbirth pollution) are available (Ahmad Lebbai 1873/1963), but are rarely used.

Moorish stereotypes of the Tamils reflected much less voyeuristic concern with the details of grooming and sexual practices. Instead, Moors complained to me about the monopoly of Tamils in the professions and the civil service, a charge more properly directed against the Jaffna Tamils, who have far outnumbered the local Batticaloa Tamils in these career paths. Moors would acknowledge that, until recent decades, the Tamils had been better educated, both in traditional Tamil culture as well as in the modern professions, but they resented the Tamils' unnecessary arrogance and ingrained attitudes of superiority. Moors attributed much of this to the rigidity of the Hindu caste system and to the inegalitarian hierarchical frame of mind upon which it is based. All Muslims, they assured me, are equal before Allah. Although my fieldwork eventually turned up some very small hereditarily ranked endogamous Moorish sub-groups (*Ostā* barber-circumcisers, *Maulānā* Sayyids), the claim of broad ritual equality among the Moors is indeed valid. In a town like Akkaraipattu, however, wealth differences seem more pronounced among the Muslims than among the Tamils.[40] Tamils are stigmatised in the eyes of the Moors for their propensity to waste time and money drinking alcohol, although some Moors are also known to imbibe surreptitiously on occasion. Finally, although they had little eyewitness knowledge of these matters, the Moors' opinion of Hindu religious practices was uniformly negative. Tamil Saivism was criticised for being polytheistic, idolatrous, and demonic, and for not being a prophetic Religion of the Book. On this issue, the local Muslims and the Christians definitely saw eye to eye.

Communal disturbances in the Batticaloa region

Popular memory recounts the many localised Tamil–Moor riots and disturbances (*kuḻapppam*, 'mix-up', *caṇṭai*, 'fight') which have plagued communal relations on the east coast throughout the 20th century and probably earlier.[41] Although I directly witnessed no local Tamil–Moor violence, I did gather oral accounts of such outbreaks. One type of incident was the post-election reprisal, typically an attack upon members of the opposite community for failure to deliver blocs of votes which had been purchased in advance with money or arrack (and sometimes purchased twice, by different candidates!). A second type of conflict would arise from an individual provocation, which was perceived as a generalised insult to the entire Tamil or Moorish community. When, for example, in the late 1960s a drunken Moorish man allegedly snipped off the braided hair of a Tamil woman who had spurned his advances in public, an innocent Moorish bystander soon lost his ear, and there were communal ambushes and roadblocks for a week. A year or so later, Moorish youths organised Akkaraipattu's very first Gandhian-inspired Shramadana community self-help project: a new road allowing Moorish cultivators

40 Neighbouring Muslim towns such as Nintavur and Sammanturai are said to have even greater concentrations of landed wealth in the hands of Moorish *pōṭiyārs*.

41 Interestingly enough, E.B. Denham, the Government Agent in Batticaloa, reported 'no trouble of any kind in this Province' at the time of the 1915 Sinhala–Muslim riots (Denham 1915: E5).

to circumambulate Tamil villages to evade ambush whenever they travel to their fields during future communal riots.

A third type of violence was related to a growing competition for land, including residential building sites. The historical tendency over the last 150 years has been for successful Moors to expand their agricultural landholdings and businesses, while upwardly mobile Tamils have favoured education and a career in the professions. Recognising the gradual decline in Tamil-owned paddy fields, the Tamils are now chagrined and resentful. Because of the determination of Moors to reside together in established Muslim enclaves, the pressure on adjoining Tamil neighbourhoods has resulted in both irresistible buy-outs and violent evictions of Tamil residents by their Moorish neighbours. For example, lower-caste Tamils have been forcibly driven out of their neighbourhoods in the Kalmunai–Sainthamaruthu area, and Moors have quickly moved in (UTHR Report 7, 1991: 49–55; and my own fieldnotes).

Based upon accounts of Hindu–Muslim rioting in North India, I had initially assumed that Tamil–Moorish conflicts in Sri Lanka would be sparked by religious provocations: Muslim cow slaughter, Hindu processions near mosques, and the like. However, the actual incidents I recorded suggest that 'religious' issues have never been a frequent trigger, not even a major underlying cause, of local Moorish/Tamil violence on the east coast. Even when religious sites have been targeted, such as the destruction of the Bhadrakali Hindu temple in Akkaraipattu by Muslims (with the acquiescence of the Sri Lankan Army) after the withdrawal of the Indian Peace-Keeping Force in 1989, the underlying motive appears to have been a desire to expand the boundaries of the Moorish residential neighbourhood near which the temple was situated.[42] With the upsurge of warfare between Tamil guerrillas and Sri Lankan armed forces in the region since 1983, Moorish seizure of agricultural lands abandoned by fleeing Tamil refugees and reprisal depredation by Tamils of exposed Moorish fields have further enflamed the inter-ethnic situation (UTHR Report 7,1991; Report 11, 1993).

Difficult as it is to take a longer view of such events, they must nevertheless be understood as part of the gradual emancipation of the Moorish community from the thraldom of pre-modern Tamil Hindu political domination, caste hierarchies, and feudalistic land tenure systems in this region (McGilvray 1982c, and book manuscript in progress). Nowadays the Moors enjoy a degree of economic prosperity and political independence from the Tamils that would have been impossible to imagine a century earlier. The wealthier, higher-caste Tamils are particularly aware of this trend, which represents the loss—or the increasing irrelevance—of their hereditary status privileges. The Moors are fully aware that many high-caste Tamils still look down upon them as their recent inferiors, and this has spurred the younger and more professionally-oriented Moors to strive for modern careers and avenues of self-respect quite independent of the Tamils.

[42] Fieldwork in Akkaraipattu in 1993 revealed that the temple I had studied intensively in the 1970s is now totally demolished. Cattle bones have been tossed into the temple well to pollute the site and to discourage the Tamils from rebuilding the temple at the same location. A land sale was one of the few options available to the temple trustees (McGilvray 1997b).

More recently, the deliberate provocation of intercommunal violence by those seeking to block the creation of any east coast Tamil–Moorish political alliance, as well as massacres and reprisals against members of both ethnic communities arising from differences over Tamil Eelam and the future of the north-eastern region, have established a climate of hatred and distrust which may poison Tamil–Moorish intercommunal amity for years to come (UTHR Report 10, 1993). The depth of misunderstanding and miscalculation was illustrated by a speech given in 1990 by Tamil Tiger spokesman Y. Yogi, scolding the Moors for failing to properly identity themselves as Tamils and justifying the mass expulsion of Muslims from Jaffna and Mannar by the LTTE as punishment for their alleged ethnic betrayal. Tragically, this was Ponnambalam Ramanathan's 1888 'ethnological' thesis yet again, but this time enforced with Kalashnikov rifles and a brutal agenda of ethnic cleansing.[43]

V

Options for the future

A low point in Muslim–Tamil relations definitely occurred in 1990, but to leave the story there would be, I think, too pessimistic. Cultural membership is always contextual and historically conditioned, and a great deal of new history is presently being made in Sri Lanka. We have already seen that Muslims in three neighbouring regions of the subcontinent were capable of forging divergent cultural styles, ethnic identities, and political strategies over the past four centuries: violent *jihād* in Kerala, literary and spiritual synthesis in Tamilnadu, 'non-Tamil' political ethnicity in Sri Lanka. Several modern observers have suggested that for all the demographic, political, and cultural reasons enumerated above, the Moors of Sri Lanka are now starting to differentiate themselves into several distinct subregional identities within the island, the most significant of which would distinguish the one-third of all Muslims concentrated in the agricultural north-east from the remaining two-thirds who live widely dispersed in the Sinhalese areas of the south-west (Ali 1992b; Ismail 1995; Sivathamby 1987).

It was the 19th and 20th century British colonial regime which provided tangible political rewards for establishing a 'racial' distinction between Moor and Tamil, thus defining the competitive arenas within which modern communal politics in Sri Lanka would be forged. After Independence came the 'interactive ethnonationalism' of Sinhalese majoritarian politics (Hennayake 1992) and shrewd accommodations by the Muslim elite defending its west-coast urban interests within Sinhala

[43] 'Muslims claim that they are neither Sinhalese nor Tamils, but are Arabs. They use this in pursuit of their selfish aims.... They are Tamils. They study in Tamil at Tamil schools. Their culture is not Arab.... We did not rape them or loot their property. We only sent them out. ... We made several promises to the Muslims.... On the contrary, they joined forces with the Sinhalese army and the Sri Lankan state and set about destroying us.... The Muslims must accept that they are Tamils. They must understand that they are descendants of Arabs who married Tamil women' (UTHR Report 7, 1991: 42–43).

For a discussion of LTTE expulsion of Muslims from the Northern Province, see Hennayake (1993) and Hasbullah (1996). For an ominous reiteration of this ultimatum to the Moors, see Mohamed (1996).

society. During the Eelam Wars of the past two decades, calculated acts of inter-ethnic sabotage by government forces and by Tamil militants have intentionally widened the division between the Moors and the Tamils into a political chasm. Yet, despite unforgivable atrocities on all sides, the general awareness of this sad history is by now so widely shared, and the sheer terror and exhaustion of the Eelam conflict is so desperately felt in the eastern war zone, that the basis for a pragmatic rapprochement between the Tamils and Moors of the Batticaloa region may still be possible (Lawrence 1997, 1998, and in press; McGilvray 1997b; Schrijvers 1998; see Krishna 1994 for a more pessimistic view).

The original Federal Party slogan of S.J.V. Chelvanayagam who sought to unite all of Sri Lanka's 'Tamil-speaking peoples' under one political umbrella was scornfully rejected by earlier Colombo-based Moorish leaders such as Sir Razik Fareed, even though there is a great deal of Tamil poetry, folklore, and religious literature by Sri Lankan Muslims from Batticaloa, Jaffna, Mannar, and elsewhere (Kandiah 1964; Saleem 1990; Sivathamby 1987; Uwise 1986, 1990). In fact, when the Eelam War first broke out in the 1980s, Tamil militant groups, including the LTTE, were able to recruit and train a significant cohort of Muslim fighters from the Eastern and Northern Provinces on the basis of regional loyalty to the idea of a 'Tamil-speaking' homeland. This militant collaboration between Tamil and Muslim youths, with its echo of the historic Moor–Mukkuvar alliance celebrated in Batticaloa legend, was shattered in 1990 when the eastern command of the LTTE, acting on local enmities and resentments, launched a series of attacks and pogroms against Muslims, including the well-publicised Kattankudy Mosque massacre (McGilvray 1997b; Sivaram 1991, 1992). Muslim cadres abruptly fled the LTTE organisation, and there seemed no hope for further dialogue.

Despite this profound Tamil betrayal, the pragmatic needs of local Muslim traders and the geographical vulnerability of both Tamils and Moors to mutual retribution soon resulted in a series of private contacts and locally-based understandings between the LTTE and Moorish village leaders and merchants which continue to the present. At the same time, working against the reestablishment of Tamil–Muslim cordiality are the various armed and thuggish 'ex-militant' 'Tamil groups (e.g., PLOTE, TELO, EPRLF) who implement the Sri Lankan Security Forces' strategy of divide and rule in the Batticaloa region (Krishna 1994: 312). At a broader level, one of the perennial obstacles to a parliamentary accord between the Muslim SLMC and the Tamil TULF parties has been the lack of minority safeguards and explicitly defined territorial rights for the Muslims within a larger federated Tamil region (Sivathamby 1987). Recently, in 1997, there were some signs of movement toward the creation of the first Moorish-majority district in Sri Lanka stretching from Kalmunai to Pottuvil in the south-eastern part of the island, just as the Māppiḷas of Kerala had carved out the newly created Mallapuram District for themselves in 1969.

At this late date, the distinct 'non-Tamil' ethnic ideology of the Moorish establishment and their fifty-year record of political collaboration with the main

Sinhalese parties, coupled with the uncompromising, short-sighted, and brutal militancy of the Tamil guerrillas, have made a rapprochement based upon a recognition of Tamil and Moorish cultural affinities and common interests on the east coast extremely difficult to achieve. First colonially-engineered competition, then ethnic party politics, and eventually civil war, have preempted whatever goodwill might have developed between the two groups under more foresighted leadership. However, because their common geohistorical destiny offers them little choice, the Tamils and Moors in the eastern Batticaloa region may eventually come to a renewed appreciation of their shared cultural roots, as well as an honest appraisal of their past prejudices. The cultural, political, and economic basis for a lasting inter-ethnic community of interest between the Tamils and the Moors is still there, at least in the geographically delimited eastern coastal region, but in the wake of massacres and reprisals, expulsions, displacements, land thefts, and masked betrayals, both deep compassion and true ethnic statesmanship on all sides will be needed to nurture it.

REFERENCES

ABEYASINGHE, T.B.H. 1986. Muslims in Sri Lanka in the sixteenth and seventeenth centuries. *In* M.A.M. Shukri, ed., *Muslims of Sri Lanka: Avenues to antiquity*, pp. 129–45. Beruwala, Sri Lanka: Jamiah, Naleemia Institute.

ABDUL MAJEED, O. 1971. *The learned Ceylon Muslims' opinion on Ahmadiyya movement* (Pamphlet). Colombo: Ceylon Ahmadiyya Muslim Association.

ABOOSALLY, M.L.M. 1975. Did Shayk Abdul Kader Jilani visit Adam's Peak in Sri Lanka? *The Muslim digest* (South Africa) September–October 1975: 167–70.

AHMAD LEBBAI, SEYYID MUHAMMAD IBN. 1963. *Fat-Hud-Dayyān: Fi Fiqhi Khairil Adyan* (A compendium on Muslim theology and jurisprudence) (trans. Saifuddin J. Aniff-Doray). Colombo: Fat-Hud-Dayyan Publication Committee. First published in Arabic–Tamil in 1873.

AL-ṬABARĪ, ABŪ JA'FAR MUHAMMAD B. JARĪR. 1989. *The history of al-Ṭabarī*, vol. 1: *General introduction and from the Creation to the Flood* (trans. Franz Rosenthal). Albany: State University of New York Press.

ALI, A.C.L. AMEER. 1980. Some aspects of religio-economic precepts and practices in Islam: A case study of the Muslim community in Ceylon during the period c. 1800–1915. Unpublished Ph.D. thesis, Perth: University of Western Australia.

———. 1981a. The genesis of the Muslim community in Ceylon (Sri Lanka): A historical summary. *Asian studies* 19: 65–82.

———. 1981b. The 1815 racial riots in Ceylon (Sri Lanka): A reappraisal of its causes. *South Asia* 4: 1–20.

———. 1984. Muslims and Sri Lanka's ethnic troubles. *Muslim world league journal* Aug–Sept. 1984: 55–58.

———. 1986–87. Politics of survival: Past strategies and present predicament of the Muslim community in Sri Lanka. *Journal institute of Muslim minority affairs* 7–8: 147–70.

———. 1992a. The quest for cultural identity and material advancement: Parallels and contrasts in Muslim minority experience in secular India and Buddhist Sri Lanka. *Journal institute of Muslim minority affairs* 13, 1: 33–58.

———. 1992b. Sri Lanka's ethnic war: The Muslim dimension. *Pravāda* 1, 11: 5–7. (Reprinted in *Tamil times*, 15 November 1992, pp. 13–14, 16.)

ANIFF, FAREED. 1990. They drive spikes into their heads. *Weekend* magazine, 6 April 1990. Colombo.

ARASARATNAM, SINNAPPAH. 1964. *Ceylon*. Englewood, NJ: Prentice-Hall.

ASAD, M.N.M. 1993. *The Muslims of Sri Lanka under British rule*. New Delhi: Navrang.

———. 1994. Muslim education in Sri Lanka: The British colonial period. *Journal institute of Muslim minority affairs* 14, 1&2: 35–45.

AZEEZ, I.L.M. ABDUL. 1907. A criticism of Mr. Ramanathan's 'Ethnology of the "Moors" of Ceylon'. Colombo: Moors' Union (reprinted 1957, Colombo: Moors' Islamic Cultural Home).

BAWA, AHAMADU. 1888. The marriage customs of the Moors of Ceylon. *Journal of the Royal Asiatic Society, Ceylon branch* 10, 36: 219–33.

BAYLY, SUSAN. 1986. Islam in southern India: 'Purist' or 'syncretic'? *In* C.A. Bayly and D.H.A. Kolff, eds, *Two colonial empires: Comparative essays on the history of India and Indonesia in the nineteenth century*, pp. 35–73. Dordrecht: Martinus Nijhoff.

———. 1989. *Saints, goddesses, and kings: Muslims and Christians in south Indian society, 1700–1900*. Cambridge: Cambridge University Press.

BOSE, SUGATA, ed. 1990. *South Asia and world capitalism*. New Delhi: Oxford University Press.

BOUCHON, GENEVIEVE. 1973. Les Musulmans du Kerala à l'epoque de la dècouverte Portugaise. *Mare Luso-Indicum* 2: 3–59.

CASIE CHITTY, SIMON. 1834. *The Ceylon gazetteer*. Ceylon: Cotta Church Mission Press (Reprinted 1989). New Delhi: Navrang.

———. 1853–1855. An analysis of the great historical poem of the Moors, entitled 'Seerah'. *Journal of the Royal Asiatic Society, Ceylon branch* 2: 90–102.

CUTLER, NORMAN. 1983. The fish-eyed goddess meets the movie star: An eyewitness account of the Fifth International Tamil Conference. *Pacific affairs* 56: 270–87.

D'SOUZA, VICTOR S. 1955. *The Navayats of Kanara: A study in culture contact*. K.R.I. monographs series 3. Dharwar: Kannada Research Institute.

———. 1959. Social organization and marriage customs of the Moplahs on the south-west coast of India. *Anthropos* 54: 487–516.

———. 1973. Status groups among the Moplahs on the south-west coast of India. *In* Imtiaz Ahmad, ed., *Caste and social stratification among the Muslims*, pp. 45–60. Delhi: Manohar.

DALE, STEPHEN FREDERIC. 1980. *The Māppiḷas of Malabar, 1498–1922: Islamic society on the South Asian frontier*. Oxford: Clarendon Press.

DALE, STEPHEN FREDERIC and M. GANGADHARA MENON. 1978. Nērccas: Saint-martyr worship among the Muslims of Kerala. *Bulletin of the School of Oriental and African Studies* 41: 523–38 (Reprinted in Asghar Ali Engineer, ed., 1995. *Kerala Muslims: A historical perspective*, pp. 174–99. Delhi: Ajanta Publications).

DE GRAEUWE, PIETER. 1676. Memorial of Pieter de Graeuwe to his successor Jan Blommert, 8 April 1676 (in Dutch). V.O.C. 1.14.17, Hoge Regering Batavia, 545. Den Haag: Algemene Rijksarchief.

DE JONG, FRED. 1986. Note sur les confréries soufies à Sri Lanka. *In* André Popovic and Gilles Veinstein, eds, *Les ordres mystiques das l'Islam: Cheminements et situation actuelle*, pp. 135–37. Recherches d'histoire et de sciences sociales 13. Paris: Editions de l'Ecole des Hautes Etudes en Sciences Sociales.

DE MUNCK, VICTOR C. 1993. *Seasonal cycles: A study of social change and continuity in a Sri Lankan village*. New Delhi and Madras: Asian Educational Services.

———. 1996. Love and marriage in a Sri Lankan Muslim community: Toward a reevaluation of Dravidian marriage practices. *American ethnologist* 23, 4: 698–716.

DENHAM, E.B. 1912. *Ceylon at the census of 1911*. Colombo: H.C. Cottle, Government Printer.

———. 1915. Report of Mr. E.B. Denham, Government Agent. Administration Reports, 1915. Part 1. Civil-Provincial Administration. Eastern Province. Ceylon.

DE SILVA, C.R. 1968. Portuguese policy towards the Muslims in Ceylon, 1505–1626. *Proceedings of the First International Conference Seminar of Tamil Studies, Kuala Lumpur 1966*, pp. 113–19. Kuala Lumpur: International Association for Tamil Research.

———. 1972. *The Portuguese in Ceylon, 1617–1638*. Colombo: H.W. Cave.

DE SILVA, KINGSLEY M. 1986a. The Muslim minority in a democratic polity—the case of Sri Lanka: Reflections on a theme. *In* M.A.M. Shukri, ed., *Muslims of Sri Lanka: Avenues to antiquity*, pp. 443–52. Beruwala, Sri Lanka: Jamiah Naleemia Institute.

DE SILVA, KINGSLEY M. 1986b. Muslim leaders and the nationalist movement. *In* M.A.M. Shukri, ed., *Muslims of Sri Lanka: Avenues to antiquity*, pp. 453–72. Beruwala, Sri Lanka: Jamiah Naleemia Institute.

———. 1988. Sri Lanka's Muslim minority. *In* K.M. de Silva, Pensri Duke, Ellen S. Goldberg and Nathan Katz, eds, *Ethnic conflict in Buddhist societies: Sri Lanka, Thailand and Burma*, pp. 202–14. Boulder: Westview.

———. 1994. *The "traditional homelands" of the Tamils, separatist ideology in Sri Lanka: A historical appraisal* (revised 2nd edn). Kandy, Sri Lanka: International Centre for Ethnic Studies.

———. 1997. Multi-culturalism in Sri Lanka: Historical legacy and contemporary political reality. *Ethnic studies report* 15, 1: 1–44.

DEWARAJA, LORNA. 1986. The Muslims in the Kandyan kingdom (c. 1600–1815): A study of ethnic integration. *In* M.A.M. Shukri, ed., *Muslims of Sri Lanka: Avenues to antiquity*, pp. 211–34. Beruwala, Sri Lanka: Jamiah Naleemia Institute.

———. 1995. The indigenisation of the Muslims of Sri Lanka. *In* G.P.S.H. de Silva and C.G. Uragoda, eds, *Sesquicentennial commemorative volume of the Royal Asiatic Society of Sri Lanka, 1845–1995*, pp. 427–39. Colombo: Royal Asiatic Society of Sri Lanka.

EFFENDI, MOHAMED SAMEER BIN HAJIE ISMAIL. 1965. Archaeological evidence of early Arabs in Ceylon. *Moors' Islamic Cultural Home, The first twenty-one years*. Anniversary souvenir, pp. 31–38. Colombo: Moors' Islamic Cultural Home.

FAIRSERVIS, WALTER A. and FRANKLIN C. SOUTHWORTH. 1989. Linguistic archaeology and the Indus valley culture. *In* Jonathan M. Kenoyer, ed., *Old problems and new perspectives in the archeology of South Asia*. Wisconsin archaeological reports 2: 133–41. Madison: University of Wisconsin.

FANSELOW, FRANK S. 1989. Muslim society in Tamil Nadu (India): An historical perspective. *Journal institute of Muslim minority affairs* 10, 1: 264–89.

———. 1996. The disinvention of caste among Tamil Muslims. *In* C.J. Fuller, ed., *Caste today*, pp. 202–26. Delhi: Oxford University Press.

GABRIEL, THEODORE P.C. 1989. *Lakshadweep: History, religion and society*. New Delhi: Books & Books.

———. 1996. *Hindu–Muslim relations in North Malabar*, 1498–1947. Lewiston, NY: Edwin Mellen Press.

GOPALAN, T.N. 1998. Muslims, friendless in Tamilnadu? *Tamil Times* 17, 4: 27–29.

GOUGH, KATHLEEN. 1961. Mappilla: North Kerala. *In* David Schneider and Kathleen Gough, eds, *Matrilineal kinship.*, pp. 415–42. Berkeley: University of California Press.

GUNAWARDANA, R.A.L.H. 1990. The people of the lion: The Sinhala identity and ideology in history and historiography. *In* Jonathan Spencer, ed., *Sri Lanka: History and the roots of conflict*, pp. 45–86. London and New York: Routledge.

HASAN, MUSHIRUL. 1997. *Legacy of a divided nation: India's Muslims since independence*. Boulder: Westview Press.

HASBULLAH, S.H. 1996. *Refugees are people*. Proceedings of the workshop on the Resettlement Program for the Forcibly Evicted Muslims of the Northern Province, Sri Lanka. Puttalam, 13–14 January 1996. Colombo: Northern Muslims' Rights Organization.

HASSAN, M.C.A. 1968. *Sir Razik Fareed*. Colombo: Sir Razik Fareed Foundation.

HELLMAN-RAJANAYAGAM, DAGMAR. 1995. Is there a Tamil race? *In* Peter Robb, ed., *The concept of race in South Asia*, pp. 109–45. Delhi: Oxford University Press.

HENNAYAKE, SHANTHA K. 1992. Interactive ethnonationalism: An alternative explanation of minority ethnonationalism. *Political geography* 11, 6: 526–49.

———. 1993. Sri Lanka in 1992: Opportunity missed in the ethno-nationalist crisis. *Asian survey* 33, 2: 157–64.

HENNAYAKE, SHANTHA K. n.d. The Muslim community in the ethnonationalist crisis of Sri Lanka. Department of Geography, Peradeniya University, Sri Lanka. Ms.

HERRING, RONALD J. 1991. From structural conflict to agrarian stalemate: Agrarian reforms in South India. *Journal of Asian and African studies* 26, 3–4: 169–88.

HUSSAINMIYA, B.A. 1986. Princes and soldiers: The antecedents of the Sri Lankan Malays. *In* M.A.M. Shukri, ed., *Muslims of Sri Lanka: Avenues to antiquity*, pp. 279–309. Beruwala, Sri Lanka: Jamiah Naleemia Institute.

IBRAHIM KUNJU, A.P. 1989. *Mappila Muslims of Kerala: Their history and culture*. Trivandrum: Sandhya Publications.

———. 1995. Origin and spread of Islam in Kerala. *In* Ali Asghar Engineer, ed., *Kerala Muslims: A historical perspective*, pp. 17–34. Delhi: Ajanta.

INDRAPALA, K. 1986. The role of peninsular Indian Muslim trading communities in the Indian Ocean trade. *In* M.A.M. Shukri, ed., *Muslims of Sri Lanka: Avenues to antiquity*, pp. 113–27. Beruwala, Sri Lanka: Jamiah Naleemia Institute.

ISMAIL, QADRI. 1995. Unmooring identity: The antinomies of elite Muslim self-representation in modern Sri Lanka. *In* Pradeep Jeganathan and Qadri Ismail, eds, *Unmaking the nation: The politics of identity and history in modern Sri Lanka*, pp. 55–105. Colombo: Social Scientists' Association.

JACKSON, K. DAVID. 1990. *Sing without shame: Oral traditions in Indo-Portuguese creole verse*. Amsterdam, Philadelphia & Macau: John Benjamins Publishing & Instituto Cultural de Macau.

KADRAMER, D.W.N. 1934. *Landmarks of ancient Batticaloa and other contributions to the Ceylon press*. Batticaloa, Sri Lanka: Catholic Orphanage Press.

KANDIAH, V.C. 1964. *Maṭṭakkaḷapput tamiḻakkam* (Batticaloa Tamil Homeland). Jaffna: Īḻakēcari Ponnaiyā Ninaivu Veḷiyīṭṭu Maṉṟam.

KEARNEY, ROBERT N. 1987. Territorial elements of Tamil separatism in Sri Lanka. *Pacific affairs* 60, 4: 561–77.

KIRIBAMUNE, SIRIMA. 1986. Muslims and the trade of the Arabian Sea with special reference to Sri Lanka from the birth of Islam to the fifteenth century. *In* M.A.M. Shukri, ed., *Muslims of Sri Lanka: Avenues to antiquity*, pp. 89–112. Beruwala, Sri Lanka: Jamiah Naleemia Institute.

KRISHNA, SANKARAN. 1994. Notes on a trip to the Eastern Province, June 25 to June 29, 1994. *Serendipity* 7: 301–303. Sri Lanka Academic Interests Group.

KURUKULASURIYA, G.I.O.M., ABDUL GAFOOR and M.A.M. HUSSEIN. 1988. *The Muslim community of Sri Lanka* (reprint of a study prepared for the Dr. Shaikh Shams Al-Fassi Foundation of Sri Lanka in 1984–85). Colombo: Marga Institute.

KUTTY, A.R. 1972. *Marriage and kinship in an island society.* Delhi: National.

LAWRENCE, PATRICIA. 1997. The changing amman: Notes on the injury of war in eastern Sri Lanka. *South Asia* 20: 215–36.

———. 1998. Grief on the body: The work of oracles in eastern Sri Lanka. *In* Michael Roberts, ed., *Collective identities revisited*, vol. 2, pp. 271–94. Delhi: Navrang.

———. In press. Violence, suffering, amman: The work of oracles in Sri Lanka's eastern war zone. *In* Veena Das, Arthur Kleinman, Mamphela Ramphele, and Pamela Reynolds, eds, *Violence, political agency, and the self.* Berkeley and London: University of California Press.

MACPHERSON, KENNETH. 1969. The social background and politics of the Muslims of Tamil Nad, 1901–1937. *Indian economic and social history review* 6: 381–402.

MACREADY, W.C. 1888–89. The jungles of Rajavanni Pattu and the ceremony of passing through the fire. *The orientalist* 3: 188–93.

MAHROOF, M.M.M. 1986a. Muslim social organisation. *In* M.M.M. Mahroof, Marina Azeez, M.M. Uwise, H.M.Z. Farouque and M.J.A. Rahim, *An ethnological survey of the Muslims of Sri Lanka from earliest times to Independence*, pp. 125–44. Colombo: Sir Razik Fareed Foundation.

———. 1986b. British rule and the Muslims (1800–1900). *In* M.M.M. Mahroof, et al., *An ethnological survey of the Muslims of Sri Lanka from earliest times to Independence*, pp. 61–95. Colombo: Sir Razik Fareed Foundation.

———. 1986c. Muslim education. *In* M.M.M. Mahroof, et al., *An ethnological survey of the Muslims of Sri Lanka from earliest times to Independence*, pp. 166–82. Colombo: Sir Razik Fareed Foundation.

MAHROOF, M.M.M. 1990. Muslims in Sri Lanka: The long road to accommodation. *Journal institute of Muslim minority affairs* 11, 1: 88–99.

———. 1991. Mendicants and troubadours: Toward a historical taxonomy of the faqirs of Sri Lanka. *Islamic studies* 30: 501–16.

———. 1994. Community of Sri Lankan Malays: Notes toward a socio-historical analysis. *Journal institute of Muslim minority affairs* 14, 1&2: 143–55.

MAHROOF, M.M.M., MARINA AZEEZ, M.M. UWISE, H.M.Z. FAROUQUE and M.J.A. RAHIM. 1986. *An ethnological survey of the Muslims of Sri Lanka from earliest times to Independence.* Colombo: Sir Razik Fareed Foundation.

MANI, A. 1992. Aspects of identity and change among Tamil Muslims in Singapore. *Journal institute of Muslim minority affairs* 13, 2: 337–57.

MANOGARAN, CHELVADURAI. 1987. *Ethnic conflict and reconciliation in Sri Lanka.* Honolulu: University of Hawaii Press.

MARIKAR, A.I.L., A.L.M. LAFIR and A.H. MACAN MARKAR, eds. 1976. *Glimpses of the past of the Moors of Sri Lanka.* Colombo: Moors' Islamic Cultural Home.

MAUROOF, MOHAMMED. 1972. Aspects of religion, economy, and society among the Muslims of Ceylon. *Contributions to Indian sociology* 6: 66–83 (reprinted in T.N. Madan, ed., 1976. *Muslim communities of South Asia: Culture and society*, pp. 66–83. New Delhi: Vikas).

———. 1986. A sociology of Muslims in southern India and Sri Lanka. *In* M.A.M. Shukri, ed., *Muslims of Sri Lanka: Avenues to antiquity*, pp. 319–36. Beruwala, Sri Lanka: Jamiah Naleemia Institute.

MCGILVRAY, DENNIS B. 1974. Tamils and Moors: Caste and matriclan structure in eastern Sri Lanka. Unpublished Ph.D. thesis, University of Chicago.

———. 1982a. Dutch Burghers and Portuguese mechanics: Eurasian ethnicity in Sri Lanka. *Comparative studies in society and history* 24, 1: 235–63.

———. 1982b. Sexual power and fertility in Sri Lanka: Batticaloa Tamils and Moors. *In* Carol P. MacCormack, ed., *Ethnography of fertility and birth*, pp. 25–73. London: Academic Press (2nd edn 1994. Prospect Heights: Waveland Press. pp. 15–63).

———. 1982c. Mukkuvar vannimai: Tamil caste and matriclan structure in Batticaloa, Sri Lanka. *In* D.B. McGilvray, ed., *Caste ideology and interaction*, pp. 34–97. Cambridge papers in social anthropology 9. Cambridge University Press.

———. 1983. Paraiyar drummers of Sri Lanka: Consensus and constraint in an untouchable caste. *American ethnologist* 10: 97–115.

———. 1988a. The 1987 Stirling Award essay: Sex, repression, and Sanskritization in Sri Lanka? *Ethos* 16, 2: 99–127.

———. 1988b. Village Sufism in Sri Lanka: An ethnographic report. *La transmission du savoir dans le monde musulman peripherique*, pp. 1–12. Lettre d'information 8. Programme de recherches interdisciplinaires sur le monde musulman peripherique. Paris: Ecole des Hautes Etudes en Sciences Sociales.

———. 1989. Households in Akkaraipattu: Dowry and domestic organization among the matrilineal Tamils and Moors of Sri Lanka. *In* John N. Gray and David J. Mearns, eds, *Society from the inside out: Anthropological perspectives on the South Asian household.* pp. 192–235. New Delhi, Newbury Park, & London: Sage Publications.

———. 1997a. Sufi circuits in/to Sri Lanka. Paper presented at the 26th Annual Conference on South Asia, University of Wisconsin-Madison. 16–19 October 1997.

———. 1997b. Tamils and Muslims in the shadow of war: Schism or continuity? *South Asia* 20: 239–53.

———. 1998. *Symbolic heat: Gender, health, and worship among the Tamils of South India and Sri Lanka.* Ahmedabad: Mapin.

MILLER, ROLAND E. 1976. *Mappila Muslims of Kerala: A study in Islamic trends.* Madras: Orient Longman.

MINES, MATTISON. 1972. *Muslim merchants: The economic behaviour of an Indian Muslim community.* New Delhi: Shri Ram Centre for Industrial Relations and Human Resources.

MINES, MATTISON. 1973. Social stratification among Muslim Tamils in Tamilnadu, South India. *In* Imtiaz Ahmed, ed., *Caste and social stratification among the Muslims*, pp. 61–71. Delhi: Manohar.

———. 1981. Islamization and Muslim ethnicity in South India. *In* Imtiaz Ahmad, ed., *Ritual and religion among Muslims in India*, pp. 65–90. New Delhi: Manohar.

———. 1983. Kin centres and ethnicity among Muslim Tamilians. *In* Imtiaz Ahmad, ed., *Modernization and social change among Muslims in India*, pp. 99–118. New Delhi: Manohar.

MOHAMED, PEER. 1996. Tamil Muslims and Tamil Eelam. *Proceedings of the international conference on the conflict in Sri Lanka: Peace with justice*. 27–28 June 1996. Canberra, Australia. http://www.tamilnet.com/conference_papers/pwj/

MOHAN, R. VASUNDHARA. 1987. *Identity crisis of Sri Lankan Muslims*. Delhi: Mittal.

MOHIDEEN, M.I.M. 1986. *Sri Lanka Muslims and ethnic grievances*. Colombo: M.I.M. Mohideen.

MOHIDEEN, M.Z. 1965. The "kudi" maraikayars of Batticaloa south. *Moors' Islamic Cultural Home: The first twenty-one years*, pp. 25–27.

MOORS' ISLAMIC CULTURAL HOME. 1965. *Moors' Islamic Cultural Home: The first twenty-one years*. Colombo, Sri Lanka

———. 1970. *Moors' Islamic Cultural Home: Silver jubilee souvenir, 1944–1969*. Colombo, Sri Lanka.

———. 1978. *Moors' Islamic Cultural Home: Souvenir III, 1970–76*. Colombo, Sri Lanka.

———. 1983. *Moors' Islamic Cultural Home: Souvenir IV, 1977–1982*. Colombo, Sri Lanka.

———. 1994. *Moors' Islamic Cultural Home: Golden jubilee souvenir, 1944–1994*. Colombo, Sri Lanka.

MORE, J.B.P. 1991. The Marakkayar Muslims of Karikal, South India. *Journal of Islamic studies* 2: 25–44.

———. 1993a. Tamil Muslims and non-Brahmin atheists, 1925–1940. *Contributions to Indian sociology* 27: 83–104.

———. 1993b. Muslim evolution and conversions in Karikal, South India. *Islam and Christian–Muslim relations* 4, 1: 65–82.

———. 1997. *The political evolution of Muslims in Tamilnadu and Madras, 1930–1947*. Hyderabad: Orient Longman.

MUJAHID, ABDUL MALIK. 1989. *Conversion to Islam: Untouchables' strategy for protest in India*. Chambersburg, PA: Anima Publications.

NAMBIAR, O.K. 1963. *The Kunjalis, admirals of Calicut*. London: Asia Publishing House.

NAMBIAR, P.K. and K.C. NARAYANA KURUP. 1968. Festival of Saint Ouadar Wali at Nagore. *Census of India 1961*, vol. IX. Madras, Part VII–B fairs and festivals, pp. 59–60 plus 8 pages of photographs.

NARAYAN, M.T. 1995. Kunjalis—the Muslim admirals of Calicut. *In* Asghar Ali Engineer, ed., *Kerala Muslims: A historical perspective*, pp. 91–102. Delhi: Ajanta.

NEVILLE, HUGH. 1887. Nāṭu Kāṭu record. *The Taprobanian*. August 1887: 127–28. October 1887: 137–41.

NISSAN, ELIZABETH. 1996. *Sri Lanka: A bitter harvest*. London: Minority Rights Group International.

NISSAN, ELIZABETH and R.L. STIRRAT. 1990. The generation of communal identities. *In* Jonathan Spencer, ed., *Sri Lanka: History and the roots of conflict*, pp.19–44. London and New York: Routledge.

OBEYESEKERE, GANANATH. 1984. *The cult of the goddess Pattini*. Chicago: University of Chicago Press.

OSSMAN, M.S. 1990. Status of Malays in Sri Lanka past–present. *Challenge for change: Profile of a community*, pp. 32–42. Colombo: Muslim Women's Research and Action Front.

O'SULLIVAN, MEGHAN. 1997. Conflict as a catalyst: The changing politics of the Sri Lankan Muslims. *South Asia* 20: 281–308.

PADMANABHA MENON, K. P. 1924. *A history of Kerala*, vol. 1. Ernakulam: Cochin Govt. Press.

PANDIAN, JACOB. 1987. *Caste, nationalism and ethnicity: An interpretation of Tamil cultural history and social order*. Bombay: Popular Prakashan.

PATHMANATHAN, S. 1976. The Nāṭu Kāṭu Paravaṇi Kalveṭṭu. *Maṭṭakkaḷappu makānāṭu ninaivu malar*. Batticaloa, Sri Lanka: International Association of Tamil Research Sri Lanka National Unit.

PEEBLES, PATRICK. 1990. Colonization and ethnic conflict in the Dry Zone of Sri Lanka. *Journal of Asian studies* 49, 1: 30–55.

PHADNIS, URMILA. 1979. Political profile of the Muslim minority of Sri Lanka. *International studies* 18: 27–48.

PEIRIS, RALPH. 1965. The effects of technological development on the population of the Gal Oya valley, Ceylon. *Ceylon journal of historical and social studies* 8, 1&2: 163–92.

PUTHENKALAM, FR. J. 1977. *Marriage and family in Kerala, with special reference to matrilineal castes*. Calgary: Journal of comparative family studies monograph series.

QUEYROZ, FR. FERNAO DE. 1930. *The temporal and spiritual conquest of Ceylon* (trans. Fr.S.G. Perera, S.J.) (3 vols). Colombo: A.C. Edwards, Acting Government Printer.

RAGHAVAN, M.D. 1971. *Tamil culture in Ceylon: A general introduction*. Colombo: Kalai·Nilayam.

RAHEEM, RAIHANA. 1975. A study of the kinship terms of the Moor community in Ceylon. Unpublished Ph.D. thesis, University of Leeds.

RAHMAT ALI, CHOUDHARY. 1943. *The millat and her minorities: Foundation of Nasaristan for Muslims of E. Ceylon* (pamphlet). Cambridge: Nasaristan National Movement.

RAM, KALPANA. 1991. *Mukkuvar women: Gender, hegemony and capitalist transformation in a south Indian fishing community*. London: Zed Books.

RAMANATHAN, PONNAMBALAM. 1888. The ethnology of the 'Moors' of Ceylon. *Journal of the Royal Asiatic Society, Ceylon branch* 10(36): 234–62.

RAO, VELCHERU NARAYAN, DAVID SHULMAN, and SANJAY SUBRAHMANYAM. 1992. *Symbols of substance: Court and state in Nāyaka period Tamilnadu*. Delhi: Oxford University Press.

RICHMAN, PAULA. 1993. Veneration of the Prophet Muhammad in an Islamic *piḷḷaittamiḻ*. *Journal of the American Oriental Society* 113, 1: 57–73.

ROBERTS, MICHAEL. 1980. From southern India to Lanka: The traffic in commodities, bodies, and myths from the thirteenth century onwards. *South Asia* 3: 36–47.

———. 1994a. Mentalities: Ideologues, assailants, historians and the pogrom against the Moors in 1915. *In* Michael Roberts, *Exploring confrontation: Sri Lanka: Politics, culture and history*, pp. 183–212. Chur, Switzerland: Harwood Academic Publishers.

———. 1994b. Ethnicity in riposte at a cricket match: The past for the present. *In* Michael Roberts, *Exploring confrontation: Sri Lanka: Politics, culture and history*, pp. 269–95. Chur, Switzerland: Harwood Academic Publishers.

ROBERTS, MICHAEL, ISMETH RAHEEM and PERCY COLIN-THOMÉ. 1989. *People inbetween*, vol. 1: *The Burghers and the middle class in the transformations within Sri Lanka, 1790s–1960s*. Ratmalana, Sri Lanka: Sarvodaya Book Publishing Services.

ROGERS, JOHN D. 1995. Racial identities and politics in early modern Sri Lanka. *In* Peter Robb, ed., *The concept of race in South Asia*, pp. 146–64. Delhi: Oxford University Press.

RUSSELL, JANE. 1982. *Communal politics under the Donoughmore constitution, 1931–1947*. Dehiwala, Sri Lanka: Tisara Prakasakayo.

SALEEM, A.R.M. 1990. *Akkaraippaṟṟu varalāṟu*. (History of Akkaraipattu). Akkaraipattu, Sri Lanka: Hiraa Publications.

SAMARAWEERA, VIJAYA. 1978. Some sociological aspects of the Muslim revivalism in Sri Lanka. *Social compass* 25: 465–75.

———. 1979. The Muslim revivalist movement, 1880–1915. *In* Michael Roberts, ed., *Collective identities, nationalisms and protest in modern Sri Lanka*, pp. 243–76. Colombo: Marga Institute.

SANYAL, USHA. 1994. *Pir, shaikh*, and Prophet: The personalisation of religious authority in Ahmad Riza Khan's life. *Contributions to Indian sociology* 28: 35–66.

SCHRIJVERS, JOKE. 1998. 'We were like cocoanut and flour in the pittu': Tamil–Muslim violence, gender and ethnic relations in eastern Sri Lanka. *Nēthrā* 2, 3: 10–39.

SHACKLE, CHRISTOPHER. 1989. Languages. *In* Francis Robinson, ed., *The Cambridge encyclopedia of India, Pakistan, Bangladesh, Sri Lanka, Nepal, Bhutan and the Maldives*, pp. 402–405. Cambridge: Cambridge University Press.

SHAIK HASAN SAHIB, S.A. 1980. *The divine light of Nagore*. Nagoor: S.K. Nazeer Ahmad.

SHAMS-UD-DI'N, A.T. 1881. Note on the 'mira kantiri' festival of the Muhammadans. *Journal of the Royal Asiatic Society, Ceylon branch* 7: 125–36.

SHARIF, JA'FAR. 1921. *Islam in India or the Qanun-i-Islam: The customs of the Musalmans of India, comprising a full and exact account of their various rites and ceremonies from the moment of birth to the hour of death*. (ed. William Crooke, trans. G.A. Herklots). Oxford University Press. (Reprinted 1972. New Delhi: Oriental Books Reprint Corp.)

SHASTRI, AMITA. 1990. The material basis for separatism: The Tamil Eelam movement in Sri Lanka. *Journal of Asian studies* 49, 1: 56–77.

———. 1998. The Estate Tamils, the Ceylon Citizenship Act of 1948, and Sri Lankan politics. *Contemporary South Asia* 7, 3, forthcoming.

SHUKRI, M.A.M., ed., 1986a. *Muslims of Sri Lanka: Avenues to antiquity*. Beruwala, Sri Lanka: Jamiah Naleemia Institute.

———. 1986b. Introduction. *In* M.A.M. Shukri, ed., *Muslims of Sri Lanka: Avenues to antiquity*, pp. 1–81. Beruwala, Sri Lanka: Jamiah Naleemia Institute.

———. 1986c. Muslims of Sri Lanka: A cultural perspective. *In* M.A.M. Shukri, ed., *Muslims of Sri Lanka: Avenues to antiquity*, pp. 337–62. Beruwala, Sri Lanka: Jamiah Naleemia Institute.

SHULMAN, DAVID. 1984. Muslim popular literature in Tamil: The *Tamīmaṉacāri Mālai*. *In* Yohanan Friedmann, ed., *Islam in Asia: Volume 1, South Asia*, pp. 174–207. Boulder: Westview.

SIVARAM, D.P. (TARAKI, *pseud.*). 1991. *The eluding peace, an insider's political analysis of the ethnic conflict in Sri Lanka*. Sarcelles, France: ASSEAY (Arts Social Sciences of Eelam Academy, France).

———. 1992. LTTE's Eelam project and the Muslim people. *Tamil times*. 15 November 1992, pp. 20, 24.

SIVATHAMBY, KARTHIGESU. 1987. The Sri Lankan ethnic crisis and Muslim–Tamil relationships—A socio-political view. *In* Charles Abeysekera and Newton Gunasinghe, eds, *Facets of ethnicity in Sri Lanka*, pp. 192–225. Colombo: Social Scientists' Association.

TAMBIAH, STANLEY J. 1986. *Sri Lanka: Ethnic fratricide and the dismantling of democracy*. Chicago and London: University of Chicago Press.

THURSTON, EDGAR and K. RANGACHARI. 1909. *Castes and tribes of southern India* (7 vols). Madras: Government Press.

UTHR (University Teachers for Human Rights, Jaffna). 1990. *Report 3: The war and its consequences in the Amparai District*. Issued 16 October 1990. UTHR(J): Thirunelvely, Jaffna, Sri Lanka.

———. 1991. *Report 7: The clash of ideologies and the continuing tragedy in the Batticaloa and Amparai Districts*. Issued 8 May 1991. UTHR(J): Thirunelvely, Jaffna, Sri Lanka.

———. 1993. *Report 10: Rays of hope amidst deepening gloom*. Issued 15 January 1993. UTHR(J): Thirunelvely, Jaffna, Sri Lanka.

———. 1993. *Report 11: Land, human rights and the eastern predicament*. Issued 15 April 1993. UTHR(J): Thirunelvely, Jaffna, Sri Lanka.

———. 1996. *Information bulletin 11: The quest for economic survival and human dignity: Batticaloa and Amparai Districts, June 1996*. UTHR(J). Internet source: JHOOLE@THUBAN.AC.HMC.EDU.

UWISE, M.M. 1986. The language and literature of the Muslims. *In* M.M.M. Mahroof, et al., *An ethnological survey of the Muslims of Sri Lanka from earliest times to Independence*, pp. 150–65. Colombo: Sir Razik Fareed Foundation.

———. 1990. *Muslim contribution to Tamil literature*. Kilakarai, Tamilnadu: Fifth International Islamic Tamil Literary Conference.

VAN SANDEN, J.C. 1926. *Sonahar: A brief history of the Moors of Ceylon*. Colombo: Van Sanden & Wright.

VATUK, SYLVIA. 1989. Household form and formation: Variability and social change among South Indian Muslims. *In* John N. Gray and David J. Mearns, eds, *Society from the inside out: Anthropological perspectives on the South Asian household*, pp. 107–39. Delhi: Sage Publications.

WADOOD, A.C.A. 1976. Sri Pada—The Muslim view. *In* Marikar, Lafir, and Macan Markar, eds, *Glimpses of the past of the Moors of Sri Lanka*, pp. 8–9. Colombo: Moors' Islamic Cultural Home.

WAGNER, CHRISTIAN. 1990. *Die Muslime Sri Lankas: Eine volksgruppe in spannungsfeld des ethnischen konflikts zwischen Singhalesen und Tamilen*. Freiburger beiträge zu entwicklung and politik 5. Freiburg: Arnold Bergstraesser Institut.

———.1991. A Muslim minority in a multiethnic state: The case of Sri Lanka. *In* Diethelm Weidemann, ed., *Nationalism, ethnicity and political development: South Asian perspectives*, pp. 93–112. New Delhi: Manohar.

WALLERSTEIN, IMMANUEL. 1976. *The modern world system: Capitalist agriculture and the origins of the European world-economy in the sixteenth century*. New York: Academic Press.

WINK, ANDRÉ. 1990. *Al hind: The making of the Indo-Islamic world*, vol. 1. *Early medieval India, and the expansion of Islam, 7th–11th centuries*. Leiden: E.J. Brill.

WOLF, ERIC. 1982. *Europe and the people without history*. Berkeley: University of California Press.

WRIGHT, THEODORE P. JR. 1966. The Muslim League in South India since Independence: A study in minority group political strategies. *American political science review* 60: 579–99.

YALMAN, NUR. 1967. *Under the Bo tree: Studies in caste, kinship, and marriage in the interior of Ceylon*. Berkeley and London: University of California Press.

YULE, HENRY and A.C. BURNELL. 1903. *Hobson-jobson: A glossary of colloquial Anglo-Indian words and phrases* (2nd edn). William Crooke, ed., London: John Murray.

15

Secularism out of its place

Paul R. Brass

A major source of the problems in recent discussions of the continued relevance to contemporary Indian political life of the secular state and the practices associated with secularism lies in the heavy burden that has been placed upon these terms. Secularism, properly speaking, is an orientation and a set of practices. However, in India, it has become an ideology seen as both contesting with Hindu communalism by those who uphold it, and as contesting against the faith of the Indian peoples by those who lately stand against it. Secularism as an orientation and a set of practices is indispensable to India's future as a liberal democracy. However, it loses its force as a binding principle of Indian unity if it is transformed into an ideology.

> Another word is thrown up a good deal, this secular State business. May I beg with all humility those gentlemen who use this word often to consult some dictionary before they use it? It is brought in at every conceivable step and at every conceivable stage. I just do not understand it. It has a great deal of importance, no doubt. But, it is brought in in all contexts, as if by saying that we are a secular State we have done something amazingly generous, given something out of our pocket to the rest of the world, something which we ought not to have done, so on and so forth. We have only done something which every country does except a very few misguided and backward countries in the world. Let us not refer to that word in the sense that we have done something very mighty [The Honourable Shri Jawaharlal Nehru] (Report 1967: 401).

I
Meanings

I believe that those of us who have commented on 'this secular State business' in India have muddied the waters still further since Nehru spoke these trenchant

Acknowledgements: I am grateful to F.G. Bailey, Harold Gould, and Gary Jacobsohn for their careful reading, comments on, and criticisms of the first draft of this paper that led to some changes in the manuscript. I am, however, solely responsible for the interpretations, arguments, and evidence presented herein.

lines. Nor will the dictionary help us easily to resolve matters—so far down the road to muddle-headedness have we gone in the past few decades. Nor is it just the term 'secular State' that we must look up, but 'secularism', doubly enshrined as faith and ideology, on the one hand, and condemned as an anti-religious, anti-national ideology, on the other hand. It is considered not only anti-religious but an insult to the faiths of the Indian people. It is considered anti-national because of its 'pseudo' character, which has allowed minorities to be 'pampered', thereby preventing the creation of a truly national state.

If we do have a look at the OED on the matter, we will find a multiplicity of meanings—not so diverse as those that litter the Indian landscape—but not enough to give us clear, firm guidelines to cut through the obscurities and obfuscations of the recent controversies on the subject. We will learn there that secular refers to the world rather than to the sacred sphere. A secular state, by implication, would be one whose concerns are with the world, not with the other-worldly. And, of course, the meaning of the term secular state derives from the attempts by certain of the American Founding Fathers, principally Jefferson and Madison, as well as many American religious leaders to establish a 'wall of separation' between church and state in both the Union and the several states.[1] The primary purpose for establishing such separation was to promote religious freedom, that is, to prevent the establishment of one religion above all others in a religiously plural society. The principle has been defended ever since both by most religious leaders in the United States and by secular political and civil liberties groups whose interests have included preservation of a social space for non-believers in a society characterised by a high degree of religious faith, and often fervour. While the principle of non-establishment ultimately became firmly established, the wall itself has not prevented fully the intrusion of religious faith and fervour into politics, state institutions and state symbols by direct and indirect means, nor the receipt by religious institutions of state patronage in the form of tax exemptions.

Secularism in the OED refers to matters of morality and education. As a moral stance, secularism refers to the idea that moral values may be created and sanctioned by men of the world as well as priests and pastors and that only those created by men of the world are good for this world. Morality has nothing to do with God and the after-life. For Jefferson himself, Jesus was a 'moral exemplar' as a man, not 'as the son of God', but his teachings had been buried in piles of 'rubbish' laid upon it by the various Christian denominations (Ellis 1997: 259). As for education, Jefferson was the architect of the idea of universal education for all the citizens of a free nation and of the idea as well as that such education, available freely to all, should be secular not religious. It is obvious that Nehru's principles were the same as Jefferson's.[2]

[1] Gary Wills has noted that Roger Williams used the term 'wall of separation' in 1644, 158 years before Jefferson's first use of the phrase in his Danbury letter (Wills 1990: 350). Jefferson did not take the term from Williams, however, since, as Wills also notes, Jefferson 'did not know or admire the work of Williams' (ibid.: 371).

[2] Jefferson was a theist, who 'rejected. . .miracles and inspired scripture' (Wills 1990: 369); Nehru confessed to no belief, only 'a sense of awe when he contemplated the mysteries of the universe', but

However, Nehru's speech in the Constituent Assembly could not have been made had Jefferson not preceded him by nearly 200 years. For, if one continues to adhere to the original principles of what is called 'secularism', it was indeed something that America gave 'to the rest of the world', though the French too at the same time—that is, on the eve of the Revolution—sought to separate church and state. It was, however, principally from the United States that secular principles spread gradually thereafter to the rest of the 'civilised' world, sometimes in diluted form. I have put the word civilised in quotation marks, but let us make no mistake about it: that is exactly what Nehru meant. He confronted those whose views he mocked in the words quoted above by saying, in effect, do you want India to be among the 'very few misguided and backward countries in the world', or do you want it to join the civilised world? Anyone saying such things today is immediately classified as Western, ethnocentrist, neo-imperialist, etcetera. Nehru himself is increasingly being viewed in those terms in India today.

I want to suggest that a major source of the problems in accepting the continued relevance of Jefferson and Nehru to contemporary Indian political life lies in the heavy burden that has been placed upon the terms secular, secularism, and secular state. It is a burden, moreover, that is not implied in either Jefferson's or Nehru's thinking on these subjects. Nehru minimised the significance of the establishment of a secular state in India as something that sprang naturally from the very achievement of statehood in the modern world. As for Jefferson, the heavily-weighted terms that are used day-in and day-out in all the Indian media, by Indian politicians, as by all of us, hardly even appear in Jefferson's writings.

Secularism, to the extent such an 'ism' exists at all, is an orientation and a set of practices based on two principles: separation of state and religious institutions, and the exclusive authority of state institutions in deciding upon the public good. As an orientation, it is challenged by organisations such as the RSS whose leaders want to create a Hindu state in India infused with Hindu religious values though they deny that they wish thereby to undermine the foundations of the Indian secular state. As a set of practices, it inhabits a world that began in India with the 19th century social reformers who challenged the sacredness of such practices as the prohibition against widow remarriage and began the process of substituting different practices more consistent with what they saw the British, as the representatives

condemned Hindu religious 'superstitions' (Smith 1963: 154). Both men believed that the principles that should guide one's practices in life and in politics derived from a moral code that could be separated from religious faith and that could also be consistent with scientific knowledge: 'the scientific spirit', as Nehru put it (ibid.), 'the system of things in which we are placed', as Jefferson put it (see Jefferson 1984: 4). Both men also found it necessary to confront as well the power of religious faith to move men and women to political action, much more so in the case of Nehru who was forced to concede how effective and valuable for the national movement were Gandhi's appeals to Hindu faith in an age of mass mobilisation. See, for example, the quotes from Nehru's *Autobiography* on this matter, cited by F.G. Bailey (1998: 190). Even Jefferson, however, resorted to a religious appeal during the 1774 agitation against the bill to close the port of Boston, when he and his fellow Virginians came to the aid of Massachusetts by 'cook[ing] up a resolution' to begin 'a day of fasting, humiliation & prayer' in protest against the bill and the prospect it presented of 'civil war', that is, war between the colonies and the mother country (Jefferson 1984: 8; Wills 1990: 359–60).

of the civilised world, condoning, namely, the remarriage of widows. They also condemned behaviours they saw as barbaric, such as justifying the practice of *sati* on religious grounds. This point of view came down to the Constituent Assembly itself where Amrit Kaur argued against the 'free "practice" of religion' in India since this would negate the gains made by social reformers and prevent further advances in abolishing such practices as 'devadasi,. . .purdah, and sati' and 'it might invalidate such secular gains as the Widows Remarriage Act'. Her view prevailed in the Constitution that established the principle that matters of 'social welfare and reform' belonged to this world, not to the other, that they were secular not religious matters (Austin 1966: 64).

Today, however, it is not such quaint customs that form the centre of political conflict over the secular orientation and secular practices. Rather, secularism has become a general rubric to describe those groups, parties, 'forces', and 'elements' that are portrayed or self-described as defending the legacy of Nehru, of Indian democracy, and sometimes of socialism against its enemies. These secular forces are depicted as counterpoised primarily against the former Jan Sangh and its inheritor, the BJP, behind which stand the RSS and the rest of the family of RSS-affiliated organisations. References to the need for solidarity amongst such forces, of course, became more and more frequent as the BJP came closer to wielding power in the states and at the Centre. For some of these forces, secularism is proclaimed as an ideology; for others it is a practice; for many it is nothing but an 'image'.[3]

I want to consider some of the multiplicity of ways in which the terms secular, secularism, and secular state are used in India and, thereby, to ferret out those that weigh too heavily upon them and condemn them to futility, hypocrisy, and rejection by India's intellectual elites, on the one hand, and those that are indispensable to political practice in a civilised democracy, on the other hand. Consider first the apparently simple distinction between 'secular interests based on occupation or class' and 'primordial groupings' (Chatterji 1988: 846). According to much thinking on this subject among India's intellectual elites, especially those on the left, demands made and policies framed on behalf of the former are secular; those made on behalf of the latter are not. For Marxists, the latter reflect 'false consciousness'; for many other intellectuals, they are 'parochial'. Many object to the mobilisation of such so-called primordial groups on the grounds that they undermine the unity of India. Nehru himself never tired of condemning 'casteism, communalism, and provincialism' as parochial interests detrimental to the achievement of the goals of national integration and economic development. But where does the question of the sacred arise in the distinction between these two types of forces? In fact, it does not arise except in the case of those movements that seek the achievement of religious goals through the political process with the aid of the state, most notably through the construction of Hindu temples by destroying Muslim mosques.

[3] Prem Bhasin, for example, referring to political events in 1970, remarked that an alliance between the newly-formed Congress (R) and the PSP would 'embellish the former's leftist and secularist image further' (1972: 45).

Most writing in the field of ethnicity and nationalism rejects the idea that the demands of ethnic groups are non-material in nature. While cultural symbols are used in such movements and considered central by many who participate in them, most also pursue material goals: access to economic privileges and political power. For some such movements, the cultural symbols may even be facades for the material and political advancement of its elites. Whether one likes or dislikes them, however, they do not belong on the other side of the secular–non-secular divide. They are anything but sacred or other-wordly. Nor does it affect the issue in the least whether the unity of India is endangered by them unless—as I am afraid it is—that unity is itself considered sacred. But insofar as that is the case, it simply bolsters my argument that the controversy over the relevance of secularism for India is confounded by forcing the term to carry far too heavy a burden.

What then about the movement to destroy Muslim mosques and replace them with newly constructed Hindu temples? There can be no doubt about this matter. Although it is evident that the entire movement has a political purpose and that it represents for many of the top leaders of the BJP, in their own words, the 'playing of the Hindu card' for the purpose of consolidating the Hindu community, creating a Hindu nation-state, and achieving power at the centre of the Indian polity, it is a movement designed to arouse the other-wordly sentiments of Hindus, to attack the religious institutions of Muslims, and to make use of the powers of the state to achieve its goals. The powers of the state government were used directly, indirectly, and duplicitously by the BJP government of Uttar Pradesh (U.P.) in making available to the VHP lands adjacent to the Babri mosque at Ayodhya for constructing a new temple to Ram, in allowing huge crowds to assemble there in violation of the spirit of the orders of the Supreme Court, and in withdrawing police and military forces from the site instead of protecting it from destruction. Every secular person in India has condemned these actions—and rightly so—for they were not only anti-secular, they were illegal, violent, and uncivilised.[4] It is evident also that these actions would have been condemned by both Jefferson and Nehru. Indeed, can anyone believe that a government under Nehru's leadership would have allowed such a thing to happen? Would not Nehru himself, who knew from his European experiences the meaning of the Nazi burning of synagogues, have resigned as prime minister if he could not have prevented it?

Unfortunately, the line of division between secular and non-secular political behaviour is not so easily drawn for all 'ethno-religious' movements. The basis for the Ayodhya movement was itself laid by the Congress under Indira Gandhi's leadership when, as Jaffrelot has noted, 'secularism and socio-economic development were supplanted by entirely different values in the nation's political discourse, and the Congress itself appealed to ethno-religious sentiments' (Jaffrelot 1996: 9).

[4] Madan has rightly noted that it is no business of an Indian secular state to 'be involved in repairing or building temples and mosques' (see Madan 1992). However, it was a government in India that helped, by its actions and non-actions, to bring down the mosque at Ayodhya. It is, therefore, now the business of the government to ensure that no Hindu temple is constructed on a site that belongs to Muslims.

Electoral appeals made on the basis of religion—and especially those that attack another's religion—are illegal under the Representation of the People Act, which has in fact from time to time been enforced in election law cases.

However, it is not at all clear that an appeal to 'Hindu pride' or criticisms of government policies said to have 'pampered' Muslims, however reprehensible, are non-secular. In fact, these slogans arise out of a different framework, in which all politically conscious Indians across the entire political spectrum are implicated, namely, the construction of a united nation out of the diverse human elements that comprise India. It is because there is no other alternative to Hindu nationalism to achieve that goal except the conversion of secularism into an ideology celebrating Indian diversities that the problems arise. For secularism cannot bear that load: it has no emotional basis to appeal to a mass public. Celebration of diversity may work in the United States—where ethnic identities have anyway become greatly attenuated—as long as ethnic group members do not demand corporate recognition in schools and other public institutions and as long as the members of all ethnic groups adhere to the American political creed that recognises in principle only individual citizens.[5] The sentiment of American patriotism thus combines in an effective merger with the emotional ties to one's ethnic or religious group.

However, the attempt to convert secularism into a principle of interreligious pluralism in India, instead of a principle of separation of state and religion, comes a cropper on several grounds. First, it provides no sentimental basis that can compete with the slogan of Hindu pride. Second, it is itself an anti-secular position, for it demands 'respect for all religions', which is none of the business of a secular state. Although it is true that the principle of separation itself arose as a consequence of interreligious pluralism in the United States, the addition to that idea of state 'respect for all religions' opens a space for the intrusion of all kinds of denominational and non-denominational practices that offend non-believers and some smaller religious sects as well. These include such practices as religious prayer in American schools or Hindu religious invocations at the beginning of meetings in district administrative offices, pledges of allegiance to the American flag that require non-believers to be loyal to God if they are to be loyal to the United States, direct state contributions to religious schools or indirect contributions through tax exemptions, exemption of temple lands in India from land ceilings legislation, and many other practices of these types in both countries. Third, it falsely credits all religions and faiths—in a characteristically Hindu manner—with tolerance, a position that cannot stand a moment's reflection.

While many aspects of Buddhist and a few of the smaller Protestant religions can perhaps be said to be tolerant and respectful of other faiths, this can hardly be said of Roman Catholicism throughout most of its history, of Islam in principle—though it has often been tolerant in practice—or of Judaism. Judaism has no respect for other faiths; it simply ignores them. Catholicism thrived for a millennium upon anti-Semitism. Lutheranism surpassed all other Christian sects for the virulence

[5] Leaving aside, of course, the special position of American Indian groups that have the status of 'nations' recognised in treaties made with the United States.

of its anti-Semitism. And Islam proclaims Mohammad—and only he—as the last prophet of God. Nor can I understand how a religion such as Hinduism, based in its very essence on principles of hierarchy, discrimination, ritual pollution, and outcasting, has come to be seen as the epitome of tolerance. In today's world, it is religious minorities and secular values that are in grave danger in societies such as Iran with established religions, or in India itself where it is dangerous for secular writers to comment on the Sikh scriptures and where Christian missions and missionaries must be on guard against militant Hindu surveillance of their activities. Further, as we have seen in the Rushdie case and less dramatically in the harassment of scholars of Sikhism outside of India, it is only in liberal secular societies that the victims of religious faith and zealotry can be protected. I find no basis in any of this—and much more that could be said of religious beliefs and practices—for the construction of a political edifice for a secular state.

Madan has condemned 'the intellectuals' for failing to draw the proper implications of their own recognition that Indians are 'moved by religion as by nothing else' and for adhering 'too seriously' instead to ideologies of 'liberalism, or Marxism, and secularism' (Madan 1992). Here again comes secularism as an ideology instead of an orientation or a practice, which must now, however, bend to the faith of the Indian peoples. Secularism must be replaced by 'a pluralist political philosophy, which offers recognition and respect to the religious-minded person as it does to the atheist...but which grants no special privileges to any group'. Secularism is seen here as an ideology that ridicules 'religion as opium or poison' and is to blame for landing 'us in Ayodhya' (ibid.). Although some secularists certainly consider religion a bane on society, it is in no way a central feature of secularism as a principle in liberal democracies. Further, Madan's position that secularism is responsible for Ayodhya is regrettably consistent with the BJP point of view. In truth, it was widespread departure from secular principles that culminated in the militant Hindu destruction of the mosque at Ayodhya.

I am at a loss to understand Madan's argument that secularism in India has been in practice anti-religious, involving ridicule of India's faiths. Although I have heard and read statements of this sort by others whom I respect, as I do Madan, I have not found in thirty-six years of travelling around India any politicians of any persuasion who have publicly ridiculed religion in this way. Nor did Nehru do so, whatever he may have felt about the matter. On the other hand, I have heard many militant Hindus condemn Islam and ridicule with laughter what they wrongly and ignorantly consider to be its fundamental precepts, and I have a book by Arun Shourie which does the same in a pseudo-sophisticated manner (see Shourie 1995). No Indian politician I have ever met would dare to condemn Hindu religion from any public platform. Moreover, I can hardly think of a handful of Hindu politicians who, in their hearts, even felt this way. On the contrary, I have countless times heard all kinds of lessons drawn from Hindu religion, philosophy, and mythology by Hindu politicians of left, right, and centre.

But, Madan would argue, it is not just a question of open attack upon religion and religious faith as such, but the very processes of secularisation that seek to 'delimit and devalue the role of religion in society' (see Madan 1997: 276). Beteille and Vanaik have dealt effectively with Madan's argument here (Beteille 1994: 559–66; Vanaik 1997: 152–62).[6] I cannot add much to their criticisms of his position. Madan's position on secularisation cannot amount to more than a railing against inevitability. He is anthopomorphising a set of processes that exist largely independently of the roles of particular actors in them. Moreover, even allowing for the obvious fact that some participants in processes of secularisation are anti-religious, religious faith continues to flourish in the United States—despite the thoroughgoing secularisation of most aspects of everyday life in a technologically advanced society and the fact that, even allowing for all the breaks in the wall of separation, the United States remains the prototypical model of the liberal democratic secular state in today's world.[7]

But then, Madan has a reply to this also. Religion is not the same in the United States and India, where it is all-encompassing and cannot be separated from the mundane aspects of daily life. This is an argument for Indian or Asian exceptionalism, which does not stand up. Religion occupies the lives of Hasidic Jews of New York as much, if not more, than the lives of any Hindu or Muslim in India, even to the extent of their closing their businesses early on Fridays, all day Saturdays, and on all Jewish holidays. But when one visits their shops or calls to buy a computer or a camera, it is strictly a matter of dollars and cents, strictly secular in other words. And how could it be otherwise? And how have the secular processes of market development in any way affected the faith of these Jews? And how has 'the construction of an Indian ideology of religious pluralism and tolerance. . .been rendered problematic' (Madan 1997: 216) by such processes when, in the land in which the whole idea 'of religious pluralism and tolerance' was invented—I mean again the United States, not India—as a companion to the secular state, such an idea remains non-problematic?

Madan agrees with Nandy that it is not only 'secularists', but 'religious zealots' who are 'against religious tolerance and religion itself' (1997: 274–75).[8] This is a strange position. It is, first of all, not 'secularists' in general, maybe not even 'secular humanists' in particular, who occupy this space. Marxists and the Soviet state certainly were opposed to religion, and Hitler also did not care much for

[6] Vanaik's summary and critique (1997) of the positions of Nandy, Madan, and Parekh is estimable as much for its clarity as its soundness.

[7] Donald E. Smith used three criteria to define the liberal democratic secular state: (*i*) the individual's right to the free practice of religion; (*ii*) the individual's relationship to the state as a citizen rather than as a member of a religious group; and (*iii*) 'separation of state and religion'. By these three measures, he remarked, the United States came 'close' to perfection, though he thought there remained 'obvious anomalies as well as important issues yet to be decided' (1963). I do not think the position of the United States has changed in a major way during the past thirty-five years, though the 'anomalies' certainly remain and, of course, there will always be 'important issues. . . to be decided'. For a radical secularist, one's satisfaction at the proximity of the United States to perfection as a secular state has to be rather limited. It is from a recognition of how fragile the structure of the secular state appears from this perspective, rather than from ethnocentric pride, that I shudder at the prospect of the dismantling of the even more fragile barriers to the triumph of communalist nationalism and Hindu religiosity in India.

[8] Madan here cites approvingly Ashis Nandy's argument (see Nandy 1990: 69–93).

conventional religion, but in no liberal democracy has it been the position of any significant group that religious tolerance or religion should be eliminated. As for the intolerance of 'religious zealots', Madan and Nandy are hoist by their own petards here. What is the history of religion in the West if not a history of religious zealotry, religious warfare, and persecution of persons of other faiths? The idea that Indian history has been at all different in this respect is another myth, shattered by the endemic warfare among the militant sects of India that long preceded the arrival of British rule (see van der Veer 1989: 133ff and *passim*), but which Madan and Nandy conveniently ignore in their idealisation of Indian religious tolerance that has to be somehow reconstructed from the true faiths of the Indian people.

Let us make no mistake about it. Madan and Nandy are making a plea for the preservation, protection, and propagation of religion in Indian public life, for its integration in the public life and business of the state. But it is true religion they wish to promote, not the religious zealotry and faith as ideology that the BJP promotes. It is Gandhian religion that unites all faiths in a common, peaceful search for transcendent truths.[9] Clearly, they reject both the principles of Jefferson[10] and those of Nehru. More important, their goal is nothing but a pipe dream in a country where politicians make a living out of instigating ethnic and religious conflicts. The only political remedies against the most dramatic recent instances of such behaviour—namely, militant Hindu efforts to consolidate a Hindu nation while encouraging anti-Muslim sentiments—can come from counter-efforts to form coalitions of caste and communal groupings in pursuit of secular goals in a society that maintains and respects diversities of all sorts. The peaceful pursuit of interreligious dialogue through the 'recovery of religious tolerance' has no meaning for those groups who have seen themselves as oppressed and discriminated against in Hindu society: Muslims, backward castes, Scheduled Castes, and Scheduled Tribes. For all these groups, secularism means tolerance, acceptance, equality, non-discrimination, not Brahmanical or Gandhian searches for transcendent interreligious truths.[11]

[9] What else are we to make of the following statements of Nandy: 'The moral of the story is this: the time has come for us to recognize that instead of trying to build religious tolerance on the good faith or conscience of a small group of de-ethnicized, middle-class politicians, bureaucrats and intellectuals, a far more serious venture would be to explore the philosophy, the symbolism and the theology of tolerance in the various faiths of the citizens and hope that the state systems in South Asia may learn something about religious tolerance from everyday Hinduism, Islam, Buddhism, and/or Sikhism, rather than wish that ordinary Hindus, Muslims, Buddhists and Sikhs will learn tolerance from the various fashionable secular theories of statecraft.' And, 'Religious tolerance outside the bounds of secularism is exactly what it says it is. It not only means tolerance of religions but also a tolerance that is religious' (see Nandy 1990: 86, 91).

[10] It will not do to cite Jefferson's proclaimed belief in the existence of 'humanistic values' embodied in the life of Jesus and Socrates as akin to Gandhi's search for the universal truths embodied in all faiths. Jefferson's writings on this matter appear to have been defensive, to combat the charge that he was a non-believer, rather than to promote a religion of 'secular humanism' (see Ellis 1997: 215).

[11] W.H. Morris-Jones pointed out that Indira Gandhi's victory in the 1971 elections—in the days when she wore the secular garb—had something to do with 'secularism', which 'meant much to the Muslims' and 'may also have meant something to scheduled and lower caste groups' (1971: 728).

II
Secularism as ideology

Secularism has become not only an ideology in India, but, as I have myself argued elsewhere, a nationalist ideology. Madan too remarks that 'the nationalism of the pre-independence days and today's secularism are essentially the same ideas' (Madan 1997: 266). I am not sure when secularism became an ideology in India, before or after independence.[12] Insofar as the pre-independence period is concerned, it is certain only that the Indian National Congress stood for the unity of all the Indian peoples against British colonialism and against either the identification of the Indian nation with the Hindu population or with the separatist Muslim ideology that led to the division of India and the creation of Pakistan. Aware of the multiplicity of divisions among the Indian peoples that they considered potentially divisive, Indian nationalist elites invented and constructed a new history of India based more on interpretation and hope than on much factual evidence that all the peoples of India shared a common civilisation, whatever their religious, linguistic, or other cultural distinctions, and that they had all been striving from time immemorial to establish an Indian state that would comprise all its peoples into one nation. On this rather feeble and highly contested construction, lacking not only evidence but any sentimental basis for mass mobilisation, the Congress managed to build a mass movement that appealed to somewhat less than half the population of India at the most. It did so by focusing the attention of its rank and file and the wider population upon the iniquity of rule by a foreign country, and, at critical moments, by allowing Gandhi to mobilise increasing numbers of Indians through direct and indirect appeals to their religious faith.

Neither of these props of Indian nationalism had anything to do with secularism. The predominant leaders of the Congress argued rather that the only workable basis for creating a united Indian nation was the construction of a 'composite nationalism' that recognised and respected the differences and diversities of the various peoples of India while seeing them all as contributions to the historic majesty of an encompassing and tolerant Indian civilisation. Secularism was the principle that would bind the various peoples of India, a principle that demanded mutual respect for differences, avoidance of any social conflicts that would distract attention from the main task of overthrowing British rule in India, and disallowing the right of any one of the distinctive cultures—especially its religious cultures—to stand for the whole. Already this was a heavier burden than the secular principle carried in its country of birth, where there was little talk of nation but, instead, of a people whose coming together depended upon disregarding the fundamental religious differences then—and still—obtaining, and eliminating the right of any one religion to 'establishment', that is, to be the official religion of the state with all the privileges of dissemination and imposition upon others that would have been involved.

[12] The Rudolphs note that 'the lesson of partition. . .was that religious politics kills', and that, 'as a result, India began its career as an independent state with a powerful commitment not only to a secular state but also to secularism as an ideology'(1987: 38).

Secularism really came into its own as an ideology in India after independence in the aftermath of the wreckage of Indian unity through the partition of the country and the assassination of Gandhi. The first forever condemned any kind of separatist or secessionist movement that might further fragment the imagined Indian nation. The second for a time limited the potential for the spread of Hindu nationalism. Since it was the appeal to religious sentiment that was seen as the principle cause of the break-up of India, a major rule of the post-independence Indian state in dealing with popular movements based upon cultural difference was that no movement whatsoever would be recognised or granted any rights or privileges if it was based upon an appeal to religious belief or upon the recognition of the corporate right of a religious community for political recognition (see Brass 1974: 17). Secularism after independence, therefore, became transformed into an ideology that banned political mobilisation of religious groups for corporate recognition, though the rights of all cultural groups, including religious groups, were to be protected in ways defined and circumscribed by Articles 29 and 30 of the Constitution of India.[13] At the same time, the secular ideology was turned into a justification for the creation of a strong centralised state, one that would ignore, restrain, or repress religious and other cultural movements deemed threatening to the unity of India and that would allow it to concentrate its efforts on the secular goals of economic development and the transformation of India into a powerful, industrialised and, increasingly as time went on, a militarised state.

In the process, the basic minimum needs of the people were ignored and upper caste dominance in Indian society was maintained. For a time during Indira Gandhi's heyday, regional forces were subdued through her political manipulations in every state in the Union until, finally, she and the secular edifice of the Indian state began to crumble and fall in the Punjab. Since her death, regional forces have multiplied and upper caste political dominance has come to an end in those states, particularly in the north, where upper castes had held sway, and in the central government as well. Intercommunal and intercaste conflict have replaced what Nigam has characterised as the 'hegemonic nationalist project' in which 'secularism' was complicit. 'Secularism's complicity with a hegemonic nationalist project' (Nigam 1996: 1168) was a function of its identification with the strong state, maintaining its dominance against all regional, religious, and caste interests that threatened its territorial integrity. In practice, this strong state became a vehicle for maintaining upper caste dominance and the right of its political leaders and bureaucrats to make huge corrupt profits from its control over the avenues to wealth in the so-called socialist state. Indeed, the myth of the secular

[13] Article 30 is the one most relevant to the question of separation of state and religion. It permits 'all minorities, whether based on religion or language', to 'have the right to establish and administer educational institutions of their choice' and prohibits the state, 'in granting aid to educational institutions', from discriminating 'against any educational institution on the ground that it is under the management of a minority, whether based on religion or language'. In effect, Article 30 goes against one of the cardinal precepts of the 'wall of separation' doctrine that prohibits state aid to educational institutions managed by religious groups.

state and its justification for state aggrandisement were themselves enhanced by the prevalence of ethnic conflict of all sorts, which at once allowed state leaders to proclaim the state's secular neutrality above the fray while justifying the need for further centralisation and enhancement of state powers, including vast increases in an array of old and new 'security' forces.[14]

It is wrong, however, to think that adherence to secular principles and practices necessarily means adherence also to an 'ideology of secularism. . .in the Enlightenment sense of the term', which Madan attributes to Nehru (Madan 1997: 270). In this respect, I disagree not only with Madan but with Gellner and Bailey. Gellner, in his usual provocative manner, went to the extent of proclaiming himself an Enlightenment 'fundamentalist'.[15] Bailey forfeited a portion of the ground on which he stood in his criticism of Madan by proclaiming secular humanism as a religious faith like any other (Bailey 1991: 229). It is here where the muddle-headedness enters and befuddles the arguments on both sides.

Secularism is a principle that has been adhered to by people of many faiths and of no faiths. Indeed, it has been argued by many people—an argument to which Madan himself refers—that the secular principle itself arises, at least in part, out of Christian religious thought, not just the Enlightenment. It loses its force as a binding principle for both people of faith and those without faith if it is transformed into an ideology for those of no faith. Moreover, the main proclaimed political enemy of the secularists in India, the RSS family of organisations, itself insists that it adheres to true secularism as opposed to the 'pseudo-secularism' of the Congress. This playing with terms is somewhat like the old argument about nonalignment in which all parties proclaimed their faith in it while accusing each other of departing from it in principle or practice. Nonalignment is now a dead issue, but secularism is not. It remains an important orientation and a set of practices in Indian politics that represent the best hope for the maintenance of the unity of India while maintaining a degree of civilised political behaviour in the country.

If I am right, then it is a great error on the part of Madan and Nandy to undermine secularism as orientation and practice in Indian politics. It is, for example, an egregious error to blame 'the weakness of the secular state' for the destruction of 'the Akal Takht in Amritsar in 1984 and the Babri Masjid in Ayodhya in 1992' because of its failure 'to overcome the challenge of communalism' (see Madan 1997: 272). It was rather deliberate deviation from secular practices on the part of political leaders and misuse of the apparatus of the state for religious purposes that were responsible for both these events. In the first case, it is well enough known that Indira Gandhi departed from her father's practices by supporting a fanatical, half-mad religious preacher to undermine Congress's principal rival in Punjab politics,

[14] Cf. D.A. Washbrook (1982: 179–80): 'Through policies which promote internal divisiveness, the territorial secular state can keep itself out of and above the fray of ethnic politics. Indeed, it can do more and stand as the independent arbiter between the claims of rival ethnicities whose members perceive themselves to have more to fear from one another than from it.'

[15] A 'humble adherent', as he put it, of 'Enlightenment Rationalist Fundamentalism' (1991: 80).

the Akali Dal. In the second case, as I have already said above, the government of Uttar Pradesh under the leadership of Kalyan Singh is directly responsible for the destruction of the mosque at Ayodhya, as is the central government and its prime minister, Narasimha Rao, who failed to protect it, as Nehru would surely have done, by dismissing the state government before, not after, the destruction of the mosque.

It is also a great error to condemn the parties and leaders that do adhere to secular practices, such as the Samajwadi Party of Mulayam Singh Yadav and the Bahujan Samaj Party of Kanshi Ram and Mayawati. Their secular credentials arise not only from the fact that they place 'material matters above matters of faith', but because of the very fact that Madan condemns, namely, that they also 'woo. . .the Muslim voters' (1997: 272). Wooing Muslim voters is not the same as recognising Islam as a state religion or as an equal religion with Hinduism in India, either of which would obviously violate secular principles.

Muslims in India have had a long list of grievances that are mostly secular in nature: discrimination in employment opportunities; discrimination against the use of the Urdu language in the face of the constitutional provisions designed to protect it; destruction of Muslim property; and killing of Muslims by the police in riots. In addition, they have had other grievances that are on the borderline between the secular and the non-secular, such as the movement to restore the minority character of the Aligarh Muslim University (AMU).[16]

On the wrong side of the secular–non-secular divide, Muslim religious and political leaders have also insisted upon the retention of their system of personal law. This indeed does represent a compromise on secular principles, for it permits a religious community to maintain a code of religiously sanctified laws[17] against the principle of the secular state that the laws, civil and criminal, apply equally to all irrespective of their faith. It should be noted, however, that it was Nehru who presided over this compromise, indeed a tacit bargain under which the loyalty of the orthodox Muslim leadership to India and to the Congress in the face of the Pakistan

[16] Comparisons are sometimes made between the AMU and Brandeis University in the greater Boston area. Although many Jews identify positively with Brandeis University, as with its namesake, and think of it in some ways as 'their university', it should be pointed out that the university is not called the Brandeis Jewish University, that its namesake was a Supreme Court justice noted for his defence of free speech, a supreme upholder of 'individualist aspirations of the American Declaration of Independence' and an adherent of 'libertarian views on expression' (Jacobsohn 1993: 165, 186), and that the University establishes no quotas or standards designed to maintain a Jewish–Christian student population ratio or any other non-secular standards or principles. It is simply a private University established by Jewish and non-Jewish philanthropists, some of whom 'were simple admirers of Justice Brandeis'. Nor is there any provision that the governing board of the University must be predominantly Jewish. I am indebted to a personal communication from Amelie Rorty for some of the information in this paragraph, including the quote.

[17] In a recent article, Asghar Ali Engineer (1998) has argued against the Muslim leadership in India that 'the Muslim personal law is not divine in the sense the Quranic injunctions are' and calls for 'reforms within the Islamic frame-work'.

movement was purchased with the understanding that they would be left in control of their religious institutions and personal laws in an independent India.[18]

The question is: how significant a deviation from secularism is this? On the one hand, it does not meet the standard set by constitutional law in the United States. On the other hand, Madan has argued that the American standard, what he calls 'unreformed secularism', cannot be applied to India. What is needed for India is equal respect by the state for all religions and an 'ideology of religious pluralism and tolerance' in society (Madan 1997: 276). The preservation of separate systems of personal law is the most significant example in India of such state respect and societal tolerance for Islam.

There is a sense, moreover, in which the acceptance of the Muslim right to maintain separate personal laws of marriage and inheritance can be reconciled with 'secularism'. The Rudolphs, for example, have argued that, in India, 'the meaning of. . .secularism historically has encompassed the celebration and constitutional protection of cultural diversity as well as the protection of equal rights of citizens in a secular state' (Rudolph and Rudolph 1987: 47). In other words, secularism in India grants group as well as individual rights. Insofar as the granting of group rights means that the state chooses to remain aloof from certain matters important to recognised groups, including religious groups, it opens the prospect that some individuals may end up being more equal than others. To use the most famous example, Mormons—and Muslims by extension from that famous case[19]—may have only one legal wife in the United States, but Muslims in India may have four. A secular state, it may be argued, need not concern itself with how many wives different groups choose to have and may disregard the fact that the practice was sanctioned by Islam's prophet, Mohammad. Hindus and other non-Muslims

[18] The Rudolphs argue that this deviation from secular principles on Nehru's part arose from his desire to assuage Muslim fears, that is, from 'a deep concern to insure that Muslims in secular India would feel not only safe but at home'. He did this, they say, by adding to their status as 'citizens with equal rights' in India the communal right to exist as 'a self-governing religious community in charge of its own personal law' (1987: 40). Although I believe the Congress's and Nehru's commitment to the Muslim clerics preceded independence, the Rudolphs' formulation also makes sense with respect to the continuation of the pre-independence bargain. Rajiv Gandhi's much-criticised turnaround in the famous Shah Bano case was, in fact, consistent with the pre-independence bargain and with Nehru's commitment to the Muslims of India. It was a reflection of his political idiocy that, on the advice of persons such as the thoroughly secularised Muslim, Arif Mohammad Khan, in his cabinet, he initially chose to accept the decision of the Supreme Court in this case, which regrettably did not restrict itself to applying the applicable criminal law to the case but added a gratuitous interpretation of the Quran to its judgement written by Chief Justice Chandrachud as well as an *obiter dictum* calling for the establishment of a uniform civil code (see Embree 1987: 58–60). See also the Rudolphs' comments on this case, in which they note that, in his turnaround, Rajiv in effect reverted to Nehru's position that allowed the Muslims of India 'some measure of self-regulation' (1987: 45).

[19] *Reynolds v. United States*, 98 U.S. 146, 166 (1879); and see the comments on this case and the same issue in an Israeli case, which should be of great interest to Indians (Jacobsohn 1993: 31–35). In the latter case, an Israeli Jew argued that he should be entitled to the right of polygamy as much as any Muslim in Israel! His plea was turned down. The court acknowledged the right of the Muslim community to regulate its own internal affairs on such matters as marriage, but not the right of non-Muslims to opt for Muslim customs in order to avoid the applicable criminal ordinance.

in India may have only one wife legally. Alimony payments also may differ for Hindus and Muslims who divorce, among many other differences. In making such discriminations, it may nevertheless be argued that the state is not establishing either Hindu religion or Islam; it is simply choosing to allow a distinctive religious group to follow its own laws in a restricted sphere. It becomes a group right rather than a religious right in which it is not the business of the state to concern itself with the divine or secular origins of the laws in question. This is, in fact, consistent with the position that the British took in withdrawing 'the state from "interference" in matters of indigenous culture and religion', though the British, as is well known, did not follow this principle consistently (see Washbrook 1982: 164–65).

But Madan wants not just non-interference by the state in distinctive groups' cultural and religious practices. Rather, he accepts the 'imperative' need for 'the notion of the secular state' in India to accommodate 'specificities of religious belief and practice' (Madan 1997: 24–25). As an unreformed—indeed a radical—secularist myself, I must say that I consider this a significant departure from secular principles, whether applied to the personal law issue or to other matters. The secular state should not enforce Muslim personal laws. It should, on the contrary, make a space for secular Muslims to have access to the civil laws, something lacking in India as it is to secular Jews and non-Jews in Israel as well. But I also think the militant Hindu demand for the establishment of a Uniform Civil Code in India is based not on the desire to purify the secular state in India, but to assimilate Muslims into a Hindu-dominated state. It is, in a word, hypocritical. Madan's position is not the same as the BJP's here. Nor is it hypocritical. He simply wants to have it both ways: respect for the separate faiths of Indians without political appeals to their desire to retain their separateness.[20]

But, in fact, the principle obstacles to a hypocritical Hindu nationalism, claiming to be genuinely secular but in fact seeking to infuse nationalism with Hindu religiosity, come from the parties of the left and of the backward and lower castes. In the case of the Communist left, adherence to secular principles is part and parcel of their entire ideology. Moreover, the Communist parties in Kerala and West Bengal have demonstrated their ability, for the most part, to prevent communal violence. They do not make appeals to the religious sentiments of Hindu or Muslim voters; they do not instigate communal riots to gain the support of one community against the other, as the Congress and the BJP have often done; and they enforce the law against riot-mongers when violence does break out, ensuring that the police act impartially.

[20] It should also be pointed out that this tolerance of the Muslim desire to maintain separate personal laws is not the same as the anti-secular position of the state of Israel, which imposes orthodox Jewish personal law upon all Jews irrespective of their adherence to orthodox Judaism or their atheism or secularism, though allowing Muslims and Christians their own system of personal laws. In short, Israel maintains a version of the Ottoman millet system, with an 'established' religion for the majority that is not, however, imposed on other religious groups. It is, in other words, a case of respect for the faiths of others, but not for the wishes of non-believers within either the dominant Jewish community, or in the non-dominant communities who remain subject to the religious laws of their respective Muslim or Christian communities.

The ideological basis for secularism among the other left parties in north India, those representing especially the interests of the backward and lower castes, is less principled than that of the Communist parties. It is based more upon the necessities of coalition building in which the Muslim vote—especially if it can be turned into a bloc vote across a whole region—must of necessity be combined with the votes of backward and lower castes in order for these parties to defeat the BJP, whose political strategy is the opposite one of consolidating the Hindu community. For the latter strategic purpose, it is convenient to incite anti-Muslim sentiments from time to time and even to instigate communal riots when the BJP is out of power. The Congress stand on these matters is nowadays the least principled of all. Under Sonia Gandhi's leadership—departing from both Indira Gandhi's strategy of pandering to Hindu sentiment and from Nehru's policy of pandering to none—the Congress has been seeking to whip up Hindu–Muslim passions on the Ayodhya issue in order to win back the Muslim vote.

The so-called 'democratic, socialist, and secular forces', therefore, contain a mixture of parties with mixed motives, some of them quite dubious. Their postures have also had mixed results. To the extent that interparty competition plays anti-Muslim and secular sentiments off against each other, Muslims become victims, against whom riotous acts of violence are often committed as a consequence. On the other hand, in West Bengal, Kerala, and Bihar, Muslim politicians either occupy significant positions of power or are protected by secular parties from being victimised.

Muslims have become a kind of kickball in Indian politics in ways that could not happen in the United States with respect to any religious or cultural group. Democrats and Republicans pander to Jewish sentiments with regard to the state of Israel in order to gain Jewish votes. But there is a consensus in the country for support to the state of Israel. Further, any kind of anti-Semitic statement or action is out of bounds in American politics. The Christian right forces do not seek to arouse anti-Jewish sentiment to achieve power—and when they even come close to doing so, it weighs heavily against them in a secular society. Most important, it is inconceivable in America that a political party could arise and stake its claim to power around the aim of turning America into a Christian nation-state in which Jews—not to mention the millions of Hindus and Muslims in the United States today—would have to acknowledge that they are political Christians in order to be entitled to full respect and rights as American citizens.

III
Secularism and the Indian nation-state

What is the real source of all this confusion and double-talk concerning the fate and future of secularism in India? It has little or nothing in fact to do with the eroding effect of secularising processes upon the conditions of India's religious communities. It arises rather from the failures of the Indian state, society, and economy to achieve most of its stated goals. As Washbrook pointed out in 1982, there has been no 'modernising transformation of the economy', at least none that could place

India even remotely in the company of the developed countries of the West or Japan or any other of the Asian economies that have become fully or partly transformed, whatever their current (1998) economic difficulties. 'In effect', Washbrook argued, 'the condition and situation of Indian society turn the generalisation of the secular territorial national identity into an improbable dream' (1982: 178–79). I believe little has changed in these respects since Washbrook wrote—except that the pursuit of that dream has intensified even as it has remained improbable.

The situation in India remains one of abject, degrading poverty, illiteracy, and ill health for the overwhelming majority of the people of the country, on the one hand, and a life of ease and comfort within India for the corrupt political and bureaucratic classes that have profited immensely from the failures of the Indian state and a life full of prospects for their children studying, working, and advancing their careers in the United States, on the other hand. In the vast middle, among the urban lower middle classes and the sons and daughters of the peasantry whose parents cannot even imagine sending their children to the United States, there is a great scramble for the limited advancement opportunities available within India, mainly still in government service. Despite the enormous bloatedness of the Indian bureaucracies and the speed at which they have increased since independence to the advantage of few but their masters and occupants, there are not enough jobs to go around to satisfy the appetites of these tens of millions of job seekers. Out of the demands of these classes have sprung a vast array of caste, language, tribal, and religious movements for the creation of separate units within or without, but mostly within the Indian Union, or for reservations of jobs and places in educational institutions within existing units, that would provide them all with the jobs they crave.

Even where the demands for recognition and maintenance of a group's distinctive cultural attributes precede or seem incidental to the demand for jobs, they are always associated with ideal and material benefits of one kind or another that will accrue to specific leadership elements within the group. If the benefits accrued are confined only to the elites who lead these movements, they soon face dissidence and revolt within the new units they create or over the compromises they have felt compelled to make. The new dissidents soon turn to violent means, are labelled terrorists by the Indian state, and are seen as grave threats to the sacred unity of the Indian nation. Those who would offer these leaders and their tens of millions of followers seeking political and economic advancement solace through interreligious faith mock them and their aspirations, some of which are completely secular, others of which arise out of cultural, including religious, differences with the spokesmen for an Indian state heretofore dominated by upper caste Hindus.

The response of the dominant elites to such demands since independence has been that the dreams of the tens of millions threaten to shatter the dreams of the founders and leaders of the Indian state for unity, economic advancement, and respect in the broader world dominated by the powerful states. Having barely succeeded in maintaining its unity, having miserably failed at economic advancement, and having utterly failed to achieve international respect in the world, India's political elites have found their scapegoats, conceptual and substantial. The conceptual scapegoat is the process of secularisation and the loss of religious tolerance. The substantial scapegoats are the Muslim community and all those other communities, such as the Sikhs and the Kashmiris and the various tribal groupings in the north-east, even the backward and lower castes of north India and elsewhere, who have demanded 'privileges', who have been 'pampered', who have been seen to push ahead of upper caste Hindus, reversing—however fancifully—the natural order of things.

In the process, the ruling party, which under Nehru at least—and for some time under his daughter as well—had adhered to secular principles, abandoned them and turned to pandering to—not the minorities—but the vast so-called majority of Hindus, thereby opening a conceptual and political space for the militant Hindu nationalists who knew better how to pander. The answer of the declining Congress and the rising BJP to the Muslim community came on 6 December 1992 in an act of destruction for which both bear responsibility, direct as well as—*and not merely as*—indirect.

The answer to the demands from the backward and lower castes has been less direct and far more complicated, containing a mixture of elements. The thrust of the response of the dominant upper caste elites, however, has been similar to the answer to the Muslims. Just as militant Hindus say that Muslims have not been discriminated against, they have been pampered and Hindus have been pushed aside to make room for them, so upper caste Hindus in general have turned the tables on the backward castes by proclaiming themselves as the true victims. This took the form, first, of the grotesque media coverage, especially by that quintessential spokesman for the glitziest of the Hindu upper classes, *India today*, of the burning-to-death of upper caste Hindu youths against the implementation of the Mandal Commission recommendations on reservations, thereby spurring other depressed and deranged youths to engage in this grisly horror of self-destruction. This was then followed by a response from the BJP which made use of these images of horror to mobilise upper caste Hindu votes by portraying the upper caste Hindus as 'victims'.[21] A further response is yet in the early stages and is associated with the continuing globalisation of the Indian economy. However slow that process in India, it is certain to provide new places for upper caste Hindus in the multinational companies and to make government positions less desirable in comparison. Indeed, to the extent that the capitalist market economy becomes dominant in India, it will marginalise government in India, as it has elsewhere in the world. The upper castes will then allow the backward and lower castes to occupy the increasingly degraded positions in government bureaucracies—degraded in comparison to those that will be available to upper castes in the multinational companies. As always, the lower castes will get the leavings.[22]

[21] On the transmogrification of 'the upper caste elite' into 'oppressed' victims during the anti-Mandal agitation, see Nigam (1996: 1168).

[22] For a similar argument, see Milner and Sahay (1997: 16): 'An optimist might say that the uprising of the Backwards and their political victories have been revolutionary; the ancient caste system is finally

India's answer to the world has been the nuclear explosions of the summer of 1998 and its defiance of the threats of the great powers and the sentiments of an entire world in protest against this grotesque, provocative, and jingoistic display of its pretensions to national greatness.

I will leave aside all the other answers that the Government of India has given, the lessons it has taught to Sikhs, Kashmiris, and others in the past fifteen years or so. What does it all amount to and what does it have to do with the issues of secularism?

What it all amounts to is that the whole debate over the relevance of secularism for India is a marginal one, subordinate to the major issue for those who continue to contest for power at the centre of the Indian polity (cf. Vanaik 1997: 152). That issue concerns what definition of the Indian nation will best consolidate its people into a united engine for the transformation of the Indian state into a colossus in the world, equal to the greatest states, a member of the Security Council of the United Nations, a nuclear power. The BJP has a clear answer to this question. It proposes to create a homogeneous Indian nation-state into which all other religious and cultural groups may enter provided they accept Hindu nationality infused with Hindu religiosity as their creed.

Standing in the way of the BJP's goal are four sets of forces: the Communist left, the parties of the backward and Scheduled Castes, the regional parties that dominate approximately half the states of the Indian Union, and what remains of the once-mighty Congress. They are all more or less secular in orientation and in practice, though only the Communist parties can be said to be consistently secular in principle. Many of the leaders of the backward and Scheduled Caste parties are rude, uncouth, and corrupt. Many of the leaders of the regional parties are also corrupt, ludicrous in some cases as well, if not rude and uncouth. The Congress—outside of Maharashtra—is a declining and pathetic organisation, led by a woman whose primary interest in politics is to prevent the exposure of the true recipients of the Bofors money. Most are willing to make alliances of all sorts, including in some cases alliances with the BJP itself for the sake of their own personal advancement.

So, there is no solid phalanx of opposition to the BJP, which has behind it a relatively solid force comprised of cadres from the RSS. Most of the parties in Indian politics today, therefore, representing the vast majority of the population of the country, support secular principles and practices, but they are fragmented, disunited, and unreliable. The BJP represents a minority of the country, but probably a majority of educated, upper caste and upper class opinion in north India and probably a significant minority in other parts of the country as well. What it lacks in popular support, it gains in organisational unity and ideological coherence. The battle for the future of the Indian polity and the dream of Indian nationhood,

dead. A pessimist might say that by shifting to a liberal economy those of upper-caste backgrounds are likely to be largely successful in reproducing their privileges.'

therefore, is evenly balanced. It is also fateful for India, South Asia, and for the world now that both India and Pakistan have nuclear weapons, whose awesome but useless power their leaders fail to truly understand or appreciate. In this great struggle, whose significance the rest of the world can no longer afford to ignore, pious hopes for the recovery of religious tolerance and for the establishment of a secular state more in tune with some imagined truth shared by all faiths are largely beside the point.

REFERENCES

AUSTIN, GRANVILLE. 1966. *The Indian Constitution: Cornerstone of a nation*. Oxford: Clarendon Press.

BAILEY, F.G. 1991. Religion and religiosity: Ideas and their use. *Contributions to Indian sociology* 25, 2: 211–31.

———. 1998. *The need for enemies: A bestiary of political forms*. Ithaca: Cornell University Press.

BETEILLE, ANDRE. 1994. Secularism and intellectuals. *Economic and political weekly* 29, 10: 559–66.

BHASIN, PREM. 1972. *Riding the wave: The first authentic account of the recent struggle for power in India*. New Delhi: Ashajanak Publications.

BRASS, PAUL R. 1974. *Language, religion and politics in north India*. London: Cambridge University Press.

CHATTERJI, RAKHAHARI. 1988. Democracy and the Opposition in India. *Economic and political weekly* 23, 17: 843–47.

ELLIS, JOSEPH J. 1997. *American Sphinx: The character of Thomas Jefferson*. New York: Knopf.

EMBREE, AINSLEE T. 1987. Religion and politics. *In* Marshall M. Bouton, ed., *India briefing*, pp. 49–75. Boulder: Westview.

ENGINEER, ASHGAR ALI. 1998. Muslim Personal Law–Codification and reform needed. Bombay: Centre for Study of Society and Secularism. 16–31 July.

GELLNER, ERNEST. 1991. *Postmodernism, reason and religion*. London: Routledge.

JACOBSOHN, GARY J. 1993. *Apple of gold: Constitutionalism in Israel and the United States*. Princeton, N.J.: Princeton University Press.

JAFFRELOT, CHRISTOPHE. 1996. *The Hindu Nationalist Movement and Indian politics, 1925 to the 1990s: Strategies of identity-building, implantation and mobilisation (with special reference to Central India)*. London: Hurst.

JEFFERSON, THOMAS. 1984. *Writings*. New York: The Library of America.

MADAN, T.N. 1992. Beyond Ayodhya: Search for new perspectives. *Times of India*, 21 December.

———. 1997. *Modern myths, locked minds: Secularism and fundamentalism in India*. Delhi: Oxford University Press.

MILNER, MURRAY and SUKRITI SAHAY. 1997. Victory without the spoils? The irony of backward caste politics in a liberalizing economy. Unpublished paper presented at the American Sociological Association, Toronto, Canada, 9–13 August.

MORRIS-JONES, W.H. 1971. India elects for change—and stability. *Asian survey* 11, 8: 719–41.

NANDY, ASHIS. 1990. The politics of secularism and the recovery of religious tolerance. *In* Veena Das, ed., *Mirrors of violence: Communities, riots and survivors in south Asia*, pp. 69–93. Delhi: Oxford University Press.

NIGAM, ADITYA. 1996. India after the 1996 elections: Nation, locality and representation. *Asian survey* 36, 12: 1157–68.

Report. 1967. *Constituent Assembly debates, official reports*, vol. II. New Delhi: Lok Sabha Secretariat, Government of India Press.

RUDOLPH, LLOYD I. and SUSANNE H. RUDOLPH. 1987. *In pursuit of Lakshmi: The political economy of the Indian state*. Chicago: University of Chicago Press.

SHOURIE, ARUN. 1995. *The world of Fatwas or the Shariah in action*. New Delhi: ASA.

SMITH, DONALD E. 1963. *India as a secular state*. Princeton, N.J.: Princeton University Press.

VAN DER VEER, PETER. 1989. *Gods on earth: The management of religious experience and identity in a north Indian pilgrimage centre*. Delhi: Oxford University Press.

VANAIK, ACHIN. 1997. *Communalism contested: Religion, modernity and secularization*. New Delhi: Vistaar.

WASHBROOK, D.A. 1982. Ethnicity and racialism in colonial Indian society. *In* R. Ross, ed., *Racism and colonialism*, pp. 143–81. The Hague: Martijnus Nijhoff.

WILLS, GARY. 1990. *Under God: Religion and American politics*. New York: Simon and Schuster.

16

The Babri Masjid and the secular contract

Harold A. Gould

This study examines the social–historical roots of the politicisation of the Babri Masjid. It suggests that the contemporary symbolic manipulation of this historic structure, culminating in its physical destruction by the Sangh Parivar in 1992, for the purpose of legitimising the propagation of a Hindu ethno-religious state, constitutes a fanciful reformulation of traditional Indian statecraft. It also suggests that the process of 'de-secularisation' of the Indian state has been aided and abetted through the years by the ostensibly secular Congress Party's periodical willingness to play the communal card whenever this suited its tactical interests.

On 6 December 1992, so-called *kar sevaks* of the Vishwa Hindu Parishad led a frenzied assault on the Babri Masjid in Ayodhya which resulted in its total destruction. It was supported by a variety of groups that espouse the transformation of India into a Hindu-dominated ethnoreligious state. The most prominent of these, of course, were the Rashtriya Swayamsevak Sangh (RSS) and its current political manifestation, the Bharatiya Janata Party (BJP).[1]

Everyone who is knowledgeable about the complex interrelationship between religion and politics in India realised at the time that the moment the Babri Masjid crashed to the ground a fundamental change had occurred in this relationship. Not only in the modern era, but in the colonial period and even in the millennium of Muslim conquest which preceded both, the basis upon which most rulers ruled India (in whole or in part) was consensual, especially with regard to their policies toward religious communities. Despite their fanatical militancy during Islam's expansionist phase, Muslim conquerors eventually learned that their powerful onslaughts could bend Hinduism but not break it. The massive cultural power of Hindu civilisation, reaching back centuries in time and spread over a land of continental proportions, gave it an enormous survival capacity. Therefore, once Islam had politically consolidated itself in India, the various and increasingly more complex and sophisticated royal courts that were established discovered that the success and survival of their kingdoms depended upon building governmental systems that incorporated Hindus into the administrative apparatus, afforded sub-autonomy to

[1] Its predecessors were the Hindu Mahasabha and the Bharatiya Jana Sangh.

Hindu vassals, and provided social space where Hindus could continue practising their cultural and religious traditions.

In modern parlance, the Muslim rulers of India concluded in the face of India's physical size, socio-religious diversity and social complexity that successful government could be achieved only through the pursuit of consensual politics. The most noteworthy example of this, of course, was to be seen in the last of the Muslim state systems to rule over a significant portion of India, that of the Mughals, from 1525 to 1857.[2] While Akbar (1556 to 1605) represented the apex of the consensual style of politics which the Mughal system evolved, the fact is that all of the Mughal emperors were compelled to practice it to varying but significant degrees. Even Aurangzeb in reality did so, despite the conventional historiographical wisdom which attributes the Mughal Empire's disintegration to his rigid application of Islamic law. While there is some truth to this, it is only a relative truth. And even then, the extent to which it is true provides an obverse validation of the thesis that consensual politics alone has always been the magic key to political harmony and successful government in India. Aurangzeb's Islamic hardline may have been responsible for driving a wedge between the Muslim and Rajput elites who together had supplied the principle muscle behind imperial authority, and played a role in driving the Mahrattas into insurrection, but the essential processes of bargaining and accommodation between the central system and the many regional systems which enjoyed vassal status within the far-flung imperium continued. It was the reason why Aurangzeb found it possible to marshal the resources needed to wage a twenty-year campaign in the Deccan trying to subdue Shivaji and his successors. In Bayly's words, 'The Mughal emperor was *Shah-an-Shah*, "King of kings", rather than king of India.' He continues:

> The emperor's power and wealth could be great, but only if he was skilled in extracting money, soldiers and devotion from other kings. He was a marshal of the kings, an entrepreneur in power. His tools were at once the siege train and the royal honors given out at the great assemblies (*darbars*) (Bayly 1988: 13–14).

Both the British East India Company state and the British Raj which followed it were compelled by structural necessity to follow the same governmental model. In fact, the East India Company initially legitimised itself in indigenous cultural terms by accepting quasi-vassal status within the Mughal political culture (Pearson 1985). As the *Diwan* of Bengal, after Plassey (1757), the Company became in effect the Delhi emperor's revenue collector for Bengal. As Company power spread to other parts of the country, the Governors-General, most particularly Warren Hastings, actively participated in the bargaining process that underlay membership in the Mughal imperium (Moon 1949). It was one of the principal means through which the East India Company consolidated this power. Following

[2] As we know, the period of full political viability of the Mughal imperium stretched from Babar (1526) to Aurangzeb (1707). From Aurangzeb's death (1707) until the removal and deportation of Bahadur Shah the Second (1859), following the Mutiny, it was mainly the Mughal political culture that endured amidst the gradual decay of the central system's coercive authority.

the Mutiny, the Raj merely replaced the Mughal court as the country's suzerain and gradually created an admixture of directly administered territories and vassalised princely states. They called it 'honouring native custom'. Within the former, the process of political reforms, catalysed by emerging nationalism, eventually led to Indian independence. But throughout this process, the principle idioms of political interaction and control remained, of necessity, bargaining and manipulation among mutually indigestible socio-cultural entities. Within the ambit of the Raj there began a transition from *Shah-an-Shah* (i.e., the management of vassal states) to a federal structure which replicated in modern institutional terms the same governmental principles.

In many ways, the Babri Masjid was from its inception emblematic of the dilemmas that confronted attempts to create and maintain systems of government which could accommodate the social, cultural and religious diversity that all Indian state systems inevitably encompassed. Until the 1992 event, however, governmental responses to confrontations between Hindus and Muslims over the site were usually attempts to effectuate compromises that would prevent violence and achieve some kind of inter-communal reconciliation.

This may have been so even at the time of the Babri Masjid's construction. The contemporary lay version of how the Babri Masjid got constructed on one of Hinduism's most hallowed sites is, of course, that Babar personally instigated the demolition of a Hindu temple situated on the *Ram Janambhumi* after 1526, and had it replaced with a mosque in order to celebrate the triumph of Islam over Hinduism. In the words of V.S. Naipal, 'In Ayodhya the construction of a mosque on the spot regarded as sacred by the conquered population was meant as an insult.'[3] But another version of the Masjid's origins is that it grew out of a visit which Babar made to Ayodhya in 1528 to pay his respects to a famous *fakir*, Quazal Abbas Qulandar, who resided there. In the words of Farzand Ahmed of Ayodhya: 'Fakir Quazal Abbas Qulandar...apparently asked Babar to demolish the temple and build a mosque where he could offer *namaz*. According to historical accounts, Babar was reluctant to do so, but the Fakir prevailed on him and his wish was carried out.'[4] If there is any validity to the latter version, then it is apparent that even in the 16th century the first Mughal ruler foresaw the political implications of such a deed.

The roots of politicisation as we understand it today commenced in the 19th century, at the threshold of the transition from East India Company to British Imperial rule. This first 'modern' incident, in the sense of having politically manipulable communal overtones, took place in February of 1855. In Michael Fisher's words, it 'sparked the final crisis for the Awadh dynasty prior to annexation . . .' (Fisher 1987). This is because Sleeman and his associates expected that it would provide the pretext they were looking for by which the East India Company could justify absorbing the politically floundering kingdom into its steadily expanding territories.

[3] *Times of India*: 'An area of awakening', 18 July 1993.

[4] *India today*: 28 February 1986, p. 114.

The precipitating incident began when a party of Sunnis, led by Shah Ghulam Husayn, attempted to oust a group of Hindus who had taken possession of the Babri Masjid. The Sunnis were repulsed by the Hindus. Several months later, however, this Sunni party renewed their efforts to evict the Hindus. Says Fisher:

> They assembled a force of from four to six hundred Muslims, men described by British observers as *faqirs*, at a mosque near the controversial spot. While the Muslims involved to this point were apparently individuals (*Sufis* and *faqirs*) with little military training, the Hindu party escalated the conflict by gathering, besides a large number of *bayragis* (Hindu wandering ascetics), the support of several of the Hindu landholders of the area. . . .British eyewitnesses. . .estimated the total number of *bayragis*, Hindu landholders with their retainers, and miscellaneous supporters at some eight thousand (ibid.: 228).

At this juncture, the Awadh army did not intervene and a pitched battle ensued in which the Muslims suffered another setback. Fisher continues:

> The Muslims later asserted that they were attacked in their mosque during a truce arranged and guaranteed by the British. The Hindu party denied any truce. Heavily outnumbered, the Muslims seem to have left the bulk of the seventy to eighty dead found on the field following the fight (ibid.: 228).

It is said that because Wajid Ali Shah was Shia while the party of Shah Ghulam Husayn was Sunni, the ruler evinced only mild sympathy for the Muslim cause and instead attempted to act as intermediary. He was reinforced in this by the fact that the district administration was headed by a Shia (Agha Ali Khan), as was most of the municipal administration. But even Shias understood that the political implications of what had taken place required some form of measured governmental action. Fisher continues:

> . . . they felt little identification with either Sunni *faqirs* or Hindu *bayragis*. They did, however, see the largely Hindu landholders as their rivals for local authority. They urged the Awadh court that 'unless the Government interferes and gives orders for rebuilding the musjid. . .the Hindoos will become inflated and elated with their success and will proceed to other and greater extremities. . .' (ibid.: 228).

Government, in other words, could not long remain passive in the face of a communal confrontation which ironically had many of the overtones present in the 1992 incident. Rancour over Muslim co-optation of Hindu sacred space was involved, as was the case in all succeeding confrontations. Divergent class interests were involved. The ongoing struggle for local control between the Shi'i-dominated district administration and the majority Hindu landholders found voice there. In the ethnoreligious domain, both the Sunni and Shi'i religious establishments in Awadh issued *fatwas* 'decreeing the official Muslim interpretation of the issues. . . carefully worded to make it an issue of the defense of Islam against polytheists. . . .' (ibid.: 229).

Statecraft demanded that consensus and reconciliation of some kind be sought, even though it would not have been impossible for Wajid Ali Shah to have blatantly sided on religious grounds with his fellow Muslims. Instead, the Awadh ruler appointed a tripartite investigative commission consisting of the district official (Agha Ali Khan), a leading Hindu landholder (the Raja of Ayodhya), and the British officer in charge of combat troops in the area. Despite this, however, the contestants were irreconcilable. They would accept no compromises, including the one that a mosque be built along an outer wall of the Masjid while the Masjid itself remained in Hindu hands.

Confrontation built, Hindus and Muslims gathered forces, and the Company officials saw in it an opportunity to seize control of the kingdom. In Fisher's words:

> When the commission—on which the Company had the decisive vote—ruled against the Muslims, the Resident exerted his influence on Wajid Ali Shah to force the ruler to subdue the *faqirs*. Further, the Resident suggested to the Governor General that this incident be manipulated to justify the Company's annexation of Awadh. He argued he '. . .should retire from Lucknow to the Company's territories, and withdraw the brigade of British troops, and formally declare the existing treaty at an end. . . .' The Resident felt certain that, suddenly deprived of his guiding presence and the major effective military force in the province at this crucial time, the Awadh administration would beg for annexation (ibid.: 229).

But to everyone's surprise, Wajid Ali Shah acted decisively and effectively: 'He moved units into position to intercept the marchers should they move toward Fyzabad. . . . To reinforce the bonds between the largely *Shi'i* army and himself, he called officers of several units facing the marchers in his *darbar*. . .and awarded them *khil'ats*. . . .*In addition to the army, Wajid Ali Shah called upon landholders to demonstrate their loyalty to his reign*' (ibid.: 233, emphasis added). Thus, while the British smugly predicted that Muslim landholders would reject such entreaties and support the *jihad*, some responded positively and, in fact, 'None of the landholders seem to have acted against the orders of Wajid Ali Shah by giving support to the marchers' (ibid.). As a result, the Malawi's march was annihilated: 'The Awadh troops stood firm and nearly all the marchers were killed. British observers estimated their dead at between three and four hundred. The Awadh army suffered casualties of thirty-three percent, testimony to the resolution shown by both sides. . .' (ibid.: 234).

Awadh was indeed annexed to Company territories a year later, an act which many say was one of the principal precipitants of the 1857 Mutiny. But the Awadh kingdom survived the Babri Masjid crisis of 1855 because its ruler in the end had remained true to principles of statecraft which had perennially recognised the importance of practising consensual politics in a multi-ethnic socio-political environment. He distanced himself from his own socio-religious community in the name of reconciling diverse ethnoreligious and class interests.

I
From the colonial era to independence

The next noteworthy milestone in the political interplay between Hindus and Muslims over the Babri Masjid occurred in the same year that the Indian National Congress was founded. A Hindu petition to build a temple on the site in 1885 was the first time the issue came within the purview of the post-Mutiny modern state. An English district judge ruled that a temple could not be built without inflaming communal passions. A railing was then built to separate the *chabutra* (17′ × 21′ platform at the spot where the *janambhumi* allegedly exists) from the Masjid. This imposed a physical boundary between Hindu and Muslim religious space which persisted until 1986 when Judge K.M. Pandey ordered the Babri Masjid unlocked and made accessible to Hindus, about which more presently.

A number of ominous confrontations occurred between 1885 and 1934. The communal confrontation over the Babri Masjid which occurred in 1934 did lead to violence. At the time, no animal slaughtering was allowed within the municipal limits of Ayodhya. However, there was a Muslim prayer ground adjacent to the city boundary and beside it a place where Muslims slaughtered goats at *Bakr Id*. In 1934, a cow was slaughtered at this spot and word went quickly out to the Hindu community that this had occurred. A congregation of *sadhus* visiting Ayodhya at the time precipitated a riot in response to this alleged deed. The Superintendent of Police at the time was a Mr. Swift who persuaded the Mahant of Bara Asthan (the largest *Akhra* in Ayodhya), who was by chance sitting in his office as the riot erupted, to accompany him to the riot scene and help put it down. Following the riot, seven cases were developed, one in each of the seven muhallas where rioting had occurred. However, the judge hearing the cases dismissed them when the testimony of some of the policemen who had allegedly witnessed the rioting proved to be suspect. Mainly, some claimed that the Bara Asthan Mahant had led the Hindu rioters, a claim which SP Swift was able to decisively refute since the Mahant had been with him all along. As in past incidents, the state's role was to strive for impartiality and public order.

However, the definitive incident, in the sense of being the immediate lineal ancestor of the 1992 tragedy, occurred on 22 December 1949, almost exactly forty-three years prior to the Masjid's destruction by Hindu fundamentalists. On this day a statue (*murti*) of Ram, and images of Sita and Lakshman 'dramatically appeared' in the Babri Masjid[5] allegedly signifying that this symbolic incarnation of Hindu kingship had returned to reclaim his sacred birth-place. This deed had, in fact, been engineered by two officers of the Uttar Pradesh provincial civil service (the Deputy Commissioner, K.K.K. Nayar, and the City Magistrate, Guru Datta Singh) who were both closet members of the Rashtriya Swayamsevak Sangh (RSS). Their motive was political image-building for themselves and for the Bharatiya Jana Sangh party (BJS) that was in the process of being formed at this time to become

[5] *Indian Express*: 6 February 1986.

the electoral vehicle for promoting right-wing Hindu interests in independent India. While they were compelled to resign from government service for their complicity in this incident, they soon surfaced as overt members of the BJS and aspirants for electoral office under its rubric.

After the images appeared in the Babri Masjid, crowds of Hindus gathered to celebrate Lord Rama's return (and correspondingly Hinduism's resurgence) while Muslim crowds materialised to oppose any Hindu seizure of the mosque. A.G. Noorani refers to two documents which reveal the official version of the 1949 incident. In the first:

> . . .a radio message sent at 10:30 a m on December 23, 1949 by the district magistrate K.K.K. Nayar to chief minister Govind Ballabh Pant, the chief secretary and the home secretary. . .read thus: "A few Hindus entered Babri Masjid at night when the Masjid was deserted and installed a deity there. Situation under control. DM and SP and force at spot. Police picket of 15 persons was on duty at night *but apparently did not act*" (Noorani 1987, emphasis added).

This message was based on a report filed earlier by police constable Mata Prasad to the Ayodhya Police Station which became the substance of the FIR submitted by sub-inspector Ram Dube of the same station on 23 December 1949 and certified by the office of the City Magistrate (Guru Datta Singh) on 11 February 1949. It says:

> According to Mata Prasad (paper No 7), when I reached to [*sic*] *Janam Bhumi* around 8 o'clock in the morning, I came to know that group of 50–60 persons had entered Babri Masjid after breaking the compound gate lock of the mosque or through jumping across the walls (of the compound) with a stair and established therein, an idol of Shri Bhagwan and painted Sita Ram, *etc*., on the outer, and inner walls with *geru* [redlom]. Hans Raj on duty asked them to defer but they did not. These persons have already entered the mosque before the available PAC (Provincial Armed Constabulary) guards could be commanded. Officials of the district administration came at the site and involved themselves in necessary arrangements. Afterwards a crowd of 5–6 thousand gathered around and while chanting *bhajans* and raising religious slogans tried to enter the mosque but were deterred and nothing untoward happened thereon because of proper arrangements.... Ram Das, Ram Shakti Das and 50–60 unidentified others entered the mosque surreptitiously and spoiled its sanctity. Government servants on duty and several others are witness to it. Therefore it is written and filed (ibid.).

Although there are discrepancies and omissions in these official accounts which effectively obscure many of the political machinations and personal ambitions which lay behind and led up to this event and its aftermath, there are unmistakable clues which indicate that some sections of the local official establishment had been far from impartial. One glaring instance is to be seen in passages from the first of the above-noted two statements which assert (*a*) that, 'DM and SP and force at spot', and (*b*) that 'Police picket of 15 persons was on duty at night but apparently did not act'. The District Magistrate was K.K.K. Nayar, one of the instigators of the plot, and the Superintendent of Police was under his command. So it was little wonder that the police picket on duty 'apparently did not act', thereby providing leeway for the conspirators to enter the mosque, plant the *murtis* and depart unmolested.

Despite the culpability of Nayar and Singh in engineering this communal confrontation, however, they appear to have panicked when it threatened to get out of hand. They rushed to cover their tracks. Within hours after it began, both men appeared on the doorstep of Babu Priyadatta Ram, Chairman of the Faizabad-cum-Ayodhya municipal board. They admitted that they had been the instigators of the incident, and even admitted that they had done it as a means of generating the kind of issue that would be beneficial to BJS party-building. They claimed they had neither intended nor anticipated the degree of inter-communal tension which had ensued. Now, faced with the ugly consequences, they implored Priyadatta Ram to invoke his influence and good offices to help defuse the situation before it led to a communal riot. Obviously their fear of the latter, Priyadatta Ram believed, arose from the fact that such a riot would lead to a judicial inquiry which would publicly reveal the partisan role which Nayar and Singh, two government officials, had played in its occurrence. This, in turn, would lead to their public disgrace and possible prosecution for felony, which would result in their disbarment from politics. Priyadatta Ram believed that neither man was genuinely contrite over what they had done, but merely afraid for their skins. Nevertheless he agreed to help because of his own desire, as a responsible elected official and an implicit supporter of the secular state, to do whatever he could to avert communal rioting on his watch.[6]

In addition to being the Chairman of the municipal board, Priyadatta Ram had warm personal relations with the U.P. Chief Minister, Pandit Pant. Nayar and Singh wanted him to use his powers and connections to work out a deal through which the Babri Masjid crisis would be put to rest as quietly as possible with minimal damage to their public reputations. Pant agreed to such an intermediary's role for Priyadatta Ram. As we shall see presently, Pant had some decided predilections of his own toward manipulating conservative Hindu religious sensibilities for political purposes, and likely was not overly perturbed about the present effort by the Hindu Right to regain control of the Masjid. However, as the Chief Minister of UP, and a leader of the party that would be the most directly challenged by the emerging BJS, Pant clearly opted for a solution that would reduce communal tensions and attempt to indefinitely postpone a decision on the ultimate disposition of the Babri Masjid.

The understanding worked out through Priyadatta Ram was that Nayar and Singh would resign from the civil service as soon as the crisis abated. Meanwhile, Guru Datta Singh, in his capacity as City Magistrate, was told to impound the

[6] My knowledge of these events comes from a long personal friendship I enjoyed with Babu Priyadatta Ram during the many years I lived in Faizabad district as a research scholar. On matters of local political history he was one of my principal informants.

property and put it into receivership pending the outcome of litigation which would ostensibly determine who had legal title to it. The designated custodian was to be Babu Priyadatta Ram, Chairman of the municipal board. It was expected that this litigation would be encouraged to go on indefinitely, thereby postponing a decision, that would provoke communal conflict whichever way it went. The fear that a definitive judicial decision would lead to such a result was certainly borne out by district judge K.M. Pandey's order on 11 February 1986 to remove the padlocks from the Masjid!

Two suits were filed in the aftermath of this stabilisation agreement. The first was filed by Gopal Singh Visharad, General Secretary of the Hindu Sabha, in early 1950. However, the suit was not allowed because Visharad had failed to give the government two months notice as is required when a suit is filed against the government. In the suit, Visharad had asked for an injunction restraining anyone from removing the idols from the Masjid.

But since there was awareness that Visharad's case might be thrown out, another Hindu Sabha supporter, Ram Chandra Das, gave two months notice to the Government that he would file a comparable suit when the notification period expired. Both suits were based on a simple allegation which met the requirements of the law: viz., 'I went to the *Janam Bhumi* a few days ago and when I went back again to worship police were there barring my entry. Therefore, there should be an injunction to remove the obstruction to my free worship there; meanwhile the *murtis* should remain where they are.'

The lawyer whom the Hindus retained in the case which followed 'the proper notification period' was, ironically, Babu Sarvjeet Lal, a Kayastha, who had been, along with Acharya Narendra Deva, one of the founders of the Congress Socialist Party in Faizabad district. In 1946, he had been elected unopposed to the U.P. Legislative Assembly from Faizabad Rural East constituency on the CON ticket (when the CSP was still a sub-party). In the 1948 by-elections he was defeated in this constituency by the Congress candidate. Subsequently, he ran as a Socialist (first on Socialist Party and later on Praja Socialist Party tickets) in 1952, 1957, and in 1969. The point is that Sarveet Lal's entire political career had been identified with the left and with upholding the sanctity of the secular state. Yet, as a lawyer in search of clients, he appears to have had no qualms about representing the Hindu Right in the Babri Masjid case. His own explanation is that everyone understood that the Babri Masjid was a political hot potato and that, resultantly, the purpose of litigation was to put off indefinitely any final judicial decision as to the structure's legal disposition. He, therefore, saw his role as abetting the determination of the state to hold communal forces at bay.

While the specific issue of which community was entitled to ownership rights over the Babri Masjid and the land (*janambhumi*) upon which it was situated lapsed into legal limbo from 1948 onward (until 1986), the foundation for the politicisation of the mosque within the framework of India's post-independence political culture had been established. This was attested by the rapidity with which groups and individuals on the Hindu Right seized advantage of it. Both K.K.K. Nayar and

Guru Datta Singh were able to parlay their celebrity as instigators of the Babri Masjid incident into significant political careers through the 50s and 60s. Each had been given the option of resigning from the provincial civil service to avoid prosecution; and because neither had thus been convicted of any crime, they were eligible to seek public office as private citizens.

Guru Datta Singh ran for the Legislative Assembly on a BJS ticket from Faizabad West constituency in 1952 and came in second. He shocked the Congress establishment in 1953 when he won the presidentship of the Faizabad-cum-Ayodhya municipal board in the only direct election ever held for this position, unseating Babu Priyadatta Ram, head of the 'Kayastha party', and scoring ahead of the Maharaja of Ayodhya as well. This victory, in fact, may well have had something to do with the U.P. government terminating this form of choosing municipal board Chairmen after this one experiment with direct election for the office. The ruling Congress government then 'superseded' the Faizabad-cum-Ayodhya municipal board in order to neutralise Jana Sangh control of its patronage machinery. Undeterred, Guru Datta next ran for Parliament in 1957 and once again came in second to the winning Congressman. In 1962, he again ran for the Legislative Assembly from Faizabad constituency (containing the city of Faizabad-cum-Ayodhya) but once again finished second to the Congress incumbent. He died before the next general election. But in the twelve years following the Babri Masjid incident, Guru Datta Singh had fashioned a significant conservative political identity for himself, rooted in his identification with the RSS, the establishment of the BJS in Faizabad district, and the role he played in transforming the Babri Masjid into a usable political resource for the Hindu Right.

K.K.K. Nayar did not remain in Faizabad district very long after his resignation from the provincial civil service. For reasons not entirely clear to me, Nayar relocated himself in Bahraich district.[7] Perhaps this was designed to distance himself from the scandal surrounding the Babri Masjid incident—to 'start fresh' elsewhere, as it were. In any event, Nayar and his wife had built a formidable Jana Sangh machine in Bahraich district by 1967 (Third General Election). In 1952, two Congress giants, Rafi Ahmad Kidwai and Jogendra Singh, won both Bahraich seats (Bahraich East and Bahraich West, respectively), while the BJS was able to do no better than third place in either. In 1957, Congress repeated its dominance in the district's two parliamentary constituencies (now called Bahraich and Kaisarganj). In 1962, however, Congress control of the district began to weaken. Two Swatantra candidates (Basant Kunwari in Kaisarganj and Kunwar Ram Singh in Bahraich) captured the parliamentary seats. Then, in 1967, K.K.K. Nayar took Bahraich constituency and his wife (Sushila Nayar) took Kaisarganj. The Congress machine had been so severely weakened that in the second election (the Fourth, in 1972) they refrained from even putting up candidates against the Nayars in either constituency.

[7] Eventually he and his wife settled in Lucknow where his widow still lives. Neither would ever consent to an interview with me despite many attempts by influential intermediaries to arrange it. The explanation I got through knowledgeable friends was that their militant Hinduism included very strong anti-foreigner feelings.

II
The BJP, the Congress and the desecularisation of Indian politics

By 1967, the BJS had become a well-established party in the Hindi heartland. In the Fourth General Election it experienced a major upsurgence in UP, winning ninety-eight seats (twice its total in 1962, which itself had been a significant achievement).[8] Exploiting the symbolism of the Babri Masjid and forging a coalition with the religious orders in Ayodhya, with Vaishyas in the city, and elite castes in the agrarian sector, a Jan Sanghi (Brij Kishore) won the Faizabad assembly seat by unseating the Congress incumbent, Madan Mohan Varma, who had been Speaker of the U.P. assembly. This was the first victory in Faizabad district by the Bharatiya Jana Sangh above the local-bodies level. Significantly it had occurred in the constituency which contained the holy city of Ayodhya where stood the Babri Masjid. The circumstances surrounding this election can be viewed in retrospect as a prototype of the grand strategy that would one day propel the Jana Sangh's successor party, the BJP, into power at the national level. It was not simply the fact that the coalition which Brij Kishore assembled at the local level consisted of the right class mix of social groups. It was also the fact that the first attempt was made during this campaign to explicitly link the Babri Masjid controversy to a wider spectrum of Hindu political mobilisation.

The context was a *hartal* that was organised on 3 December 1966, by the BJS to memorialise the demise of sadhu Rishi Sarup who had died in Delhi while fasting against cow slaughter. Following the sadhu's death, over 400 supporters of the anti–cow-slaughter movement gathered at Nigambodh Ghat and demanded that the sadhu's body be transported to Diwan Hall, near Lajpat Rai Market, so that his disciples could pay him their last respects. When the authorities refused, claiming that the sadhu had not actually died while on fast, a mob gathered, took control of his body, placed it on a truck and set out for Gurmukteshwar. They were intercepted by the police and the devotees were forced to flee leaving the sadhu's body behind in the truck.

The death of this sadhu in Delhi, and the events which followed, reverberated in many U.P. towns in the form of BJS-led agitations and general strikes. In Faizabad-cum-Ayodhya, *the cow-slaughter issue was melded with demands for the opening of the Babri Masjid* into a comprehensive ideological package by the Jana Sangh candidate in his successful campaign for the assembly seat. A deputation of sadhus and others had travelled from Faizabad to Delhi to take part in the anti–cow-slaughter demonstrations there so that they could connect this issue with the *janambhumi* issue in Ayodhya. In this sense, Brij Kishore proved to have been a pioneer of sorts. However, while successful locally, the time had not come for this model to be effectively projected onto a national or indeed even a regional

[8] See Andersen (1987); Graham (1990); and my review of Graham in *Economic development and cultural change* 42, 2: 465–67 (1994).

scale. The sociological and ideological ingredients were there, but universalisation processes had at this point not gathered enough political momentum.

What were the developments that eventually did set these processes in motion? Clearly, their referents were a series of major changes that occurred in India between the 1960s and 1980s which created a socio-cultural milieu facilitating the transformation of the Babri Masjid/*Ram janambhumi* controversy from a relatively localised preoccupation into a national *cause célèbre*. These were: (1) a scalar increase in the complexity of the national political economy; (2) a major restructuring of the agrarian system; (3) the melding of caste ethnicity with emerging class differentiation; (4) the ramification of mass-media culture into the remote reaches of the society. The contest between the BJP, the Janata Dal (in its various manifestations), and the Congress from the start had class as well as ethnoreligious dimensions. Since the Green Revolution, India has been evolving an increasingly centralised, integrated national political economy in which clusters of castes (the primary social structural legacy of pre-industrial society) have found themselves sharing particular relationships to the means of production and power. The Backward Castes are a case in point. Beneficiaries of the transformation of the agrarian system from feudal to modern market-oriented agriculture, they have increasingly formed the backbone of the so-called *Kisan* parties, such as today's United Front and its predecessors, reaching back to Charan Singh's Samyukt Vidhayak Dal in U.P., which had started it all on a systematic basis more than thirty years ago. Dalits, the current term for politicised Scheduleds, have combined for political purposes in a manner comparable to the Backwards, under the rubric of parties like the Indian People's Front (IPF) and the Bahujan Samaj Party (BSP).[9]

The 1980s were a crucial turning point in this process. Toward the end of Mrs Gandhi's tenure in office and especially following her assassination, pressures mounted to de-bureaucratise the Indian economy and give market forces a freer reign. The first culmination of this new turn was, of course, during Rajiv Gandhi's term in office when much was made of his 'management style' of running the country and the economy. 'Image management', and 'spin-doctoring', i.e., the manipulation of publics through television, video tapes, cinema and other forms of mass-media technology, became an integral aspect of political strategies designed to win national elections and obtain public support for new economic policies.[10]

[9] At the time of the Tenth General Election (1991), I noted the emergence of the Scheduleds as a distinctive political force:

> Another symptom of a growing nationally integrated class system is the increasing political visibility and viability of Dalit-based political organization. Behind this lies the steady erosion of hierarchical paternalism as agrarian society succumbs to market-driven, labor-intensive food production. The Bahujan Samaj across much of the Hindi Belt and the IPF in Bihar are striking manifestations of the politicization of this major socio-economic change in the occupational system (Gould 1993: 309).

[10] See Gould 1993; see also Rudolph (1993: 165), who speaks of the origins of the media factor: 'Rajiv Gandhi was India's first TV prime minister, i.e., he had TV access to a majority of the population.'

Importantly, the time when these changes were occurring in the country's political culture coterminated with (indeed catalysed) the development of a class cleavage between Elite Castes and Backward Castes that reverberated with special intensity across the Hindi heartland. The specific trigger for this outburst of class rivalry was the V.P. Singh–led Janata Dal government's (November 1989 to November 1990) determination to implement the Mandal Commission Report issued in the mid-1980s. (The Report had recommended that 27 per cent of all central government jobs be reserved for Backward Castes in addition to 21 per cent for Scheduleds.) This was a deliberate strategy designed to simultaneously exploit both class ethnicity to garner support from the Backward and Scheduled Castes on economic grounds, and communal identity to attract Muslims on ethnoreligious grounds. The aim was to make the Janata Dal the party of the 'under-represented majority' by luring these groups away from their traditional allegiance to the Congress and offering them a haven from the reactionary elitism of the BJP.

Violent protests, including self-immolations, by members of the upper castes ensued because it was (rightly) seen that such quotas constituted a threat to their heretofore privileged access to positions in government service, access to institutions of higher learning, seats in medical schools, etc. This, in turn, opened the way for intensified counter-mobilisation by the Janata Dal leadership on behalf of their Backward and Scheduled Caste clienteles who stood to benefit socially, economically and politically from the implementation of Mandal.

It was a crucial turning point in contemporary Indian political evolution. The broad class cleavage that was opened up at this time enabled the opponents of secularism as originally embodied in the Indian Constitution to move from a position of marginality in Indian politics to a position of respectability. Put simply, right-wing Hindu nationalism, long the enemy of any concept of the state in which Muslims and Hindus enjoyed equal status under the law and in cultural esteem, acquired a mass following by pandering to the status trepidations of urban middle-class and Elite Caste Hindus (in actuality overlapping categories of people) who felt threatened by Mandal, Muslims and upwardly mobile middle and lower castes. Its leadership emanated from that segment of the Indian population which had throughout the country's modern history refused to reconcile itself either to communal accommodation with India's Muslims or the establishment of the secular state. In the 1980s, the Bharatiya Janata Party merely became the latest political legatee of what Pandey (1991) has called 'the militant Hindu construction' originated by M.S. Golwalkar and given original political expression by the old Hindu Mahasabha. Responding to the increased scale of contemporary mass society, the Bharatiya Janata Party consolidated within its organisational ambit the old Bharatiya Jana Sangh party, the RSS, the Vishwa Hindu Parishad, the Bajrang Dal and various other right-wing Hindu action groups of past and present vintage. It brought into the political mainstream for the first time since Mahatma Gandhi's assassination, under the rubric of Hindutva, a doctrine which fundamentally rejected the premises of the secular state and proposed in its place the establishment of an enthnoreligious state.

III

Congress's role in the promotion of anti-secular processes

Apart from the broad socio-economic process alluded to above that underlay it, this gravitation of counter-secular ideology toward the political mainstream was abetted by the fact that, even in Nehru's day, there had been much ambivalence in the Congress Party itself on the issue of what secularism should mean, especially with regard to what policies should be adopted toward the country's 'mega-minority', the Muslims. In certain respects, this ambivalence helped pave the way for the Babri Masjid's destruction in 1992, and certainly influenced its political aftermath, as indeed it had paved the way for the *murtis* incident in 1949.

Speaking of the latter first, it is often forgotten that the conservative wing of Congress routinely employed counter-secular tactics in the late 1940s and early 1950s to destroy the legitimacy of its own left wing—viz., the dissident Congress Socialists—as well as to try and politically neutralise Jawaharlal Nehru (see Brass 1965; Gould 1994; Weiner 1957). Precedents were set for politicising the Babri Masjid as early as 1948 when the U.P. Congress cynically employed Hindu religious symbolisms and 'Red-baiting' tactics as part of their strategy for defeating the twelve Congress Socialist candidates who fought by-elections in U.P. after resigning from the party. In general, the Pandit Pant–led Congress repeatedly tarred these Socialists with the 'atheist' label (because they were avowed Marxists, although anti-Stalinist), thus appealing to the religious prejudices of an unsophisticated, largely peasant electorate. The tactic was employed with special ruthlessness against Acharya Narendra Deva, the father of the Socialist party, because of the powerful factional status he had enjoyed in Congress before he left it (his faction had actually been dominant over Pant's) and because the constituency from which he ran for the Legislative Council was Faizabad–Sitapur–Bahraich Urban.[11] Faizabad was the Acharya's home town which, of course, contained the holy city of Ayodhya, the embodiment of Hindu orthodoxy.

To develop and exploit this resource for political purposes, Congress chose a 'political holy man', Baba Raghava Das (see Brass 1965), to run against Narendra Deva. Purshottamdas Tandon and Pandit Pant led a parade of Hindu traditionalists harboured by the Congress right wing to Ayodhya where they hammered relentlessly at the Acharya's alleged godless Marxism, even going to the extent of noting that he no longer wore the *chhot*, the tuft of hair at the back of the head that denotes Hindu religiosity. Also important is the fact that the manager of this campaign was a fellow Congress Socialist, Gopal Narain Saxena, who had decided not to leave the party with his fellow leftists and then concluded that pragmatic political considerations took precedence over principle when the chips were down. Analysts of this campaign agree that the small margin by which Narendra Deva was defeated in the 1948 by-elections was almost certainly attributable to the 'Ayodhya factor'—i.e., the utilisation of whatever combination of factional and symbolic (including counter-secular) resources it took to win.

[11] This election was conducted under the rules of the 1935 Government of India Act.

Conscientious attempts by the Hindu Right to politicise Ayodhya, and most particularly, the Babri Masjid, followed closely on the heels of Congress's successful campaign against Acharya Narendra Deva through which Baba Raghava Das became the sitting MLC from Faizabad. Although the 'Gorakhpur Gandhi' seems not to have blatantly exploited the political implications of his religiosity, his example was certainly not lost on other, less idealistic, Hindu-oriented aspirants to political careers, such as K.K.K. Nayar and Guru Datta Singh. The Congress itself had let the genie out of the bottle. But the political damage proved to be minimal at this point in time because Congress enjoyed such pervasive dominance as the party which had led the country to independence (see Gould 1994).

It was in the 1980s that the chickens of political morality came home to roost. The Congress, as they had done forty years ago in order to counter the Socialist left, once again opted for the tactics of 'limited de-secularisation', this time in order to try and checkmate the Hindu right. The massive political mandate achieved by Rajiv Gandhi in the Eighth General Election (1984) was showing signs of erosion by 1986. A number of factors were responsible for this. Rajiv's increasingly apparent political ineptitude and the widening spectre of corruption (exemplified by the Bofors scandal) had resulted in V.P. Singh's defection from the Congress and the establishment of a rival political force. The BJP was on the rise. Taking advantage of the growing Hindu backlash over the Sikh and Kashmir insurgencies and Elite Caste alarm over the increased assertiveness of the Backward and Scheduled Castes, its leaders, most particularly the L.K. Advani wing of the party, had discovered the Babri Masjid as an integrative symbol around which mass mobilisation could be developed. It was this strategy that enabled the party to achieve a political critical mass.

The transformation of the Babri Masjid from a local or at most regional issue to one of national proportions required a dramatic amplification of the current level of public awareness for which the forces of the Hindu right could take credit. This opportunity occurred on 11 February 1986, ironically but unsurprisingly (in the light of its past conduct) with Congress collusion. On this date a Faizabad lawyer, Umesh Chandra Pandey, seemingly came out of the blue and moved an appeal before District and Sessions Judge K.M. Pandey against the rejection of his plea by the town *munsif* that the gates of the Babri Masjid be unlocked.[12] When Judge Pandey vacated the *munsif*'s ruling and ordered that the Babri Masjid be unlocked, the floodgates of ethnoreligious turmoil over the mosque were flung open once again. Returning the Babri Masjid to Hindu access was touted by the BJP and its allies as a triumph, as the first step toward the achievement of Hindutva, i.e., the eventual de-secularisation of Indian society and the establishment of an ethnoreligious state. The latter could now be pursued through mass mobilisation, using the full force of the contemporary media, under the aegis of the combined political resources of the Bharatiya Janata Party, the Vishwa Hindu Parishad, the

[12] As Pandey described the logic behind his initiative: (*a*) Litigation was consigned to irrelevance by Judge Pandey's order because no judgement years down the road could ever be expected to reverse the access Hindus now have to the shrine. (*b*) A Ram temple will surely be eventually constructed at the site.

RSS, and the Bajrang Dal. All of the fears and concerns which had haunted Babu Priyadatta Ram and others who were responsible for putting this dispute in limbo thirty-seven years earlier had dramatically materialised!

Prior to this sequence of events a scenario unfolded which Congress helped to orchestrate and which, by doing so, profoundly compromised Congress's standing as the bulwark of Nehruvian secularism. It began with Arun Nehru, at the time one of Rajiv Gandhi's closest associates, having a letter delivered to Judge Pandey intimating that Congress would not object to his ordering the unlocking of the Babri Masjid. At the same time, an agreement was concluded between the BJP and Congress by Buta Singh and Narain Datta Tiwari (the then Chief Minister of Uttar Pradesh) approving of a *Shilanya* Ceremony (the laying of a cornerstone) that would be conducted by the BJP/VHP after the Babri Masjid had been reopened, thus affording symbolic legitimation of its eventual replacement on the *janambhumi* by a Ram *mandir*. The Congress contact was with one of two VHP factions, one that was on friendly terms with Hindu-oriented Congressites. The other, more orthodox and militant faction did not trust Congress and claimed that Congress was merely trying to use the VHP for its own purposes—viz., to try and co-opt a portion of the Hindu Right's constituency. The latter were correct, of course, and it is herein that the irony of this entire episode lies. The Congress leadership had grown panicky over its perceived eroding political dominance and believed that the party must move toward the right on socio-religious issues in order to stem the rot. The anti-Congress faction had the upper hand in the VHP and in their propaganda simply took ideological advantage of the opening which Congress had provided for them. The BJP then skilfully entered the fray by organising marches and demonstrations (such as the famous *Rath Yatra* led by L.K. Advani), utilising modern media technology to propagate its ideology and symbols wherever possible.

The latter process was enormously abetted by a media event for which the BJP and its allies bore no direct responsibility. As the political atmosphere was heating up, Doordarshan ran a highly sophisticated dramatisation of the *Ramayana* whose episodes continued for eighteen months commencing in January of 1987, and then followed it up with a ninety-one–episode version of the *Mahabharata*! The entire country became transfixed by these presentations of Hinduism's two most renowned epics about traditional kingship and moral struggle during India's mythological Golden Age. Not unlike fascist-style political organisations everywhere, the BJP lost no time in connecting its own revivalistic imageries to those that millions of Indians were watching on their television screens. It undoubtedly fertilised the symbolic environment in which the Sangh Parivar was operating.

IV
Conclusions

As noted at the beginning of this essay, the destruction of the Babri Masjid on 6 December 1992, shortly after Congress returned to power with P.V. Narasimharao as Prime Minister, marked the end of an era. Secularism as an unchallenged, or at least *unchallengeable*, basis for the Indian state disintegrated along with Babar's almost five-centuries-old mosque. In the past, even before the birth of the modern Indian state, or indeed even before the colonial state, governments which had political authority over Ayodhya consistently tried to be as even-handed as possible in dealing with any controversy concerning ownership claims on the Babri Masjid/*Ram janambhumi*. This was consistent with the time-honoured principle of *shah en shah*—viz., accommodating diversity when failure to do so threatened to tear the state asunder. Wajid Ali Shah suppressed Muslim zealots in 1856 when their actions offended the religious sensibilities of Hindu landholders whose political quiescence was important to the state. The colonial authorities acted similarly when communal confrontations flared which threatened the status quo. All Indian governments prior to 1986 did likewise despite the fact that the composition of these governments and their citizenry was overwhelmingly Hindu. When trouble arose over the mosque, government action endeavoured to head off inter-cultural violence and seek compromise among the contending parties.

In his masterful study of secularism and fundamentalism in India, Madan (1997) has vividly characterised the fundamental change which occurred in how government dealt with communally charged social confrontation at the practical political level. Says he:

> The destruction of the Babri mosque in Ayodhya in December 1992 by right-wing Hindu extremists, including prominently the so-called RSS family (*sangh parivar*), was an unprecedented and crippling blow to Indian secularism. . . .[T]he Indian state, at the state and national levels, became an accomplice, through acts of omission and commission, in *this act of betrayal of both traditional cultural pluralism and modern secularism* (Madan 1997: 259, emphasis added).

Stated in more systematic terms, the manner in which governments prior to 1986 dealt with the Babri Masjid was emblematic of a broad principle of statecraft that had always made sense in the face of the country's elaborate cultural diversity: Ruling elites found it more politically effective to construct 'ethno-accommodative states' than 'ethnoreligious states'. The former kept the peace; the latter fomented ethnic violence and rebellion. In this sense, the modern secular state *in the Indian context* was both a logical and moral extension of the ethno-accommodative state which had always been the preferred model for enlightened ruling elites. This is something which both Mahatma Gandhi and Jawaharlal Nehru, each in his own way, instinctively understood.

The period between 1986 and 1992 changed everything. For the first time since independence, a secular government compromised its unambiguous affirmation of secular (i.e., ethno-accommodative) principles and colluded with the proponents of the ethnoreligious state. This went far beyond the pandering to communal sentiments in which Pandit Pant and other Congressmen of this era engaged. While the Hindu Right and their well-wishers in Congress contended that what they were doing represented a return to 'traditional' political values, the fact is that it represented a fundamental change in the traditional political value system as it had always operated at the *de facto* level, for it meant abnegating the 'ethno-accommodative contract' which had for centuries driven governmental policies pertaining to relations between the major socio-cultural and socio-religious communities. The Sangh Parivar's claim that its advocacy of the ethnoreligious state represented the restoration of an original Hindu culture and statecraft is a classic manifestation of the *ex post facto* invention (or reworking) of a tradition to fit contemporary political stratagems. This process is as old as the Bronze Age.[13]

By acceding to the unlocking of the Babri Masjid and then remaining passive when the mosque was torn down by the Vishwa Hindu Parishad, Congress helped to facilitate this reworking of tradition to accommodate the Sangh Parivar's political agenda, and by doing so cut the moral ground out from under itself. From that point, the Babri Masjid as a kind of metaphor for the sanctity of all cultural communities within the ambit of the ethno-accommodative state was ended. Its destruction was then only a matter of time, along with Congress's continuation of its status as the custodian and defender of the secular contract.

Pradip K. Datta (1991: 2523) described the consequences of what he termed the 'attempted appropriation of political Hinduism by the Congress' as follows:

> . . .[W]hat they received was a tremendous propagation of Hindu identity through Rajiv Gandhi's turn to a 'soft-sell' Hinduism combined with a craving for hi-tech. This particular mix not only removed the idea of political Hinduism from

[13] See Hobsbawm and Ranger 1988. '"Tradition"', declare the authors, 'must be distinguished clearly from "custom" which dominates so-called "traditional" societies.' With regard to 'tradition', 'insofar as there is. . .reference to a historic past, the peculiarity of "invented" traditions is that the continuity with it is largely fictitious' (p. 2). This point is especially apropos with regard to the factual basis for the current claims of Hindu nationalists that the *Ram janambhumi* has been a functioning sacred site since the time of Raja Ram himself. Groups representing Hindu interests assert, of course, that there was indeed a temple situated at the *janambhumi* which was pointedly demolished and replaced by a mosque in order to symbolise the triumph of Islam over the Hindu 'infidels'. Their opposite number, the Muslims, unsurprisingly dispute the claim that a Hindu temple preceded the Babri Masjid. They contend that archaeological evidence shows that the area was uninhabited before 700 B.C. (the period when believers say Rama was supposedly born); and that, in any event, there is no proof that Lord Rama was a historical figure. Historians themselves are unable to provide an objective picture of what actually existed in and around Ayodhya, including the location and significance of the *janamsthan*, through the centuries leading up to the Mughal conquest and its aftermath. Some suggest that Ayodhya's 'development as a major center of Rama worship is relatively recent' (Gopal 1990: 26). If so, this would presumably reinforce the Muslim position concerning the possible existence of a temple on the site in Babar's time.

Further reinforcement of this viewpoint is provided by narratives emanating both from Hindu and Muslim, indeed even from foreign, traditional sources. None refer to the presence of any pre-Muslim structure on the *janambhumi* site and moreover fail to associate Ayodhya with any form of Rama worship until well into the second millennium A.D. 'The early places of Hindu worship in Ayodhya were either of Vaishnava or Shaiva provenance', declares Gopal (1990). 'Even the inscriptions from the fifth to eighth centuries AD do not associate Ayodhya with the worship of Rama. Hsuan Tsang also does not mention any place of Rama worship, even though he has recorded the existence of "ten Deva temples" (Vaishnava temples?) in Ayodhya in the seventh century AD'(ibid.: 26).

its resonances of conservatism, but also made it an openly acceptable way of conceptualizing the nation, an act that repudiated Nehruvian secularism from within his family and party.

The longer range results are there for all to see. Since the unlocking of the Babri Masjid and its subsequent destruction, the Bharatiya Janata Party has steadily grown in stature and power from a Hindi-belt political organisation to a national political party. In March 1998 it came to power as the dominant component of a coalition of parties that subscribe to the proposition that an ethnoreligious state which in some measure defines itself as 'Hindu' is now a political reality. What the consequences of this shift from an ethno-accommodative contract with the Indian people to an ethnoreligious contract forebode remain to be determined. But one suspects that India will never be the same as it was; that the Nehruvian and Gandhian visions are gone forever. This will be especially so if the present tenuous hold which the BJP has on power is successfully expanded in the future to an absolute majority, at which point the party's right wing will very likely find itself in a position to push harder for implementation of what Gyan Pandey (1991) has called the 'militant Hindu construction'. Should this happen, the chances for the fractionalisation of India, so often predicted in the past, could greatly increase. As long as the Babri Masjid remained standing, and the potential solution to the controversy over how Hindus and Muslims might share the same sacred space remained a juridical matter, the ethno-accommodative state, and its contemporary manifestation, the secular state, with all the civil guarantees attendant upon it, remained intact. The Babri Masjid is no more because the moral contract that sustained and protected it for almost five centuries has been supplanted by one which seems destined to allow far less latitude for diversity and inter-cultural accommodation.

REFERENCES

ANDERSEN, WALTER. 1987. *Brotherhood in saffron: A study of Hindu revivalism.* Boulder, CO: Westview Press / New Delhi: Sage Publications.

BAYLY, C.A. 1988. *Indian society and the making of the British empire. The new Cambridge history of India* II (I). Cambridge: Cambridge University Press.

BRASS, PAUL R. 1965. *Factional politics in an Indian state: The Congress party in Uttar Pradesh.* Berkeley: University of California Press.

DATTA, PRADIP K. 1991. VHP's Ram at Ayodhya: Reincarnation through ideology and organization. *Economic and political weekly* 26, 44: 2523.

FISHER, MICHAEL. 1987. *A clash of cultures: Awadh, the British and the Mughals.* Delhi: Manohar.

GOPAL, S. 1990. *Anatomy of a confrontation: The Babri Masjid–Ram Janambhumi issue.* New Delhi: Penguin.

GOULD, HAROLD A. 1993. Mandal, Mandir and Dalits: Melding class with ethnoreligious conflict in India's tenth general election. *In* Harold A. Gould and Sumit Ganguly, eds, *India votes: Alliance politics and minority government in the ninth and tenth general elections*, pp. 293–340. Boulder, CO: Westview Press.

———. 1994. *Grass-roots politics in India: A century of political evolution in Faizabad district.* New Delhi: Oxford University Press and IBH.

GRAHAM, BRUCE. 1990. *Hindu nationalism and Indian politics: The origins and development of the Bharatiya Jana Sangh*. Cambridge: Cambridge University Press.

HOBSBAWM, ERIC and TERRENCE RANGER, eds. 1988. *The invention of tradition*. Cambridge: Cambridge University Press.

MADAN, T.N. 1997. *Modern myths and locked minds: Secularism and fundamentalism in India*. Delhi: Oxford University Press.

MOON, PENDEREL. 1949. *Warren Hastings and British India*. New York: Macmillan.

NOORANI, A.G. 1987. The Babri masjid case. *Economic and political weekly* 22, 3: 71–72.

PANDEY, GYANENDRA. 1991. Hindus and others: The militant Hindu construction. *Economic and political weekly* 26, 52: 2997–3009.

PEARSON, M.N., ed. 1985. *Legitimacy and symbols: The south Asian writings of F.W. Buekler.* Ann Arbor, MI: Centre for South and Southeast Asian Studies, University of Michigan.

RUDOLPH, LLOYD. 1993. The media and cultural politics. *In* Harold A. Gould and Sumit Ganguly, eds, *India votes: Alliance politics and minority government in the ninth and tenth general elections*, pp. 159–79. Boulder, CO: Westview Press.

WEINER, MYRON. 1957. *Party politics in India: The development of a multi-party system.* Princeton: Princeton University Press.

17

The twilight of certitudes: Secularism, Hindu nationalism and other masks of deculturation[1]

Ashis Nandy

Politics of religious and ethnic violence is basically the politics of secularism and secularisation. As a society gets more secularised, the attraction of secularism diminishes in those anxious about losing touch with all transcendental values and sacred symbols. They then begin to look for readymade, packaged forms of religion that would simultaneously serve as manageable forms of religion in a modern society and as a political ideology seemingly resisting the desacralisation of life. However, this is a double-bind, for such new religious packages are themselves a part of the process of secularisation. Indeed, they strengthen the process of secularisation by extending it to the sphere of religion, and even religious strife, further marginalising traditional faiths. The violence associated with such secularised religious ideologies springs both from the fear of losing one's faith and identity and hostility towards official secularism, usually vended as an alternative proselytising religious faith free from the constraints of time and space.

What follows is basically a series of propositions. It is not meant for academics grappling with the issue of ethnic and religious violence as a cognitive puzzle, but for concerned intellectuals and grass-roots activists trying, in the language of Gustavo Esteva (1987), to 'regenerate people's space'. Its aim is threefold: (*a*) to systematise some of the available insights into the problem of ethnic and communal violence in South Asia, particularly India, from the point of view of those who see communalism and secularism not as sworn enemies but as the disowned doubles of each other; (*b*) to acknowledge, as part of the same exercise, that Hindu nationalism, like other such ethnonationalisms, is not an 'extreme' form of Hinduism but a modernist creed which seeks, on behalf of the global nation-state

[1] This is a new incarnation of a paper published in *Alternatives* 22 (Spring 1997) and in a revised form in *Postcolonial studies* 1, 3 (1998). It draws upon a Keynote Address delivered at the XVII International Congress of History of Religions, Mexico City, 5–12 August 1995, and upon brief notes written for Ved Bhasin and Om Prakash Saraf, eds., *Challenges facing India: Essays in honour of Balraj Puri* (New Delhi: Konark, 1994), and the *Revue Internationale de theologie* 262 (1995). The present version has been written for the festschrift in honour of Triloki Nath Madan, whose works have enormously deepened our understanding of the role of religion in public life.

system, to retool Hinduism into a national ideology and the Hindus into a 'proper' nationality; and (*c*) to hint at an approach to religious tolerance in a democratic polity that is not dismissive of the ways of life, idioms and modes of informal social and political analyses of the citizens even when they happen to be unacquainted with—or inhospitable to—the ideology of secularism.

One qualification at the beginning. This is the third in a series of papers on secularism, in which one of my mains concerns has been to examine the political and cultural-psychological viability of the ideology of secularism and to argue that its fragile status in South Asian politics is culturally 'natural' but not an unmitigated disaster. For there are other, probably more potent and resilient ideas within the repertoire of cultures and religions of the region that could ensure religious and ethnic co-survival, if not creative inter-faith encounters. Few among the scores of academic responses to the papers—some of them hysterically hostile—have cared to argue or examine that part of the story, which I once foolishly thought would be of interest even to dedicated secularists. They were more disturbed by my attempts to identify the spatial and temporal location or limits of the ideology of secularism. Evidently, for some academics, the ideology of secularism is prior to the goals it is supposed to serve. Much less provoked were those who had some direct exposure to religious or ethnic strife either as human rights activists, first-hand observers or victims, for whom the papers were written in the first place. For even when uncomfortable with M.K. Gandhi's belief that 'politics divorced from religion becomes debasing' (Iyer 1986: 374), they seemed to intuitively gauge the power of Raimundo Panikkar's (1993: 189) pithy formulation: 'the separation between religion and politics is lethal and their identification suicidal.'

I

The paradox of secularism

Secularism as an ideology can thrive only in a society that is predominantly non-secular. Once a society begins to get secularised—or once the people begin to feel that their society is getting cleansed of religion and ideas of transcendence—the political status of secularism changes.[2] In such a society, people become anxiously aware of living in an increasingly desacralised world and start searching for faiths, to give meaning to their life and retain the illusion of being part of a traditional community. If faiths are in decline, they begin to search for ideologies linked to faiths, in an effort to return to forms of traditional moral community that would negate or defy the world in which they live. If and when they find such ideologies, they cling to them defensively—'with the desperate ardour of a lover trying to converse life back into a finished love', in the language of Sara Suleri. What sometimes happens to communities can also happen to sections of a community or to individuals. Thus, in recent years many expatriate South Asians in the West have become more aggressively traditional, culturally exclusive and

[2] The decline of faith I am speaking of has its rough counterpart in the erosion of beliefs surveyed in a somewhat different context by Dogan (1995) and Inglehart (1995). See also Inglehart (1991).

chauvinistic. As their cherished world becomes more difficult to sustain, as their children and they themselves begin to show symptoms of getting integrated in their adopted land, they become more protective about what they think are their faiths and cultures.

The enthusiasm of some states to aggressively impose secularism on the people sharpens these fears of deracination. Already sensitive about the erosion of faiths, many citizens are particularly provoked by a secularising agenda imposed from the top, for that agenda invariably carries with it in this century a touch of contempt for the believers. Such secularism is:

> essentially a religious ideology, not based on any scientifically demonstrable propositions. ... It is the religion of a divinised human rationality of a particular kind, making critical rationality the final arbiter. This religious ideology is then imposed on our children in schools—from which all other religions are proscribed. ... This religion spread in the UK and the USA for two generations. Sunday schools were established. Catechisms of the new religion were published. With the rise of Nazism and the Second World War it fizzled out, and merged with modern liberalism, which is also the religion of the new civilisation now sweeping Europe. ... Secularism creates communal conflict because it brutally attacks religious identity, while pretending to be tolerant of all religions (Gregorios 1995: 24–25, 27).[3]

When Indian public life was overwhelmingly non-modern, secularism as an ideology had a chance. For the area of the sacred looked intact and safe, and secularism looked like a balancing principle and a form of legitimate dissent. Even many believing citizens described themselves as secular, to keep up with the times and because secularism sounded like something vaguely good. Now that the secularisation of Indian polity has gone far, the scope of secularism as a creed has declined. For signs of secularisation are now everywhere; one does not have to make a case for it. Instead, there has grown the fear that secularisation has gone too far, that the decline in public morality in the country is due to the all-round decline in religious sensibilities. Many distorted or perverted versions of religion circulating in modern or semi-modern India owe their origins to this perception of the triumph of secularisation rather than to the persistence of traditions.

As part of the same process, many 'non-secular' ideologies and movements have become more secular in style and content. They *do* try to look religious, for the sake of their constituency, but they can pursue political power in a secularised polity only through secular politics, secular organisations and secular planning. They increasingly resemble the jet-setting gurus and *sadhu*s who, while criticising the 'crass materialism of the West', have to use at every step Western technology, Western media and Western disciples to stay in business. A popular way of recognising this in India is to affirm that the politicians misuse religion. But that affirmation usually fails to acknowledge that only a person or a group at least partly repudiating the sanctity of religion can 'misuse' religion or 'use' it only

[3] On the contempt for the believers that lies at the heart of secularism and the capacity this contempt has to legitimise Western dominance over all traditional societies, see Sardar and Davies (1990).

instrumentally.[4] In this sense, the Bharatiya Janata Party and the Shiv Sena, though called fundamentalist, are two of the most secular parties in India, for they represent most faithfully the loss of piety and cultural self-doubts that have come to characterise a section of urban, modernising India. While other parties observe, even if by default, some limits in their instrumental use of religion, there seems to be no such restraint in the BJP or the Shiv Sena. The people these parties mobilise may sometimes be driven by piety—in Shiv Sena's case even that is doubtful—but their leaders view that piety as only a part of their political weaponry.

Even religious riots or pogroms are becoming secularised in South Asia. They are organised the way a rally or a strike is organised in a competitive, democratic polity and, usually, for the same reasons—to bring down a regime or discredit a chief minister here or to help an election campaign or a faction there. Some political parties in India today have 'professionals' who specialise in such violence and, like true professionals, do an expert job of it. Often these professionals, though belonging to antagonistic religious or ethnic communities, maintain excellent personal, social and political relationships with each other. Fanaticism, they apparently believe, is for the hoi polloi, not for the serious politicians playing the game of ethnic politics.[5] It is not difficult today to find out the rate at which riots of various kinds can be bought, how political protection can be obtained for the rioters and how, after a riot, political advantage can be taken of it.

There is even a vague consensus among important sections of politicians, bureaucracy and the law-and-order machinery on how such specialists should be treated. Despite hundreds of witnesses and detailed information, hardly anyone has ever been prosecuted for complicity or participation in riots in India and, for that matter, in the whole of South Asia. The anti-Sikh riot in Delhi in 1984 was only a more dramatic evidence of such consensus. Though more than 3,000 Sikhs were killed in the three-day pogrom in India's capital, till 1995 the instigators and active participants in it had not only escaped prosecution but had risen high in the

[4] The great European witch-hunt, it has been frequently pointed out, peaked not during the period when the European Christendom and the Church were secure, but when modernity had weakened their bases. Speaking of the belief in witches in the 16th and 17th centuries, H.R. Trevor-Roper says, 'it was not, as the prophets of progress might suppose, a lingering ancient superstition, only waiting to dissolve. It was a new explosive force, constantly and fearfully expanding with the passage of time' (Trevor-Roper 1967: 90–192). See also Cohn (1975).

[5] In the context of the films of Woody Allen, Barbara Schapiro speaks of the 'clever, manipulative technique by which Allen attempts to control his critics by demonstrating an awareness of his own potential weaknesses. … The character displays awareness of his problem while in the very act of demonstrating the problem, and that self awareness, of course, creates the humour' (Schapiro 1986). I am speaking here of an analogous process which produces, instead of humour, tragedy for millions.

However, there is some scope for irony, if not humour, within such tragedies. Recently, when Brijbhushan Sharan Singh, an MP of the Bharatiya Janata Party, the powerful political front of the Hindu nationalist formations, was accused of harbouring criminals having terrorist connections and protecting them from law, the criminals turned out to be associates of the notorious don of Bombay, Dawood Ibrahim. Likewise, when BJP president Lal Krishna Advani was accused of being involved in criminal money-laundering, the main source of payments to him was said to be one Ameerbhai. The party has established its secular credentials the hard way!

political hierarchy. At least two have been in the union cabinet and another three have been Congress Party MPs from the capital. It does not need much political acumen to predict that the same fate awaits the self-declared instigators and perpetrators of the anti-Muslim violence in Bombay in January 1993.

On the other hand, though by now human rights activists and students of communal violence have supplied enough data to show that riots are organised, they have rarely pushed this point to its logical conclusion. Riots *have* to be organised because the ordinary citizens—the 'illiterate', 'superstitious' South Asians, uncritically allegiant to their primordial identities—are not easy to rouse to participate in riots. To achieve that end, you need detailed planning and hard work. It is not easy to convert ordinary citizens into fire-spitting fanatics or killers; they may not be epitomes of virtue, but they are not given to bloodcurdling Satanism either. Not even when lofty modern values like history, state and nationalism are invoked.[6] South Asian loves and hates, being often community based, are small-scale. In the case of communal violence, the most one can accuse them of is a certain uncritical openness to the rumours floated before riots, which helps them make peace with their conscience and their inability to resist the violence.

Yet, they do resist. Each riot produces instances of bravery shown by persons who protect their neighbours at immense risk to their own lives and those of their families (Hasan 1995; Nandy et al. 1995). Often entire families and communities participate in the decision to resist. There is no empirical basis whatever to explain away this courage as a function of individual personality while, at the same time, seeing the violence it opposes as a cultural product. In South Asia as much as in Nazi Germany, those who resist such violence at the ground level derive their framework from their religious faith (cf. Fogelman 1996: 91–92). I have been hearing since my childhood literally hundreds of caustic accounts of the victims of the great Partition riots—about their suffering in 1946–47. In most cases, the experiences have made them bitterly anti-Muslim, anti-Sikh or anti-Hindu. Despite the bitterness, however, most accounts include a story of someone from the other community who helped the family. The loves and hates of everyday life, within which are usually fitted ethnic and religious prejudices and stereotypes, may be small-scale but they are not always petty.

The resistance is stronger where communities have not splintered into atomised individuals. Not only do riots take place more frequently in the cities, but they are also harder to organise in villages. The village community is breaking down all over the world, but it has not broken down entirely in South Asia. Even the smaller towns in South Asia have often escaped massification. It is no accident that, despite the claim of some Hindu nationalists that more than 350,000 Hindus had already died fighting for the liberation of the birthplace of Rama,

[6] Probably the rational-legal values of an individualised, mass society have not yet made inroads into the interstices of South Asian personality, and the values and faiths most South Asians live by cannot be mobilised that easily for collective action cutting across sects or denominations. Urbanisation and massification are changing this profile, but the changes as yet affect a minority.

Ramjanmabhumi, during the previous 400 years, the residents of Ayodhya themselves lived in reasonable amity till the late 1980s. The Sangh Parivar sensed this; till the mid-1980s, the case for demolishing the Babri mosque at Ayodhya was not taken up by any of the noted Hindu nationalists, from V.D. Savarkar, Balkrishna Munje and Keshav Hedgewar to Bal Thackeray, Lal Krishna Advani and Murli Manohar Joshi. The Babri mosque was turned into a political issue only after India's urban middle class attained a certain size and India's modernisation reached a certain stage (Nandy et al. 1995).

The first serious riot in the sacred city of Ayodhya took place on 6–7 December 1992. For seven years, despite all efforts to mobilise the locals for a riot, no riot had taken place.[7] This time, it was organised by outsiders and executed in many cases by non-Hindi-speaking rioters with whom the local Hindus could not communicate. These outsiders were not traditional villagers, but urbanised, semi-educated, partly Westernised men and, less frequently, women. They broke more than a hundred places of worship of the Muslims in the city to celebrate the 'fall' of the unprotected Babri mosque (Nandy et al. 1995: *passim*).

In the final reckoning, the demolition of the Babri mosque in 1992 was proof that the secularisation of India had gone along predictable lines.

II
The politics of secularism

Over the last fifty years or so, the concept of secularism has had a good run. It has served, within the small but expanding modern sector in India, as an important public value and as an indicator of one's commitment to the protection of minorities. Now the concept has begun to deliver less and less. By most imaginable criteria, institutionalised secularism has failed. Communal riots have increased more than tenfold and have now begun to spread outside the perimeters of modern and semi-modern India (Nandy et al. 1995: ch. 1). In the meanwhile, the ruling culture of India, predominantly modern and secular, has lost much of its faith in—and access to—the traditional social and psychological checks against communal violence.

In this respect, one is tempted to compare the political status of secularism with that of modern medicine in India. Traditionally Indians used a number of indigenous healing systems, and did so with a certain confidence and scepticism. These systems were seen as mixed bags; they sometimes worked, sometimes not. But they were not total systems; they did not demand full allegiance and left one with enough autonomy to experiment with other systems, including the modern ones. Slowly, well-meaning reformers broke the confidence of their ignorant compatriots in such native superstitions. In the second half of the 19th century, modern medicine was introduced into India with great fanfare. It was introduced usually

[7] In the case of both Kashmir and the Punjab, despite the bitterness produced by the militants and the agencies of the state and despite some determined efforts to precipitate riots, there have been no communal riots till now.

with the backing of the state and sometimes with the backing of the coercive apparatus of the state, not merely as a superior science but also as a cure for the irrational faith of the natives in the traditional systems of healing (see for instance Apffel-Marglin 1990). People were constantly bombarded with the message that the older systems were bogus or, at best, inefficient; that they should, therefore, shift to the modern, 'truly universal' system of medicine.

Once the confidence of a sizeable section of Indians in the older, more easily accessible healing systems was destroyed, the inevitable happened. Most of those who converted to modern medicine found it prohibitively costly, more exclusive, often inhuman and alienating. They also found that their proselytisers had other priorities than to give them easy access to modern medicine. In the meanwhile, the converts had lost some of their faith in the traditional systems of healing. Many of the practitioners of the traditional systems, too, had lost confidence in their vocation and had begun to pass themselves off as deviant practitioners of modern medicine; they had begun to copy the allopaths in style and, more stealthily, in practice.

Similarly, the concept of secularism was introduced into South Asian public life by a clutch of social reformers, intellectuals and public figures—seduced or brainwashed by the ethnocidal, colonial theories of social evolution and history—to subvert and discredit the traditional ideas of inter-religious understanding and tolerance. These traditions had allowed the thousands—yes, literally thousands—of communities living in the subcontinent to co-survive in reasonable neighbourliness for centuries. The co-survival was not perfect; it was certainly not painless. Often there were violent clashes among the communities, as is likely in any 'mixed neighbourhood'. But the violence never involved such large aggregates or generic categories as Hindus, Muslims, Sikhs, Tamils or Sinhalas. Conflicts were localised and sectored, and were almost invariably seen as cutting across religious boundaries, for such boundaries were mostly fuzzy.[8] More important, both the conflicts and their resolutions were explained and negotiated in languages that were reasonably transparent to a majority of the peoples living in the region (Nandy 1999). To the reformers, thinkers and politicians—brought up on the colonial state's classification of Indians into broad European-style religious categories—this 'living past' looked like an anachronism, an embarrassment and a sure prescription for ethnic and religious strife. To them, some of the clashes between sects, denominations or ethnic groups in the earlier centuries began to look in retrospect like clashes between entire religious communities. Simultaneously, the categories that sustained such inter-religious adaptations

[8] See Singh's (1992, vol. 1) work, part of a voluminous and authoritative survey that almost incidentally shows that even in the 1990s, nearly fifty years after the Hindu–Muslim divide has become the most dangerous cleavage in the subcontinent, of the 2,800-odd communities identified as Hindu and Muslim, more than 400 cannot be identified as exclusively Hindu or Muslim. There are probably something like 600 such communities which live, not with multiculturalism without, but with multiculturalism within South Asia. In a personal communication, Singh estimates that the proportion of such fuzzy-bordered communities had been much higher in earlier times. For a fascinating case study of what this means in practice, see Apffel-Marglin (1995) and Mayaram (1995, 1996).

or tolerance—or, to put it modestly, the categories that contained communal animosities within tolerable limits—were systematically devalued, attacked and ridiculed as parts of an enormous structure of irrationality and self-deceit, and as sure markers of an atavistic, retrogressive way of life.

In place of these categories, the concept of secularism was pushed as *the* remedy for all religious conflicts and fanaticism, something that would do away with the constant religious violence and bloodletting that had reportedly characterised the region from time immemorial. 'Reportedly' because no one produced an iota of empirical evidence to show that such conflicts existed on a large scale and involved religious communities as they are presently defined.[9] That did not cramp the style of the properly educated South Asian liberals and progressives. They seemed convinced that the data did not exist because their societies were ahistorical; had a proper scientific, objective history existed, it would have shown that pre-modern South Asia had been a snake pit of religious bigotry and blood lust.

That innocent social-evolutionist reading today lies in tatters. Yet, the dominance of the ideology of secularism in the public discourse on religious amity and ethnic plurality in India continues. Why? Why do even the Hindu nationalists uphold not religion but genuine secularism (as opposed to what they call the pseudo-secularism of their political enemies)? Above all, who gets what from secularism and why? Any attempt to even raise this question triggers deep anxieties; it seems to touch something terribly raw in the Indian bourgeoisie. As if secularism was a sacred transhistorical concept, free from all restraints of space and time, and any exploration of its spatial and temporal limits was a reminder of one's own mortality. As if those disturbed by the questions knew the answers, but did not like to be reminded of them. I shall risk political incorrectness here and obstinately turn to these very questions.

First, once institutionalised as an official ideology, the concept of secularism helps identify and set up the modernised Indians as a principle of rationality in an otherwise irrational society and gives them, seemingly deservedly, a disproportionate access to state power. After all, they are the ones who have reportedly freed themselves from ethnic and religious prejudices and stereotypes; they are the ones who can even be generous and decide who among the majority of Indians who do not use the idiom of secularism are 'objectively' secular. Secularism for them is often a principle of exclusion. It marks out a class that speaks the language of the state, either in conformity or in dissent. On this plane, secularism is emblematic of a person or group willing to accept two corollaries of the ideology of the Indian state: the assumption that those who do not speak the language of secularism are unfit for full citizenship, and the belief that those who do have the sole right to determine what true democratic principles, governance and religious tolerance are.[10] The main function of the ideology of secularism here is

[9] For a concise, if non-committal, coverage of this part of the story, see Bayly (1985).

[10] A cute, if chilling example of this attitude is Bannerji (1993).

to shift the locus of initiative from the citizens to a specialist group that uses a special language.

To be more generous to this sector and its mentors in the mainstream global culture of scholarship, secularism has become mainly modern India's way of 'understanding' the religious tolerance that survives outside modern India. It has become a concept that names the inexplicable and, to that extent, makes it more explicable. Its necessity depends on modern India's loss of touch with Indian traditions and loss of confidence in the traditional codes of religious tolerance that constitute an alternative vantage ground for political intervention in a democratic polity. Hence the modern Indian's fear of the void that the collapse of the concept of secularism might produce.

Many secularists are secular on ideological or moral grounds. They consider their ideology to be compatible with radical or leftist political doctrines and seem oblivious of its colonial connections and class bias. Evidently, class analysis for them, unlike charity, does not begin at home. Some of them have personally fought for religious and ethnic minorities, but now face the fact that, with the spread of participatory mass politics, they are being reduced to a small minority among the very section within which they expected to have maximum support—the Westernising, media-exposed, urban middle classes. They can neither give up their faith in secularism, because that would mean disowning an important part of their self-definition, nor shake off the awareness that it is doomed, at least in ground-level politics.[11] Such politics is already getting too secularised to be able to sustain secularism as a popular ideology.

Second, the ideology of secularism not merely fits the culture of the Indian state, it invites the state to use its coercive might to actualise the model of social engineering the ideology projects. Secularism and statism in India have gone hand in hand—perhaps the main reason why Hindu nationalism, statist to its core, has not given up the language of secularism.[12] The goal of both is to retool the ordinary citizen so that he or she, though given democratic rights, would not exercise the rights except within the political limits set by South Asia's Westernising élite, constituting the steel-frame of the region's Wog empires. Secularism, too, has its class affiliations; it too has much to do with who gets what and when in a polity. Tariq Banuri (1993: 8) compares the dominant position of the ego in

[11] For a profile of Westernising, media-exposed urban India as the site of rivalry between the secularists and the Hindu nationalists, see Nandy et al. (1995).

[12] Theologian Jyoti Sahi (1998) claims that both the modern state and secularism owe their origins to the Judaeo-Christian worldview, and secularism particularly has no theological status outside Christianity.

> Monotheism has created its own understanding of the state and its relation to the nation. ... The concept of a nation state based on a religious identity derives from a Judeo-Christian background, but now has been adopted by other faith systems, giving rise to a very new idea like a Hindu Nation State. ... The concept of a secular state has also come from a Christian debate on the relation of church to State. ... Hinduism and Buddhism have never discussed or defined this kind of distinction; in fact the sacred and the profane are interwoven. ... even in Islam there is no clear distinction drawn between the sacred and profane, or religious and secular.

Freudian psychology with the dominant position of the nation-state in the contemporary ideas of political development. To complete his evocative metaphor, one must view secularism as a crucial defence of the ego.

Banuri's metaphor also supplies a clue to the fanaticism of many secularists in India, eager to fight the cause of secularism to the last Muslim or Sikh. It is their version of a passionate commitment to interests or, if you like, an irrational commitment to rationality (a typical 19th- and 20th-century psychopathology in which allegiance to an ideology outweighs the welfare of the targeted beneficiaries of the ideology). Such romantic realism is the underside of what Banuri calls 'the overly enthusiastic pursuit of national integration'(Banuri 1993: 1). Thoughtfully carrying the white man's burden after the demise of empires in the subcontinent, these secularists seem particularly unhappy at the South Asian failure to internalise the psychological traits and social skills congruent with the ideology of secularism. Underlying the unhappiness, however, is a certain glee at the persistence of religious belligerency. It is proof that the average South Asian's internship to qualify for full citizenship is not yet complete and it justifies further postponement of the day when the plebeians would be allowed to 'legitimately' claim their full democratic rights and exercise the power of numbers.

The third reason for the survival of secularism as an important ideological strain in Indian public life is for some reason even less accessible to political analysts, journalists and thinkers. Though the culturally rootless constitute a small, if audible, section of the population, to many of them, secularism is a way of communicating not just with the modern world but also with compatriots trying to enter that world. These neophytes do not have much to do with the European associations and cultural baggage of the term 'secularism'. But they have stretched the meaning of the term for their own purposes and adapted it in such a fashion that it manages to communicate something to others who have to cope, however unwillingly, with Indian realities.[13] They seem satisfied that such secularism allows one to break the social barriers set up by castes, sects and communities, and helps one converse not only with the political and social élite, but also with the metropolitan intellectuals and professionals. Secularism for them is a marker of cosmopolitanism. Many Indian politicians—when they pay lip-service to the standard, universal concept of secularism—have one eye on the response of the national media, the other on their clever competitors who have profited from the secular idiom.

Finally, there are the self-avowed 'genuine secularists'—political actors and ideologues who have an instrumental concept of secularism. They see secularism partly as a means of mounting an attack on the traditional secularists and partly as a justification for majoritarian politics. (The fact that this majoritarianism appeals only to an urban, deracinated minority is a frustrating experience which

[13] I am afraid that much of the recent academic defence of secularism, however elegantly formulated, is totally irrelevant to South Asian political life from this point of view. See, for instance, Bilgrami (1995: 1–29), and Sen (1996). It is a pity that the academic viability of many ideas in the mainstream global culture of universities does not ensure their political survival in the tropics.

probably contributes significantly to organised violence against constructed 'others' in South Asia.) These are the people who often use, participate in, or provoke communal frenzy, not on grounds of faith but on grounds of secular political cost calculations. Occasionally, in place of political expediency, they are motivated by political ideology and that ideology may *appear* to be based on faith. But on closer scrutiny it turns out to be only a secularised version of faith or arbitrarily chosen elements of faith packaged as a political ideology.[14] I accept the self-definition of the genuine secularists simply because their world *is* entirely secular. They use religion rationally, dispassionately and instrumentally, untouched by any theory of transcendence. They genuinely cannot or do not grant any intrinsic sanctity to the faith of even their own followers.

At one time, secularism *had* something to contribute to Indian public life. That context presumed a low level of politicisation, a personalised, impassioned quality in collective violence, its expression and execution (Nandy 1988: 189). As ethnic and religious violence has become more impersonal, organised, rational and calculative,[15] it has come to represent, to rework my own cliché, more a pathology of rationality than that of irrationality. As part of the same process, the ideology of secularism too has become ethnocidal and dependent on the mercies of those controlling or hoping to control the state. It is has become chronically susceptible to being co-opted or hijacked by the politically ambitious. Corollarily,

[14] There has been some discomfort about the distinction between faith and ideology that I have drawn in this and other papers on the subject. As should have been obvious from the context, my use of the concept of ideology is not Marxian or Mannheimian but conventional social-psychological and cultural-anthropological. However, I now find that at least one respected scholar-activist and historian of religion has arrived at the same dichotomy, starting from altogether different concerns. The distinguished dissenter and philosopher of Islam, Abdolkarim Soroush, claims that 'Islam, or any other religion, will become totalitarian if it is made into an ideology, because that is the nature of ideologies' (quoted in *Communalism combat* [1997: 24]). A similar distinction informs Lipner (1999) and Mehta (1999).

I should clarify here that, following the conventions of contemporary social psychology, I make no assumption regarding the truth or falsity of the consciousness that underlies faith or ideology. I am merely underscoring the psychological organisational principles of two distinct forms of consciousness, one of which includes a theory of transcendence, while the other does not or is not supposed to. The distinction echoes the differences in emotive tone of most collective violence in our times and the more hate-filled religious violence that marked earlier centuries. Ethnic cleansing carries the psychological stamp of the modern farmer's attitude towards pest control rather than that of a crusade or *jihad* (see below). This is a difference to which others also, notably Hannah Arendt and Robert J. Lifton, have drawn our attention. See also Nandy (1990). I thank Sumit Sarkar and Nivedita Menon for drawing my attention to this issue.

[15] According to Zygmunt Bauman,

> The most shattering of lessons deriving from the analysis of the 'twisted road to Auschwitz' is that—in the last resort— *the choice of physical extermination as the right means to the task of* Entferung *was a product of routine bureaucratic procedures*: means–ends, calculus, budget balancing, universal rule application. ... The 'Final Solution' did not clash at any stage with the rational pursuit of efficient, optimal goal-implementation. On the contrary, *it arose out of a genuinely rational concern, and it was generated by bureaucracy true to its form and purpose* (quoted in Ahmed [1995: 4]).

religion as the cultural foundation of the existence of South Asian communities has increasingly become a marker of the weak, the poor and the rustic.

As a result, modern India, which sets the tone for the culture of the Indian state, now fears religion. That fear of religion, part of a more pervasive fear of the people and of democracy (which empowers the majority of Indians who are believers), has thrown up the various readymade, packaged forms of faith for the alienated South Asians—Banuri calls them Paki-Saxons—who populate urban, modernised South Asia.[16] For that feared, invisible majority, on the other hand, the religious way of life continues to have an intrinsic legitimacy. For that majority seems to believe, with Hans-Georg Gadamer, that 'the real force of morals ... is based on tradition. They are freely taken over but by no means created by a free insight grounded on reasons.'[17] If that religious way of life cannot find a normal play in public life, it finds distorted expression in fundamentalism, revivalism and xenophobia. That which is only a matter of Machiavellian politics at the top does sometimes acquire at the ground level the characteristics of a *satyagraha*, a *dharma yuddha* or a *jihad*.

I do not mean to identify secularism as a witches' brew in South Asia. Perhaps in parts of the region where political participation has not outstripped the legitimacy of the nation-state, secularism still has a political role, exactly as it had a creative role to play in India in the early years of Independence. But its major implications are now ethnocidal and statist, and it cedes—in fact, lovingly hands over—the entire domain of religion, in societies organised around religion, to the genuine secularists—the ones who deal in, vend or use as a political technology secularised, packaged versions of faith. Secularism today is threatening to become a successful conspiracy against the minorities.

Is secularism doomed to political impotency in the Southern world where historicisation of consciousness and individuation are not complete? What is the fate of secularists who are dedicated crusaders for communal peace and minority rights? There is no reliable answer to the questions but some secularists, I suspect, *will* survive the vicissitudes of South Asian politics. They are the ones in whom there is no easy, cheerful assumption that one day they would abolish categories such as Hindu, Muslim, Buddhist and Sikh, including their myriad

[16] These packaged forms go with various circus-tamed versions of religion, meant for easy consumption. In India, these versions are bookish, high-cultural, pan-Indian, and go well with modern cults, political skullduggery and fashionable, jet-setting gurus—both within India and among the decultured, uprooted, expatriate Indians and the Indophiles in the West. Those given to this modern version of religion find all other spiritual experiences low-brow, corrupted and, thus, meaningless, uncontrollable and fearsome. That fear of the religion of the uncontrollable kind (to which the majority of Indians of all faiths give their allegiance) is a part of the fear of the vernacular, the democratic and the plural. It is the fear that a majority of Indians are religious in a way that is not centrally controllable and does not constitute a 'proper' religion in contemporary times.

[17] Hans-Georg Gadamer, quoted in Chakrabarti (1996: 15). Of course, neither Gadamer nor Chakrabarti seems aware that this is also a typical Gandhian formulation.

subdivisions, and have the luxury of working with newly synthesised categories such as Indian, Sri Lankan or Pakistani. They do what they do—by way of defending the human and cultural rights of the minorities—not so much as a well-considered, ideological and cognitive choice, but as a moral reaction set off by a vague sense of rebellion against the injustice and cruelty inflicted on fellow citizens. The social evolutionary project sits lightly on such secularists. They do not really expect the world to be fully secularised over time. Nor do they expect the 'rationality' of modern science to gradually supplant the 'irrationality' of religion (somewhat like Sigmund Freud who, propelled simultaneously by the optimism of the Enlightenment and a tragic vision of life, hoped that the human ego would gradually win over more and more territory from the id, without fully giving up the belief that the dialectic between the two was an eternal one. I am sure Banuri will accept this qualification of his metaphor).

Apparently, it is not much of an inheritance with which to enter the next millennium. However, I like to believe that inheritance is not trivial either, for it has something to do both with the very core of our humanness and with the key civilisational categories that distinguish this part of the world. It cannot be written off as ethically pointless or politically futile.

I have said that a huge majority of South Asians knows neither the literal meaning of the word 'secularism' nor its connotative meaning derived from the separation of the state from the Church in post-medieval Europe; and, sadly, in an open polity, the choices of this majority matter. I have also pointed out that most properly educated Indians love to believe that life in pre-colonial India was nasty, brutish and short; that communal violence was a daily affair till the imperial state forcibly imposed some order on the warring savages. Strangely, many secular South Asians are not comfortable with that 'history' either. They feel compelled to remind us, often in maudlin detail, how gloriously syncretic India was before religious fanaticism spoilt it all.[18] Only, they do not stop to ask if that syncretism was based on secularism or on some version of 'primitive proto-secularism', and if those who did so well without the ideology need it now.

These secularists seem oblivious that mass politics in an open polity demands an accessible political idiom, even when that idiom seems crude and unbecoming of the dignity of a modern state or looks like a hidden plea to return to the country's brutal, shabby past. That is why, at times of communal and ethnic violence when the state machinery and the newspaper-reading middle classes harp on the codes of secularism, at the ground level, where survival is at stake, the traditional codes of tolerance are the ones that matter, however moth-eaten they may otherwise look (Nandy et al. 1995).

Two formulations at the end. First, that religion is the foundation of social life is true mainly for the weak, the poor and the rural. This is the kind of religion that

[18] For a random example, see the superbly executed television series made by Saeed Naqvi and shown on Doordarshan during 1992–94.

modern India fears. Second, the opposite of religious and ethnic intolerance is not secularism but religious and ethnic tolerance. Secularism is merely one way of ensuring that tolerance. However, in societies where most citizens have been uprooted from traditional lifestyles, secularism *can* become the counterpoint of religious chauvinism, because both begin to contest for the allegiance of the decultured, the atomised and the massified. In other societies, religious fanaticism mainly contests the tolerance that is part of religious traditions themselves.

That is why in South Asia secularism can mostly be the faith of—and be of use to—the culturally dispossessed and the politically rootless. In favourable circumstances, it can make sense even to the massified in the growing metropolitan slums, but never to the majority living its life with rather tenuous links with the culture of the nation-state. True, when such a concept of secularism is made profitable by the state and the élite—that is, if lip-service to the concept pays rich enough dividends—many begin to use it, not in its pristine sense but as an easy, non-controversial synonym for religious tolerance. If such a reward system functions long enough in a society, the political institutions may even begin to project the view that religion is essentially a drag on the civil society. The primary function of secularism then becomes the management of the fear of religion and the religious.

To function thus, the ideology of secularism must presume the existence of an individual who clearly defines his or her religious allegiance according to available census classifications and does not confuse religion with sect, caste, family traditions, *dharma*, culture, rituals and *deshachara* or local customs. That is, the ideology presumes a relatively clear, well-bounded self-definition compatible with the post-17th-century ideal of the individual, comfortable in an impersonal, contractual-relations-dominated society. There is nothing terribly wrong with such a presumption and many people might in fact wish to live in such an individualistic society, seeing in it the scope for true freedom. Only, they have to take into account two political developments, working at cross purposes.

On the one hand the majority, impervious to the charms of the official ideology of secularism, now has *some* access to political power. And with quickening politicisation in this part of the world and large-scale efforts to empower newer sections of people by parties and movements of various kinds, this access is likely to increase. So, the contradiction between the ideology of secularism and the democratic process is likely to sharpen further in the future. The secularist project may then have to depend even more on the coercive power of the state to be implemented. Not merely to keep in check the enemies of secularism, but also to thought-police history (through the production of official histories, history textbooks, time capsules and other such sundry tricks of the trade to which both India's intellectual left and the liberals are privy).[19] This should not be much of a

[19] That is partly the reason why even the Bharatiya Janata Party, being ideologically committed to unqualified statism, is unable to shed the idiom. It has to define its position as loyalty to 'true' secularism, in opposition to what it calls the 'pseudo-secularism' of other parties dependent on minority vote banks.

shock to the Indian secularists. Secularism has always had a statist connection, even in the West, and most South Asian, especially Indian, secularists are confirmed statists. As the legitimacy of the state as a moral presence in society declines, this state connection may produce new stresses within the ideology of secularism.

On the other hand, there is now a powerful force that may find meaning in the secularist worldview. Modern India—by which I mean the Westernised, media-exposed India, enslaved by the urban-industrial vision—is no longer a small, insignificant oasis in a large, predominantly rural, tradition-bound society. One fourth of India is a lot of India. In absolute terms, modern India is itself a society nearly four times the size of its erstwhile colonial master, Britain. It is—to spite Thomas Macaulay, that intrepid, romantic ideologue of the *raj*—no longer a buffer between the rulers and the ruled. It is the world's fourth largest country by itself.

This India does have an adequate exposure to the ideology of the state to be able to internalise the concept of secularism, and sections of it are willing to go to any length to ensure that the concept is not questioned. But that by itself is not particularly surprising. There are a lot of Indians now who are willing to sacrifice the unmanageable, chaotic, real-life Indians for the sake of the idea of India. They are miserable that while the Indian democracy allows them to choose a new set of political leaders every five years, it does not allow them to choose once in a while the right kind of people to populate the country. Instead, they have to do with the same impossible mass of 950 million Indians—uneducable, disorganised, squabbling and, above all, multiplying like bed bugs. For in the Indianness of Indians who are becoming empowered lies, according to many learned scholars, the root cause of all the major problems of the country.

III

Hindu nationalism and the future of Hinduism

When a secularising society throws up its own versions of religion, extremist or otherwise, to cater to the changing psychological and cultural needs of the citizenry, what is the link between these versions and the faith that serves as their inspiration? The relationship between Hindutva, the encompassing ideology that inspires all Hindu nationalist movements in India, and Hinduism provides the semblance of an answer.

Speaking pessimistically, Hindutva will be the end of Hinduism. Hinduism is what most Indians still live by. Hindutva is a response of the mainly Brahminic, middle-class, urban, Westernising Indians to their uprooting, cultural and geographical. According to V.D. Savarkar, the openly agnostic, Westernised nationalist who coined the term, Hindutva is not only the means of Hinduising the polity but also of militarising the effeminate, disorganised Hindus. It is a critique—and an answer to the critique—of Hinduism as most Indians know the faith, and an attempt to protect, within Hinduism, the flanks of a minority consciousness—including the fears and anxieties—that the democratic process threatens to marginalise.[20]

Though I have stressed earlier the pathology of rationality that characterises this minority consciousness, there is also in it an element of incontinent rage. It is the rage of Indians who have decultured themselves, seduced by the promises of modernity, and who now feel abandoned. With the demise of imperialism, Indian modernism—especially that subcategory of it that goes by the name of development—has failed to keep these promises. Hence the paradoxical stature of Hindutva; it is simultaneously an expression of status anxiety and a claim to legitimacy. On one plane, it is a *savarna purana* that the lower middle class ventures while trying to break into the upper echelons of modern India; on another, it is an expression of the fear that they may be pushed into the ranks of the urban proletariat by the upper classes, not on grounds of substance, but 'style'. The 'pseudo-secularists' represent for them the ambition; the Muslims (in India, consisting mostly of communities of artisans getting proletarianised) the fear. Hence, the hatred for both.

It is as a part of the same story that Hindutva represents in popular, mass-cultural form some of the basic tenets of the worldview associated with secularism and the secular construction of the Muslim. Built on the tenets of religious reform movements in the colonial period, Hindutva cannot but see Hinduism as inferior to the Semitic creeds—monolithic, well-organised and capable of being a sustaining ideology for an imperious state. And, being a mass-cultural ideology, it *can* do to Hinduism what the secularists have always wanted to do to it. Hindutva on this plane is a creed which, if it succeeds, might end up making Nepal the world's largest Hindu country. Hinduism will then survive not as a faith of a majority of Indians, but in pockets, cut off from the majority who will claim to live by it—perhaps directly in Bali, indirectly in Thai, Sri Lankan and Tibetan Buddhism and, to the chagrin of many Hindu nationalists, in South Asian and Southeast Asian Islam. The votaries of Hindutva will celebrate that death of Hinduism. For they have all along felt embarrassed and humiliated by Hinduism as it is. Hence, the pathetic, counterphobic emphasis in Hindutva on the pride that Hindus must feel in being Hindu. Hindutva *is* meant for those whose Hinduism has worn off. It *is* a ware meant for the supermarket of global mass culture where

[20] This critique of Hinduism, often masquerading as a personological critique of the Hindus, is central to Hindutva. For a useful discussion of this part of the story, see Badrinath (1991). A flavour of the intellectual and cultural climate that produced Hindutva can be had from Keer (1966). For a succinct comment on the Rashtriya Swayam Sevak Sangh as a lower-middle-class, political expression of the ideology of Hindutva and its relationship with Hinduism, see Rao Jr. (1998).

The line drawn between Hinduism and Hindutva is visible at the ground level, when communal violence spreads to or breaks out in rural India, where communities have not yet fully broken down and where the ideology of Hindutva faces resistance from everyday Hinduism. Some have academic objections to such a separation, but I doubt if those who offer such resistance would worry about that. They will draw sustenance either from the 'low-brow' Hinduism of everyday life, as described, for instance, by Apffel-Marglin (1995) and Mayaram (1996), or even from some of the pillars of Brahminic/classical orthodoxy, such as Shankaracharya Chandrasekharendra Saraswati (1996).

all religions are available in their consumable forms, neatly packaged for buyers. Predictably, its most devoted consumers can be found among the expatriate Hindus of the world.

Many years ago, H.R. Trevor-Roper raised an important question in the context of the great European witch-hunt: did the inquisitors discover a new 'heresy' beneath the faith of the heretics or did they invent it? (Trevor-Roper 1967: 115–27). Trevor-Roper reached the conclusion that, on the whole, the witch-craze did not grow out of the social and religious processes operating in medieval Europe; it 'grew by its own momentum' from within modernising Europe (ibid.: 119). The growth of Hindutva has depended heavily upon invented heresies that are organised around themes that have no place in Hindu theology: the modern state, nationalism and national identity. It has borrowed almost nothing from existing Hindu theology in its construction of the non-Hindus; it has followed its own trajectory in the matter. This is another crucial difference between Hindutva and Hinduism. It is pity that, to some extent, the same can be said about some of the more fanatical opponents of Hindutva in the modern sector, too. That fanaticism comes from a tacit recognition that, beneath the skin, they are each other's doubles. Only, while the ideologues of Hindutva have already found Indian analogues of *The protocols of the Elders of Zion*, some opponents of Hindutva are still desperately looking for them.[21]

Speaking optimistically, Hindu nationalism has its territorial limits. It cannot spread easily beyond the boundaries of urban, Westernising India. Nor can it easily penetrate those parts of India where Hinduism is more resilient and the Hindus less prone to project on to the Muslim the feared, unacceptable parts of their self. Hindutva cannot survive where the citizens have not been massified and speak only the language of the state.

To those who live in Hinduism, Hindutva is one of those pathologies that periodically afflict a faith. Hinduism has, over the centuries, handled many such pathologies; it still retains the capacity, they feel, perhaps over-optimistically, to handle one more. It will, they hope, consume Hindutva once a sizeable section of the modernised Hindus finds an alternative psychological defence against the encroaching forces of the market, the state and the urban-industrial vision.

Whether one is a pessimist or an optimist, the choices are clear. They do not lie either in a glib secularism talking the language of the state or in pre-war versions of nationalism seeking to corner the various forms of increasingly popular ethnic nationalism breaking out all over South Asia. The choice lies in alliance with forces that have risen in rebellion against the social forces and the ideology of dominance that have spawned Hindutva in the first place. As the world built by 19th-century imperialism collapses around us, Hindutva, too, may die a natural

[21] For a while, they found it in Golwalkar's book, *We* (1939). Things became a little convoluted when his disciples disowned it and claimed that Golwalkar, too, had disowned it. That was not what self-respecting fascists were expected to do and it was considered almost a betrayal by important sections of the Indian left.

death. But then, many things that die in the colder climes in the course of a single winter survive in the tropics for years. Stalinism has survived better in India than even in the Soviet Union and so probably will imperialism's lost child, Hindutva. Maybe its death will not be as natural as that of some other ideologies. Maybe post-Gandhian Hinduism—combined with a moderate, modest, and what Ali Mazrui calls ecumenical state—will have to take advantage of the democratic process to help Hindutva to die a slightly unnatural death. Perhaps that euthanasia will be called politics.

REFERENCES

AHMED, AKBAR S. 1995. Ethnic cleansing: A metaphor for our time. *Ethnic and racial studies* 18, 1: 1–25.

APFFEL-MARGLIN, FRÉDÉRIQUE. 1990. Smallpox in two systems of knowledge. *In* Frédérique Apffel-Marglin and Stephen A. Marglin, eds., *Dominating knowledge: Development, culture and resistance*, pp. 145–84. Oxford: Clarendon Press.

——. 1995. On pirs and pandits. *Manushi: A journal about women and society* 91, 1: 17–26.

BADRINATH, CHATURVEDI. 1991. *Dharma, India and the world order: Twenty essays*. New Delhi: Centre for Policy Research.

BANNERJI, SUMANTA. 1993. Sangh Parivar and democratic rights. *Economic and political weekly* 28, 34: 1715–18.

BANURI, TARIQ. 1993. Official nationalism, ethnic conflict and collective violence. Unpublished manuscript, Islamabad: Sustainable Development Policy Institute.

BAYLY, C.A. 1985. The pre-history of 'communalism'? Religious conflict in India, 1700–1860. *Modern Asian studies* 19, 2: 177–203.

BILGRAMI, AKEEL. 1995. *Secularism, nationalism and modernity*. Paper no. 29. New Delhi: Rajiv Gandhi Institute for Contemporary Studies.

CHAKRABARTI, ARINDAM. 1996. Rationality in Indian philosophy. Lecture given at the Devahuti–Damodar Library, 13 July. Mimeograph.

COHN, NORMAN. 1975. *Europe's inner demons*. New York: Basic Books.

Communalism combat. 1997. Volume 37, October issue: 24.

DOGAN, MATTEI. 1995. Decline of religious beliefs in Western Europe. *International social science journal* 47, 3: 405–17.

ESTEVA, GUSTAVO. 1987. Regenerating people's space. *Alternatives* 12, 1: 125–52.

FOGELMAN, EVA. 1996. Victims, perpetrators, bystanders, and rescuers in the face of genocide and its aftermath. *In* Charles B. Strozier and Michael Flynn, eds., *Genocide, war and human survival*, pp. 87–98. New York: Rowman and Littlefield.

GOLWALKAR, M.S. 1939. *We or our nationhood defined*. Nagpur: Bharat Publications.

GREGORIOS, PAULOS MAR. 1995. Speaking of tolerance and intolerance. *India International Centre quarterly* 22, 1: 22–34.

HASAN, TARIQ. 1995. How does it matter who is the victim? *The Times of India*, 3 April 1995, New Delhi.

INGLEHART, RONALD. 1991. *Culture shift in advanced societies*. Princeton: Princeton University Press.

——. 1995. Changing values, economic development and political change. *International social science journal* 47, 3: 405–17.

IYER, RAGHAVAN, ed. 1986. *The moral and political writings of Mahatma Gandhi*. Oxford: Clarendon Press.

KEER, DHANANJAY. 1966. *Veer Savarkar*. Bombay: Popular.

LIPNER, JULIUS J. 1999. *Brahmabandhab Upadhyay: The life and thought of a revolutionary*. Delhi: Oxford University Press.

MAYARAM, SHAIL. 1995. Ethnic co-existence in Ajmer. Unpublished manuscript, Project on Culture and Identity. Colombo: International Centre for Ethnic Studies and Delhi: Committee for Cultural Choices.

——. 1996. Representing the Hindu–Muslim civilisational encounter: The Mahabharata of a community of Muslims, Unpublished manuscript. Jaipur: Institute of Development Studies.

MEHTA, PRATAP BHANU. 1999. Hollow Hinduism: The VHP's self-defeating vision. *The Times of India*, New Delhi, 18 February.

NANDY, ASHIS. 1988. The politics of secularism and the recovery of religious tolerance. *Alternatives* 13, 3: 177–94.

——. 1990. Introduction: Science as a reason of state. *In* Ashis Nandy, ed., *Science, hegemony and violence: A requiem for modernity*, pp. 1–16. Tokyo: UN University Press and Delhi: Oxford University Press.

——. 1999. Time travel to another self: Searching for the alternative cosmopolitanism of Cochin. Unpublished manuscript, written for the Multiculturalism Project. Colombo: International Centre for Ethnic Studies.

NANDY, ASHIS, SHIKHA TRIVEDY, SHAIL MAYARAM and ACHYUT YAGNIK. 1995. *Creating a nationality: The Ramjanmabhumi movement and fear of the self.* New Delhi: Oxford University Press.

PANIKKAR, RAIMUNDO. 1993. The challenge of modernity. *India International Centre Quarterly* 20, 1–2: 183–92.

RAO JR., PARSA VENKATESHWAR. 1998. The real RSS: Not Hindu, cultural or nationalist. *The Times of India*, New Delhi, 8 July.

SAHI, JYOTI. 1998. Response to Asghar Ali Engineer's 'Imaging and imagining religious symbolism in mass media'. Paper presented at the conference on Globalisation of Mass Media: Consequences for Indian Cultural Values, 29 June–1 July. Bangalore: United Theological College.

SARASWATI CHANDRASEKHARENDRA. 1996. *Hindu dharma: The universal way of life*. Bombay: Bharatiya Vidya Bhavan.

SARDAR, ZIAUDDIN and MERRYL WYN DAVIES. 1990. *Distorted imagination: Lessons from the Rushdie affair*. London: Grey Seal, and Kuala Lumpur: Berita.

SCHAPIRO, BARBARA. 1986. Woody Allen's search for self. *Journal of popular culture* 18, 1: 47–62.

SEN, AMARTYA. 1996. Secularism and its discontents. *In* Kaushik Basu and Sanjay Subramanyam, eds., *Unravelling the nation: Sectarian conflict and India's secular identity*, pp. 11–43. New Delhi: Penguin.

SINGH, KUMAR SURESH. 1992. *People of India: An introduction*. New Delhi: The Anthropological Survey of India.

TREVOR-ROPER, H.R. 1967. The European witch-craze in the sixteenth and seventeenth centuries. *In* H.R. Trevor-Roper, ed., *The European witch-hunt in the sixteenth and seventeenth centuries and other essays*, pp. 90–192. New York: Harper.

18

Self as other: Amar Singh's diary as reflexive 'native' ethnography

Lloyd I. Rudolph

In this essay I try to show how Amar Singh's reflexive writing about himself in his forty-four-year diary (1898–1942) constructed a 'self as other' ethnography of turn-of-the-century princely and British India. Through the medium of his diary he becomes a participant, an observer, an informant, a narrator and an author. I set the stage for Amar Singh's 'self as other' ethnography by examining the separation and alienation in anthropological discourse of self and other. Common to ethnography since Malinowski invented participant-observer field work, the separation was questioned, then challenged by postcolonial Indian and by postmodern Western anthropologists. I then show how Amar Singh, a self-conscious and critical 'native' self, constitutes the other in constituting himself. It is a story about how a native came to represent, speak for and know himself.

Amar Singh began at 20 to write on a daily basis. His diary extends over forty-four years, from 1898 until 1942. Its last entry is dated 1 November 1942. He died that night. These days, the eighty-nine quarto-size bound volumes averaging 800 manuscript pages can be found at Kanota Fort, 10 miles east of Jaipur off the Agra road, where Mohan Singh, his nephew and heir, keeps them in glass-fronted Victorian cabinets in one of the several rooms Amar Singh called his library.

In the essay that follows I try to show why and how Amar Singh, a diarist writing reflexively about himself, constructed a 'self as other' ethnography of turn-of-the-century princely and British India. Through the medium of his diary he becomes a participant, an observer, an informant, a narrator and an author. I set the stage for Amar Singh's 'self as other' ethnography by examining the separation and alienation of self and other in anthropological discourse. Common to ethnography since Malinowski invented participant-observer field work, the separation was questioned, then challenged by postcolonial Indian and by postmodern Western anthropologists. I then show how Amar Singh, a self-conscious

Acknowledgements: Aspects of this essay, which was originally published in *Modern Asian studies* 31, 1(1997), will be part of the introduction that Susanne Hoeber Rudolph and I are preparing for our edited version of the early years (1898–1905) of Amar Singh's diary. I am grateful to *Modern Asian studies* for permission to reprint the essay in this *festschrift* volume in honour of T.N. Madan.

and critical 'native' self, constitutes the other in constituting himself. It is a story about how a native came to represent, speak for and know himself.

I
Introducing the subject: Amar Singh's provenance and career

Before turning to Amar Singh, the 'self' and 'other' of this essay, I want to locate the 'subject' and author, Amar Singh, in space and time by saying something about his provenance, his early life and his career. What kind of a person was he?[1]

In 1849 Jivraj Singh, Amar Singh's great-grandfather, a Rajput of the Champawat lineage whose clan, the Rathores, ruled Jodhpur, and Thakur of Peelwa, an impecunious Jodhpur *thikanna* (estate), travelled by camel from Jodhpur to Jaipur, a 250-mile journey, to carry a condolence message from the Thakur of Pokran to the Thakur of Chomu.[2] Jivraj Singh's journey opened the way for him to seek his fortune in Jaipur state.

According to family stories, Jaipur's 16-year-old maharaja, Ram Singh, caught sight of a fine-looking man on a camel from the balcony of one of the royal gardens that line the road coming from Agra to a Jaipur city gate. Dressed and bearded in the Jodhpuri manner the 50-year-old Jivraj Singh's appearance, demeanour and skill are said to have impressed the young maharaja. He summoned the rider, asked after his origins, and invited him to stay with him in the palace to teach him how to ride a camel. Jivraj became the maharaja's companion and a member of his household staff.[3]

[1] Susanne Rudolph and I have written at greater length about Amar Singh as subject and agent (see L.I. Rudolph and S. Rudolph 1994, forthcoming; S.H. Rudolph and L.I. Rudolph 1975, 1976, 1980, 1988).

[2] A marriage had linked leading *jagirs* (landed estates) of Jodhpur and Jaipur, Pokran and Chomu. When, in 1849, the Pokran spouse—mother of the then Thakur of Chomu—died, the Thakur of Pokran was unable to pay the required condolence visit to Chomu. In his place, to represent him, he sent his kinsman and fellow Champawat, the 50-year-old Thakur of Peelwa, Jivraj Singh.

[3] Over the next thirty years, until his death in 1880, Ram Singh established a reputation in British and princely India as an outstanding prince, intelligent, learned, skilful and 'progressive'.

Ram Singh promoted the arts, education and health and reformed his state's administration. He built a theatre (now a cinema hall) where 'Parsi' companies from Bombay performed, an opera hall (now the home of the Rajasthan *vidhan sabha* [state assembly]), a hospital and an art and natural history museum set in a municipal garden, subsequently named for him (the Ram Niwas garden).

Sir Pratap Singh, Amar Singh's mentor and patron at Jodhpur, 'exiled' himself to Jaipur in 1873 in part to learn from Ram Singh how to rule a princely state but also to escape hostile bureaucratic and court politics at Jodhpur. Between 1878 and 1922 Sir Pratap served on four occasions as regent of Jodhpur state. Pratap Singh and Narain Singh, Amar Singh's father and head of Ram Singh's household service during Sir P's 'apprenticeship', became close friends. Their friendship provided the circumstance for Narain Singh to send his 10-year-old eldest son and heir to the Jodhpur court in 1888 for education and training.

For the progressive quality of Ram Singh's rule see Roy (1978) and Stern (1988).

Jivraj Singh made a place for himself and three of his sons at the Jaipur court and in the administration of Jaipur state.[4] Amar Singh's grandfather, Zorawar Singh, became a minister, Thakur of Kanota, and a *tazimi sardar*, an honoured member of the Jaipur court. Zorawar Singh's eldest son, Amar Singh's father Narain Singh, became an intimate of Ram Singh and head of his household administration. Some years after Ram Singh's death in 1880,[5] he found service outside Jaipur state as the guardian of the minor Alwar maharaja, Jai Singh.[6]

Born in 1878, Amar Singh is Narain Singh's eldest son. As such he is destined to become Thakur of Kanota—lord of a manor, master of a ten-village estate and of a 100-person joint family household, and an important person in Jaipur court society. Circumstances lead him to a military career.[7]

In 1888, at 10, he is sent to Jodhpur to be educated by Narain Singh's friend and age-mate, Sir Pratap Singh, regent of Jodhpur, celebrated as 'India's leading prince', commander of Jodhpur's state forces, and a pre-eminent polo player and sportsman. In 1898, at 19, Amar Singh joins the Jodhpur Lancers as a squadron commander and ADC to Sir Pratap and begins his diary.

In 1900 we find Amar Singh on imperial service overseas with the Jodhpur Lancers in China during the Boxer rebellion (1900). From 1901 to 1905 he is a cadet in the Imperial Cadet Corps (ICC) where he is trained in the Sandhurst manner to be a military officer. Upon graduation in 1905, Amar Singh is commissioned in the India Land Forces (ILF) and assigned as a staff officer with the Indian Army at Mhow, a divisional and command headquarters. He serves at Mhow for nine years as a staff officer, the only Indian in a British officers' mess.

At the outbreak of World War I in 1914 the British government for the first time commits the Indian Army to fight in a European war. Amar Singh, still an ILF officer on staff duty in the Indian Army, is sent with the Sirhind Brigade of the 7th Meerut Division to Flanders where, from October 1914 until the spring of

[4] Fateh Singh, the youngest of the three, became Thakur of Naila and 'prime minister' of Jaipur state (1873–80), and Shambu Singh, the eldest, became Thakur of Gondher and a minister in various departments of Jaipur state.

[5] Narain Singh served Maharaja Madho Singh for a time as Nazim (governor) of Jhunjhunu, the unruly northern region of Jaipur state. When Madho Singh lost confidence in him, Narain Singh, with help from the raj's political department, found service in Alwar.

[6] Jai Singh became famous—and notorious—as a brilliant ruler who practised and patronised Hindu learning and persecuted Meo Muslims in Alwar. Meo revolts led to his deposition and exile. For Jai Singh's changing self-image, e.g., from a Westernised prince to a Hindu nationalist and 'Raj Rishi', see Shail Mayaram (1994: ch. 2).

[7] The circumstances that led Amar Singh to a military career and the early phases of that career—imperial service with the Jodhpur Lancers as part of the allied expeditionary force sent to China in 1900 to deal with the Boxer rebellion and as a cadet in the Imperial Cadet Corps (1901–05)—are detailed in Lloyd I. Rudolph and Susanne Hoeber Rudolph (forthcoming). For a history of the Imperial Cadet Corps, see Sundaram (1996: ch. 3).

1915, the Indian Corps plays an indispensable part in stopping the German advance on the Marne.[8]

In 1905, when Lord Curzon, the viceroy, tries for King's Commissions for graduates of the Imperial Cadet Corps, he fails because it entails 'a black man commanding a white man which no one will look at' (Dilks 1967–70: 244).[9] But on 25 August 1917, in an unprecedented act that (temporarily) integrates the hitherto racially segregated Indian Army, Amar Singh is one of nine Indian ILF officers (all graduates of the Imperial Cadet Corps) given King's Commissions.[10]

Amar Singh goes on retirement leave from the Indian Army as a major in 1921. At 44, in 1922, he begins a second military career in Jaipur state, raising and commanding the Jaipur Lancers, commanding Jaipur state forces and serving as defence minister. An elder statesman and senior figure at court when he retires in 1936, Amar Singh remains until his death, on 1 November 1942, a confidant and adviser to Maharaja Man Singh.[11]

Like his mentor, master and patron, Sir Pratap Singh, off-and-on regent or prime minister of Jodhpur between 1878 and 1922, Amar Singh becomes a sportsman—rider, hunter, polo player, pigsticker—as well as a soldier. Unlike Sir Pratap he reads avidly, often sixty books a year. Writing his diary occupies him

[8] Amar Singh sees combat and is mentioned in dispatches. For an account of the role of the Indian Army during the early phases of the war see Mason (1987: ch. 17). Sent to Basra (in modern Iraq at the confluence of the Tigris and Euphrates rivers) in 1916 he sees action against Ottoman forces (see Barker 1967).

[9] As viceroy, Curzon had launched the Imperial Cadet Corps scheme in 1901 to open military careers to princes and nobles. In 1905, when the first class graduated, Curzon was blocked by opposition in India—inter alia from Commander-in-Chief Lord Kitchener—and Britain—inter alia from Prime Minister Lord Salisbury—from granting King's Commissions to the first batch of graduating cadets. Curzon created a new service, the Indian Land Forces, to accommodate graduating cadets.

For an insightful, detailed account of the background and career of the Imperial Cadet Corps in the context of raj-British ideological and bureaucratic politics, see Sundaram (1996: ch. 3). L.I. Rudolph and S. Rudolph (forthcoming: part 4) contains Amar Singh's diary account of his seven terms (1902–05) in the ICC.

[10] First proposed as an act of grace and gratitude in 1915 by Austen Chamberlain, then secretary of state for India, but strongly opposed in India and Britain, the granting of KCOs to Indians occurred just five days after the 'historic declaration' of 20 August 1917 committing Britain to responsible government in India.

[11] For an account inter alia of Amar Singh's military career in Jaipur and his relationship with Maharaja Man Singh, see Crewe (1985). Crewe makes extensive use of Amar Singh's diary in writing Man Singh's biography.

Philip Mason's otherwise masterful study (1987) does not attend to princely state forces or their imperial service units. He argues that 'the real reason for segregated units [after the 1918 commitment to Indianise the Indian Army's officer corps] was dislike [by British officers] of serving under a "native".... No one could disguise the fact that most Englishmen believed that hardly any Indians were really good enough to lead Indian troops' (ibid.: 456). Byron Farwell's *Armies of the Raj* (1989) devotes a chapter to 'Indian princes and their armies' in which Sir Pratap Singh of Jodhpur is featured. Chandra Sundaram's 'Little grace in the giving' (1996) examines princely state dimensions of the Indian Army's Indianisation.

For further background to Amar Singh's experiences in the Imperial Cadet Corps and the Indian Army see Cohen (1971); Ellinwood (1987); L.I. Rudolph and S. Rudolph (1994).

above all else. In a sea of boredom and philistinism and surrounded by Rajputs who believe that reading threatens their martial virtues, he keeps himself alive and amused by writing in secret to and about himself.[12]

II
The diary as context and medium for 'self as other' ethnography

What does this diary kept by a 'native' of princely and British India have to do with 'self', 'other', and ethnography? Diaries are often taken to be daily accounts about a self, but what is meant by self is not self-evident.[13] Is the self in a diary being constructed or revealed? Is the experience of writing a diary a way of constituting a subject—a narrative self—or establishing an object—a narrative other?

And what of ethnography? Ethnography used to be understood as an account of an 'other'. In the 1980s, the other in Malinowski's canonical ethnography[14]

[12] These themes are more fully developed in S.H. Rudolph and L.I. Rudolph (1988).

[13] In recent years there has been a renewal of philosophical and psychological interest in the self concept (see Csikszentmihalyi 1993; Lifton 1993; Ricoeur 1992; Taylor 1989). My endeavour is to locate, a self concept in anthropology's preoccupation with the 'self and other' relationship. While related to aspects of Ricoeur's, Taylor's and Lifton's treatments of the self concept, I do not propose in this paper to address directly the hermeneutic, moral, psychological or historical concerns found in their works.

Ricoeur frames his study by presenting three 'philosophical intentions'. The third bears some relationship to my 'self as other' story by distinguishing selfhood from sameness through an analysis of 'the dialectic of the *self* and the *other than self*' (1992: 3). When Taylor speaks of 'the self [being] partly constituted by its self-interpretations' (1989: 34) he seems close to my account of reflexivity in Amar Singh's 'self as other' ethnography. Similarly, Lifton's account of a 'protean' concept of self seems to resemble how Amar Singh responds to his liminal positioning between Rajput princely India and raj British India.

None of these accounts of 'self' seems willing to accept what might be called an a priori conception of self, i.e., universal, ahistorical, acontextual. I have in mind the a priori sameness found in 'liberal' versions that feature a self-interested, instrumental/utilitarian self, and in neo-classical economics and rational choice versions that feature a Descartian solipsistic *cognito* rationalism.

[14] For an internal critique of Malinowski's fou nding of field work ethnography see Young (1979a). According to Young

> none of Malinowski's mentors…had managed to fulfill to the letter [the perceived need for] first hand, intensive research.… Until this time [1914], most ethnographic information had been collected by amateurs.…It was clear…that academic opinion in Britain at the time was favourably disposed to innovations in ethnographic method, and Malinowski, through his Trobriand fieldwork, amply provided them. It was, in short, a matter of the right man being in the right place at the right time; though such was the man's charismatic influence that he was able to persuade a whole generation of his followers that 'social anthropology began in the Trobriand Islands in 1914' [Leach 1957: 124] (Young 1979a: 7).

Malinowski repressed the dilemmas of subjectivity vs objectivity, self vs other. Young speaks of

> the somewhat incompatible demands between scientific 'objectivity' and the personal involvement of the field-worker's 'subjectivity'. Despite his incorrigible self-dramatisation and his claim that 'the facts of anthropology attract me mainly as the best means of knowing myself'…, Malinowski did

was increasingly challenged, first as an artifact of a now faded colonial era,[15] then as a spurious construct of 'Orientalist' discourse,[16] then as a generic way of talking about difference. The subject (self) began to merge with the object (other), the subjective with the objective. How did this come about?

As I read and re-read the diary, it became apparent that Amar Singh found out about and constructed himself in a variety of contexts, who he had been, who he meant to be, who he might become. He observes, describes, queries and analyses his own and others' motives, intentions and conduct. He tells us about customs and manners and his and others' expectations in his family, at weddings and funerals, at court and in raj society; about how and why rules and roles are enacted, contested or constituted among the generations and between the genders and the races; about his and others' intentions, judgements and strategies; about how what is said, thought and done is shaped in part by what others say and do. Amar Singh learns about himself and his world through observation and reflection. His youth sharpens his ethnographic eye. He is still shaping an identity, making cultural judgements and choices, for example about what kind of Rajput he wants to be and what he wants to learn from English models. The diary

---

> not propose any theory which included the observer in its frame of reference. This was at least partly due to his basic orientation: the field of enquiry was wholly external to himself. He [does not mention]...the 'personal equation' of the investigator...and he counsels [against] the keeping of an 'ethnographic diary' of events as a corrective measure.... Paradoxically, however, the field diaries which Malinowski himself kept...constitute an entirely different form of document—one which, in laying bare his prejudices, gives the lie to his public image and puts his sincerity severely to the test.

Young soon quotes the by now notorious remark from Malinowski's posthumously published diaries: 'As for ethnology: I see the life of the natives as utterly devoid of interest or importance, something as remote from me as the life of a dog....'

For those interested in what Malinowski knew and thought about philosophical issues before he went to the Trobriand Islands see Thornton and Skalnik (1993). The editors observe that Malinowski's '...specific intellectual debts can be traced for the first time to Friedrich Nietzche, Ernst Mach and James George Frazer....' (ibid.: ix).

[15] See Srinivasan (1993) for the imperial/colonial setting of British anthropology and its 'theory' of the other in a science of man that, according to Srinivasan's reading, served to bolster Britain's ambitions for world hegemony.

[16] The kind of paternalistic, reverse mirror image knowledge that Edward Said (1979) alleged characterised much of Western scholarship about the 'Orient'—mainly the Middle East but also implicating India and China. Said recaptures the idea in *Culture and imperialism* (1993), when he writes: 'Conrad seems to be saying [in *Nostromo*], "We Westerners will decide who is a good native or a bad, because all natives have sufficient existence by virtue of our recognition. We created them, we taught them to speak and think...."' (ibid.: xviii). But *Culture and imperialism* is a different book from *Orientalism.* 'Yet it was the case nearly everywhere in the non-European world,' Said says in his 1993 account,

> that the coming of the white man brought forth some sort of resistance. What I left out of *Orientalism* was that response to Western dominance which culminated in the great movement of decolonisation. Along with armed resistance...there also went considerable efforts in cultural resistance.... [that] in the overwhelming majority of cases...finally won out' (ibid.: xii).

Amar Singh's 'self as other' ethnography is inter alia about this resistance.

provides an arena for defining selves, a medium for puzzling over choices, and a place for recording how and why they are explored and tried out. We learn from the pages of the diary about how culture shapes the self and how the self shapes culture, about culture in the making as well as in the doing.[17]

This article is named 'self as other' in part because the way Amar Singh represents himself and his world resembles how anthropologists as ethnographers seek to know, represent and write about the 'other'[18]. But there are crucial differences between the ways Amar Singh and anthropologists do ethnography. The diary's text reveals, at one and the same time, a participant, an observer, an informant, a narrator and an author. The obfuscating mediations that plague anthropology—the absence of transparency and the presence of subjectivity and projection that affect observation and knowing; informants' fortuitous or calculating resistance and compliance; the fictions of authorial rhetoric—drop from view in the ethnography of 'self as other' diary writing.

III
Getting started

On 3 September 1898, five months after opening his 'Memorandum Book', and still on the lined paper of an ordinary copy book, Amar Singh inscribes at the head of a page, 'The Diary, 1898'. His teacher, Barath Ram Nathji, in tune with the European vogue for diaries as a means for 'understanding and self-control',[19]

[17] To say 'culture in the making as well as in the doing' opens up a line of inquiry and interpretation that cannot be explored in the space available. To view culture as constituted as well as given suggests that it is wise to avoid dichotomies such as culture vs psychology or structure vs agency as determinants of reality or truth. I am suggesting that all four terms are involved in mutually determining processes and interactions. For a close approximation in the literature of what I have in mind here see Richard Shweder's chapter on 'Cultural psychology: What is it?' (1991), where he remarks, inter alia, 'Psyche refers to the intentional person. Culture refers to the intentional world. Intentional persons and intentional worlds are interdependent things that get dialectically constituted and reconstituted through the intentional activities and practices that are their products, yet make them up...' (ibid.: 101).

[18] I say 'resemble' because Amar Singh was not a professionally trained anthropologist. I return to the question of Amar Singh's ethnography from time to time, particularly on pages 439–43.

[19] The phrase is from 'Backstage' by Alain Corbin in Perrot (1990). An account of the rise of the diary in Europe is given in Perrot (1990: 497–502, 265–68).

'The great diarists of the first half of the nineteenth century', Corbin (1990) tells us, 'pursued their goal of illumination without the least shadow of literary ambition'. It was the desire for 'inner illumination coupled with the obsession with loss [that] gave rise to a practice...' no longer justified, as it had been early in the century, by dialogue with the Creator. One of the many factors that contributed to the rise of diaries was, according to Maine de Brian, a way of founding 'the science of man.... The quest for self was spurred by all the historical factors that deepened the individual's sense of identity.' The most prominent, according to Corbin, was 'the insecurity that stemmed from social mobility' (ibid.: 500).

Diaries are also, according to Anne Martin-Fugier in her section on 'Bourgeois rituals', reference books, a way of creating a history of the self, a way to record 'confidential observations' and the 'passage of time', in a word to 'write the history of [one's] life...' (1990: 265).

encouraged him to keep one. The early diary, like the 'Memorandum Book' that preceded it, seems to reflect inter alia Amar Singh's desire to improve himself in this way.[20] Living as he does in a liminal space between princely Rajput and British imperial society, he uses his diary, too, to explore problematics of identity, power and manners.[21]

Amar Singh's ethnography is located in his pursuit of understanding and self-control and in his effort to know and make himself under liminal conditions. It is not the ethnography of a trained and certified ethnographer; in 1898, when he begins his diary, Malinowski had not yet invented professional ethnography (Young 1979a) so he couldn't even have imagined himself as an 'ethnographer'.

Amar Singh is less concerned in his diary about inner states, the kind of moral ruminations that 18th century diaries featured, than he is with the meaning of practice, with the what, how and why of conventional conduct and social relationships. His accounts resemble an ethnographer's notebooks, the 'field notes' that record rituals, kinship terms and dynamics, social networks, financial arrangements, exchanges of gifts.

Amar Singh devotes 127 foolscap pages, for example, to the marriage of his sister-in-law at Satheen, an estate in Jodhpur. His essay is organised under five Roman numeral headings each followed by many Arabic numeral sub-heads: 'The Arrangements; The Reception; The Camp; The Nota; The Pudhla; The Toran; The Adoption; The Question of Giving Leave; The Dowry; The Siropaos Refused; The Argument About Horses; The Khejarla Feast; Feeding the Jan'. If the difference between a professional and an amateur is, as Helmholtz said, only that the amateur lacks a firm and reliable work procedure (Weber 1972), Amar Singh qualifies as something of a professional. If what is meant by being a professional extends to certified induction into theory and method, then we should count Amar Singh as an amateur. Either way, he does something very like what the post-Malinowski discipline of anthropology came to call ethnography.

He reports the Satheen wedding as outsider and insider, observer and participant. As outsider, he renders, in T.N. Madan's phrase, the familiar unfamiliar by distancing himself from the familiar. Much of his account is written as if what he is observing is strange and problematic. But he also writes as if he is an insider. He is a participant, a family member, who is engaged and must make judgements and choices. He shows a special zest for acerbic moments when rules are being contested and expectations challenged, recording his own among the opposed interpretations. Here is how he sums up the problem of interpretation:

> There was no end of experiences. Every argument was an experience. It gave me an idea of how things are done and what things are required. Now I can go with anyone and get him married without anyone's help or advice and I can do

[20] For an account of this and other reasons for Amar Singh becoming and remaining a diarist see S.H. Rudolph and L.I. Rudolph (1988).

[21] See Susanne Hoeber Rudolph and Lloyd I. Rudolph (1984) for a micro-analysis of the British empire's hegemonic project in India.

it with credit too, but before this occasion I could not have for I never watched carefully how things went and people managed. . . . When my sister and cousin were married I was simply running about or enjoying myself. This time my advice was sought and I had to be careful what I said.

Anthropologists have often found the kind of combination Amar Singh represents in key informants, what might be called natural ethnographers, persons at once keenly perceptive and deeply knowledgeable, upon whom they rely for a great deal of what becomes their ethnographic account. Amar Singh resembles both the informant-as-natural-ethnographer who tells what he knows and the anthropologist-as-ethnographer who writes down and reflects on what the informant knows. He is aware that those who see rarely observe; that ethnographic knowledge depends on learning from seeing:

> The more we see the more we [can] learn. . . . My father is considered the best man to take advice on any subject. Why is that so? It is because he has seen several things but he has not merely seen them—he has observed them carefully. His brothers and cousins have seen the same things but they have not observed and the result is they have not learned.[22]

Amar Singh's ethnography addresses questions about knowing and writing that have troubled anthropology over the past decade or so.[23] Anthropologists spend as much time these days contesting ethnography's past, present and future as they spend doing it, perhaps for good reason. In what follows I tell an India-related version of ethnography's career that positions the diary's 'self as other' ethnography.

IV

Constructing the other: Some stories about culture and ethnography

Ethnography used to be the staple of anthropology. There was an 'other' or 'them', alien, distant, isolated, usually exotic and 'primitive'[24] and almost always

[22] All references are to Jaipore, Friday, 7th October, 1904, continued on October 9, 12, 14, 16, and 19, NOTES ABOUT MY LAST VISIT TO SATHEEN, V. The Marriage, 26. Impressions and Experiences.

[23] For recent versions of the troubled career of ethnography that I find attractive, see Shweder (1991: esp. Introduction and ch.1), and Rosaldo (1989: esp. ch. 1).

[24] See Torgovnick (1989). Since the mid-19th century, Torgovnick argues, cultural self-consciousness in the West has been an evolving consequence of Western thinkers—both literary and social scientific—coming to grips with what they identified and designated as primitive. The 'fantastical' views of the primitive have contributed to the effort to find and know 'us', to understand our form of life, to establish a Western civilisational identity. Among those who created mirrors of the primitive which revealed who and what we are were social scientific figures such as Sigmund Freud, Bronislaw Malinowski, Claude Lévi-Strauss and Margaret Mead. It is not, ultimately, the ethnographic truth about cultures designated primitive that matters for identity but rather that 'we' have a concept of the primitive and that it pervades ethnographic discourse about and constructions of the other. Primitivism allows us to 'project feelings about the present and to draw blueprints of the future'; it is both a convenient and necessary invention.

relatively powerless, and an 'us', civilised and powerful. Because they were perceived as different, 'their' culture was visible, palpable, 'ours' invisible, hidden by our cultural (and political) hegemony and by the ubiquity of the quotidian and the conventional. 'In "our" own eyes', Renato Rosaldo writes, '"we" appear to be "people without culture". By courtesy, "we" extend this noncultural status to people who ["we" think] resemble "us".' Cultural visibility and invisibility '...derive in large part from tacit methodological norms that conflate the notion of culture with the idea of difference'. The 'people without culture' studied the 'people with culture' (Rosaldo 1989: 198–204).[25]

Early in the 20th century emissaries from the civilised, imperial world, the people without culture—travellers, adventurers, missionaries, scholars—assumed the guise of anthropologists. Post-Malinowski, they understood themselves as 'human scientists' (those scientists who studied the science of man). Like the 'scientist' depicted by Weber in 'Science as a Vocation', they were 'called' to anthropology. The trope 'science' was thought to neutralise their subjectivity, distancing and alienating them from the 'other'. They observed from nowhere; they were neutral instruments in a laboratory setting. Malinowski, Michael Young tells us, 'did not propose any theory which included the observer in its frame of reference...the field of enquiry was wholly external to himself' (Young 1979a: 11). The gaze of the human scientists yielded observations that went into notebooks as objective ethnographic knowledge. But they were meant to be a special kind of scientific instrument, a participant observer, both engaged and analytic,[26] capable of seeing inside, grasping, in Malinowski's (1961: 25) phrase, 'the native's point of view', as well as seeing outside, observing what natives did, how they behaved. T.N. Madan has called this dual seeing 'living intimately with strangers' (Madan 1975). In practice, anthropologists came to know the natives' point of view mostly through interrogating informants and told 'us', who had not been there, all about it as authors of published accounts.

The 'us' in the early days of ethnography were 'Europeans' from imperial metropoles, the 'them', natives living under colonial domination in what were deemed cultural isolates, denizens of remote islands, villagers living behind mud walls, tribals hidden away in the bush, the mountains or the forest. Natives were objects to be studied, subjects of alien rulers, peoples whom colonial administrators had to control and, in time, improve morally and materially—the white man's burden in Kipling's unintendedly ironic phrase.

[25] The attention to difference in the study of culture, Rosaldo (1989) argues '...results in a peculiar ratio: as the "other" becomes more culturally visible, the "self" becomes correspondingly less so'. On this reading, subordinate groups have an authentic culture but dominant groups can't discern their own way of life as distinctive and configured. Power associated with class position—or, we might add, colonial dominance—tends to make culture invisible. The result is that 'the more power one has, the less culture one enjoys, and the more culture one has, the less power one wields' (ibid.: 202).

[26] Characterising participant observation as a state of being simultaneously engaged and analytic—'subjective objectivity'—can be found in an early essay by Clifford Geertz (1968).

Partially positioned in this way, ethnographic anthropology started its career in the shadow of colonial administration. Power helped to generate and shape ethnographic knowledge and ethnographic knowledge helped those with power to rule.[27] Even Claude Lévi-Strauss, whose structuralist anthropology purported to eliminate the separation between the powerful, civilised European self and powerless, primitive others, regarded himself as a special kind of European whose calling it was to penetrate difference and reveal universal mental categories of the 'human condition'. Beyond myths[28] and observed cultural differences recorded in ethnographies of as yet unspoiled 'primitive' peoples lay the 'savage mind' whose codes revealed universal categories of human thought and action. Primitive others could represent their cultures but not know themselves; that was left to those specially called to structuralist anthropology.[29]

In the autobiographical chapter of *Tristes tropiques* entitled 'The making of an anthropologist', Lévi-Strauss tells us that

> the anthropologist tries to study and judge mankind from a point of view sufficiently lofty and remote to allow him to disregard the particular circumstances of a given society or civilization.... an almost monk-like tendency inspires him to withdraw...into study and to devote himself to the preservation and transmission of a heritage independent of the passing moment...his aim is commensurable only with the time span of the universe....'[30]

[27] The oft-told story of anthropology's links to colonialism will not be re-told here. Those, who have not read Rudyard Kipling's 'The Head of the district' or, from a quite different perspective, George Orwell's 'Shooting an elephant' might want to do so. For an account by an ex-colonial master that shows how, like Joel Chandler Harris's character, Brer Rabbit, in his Uncle Remus tales, the natives manipulate and sometimes control their colonial masters, see Philip Mason, *The wild sweet witch,* and *Call the next witness.*

The story of Anglo-American anthropology's origins and early development as a 'discipline' is best told by George W. Stocking, Jr. in his *Victorian anthropology* (1987). See also Stocking (1976).

For an account that reads post-Malinowski ethnographic field workers and their 'science' as constructions of imperial hegemony and its postcolonial legacy, see Srinivasan (1993).

[28] Because I am concerned in this essay with self–other relationships I focus on Lévi-Strauss's orientation to primitive others as in *Tristes tropiques* rather than on the ahistorical universalism of his four volumes (*The raw and the cooked; From honey to ashes; The origin of table manners; The naked man*) on myths. For an appreciation and critique of his work on myth see Champagne (1987). Champagne tells us in his chapter on 'De-mythologizing' that 'The myths collected by Lévi-Strauss belong to a sort of collective unconscious, almost Jungian in psychological universality.' That common bond,

> that gluey matter, was not easily recognized, even by Lévi-Strauss himself. He was accused...of identifying many kinds of logic operating within various groups of myths. At one point, however, he did bring together several observations that approximate the unity in myths: 'We know, in fact that myths are transformed...in space. The transformations thus respect a kind of conservation principle of mythical matter...' (Champagne 1987: 41–42).

[29] Didier Eribon challenges Lévi-Strauss: 'According to the critics, the Westerner nonetheless maintains supremacy over the culture he is observing.' Lévi-Strauss replies: 'It's not a question of the supremacy of the observer, but of the supremacy of observation. In order to observe, one must be on the outside.... Knowledge lies on the outside' (Eribon 1991: 154).

[30] Lévi-Strauss's reference to the universe seems to have a 'modern' provenance. The modern era, whose 300-year career Stephen Toulmin says began in the early 17th century and took shape within

Like music and mathematics,[31] anthropology is 'one of the few genuine vocations. One can discover it in oneself, even though one may have been taught nothing about it.' Non-Europeans, he implies, cannot achieve the elevation of mind and self-discipline, the civilisation, to join the 'monastic brotherhood' that studies the 'common structure of the mind' that for him is anthropology (Lévi-Strauss 1973: 54–55).[32] In 1960, five years after the publication of *Tristes tropiques*, he concluded his inaugural lecture on assuming the Chair of Social Anthropology at the Collége de France by telling his colleagues that anthropology reveals 'its true colours' when it ceases to treat the primitive other as an object by spreading 'humanism to all humanity'.

> [T]hose 'primitives'...those Indians of the tropics and their counterparts throughout the world who have taught me their humble knowledge (in which is contained...the essence of the knowledge which my colleagues have charged me to transmit to others) soon, alas, ...are all destined for extinction ....To them I have incurred a debt which I can never repay, even if...I were able to give some proof...of the gratitude which I feel towards them by continuing to be as I was among them...their pupil, their witness (1967: 52–53)

After World War II and decolonisation, 'them', the other, the 'people with culture' whose powerlessness gave them 'cultural visibility', had not yet become

---

the assumptions and axioms of Descartes, Newton (via Copernicus and Galileo) and Hobbes (see Toulmin 1990), tended to link 'the Natural and Social Orders in a single picture' by looking

> for models in the physics of their time, seeking a Stable Order of Society behind the flux of historical events, as astronomers had found a Stable Order of Nature behind natural phenomena....The belief that Society forms a stable, homeostatic system, which was fundamental to eighteenth-century modes of thought and practice, gave the language of Social Order a seemingly 'scientific' underpinning.... This physical analogy [to the solar system universe] had deep methodological effects on the social sciences.... Scientific students of society were pure observers, like watchers of stars and planets; their standpoint was as detached from the social facts they reported as the astronomer's was from the planetary facts he recorded.... Today, however, such a detached view of objectivity is hardly relevant, even in physics (Toulmin 1994: 5).

[31] Champagne suggests how Lévi-Strauss privileges music and math:

> The affinity between music and human thinking was an especially obsessive matter for Lévi-Strauss....The mathematical precision of musical notation united with the humanistic pursuit of song and dance to provide a potentially rich discipline from which to learn how to link science and humanism.... Mathematics gave him the instruments, by means of its formulas, to separate the elements of myth and then to reassemble them into a coherent deduction, an approximation of human meaning in an anthropological artifact (1987: 69, 95).

[32] Marianna Torgovnick's chapter interpreting *Tristes tropiques*, entitled 'Remembering with Levi-Strauss', in *Gone primitive* finds that 'Like Freud, Lévi-Strauss scripts the primitive in an us/them vocabulary that writes himself into the majority 'us' of European culture' (Torgovnick 1989: 217). 'The anthropologist in the manner of Lévi-Strauss', Susan Sontag finds, 'is a new breed altogether ....Essentially he is engaged in saving his own soul, by a curious and ambitious act of intellectual catharsis' (1970: 190).

extinct. They could still be found in what came to be called 'third world' countries as well as among another new category, 'minorities' at home, marginalised, dispossessed underclasses and downwardly mobile or displaced elites, e.g., WASPS in America, gentry and aristocracy in Britain.[33] In the anthropological canon of the classical era, natives, the other, were not supposed to be ethnographers; informants perhaps but not ethnographers. They could be observed enacting their culture, fulfilling cultural 'obligations', behaving in culturally appropriate ways, but they were not expected to be self-conscious or reflective, capable of subjectivity, choice or contestation. We constructed them, and told them who they were and how they should behave.

In the not-so-distant past, before 'authenticity'[34] challenged outsiders' epistemological claim that only they could know the other, anthropologists fancied that they had a professional licence, a guild monopoly, a scientific calling to study, know and write about the other. Today, as we traverse the 1990s, the anthropologist's monopoly claim has been reversed; the natives abroad and minorities at home now insist that only they, the reflexive (and not-so-reflexive) other, can know and speak for themselves. But their monopoly claim is recent.

When Amar Singh wrote his diary, natives were not expected to be, indeed were thought incapable of being, reflexive—much less capable of speaking for, representing or governing themselves. Natives abroad (and minorities at home) were sometimes 'restless' and could be 'uppity', indeed even rebellious, but generally it was expected that they would conduct themselves according to cultural scripts written by ethnographers. There were anomalies and exceptions but they did not bring about a 'scientific revolution' or a paradigm shift; 'normal science' in the 'classic period' of anthropology required field work among natives, alien, primitive others, that yielded the required ethnographic monograph, i.e., the objective knowledge and hopefully monumental truth about the other.[35]

[33] See for example Lloyd Warner's (1941–47) studies of Newburyport, Massachusetts, in his Yankee city series, Robert and Helen Lynd's (1929, 1937) of 'Middletown' (Muncie, Indiana), and Rupert Wilkinson's *Gentlemanly power* (1964), for early studies of downwardly mobile elites in America and Britain. For more on Warner and the Lynds see footnote 35.

[34] For an account and rebuttal of authenticity's epistemological and ontological claim that only a native can know a native, that it takes a native or African American to know and tell about native or African American, see Henry Louis Gates, Jr. (1991).

[35] T.N. Madan, an early reflexive 'other', but not one who made monopoly claims, in an autobiographical account of how he came to study his own community in India, implicitly sees himself as an anomaly when he remarks that 'social anthropology took a very long time to realize the potential of' studying one's own society (1975: 153). He cites two of Malinowski's students, Jomo Kenyatta, 'an African tribal chief', and Fei Hsiao-Tung, 'a Chinese Mandarin', whose studies were published in 1938 and 1939, as examples, in Malinowski's words, of anthropologies 'of one's own people... the most arduous, but also the most valuable achievement of a field worker' (quoted in Madan 1975: 152).

David Riesman, in reference to Helen Merrill Lynd and Robert S. Lynd's studies of 'Middletown', e.g., Muncie, Indiana (1929, 1937), spoke of 'anthropology coming home'. Lloyd Warner's studies of Newburyport, Massachusetts (1941–47), and John P. Marquand's 1961 novel, *Point of no return*, which meant to show how little Warner's behavioural explanations explained, come to mind as reflexive studies of 'us' by 'us'. Both the Lynds and Warner studied downwardly mobile WASPS whose culture became more visible as their power decreased.

V
'Native' ethnography?

How do we move practically and epistemologically from the self constructing an other to the 'self as other', from the ethnographer and the native to the native as ethnographer? The story of how T.N. Madan came to do a field-work ethnography of his own community will help us to see how and why this could occur.[36] It was already innovating—and at the time anomalous—when in 1952 M.N. Srinivas published a study based on field work of an 'other' in Indian society, *Religion and society among the Coorgs of south India.* By virtue of his Oxford Ph.D. in Anthropology[37] and appointment in 1948 to a newly created lecturership in Indian sociology, Srinivas had become an 'us', a Western-trained anthropologist, in relation to 'them', the Coorg 'other' in Indian society. As T.N. Madan put it,

[36] T.N. Madan's *Family and kinship: A study of the Pandits of rural Kashmir* (1965) was based on participant-observer field work in his own community.

Madan's decision to study Kashmiri Pandits ran counter to an early postcolonial norm articulated by M.N. Srinivas, by the mid-1950s the 'doyen' of Indian anthropologists. In the face of limited resources and a related but more vague sense that anthropology should serve national development goals, Srinivas advised his students and colleagues to do field work '.... in a section of [Indian] society different from that to which he [*sic*] belongs' (Srinivas 1966: 155). The 'other' it seems could be found at home.

According to Srinivas, India's 'sharp stratification system. . . [and] regional diversity. . . [can] compensate. . . for the non-availability of [the] resources. . .' (Srinivas 1966: 155–56). British anthropologists could command to do field work in distant, alien places. Field work could and should be done in Indian society. André Béteille, from Bengal, and Srinivas's most distinguished student, earned his credentials by doing participant-observer field work in a Tamil village where he found 'class' as well as caste (see Béteille 1965).

Of course, anthropology as an academic discipline had begun in India several generations before Independence in 1947, but it was as officially useful descriptive ethnography ('the castes and/or tribes' of x, y or z place) or sociology (again castes or tribes were the principal subjects) rather than as Malinowski-style field work. Patrick Geddes established the first Indian Department of Sociology at the University of Bombay in 1919. In 1924 Geddes was succeeded by G.S. Ghurye, who was trained at the London School of Economics and at Cambridge University where he studied with W.H.R. Rivers who appreciated but did not teach or practise Malinowski-style field work. For an insightful analytic account of anthropology's career in India before and after Independence see T.N. Madan (1994: 3–107), and Amrit Srinivasan's more polemical version of the pre-Independence story (1993).

M.N. Srinivas, who *was* committed to field work, established the first postcolonial Departments of Sociology, initially at the M.S. University of Baroda, then at Delhi University in 1959. With his move to Delhi, Anthropology/Sociology can be said to have 'arrived' literally and figuratively at the 'centre'. Second only to Economists, Anthropologists/Sociologists became the gurus not only of 'development' and 'rule' but also of ongoing debates about values and identity.

[37] Srinivas's Oxford dissertation was based on data collected earlier for the first of two Ph.D.s, a 900-page Bombay University dissertation done in 1944 under G.S. Ghurye who had suggested the Coorg topic to him. After Radcliffe-Brown's retirement, Srinivas completed the dissertation under Evans-Pritchard. The Oxford dissertation and the 1952 book retained Radcliffe-Brown's functionalist theory, including a functionalist theory of religion and its relation to society. See T.N. Madan's chapter in *Pathways*, 'An introduction to M.N. Srinivas's oeuvre', for a more detailed analystic and evaluative account of Srinivas's career and contributions (1994: 37–51).

> Srinivas apparently operated in the village as any other anthropologist from outside the cultural region, if not India, might have done. The tools of his study and analysis... were those designed for the study of 'other cultures'. There is a sense in which he *was* an outsider in Rampura: an urban, 'England returned'..., highly educated Indian. Add to this his caste status of a Brahman, and you have a clue to the social distance and the cultural surprise that seem to have characterized his situation in the village (Madan 1994: 48).

The Coorgs, an 'evolved', i.e., 'Hinduised' people in south-western India said to be of tribal origin, were an 'other' by 'Western' and arguably by 'Indian' standards. But neither in doing his Coorg book nor in writing his book on caste mobility (Srinivas 1966) did Srinivas imagine that he should—or could—do field work on his own Mysore-Tamil Brahmin community.[38]

How did it happen that T.N. Madan, unlike Srinivas and his students, conducted participant-observer field work among his own Kashmiri Pandit community? How did a 'native' anthropologist manage the move from studying the 'other' in India to studying the self?

Madan read for his Master's degree between 1949 and 1951 at Lucknow with D.N. Majumdar, an anthropologist, and D.P. Mukerji, a social theorist. Mukerji ran down field work as 'a preoccupation with the minutiae of a people's daily life', praised the study of history and philosophy and spoke of the higher relevance for anthropology of 'cultural reconstruction', but Majumdar told him that 'he could not hope to make a professional career out of anthropology without [field work].' Recognising that 'there was no escape' but that his reluctance to deal with strangers could at least be postponed, Madan registered to do a dissertation on tribals 'from published sources'.

About a year later, in 1952, Majumdar asked Madan to join a group of M.A. students on a two-week field trip to Ranchi to study Oraons, a nearby tribal community.

> It was a depressing, and even traumatic, experience... what upset me was our own behaviour. Everybody was asking people questions about their most intimate relationships and fondest beliefs, without any regard for their feelings or

[38] T.N. Madan, in a letter dated 6 April 1993 commenting on a draft of this article, pointed out that Srinivas 'actually says in the last chapter of his *Social change* book, that the anthropologist must begin away from home'. Madan queries this view in his recently published *Pathways*. There he questions whether M.N. Srinivas as well as Lévi-Strauss and Louis Dumont are right in believing that the only way for anthropologists to acquire the allegedly requisite 'anthropological doubt' for studying their own culture is through participant-observer study of a remote ('the remoter the better') culture. Madan doubts that 'the only way one can learn about other [remote] cultures is through personal field work. This is the well-known mystique of "participant observation" and plays down both the volume of extant, good ethnographical literature and what one can learn from studying it' (1994: 159).

Madan seems to agree with Srinivas, Lévi-Strauss and Louis Dumont that 'self ethnography' of the kind he did among his own community of Kashmiri Pandits requires knowledge of an 'other', but holds that such knowledge can be acquired from books—i.e., quality descriptive ethnographies—as well as from the personal field work that these luminaries insist upon.

> convenience.... I had the uncomfortable feeling there was something indecent about such field trips.... [and that] anthropological field work was in a certain sense degrading to the unwilling subject of observation by a stranger.... (Madan 1975: 134).

It was 1952, just five years after Independence. Here he was, an erstwhile subject of the raj and an ex-native (perhaps an ex-native gentleman) being asked to study primitive tribals who constituted part of newly independent India's internal colonial problem. Madan attributes his difficulties about doing field work to a sense of 'awkwardness in dealing with strangers' and 'temperamental inadequacy as a field worker'. Too shy and too embarrassed to intrude on Oraon privacy, he wanted nevertheless to get his professional credential, which meant enduring the required rite of passage, field work. '[C]ould I not', he asked himself, 'study my own cultural group among whom I would not be an outsider?' 'Gradually, almost imperceptibly, it occurred to me that a solution lay in studying my own community, the Kashmiri Pandits.... It is clear to me now, though it was not then, that I was transforming the familiar into the unfamiliar by the decision to relate to it as an anthropologist' (1994: 157).

In 1954 he was told by S.F. Nadel, a 'psychologist-anthropologist on an academic visit to Lucknow University, that he could see no objection to his studying aspects of his community of birth' (rather than 'the strange and the exotic') provided he had adequate training in formal anthropology and field methods 'to overcome the limitations of subjective bias' (1994: 157). 'Obviously, he thought that my birth and upbringing in an urban milieu, and my subsequent university education, would have created sufficient cultural distance between me and the peasants [*sic*] I wanted to study. He accepted me as a doctoral student at the Australian National University' (ibid.).

In 1956, when Madan arrived at ANU to take up a research scholarship to study 'kinship values' among the Pandits of rural Kashmir, he discovered that Nadel had just died. His new advisers, Edmund Leach and Derek Freeman, tried to convince him that structure, not values, determined culture and that knowledge of structure yielded objective truth. Madan listened but remained resolute in his commitment to study family and kinship through participant-observer field work among his own community.

Madan did not justify his study of his own community by claiming, as is current fashion, that authenticity required a Kashmiri Pandit to know and write about kinship among Kashmiri Pandits. Instead, he framed his study in terms of conventional field-work doctrine. 'My own experience', he tells us, 'had been limited... by the fact that I had grown up in an urban neighbourhood [of Srinagar] in which only one other household was related to ours but did not belong to the same family as we did.' And he was to do his field work in a rural village, not quite a cultural isolate but close enough. There he relied on informants, particularly on Sarvanand, 'a born ethnographer', a bachelor, lonely, shy, intelligent, with a prodigious memory, knowledge of the 200-year-old history of the hamlet of Umanagri, and on a written record of notable events during his own lifetime (1975: 138, 140–41).

In his 1975 essay, 'Living intimately with strangers', Madan explained to himself and his anthropologist colleagues that an ethnographic anthropologist can go home again *if* he can render the familiar unfamiliar. He recognised that 'detachment' distinguished his way of knowing from the 'empathy' called for by participant observation among an 'other'. What he did was closer to 'objective subjectivity' than it was to the 'subjective objectivity' or the earlier 'observation' of an anthropology that claimed to be human science. Madan was on the way to establishing a space for the practice by anthropologists of what Michael Herzfeld, a European anthropologist who 'went home again' to Greece, has identified as reflexivity: anthropological theory, Herzfeld says, 'was seen to be about exotic Others. It seems to me that it's not a coincidence that the rise of Europeanist anthropology as a serious force has come about simultaneously with the rise of reflexivity in the discipline' (Herzfeld 1987).[39]

By 1994 Madan had travelled further; 'my title "On Living Intimately with Strangers"', he wrote, 'had been a sincere bow to anthropological orthodoxy, not a clear clue to the content of the essay or its central argument.... the title of my paper', he continued, 'might have been "On Living Strangely with Intimates" [because]...an excessive emphasis on the otherness of those studied only results in their being made the objects of study rather than its subjects.' Studying not only his own society but more importantly his own community of Kashmiri Pandits led him in time to the more general view that anthropologists should '... not divide humankind into "ourselves" and "others"....' Instead we should 'see ourselves in others and others in ourselves... [through] a mutual interpretation of cultures. It is only through such mutual interpretation', he continued, '...that one may develop that critical self-awareness towards which...all anthropologists—and not only those engaged in the study of their own cultures—should aspire' (1994: 159–60).

Madan's story brings us closer to an understanding of Amar Singh's 'self as other' ethnography. After concluding that he did not have to be 'a pseudo-European' 'touched by Western consciousness and transformed into a "modern

[39] Herzfeld is characterising his position in *Anthropology through the looking-glass* (1987), where he examines 'the marginal position of Greek ethnography— and European ethnography generally— in the field of anthropology, arguing that contemporary Greek identity and theoretical anthropology share parallel ideological pressures and conflicts related to the issue of self and other, of insider and outsider'. Explaining the title of his book, Herzfeld recently commented that

> I do see Greece as a looking-glass in which anthropology can view itself. The book attempts to shed some light on Greek society and culture and to show how the tension between anthropological theory and ethnography is equivalent to the tension between the idealized neoclassical reading of Greek culture and the actual, intimate experience of everyday life in Greece, where people are deeply concerned about questions like whether they should be considered 'Europeans' or 'Orientals...' (interview with Michael Herzfeld on the occasion of being awarded the 1994 J.I. Staley prize in *Ideas in anthropology; 1994 Annual Report of the School of American Research*, pp. 34–35).

scholar"...to do anthropology at home'; carry on personal field work among a remote other before he could recognise himself and be recognised by his professional colleagues as an anthropologist; or recognise the 'self and other' dichotomy as a requisite for doing ethnography, Madan found 'critical self-awareness', what I am calling reflexivity, to be the essential condition for ethnographical inquiry and knowledge.

Although T.N. Madan's story opens the way to Amar Singh's ethnography of princely and British India, we are still faced with a difficulty. 'Critical self-awareness' is vouchsafed to anthropologists; they are in a position to acquire the 'distance', the 'sense of surprise', the 'anthropological doubt' required for 'critical self-awareness'.[40] What makes this possible? Having dispensed with an anthropology that privileges European selves over native others, i.e., separates and alienates the self and other, and an anthropology that requires field work as a professional credential and a necessary condition to study the self, Madan tells us that the distance, surprise and doubt that define a critically aware or reflexive anthropologist depend on a command of anthropological literature and theory.

> The message [is]...clear: the ideas of the people must be the starting point of any anthropological inquiry, but ideology never tells us everything. To fill the gaps one must confront it with what people do and *with ideas derived from anthropological literature, theory as well as ethnography* (emphasis added) (1994: 158).

But then Madan disavows this 'bow to anthropological orthodoxy'. James Clifford was right, he tells us, to speak of 'the great lies that make up the truth of anthropology' (Madan 1994: 160; see also Clifford and Marcus 1986: 7). For an Indian other, anthropological truth about India is mainly the invention of European colonial selves. 'The invented image', Madan says, 'takes root in the mind [of the other] and becomes the "intimate enemy"[41]...' whose 'seductive power' keeps native others enthralled and results in 'the loss of self'. 'In anthropological literature India is the land of karma, caste, and renunciation' (Madan 1994). Madan cannot accept this view. 'My own upbringing and experience as a Hindu Indian', he says, 'speaks to me in another idiom—the idiom of moral responsibility rather than karmic choicelessness, of the family rather than caste, and plentitude rather than renunciation' (ibid.: 160–61).[42]

Non-Western peoples, 'by having cultural "otherness" held out as their most characteristic feature', have had their societies and histories misrepresented. Because non-Western societies have 'been studied but not listened to' by a hegemonic anthropological enterprise, their societies have been reduced to 'a single version of "truth"...'(1994: 163).

[40] These themes are developed in 'On critical self-awareness' from accounts of the work of Lévi-Strauss and Louis Dumont.

[41] The reference is to Ashis Nandy's *The intimate enemy* (1983).

[42] Madan elaborated an alternate view of Indian society and culture to that found in the European colonial canon in his *Non-renunciation* (1987).

That truth has been based on deceptions. Non-Western societies, Madan argues, have had '...their traditions tampered with, eroded and invented, often with the help of anthropologists and historians'. Essentialised as 'third world' 'developing societies', non-Westerners have been told that they are locked into 'a permanent transition...' and are positioned to be economically, politically and culturally dependent. 'Dazzled by what technology and the "market", and the power of the state, have to offer, unmindful of the stupendous costs (such as the destruction of the environment and loss of cultural autonomy), non-Western societies make choices that constitute their self-deception' (Madan 1994).

Madan concludes his liberating repudiation of anthropological literature and theory as a necessary condition for being an anthropologist by suggesting that being deceived is possible but not necessary, that there are ways to avoid deception. 'Can people', he asks, 'who live and experience their culture, not in an unquestioning attitude, but self-consciously, in critical self-awareness, and in a similar awareness of others, be ever deceived?'(1994: 165–66).

The odyssey from ethnography as the special preserve of anthropologists to ethnography as a possibility of the human condition opens the way for the final move, an account of Amar Singh's 'self as other' ethnography.

VI
'Self as other' ethnography

Amar Singh was not a professionally trained anthropologist. Unlike T. N. Madan, he could not place himself in the intellectual history of ethnography. Like Molière's Monsieur Jourdain who didn't know he was speaking prose, Amar Singh, when he began writing in 1898, didn't know he was writing ethnography. In any case, doing ethnography in the Edwardian era before Malinowski invented ethnographic field work in 1914–15[43] made him something of an anachronism and, as a 'native' certainly an anomaly. Although Amar Singh read fifty or sixty books a year, he didn't read any expressly labelled or claiming to be 'anthropology'.

[43] See Young (1979a). Young quotes W.H.R. Rivers's call as of 1913 for

> intensive field work... [wherein] the worker lives for a year or more among a community of perhaps four or five hundred people and studies every detail of their life and culture; in which he comes to know every member of the community personally...[and] studies every feature of life and custom in concrete detail and by means of the vernacular language.... It is only by such work that it is possible to discover the incomplete and even misleading character of much of the vast mass of survey work which forms the existing material of anthropology (Young [1979a: 7], quoted from Kuper [1973: 20]).

Young continues:

> Now none of Malinowski's mentors [Westermarck, Seligman, nor yet Rivers himself] had managed to fulfill to the letter this prescription for first hand, intensive research, and no one knew what its consequences would be....[Malinowski] was able to persuade a whole generation of his followers that 'social anthropology' began in the Trobriand Islands in 1914 (1979a: 7).

I would not have called what Amar Singh wrote in his diary 'self as other' ethnography if I had not lived through and reflected on the collapse in the 1980s of ethnography as a way of knowing and a form of knowledge. Anthropology's fall from innocence and grace followed from eating the fruit of discourse, seeing the partial truths of deconstruction and hearing the rhetoric in the authorial voice. The immaculate conception of knowledge and the scientific style of telling lost credibility as the natives became restless, gained power and voice and claimed to be part of us, denizens of the modern world. Scholar anthropologists were revealed as authors and rhetoricians whose work was more literary and philosophic than scientific. Their subjectivity, critics argued, coloured what they saw, heard and 'represented' and their language relied on the arts of persuasion.[44]

This is one of the ways that Amar Singh the diarist-ethnographer speaks to the multifaceted crisis of contemporary anthropology. According to Clifford Geertz,

> the ability of anthropologists to get us to take what they have to say seriously has less to do with either a factual look or an air of conceptual elegance than it has to do with their capacity to convince us that what they have to say is a result of having actually penetrated (or, if you prefer, been penetrated by) another form of life, of having, one way or another, truly 'been there'.... Persuading us that this offstage miracle has occurred...is where the writing comes in (1988: 4–5).

Amar Singh does not have to convince us that he truly has been there. He is there, in princely and British India, speaking in an 'authentic voice' (his own) about forms of life of which he is a part. As a result his writing is not burdened by the need to produce an 'offstage miracle' that convinces us that he commands another form of life.

If there is a miracle it occurs on stage in sharing through his diary accounts the experience of the self as other. We have been spared the mediations that separate an anthropologist *from* a form of life but not the mediations involved in constructing a diarist-ethnographer *within* a form of life. The 'self as other' disposes of one conundrum only to reveal another: why and how does the self as diarist-ethnographer construct his own form of life?

It was diary writing and a liminal location between princely and British India that helped Amar Singh to distance himself from the familiar. Although not

[44] 'It is clear', Clifford Geertz tells us, 'that in...[Foucauldian] terms, anthropology is pretty much entirely on the side of 'literary' discourses rather than 'scientific' ones...ethnographies tend to look at least as much like romances as they do like lab reports...' (1988: 8).

Amar Singh's ethnography is more in accord with Michael M.J. Fisher's characterisation of today's anthropology:

> Anthropological accounts step into an ongoing stream of representations. Anthropology in the late twentieth century is no longer the 'discovery' of terra nova or undescribed cultures, but rather a method of informed critique, pursued often by placing into strategic and disjunctive juxtaposition different representations or perspectives so as to throw light upon the social context of their production and meaning, and to draw out their implications (M.M.J. Fisher 1993: 187).

a professional anthropologist capable of occupying 'the lofty and distant point of vantage' that Lévi-Strauss claimed for his special breed, his reflexivity and liminal position made it possible for him to render the familiar unfamiliar.

Amar Singh wrote—and read—in the first instance for amusement and pleasure, to get outside of and beyond the isolation and boredom of Rajput society.[45] He recognises himself as different from his fellow Rajputs, those who believe that 'he who reads a book will never ride a horse.' He reads—and writes—yet rides a horse, and well.

One day when the Jodhpur Lancers were in China during the Boxer rebellion, Sir Pratap Singh asked 'where I was during the whole of the day yesterday. . . . I explained that I. . . was in my room reading books. . .' Sir Pratap, Amar Singh explains, expected his staff 'to loaf about after him doing nothing but staring at his face. Now this is too hard for me. . . who love reading as much as anything in the world.' He is often annoyed at the Imperial Cadet Corps by prattling classmates who interrupt his writing or reading. 'I like Lichman Singh,' he wrote in July 1905, 'because he is not a bore. If I am busy I go on with my work and he does not mind.' He goes to great lengths to find or make secluded working space; a railroad retiring room in the middle of the night pleases him greatly. At Mount Abu, Rajasthan's hill station where princes and their courtiers mix with raj officials during the hot weather, he seeks refuge in a bathroom. 'How can a man enjoy his life,' he asks, 'when he has to shut himself in a bath room to escape the constant noise of the room and concentrate his mind on reading and writing?' Locked away in a bathroom, he devotes

> hours and hours writing my notes. . . . The room was a quite small one and the table an awful thing. It was small and rickety with room hardly enough to put my diary and inkpot on. I had to put it against a wall to prevent it from moving up and down. . . . The others never would get a [proper] table though I begged of them repeatedly to do so. They merely laughed. Even this table I brought against their will. They were an idle lot indeed. They never realized how much I wanted this piece of furniture.[46]

In the pages of his diary Amar Singh constructs a self who thinks and writes about the books he reads, conversations he has, persons and events he experiences and the behaviour he observes. His diary self became his best friend. To amuse himself in a world of courtiers, sycophants and philistines he creates a self, an alter ego, whose pleasure in books and ideas and imagination about different worlds provide mirrors for the mind that help him to be self-aware and reflexive.

Amar Singh's diary self becomes a convenient, even compelling fiction, a fiction that is in turn constitutive, enabling, and empowering. Amar Singh becomes quite attached to his alter ego and best friend: 'To destroy the diary', he

[45] A more extended version of the argument can be found in S.H. Rudolph and L.I. Rodolph, (1988).

[46] Quotations are from diary entry Shanhai Khan, December 18, 1900 and Jaipore, Friday, 7th July 1905 (continued at July 11) NOTES ABOUT MY LAST VISIT TO MOUNT ABU.

wrote in October 1904, 'would cut me to the heart, as this is a thing I have written with great delight and interest. Then it is my ambition', he continued, 'to keep on writing so long as I live in order that people can have an idea of what sort of life I led and what my ideas were. . . .'[47]

Liminality too helped Amar Singh to become and remain a diarist who could distance himself from, yet engage reflexively with, Rajput and British forms of life. Like the young moving toward adulthood and the travellers, pilgrims, creators, apologists, confessors and prisoners whose diaries find a place in Thomas Mallon's *A book of one's own: People and their diaries* (1984), he was continuously and sharply aware of living between as well as in two worlds, the Rajput world of princely India and the English world of the British raj. Sorting out how each worked, the rules, what Montesquieu and Tocqueville called *moeurs*, that governed conduct in each, preoccupied his early years. He often seems to be telling an invisible Englishman about how Rajputs live and an invisible Rajput, usually himself, how Englishmen live.[48]

Like boredom and the need for amusement, coping with liminality provokes him to write, but unlike them liminality often equips him with a double vision, one Rajput, the other English. Here is a passage about his wife's younger sister's wedding at Satheen:

> My sister-in-law has already won the favor of her husband. They are both very pleased and contented with one another and I think the wife will soon assert her superiority. . . . The thakoor spends a lot of time in her company and does anything she wants him to do. This may not be a strange thing for Europeans who always fulfill their wife's wishes, but among the Indians it is not always so. The husbands as a rule are either tyrants or slaves but mostly the former.[49]

After a long and painful discussion with his father about his recently married sister's seizures—seizures that she and those around her attribute to possession by an evil spirit (a *bootni*)—Amar Singh gives another of his double-visioned accounts, this time of his father's difficulties in acquainting his daughter with what he believes to be the cause of her seizures.

[47] Dehra Doon, Friday 21st October 1904. NOTES ABOUT MY LAST VACATIONS, XXVI. Some Anecdotes.

[48] The meaning and consequences of liminality, thought of here as reflexive self-representation in the context of living between cultures, is theorised and illustrated with evidence from the Amar Singh diary in L.I. Rudolph and S.H. Rudolph (1994). Michael H. Fisher analyses the remarkable careers and writing of Shaikh Din Muhammad (1759–1851) (see M.H. Fisher 1994). At 24, in 1784, he emigrated from 'Bengal' to Cork, Ireland and early in the 19th century to London and Brighton. Fisher frames his analysis of SDM's remarkable literary self-representations in terms of Mary Louise Pratt's concepts of 'contact zones' and 'transculturation' (Pratt 1992), terms I find reminiscent of liminality. Fisher provides a valuable bibliography (in his footnote 55) of 18th and 19th century 'transcultural' travel and autobiographical writing by colonial subjects.

[49] Jaipore, Friday, 7th October 1904 (continued 9, 12, 14, 16, and 19) NOTES ABOUT MY LAST VISIT TO SATHEEN, V. The Marriage, 27. Epilogue.

> My father's conclusion was that my sister is pregnant.... while under this condition women often get sick, and the present sickness is one, though a rare case. This was not a matter that my father could say personally to his daughter.... He sent for the slave girls that had come from Jaipore...these were the only ones [in my sister's house] to whom my father could talk.... All this trouble arises through the Rajpoot etiquette [which forbids such a discussion between father and daughter]. Englishmen talk straight off to their daughters and sisters....[50]

VII
A diary as ethnography

Amar Singh's 'self as other' ethnography depends on the distance and reflexivity his diary allows. The secrecy of private space seems to generate reflexivity. To be a diarist and write as a diarist entails writing in secret for the self. Away from public gaze and censure, a diarist can see, hear, and say things not allowed or not recognised by conventional society. Secrecy for the diarist can be like 'science' for the anthropologist studying the other, a way of realising objective subjectivity. On this reading, the diary becomes the ethnography of secrets of and about the self.[51] Personal diaries began in Europe[52] as secret documents, theatres for the self without an audience. Like most early diarists, Amar Singh wrote in secret; what he wrote was '...not suitable for public scrutiny' (Nussbaum 1988: 134). According to Felicity Nussbaum, those likely to write diaries in the 18th century were 'individuals with secrets to tell....', i.e., persons like Amar Singh who were dependent, subject to masters with authority. Like the women and dissenters who

[50] Tuesday, 2nd December 1902.

[51] Diarists wrote, Felicity Nussbaum tells us in 'Toward conceptualizing diary', on

> the perplexing boundary between the private and public worlds....it is in that privatization of self, that division between public and private self, that journal is born. More permanent than spoken speech, it is a private working out of what cannot and is not ready to be published.... [A private and personal revelation, the diary records what cannot] ...be spoken to anyone except the self....a confession to the self with only the self as auditor and without public authority.... [On the other hand, writing a diary] ...becomes necessary at the point when the subject begins to believe that it cannot be intelligible to itself without written articulation and representation....[It is a way]...to expose the subject's hidden discourse, perhaps in the hope of 'knowing' the self when the subject is still sole censor and critic of his or her own discourse. Before diaries were published, they provided a way to keep the truth about oneself out of the tangled skein of power... (1988: 134–35).

[52] Susanne Rudolph and I in 'Becoming a diarist...' (1988) discuss the limited sense in which diaries were written or known in pre-British India. Amar Singh, like educated Indians and Britishers of his time, is innocent of subcontinental diaries such as the *Baburnama* or the *Tuzhuki Jehangiri.* Barath Ram Nathji, who holds an Indian university degree and has travelled in Britain and on the Continent, encourages Amar Singh to keep a diary in part because he knows as an educator that English public schools are using them as a means of discipline and self-control.

wrote diaries in 17th and 18th century Europe, the young Amar Singh feared discovery by powerful persons in his environment.[53]

When early in the diary's history his father, writing to him at the Jodhpur court from the Jaipur court, tells Amar Singh to destroy his letter, Amar Singh goes further. He cuts out several pages of his diary about his age-mate, the Jodhpur maharaja Sardar Singh, for fear of the consequences if their contents became known. His father's injunction to destroy his letter makes him aware that speaking his mind in the diary could, if its secrecy was breached, bring dangerous knowledge to light. (A few months later, his confidence restored, he writes another essay assessing Sardar Singh's character.) Some years later, his patron and mentor Sir Pratap Singh, formerly regent at Jodhpur but now maharaja of Idar, is arranging to have his biography written. He asks Amar Singh to help by making his diary available. Amar Singh declares himself ready to destroy his diary rather than have it fall into Sir Pratap's hands. He evades and procrastinates long enough to scuttle the request.

Amar Singh, too, had 'secrets' to tell about himself, and about his contemporaries' lives, secrets that they were unable to recognise or unwilling to acknowledge publicly. Amar Singh may not have had the 'distance' that a trained ethnographer engaging in participant observation might claim, but his position as a diarist writing reflexively in secret enabled him to render the familiar unfamiliar. He saw and wrote at a distance from within.

VIII
Selves as ethnographers

With these thoughts in mind about how diaries can distance their authors from the forms of life which they share, I want to return to the question of how Amar Singh's diary can be read as ethnography. I do so by resuming the story of the collapse in the 1980s of anthropologists' ethnography as way of knowing and as form of knowledge. James Clifford's introduction to *Writing culture* (Clifford and Marcus 1986: 3) frames the essays that follow by telling us about the 'crisis in anthropology' created by the problem of writing ethnography in a 'post-anthropological' and 'post-literary' era. I say writing ethnography and not writing about ethnography because ethnography is not out there to be known and then represented in written accounts. Its 'being'—its existence—entails writing. As Clifford remarks, '...one of the principal things ethnographers do—that is write—[is]... central to evaluation of the results of scientific research' (ibid.: 24).

[53] According to Felicity A. Nussbaum the diary in 17th and early 18th century Europe 'was largely a private document' but by the 19th century it had become both a private and a public document (1988: 131). I have already alluded to Alain Corbin's and Anne Martin-Fugier's accounts of the rise of the diary in Michelle Perrot (1990).

Thomas Mallon in *A book of one's own: People and their diaries* argues that 'no one ever kept a diary for just himself.' Diaries can't be written without a public meaning because 'the words have to start going someplace....' Mallon is confident too that diaries will be read. It may be a great-great-granddaughter or the person to whom she sold the house 'but an audience will turn up'

The 'ideology' of 'transparency of representation' and 'immediacy of experience' reflected in language such as field notes, maps and '"writing up"' results has lost credibility. 'Literary processes—metaphor, figuration, narrative—affect the ways cultural phenomena are registered, from the first jotted "observations", to the completed book, to the ways these configurations "make sense" in determined acts of reading' (Clifford and Marcus 1986: 2, 4). What counts as 'realist' in ethnography '...is now a matter of both theoretical debate and practical experimentation'. We can no longer claim we know or can communicate the whole truth. The higher realism, according to Clifford, involves a 'rigorous partiality' that recognises that 'no one can write about others...as if they were discrete objects or texts...' because the apprehension of culture is 'interactive and historical', i.e., subject to the contingencies of language, rhetoric and power (ibid.: 25).

Clifford illustrates 'higher realism' by telling us a story about a Cree hunter. When put under oath in a Canadian court to tell the truth, the whole truth, and nothing but the truth about his way of life in connection with a case about his people's hunting lands, he said, 'I'm not sure I can tell the truth...I can tell what I know' (Clifford and Marcus 1986: 8). As the following story from the diary suggests, this is the kind of truth, i.e., 'rigorous partiality', we find in Amar Singh's 'self as other' ethnography. Amar Singh, who has just completed the first full year of his diary, is responding to a rebuke from his respected teacher, now friend, Ram Nathji. In a note pencilled in at the end of the 1899 volume, Ram Nathji asks Amar Singh how he can have written so much about 'butchery' (hunting boars—pig sticking—and tigers) when Jodhpur was experiencing the worst famine in a century.

> I ought surely to have written about the famine but you must bear in mind that no opportunities were given me to study or watch it and consequently I could not write anything...fearing that I might put in something quite out of place. What I have written is of which I am an eye witness or have heard from very reliable sources.[54]

Amar Singh seems clear about telling what he knows—things he can study and watch—and not telling about those he can't.

[54] Comments Written on End Papers of Ms Volume I.

The full text of Amar Singh's response to Ram Nathji's comments at the end of the bound volume for 1899 are given below. Ram Nathji was the only person allowed to read the diary. He did so for the first three years, pencilling in comments in the margins and writing a summary comment at the end.

My dear Master Sahib,

I am indeed very grateful for the trouble you have taken to read the whole of my diary and [to] have written remarks on it. I feel very much honoured by it. You know this perfectly, that you are the only man who has yet been at liberty to do what you like with these pages which, though quite rot and a record of butchery [accounts of hunting expeditions] as you say, can yet put me to great inconvenience if known to bad characters. I ought surely to have written about the famine but you must bear in mind that no opportunities were given me to study or watch it...What I have written is of which I am an eye witness or have heard from very reliable sources.

Can an ethnographer tell what he knows if he writes from *within* rather than from outside a cultural context? The participant-observer canon holds that ethnographers achieve distance by being outsiders who are empathetic even while being objective, i.e., they should participate in the inner life of the other but remain objective by observing (not being) the other. Should Amar Singh's 'self as other' diary accounts qualify as ethnography?

Clifford argues that in recent decades the participant-observer subjective objectivity distancing dichotomy eroded, then washed away. In his view, the dichotomy between the self and other, the ethnographer and the natives, expressed in the 'rhetoric of experienced objectivity', gives way to first-person field-work accounts that replace third-person accounts of the theatre of the other (Clifford and Marcus 1986: 14).

In 'polyphonic' 'dialogic' textual production both ethnographer and subject are on stage in a reconstituted theatre of the other. They engage each other, sharing the conversation built into a script. But they do not share the production of the script's text. Despite the appearance on stage of reciprocity and mutual determination, the writing of the play, however literary and 'partial' it may be, remains the task of the ethnographer. Politically, Clifford argues, he or she retains authority over the text about an other. But Amar Singh, a reflexive diarist writing about his culture from within, realises a more symmetrical relationship by uniting self and other. He can be observer, informant, narrator and author rolled into one. He writes the play and speaks its lines; it is his text, his script, and his performance.

REFERENCES

BARKER, A.J. 1967. *The neglected war: Mesopotamia 1914–1918.* London: Faber and Faber.

BÉTEILLE, ANDRÉ. 1965. *Caste, class and power: Changing patterns of stratification in a Tanjore village.* Berkeley, CA: University of California Press.

CHAMPAGNE, ROLAND A. 1987. *Claude Lévi-Strauss.* Boston: Twayne Publishers.

CLIFFORD, JAMES and GEORGE MARCUS, eds. 1986. *Writing culture: The poetics and politics of ethnography.* Berkeley, CA: University of California Press.

COHEN, STEPHEN P. 1971. *The Indian army: Its contribution to the development of a nation.* Berkeley, CA: University of California Press.

CORBIN, ALAIN. 1990. Backstage. *In* Michelle Perrot, ed., *A history of private life, Volume IV: From the fires of revolution to the Great War*, pp. 497–502. Cambridge, MA: The Belknap Press of Harvard University Press.

CREWE, QUENTIN. 1985. *The last maharaja: A biography of Sawai Man Singh II, Maharaja of Jaipur.* London: Michael Joseph.

CSIKSZENTMIHALYI, MIHALY. 1993. *The evolving self: A psychology for the third millennium.* New York: Harper Collins.

DILKS, DAVID. 1967–70. *Curzon in India, Volume I: Achievement.* London: Hart-Davis.

ELLINWOOD, DEWITT C. 1987. The Indian soldier and national consciousness: 1914–39. *Quarterly review of historical studies* 27, 1: 4–24.

ERIBON, DIDIER. 1991. *Conversations with Claude Lévi-Strauss.* Chicago: The University of Chicago Press.

FARWELL, BYRON. 1989. *Armies of the Raj: From the great mutiny to independence, 1858–1947.* New York: Norton.

FISHER, MICHAEL H. 1994. *Indian autobiography from the frontier: Travelling from Patna to Brighton.* Unpublished paper. Oberlin, Ohio.

FISHER, MICHAEL M.J. 1993. The Jewish, Spanish, Turkish, Iranian, Ukrainian, German unconscious of Polish culture—or—one hand clapping: Dialogue, silences, and the mourning of Polish romanticism. *In* George, Marcus, ed., *Perilous states: Conversations on culture, politics and nation.* Chicago: The University of Chicago Press.

GATES, JR., HENRY LOUIS. 1991. 'Authenticity' or the lesson of Little Tree. *New York Times Book Review,* November 24.

GEERTZ, CLIFFORD. 1968. Thinking as a moral act: Dimensions of anthropological fieldwork in the New States. *Antioch Review* 28, 2: 139–58.

——. 1988. *Works and lives: The anthropologist as author.* Stanford, CA: Stanford University Press.

HERZFELD, MICHAEL. 1987. *Anthropology through the looking-glass: Critical ethnography in the margins of Europe.* Cambridge, UK: Cambridge University Press.

HOBBES, THOMAS. 1990. *Cosmopolis: The hidden agenda of modernity.* New York: Free Press.

KUPER, A. 1973. *Anthropologists and anthropology: The British school, 1922–1972.* London: Allen Lane.

LÉVI-STRAUSS, CLAUDE. 1967. *The scope of anthropology.* London: Jonathan Cape.

——. 1973. *Tristes Tropiques* (trans. from the French by John and Doreen Weightman). London: Jonathan Cape.

LIFTON, ROBERT. 1993. *The protean self: Human resilience in an age of fragmentation.* New York: Basic Books.

LYND, HELEN MERRILL and ROBERT S. LYND. 1929. *Middletown: A study of contemporary American culture.* New York: Harcourt Brace.

——. 1937. *Middletown in transition: A study in cultural conflicts.* New York: Harcourt Brace.

MADAN, T.N. 1965. *Family and kinship: A study of the Pandits of rural Kashmir.* Bombay: Asia Publishing House.

——. 1975. On living intimately with strangers. *In* André Béteille and T.N. Madan, eds., *Encounter and experience: Personal accounts of field work,* pp. 131–56. Delhi: Vikas Publishing House.

——. 1987. *Non-renunciation: Themes and interpretations of Hindu culture.* Delhi: Oxford University Press.

——. 1994. *Pathways: Approaches to the study of society in India.* Delhi: Oxford University Press.

MALINOWSKI, BRONISLAW. 1961. *Argonauts of the Western Pacific.* New York: Dutton.

MALLON, THOMAS. 1984. *A book of one's own: People and their diaries.* New York: Ticknor and Fields.

MARCUS, GEORGE E. 1993. *Perilous states: Conversations on culture, politics and nation.* Chicago: University of Chicago Press.

MARQUAND, JOHN P. 1961. *Point of no return.* Boston: Little Brown.

MARTIN-FUGIER, ANNE. 1990. The Bourgeois rituals. *In* Michelle Perrot, ed., *A history of private life, Volume IV: From the fires of revolution to the Great War,* pp. 265–68. Cambridge, MA: The Belknap Press of Harvard University Press.

MASON, PHILIP. 1987. *A matter of honour: An account of the Indian army, its officers and men.* London: Macmillan/PERMAC.

MAYARAM, SHAIL. 1994. Powerful regimes, cultural critiques: The Meos of north India. Ph.D. dissertation, University of Delhi.

NANDY, ASHIS. 1983. *The intimate enemy: Loss and recovery of self under colonialism.* Delhi: Oxford University Press.

NUSSBAUM, FELICITY A. 1988. Toward conceptualizing diary. *In* James Olney, ed., *Studies in autobiography,* pp. 134–35. New York: Oxford University Press.

PERROT, MICHELLE, ed. 1990. *A history of private life, Volume IV: From the fires of revolution to the Great War* (trans. Arthur Goldhammer). Cambridge, MA: The Belknap Press of Harvard University Press.

PRATT, MARY LOUISE. 1992. *Imperial eyes: Travel writings and transculturation.* London: Routledge.

RICOEUR, PAUL. 1992. *Oneself as another.* Chicago: University of Chicago Press.

ROSALDO, RENATO. 1989. *Culture and truth: The remaking of social analysis.* Boston: Beacon Press.

ROY, ASHIM KUMAR. 1978. *History of the Jaipur city.* Delhi: Manohar.

RUDOLPH, LLOYD I. and SUSANNE RUDOLPH. 1994. Setting the table: Amar Singh aboard the SS Mohawk. *Common Knowledge* 3, 1: 158–77.

——, eds. Forthcoming. Reversing the gaze: The Amar Singh diary as a narrative of imperial India. New Delhi: Oxford University Press and Boulder, CO: Westview Press (with Mohan Singh Kanota).

RUDOLPH, SUSANNE HOEBER and LLOYD I. RUDOLPH. 1975. A bureaucratic lineage in Princely India: Elite formation and conflict in a patrimonial system. *Journal of Asian studies* 34, 3: 717–53. (Republished in Rudolph and Rudolph 1984.)

——. 1976. Rajput adulthood: Reflections on the Amar Singh diary. *Daedalus* Spring. (Republished in Rudolph and Rudolph 1984.)

——. 1980. Authority and the transmission of values in the Rajput joint family. *In* Mel Albin, ed., *New directions in psychohistory: The Adelphi papers in honor of Erik Erikson*, pp. 143–60. Lexington, MA: D.D. Heath and CO. (Republished in Rudolph and Rudolph 1984.)

—— 1984. *Essays on Rajputana: Reflections on history, culture and administration.* New Delhi: Concept Publishing Co.

——. 1988. Becoming a diarist: The making of an Indian personal document. *Indian social and economic history review* 25, 2: 113–32.

SAID, EDWARD. 1979. *Orientalism.* New York: Vintage Books.

——. 1993. *Culture and imperialism.* New York: Alfred Knopf.

SHWEDER, RICHARD. 1991. *Thinking through culture: Expeditions in cultural psychology.* Cambridge, MA: Harvard University Press.

SONTAG, SUSAN. 1970. The anthropologist as hero. *In* E. Nelson Hayes and Tanya Hayes, eds., *Claude Lévi-Strauss: The anthropologist as hero.* Cambridge, MA: The MIT Press.

SRINIVAS, M.N. 1952. *Religion and society among the Coorgs of South India.* Oxford: The Clarendon Press.

——. 1966. *Social change in modern India.* Berkeley: University of California Press.

SRINIVASAN, AMRIT. 1993. The subject of fieldwork: Malinowski and Gandhi. *Economic and political weekly* 28, 50: 2745–52.

STERN, ROBERT. 1988. *The cat and the lion: Jaipur state in the British Raj.* The Hague: Brill.

STOCKING, JR. GEORGE W. 1976. Ideas and institutions in American anthropology: Thoughts toward a history of the interwar years. *In* George W. Stocking, ed., *Selected papers from the American anthropologist, 1921–1945*, pp. 1–53. Washington, D.C.: American Anthropological Association.

——. 1987. *Victorian anthropology.* New York: Free Press.

SUNDARAM, CHANDRA. 1996. Little grace in the giving: The Indianization of the Indian Army's Officer Corps 1817–1925. Ph.D. dissertation, McGill University.

TAYLOR, CHARLES. 1989. *Sources of the self: The making of the modern identity.* Cambridge, MA: Harvard University Press.

THORNTON, ROBERT J. and PETER SKALNIK, eds. 1993. *The early writings of Bronislaw Malinowski.* Cambridge, UK: Cambridge University Press.

TORGOVNICK, MARIANNA. 1989. *Gone primitive: Savage intellects, modern lives.* Chicago: The University of Chicago Press.

TOULMIN, STEPHEN. 1990. *Cosmopolis: The hidden agenda of modernity.* New York: Free Press.

——. 1994. The twilight of sovereignity: Subject/Citizen/Cosmopolitan. *Graven images: A journal of culture, law and the sacred* 1: 5.

WARNER, LLOYD. 1941–47. *Yankee city series*, 4 vols. New Haven: Yale University Press.

WEBER, MAX. 1972 [1946]. Science as a vocation. *In* H. Gerth and C.W. Mills, eds., *From Max Weber: Essays in sociology*, pp. 129–56. New York: Oxford University Press.

WILKINSON, RUPERT. 1964. *Gentlemanly power.* New York: Oxford University Press.

YOUNG, MICHAEL W. 1979a. Introduction. *In* Michael W. Young, ed., *The ethnography of Malinowski: The Trobriand Islands 1915–1918*, pp. 1–20. London, Boston and Henley: Routledge and Kegan Paul.

——, ed. 1979b. *The ethnography of Malinowski: The Trobriand Islands, 1915–1918.* London: Routledge and Kegan Paul.

T.N. Madan: A biographical note and bibliography

Biographical note

Triloki Nath Madan's professional career in social anthropology effectively covers the five decades since Indian independence. Born on 12 September 1933, Madan was introduced to anthropology and sociology while studying for his M.A. degree at the University of Lucknow in the early 1950s. There he was exposed to the very different disciplinary orientations of his distinguished teachers, Radhakamal Mukerjee, D.P. Mukerji and D.N. Majumdar, and came into contact with many of the pioneers of anthropological and sociological studies in India: A. Aiyappan, Nirmal Kumar Bose, S.C. Dube, Louis Dumont, Irawati Karve and M.N. Srinivas.

In 1956, Madan joined the Australian National University as a Ph.D. research scholar, working under the supervision of W.E.H. Stanner and Derek Freeman, and in close touch also with J.A. Barnes. His Ph.D. dissertation, which was subsequently published as *Family and kinship among the Pandits of rural Kashmir* (1965), was acknowledged as the first comprehensive study of the dynamics of the north Indian household, and was very well received by the profession. It was also methodologically innovative. Uncomfortable with the methods and perspectives of contemporary anthropology conceived as the study of 'primitive' tribal societies and 'other' cultures, Madan had self-consciously sought to expand the scope of anthropology to encompass the study of 'one's own' society. He argued that 'living strangely with intimates' should be as acceptable a procedure of anthropological field research as the conventional 'living intimately with strangers' (1975).

Following his Ph.D., Madan took up successive teaching posts at the University of Lucknow, the School of Oriental and African Studies, London, and the Karnatak University, Dharwar. In 1966 he joined the Institute of Economic Growth, Delhi, as Professor of Sociology, continuing in this position till his retirement in 1996. Simultaneously with his move to the IEG, Madan was invited to assume the editorship of the second series of the journal, *Contributions to Indian sociology*, founded by Louis Dumont and David Pocock in 1957. He relinquished this position in 1991 after twenty-five years at the helm, while continuing his association with the journal as a member of the Editorial Board.

In the meantime, Madan expanded the substantive scope of his research to cover new areas—modern occupations and professions, medical practice, comparative Asian development, ethnicity and nation-building, and religion. The study of religion in historical and contemporary contexts, the sociological interpretation of communalism and religious fundamentalism, and the deconstruction of the idea of Indian 'secularism' are themes that have increasingly occupied his attention, culminating in the publication of his book, *Modern myths, locked minds* (1997), which was awarded the Hem Ram Chaturvedi Memorial Award for the best published work on the relationship of religion and society in India for 1996–98.

Madan's study of the Pandit family was executed firmly within the structural-functional anthropological tradition, to which it was an important South Asian contribution. But increasingly he came to believe that anthropology must take account not only of observed behaviour, but also of values and ideologies. Inspired by the work of Louis Dumont,

Madan's subsequent writing has sought to engage with people's own ideas and cultural values—as in his well-known essay on the ideology of the householder among the Pandits (1981)—and to bring under scrutiny sources of data such as religious texts and works of fiction that are often considered beyond the sociological 'pale' (see his *Non-renunciation* [1987]).

Besides his many contributions to South Asian ethnography, Madan has held several important administrative posts, including that of Coordinator of the UNESCO project on the medical profession in Asia (1975–77), Member Secretary of the Indian Council of Social Science Research (1978–81), Director of the Institute of Economic Growth, Delhi (1986–89), Member of the Advisory Committee on Medical Research of WHO for South and Southeast Asia (1981–84), and Member of the Advisory Committee of the Fundamentalism Project of the American Academy of Arts and Sciences (1989–93). Among his many awards and honours are his Honorary Fellowship of the Royal Anthropological Institute of Great Britain and Ireland, one of just fifty fellowships worldwide, the University Grants Commission Pranavananda Award (1994) for his contribution to sociology in India, his Docteur Honoris Causa (Ethnologie) of the University of Paris X (1994) and the Radhakrishnan Chair in Humanities and the Social Sciences at the University of Hyderabad (1995). Following his retirement from the IEG, the Indian Council of Social Science Research awarded him its highest honour, a National Fellowship.

From the 1970s, Madan has had visiting assignments at a number of foreign universities, including the University of Illinois, Champaign-Urbana; the Australian National University, Canberra; the Ecole des Hautes Etudes en Sciences Sociales, Paris; Harvard University; the University of Chicago; the University of Washington, Seattle; the University of Texas, Austin; and Smith College, Northampton. The academic and personal links that he forged during these assignments are reflected in many of the contributions to this book.

In addition to his long stint as Editor of *Contributions to Indian sociology*, Madan has been a member of the editorial advisory boards of a number of leading national and international journals, among them *The Eastern anthropologist, Ethnic and racial studies, International sociology, Modern Asian studies, Journal of the Indian Council of Philosophical Research*, and *Social science and medicine*. He is currently Editor-in-Chief of the new *Indian social science review*, and General Editor of the well-known series, *Oxford in India Readings in Sociology and Social Anthropology*.

A bibliography of Madan's published writings follows this biographical note. This should prove useful not only for researchers seeking to construct T.N. Madan's intellectual biography within the context of the development of Indian sociology and anthropology in the post-independence era, but also for those aspiring to follow in his footsteps in the several fields of study in which he has led the way.

Bibliography

Books

1956 *An introduction to social anthropology* (co-authored with D.N. Majumdar). Bombay: Asia Publishing House. Eleven impressions. Reprinted, New Delhi: National Publishing House, 1986. Fourteenth impression, 1998.

1962 *****Indian anthropology: Essays in memory of D.N. Majumdar* (co-edited with Gopala Sarana). Bombay: Asia Publishing House.

1965 *****Family and kinship: A study of the Pandits of rural Kashmir*. Bombay: Asia Publishing House.

1974 *Sāmājik mānavashāstra parichay*. New Delhi: National Publishing House. Hindi translation of Madan (1956) by Gopal Bhardwaj. Twelfth impression, 1998.

1975 **Encounter and experience: Personal accounts of fieldwork* (co-edited with André Béteille). New Delhi: Vikas; Honolulu: University Press of Hawaii.

1976 **Muslim communities of South Asia: Society and culture* (editor). New Delhi: Vikas.

1980 **Doctors and society: Three Asian case studies: India, Malaysia, Sri Lanka* (in collaboration with Paul Wiebe, Rahim Said and Malsiri Dias). New Delhi: Vikas (on behalf of UNESCO).

1982 *Way of life: King, householder, renouncer. Essays in honour of Louis Dumont* (editor). New Delhi: Vikas; Paris: Editions Maison des Sciences de l'Homme. Reprinted, Delhi: Motilal Banarsidass, 1988.

1983 **Culture and development*. D.N. Majumdar Lectures, under the auspices of the Ethnographic and Folk-Culture Society, Lucknow. Delhi: Oxford University Press.

1987 *Non-renunciation: Themes and interpretations of Hindu culture*. Delhi: Oxford University Press. Reprinted, 1988. Paperback edition, 1996.

1988 *Choice and morality in anthropological perspective: Essays in honour of Derek Freeman* (co-edited with George N. Appell). Albany, NY: State University of New York Press.

1989 *Family and kinship: A study of the Pandits of rural Kashmir*. Second enlarged edition. Delhi: Oxford University Press.

1990 *A l'opposé du renoncement: Perplexitiés de la vie quotidienne hindoue*. Paris: Editions Maison des Sciences de l'Homme. Translation of Madan (1987) by Denise Paulme-Schaeffner and Bernard Juillerat. New Preface.

1991 *Religion in India* (editor). Delhi: Oxford University Press. Second, enlarged, paperback edition, 1992. Fifth impression, 1999.

1994 *Pathways: Approaches to the study of society in India*. Delhi: Oxford University Press. Paperback edition, 1995. Second impression, 1999.

1995 *Muslim communities of South Asia: Culture, society, and power*. Revised enlarged edition. New Delhi: Manohar. Reprinted with additions and alterations, 2000 (forthcoming).

1997 *Modern myths, locked minds: Secularism and fundamentalism in India*. Delhi: Oxford University Press. Reprinted, 1998. Paperback edition, 1998.

Title out of print

Selected papers and shorter articles*

1953 Kinship terms used by the Pandits of Kashmir. *The eastern anthropologist* 7, 1: 37–46.

1961 Dhirendra Nath Majumdar 1903–1960. *American anthropologist* 63, 2 (Pt. I): 369–74.

1961 Majumdar's contributions to anthropology in Uttar Pradesh: A note. *Research bulletin of the Faculty of Arts*, University of Lucknow, 1: 3–10.

—— Herath: A religious ritual and its secular aspects. *In* L.P. Vidyarthi, ed., *Aspects of religion in Indian society*, pp. 129–39. Meerut: Kedarnath Ramnath.

1962 Is the Brahmanic gotra a grouping of kin? *Southwestern journal of anthropology* 18, 1: 59–77.

—— The Hindu joint family. *Man* 62, art. 145: 88–89.

—— The joint family: A terminological clarification. *International journal of comparative sociology* 3, 1: 7–16.

1963 Proverbs: The 'single-meaning' category. *Man* 63, art. 114: 93.

—— A further note on Pandit kinship terminology. *In* L.K. Bala Ratnam, ed., *Anthropology on the march*, pp. 268–74. Madras: Social Science Association.

1965 Pakistan: Races, languages, religions and cultures. *Encyclopaedia Britannica* 17: 75–76. London.

—— Social organization. *In* V.B. Singh, ed., *Economic history of India 1857–1956*, pp. 59–87. Bombay: Allied Publishers.

—— Caste: Facts and the future. *Seminar* 70: 34–37.

1966 Politico-economic change and organizational adjustment in a Kashmiri village. *The journal of Karnatak University* (social sciences) 2: 20–34.

—— For a sociology of India. *Contributions to Indian sociology* 9: 9–16.

—— Dhirendra Nath Majumdar. Biographical memoirs of the Fellows of the National Institute of Sciences of India 1: 165–80. New Delhi.

1967 Political pressures and ethical constraints upon Indian sociologists. *In* G. Sjoberg, ed., *Ethics, politics and social research*, pp. 162–79. New York: Schenkeman.

—— The changing political functions of caste. *In* Baljit Singh and V.B. Singh, eds., *Social and economic change*, pp. 208–25. Bombay: Allied.

—— For a sociology of India: Some clarifications. *Contributions to Indian sociology (n.s.)* 1: 90–93.

* This selection of Professor Madan's papers excludes some items described by him as 'forgettable' Also excluded are book reviews (over 200 in number) and many articles published in newspapers, newsletters and magazines. A number of the papers listed here have been reprinted (some of them more than once); such reproduction has been noted only in a couple of cases. *Editors.*

1968 D.N. Majumdar. *In* D.L. Sills, ed., *International encyclopedia of the social sciences* 9: 540–41. New York: Macmillan–Free Press.

1969 Caste and development. *Economic and political weekly* 4, 5: 285–87, 289–90.

—— Who chooses modern medicine and why. *Economic and political weekly* 4, 37: 1475–77, 1479–81, 1483–84.

—— Urgent research in social anthropology in Kashmir. *In* B.L. Abbi and S. Saberwal, eds., *Urgent research in social anthropology*, pp. 101–5. Simla: Indian Institute of Advanced Study.

1971 Development and the professions in Asia: [Three] Working Papers (co-authored with P.C. Verma). *In* Ratna Dutta and P.C. Joshi, eds., *Studies in Asian social development*, pp. 145–83. New Delhi: Tata McGraw-Hill.

1971 On the nature of caste in India: Introduction. *Contributions to Indian sociology (n.s.)* 5: 1–13, 79–81.

1972 Doctors in a north Indian city: Recruitment, role perception and role performance. *In* Satish Saberwal, ed., *Beyond the village*, pp. 77–110. Simla: Indian Institute of Advanced Study.

—— Caste and community in the private and public education of Mysore state. (co-authored with B.G. Halbar). *In* S.H. Rudolph and L.I. Rudolph, eds., *Politics and higher education in India*, pp. 121–47. Cambridge, MA: Harvard University Press.

—— Two faces of Bengali ethnicity: Muslim Bengali or Bengali Muslim. *The developing economies* (Tokyo) 10, 1: 74–85.

—— Religious ideology in a plural society: The Muslims and Hindus of Kashmir. *Contributions to Indian sociology (n.s.)* 6: 106–41. Reprinted as: The social construction of cultural identities in rural Kashmir, *in* T.N. Madan, ed., *Muslim communities of South Asia*, pp. 241–87. New Delhi: Manohar, 1995.

—— Research methodology: A trend report. *In* M.N. Srinivas, M.S.A. Rao and A.M. Shah, eds., *A survey of research in sociology and social anthropology*, vol. 3, pp. 282–315. Bombay: Allied.

—— Twenty-five years of Indian anthropology: A profile (co-authored with Mukul Dube). *In* K.S. Mathur and S.C. Verma, eds., *Man and society.* Silver jubilee number of *The eastern anthropologist*, pp. 79–94.

1973 Magnitude and structure of the professions in India: A study of interstate variation (co-authored with P.C. Verma). *Indian journal of labour economics* 15, 3–4 [1972–73]: 207–41.

1973 Social change in contemporary India. *In* K.S. Mathur et al., eds., *Studies in social change*, pp. 1–10. Lucknow: Ethnographic and Folk-Culture Society.

1974 The dialectic of ethnic and national boundaries in the evolution of Bangladesh. *In* S. Navlakha, ed., *Studies in Asian social development*, pp. 158–83. New Delhi: Vikas.

1974 The gift of food. *In* B.N. Nair, ed., *Culture and society*, pp. 84–96. Delhi: Thomson.

—— The teaching of sociology in India: Some comments. *Sociological bulletin* 23, 1: 113–18.

1975 Structural implications of marriage in north India: Wife-givers and wife-takers among the Pandits of Kashmir. *Contributions to Indian sociology (n.s.)* 9, 2: 217–43.

—— On living intimately with strangers. *In* André Béteille and T.N. Madan, eds., *Encounter and experience: Personal accounts of fieldwork*, pp. 131–56. New Delhi: Vikas.

—— Introduction (co-authored with André Béteille). *In* André Béteille and T.N. Madan, eds., *Encounter and experience: Personal accounts of fieldwork*, pp. 1–12. New Delhi: Vikas.

1976 The Hindu family and development. *Journal of social and economic studies* (Patna) 4, 2: 211–31.

—— The Hindu woman at home. *In* B.R. Nanda, ed., *Indian women: From purdah to modernity*, pp. 67–87. New Delhi: Vikas.

—— Toward a humanised medicine. *Indian journal of medical education* 15, 1: 1–7.

1977 The quest for Hinduism. *International social science journal* 29, 2: 261–78.

—— Indian society: The rural context. *In* S.C. Dube, ed., *India since independence*, pp. 48–84. New Delhi: Vikas.

—— Dialectic of tradition and modernity in the sociology of D.P. Mukerji. *Sociological bulletin* 26, 2: 155–76. Reprinted with minor changes in *Social science information* 17, 6(1978): 777–99.

1978 M.N. Srinivas's earlier work and *The remembered village:* An introduction. *Contributions to Indian sociology (n.s.)* 12, 1: 1–14.

1979 Linguistic diversity and national unity: Dimensions of a debate. *In* C.H. Hanumantha Rao and P.C. Joshi, eds., *Reflections on economic development and social change*, pp. 393–410. Delhi: Allied.

—— Introduction to the Indian edition [of] T. Scarlett Epstein, *Capitalism, primitive and modern: Some aspects of Tolai economic growth*, pp. vii–xii. Delhi: Hindustan.

1980 Indigenous anthropology in non-western countries: A further elaboration. *Current anthropology* 21, 5: 653–55.

—— Indigenisation in perspective. *In* Jan J. Loubser, ed., *The indigenisation of social sciences in Asia*, pp. 22–28. Copenhagen: IFSSO Occasional Papers No. 1.

1981 Moral choices: An essay on the unity of asceticism and eroticism. *In* A.C. Mayer, ed., *Culture and morality*, pp. 126–52. New Delhi: Oxford University Press.

—— The ideology of the householder among the Pandits of Kashmir. *Contributions to Indian sociology (n.s.)* 15, 1–2: 223–49. Reprinted *in*

T.N. Madan, ed., *Way of life: King, householder, renouncer. Essays in honour of Louis Dumont*, pp. 223–50. New Delhi: Vikas, 1982. Reprinted with minor changes in A. Ostor, L. Fruzzetti and S. Barnett, eds., *Concepts of person*, pp. 99–117, 239–42. Cambridge, MA: Harvard University Press, 1983.

1981 For a sociology of India. *Contributions to Indian sociology (n.s.)* 15, 1–2: 405–18.

1982 Anthropology as the mutual interpretation of cultures. *In* Hussain Fahim, ed., *Indigenous anthropology in non-western countries*, pp. 4–18. Durham, NC: Carolina Academic.

1983 The historical significance of secularism in India. *In* S.C. Dube and V.N. Basilov, eds., *Secularization in multi-religious societies*, pp. 11–20. New Delhi: ICSSR–Concept.

1983 Cultural identity and modernization in Asian countries: Some Indian questions soliciting Japanese answers. *In: Proceedings of Kokugakuin University Centennial Symposium*, pp. 130–37. Tokyo: Kokugakuin University.

1984 Coping with ethnic diversity: A South Asian perspective. *In* David Maybury-Lewis, ed., *The prospects for plural societies*, pp. 136–45. The 1982 Proceedings of the American Ethnological Society. Washington, D.C.: American Ethnological Society.

1985 Concerning the categories śubha and śuddha in Hindu culture: An exploratory essay. *Journal of developing societies* 1, 1: 11–29. Reprinted *in* J.B. Carman and F.A. Marglin, eds., *Auspiciousness and purity*, pp. 11–29. Leiden: E.J. Brill, 1985.

—— At ta aur anāgat: Samājshāstra ke bhārat ya sandarbh mein (in Hindi). *Samājikī* 6, 2: 1–8.

1986 Secularisation and the Sikh religious tradition. *Social compass* 33, 2–3: 25–73.

—— Foreword. *In* Charlotte Vaudeville, *Bārahmāsā*, pp. v–vii. Delhi: Motilal Banarsidass.

1987 Community involvement in health policy: Socio-structural and dynamic aspects of health beliefs. *Social science and medicine* 25, 6: 615–20.

—— Secularism in its place. *Journal of Asian studies* 46, 4: 747–60.

1988 Kashmir; Srinagar. *In* Ainslee T. Embree, ed., *Encyclopedia of Asian history* 2: 278–80; 4: 9. New York: Charles Scribner's Sons.

—— J. Krishnamurty: The teaching. *New Quest* 67: 5–13.

—— The son as saviour: A Hindu view of choice and morality. *In* G.N. Appell and T.N. Madan, eds., *Choice and morality in anthropological perspective: Essays in honour of Derek Freeman*, pp. 137–56. Albany: State University of New York Press.

1989 Foreword. *In* John N. Gray and David J. Mearns, eds., *Society from the inside out*, pp. 9–12. New Delhi: Sage.

1989 Society—Introduction: How people live. *In* Francis Robinson, ed., *The Cambridge encyclopedia of India, Pakistan, Bangladesh, Sri Lanka, Nepal, Bhutan and the Maldives*, pp. 364–75. Cambridge: Cambridge University Press.

—— Religion in India. *Daedalus* 118, 4: 115–46.

1990 India in American anthropology. *In* Sulochana R. Glazer and Nathan Glazer, eds., *Conflicting images: India and the United States*, pp. 179–202. Riverdale, MD: Riverdale.

1991 The double-edged sword: Fundamentalism and the Sikh religious tradition. *In* Martin R. Marty and R. Scott Appleby, eds., *Fundamentalisms observed*, pp. 594–627. Chicago: The University of Chicago Press.

1991 Relevance in social anthropology: Some observations. *In* B.G. Halbar and C.G. Hussain Khan, eds., *Relevance of anthropology: The Indian scenario*, pp. 283–87. Jaipur: Rawat Publications.

—— The concept of secularism. *In* M.S. Gore, ed., *Secularism in India*, pp. 17–28. Allahabad: Vindhya Prakashan for Indian Academy of Social Science.

—— Auspiciousness and purity: Some reconsiderations. *Contributions to Indian sociology (n.s.)* 25, 2: 287–94.

—— Introduction. *In* T.N. Madan, ed., *Religion in India*, pp. 1–22. Delhi: Oxford University Press.

1992 Dying with dignity. *Social science and medicine* 35, 4: 425–32.

—— Fundamentalism. *Seminar* 394: 23–25.

1993 Whither Indian secularism? *Modern Asian studies* 27, 3: 667–97.

1994 D.P. Mukerji 1894–1961: A centenary tribute. *Sociological bulletin* 43, 2: 133–42.

—— Religious pluralism and Maulana Azad. *Religion and politics today*, vol. 1, pp. 121–33. New Delhi: Rajiv Gandhi Institute for Contemporary Studies.

—— On being a Hindu in India: The burden of cultural identity. *Cultural survival quarterly* Summer/Fall: 69–71.

—— Secularism and the intellectuals. *Economic and political weekly* 29, 30: 1095–96.

1995 Religion and social change: Some conceptual issues. *Asia journal* (Seoul) 2, 1: 1–14.

—— From orthodoxy to fundamentalism: A thousand years of Islam in South Asia. *In* Martin E. Marty and R. Scott Appleby, eds., *Fundamentalisms comprehended*, pp. 288–320. Chicago: The University of Chicago Press.

—— The plague in India, 1994. *Social science and medicine* 40, 9: 1167–68.

—— Introduction. *In* T.N. Madan, ed., *Muslim communities of South Asia*, pp. xi–xxii. New Delhi: Manohar.

1996 Westernization: An essay on Indian and Japanese responses. *In* A.M. Shah et al., eds., *Social structure and change,* vol. 1: *Theory and* *method: An evaluation of the work of M.N. Srinivas*, pp. 146–67. New Delhi: Sage.

1996 Anthropology as critical self-awareness. *In* D.L. Sheth and Ashis Nandy, eds., *The multiverse of democracy: Essays in honour of Rajni Kothari*, pp. 242–65. New Delhi: Sage.

1997 Religion, ethnicity, and nationalism in India. *In* Martin E. Marty and R. Scott Appleby, eds., *Religion, ethnicity, and self-identity: Nations in transition*, pp. 53–71. Hanover, NH: University Press of New England.

1998 Discovering anthropology: A personal narrative. *In* Meenakshi Thapan, ed., *Anthropological journeys*, pp. 143–62. New Delhi: Orient Longman.

—— Coping with ethnicity in South Asia: Bangladesh, Punjab and Kashmir compared. *Ethnic and racial studies* 21, 5: 969–89.

—— Religione e politica in India. Cultura politica, revivalismo, fondamentalismo e secolarismo. *In: l'India contemporanea* 1: 49–65. Torino: Edizioni Fondazione Giovanni Agnelli.

—— Mohandas Karamchand Gandhi; Hinduism; India. *In* Robert Wuthnow, ed., *The encyclopedia of politics and religion* 1: 289–90; 319–28; 361–65. Washington, D.C.: Congressional Quarterly, Inc.

1999 Religion and politics in India: Political culture, revivalism, fundamentalism and secularism. *In* V.A. Pai Panandiker and Ashis Nandy, eds., *Contemporary India*, pp. 318–36. New Delhi: Tata McGraw-Hill.

—— Louis Dumont 1911–1998: A memoir. *Contributions to Indian sociology (n.s.)* 33, 3 (in press).

—— Perspectives on cultural pluralism. *Seminar* (in press).

Forthcoming in 2000/2001

Religions of India: Plurality and pluralism. *In* Veena Das, ed., *Encyclopaedia of sociology and social anthropology*. Delhi: Oxford University Press.

The caste system. *Encyclopaedia Britannica*.

The householder tradition. *In* Gavin Flood, ed., *The Blackwell companion to Hinduism*. Oxford: Basil Blackwell.

Religious nationalism and the secular state. *In* Neil J. Smelser and Paul B. Baltes (gen. eds.), *International encyclopaedia of social and behavioural sciences. Modern cultural concerns* (section ed., Richard A. Shweder). Oxford: Elsevier.

About the editors and contributors

Editors

Veena Das is Professor of Sociology at the Delhi School of Economics, and Professor of Anthropology at the New School for Social Research, New York. She is also Editor of *Contributions to Indian sociology.* Among her previous publications are *Critical events: An anthropological perspective on contemporary India* (1995); *Social suffering* (co-edited, 1997); and *Violence and subjectivity* (1999). She was recently elected to the American Academy of Arts and Sciences.

Dipankar Gupta is Professor of Sociology at the Jawaharlal Nehru University, New Delhi, and Editor of *Contributions to Indian sociology*. He is the author of *Nativism in a metropolis: The Shiv Sena in Bombay; The context of ethnicity: Sikh identity in a comparative perspective; Rivalry and brotherhood: Politics in the life of farmers of Northern India*; and *Political sociology in India*. He has also edited *Social stratification* and (with K.L. Sharma) *Country–town nexus*.

Patricia Uberoi is Reader in Social Change and Development at the Institute of Economic Growth, Delhi, and Editor of *Contributions to Indian sociology*. Her research interests include issues of family, gender and popular culture in both India and China. She has previously edited *Family, kinship and marriage in India* (1993) and *Social reform, sexuality and the state* (1996).

Contributors

Frédérique Apffel-Marglin is Professor of Anthropology and Co-ordinator of the Center for Mutual Learning at Smith College. She carried out fieldwork in Orissa from 1975 to 1992, and was a co-director in several projects on Critiques of Technology Transfers at UNU/WIDER (World Institute of Development Economics Research, United Nations University) between 1985 and 1992. Since 1994 she has been Director of the Project of Centers for Mutual Learning (CML), and in 1996 started the CML at Smith with her colleague Kathryn Pyne Addelson. Since 1994 she has also been collaborating with several Andean grass-roots organisations in Peru and Bolivia.

Lawrence A. Babb is Professor of Anthropology and Willem Schupf Professor of Asian Languages and Civilisations at Amherst College. He has completed field research in central and northern India among both Hindu and Jain communities. His most recent book is *Absent Lord: Ascetics and kings in a Jain ritual culture* (1996).

Paul R. Brass is Professor Emeritus of Political Science and South Asian Studies in the Jackson School of International Studies at the University of Washington, Seattle. He has published numerous books and articles on comparative and South

Asian politics, ethnic politics and collective violence. His most recent books are: *Theft of an idol: Text and programs* (1996); and *The politics of India since independence* (2nd edn., 1994). His other books include *Ethnicity and nationalism: Theory and comparison* (1991); *Caste, faction, and party in Indian politics* (2 vols., 1983 and 1985); *Language, religion, and politics in north India* (1974); and *Factional politics in an Indian state: The Congress Party in Uttar Pradesh* (1965), as well as several other edited and co-authored volumes. He is currently working on a book on Hindu–Muslim communalism and collective violence in India.

Lionel Caplan is Emeritus Professor of South Asian Anthropology, School of Oriental and African Studies, London. He is the author of several books on Nepal, the most recent being *Warrior gentlemen: 'Gurkhas' in the western imagination* (1995). Previous research on the Indian Christian community in south India resulted in a number of publications, including *Class and culture in urban India: Fundamentalism in a Christian community* (1987). His current research focuses on colonial and post-colonial issues as they relate to the Anglo-Indian community, on which he has published several papers.

Diana L. Eck is Professor of Comparative Religion and Indian Studies at Harvard University. She has previously published *Banaras: City of light* and *Darśan: Seeing the divine image in India*, and has been working on a long book on *India's sacred geography*. In the meantime, she has launched an American research team called the Pluralism Project to map the changing religious landscape of the US in the light of the new post-1965 immigration. The Project's multimedia CD-ROM, on 'Common ground: World religions in America', brings America's religious communities to life through texts, time-lines, images, music and voices.

Harold A. Gould is Visiting Professor of South Asian Studies at the Center for South Asian Studies of the University of Virginia, Charlottesville. He is also Professor Emeritus (Anthropology), University of Illinois, Champaign-Urbana. He is currently engaged in research on grassroots political behaviour in India and on aspects of US–Indian relations. His books include *The Hindu caste system*, vol. 1: *The secularisation of a social order* (1987); *The hope and the reality: US–Indian relations from Roosevelt to Reagan* (co-edited with Sumit Ganguly, 1992); and *Grass-roots politics in India: A century of political evolution in Faizabad District* (1994).

Ravindra K. Jain is Professor of Social Anthropology/Sociology at the Jawaharlal Nehru University, New Delhi. He was University Lecturer in the Social Anthropology of South Asia and Fellow of Wolfson College, Oxford University (1966–74), and T.H.B. Symons Fellow in Commonwealth Studies (1995–96). His publications include *South Indians on the plantation frontier in Malaya* (1970); *Text and context: The social anthropology of tradition* (edited, 1977); *Indian communities abroad: Themes and literature* (1993); and a number of articles in international journals.

R.S. Khare is Professor of Anthropology at the University of Virginia, Charlottesville, USA. He currently heads the Center on Critical Human Survival Issues at the University, and his recent publications include *Cultural diversity and social discontent (1998); Anthropological studies on contemporary India*; and *Perspectives on Islamic law, justice and society*.

Arthur Kleinman is Maude and Lillian Presley Professor of Medical Anthropology at Harvard University. An anthropologist and psychiatrist who has conducted field research in East Asia and North America for over thirty years, his major publications include *Patients and healers in the context of culture* which won the Wellcome Prize of the Royal Anthropological Institute; *The illness narratives* (1988); *Rethinking psychiatry* (1988); and *Writing at the margin: Discourse between anthropology and medicine*. He is currently conducting research on suicide, depression, and end-of-life care in China.

McKim Marriott has researched Indian culture for five decades through his own residence in small communities of Uttar Pradesh and Maharashtra, and through the work of many students and associates throughout South Asia. His home base is at the University of Chicago in its Social Sciences College, its Department of Anthropology, and its Committee on Southern Asian Studies.

Dennis B. McGilvray is Associate Professor in the Department of Anthropology at the University of Colorado at Boulder. His fieldwork and publications on the Tamils and Muslims of eastern Sri Lanka have focused upon the structure of matrilocal households, matrilineal caste hierarchies and colonial politics, ethnomedical constructions of gender and sexuality, Eurasian (Burgher) ethnicity, non-Sanskritic goddess cults, the spread of popular Sufism, and the recent impact of the Eelam Wars on Tamil–Muslim relations. His recent photographic book is *Symbolic heat: Gender, health, and worship among the Tamils of South India and Sri Lanka* (1998).

Ashis Nandy is a political psychologist, futurist and social theorist. He is Fellow and former Director of the Centre for the Study of Developing Societies, Delhi; Chairperson of the Committee for Cultural Choices; and Fellow in South Asian Alternatives. He is also a member of the International Network for Cultural Alternatives to Development; the Executive Board of the Commonwealth Human Rights Initiative; and the Advisory Board of The Transnational Foundation for Peace and Future Research. His previous publications include *Alternative sciences; At the edge of psychology; The intimate enemy; Traditions, tyranny and utopias; The Tao of cricket; The illegitimacy of nationalism*; and *The savage Freud and other essays on possible and retrievable selves*. He has also published *The blinded eye* (co-authored) and *Creating a nationality* (co-authored), and *The multiverse of democracy* (co-edited) and *The secret politics of our desires* (co-edited).

Patrick Olivelle is Chairperson, Department of Asian Studies, and Director, Center for Asian Studies, at the University of Texas at Austin, where he is

Professor of Sanskrit and Indian Religions. Among his recent publications are *The Saṃnyasa Upanisads: Hindu scriptures on asceticism and renunciation* (1992); *The Āśrama system: History and hermeneutics of a religious institution* (1993); *Rules and regulations of Brahmanical asceticism* (1994); *Upaniṣads* (1996); *Pañcatantra: The book of India's folk wisdom* (1997); *The early Upaniṣads: Annotated text and translation* (1998); and *Dharmasūtras: The law codes of Āpastamba, Gautama, Baudhāyana, and Vasiṣtha* (1999).

Lloyd I. Rudolph has AB, MPA and Ph.D. degrees from Harvard University and is Professor of Political Science and Member of the Committee on Southern Asian Studies, University of Chicago. Formerly Chairperson of the Committee on International Relations, he has spent ten research years in India and is author or co-author of *In pursuit of Lakshmi: The political economy of the Indian state; The modernity of tradition: Political development in India; Education and politics in India: Cultural policy in India; The regional imperative; Essays on Rajputana: The idea of Rajasthan*; and *Gandhi*, as well as *Reversing the gaze: Amar Singh's diary as narrative of imperial India* (forthcoming).

Don Seeman is Lecturer in the Department of Sociology and Social Anthropology at the Hebrew University of Jerusalem. He completed his doctorate in Anthropology at Harvard in 1997, and was a post-doctoral fellow in the Department of Social Medicine at Harvard Medical School. His research interests include the social and cultural context of infectious disease among transnational migrants, and the relationship between illness experience, religious healing and national identity in Israel.

Stanley J. Tambiah is Esther and Sidney Rabb Professor of Anthropology at Harvard University. He began his fieldwork in the 1950s in Sri Lanka, the island of his birth. Since 1960 he has concentrated on Thailand, about which country he has written three monographs dealing with the relations between religion (Buddhism), society and politics. Since 1983 he has revived his interest in Sri Lanka, and more generally in South Asia, and has focused on ethnonationalist conflict and violence. His many publications include *World conqueror and world renouncer* (1976); *Magic, science, religion and the scope of rationality* (1990); and *Leveling crowds: Ethnonationalist conflict and collective violence* (1996). He has served as President of the Association of Asian Studies and as a member of the US National Academy of Science. He was awarded the Huxley Memorial Medal by the Royal Anthropological Institute (1977), and the Balzan Prize (1997).

Index

Abdul Majeed, O., 308n1, 349
Abeyasinghe, T.B.H., 310, 311n, 349
Aboosally, M.L.M., 317, 349
Addelson, Kathryn Pyne, 77n4, 92
Africa, 196, 199, 202; South, 198, 201, 203–5, 212, 213
Agra, 220, 223, 226, 230, 233, 237, 256, 257, 421
Agrasen, King, 246, 247, 257–59, 259n, 260, 262, 263; Jayantī, 247, 262, 263
Agravāl (caste), 245–47, 255–63; origin of, 245, 247, 255, 258, 260–63
Agravāl, Cunnīlāl, 259n, 260n, 264
Agrawal, Anuja, 180n28, 192
Agroha, 245–47, 246n2, 255–63
Ahir(s), 128, 268, 271, 273, 274, 276–78
Ahmad Lebbai, Seyyid Muhammad Ibn, 342–44, 343n38, 344n, 349
Ahmed, Akbar S., 411n15, 418
Aiyengar, T.V. Rangaswamy, 26, 27, 45
Akbar, Emperor, 222, 223, 223n5, 230, 234, 235, 237, 239, 258, 382
Ali, A.C.L. Ameer, 308n2, 309, 310, 315n11, 317–21, 323–25, 327, 327n31, 328, 330, 331, 347, 349
Alter, Joseph S., 143, 158, 180n28, 192
Ambedkar, B.R., 126n17, 132–34, 132n, 133n27, 134n, 135, 272
amir(s), 220, 227, 228, 229n, 231, 234. *See also mansabdar*(s)
ancestor(s), 119, 145, 252, 255, 260, 261, 261n, 308n1, 386
Anderson, Benedict, 24n, 27, 45, 199
Anglo-Indian(s), 283–305
Aniff, Fareed, 333, 349
anthropology, 9, 18, 427–32, 434n36, 435, 437, 437n, 438, 439, 439n; medical 97–99, 104, 105
Apffel-Marglin, Frédérique, 15, 16, 72, 75–93, 152, 160, 407, 407n, 416, 418
Appadurai, Arjun, 165, 165n2, 166n5, 168, 170n15, 183, 192, 196, 207, 208, 215, 284, 303
Arab(s), 307–57; traders 310, 313, 324
Arasaratnam, Sinnappah, 310, 349
Arnold, D., 286, 287, 303
Asad, M.N.M., 323, 325, 325n27, 350
Asad, Talal, 209, 216
Asia, 98, 219, 224, 230; South, 11, 137, 147, 148n, 242, 243, 309, 367n9, 378, 401, 404, 405, 407n, 408, 411, 412, 417; Southeast, 196, 197, 199, 242, 243, 309, 310, 317
Assayag, Jackie, 154, 155, 158
Aurangzeb, 43, 220, 222, 222n4, 223nn5, 6, 224, 236n, 382, 382n
Austin, Granville, 362, 378
Australia, 198, 199, 204, 207, 208, 288n8, 293
auspiciousness (*śubha*), 50n3, 72
avatarana/avatara(s), 23, 31, 36, 154, 155, 257
Ayodhya, 13, 24, 29, 43, 365, 374, 381, 383, 386–88, 390, 391, 394, 395, 397, 398n, 406; Babri Mosque at, 363, 363n, 370, 371
Azeez, I.L.M. Abdul, 324, 324n24, 325, 325n26, 326, 350

Babb, Lawrence A., 16, 245–65
Babar/Babur (Mughal emperor), 222, 383, 397
Babri Masjid, 13, 281, 381–400, 406; destruction of, 394, 396, 397, 406
Backward Caste(s), 268, 281, 367, 373, 374, 376, 377, 392, 393, 395
Badrinath, Chaturvedi, 416n, 418
Bahadur Shah (Mughal emperor), 223n5, 382n
Bahujan Samaj Party (BSP), 268, 272–76, 281, 371, 392, 392n9
Bailey, F.G., 267, 282, 361n, 370, 378
Banaras/Banares, 23, 24, 27, 29, 34, 238, 256. *See also* Kashi
Bannerji, Sumanta, 408n10, 418
Banuri, Tariq, 409, 410, 412, 413, 418
Bardhan, Kalpana, 121, 135, 150, 158
Barth, Fredrik, 196, 200, 201, 216
Baxi, Upendra, 113, 115n, 132, 133, 135, 300, 305

Bayly, C.A., 382, 399, 408n9, 418
Bayly, S., 284, 303, 310, 315–17, 319n18, 344, 350
Bayrou, Francois, 77, 78, 82; 89, 92
Beck, Brenda E.F., 155, 158
belief, 16, 81, 85, 267, 337, 360n2, 365–69, 367n10, 402, 402n, 404n4, 408, 413, 432, 435. *See also* religion
Bell, Rev. A., 288, 303
Belmont, Nicole, 76, 92
Bengal, 45, 220, 223, 224, 228, 233, 239, 382
Bennett, Lynn, 146, 150, 158
Benveniste, Emile, 84, 92
Bernier, Francois, 17, 18, 219–44
Berreman, G.D., 48, 48n, 73
Berry, M.E., 292, 303
Béteille, André, 365, 366, 378, 434n36, 446
Bevan, Major H., 286n3, 303
Bhabha, Homi, 211, 216
Bhagvad Gita, 124, 126n16
Bharat, Shalini, 165n2, 192
Bharatiya Jana Sangh Party, 386, 388, 390, 391, 393
Bharatiya Janata Party (BJP), 268–70, 272–74, 276–78, 280, 362, 363, 365, 367, 373, 374, 376, 377, 381, 391–93, 395, 396, 399, 404, 404n5, 414
Bharucha, R., 172, 193
Bhasin, Prem, 362, 378
Bhatia, B.M., 130, 135
Bhattacharjee, Anannya, 165n2, 167, 193
Bhave, Vinoba, 126n
Biardeau, M., 89
Bihar, 19n, 34, 42, 200, 223, 233, 267, 268, 271, 276–79, 282, 374
Bilgrami, Akeel, 410n, 418
biomedicine/biomedical practice, 16, 102, 104, 105, 107, 108
Blake, Stephen P., 235, 238n, 243
Bodenheimer, Edgar, 125n, 135
Bollywood (Bombay commercial cinema), 125, 169, 170, 173n22, 185n33. *See also* cinema, Indian popular
Bombay, 27, 268–70, 293n17, 325, 405, 422n3
Bondurant, Joan V., 132, 135
Bonner, Rahul, 145, 154, 158
Bose, Pradip Kumar, 280, 282
Bose, Sugata, 313, 350
Bottomley, G., 196, 217
Bouchon, Genevieve, 310, 350
Bouglé, C., 280, 282
Boyle, Robert, 76–80, 76n2, 77n3
Brah, Avtar, 215, 216
Brahma Purana, 29n, 36
Brahman/Brahmin(s), 31n, 43, 48, 49, 55, 64, 65n28, 67, 68n33, 71, 71n, 82, 88, 89, 112n, 122, 123, 128, 248–55, 256, 260, 261, 269, 271–74, 277, 280, 435; Gaur, 258; Khaṇḍelvāl, 249, 249n7
Brandis, Dietrich, 75, 80, 81, 86
Brass, Paul R., 19, 19n, 20, 284, 296, 304, 359–79, 394, 399
Breckenridge, Carol A., 208, 209, 216, 284, 303
Brennan, Nancy L., 301, 304
Buddhism/Buddhist(s), 25, 45, 98, 103, 132, 133n27, 308, 310, 317, 323, 330n, 333, 341, 364, 367n9, 409, 412, 416
bureaucracy, 113n, 231, 233, 238n, 302, 404

Cakreśvarī Devī (the goddess), 254, 255, 261
Canada, 202, 204
capitalism, 203, 206, 209, 231
Caplan, Lionel, 14, 15, 283–305
Caplan, P., 297, 304
Carman, John, 72, 73, 88, 92
Carstairs, G. Morris, 150, 158
caste(s), 16, 17, 47–49, 82, 88, 89, 91, 111, 113, 114, 115, 115n, 116, 118n8, 126–31, 132n, 142n10, 148, 148n, 200, 201, 204, 231, 233, 241, 245–50, 248n, 250, 253, 255, 259–62, 262n, 263n, 281, 314, 319, 315n11, 332, 333, 375, 392, 414, 434n36, 438; Ahir, 128, 268, 271, 273, 274, 276–78; and politics, 16, 267–82; and purity, 47–73; backward, 268, 367, 373, 374, 376, 377, 392, 393, 395; dominant, 116, 232, 271, 314; Gujar, 272, 279–82; hierarchy, 16, 89, 91, 119, 132, 134n, 267n, 332, 333, 346, 435; high/higher, 132, 204, 271, 284, 332, 341, 342, 346, 369, 376, 376n21, 377, 377n, 391, 393, 395; identity, 16, 267, 268, 280, 281, 369; Jat, 271, 272, 279–82; Kurmi, 128, 271, 273, 274, 279, 281; lower, 314, 323, 323n23, 346, 367n11, 373, 374, 376, 393; Rājpūt, 255, 259; system, 47–50, 72, 132, 268, 280, 281, 376n22; trading, 245, 246, 248, 249, 252, 255, 260; Untouchable, 118n, 122, 123, 128, 272 (*See also* Backward Caste[s]); Yadavas, 112n, 128, 268, 276–79, 281, 282

Casie Chitty, Simon, 316, 318, 320, 350
Chakrabarti, Arindam, 412n17, 418
Chakravarty, Sumita S., 164, 166, 167n7, 170n15, 173n22, 184n, 188n, 193
Chandola, Anoop, 155, 158
Chandra, Sudhir, 256n22, 264
change, social/cultural, 12, 97, 100, 101, 130, 130n23, 133, 134, 148, 196, 204, 250, 254, 331, 381, 392, 397, 398
charity, 15, 127, 128, 128n19, 129, 134; Anglo-Indian, 15, 283–305; Churches as source of, 286, 291, 292. *See also* gift
Chatterjee, Partha, 156, 158, 195, 196, 216
Chatterjee, Saibal, 172, 193
Chatterji, Rakhahari, 362, 378
China, 98, 100, 101, 197, 202, 208, 225, 233, 423, 423n7, 426n16, 441
Chopra, Aditya, 163, 167, 169, 169nn12, 13, 14, 170, 172, 173n22, 178, 180, 185, 185n32
Chopra, Yash, 169, 169n12, 173n22, 184n
Chousalkar, Ashok S., 121, 135
Christian(s)/Christianity, 25, 45, 76, 78, 127, 128, 214, 295, 296, 307, 313, 313n9, 323, 345, 360, 365, 370, 373n, 374, 409n12
cinema, Indian popular, 163, 164, 168,170n15
civilisation, 13, 97, 137, 155,195, 201, 202–6, 215, 368, 431, 432
Clarke, C., 198, 216
Clarke, T.G., 288n8, 304
class, 128, 173n22, 212, 284, 314, 333, 384, 385, 391–93; backward 297; lower middle, 375, 416, 416n; middle, 208, 299, 300, 309n4, 318, 330, 367, 393, 406, 409, 413, 415; upper, 317, 377, 416
Clifford, James, 210, 216, 438, 444–46
Cohen, Stephen P., 424n11, 446
Cohn, Bernard, 202, 204, 216, 238, 239, 243
colonialism, 81, 197, 205, 207, 212, 214, 368
communalism, 13, 19, 359, 362, 370, 381, 391–93, 401
Communism/Communist Party, 90, 278, 314, 373, 374, 377
conflict(s), 12, 18, 19, 77, 111, 113, 115, 129, 131, 132, 150, 212, 256, 309, 309n5, 341, 345, 407, 409, 437; political, 19, 129, 362, 368, 369; religious, 112n, 129, 134, 367, 370, 389, 403, 408
Congress Party, 268–70, 272, 276–78, 280, 314, 316, 363, 368, 370, 371, 372n18, 373, 374, 376, 377, 381, 386, 389–96, 398; Congress Socialist Party, 389, 394
cosmos/cosmology, 13, 25, 25n, 28, 29, 33, 34, 36, 84, 118, 127, 238, 248
Courtright, P.B., 146, 151, 158
Crewe, Quentin, 424n11, 446
Crooke, W., 262n, 264
culture, 11, 12, 14, 17–20, 50, 121, 137, 196, 198, 200, 201, 205, 211, 212, 214, 243, 318, 341, 347n, 368, 392, 402, 403, 412, 414, 427n17, 429–33, 446; global, 409, 410n, 416; political, 19, 20, 214, 263, 296, 389; Tamil, 284, 316, 345
custom(s), 11, 83, 113, 116, 116n, 117n6, 120, 223n6, 241, 362, 383, 414, 426, 439n

Dale, Stephen Frederic, 310, 314, 350
Dalit(s), 128, 132, 133, 134, 392, 392n9. *See also* caste
Daniel, E. Valentine, 138, 158
Daniel, Sheryl B., 146, 157, 158
Darak, Śivkaraṇ Rāmratan, 250, 251, 251nn12, 13, 264
Das, Arvind, 183, 186, 193
Das, Veena, 9–21, 48n, 73, 97, 104, 109, 144, 145, 148, 151, 157, 158, 180n27, 190n39, 193
Datta, Pradip K., 398, 399
David, Kenneth A., 144, 145, 157, 158
Davies, Merryl Wyn, 403, 419
Davis, Marvin G., 144, 150, 158
debt(s)/*rna*, 14, 61, 111, 117–20, 133
deity, 38n9, 81, 85, 86, 151–54, 247, 251, 256
de Jong, Fred, 326, 350
Delhi, 220, 226, 230, 245, 246, 257, 289n11, 382, 391
democracy, 112n, 113, 123, 135, 196, 231, 243, 359, 362, 365–67, 366n7, 412, 415
Denham, E.B., 308, 318, 345n41, 350
Derne, Steve, 157, 158
Desai, A.R., 113, 135
Deshpande, Madhav, 70, 73
de Silva, C.R., 310, 350
de Silva, Kingsley M., 309, 324, 327, 328, 351
despotism, 219, 222, 223, 225, 226, 234, 242
Dewaraja, Lorna, 310, 319, 328, 351
De Wit, J.W., 297n20, 304
Dhalla, Paul E.H., 213, 216

dharma (morality), 10, 47–73, 111, 114–17, 118n7, 119–22, 123, 125n14, 126, 127–31, 134, 241, 414
Dharmasastra(s), 10, 49, 70, 71, 111, 138
Dhruvarajan, Vanaja, 145, 151, 157, 158
diaspora, Indian, 10–14, 45, 165nn2, 3, 195–218; cinematic representation of, 163–65, 187–89
Dickey, Sara, 164, 172, 193, 284, 296, 304
Dilks, David, 424, 446
Dirks, Nicholas, 48, 73, 89, 92, 284, 304
Doniger, Wendy, 26, 45, 138n, 145, 154, 158
Doraiswamy, Rashmi, 172, 193
doṣa (humours), 138, 155
Douglas, Mary, 10, 20, 66, 68, 69, 71–73
Draupadi, 86, 87, 90
Drummond, Lee, 211, 212, 216
D'Souza, A.A., 286, 304
D'Souza, Victor S., 314, 315n11, 317, 318, 350
Dumont, Louis, 47–49, 48n, 49n, 56n, 58n18, 68, 68n34, 71, 73, 89, 180, 193, 202, 216, 435n, 438n40
Durkheim, Emile, 203, 216
duty (*kartavya*), 111, 117–20, 121, 124, 127, 296, 332

East India Company, 382, 385
Eck, Diana L., 12, 13, 23–46, 256n25, 264
Egnor, Margaret Trawick, 145, 155, 157, 158
Ellinwood, Dewitt C., 424n11, 446
Ellis, Christine M. Cottam, 246, 264
Embree, Ainslee T., 372n18, 378
Engineer, Asghar Ali, 371n17, 378
Erndl, Kathleen M., 154, 158
Esteva, Gustavo, 401, 418
Ethiopia, 106–8, 225
Europe, 34, 75–77, 79, 91, 199, 202, 209, 223n6, 224, 302, 413, 417, 427n19, 443, 444
everyday life, 9, 10, 17, 19, 20, 405, 416n, 437n

Fairservis, Walter A., 341, 351
faith, 142n10, 219, 359, 360, 361n, 364–67, 367n9, 368, 370, 371, 373n, 378, 401, 402, 402n, 403, 405, 405n, 406, 407, 409n12, 411, 411n14, 412, 414–17; Muslim, 310, 313, 326
family, 10, 11, 70, 72, 79, 98, 99, 101, 106–8, 113, 117, 118n8, 122, 122nn10, 12, 123, 125, 130, 132, 137–61, 162–194, 227, 237, 237n, 238n, 249, 262, 272, 283, 288, 290, 291, 293, 314, 326, 340, 405, 424, 426, 428, 436, 438; joint/extended, 137, 150, 156, 190, 238n, 423; Moorish, 318, 333; roles, 143–47, 155, 182; values, 163, 166–69, 169n11, 183, 189, 190
famine (drought), 115–17, 121, 122n10, 124, 129, 130n23; Bengal 12, 131; relief 124, 130, 130n23
Fanselow, Frank S., 315, 316, 319, 319n18, 351
Farwell, Bryon 424n11, 447
feminism, 165n2, 167
femininity, Indian, 137–57, 160
Ferguson, James, 207, 216
festival(s), 75, 76, 82–88, 90, 116, 228, 250, 257, 314, 324; Karva Chauth, 173n20, 183
Fiji, 197–99, 204, 212
Fisher, Michael, 384, 399
Fisher, Michael M.J., 440n, 447
Fitch, Ralph, 221, 222n3
Fogelman, Eva, 405, 418
food, 14, 111–36, 144, 145, 291, 298, 299, 302
Foster, Sir William, 220, 221n, 222n3, 243
Foucault, M., 288, 304
France, 77, 78, 98, 219, 222–25, 227, 292, 230
Frankel, Francine R., 267, 267n, 282
Freeman, Derek, 436
Freud, Sigmund, 413, 429n24, 432n32
Friend-in-Need Society (FINS), 286–90, 286n5, 289n10, 296, 300, 302
fundamentalism, 10, 19, 75, 412. *See also* religion; secularism
Fürer-Haimendorf, C. von, 48, 48n, 73
Furnivall, J.S., 13, 14, 20, 202, 216

Gabriel, Theodore P.C., 314, 314n, 318, 327n33, 351
Gadgil, Madhav, 75, 92
Gandhi, Indira, 363, 367n11, 369, 370, 374
Gandhi, Mahatma, 115, 119, 126, 128, 128n20, 132, 361n, 367n10, 368, 369, 393, 397, 402
Ganga, 27, 31, 32, 36, 37, 39, 45, 257
Geertz, Clifford, 102, 104, 109, 210, 216, 430n26, 440, 440n, 447
Gellner, Ernest, 370, 378
Ghai, Subhash, 163, 168n9

Ghoshal, U.N., 124, 135
Ghosh, Amitav, 197
Ghurye, G.S., 434nn36, 37
gift(s), 148, 229, 240, 256, 283–305; exchange 14, 15, 82, 83, 428
Gilroy, Paul, 211, 216
globalisation, 12, 13, 162–94, 195–217, 376. *See also* diaspora
Gluckman, Max, 88, 89, 92
Gold, Ann Grodzins, 40, 46, 140n, 145, 146, 148, 148n, 151, 152n, 155, 157, 159, 161
Goldhagen, Daniel J., 100, 109
Golwalkar, M.S., 417n, 418
Gonda, Jan, 38, 38nn9,10, 46, 62, 62n, 73
Good, Anthony, 148, 150, 159
Good, Byron J., 102, 104, 109
Gopal, S., 398n, 399
gotra(s) (exogamous patriclan), 248n, 249, 254, 254n19, 257, 258, 261–63, 262n; Agravāl 247, 261, 262n
Gould, Harold A., 13, 381–400
Gourishankar, V., 284, 295, 305
Govers, Cora, 199, 218
Graham, Bruce, 391n, 400
Greenough, Paul R., 121, 122n10, 124, 130, 130n23, 131, 135
Gregorios, Paulos Mar, 403, 418
Guha, Ramachandra, 75, 92
Guha, Ranajit, 91n14
Gujar(s), 272, 279–82
Gujarat, 29–32, 201, 222n3, 223, 234, 239, 240, 241
Gulati, Leela, 165n2, 193
Gunawardena, R.A.L.H., 324n25, 351
Gupta, Akhil, 207, 215, 216
Gupta, Badlu Ram, 262, 264
Gupta, Campālāl, 258, 262, 263n, 264
Gupta, Dipankar, 16, 172, 193, 267–82
Guyana, 187, 198, 211, 212, 215

Habib, Irfan, 232, 233, 234, 236, 243
Hancock, Mary, 154, 159
Harlan, Lindsey, 146, 151, 152, 155, 157, 159, 261, 264
Harrison, B., 287, 300, 304
Harriss, B., 297n21, 304
Hartz, Louis, 204, 207, 216
Hasan, Mushirul, 314, 315, 351
Hasan, Tariq, 405, 418
Hasbullah, S.H., 331, 347n, 351
Hassan, M.C.A., 327, 328, 351
Hawes, C.J., 285, 288, 289, 304
Haynes, D.E., 287, 292, 304
healing, 16, 96, 98, 102, 406, 407
Heesterman, J.C., 48n, 89, 92, 131n, 135
Hellman-Rajanayagam, Dagmar, 324n25, 351
Hennayake, Shantha K., 330, 347, 347n, 351
Hershman, Paul, 150, 159
Herzfeld, Michael, 437, 437n, 447
Hick, John, 102, 109
hierarchy, 47–49, 51, 68n34, 88–90, 91, 146, 219, 302, 318, 365; caste 16, 47–49, 49n, 51, 89, 91, 333
Hiltebeitel, Alf, 42, 46
Himalaya, 26–28, 30, 31, 35, 36, 39, 41–43
Hindu(s), 10, 11–14, 17, 23, 24n, 25, 26, 29, 30, 34, 35, 37, 45, 50n5, 83, 84, 90, 91, 111–36, 138, 138n5, 154, 199, 204, 209, 221–23, 231, 236n, 239, 248, 250, 252, 267, 280, 281, 313, 318, 323, 331–34, 337, 339, 343, 344, 363, 364, 366–68, 367n9, 372–74, 381–87, 389, 393, 395, 397–99, 398n, 404n5, 406, 407, 407n, 412, 415–17, 423n6, 438; cosmology, 23–46; dominant high/upper caste/elite, 314, 323, 324, 375, 376, 393; fundamentalist, 215, 359, 386, 393, 397; kings/kingdoms, 91n13, 313, 314, 316, 317, 319, 361, 386; militant, 365, 367, 373, 376, 390, 398; nationalism/nationalist, 19, 27, 34, 364, 369, 373, 393, 401–19, 415–18, 423n6; sacred geography, 12, 23–46; Tamil, 199, 307, 317, 319, 332, 337, 339, 344; temples, 29, 30, 32, 316, 332, 346, 362, 363, 363n
Hinduism, 25, 26, 27, 47–74, 111, 115, 117, 126n17, 127, 128n20, 337, 361n, 365, 367n9, 377, 381, 383, 387, 394, 396, 401, 409n12, 415; caste system (*See caste*)
Hindutva, 20, 134, 415–18, 416n. *See also* Hindu: fundamentalist
Hinnells, J., 284, 287, 301n, 304
Hitchcock, John T., 144, 160
Hobbes, Thomas, 77n3, 79
Hobsbawm, Eric, 104, 109, 398n, 400
household, 9, 11, 137–62. *See also* family
householder, 39, 56, 66n31, 95, 131n
human rights, 14, 114, 115, 126, 132, 133, 134, 214, 243; movement, 114, 115, 123, 134, 195

hunger, 14, 112–17, 116n, 120, 123, 126, 127, 128n19, 129, 130n23, 132, 134
hybridity and creolisation, 210–13

Ibrahim Kunju, A.P., 314, 317, 352
identity, 13, 14, 17, 195, 196, 199, 208, 246, 247, 250, 260, 303, 308n3, 426, 428, 429n24; Agravāl, 16, 245–65; caste, 245–65, 267–82; diasporic, 163–94, 195–218; Indian, 166, 167, 167nn7, 8, 168, 169, 174, 178, 186, 189, 417; Moorish, 307–57; Muslim/Islamic, 307, 324, 326; religious, 172, 173, 393, 398, 401, 403, 409n12
illness, 95, 97, 101, 103, 104, 107
impure/impurity, 10, 47, 49, 50, 58, 59, 62, 67, 69–72, 88, 89, 141, 142, 142n10
Inden, Ronald B., 144, 145, 157, 159
India, 11, 13–16, 18–20, 19n, 23–41, 43–45, 48, 50, 50nn3, 5, 71, 76, 76n1, 91, 112–14, 112n, 117, 124, 126–33, 126n18, 129n, 134, 135, 195–99, 202, 204, 208, 211, 219–22, 220n1, 221n, 226, 231, 236n, 241–43, 246, 248, 248n, 255, 256, 258, 267n, 268, 281, 283–87, 295, 296, 310, 313, 314, 342, 346, 359, 361–78, 381, 382, 392, 405, 406, 408–10, 412, 412n16, 413, 415, 417, 423, 424nn8, 9, 10, 11, 425n13, 426n16, 428n21, 429, 433, 434n36, 435, 438; and the West, 189, 191, 192; British, 75, 421, 422n3, 425, 438, 440, 443; modern, 45, 75, 111, 112n, 132, 134, 404, 406, 409, 414–16, 421; South, 155, 296, 318, 319; unity of, 362, 363, 369, 370
individualism, 97, 98, 114
injustice, 17, 116, 120, 125, 127, 132, 224, 413
Islam, 25, 45, 214, 308, 309, 310, 313, 314, 316, 328, 332, 340, 341, 342, 344, 364, 365, 371–73, 381, 383, 384, 398n, 411, 411n14, 412
Islamisation, 310, 316
Ismail, Qadri, 313n8, 324, 326, 328, 347, 352
Israel, 106, 373, 373n, 374
Iyer, Krishna V.R., 132, 135
Iyer, Raghavan, 402, 418

Jacobson, Doranne, 144–46, 157, 159
Jaffrelot, Christophe, 363, 378
jagir, 229, 234, 234n, 236, 237, 238, 239, 240, 241
Jahangir (Mughal emperor), 220, 223, 223n5, 237
Jain(s)/Jainis, 25, 29, 32, 251–55
Jain, Kailash Chand, 249n6, 264
Jain, Ravindra K., 13, 14, 165n3, 193, 195–217
Jaipur, 247, 249, 251n11, 253, 262, 421–24, 422nn2, 3, 423nn4, 5, 444
jajmani system, 86, 120, 127, 128
Jameson, Frederick, 203, 206, 216
Janata Dal (JD), 268, 273, 274, 276–79, 392, 393
Jat(s), 271, 272, 279–82
Jatava, D.R., 132n, 133n26, 135
Jayawardena, C., 199, 211, 212, 217
Jefferson, Thomas, 360, 360nn1, 2, 361, 361n, 363, 367, 367n10, 378
Jews/Judaism, 23, 100, 364, 366, 371n16, 372n19, 373, 373n, 374
Jones, G.W., 198, 217
Jupp, James, 213, 217
jyotirlinga (the linga of Shiva), 24, 28, 35, 40, 41, 43

Kakar, Sudhir, 137, 150, 154, 156, 159, 164, 193
Kale, Madhavi, 213, 217
karma, 18, 111, 115, 117–20, 118n7, 119, 120, 122, 125, 126n16, 127, 128, 132n, 133n27
Kandiah, V.C., 332n, 348, 352
Kane, P.V., 51n, 73, 111, 122n10, 135
Kāshī, 28, 41, 43. *See also* Banaras
Kāshī Vishvanāth temple, 28, 29, 41, 45
Keer, Dhananjay, 133, 135, 416n, 418
Kemper, Steven E.G., 146, 159
Kerala, 17, 19n, 31, 44, 307, 309, 310, 313, 314, 317, 326n28, 328, 332, 333, 348, 374
KHAM (Kshatriya, Harijan, Adivasis, Muslim), 280, 281
Khaṇḍelvāl, M.C., 249, 265
Khaṇḍelvāl, Bramhins, 249, 249n7; Jain, 248, 253–55, 255n, 260, 261; Vaiśya, 248–50, 252, 255, 255n, 260; origin mythology, 248, 249, 255
Khare, R.S., 14, 15, 48n, 50n5, 73, 111–36, 145, 159, 300, 304
kinship, 12, 14, 81, 131, 137–62, 200, 283, 293, 307, 317, 318,

318nn14, 15, 428, 436. *See also* family; marriage
Kipling, Rudyard, 430, 431n27
Klass, Morton, 200, 217
Kleinman, Arthur, 16, 95–110, 299, 304
Knipe, David M., 152n, 159
Kolenda, Pauline M., 145, 150, 159
Kondos, Vivienne, 138n3, 148, 159
Kosseleck, Rhinehart, 19n
Kothari, Rajni, 115, 135
Kothari, Smitu, 113, 115n, 132, 136
Krishna, Daya, 116, 136
Krishna, Lord, 29, 31, 39, 41, 43, 154, 155
Krishna, Sankaran, 348, 352
Ksatriya(s), 67, 128, 239, 248, 251, 255, 259, 260. *See also* caste
Kulke, Herman, 91n13, 92
Kuper, A., 439n43, 447
Kurmi (caste segment), 128, 271, 273, 274, 279, 281
Kurtz, Stanley N., 150, 154, 159
Kurukulasuriya, G.I.O.M., 320, 342, 352
Kutty, A.R., 314n, 352

Lamb, Sarah Elizabeth, 145, 146, 150–52, 157, 159
Lannoy, R., 204, 217
Larson, Gerald James, 138, 140, 160
Lath, Mukund, 253n16, 265
Latour, Bruno, 15, 20
Lawrence, Patricia, 348, 352
Lawrence, Sir H.M., 288n9, 304
Leach, Edmund, 48n, 49, 73, 425n14
Lechte, John, 196, 217
Leeuwen, Marco H.D., 295, 298, 300, 304
Lele, Jayant, 269, 271, 282
Leslie, I. Julia, 152, 160
Lewis, I.M., 102, 109
Lienhardt, Godfrey, 102, 109
Littlewood, Ronald, 102, 109
Lévi-Strauss, Claude, 429n24, 431, 431nn28, 29, 432, 432nn31, 32, 435n, 438n40, 441, 447
Lifton, Robert, 425n13, 447
Lijphardt, Arend, 242, 243
lineage, 145, 257, 258, 259, 260, 314, 422
linga(s), 28, 31, 35, 37, 39, 41, 42, 43
Lingat, Robert, 117, 136
Lipner, Julius J., 411n14, 418
Lord Curzon, 424, 424n9
Love, H.D., 286, 304
LTTE, 309, 331, 340, 347, 347n, 348
Lucknow, 112n, 116n, 118n8, 122, 127, 128n19, 132n, 133n26, 385, 390, 435
Luhrmann, T.M., 301n, 304
Lynch, Owen M., 143n11, 160

MacIntyre, Alisdair, 206, 211, 217
Macleod, Norman, 23, 46
Macrae, J., 287n7, 305
Macready, W.C., 324, 352
MacPherson, Kenneth, 315, 316, 352
Madan, T.N., 18–21, 47–49, 48n, 50n3, 70, 72–74, 76, 77, 77n5, 88, 89, 90, 92, 95, 96, 109, 110, 137, 146, 160, 164, 193, 242, 246, 265, 283, 305, 363n, 365–68, 366n, 370–73, 378, 397, 400, 428, 430, 433n35, 434–39, 434nn36, 37, 435n, 438n42, 447
Mahabharata, 29, 33, 35, 39, 40, 86, 86n, 90, 119–21
Maharashtra, 24, 28, 36, 41, 267–72, 276, 377
Māheśvarī(s), 248, 250–53, 255, 260, 261
Mahroof, M.M.M., 308n1, 316, 318, 322n, 326n29, 327n32, 333, 352, 353
Malinowski, Bronislaw, 421, 425, 425n14, 426n14, 428, 429n24, 439, 439n
Malamoud, C., 64n27, 74
Malaysia, 198–200
Mani, A., 316, 318n15, 353
Māppiḷas of Kerala, 307, 309, 310, 313, 314, 316, 318, 328, 348
mansabdar(s) (petty amir[s]), 229n, 231, 234–37, 234n, 236n
Manu, 51n, 52, 53, 55–57, 58n18, 59, 65, 66, 138n3
Maratha(s), 269, 270, 271, 280
Marcus, George, 438, 444–46
marriage(s), 146n15, 147, 148, 149, 150–53, 166, 179, 187, 191, 209, 247, 248, 256, 262, 286n4, 293, 313n9, 314, 315, 318, 319n18, 332, 340, 341, 361, 362, 372n19, 377, 422n2, 428; love 164, 164n, 176, 192
Marriott, McKim, 10, 11, 48, 50nn3, 5, 74, 137–61, 204, 217
Mason, Philip, 424n11, 431n27, 446
Mauritius, 197, 198, 204, 212, 215
Mauroof, Mohammed, 316, 317, 319, 319n18, 326n29, 353
Mayaram, Shail, 407n, 416n, 419, 423n6, 447
Mayer, A.C., 296n, 305

Menon, Usha, 145, 148, 156, 157, 160
McGilvray, Dennis B., 17, 307–57
Mehta, Pratap Bhanu, 411n14, 419
Mendelsohn, O., 300, 305
Midgely, J., 287, 288, 298n, 301, 302, 305
migration, Indian, 165, 165n2, 166. *See also* diaspora
Miller, Roland E., 313n, 314, 353
Milner, Murray, 376n9, 378
Mines, Dianne Paull, 58n18, 74, 151, 160
Mines, M., 284, 295, 296, 305
Mines, Mattison, 315–18, 319n18, 353, 354
Minturn, Leigh, 144, 151, 160
Misri, Urvashi, 144, 148, 160
mobilisation, political, 362, 368, 369, 376, 391, 393
modernity, 9, 10, 14, 15, 126, 126n18, 132, 134, 195, 208, 245, 248, 404n4, 416
Mohamed, Khalid, 167, 169, 170, 177, 180n26, 184n, 186, 193
Mohan, R. Vasundhara, 309, 326, 328, 342, 354
Mohanty, J.N., 20, 21
Mohideen, M.I.M., 310, 330, 333, 354
Mookerji, Radhakumud, 34, 38, 46
Moon, Penderel, 382, 400
Moore, Barrington Jr., 225n, 230, 231, 243
Moore, Melinda Ann, 145, 160
Moors (Tamil-speaking Muslims), 307–57
More, J.B.P., 315, 315nn11, 12, 316, 319n18, 332, 354
Moreland, W.H., 225n, 243
Moreno, Manuel, 155, 160
Morris-Jones, W.H., 367n11, 378
Motwani, Jagat K., 198, 217
movement, 118, 126, 131, 134, 155, 195, 196, 199, 204, 205, 215, 226, 238, 243, 316, 322, 327, 331, 341, 362, 363, 368, 369, 371, 372, 391, 403, 414, 415; ethnic, 124, 199, 327, 331, 369; human rights, 114, 115, 123, 134, 195; religious, 91, 208, 215, 253n16, 331
multiculturalism, 167, 195–217
murti(s) (idols), 30, 31, 34, 42, 386–89, 394
Muslim(s), 23, 45, 83, 86, 123, 127–29, 204, 214, 239, 240, 243, 270, 276, 277, 281, 307–57, 362–64, 366–68, 367nn9, 11, 371–76, 373n, 382–86, 393, 394, 398n, 399, 405, 407, 407n, 410, 412, 416, 417, 423n6 (*See also* Islam); elites, 313n8, 315, 320, 323, 326n29, 347, 382; identity, 17, 313–20; Personal Laws, 241, 372, 373, 373n; Shia, 226, 227, 235, 330, 384 (*See also* Islam)
Muslim League, 314, 316, 326
Muthiah A., 198, 217
myth(s)/mythology, 23, 26, 27, 33, 34, 37, 42, 44, 45, 232, 246–56, 258, 367, 369, 431, 431n28, 432n31; Agravāl origin, 245–48, 255, 256, 258

Nadarajah, M., 165, 165n3, 193
Naipaul, V.S., 197, 215, 383
Nandy, Ashis, 19, 20, 164, 193, 366, 366nn6, 8, 367, 367n9, 370, 378, 401–19, 438n41, 447
Narayana Rao, Velcheru, 157, 160
Nayyar, Deepak, 197, 217
Nehru, Jawaharlal, 132, 359–63, 360n2, 361n, 365, 367, 370, 371, 372n18, 374, 376, 394, 397
Nicholas, Ralph W., 145, 157, 159
Nigam, Aditya, 369, 376n21, 378
Niranjana, Tejaswini, 197, 198, 209, 215, 217
Nissan, Elizabeth, 309n5, 323, 354
Noorani, A.G., 387, 400
NRI (Non-Resident Indian), 165, 165n3, 166, 170, 170n15, 176, 183, 185, 189, 197, 198, 215
Nussbaum, Felicity A., 443, 443n51, 444n, 447

Obeyesekere, G., 103, 104, 110, 319n17, 354
O'Flaherty, Wendy Doniger, 150, 160
Oldenburg, Veena Talwar, 151, 160
Olivelle, Patrick, 10, 47–74
Orissa, 28, 36, 75, 76, 82, 83, 85, 88, 91n14, 268
orphanage(s), Christian, 287–89
O'Sullivan, Meghan, 330, 354

Padmanabha Menon, K.P., 318, 354
Pandey, Gyanendra, 250n10, 265, 393, 399, 400
Pandian, Jacob, 315n12, 319n18, 354
Pandit(s), Kashmiri, 10, 70, 434n36, 435–37
Panikkar, Raimundo, 402, 419
Parekh, Bhikhu, 117n5, 136, 366n6
Parry, J., 284, 305
participant observation, 421, 428, 435, 435n, 436, 446
Pathan(s), 226, 227, 229, 315
Peabody, Norbert, 242, 243

Pearson, M.N., 235, 236n, 239nn17, 18, 240, 241, 244, 382, 400
Pearson, Veronica, 101, 110
Peebles, Patrick, 333, 355
Penny, F., 286, 287, 305
Perrot, Michelle, 427n19, 444n, 447
Phadnis, Urmila, 320n, 328, 342, 355
philanthropy, 111–36, 283, 284, 287, 292, 295–97, 299, 302, 303. *See also* charity; gift
Pieris, Ralph, 333, 355
pilgrim(s)/pilgrimage, 12, 23–46, 107, 152n, 154, 245, 246, 247, 256, 256n25, 316, 317
pitha(s), 26, 33, 34, 35, 39n12
pluralism, 11, 12, 13, 195, 205, 239, 243, 364, 366, 372
pollution, 10, 49, 50, 67, 88, 344, 344n, 365. *See also* purity
poverty, 14, 116, 116n, 123, 284, 285, 287, 294–97, 299, 301–3, 375
power, 18, 48, 49, 49n, 53, 69, 71, 80, 89, 99, 126, 143, 212, 219–43, 316, 341, 342, 402, 414, 428, 430n25, 431, 433n35, 438, 440, 443n51, 445; political, 232, 267–82, 314, 359–381, 383–99, 403, 414, 439
Prabhu, Pandharinath H., 191, 193
Prasad, M. Madhava, 164, 166, 169n12, 170, 170n17, 172n18, 173, 183, 190n40, 193
Price, Charles S., 207, 217
Price, P.G., 284, 305
priest, 86, 88n, 143n11, 249, 253, 258, 261
Prochaska, F., 287, 287n6, 288, 290n, 291n15, 300, 301, 305
psychotherapy, 98, 99
Public Distribution of Food, 15, 113, 114, 116, 120, 120n, 128, 129,129n,
Pugh, Judy Fayrene, 138n3, 160
Punjab,19n, 37, 45, 129, 223, 257, 369, 370, 406n
purity, 9, 10, 47–74, 88, 89, 142, 142n10, 143, 145, 146, 150, 262
Purī, 31, 32, 39, 39n12, 40, 82, 88n, 91n13
Puthenkalam, Fr. J., 318n15, 355

Queyroz, Fr. Fernao De, 311, 311n, 355
Quigley, D., 48, 68n34, 74

Raheja, Gloria Goodwin, 88, 89, 93, 140n, 145, 146, 148n, 150, 155, 157, 160, 161, 284, 305
Raja Parba (festival), 83–90, 85n, 88n
Rajadhyaksha, Ashish, 169n12, 193
Rajasthan, 16, 19n, 30, 40, 43, 242, 246, 248, 249, 258, 421, 422n3, 441
Rajput(s), 152, 252, 254, 255, 259, 260, 271–74, 277, 281, 382, 422, 425, 425n13, 426, 428, 441, 442, 443
Rāma (Lord), 25, 26, 27, 39, 39n11, 40, 43, 115, 132, 363, 386, 398n; *janmabhumi* 25, 29, 236, 236n, 381–99, 405, 406
Ram, Kalpana, 332, 355
Ramanathan, Poonambalam, 323, 355
Ramanujan, A.K., 50n5, 74, 89, 93, 140n, 150, 154, 157, 161
Rāmeshvaram, 27, 30, 32, 35, 39, 39n11, 40, 41, 43, 44
Rangacharya, Adya, 146, 161
Rangoonwala, Firoze, 166, 173n22, 185n33, 193
Rao Jr., Parsa Venkateshwar, 416n, 419
Rao, Velcheru Narayan, 315n12, 316, 355
Rashtriya Janata Dal (RJD), 268, 276–79, 282
Rashtriya Swayamsevak Sangh (RSS), 361, 362, 370, 377, 381, 386, 390, 393, 396, 397, 416n
Rayaprol, Aparna, 165n3, 166n5, 193
Reddock, Rhoda, 210, 217
reform/reformer(s), 17, 114, 126, 128, 128n20, 132–35, 247, 362, 383
Rege, M.P., 119, 136
religion, 25, 47–72, 80, 91, 95–110, 111–35, 214, 221, 236, 236n, 237, 242, 245–64, 303, 308, 323, 325n26, 345, 360, 362, 364–67, 368, 372, 373n, 401, 402, 403, 408, 411n14, 412, 412n16, 413, 415 (*See also* Hinduism; Islam); and politics, 76, 77n3, 156, 235, 359–78, 381, 402, 404 (*See also* secularism)
renunciation, 18, 131n, 332, 438
Republican Party of India (RPI), 268–70, 272; victory 269
Reynolds, Holly Baker, 157, 161
Rex, John, 205, 213, 217
Ṛg/Rig Veda, 33, 37, 38n10, 49n, 68
Richards, J.F., 234, 244
right(s), 118, 129, 224, 331, 325, 366n7, 368, 369, 369n, 372, 372nn18, 19, 373, 408, 409, 412, 413; human, 14, 114, 115, 126, 132, 134, 214, 243; to food 111–36

rite(s), 42, 43, 56, 63, 81, 88, 144, 151, 245, 247, 248, 254, 255, 257, 262; of passage, 253, 261, 341, 343; sacrificial 247, 262, 250
ritual, 10, 25, 29, 35, 37n8, 51, 53, 59, 61, 67, 69, 72, 76, 84, 85, 87, 88, 105, 108, 116, 131, 146, 148, 150–52, 235, 243, 257, 262, 263, 332, 334, 337, 414, 428; pollution, 59, 62, 344, 344n, 365. *See also* Hinduism; Islam; religion
Roberts, Michael, 313, 319n17, 326, 326n28, 327, 327n31, 330, 355
romance, 163, 164, 174–80. *See also* marriage
Roe, Sir Thomas, 220, 221, 221n
Rogers, John D., 323, 323n23, 324n25, 355
Rosaldo, Renato, 429n23, 430, 430n25, 448
Rosebury, William, 209, 210, 217
Rudner, D.W., 284, 292, 305
Rudolph, Lloyd I., 18, 368n, 372, 372n18, 378, 392n10, 400, 421–49
Rudolph, Susanne Hoeber, 368n12, 372, 372n18, 378, 422n1, 423n7, 424nn9, 11, 425n12, 441n45, 442, 443n52

sacred, grove, 75–92
sacrifice, 12, 16, 30, 33, 64n27, 65, 82, 88n, 153, 154, 245–65, 260n, 263n, 415
Safran, William, 215, 217
Sāh, Bakhatrām, 253, 253n16, 265
Śaiva/Śaivism, 249n6, 250, 253, 345
Samajwadi Party (SP), 268, 274, 371
Samaraweera, Vijaya, 323, 326, 355
satī, 28, 33, 34 152, 153, 155, 246n2, 251, 362
Savyasaachi, 83, 93
Scheduled Caste(s), 270–77, 281, 282, 297, 367, 367n11, 377, 393, 395. *See also* caste: lower/Untouchable
Scheduled Tribes, 276, 277, 279, 367
Schrijvers, Joke, 342, 348, 355
Scott, James C., 80, 90, 93
Seabrook, J., 295, 305
secularisation, 77, 77n5, 80, 81, 272, 366, 403, 406
secularism, 10, 13, 19, 75–93, 359–79, 396, 399, 401–19
Seeman, Don, 16, 95–110
Sen, Amartya, 117, 117n6, 130, 136, 410n, 419
Sethi, Harsh, 132, 136
Shah, A.M., 137, 161, 165, 193, 239n15, 244
Shah Jahan (the Mughal emperor), 220, 222, 222n4, 223, 223n5
Shapin, Steven, 76, 77, 77n3, 79, 80, 93
Sharif, Ja'far, 317, 356
Shastri, A.K., 39n12, 46
Shastri, Amita, 328, 333, 356
Shiva, Vandana, 91, 93
Shiva/Siva, 27, 30, 32, 33–6, 38, 40, 41, 43, 45, 250, 251, 252, 256
Shiv Sena, 268, 269, 280, 404
Shourie, Arun, 365, 379
Shukri, M.A.M., 309, 317, 322, 326n29, 356
Shulman, D., 284, 305, 355, 356
Siddiqi, Majid H., 281, 282
Sikh(s)/Sikhism, 127–30, 173, 173n22, 215, 365, 367n9, 376, 377, 395, 404, 405, 407, 410, 412
Silburn, Lillian, 84, 93
sin, 35, 50n6, 57, 66–68
Singer, Milton, 48n, 204, 217
Singh, H.D., 268, 282
Singh, Kumar Suresh, 130, 136, 407n, 419
Sinha, Jadunath, 146, 161
Sivaram, D.P., 331, 348, 356
Sivaramakrishnan, K., 75, 80
Sivathamby, Karthigesu, 347, 348, 356
Smith, Brian K., 49n, 74, 138n3, 158, 248, 265
Smith, Donald E., 361n, 366n7, 379
Smith, M.G., 205, 217
Simth, Vincent, 130, 136
social justice, 14, 114, 115, 132–35
Sri Lanka, 17, 104, 198, 199, 252, 253, 256, 307–49
Srinivas, M.N., 267n, 282, 434, 434n36, 37, 435, 435n, 448
Srinivasan, Amrit, 426n15, 431n27, 434n36, 448
Stanley, John M., 154, 161
status, socio/economic, 49n, 88n, 89, 97, 118, 119, 128n20, 131n, 211, 212, 220, 227, 229, 232, 225, 261, 280, 299, 315, 325, 333, 364n, 372n18, 394, 398, 402. *See also* caste
Steed, Gitel Poznanski, 151, 161
Stern, Henri, 239n16, 244
Stern, Robert, 422n3, 448
Stirrat, R.L., 323, 354

suffering, 16, 96, 97, 98, 100–105, 108, 115
Sundaram, Chandra, 423n7, 424n9, 448

Tambiah, Stanley J., 17, 18, 58n18, 74, 219–44, 309n5, 356
Tambs-Lyche, Harald, 200, 201, 218
Tamilnadu, 17, 19n, 24, 25, 28, 30, 39, 42, 43, 291nn13, 14, 314–18, 315nn11, 12, 332, 347
Temple, Richard Carnac, 246, 265
Thomas, Rosie, 164, 166, 167n7, 170n17, 180n27, 185, 187n35, 193, 194
Thompson, E.T., 202, 218
Thurston, Edgar, 313n9, 315, 318, 356
Timberg, Thomas A., 246n1, 265
Tinker, Hugh, 214, 218
tirtha(s), 23, 25, 26, 28–36, 38, 39 256. *See also* pilgrimage
Tiwari, J.N., 34, 46
Tod, James, 241, 242, 244
tolerance, religious, 77, 78, 95, 235, 242, 243, 365, 367, 372, 373n, 376, 378, 407, 408, 413, 414
Toulmin, Stephen, 77–79, 81, 93, 432n30, 448
tradition(s), 11, 12, 13, 25, 29, 39, 112n, 114, 126, 132, 134, 135, 200, 203, 204, 206, 220, 249, 250n10, 256, 313, 316, 318, 398, 403, 412; Hindu, 25, 27, 112, 118n8, 120, 126n18; Indian, 47, 112, 113, 116, 123, 131, 132, 134, 135, 167, 167n7, 168, 170, 180–83, 409; religious, 25, 287, 382, 414; Tamil, 341, 342. *See also* Hinduism; Islam; Jainism; Sikhism
Trawick, Margaret, 146–48, 154, 161
Trevor-Roper, H.R., 404, 417, 419
Trinidad & Tobago, 197, 198, 200, 201, 204, 209, 212, 213, 215
Turner, Victor, 88, 89, 93

Uberoi, Patricia, 10–12, 126n18, 163--94
Uniform Civil Code, 372n18, 373
United States, 80, 81, 98–101, 104, 197, 202, 204, 207, 208, 364, 364n, 366, 366n7, 372, 374, 375, 403
Untouchables/Dalits, 128, 133n27, 134n. *See also* caste: lower
Uttar Pradesh, 19n, 118n8, 128, 129, 200, 267, 268, 271–76, 279–81, 363, 371, 386, 388, 390–92, 394–96
Uwise, M.M., 307, 309, 316, 348, 356

Vaiśya(s), 67, 128, 239, 245–63, 263n
Vanaik, Achin, 366, 366n6, 377, 379
Van der Veer, Peter, 367, 379
Van Gennep, Arnold, 253, 265
Van Sanden, J.C., 317, 356
Varanasi. *See* Banaras, Kāshı
varna(s), 49, 49n, 58n18, 68, 68n33, 72, 128, 248, 260. *See also* caste
Vasudevan, Ravi S., 166, 194
Vatuk, Sylvia, 150, 151, 161, 315, 357
Vatuk, Ved Prakash, 150, 161
Vermeulen, Hans, 199, 218
Vertovec, Steven, 214, 218
violence, 16, 143, 145, 245–65, 340, 374, 383, 397, 404, 411, 411n14; communal, 316, 347, 373, 405, 406, 413, 416n; ethnic, 331, 345, 346, 397, 401, 408, 411
virgin/virginity, 144, 145, 147–52, 176–77, 186
Vishnu (Lord), 30, 31, 33, 39, 40, 42, 43, 45
Vishwa Hindu Parishad (VHP), 35, 363, 381, 393, 395, 396, 398

Wadley, Susan Snow, 140, 144, 145, 151, 157, 161
Wagner, Christian, 323, 326, 330, 342, 357
Walzer, Michael, 111, 136, 242, 244
Washbrook, D.A., 370n14, 373, 374, 375, 379
Waugh, Linda, 140, 161
Weber, Max, 102, 110, 238n, 428, 430, 448
Weinberger-Thomas, Catherine, 152, 161
Weiner, Myron, 394, 400
Werbner, P., 295, 305
White, D.L., 284, 293n17, 305
widow(s)/widowhood, 145, 150, 151, 152, 153, 155
Williams, Brackette, F., 212, 213, 218
Wills, C.U., 242, 244
Wills, Gary, 360nn1, 2, 379
Wittgenstein, Ludwig, 10n, 11, 21
Wadood, A.C.A., 324, 357
worship, 42, 87, 88, 91, 137, 154, 254, 286, 331, 334, 339, 389

Wright, Theodore P. Jr., 314, 316, 357
Wulff, Donna Marie, 154, 162

Xiong, W., 101, 110

Yadav, Maulayam Singh, 268, 274, 281
Yadav(s), 112, 128, 268, 276–79, 281, 282
Yadav, Laloo, 268, 276, 277
Yalman, Nur Osman, 146, 162, 317, 357
Young, Michael W., 425n14, 426n14, 428, 430, 439, 449
Young, R.J.C., 302, 305

zamindar, 232–34, 238, 240
Zimmermann, Francis B., 138, 162